Introduction to Mathematical Economics

Mark Casson
University of Reading

Nelson

Thomas Nelson and Sons Ltd
36 Park Street London WIY 4DE

Nelson (Africa) Ltd
PO Box 18123 Nairobi Kenya

Thomas Nelson (Australia) Ltd
171–175 Bank Street South Melbourne Victoria 3205

Thomas Nelson and Sons (Canada) Ltd
81 Curlew Drive Don Mills Ontario

Thomas Nelson (Nigeria) Ltd
PO Box 336 Apapa Lagos

First published in Great Britain by
Thomas Nelson and Sons Ltd, 1973

ISBN 017 711203 4 (boards)
017 712203 X (paper)

Printed in Great Britain by
William Clowes & Sons, Limited
London, Beccles and Colchester

Introduction to Mathematical Economics

Contents

8 Integration

9 Programming methods for the solution of optimization problems

Part 3 Matrix algebra

10 Equilibrium conditions for interacting markets

11 Introduction to matrix algebra

12 Simultaneous linear equations: existence, uniqueness and feasibility of the solution

13 The matrix multiplier and the stability of equilibrium

14 Characteristic values

To my parents

Foreword

Economics is becoming an increasingly mathematical subject. Writings which twenty years ago would have been regarded as highly mathematical are now viewed as part of the literary approach to the subject; and the most literate of contemporary economists would have seemed highly numerate to the preceding generations. It is for this reason that Mr. Casson's book is to be welcomed. Its purpose is to provide the basic minimum of mathematics for the undergraduate economics degree for students without a great deal of previous training but with a desire to understand the subject. The book will also be useful in such related degrees as business studies. The author has had a great deal of experience of teaching at this level, and has gone to a great deal of trouble (involving several rewrites!) to encompass that in this book. This is especially shown by the many worked examples which he has provided, and the care and clarity of his exposition.

M. H. Peston
Queen Mary College
London

Preface

This book has grown out of a course of lectures given to economics students at Reading University over the past four years. The course is primarily intended for students who have not done any mathematics since O level, although it is also attended by students with A level, and the mathematical knowledge presumed is that of a student who has already forgotten much of the O level mathematics syllabus. The level of ability presumed is that of a student who has dropped mathematics because he or she has become convinced that they are no good at it, which often means that a student is very able but has been badly taught. One of the aims of this book is to remove the psychological block which many students experience with mathematics, and to attempt to counter the attitude that 'I gave up maths as soon as I could, I've got by very well without it since, so why do I need to start learning it again now?' The book sets out to explain why mathematics is useful to the economist by developing a wide variety of applications to immediate questions of economic policy. The applications are not usually in the field of abstract economic theory because theories themselves need to be justified in terms of their relevance to policy making—and with contemporary economic theory this is often difficult to do. The emphasis is much more on the advantages of quantitative thinking in applied economics.

Each new mathematical technique is introduced by a series of worked examples, together with a brief statement of the purely mathematical results and an intuitive explanation of why the results hold. In this way it is hoped to avoid confusion between the general results and their specific applications, while at the same time showing how the mathematics can be used to solve a variety of practical problems. At the end of each chapter is a short bibliography referring both to the mathematical methods and to the economic applications. There is also a set of problems, referenced with respect to each section within the chapter. Answers to the purely mathematical problems are given at the end of the book; some of the more challenging problems in economic applications may be useful for class use, and the answers to these are not given.

Most members of the Reading economics department have at some time or other been kind enough to read through part of the text. I am particularly grateful to Professor Hart and Nick Robinson for much detailed advice on the content and presentation of the material, and also to John Mellors for editing several obscure passages in the final draft. Professor Peston read through the entire penultimate draft, and as a result of his criticisms the book is now at least one hundred pages longer! Sue Galley and Sarah Macfarlane did their best to ensure mathematical rigour in the exposition. Alan Thorley prepared most of the problems, and whatever amusement is derived from reading—if not solving—them is due to him. Reading students past and present have had the opportunity of criticizing successive drafts, and I am grateful to them not only for many points of substance but also for correcting pluses to minuses, superscripts to subscripts, and so forth. Jane Caldicott, Margaret Lewis, Barbara Wall and Pat Wylie have spent many long hours typing and retyping the various drafts with remarkable accuracy, and to them I am very grateful. I should also like to thank Martin Lewin and the other editors concerned with the book for the care and effort which has gone into its presentation.

MARK CASSON

Part 1
Introduction

Chapter 1

Use of mathematics in economics

Nowadays a great many students find it necessary to learn mathematics in order to understand the technical literature on their subject. Such students do not usually find the manipulation of numbers or the remarkable results of algebra and geometry intrinsically interesting. They simply wish to understand those parts of mathematics which are relevant to their own needs. This book is intended for them.

The presentation of the material reflects two beliefs. First, that the student who is led through a number of simple examples will soon appreciate that many of the difficulties of the subject are only apparent—a little practice usually suffices to give him a grasp of the techniques involved. Second, that intuition is a considerable help both in understanding why certain mathematical techniques work and in learning to appreciate the scope and limitations of mathematical methods.

On finishing this book, the student who has read it thoroughly will have devoted a considerable amount of time to learning mathematical methods. Assuming that his basic aim is to understand economics it is useful to begin by showing why this is time well spent. Four main fields of economics may be distinguished to illustrate the substantial contribution that mathematics makes to the study of economics.

1.1 Use of pure mathematics in economic theory

It is surely no coincidence that many of the greatest economists of the last hundred years were trained as mathematicians—Alfred Marshall, William Stanley Jevons, Irving Fisher, Knut Wicksell and John Maynard Keynes, for example—while others, equally notable, combined the study of economics with that of logic—John Stuart Mill, Francis Ysidro Edgeworth, John Neville Keynes and Roy Harrod are perhaps the best known. It is interesting that each of these men—with the possible exception of Edgeworth and Jevons—made their major contributions to economics in fields outside what today would be called mathematical economics; their contribution was not so much in introducing specific mathematical methods into economics as in extending the frontiers of conventional economics by careful and well-reasoned argument.

Why should mathematicians be so successful in making non-mathematical contributions to economic theory? One possible explanation is that the language of mathematics is a particularly suitable medium for abstract thought of the kind required in economics. In order to examine the working of any economy it is necessary to identify certain important features of it and isolate these from those aspects of lesser importance. The selection of the features to be abstracted requires good judgement, but the analysis of what is abstracted requires a much rarer quality: the ability to see the abstract relationships with new eyes, to see their logical structure and to appreciate the interplay of the relationships within the system as a whole. Once the economist has identified what he believes to be the key relationships, the extent of his progress is determined by the facility with which he can make deductions from the logical structure of his abstract theory and then transform these deductions into statements about the real world. It is largely because mathematics facilitates abstract reasoning of this kind that it is so useful in economic theory. But why should mathematics have such an advantage over ordinary language as a vehicle for abstract thought?

(a) The vocabulary of mathematics is precise and free from misleading connotations

In ordinary language the same word may have several meanings, each slightly different, but none so different as to make clear the precise meaning in a particular context. Besides being ambiguous, many words have value-loaded connotations, even when used in a technical sense. Consider, for example, the use of the word 'equilibrium' in economics. A statement that the economy is in 'equilibrium' suggests to many people a highly desirable state of affairs—of economic efficiency, personal contentment and social harmony—while 'disequilibrium' suggests a distinctly unpleasant situation. However, it is quite possible, as Keynes pointed out, to have a state of equilibrium in a slump and a state of disequilibrium when there is full employment. The vagueness and value-loaded connotations of the term 'equilibrium' are reflected in its widespread misuse in economics. Thus in connection with markets the term has been used to suggest a state of affairs in which (i) the plans of both buyers and sellers are realized, or (ii) there is no need for the plans of buyers and sellers to be revised, or (iii) there are no forces tending to change prices and quantities traded, or (iv) prices and quantities traded are constant over time. Yet equilibrium in one of these senses by no means implies equilibrium in the other senses. In mathematical language a state of equilibrium may be defined by an equation between a set of precisely defined variables; such a definition is unambiguous and devoid of misleading connotations.

(b) The language of mathematics simplifies the presentation and understanding of complicated arguments

Most economists would agree that the working of even the simplest economy involves very many interactions. Analysis of these interactions becomes exceedingly difficult when all stages of the analysis have to be expressed in ordinary language; the literary task of presenting the analysis becomes tedious, and comprehension becomes difficult as arguments become tangled in an intricate web of grammar.

One familiar remedy is to summarize a complicated analysis with the aid of schematic diagrams, flow charts, graphs, etc. In economics the subject-matter is often so complex that a simple diagram is inadequate, and recourse must be had to mathematical equations if the subject is to be summarized in a manageable way. It has been found that mathematical representation not only elucidates discussion but can also high-light useful analogies with the biological and physical sciences. Such analogies often suggest methods of solving apparently intractable problems.

(c) 'Economic man' is a mathematician

Much of economic theory is based (for want of a better assumption) on the hypothesis that individuals behave rationally. The concept of 'economic man' is a gross oversimplification in psychological terms, but nevertheless in their everyday economic behaviour many individuals resemble the portrait quite remarkably. The choice of a course of action by a rational individual is an exercise in applied logic; when the choice is a quantitative one—relating to 'how many?' or 'how much?'—it becomes a mathematical exercise as well. Since 'economic man' behaves as though he were a logician-cum-mathematician, it is not surprising that many of the laws of economics, most of which rest upon the assumption of rationality, have been discovered by minds trained in logic and mathematics.

1.2 Use of applied mathematics in economic policy making

The methods of applied mathematics have been evolved mainly for the purpose of analysing relations between quantities with numerical values. Most of the key factors in which economists are interested—price, output, employment, income, balance of trade, etc.—can be measured numerically. It is not surprising, therefore, that those economists interested in studying the relationships between key economic quantities have made use of the methods of applied mathematics. One advantage of studying a relationship involving numerical values is that, once the precise form of the relationship has been discovered, it is possible to forecast the future state of the economy—provided that the relationship is stable over time. In the light of such forecasts objective economic policies can be formulated that move the economy towards selected targets.

For example, suppose that one Sunday morning at 4 a.m. your telephone rings; it is the Chancellor of the Exchequer. The Chancellor wishes to know how to reconcile balance of payments stability with full employment, and requires your answer by Monday morning. A quick examination of the *Blue Book of National Income and Expenditure* shows that (see Table 1.1) in 1970 the balance of trade was in surplus, but the loss of income due to unemployment was, in absolute terms, quite considerable. To answer the Chancellor's question in terms of, say, an economic policy for 1973, it is necessary to forecast the state of the economy in that year, and this requires some knowledge of the way in which key economic quantities are related to one another. Suppose a study of data for post-war years leads you to believe that

(i) exports will increase by 5% per annum over the period 1970–3;

(ii) imports in 1973 will be equal to 35% of the national income, i.e. of goods required to satisfy home demand, 35% by value will be purchased from foreigners;

Table 1.1 Key economic quantities for the UK in 1970

	£,000m
National income	29·4
Estimate of national income at full employment	30·0
Loss of income due to unemployment	0·6
Exports	8·6
Imports	8·4
Balance of trade = Exports − Imports	0·2

SOURCE *National Income and Expenditure 1971*, London: HMSO, Table 14. All figures at 1963 prices. The estimate of national income at full employment is obtained by adjusting the national income figure using the rate of unemployment derived from *Annual Abstract of Statistics 1971*, London: HMSO, Table 142.

(iii) due to stagnation of investment, the national income which is attainable with full employment of resources will remain unchanged from the 1970 value.

On the basis of these assumptions, together with the figures given in Table 1.1 above, a forecast may be drawn up for 1973. For reasons which will soon be evident, the forecast is expressed in terms of the (unknown) value of national income in 1973, which is denoted by the letter Y. The forecast is shown in Table 1.2. Substituting in turn different numerical values for Y into this table

Table 1.2 Forecast of key economic quantities for the UK in 1973

	Relationship used	*Forecast value (£,000m)*
National income	Denoted Y	Y
Estimate of national income at full employment	= 1970 value	30·0
Exports	= Exports in 1970 × $(1{\cdot}05)^3$	10·0
Imports	= 0·35 × Nat. inc. in 1973	$0{\cdot}35Y$
Balance of trade	= Exports − Imports	$10{\cdot}0 - 0{\cdot}35Y$

shows that if national income in 1973 were high enough to eliminate unemployment (i.e. $Y = 30{\cdot}0$) then the balance of trade would be unfavourable ($= 10{\cdot}0 - 0{\cdot}35 \times 30{\cdot}0 = -0{\cdot}5$); if, on the other hand, the national income in 1973 were relatively low (say $Y = 28{\cdot}0$) then the balance of trade would be favourable ($= 10{\cdot}0 - 0{\cdot}35 \times 28{\cdot}0 = +0{\cdot}2$) but the loss of income due to unemployment would be alarmingly high ($= 30{\cdot}0 - 28{\cdot}0 = 2{\cdot}0$). Suppose that the Chancellor is able to control the level of national income by his Budget measures, changes in Bank Rate, etc. His problem is to choose the level of national income which will, if possible, achieve the twin targets of full employment and a favourable balance of trade. Unfortunately, the numerical examples above suggest that there is a trade-off between full employment and a favourable balance of payments, an improvement in the employment situation being associated with a deterioration in the balance of trade. By using some simple algebra this trade-off can be expressed quantitatively.

Let B = balance of trade in 1973
Let L = loss of income due to unemployment in 1973

We have already defined

Y = national income in 1973.

Comparing the first two lines of Table 1.2 shows that

$$L = 30 - Y$$

The final line of Table 1.2 may be expressed algebraically as

$$B = 10 - 0{\cdot}35Y$$

The first equation implies that

$$Y = 30 - L$$

Substituting for Y in the second equation above shows that

$$B = 10 - 0{\cdot}35(30 - L) = -0{\cdot}5 + 0{\cdot}35L$$

The graph of this equation is shown in Fig. 1A below. The graph indicates that for every additional £1m of income that is earned by reducing unemployment, the balance of payments worsens by £0·35m. Clearly, if the Chancellor is able to

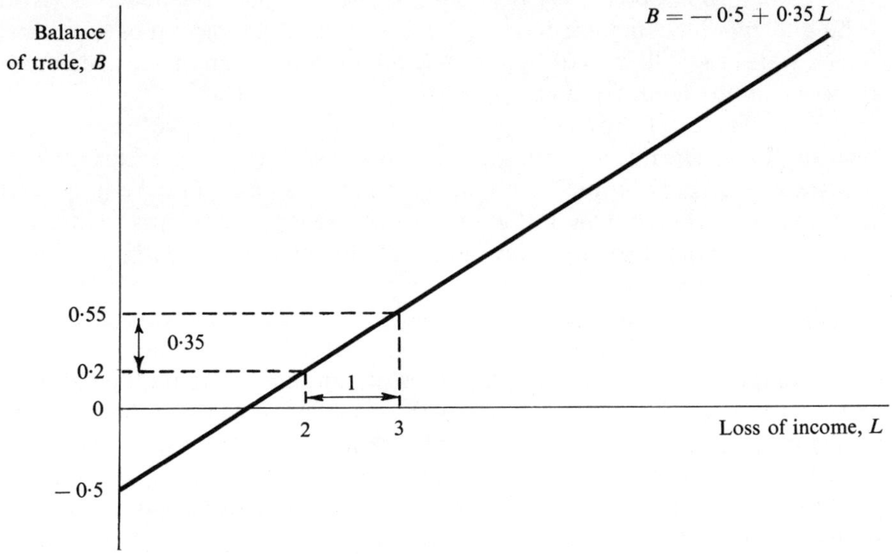

Fig. 1A Forecast relationship between balance of trade and loss of income due to unemployment in 1973

regulate only the level of national income then there is no simple way to reconcile a high level of employment with a favourable balance of payments. But at least the economist can explain to the Chancellor the nature of his dilemma and, by using simple mathematics, determine the relative magnitudes of the sacrifices, i.e. income and financial reserves foregone, which result from pursuing a particular policy.

1.3 Use of mathematics to analyse economic statistics

Elementary mathematics is very useful for summarizing and interpreting economic and social statistics. More advanced mathematics is used in econometric theory, which is concerned with ways of estimating relationships between key economic quantities.

A great deal of statistical information is available nowadays, most of it from official sources which cover the spectrum from reports on the ten-year censuses of population, production and distribution to monthly bulletins summarizing the financial state of the economy. Most of the figures available from these sources need preliminary analysis—conversion to ratios, means, etc.—before they can be easily interpreted. In order to avoid mistaken inferences it is important that, in addition to knowing the correct formulae for percentages, means (arithmetic and geometric), variances and so forth, something is also known of the way in which these quantities vary as a result of variation in the figures from which they are computed. Only in this way is it possible to avoid using the wrong technique to analyse data from a particular source. In order to understand thoroughly the dangers of misusing statistical technique, and also the qualifications which are necessary when applying a particular statistical method, it is essential to be familiar with certain results of mathematical probability theory; this book does not develop these results, but it develops the techniques by which they are derived. The use of simple mathematics to interpret official statistics is illustrated by the following examination of the distribution of income in the United Kingdom.

Table 1.3 shows the share-out of the 'national cake' in two years, 1960 and 1970. The unwary investigator could easily misinterpret this table. By failing to read the footnote he might infer that the national cake had nearly doubled in ten years; but all the figures are in current prices, and more than one-half of the apparent increase is accounted for by inflation. By failing to understand the distinction between a simple rate of growth and a compound rate of growth, he might easily make matters worse by evaluating the annual rate of growth of the national cake as a simple rate instead of using the more appropriate compound rate. (The simple rate is obtained by dividing the difference between the totals by ten and expressing the result as a fraction of the 1960 total, while the compound rate is obtained as the difference between the tenth root of the ratio of the totals and unity; see Chapter 17.) Working in terms of current prices would tend to overstate the growth of the national cake and calculating a simple rate of growth when a compound rate is appropriate would make the overstatement even greater; the net result would be a conclusion which was hopelessly wrong.

Table 1.3 A comparison of shares in the gross national product of the UK in 1960 and 1970

	£,000m	
	1960	*1970*
Income from employment	15·2	30·5
Income from self-employment	2·0	3·3
Rent	1·3	3·0
Dividends and interest	1·1	1·6
Undistributed profits	3·5	5·3
Total	23·0	43·8

SOURCE *National Income and Expenditure 1971*, London: HMSO. Tables 1 and 9.
NOTE All figures at current prices. Undistributed profits include the gross trading surplus of public authorities after deduction of rent, dividends and interest. The total differs from gross national product, due to net transfers abroad and stock appreciation. Because of rounding errors the totals are not equal to the sums of the components.

To draw sound inferences from Table 1.3 it is best to proceed along the following lines. First of all calculate for each year separately the percentage of the total product distributed to each sector (see Table 1.4). For each type of income compare the percentage in 1960 with the percentage in 1970, taking the difference between the two. The final column of Table 1.4 shows quite clearly that over the decade there has been a significant rise in the share of income going to employees and a significant drop in the proportion of income retained by firms and public corporations as undistributed profits. The proportion of

Table 1.4 An analysis of changes in the distribution of income in the UK between 1960 and 1970

	% of total income		
	1960	*1970*	*Change*
Income from employment	$\frac{15{\cdot}2}{23{\cdot}0} \times 100 = 66$	$\frac{30{\cdot}5}{43{\cdot}8} \times 100 = 70$	+4
Income from self-employment	$\frac{2{\cdot}0}{23{\cdot}0} \times 100 = 9$	$\frac{3{\cdot}3}{43{\cdot}8} \times 100 = 8$	−1
Rent	$\frac{1{\cdot}3}{23{\cdot}0} \times 100 = 6$	$\frac{3{\cdot}0}{43{\cdot}8} \times 100 = 7$	+1
Dividends and interest	$\frac{1{\cdot}1}{23{\cdot}0} \times 100 = 5$	$\frac{1{\cdot}6}{43{\cdot}8} \times 100 = 4$	−1
Undistributed profits	$\frac{3{\cdot}5}{23{\cdot}0} \times 100 = 15$	$\frac{5{\cdot}3}{43{\cdot}8} \times 100 = 12$	−3
Column total	101	101	0

NOTE The column totals do not equal 100 because of rounding errors in the individual entries.

income earned from rent has increased while the proportion earned from self-employment, and from dividends and interest has declined. Not all these conclusions are equally reliable; the statistic in the final column is obtained by taking the difference between two percentages, and a critical examination of its reliability would require a degree of mathematical sophistication well beyond the scope of this introductory chapter.

More advanced mathematical methods can be used to estimate relationships between two or more economic quantities on the basis of information on their past behaviour. The following example indicates the nature of the methods used.

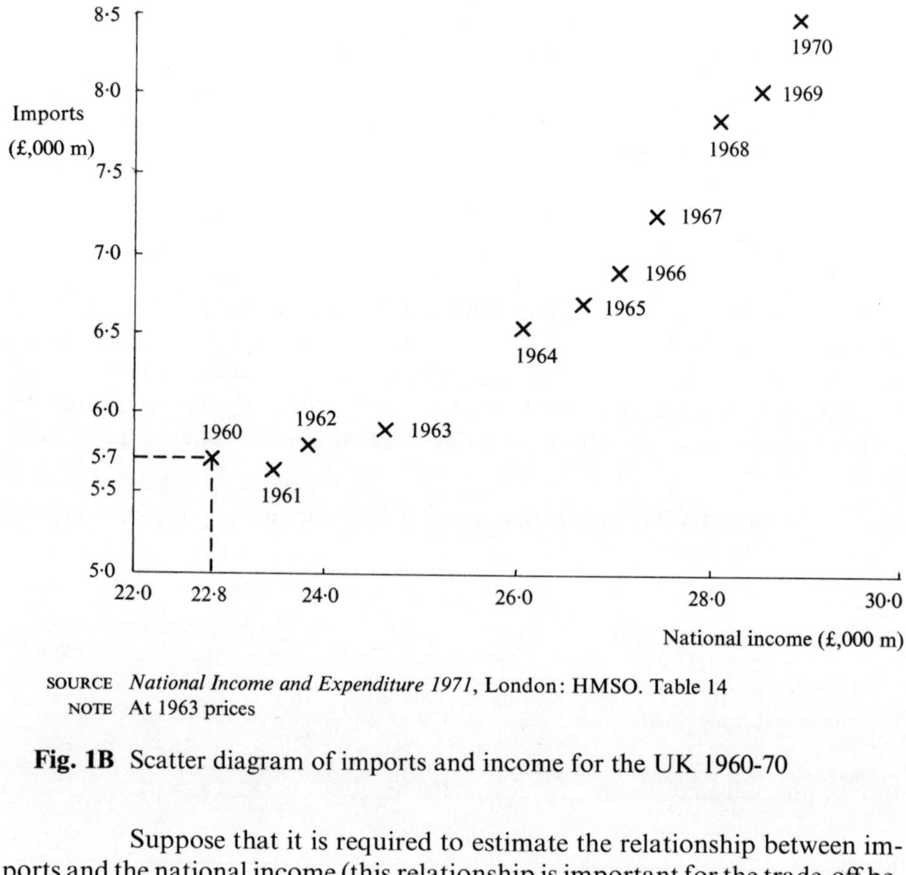

SOURCE *National Income and Expenditure 1971*, London: HMSO. Table 14
NOTE At 1963 prices

Fig. 1B Scatter diagram of imports and income for the UK 1960-70

Suppose that it is required to estimate the relationship between imports and the national income (this relationship is important for the trade-off between the balance of payments and unemployment; see Section 1.2). If annual data on imports and income are collected for, say, the decade 1960–70, then a scatter diagram (Fig. 1B) may be drawn up by plotting on graph paper a point for each of the eleven years, the height of each point being a measure of the imports that year and the horizontal displacement of the point being the corresponding measure of national income. For example, on looking at the bottom left-hand point in the diagram, we see that in 1960 imports were 5·7 (£,000m) and national income was 22·8 (£,000m). If it is believed that the true relationship between imports and income is a straight-line relationship (sometimes called a linear relationship) then to infer from the data the precise formula which relates imports to income it is necessary to fit a straight line to the scatter of points. The problem is that the points in a scatter diagram do not usually lie on the same straight line, so that it is necessary to measure the straight-line relationship by choosing a line which, in some sense, fits the points most closely. It has been discovered, as the result of mathematical reasoning, that in many cases the best way to measure a straight-line relationship is to select the line which, in the context of the scatter diagram, minimizes the sum of the squares of the vertical discrepancies between the points and the fitted line. This 'least squares' criterion may be visualized as follows. For each point the square of the vertical discrepancy between it and the fitted line is equal (by simple geometry) to the area of a square (drawn on the scatter diagram), one of whose sides is equal in length to the absolute value of the vertical discrepancy. It follows that if a square is drawn so that one of its sides connects vertically a point to the line then the area of the square is equal to the square of the vertical discrepancy between the point and the line. Consequently the sum of the squares of the vertical discrepancies between the points and the line is equal to the total area of the squares, when one such square is drawn for each point. The line for which this total area is a minimum is shown in Fig. 1C; it is the line—chosen from all possible straight lines—for which the total shaded area in the figure is a minimum, i.e. any other line fitted to the same scatter of points would have associated with it a larger shaded area and would, if our criterion is correct, be inferior as a measure of the true straight-line relationship. Chapter 12 gives a simple algebraic formula by which the equation of the line can be found. It suffices to note here that an equation obtained in this way may provide valuable insights into the relationship between two or more economic variables and provide a basis for making forecasts of the future values of such variables.

1.4 Use of mathematics to solve economic problems in commerce, government and industry

Recent years have seen a rapid increase in the application of mathematical methods to solve a diversity of economic problems. These problems range from broad policy questions—such as those arising in the planning of urban transport systems or the health and education services—to more mundane, but equally important, problems of organizational efficiency—inventory replacement policy, vehicle scheduling and the like.

Most of these problems are distinguished by the great complexity which is inevitable whenever the problem is specified realistically. We give below a highly simplified example of the application of mathematical technique to an economic problem within the field of transport planning.

Many years ago two railways were built from London to the south-east coast (see Fig. 1D). One was the London, Chatham and Dover Railway, which ran to Dover via Chatham and Canterbury, with a branch from Faversham to Ramsgate; the other was the South Eastern Railway, which ran to Dover via

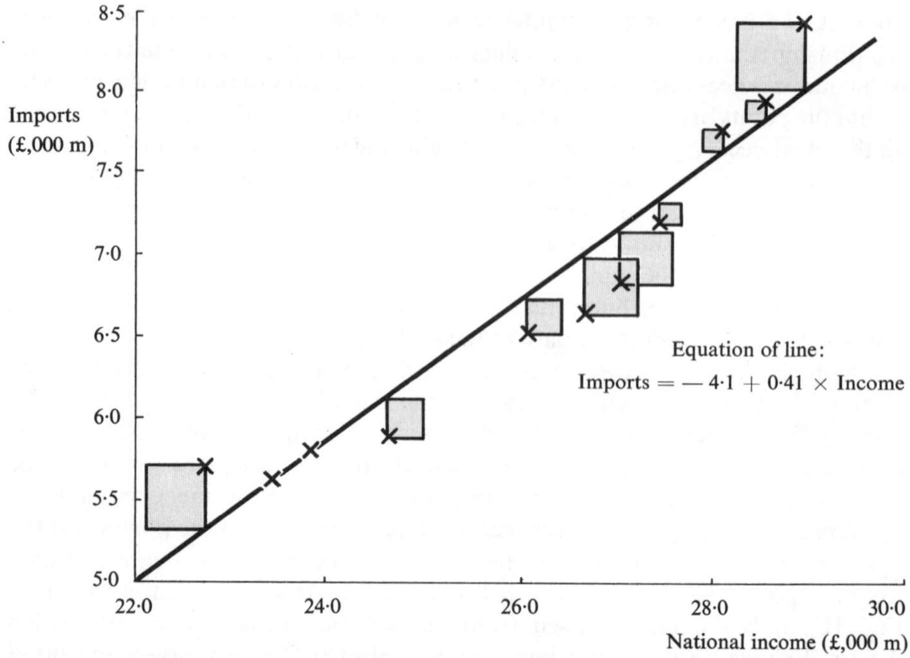

NOTE The height of each shaded area is equal to the absolute difference between the actual value of imports in a particular year and the value of imports which the *fitted line* indicates should correspond to the current value of income. By elementary geometry each shaded square has an area equal to the square of its height. The total shaded area in the figure is therefore equal to the sum of the squares of the discrepancies between the actual values of imports and the values of imports indicated by the fitted line. The line shown is the line which, out of all possible straight lines, has the least total shaded area associated with it. The equation of the line can in fact be calculated by a simple formula.

Fig. 1C Relationship between imports and income estimated from annual UK data 1960-70

Tonbridge, with a branch from Ashford to Canterbury and Ramsgate. Today British Rail operates passenger services over these lines by four different routes:

Route

1 London – Chatham – Ramsgate
2 London – Chatham – Canterbury – Dover
3 London – Tonbridge – Canterbury – Ramsgate
4 London – Tonbridge – Dover.

Suppose a market researcher reports that in order to attract sufficient traffic at reasonable fares there must be at least

(a) 12 trains a day between London and Dover
(b) 12 trains a day between London and Ramsgate
(c) 8 trains a day between London and Canterbury
(d) 16 trains a day between London and Chatham
(e) 6 trains a day between London and Tonbridge.

What must be the daily frequency of trains on each route if all these requirements are to be met?

To begin with, let us investigate whether it is possible to satisfy each of the requirements *exactly*. Let f_1 be the daily frequency of trains on route 1, f_2 be the daily frequency on route 2, and so on; the numbers f_1, f_2, f_3, f_4 are the number of trains per day on routes 1, 2, 3 and 4 respectively.

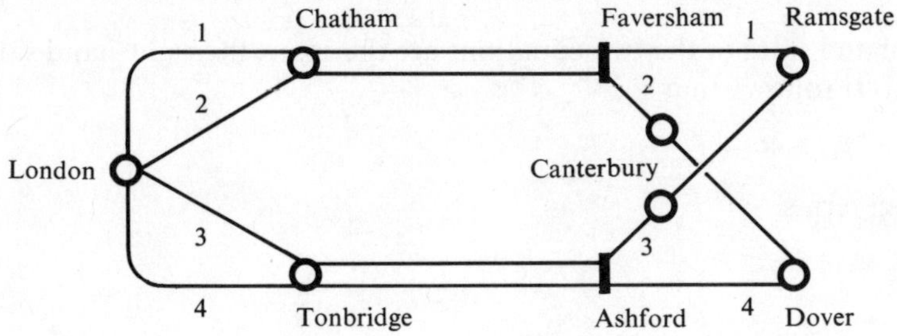

Fig. 1D Train services from London to the south-east coast

The first requirement is that there must be twelve trains a day between London and Ramsgate. Routes 1 and 3 connect London and Ramsgate; the total frequency of trains between London and Ramsgate will be equal to the sum of the frequency on route 1 and the frequency on route 3, i.e. the total frequency between London and Ramsgate is $f_1 + f_3$. The first requirement may therefore be written algebraically as

$$f_1 + f_3 = 12$$

The second requirement, for trains between London and Dover, requires that the frequencies of trains on routes 2 and 4 satisfy the algebraic equation

$$f_2 + f_4 = 12$$

Each of the other requirements has a corresponding equation; the set of five equations may be written in the form of a tableau:

$$\begin{array}{llllll}
(1) & f_1 & & + f_3 & & = 12 \\
(2) & & f_2 & & + f_4 & = 12 \\
(3) & & f_2 & + f_3 & & = 8 \\
(4) & f_1 & + f_2 & & & = 16 \\
(5) & & & f_3 & + f_4 & = 8
\end{array}$$

A mathematician would describe this tableau as a set of five simultaneous equations in the four unknowns f_1, f_2, f_3, f_4. To solve the problem we need to find, if possible, particular values of f_1, f_2, f_3, f_4 which satisfy all five equations. One way of tackling the problem is as follows (a better way is described in Chapter 12). By subtracting f_3 from both sides, equation (1) may be written

$$f_1 = 12 - f_3$$

and substituting this result into equation (4) we get

$$(12 - f_3) + f_2 = 16$$

Rearranging terms gives

$$f_2 = (16 - 12) + f_3 = 4 + f_3$$

Compare this result with the equation (3), which can be written

$$f_2 = 8 - f_3$$

Since the left-hand sides of the two equations are the same, the right-hand sides must be equal. It follows that

$$4 + f_3 = 8 - f_3$$

or, rearranging terms,

$$2f_3 = 4$$

$$\text{so that } f_3 = 2$$

Equation (1) implies that if $f_3 = 2$ then $f_1 = 10$ and equation (3) implies that if $f_3 = 2$ then $f_2 = 6$. Equation (2) implies that if $f_2 = 6$ then $f_4 = 6$. Equation (4) is now satisfied since $f_1 + f_2 = 10 + 6 = 16$, and so is equation (5), since $f_3 + f_4 = 2 + 6 = 8$. We therefore conclude that British Rail can meet all the requirements exactly by running 10 trains a day to Ramsgate via Chatham (route 1), 6 trains a day to Dover via Chatham (route 2), 2 trains a day to Ramsgate via Tonbridge and Canterbury (route 3) and 6 trains a day to Dover via Tonbridge (route 4).

Chapter 2

Elementary mathematical concepts

This chapter gives a brief review of elementary mathematical concepts, revising what is usually covered at school. The topics are numbers, variables, absolute values, sums, powers and roots, functions, graphs, continuity, equations, geometric series and limits.

2.1 Numbers

It is useful to distinguish four different types of number.

Integers

Positive integers are the numbers ordinarily used for counting: 1, 2, 3, 4, 5, ... Positive integers are sometimes known as whole numbers. The corresponding negative numbers, -1, -2, -3, -4, -5 are negative integers. The set of all integers consists of the positive integers, the negative integers and the number zero: ..., -3, -2, -1, 0, 1, 2, 3, ...

Rational numbers

A number is rational if it can be expressed as a ratio of integers. Examples of rational numbers are 3/2, 4/9, 8/25. Dividing the integers by the number 1 shows that integers are themselves rational numbers.

Real numbers

Real numbers are numbers which can be expressed in a form such as decimals, e.g. 4·615, 8·0, $-12{\cdot}48375$. A real number may possibly have an infinite number of decimal places, e.g. $1/3 = 0{\cdot}333$ (recurring), $1/9 = 0{\cdot}111$ (recurring), $\sqrt{2} = 1{\cdot}414\ldots$. All rational numbers are real numbers, but the converse is not true. A real number which is not a rational number is known as an irrational number (examples are $\sqrt{2}$ and π).

Complex numbers

A more general form of number is the complex number. Complex numbers have important properties which are not shared by real numbers, e.g. every complex number has a square root which is a complex number, whereas a negative real number has no square root which is a real number. For further details see Chapter 19.

2.2 Variables and their notation

A variable is simply a quantity which can take on different numerical values, i.e. a variable is something whose value varies. For example, the demand for a commodity is a variable, since at different prices different amounts of a commodity are demanded. A variable is usually denoted by a letter, e.g. the demand for a commodity is usually denoted by D, its price by P, and so on. The statement that demand is equal to 50 units is written mathematically

$$D = 50$$

Sometimes we wish to say, not that demand is equal to a given value, but that demand exceeds some value, or is less than some value. Such statements are written mathematically using the inequality signs $>$ meaning 'greater than' and $<$ meaning 'less than'. For example, demand exceeds 60 units is written

$$D > 60$$

Price is less than £5 is written

$$P < 5$$

where P is measured in £ units. The inequalities $>$ and $<$ are known as *strong inequalities* because they rule out the possibility of equality. To express the fact that a variable is greater than *or equal to* some value, or is less than *or equal to* some value we use the respective inequalities $\geqslant$ and $\leqslant$; these are known as *weak inequalities*. To illustrate,

$$P \geqslant 6$$

means that price is greater than or equal to £6. Similarly

$$D \leqslant 40$$

means that demand is less than or equal to 40 units.

Inequality signs can be used to describe both the upper and lower bounds between which a quantity varies. For example,

$$40 < D < 80$$

reads '40 is less than D and D in turn is less than 80' which implies that D varies between 40 and 80 exclusive. Similarly

$$20 \leqslant P \leqslant 100$$

reads '20 is less than or equal to P and P in turn is less than or equal to 100', which implies that P varies between 20 and 100 *inclusive*.

Sometimes it is convenient to index variables by using subscripts or superscripts. For example, if there are three commodities it is often convenient to index them 1, 2, 3 and to denote the respective demands for the commodities by D_1, D_2, D_3 and their prices by P_1, P_2, P_3. Sometimes we go even further and denote some special price by, say, a superscripted asterisk, e.g. P_2^* may denote the 'equilibrium price' of the second commodity. There is no need for subscripts and superscripts to cause confusion provided that the notation is clearly explained when it is first introduced.

2.3 Some useful things to know about absolute values, sums, powers and roots

It is useful at this stage to collect together results which are needed in Sections 2.4–2.6 below. Readers who are in a hurry are advised to skip this section and refer back to it when necessary.

(a) Absolute values

The absolute value of a number is the magnitude of the number independent of its sign, for example, the absolute value of 4 is 4, the absolute value of -2 is 2. The absolute value of a real number x is denoted $|x|$. By definition

$$|x| = \begin{cases} x \text{ if } x > 0 \\ -x \text{ if } x < 0 \\ 0 \text{ if } x = 0 \end{cases}$$

A useful property of the absolute value is that for any two real numbers x, y the absolute value of the product is equal to the product of the absolute values,

$$|xy| = |x| . |y|$$

The sums and differences of absolute values satisfy only inequalities, viz:

$$|x + y| \leqslant |x| + |y|$$
$$|x - y| \leqslant |x| + |y|$$

Note that the inequality for a sum is the same as the inequality for a difference. For future reference we note that the absolute value of a real number is equal to its 'modulus' as defined in Chapter 19.

(b) Sums

For convenience, the sum of n terms

$$x_1 + x_2 + \cdots + x_N$$

is denoted

$$\sum_{i=1}^{N} x_i$$

The subscript i is used as an index; i takes on all the integer values within a specified range. The lower limit of the range is written beneath the Σ and the upper limit is written above.

The following examples should clarify the use of these conventions.

Examples

$$\sum_{i=2}^{5} x_i = x_2 + x_3 + x_4 + x_5$$

$$\sum_{i=1}^{4} x_i y_i = x_1 y_1 + x_2 y_2 + x_3 y_3 + x_4 y_4$$

$$\sum_{i=-2}^{1} x_i x_{i-1} = x_{-2} x_{-3} + x_{-1} x_{-2} + x_0 x_{-1} + x_1 x_0$$

$$\sum_{i=1}^{3} x_i^2 = x_1^2 + x_2^2 + x_3^2$$

Useful properties of sums are that for any positive integer N and any real number a,

(1) $$\sum_{i=1}^{N} a x_i = a \sum_{i=1}^{N} x_i$$

(2) $$\sum_{i=1}^{N} (x_i/N) = (1/N) \sum_{i=1}^{N} x_i$$

(3) $$\sum_{i=1}^{N} (x_i - a)/N = \left(\sum_{i=1}^{N} x_i/N \right) - a$$

(4) $$\sum_{i=1}^{N} (x_i - a)^2/N = \left(\sum_{i=1}^{N} x_i^2/N \right) - 2a \left(\sum_{i=1}^{N} x_i/N \right) + a^2$$

(5) $$\sum_{i=1}^{N} (x_i - \bar{x})^2/N = \left(\sum_{i=1} x_i^2/N \right) - \bar{x}^2$$

where $\bar{x} = \sum_{i=1}^{N} x_i/N$

Properties (1), (3) and (4) are obtained by expanding, factorizing and collecting terms; (2) is a consequence of (1) and (5) is obtained from (4) by substituting $a = \Sigma_{i=1}^{N} x_i/N$. These formulae are useful in statistics; if $x_1, \ldots, x_n$ is a set of N measurements then (2) is the formula for an arithmetic mean, (3) is the first moment about a, (4) is the second moment about a and (5) is the variance.

(c) Powers and roots

The quantity x^n is known as 'x raised to the power n' and is the result of multiplying together n terms each equal to x. It is easily verified that the product of two powers of x is equal to x raised to the sum of the powers,

(1) $$x^a x^b = x^{a+b}$$

The proof is straightforward: since $x^a = x.x \ldots x$ (a times) and $x^b = x.x \ldots x$ (b times), $x^a.x^b = [x.x \ldots x$ (a times)]. $[x.x \ldots x$ (b times)] $= x.x \ldots \ldots x$

$(a + b)$ times $= x^{(a+b)}$. Another result is that the ratio of two powers of x is equal to x raised to the difference between the powers,

$$(2) \qquad x^a/x^b = x^{a-b}$$

If a exceeds b then this result is proved by writing $x^a/x^b = [x.x \ldots x$ (a times)]/ $[x.x \ldots x$ (b times)] and cancelling terms top and bottom to get $[x.x \ldots x$ ($a - b$ times)]. If b exceeds a then this proof does not work because the terms which remain after cancellation are in the denominator. However, if we define the reciprocal $1/x^n$ as the power x^{-n} then the result can be shown to be valid: since b exceeds a, $x^a/x^b = [x.x \ldots x$ (a times)]/$[x.x \ldots x$ (b times)] $= 1/[x.x \ldots x$ ($b - a$ times)] $= 1/x^{b-a} = x^{-(b-a)} = x^{a-b}$. It remains to examine the case in which a is equal to b. In this case it is obvious that $x^a/x^b = 1$. To make the rule $x^a x^b = x^{a-b}$ valid we must therefore define $x^0 = 1$. We conclude that equation (2) is valid on the understanding that

$$(3) \qquad 1/x^n = x^{-n}$$
$$(4) \qquad x^0 = 1$$

Another useful result is that the power of a power of x is equal to x raised to the product of the powers,

$$(5) \qquad (x^a)^b = x^{ab}$$

The proof is that $(x^a)^b = [x.x \ldots x$ (a times)] (b times) $= [x.x \ldots x$ (ab times)] $= x^{ab}$.

The quantity $\sqrt[n]{x}$ is known as the 'nth root of x'. If $y = \sqrt[n]{x}$ then y raised to the power n is equal to x, i.e.

$$(6) \qquad \text{if} \quad y = \sqrt[n]{x} \quad \text{then} \quad y^n = x$$

The nth root of a number may be expressed as the number raised to the power $1/n$. This result is a consequence of (5) and (6): from (6) it follows that

$$(\sqrt[n]{x})^n = x$$

Setting $a = 1/n$, $b = n$ in (5) gives

$$(x^{1/n})^n = x$$

Comparing these two equations shows that

$$(7) \qquad \sqrt[n]{x} = x^{1/n}$$

Combining equations (5) and (7) gives a definition of a fractional power:

$$(8) \qquad \sqrt[n]{x^m} = (x^m)^{1/n} = x^{m/n}$$

Equation (8) shows that $x^{m/n}$ is equal to the nth root of x raised to the power m.

Finally, a most important result is that *an even power of any real number is necessarily non-negative*. This is a consequence of the well-known fact that a square of a number is non-negative (if $x > 0$ then $x^2 > 0$, if $x = 0$ then $x^2 = 0$ and if $x < 0$ then $x^2 > 0$, so that $x^2 \geqslant 0$). Setting $a = 2$ in equation (5) shows that an even power of x can be expressed as an integer power of x^2:

$x^c = (x^2)^{c/2}$ where $c/2$ is an integer since c is even. Since x^2 is non-negative, $(x^2)^{c/2} = x^c$ is non-negative, which proves the result.

Example Experiments suggest that the effect of fertilizer on crop yield can be described by the equation

$$C = a\sqrt[3]{F^2}$$

where C is crop yield (bushels per acre) and F is fertilizer application (weight of fertilizer per acre). How does the productivity of fertilizer vary with (i) total fertilizer application, (ii) crop yield?

(i) The productivity of fertilizer is measured by the crop yield per unit fertilizer application, C/F. Writing $C = aF^{2/3}$ we find

$$C/F = aF^{2/3}/F = aF^{-1/3} = a/\sqrt[3]{F}$$

We conclude that the productivity of fertilizer decreases as the reciprocal of the cube root of the fertilizer application. This indicates that the productivity of fertilizer decreases slowly as the application is increased.

(ii) Since $\sqrt[3]{F^2} = C/a$ it follows that

$$F = (F^{2/3})^{3/2} = (C/a)^{3/2}$$

whence

$$C/F = C/(C/a)^{3/2} = a^{3/2}C^{-1/2} = \sqrt{(a^3/C)}$$

We conclude that the productivity of fertilizer varies as the reciprocal of the square root of crop yield, so that productivity decreases as crop yield increases.

2.4 Functions

An economist, working for a firm, draws up a demand schedule for the firm's product, showing how much of the product will be demanded at various prices. This demand schedule might be tabulated as shown in Table 2.1. To present

Table 2.1

Price (£)	*Demand* (*number of units of the product demanded*)
2	116
4	92
6	68
8	44
10	20

such a table in its entirety can be very laborious; furthermore there may be certain general characteristics of the demand for the commodity which it is difficult to appreciate from the table. For example, an inspection of Table 2.1 reveals that demand is systematically related to price in a very simple way. Let D

denote the demand for the commodity (in number of units) and let P denote the price of the commodity (in £); the figures for demand and price given in Table 2.1 are related by the simple equation

$$D = 140 - 12P$$

That this equation is consistent with the figures in Table 2.1 is demonstrated by the calculations shown in Table 2.2. The first line of Table 2.2 tells us that when

Table 2.2

Price	*Demand*
2	$140 - 12 \times 2 = 116$
4	$140 - 12 \times 4 = 92$
6	$140 - 12 \times 6 = 68$
8	$140 - 12 \times 8 = 44$
10	$140 - 12 \times 10 = 20$

$P = 2$ the value of D is $140 - 12 \times 2$. The table as a whole tells us that when P takes on any of the values 10, 8, 6, 4 or 2, the value of D is $140 - 12P$. Consequently the entries in Table 2.1 may be summarized by the equation

$$D = 140 - 12P$$

This is a very convenient way of describing the demand schedule. By making use of more complicated equations a wide variety of economic relationships can be conveniently represented in a mathematical form.

Table 2.1 establishes a correspondence between certain values of demand and certain prices of the product. In mathematical language we say that demand and price are *variables*, since the value that either demand or price takes on many vary. The table illustrates the most general concept of a *function*: it shows a correspondence between certain values of one variable (demand) and certain values of another variable (price). An economist would say simply that 'demand is a function of price', meaning that demand *depends upon* price and that price *determines* demand—in functional notation, $D = f(P)$, which means that the variable on the left, D, is a function of the variable in the bracket, P. On the other hand, a mathematician would say both that demand is a function of price, and that price is a function of demand. The difference arises because the economist looks behind the table of figures at the would-be consumers of the product: so far as these consumers are concerned, the price of the product determines the amount of the commodity they intend to purchase; the mathematician abstracts from these considerations and looks only at the table of figures: two quantities, demand and price, are related, in the sense that for each value of price there is a corresponding value of demand, and vice versa, so that demand may be regarded as a function of price, or price may equally be regarded as a function of demand.

In Table 2.1 the price of the commodity, P, takes on only the values

2, 4, 6, 8, 10. Table 2.2 shows that when P takes on these values the demand, D, takes on values which may be calculated from the equation

$$D = 140 - 12P$$

Now as it stands, this equation can be used to calculate values of D for any value of P. Of course, we know only the demand at five different values of P, and we cannot infer that because this equation gives the demand at five values of P it will also give the true demand for any value of P; however, it seems reasonable to suppose that an approximation to the true value of demand could be obtained from this equation for any price in the range, say, £2–£10. In general, a function which is tabulated for only a few values, as shown in Table 2.1, can often be usefully approximated by a function defined for a whole range of values. If a variable, such as P, can take on any value within a range, say from 2 to 10 inclusive, then it is said to vary continuously over that range. If a variable, such as P, varies continuously over some range then it is impossible to tabulate every value of P and the corresponding value of D. Consequently, the function $D = f(P)$ will no longer be described by a table of numbers but by an equation which is valid over a certain range of values of P: for example, we might write for $D = f(P)$,

$$D = 140 - 12P, \qquad 10 \geqslant P \geqslant 2$$

The expression $10 \geqslant P \geqslant 2$ means that 10 is greater than or equal to P, and P is greater than or equal to 2, i.e. P can take on any value between 2 and 10 inclusive.

2.5 Graphs

A number of mathematical functions, which together can be used to represent a wide variety of economic relationships, are plotted graphically in Figs 2A–2D below. When there are two variables, x and y, and y is a function of x, $y = f(x)$, then x is called the 'argument' of y. When the function $y = f(x)$ is plotted graphically it is usual to measure the values of x along a horizontal axis, and the values of y along a vertical axis.

Figure 2A illustrates the graph of the linear function

$$y = 40 + 5x$$

A function $y = f(x)$ is linear if its graph is a straight line.[1] All linear functions $y = f(x)$ are of the form

$$y = a + bx$$

where a is known as the 'intercept' and b is known as the 'gradient'. This terminology can be explained by referring to Fig. 2A. The function $y = 40 + 5x$, whose graph is shown in Fig. 2A, has an intercept $a = 40$ and a gradient $b = 5$ (compare the function $y = 40 + 5x$ with the general function $y = a + bx$). In the figure, it is seen that the graph of the function cuts the y axis at the point

1 A more general definition of linearity is given in Chapter 14.

marked 40. The point where the graph cuts (or 'intercepts') the y axis is, appropriately, known as the intercept, and so the intercept of the function shown in the figure is 40. In general, the graph of the linear function $y = a + bx$ will intercept the y axis at the point marked a; consequently, a is known as the intercept of the linear function $y = a + bx$. The word 'gradient' is used because of an analogy between the graph of the linear equation and the profile of a steadily rising hill. The gradient of a hill might be given as, say, 1 in 10; this means that, when climbing the hill, for every 10 feet moved horizontally one moves 1 foot vertically; again, a gradient of 5 in 1 means that for every foot moved horizontally, one moves up 5 feet vertically. It is readily seen from the figure that for every incremental unit movement horizontally (parallel to the x axis), a point on the graph moves 5 units vertically (parallel to the y axis),

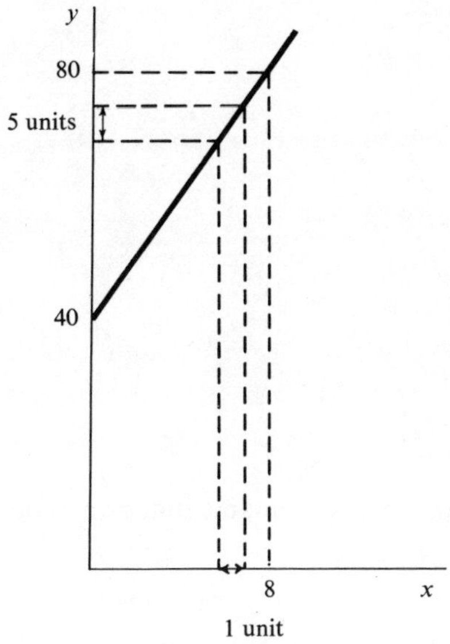

NOTE The scales on the x and y axes differ

Fig. 2A Graph of the function $y=40+5x$

i.e. the graph plotted in Fig. 2A is the profile of a 5 in 1 hill. We say that a 5 in 1 hill has a gradient of $5/1 = 5$, that a 1 in 10 hill has a gradient of $1/10 = 0{\cdot}1$, and so on. From this definition of a gradient, it follows that, in general, the gradient of the graph of the linear function $y = a + bx$ is b. Hence b is said to be the gradient of this linear function.

The linear function $y = 40 + 5x$ could represent the cost schedule of a firm. Let x be the output of the firm in one year (measured in physical units) and let y be the costs of the firm incurred in one year (in £). When the firm produces no output ($x = 0$) the costs of the firm are £40 (since $y = 40$ when $x = 0$). This £40 cost is the 'fixed cost' or 'overhead cost' of the firm, and is incurred independently of the level of output, x. The remaining costs depend on the level of output, x; they are known as variable costs. It is seen from the cost function, $y = 40 + 5x$, that whatever the level of output, producing one additional unit of output incurs an additional cost of £5. We shall see, later, how other aspects of the cost structure of the firm can be deduced from just the one function representing the dependence of costs on output.

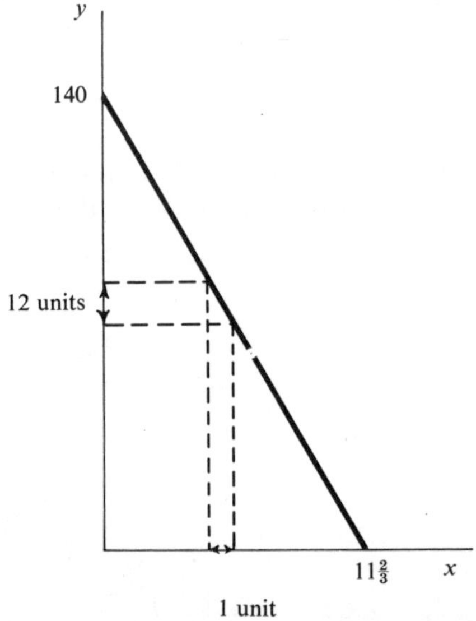

NOTE The scales on the x and y axes differ

Fig. 2B Graph of the function $y = 140 - 12x$

Figure 2B illustrates the graph of the demand function which was described earlier:

$$y = 140 - 12x$$

Here, y represents demand and x represents price.(2) This, again, is a linear function, since it is of the form

$$y = a + bx$$

with an intercept $a = 140$ and a gradient $b = -12$. The gradient is negative; the meaning of this is illustrated in the figure: the graph of the linear function now slopes steadily *downwards* from left to right. An increase of one unit in the price, x (measured horizontally) causes a fall of 12 units in the demand, y (measured vertically). If a fall of 12 units is interpreted as a negative increase—i.e. an increase of -12 units—then the gradient of the graph is calculated to be $-12/1 = -12$. Consequently, a graph which rises from left to right has a positive gradient, a graph which falls from left to right has a negative gradient.

2 Economists usually graph a demand function $y = f(x)$ by plotting demand, y, *horizontally* and price, x, *vertically*. In every other instance they follow the convention given at the beginning of this section: the function $y = f(x)$ is graphed by plotting y vertically and x horizontally.

Table 2.3 Economic relationships which can be represented by the graphs in Figs 2A–D

		Interpretation of		
Figure	*Function*	*y*	*x*	*the function* $y = f(x)$
2A	$y = 40 + 5x$	Cost	Output	Cost curve of a firm
		Output	Price	Supply curve of a commodity
		Demand	Income	Consumption function for a commodity
2B	$y = 140 - 12x$	Demand	Price	Demand curve for a commodity
		Investment	Rate of interest	The marginal efficiency of investment schedule
2C	$y = -40 + 6\frac{2}{3}x - \frac{1}{12}x^2$	Profit	Output	Profit function of a firm
		Net savings	Age	Effect of age on the savings decision of an individual
2D	$y = 40/x + 5$	Average cost	Output	Average cost curve of a firm
		Speculative demand for money	Rate of interest	Keynesian speculative demand for money schedule

Let us suppose that the firm whose demand curve is shown in Fig. 2A is the same as the firm whose cost curve is shown in Fig. 2B. By using only the information contained in the demand curve and the cost curve it is possible to determine the output, or outputs, at which the firm's profit will be a maximum. This has the following implication: if the aim of the owners and managers of the firm is to maximize profit, and if they are able to do this, then the output that the firm will produce is determined only by the firm's demand schedule and cost schedule. Economists quite often assume that the aim of the owners and managers of a firm is to maximize profit. Economists are well aware of the qualifications which are necessary for such an assumption to be realistic; however, it is a very simple assumption, and its implications for economic behaviour are readily deduced by mathematical methods.

Let us see how we can calculate the output, or outputs, at which profit is a maximum. Profit is defined as the difference between revenue and costs. We know how costs depend upon output; if we can find how revenue depends upon output, we can find how the difference between revenue and costs depends upon output, i.e. how profit depends upon output. Having found how profit depends upon output, we can readily find the output or outputs at which profit is a maximum.

We can find how revenue depends upon output in the following way. The revenue is equal to the total number of units sold, Q, multiplied by the price of each unit, P. Suppose that the firm charges a price which is just sufficient to ensure that the output is sold. Then the price charged by the firm must be such that the demand, D, is equal to the output, Q. The demand is given by

$$D = 140 - 12P$$

so that $D = Q$ only if

$$Q = 140 - 12P$$

By rearranging terms in this condition, it becomes

$$12P = 140 - Q$$

On dividing both sides by 12,

$$P = 11\tfrac{2}{3} - \tfrac{1}{12}Q$$

Consequently all the output (Q units) will be sold only if $P = 11\frac{2}{3} - \frac{1}{12}Q$. The total revenue will then be

$$\begin{aligned}\text{Revenue} &= P.Q \\ &= (11\tfrac{2}{3} - \tfrac{1}{12}Q)Q \\ &= 11\tfrac{2}{3}Q - \tfrac{1}{12}Q^2\end{aligned}$$

Costs depend upon output in the way described above, so

$$\text{Cost} = 40 + 5Q$$

It follows that

$$\begin{aligned}\text{Profit} &= \text{Revenue} - \text{Cost} \\ &= 11\tfrac{2}{3}Q - \tfrac{1}{12}Q^2 - (40 + 5Q) \\ &= -40 + 6\tfrac{2}{3}Q - \tfrac{1}{12}Q^2\end{aligned}$$

The graph of profit, y, against output, x, is plotted in Fig. 2C. The function

$$y = -40 + 6\tfrac{2}{3}x - \tfrac{1}{12}x^2$$

is an example of a 'quadratic function'. A quadratic function contains a term in x^2, and possibly a term in x or a constant term, or both, but no other terms besides. The general formula of a quadratic function is

$$y = a + bx + cx^2$$

We have shown so far that for the firm we are considering profit is a quadratic function of output. Having obtained profit as a function of output we can, in principle, determine the output which makes the profit a maximum. It is seen from Fig. 2C that profit is a maximum when the output is 40 units. At this output the profit is £$93\frac{1}{3}$. In fact, there is a very simple, nongraphical way of finding the maximum of a function such as the one described above. This method will be described in Chapter 4.

We conclude this digression by examining how the average cost of a unit of output depends on the firm's level of output. Is it true, for the firm we are studying, that, as is often asserted, the average cost of a unit of output is lower, the higher the level of output? This average cost is obtained by apportioning to

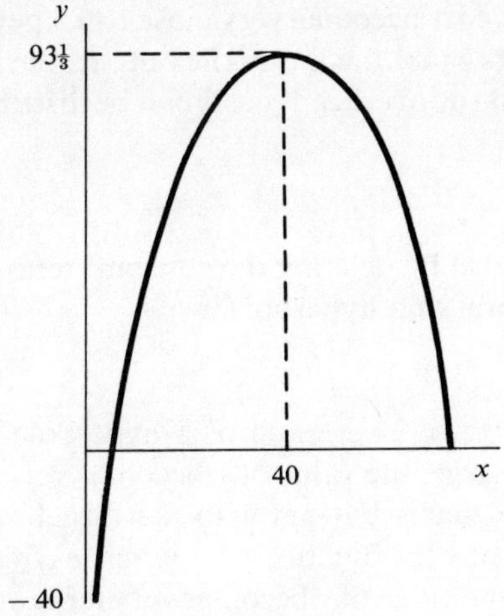

Fig. 2C Graph of the function
$y = -40 + 6\frac{2}{3}x - \frac{1}{12}x^2$

each unit of output an equal share in the total costs of the firm. If Q units of output are produced, then the average cost of one such unit is equal to the total costs of the firm divided by Q. It follows that

$$\begin{aligned} \text{Average cost} &= \text{Total cost}/Q \\ &= (40 + 5Q)/Q \\ &= 40/Q + 5Q/Q \\ &= 40/Q + 5 \end{aligned}$$

The graph of average cost as a function of output is plotted in Fig. 2D. The graph shows that the average cost decreases steadily with output, and that as

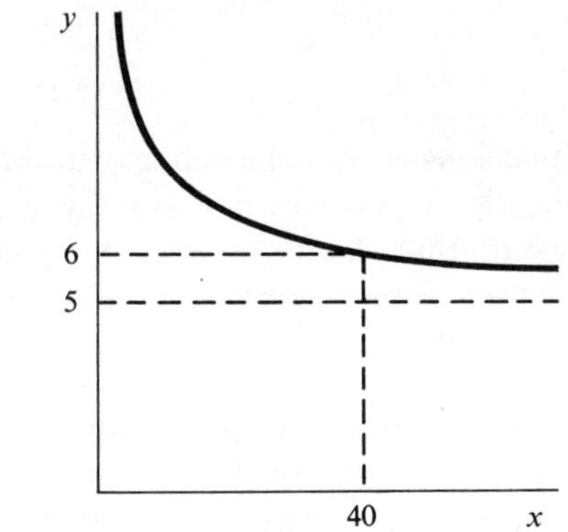

NOTE The scales on the x and y axes differ

Fig. 2D Graph of the function
$y = 40/x + 5$

output becomes very large, the average cost becomes very close to £5 per unit. The average cost decreases in this way because the larger the output, the larger the number of units over which the fixed (or overhead) costs can be distributed. The function

$$y = 40/x$$

which is obtained from the function above by deleting the constant term, is an example of a hyperbola. The general form of a hyperbola is

$$y = a/x$$

where a can take on any value except zero. The graph of a hyperbola has a characteristic form. As x becomes very large, the value of y becomes very small and the graph steadily approaches the x axis but never in fact touches it or intersects it: we say that for large values of x the function $y = a/x$ is 'asymptotic to' the x axis. As x becomes very small, the value of y becomes very large and the graph steadily approaches the y axis without either touching it or intersecting it, i.e. for small values of x the function $y = a/x$ is asymptotic to the y axis.

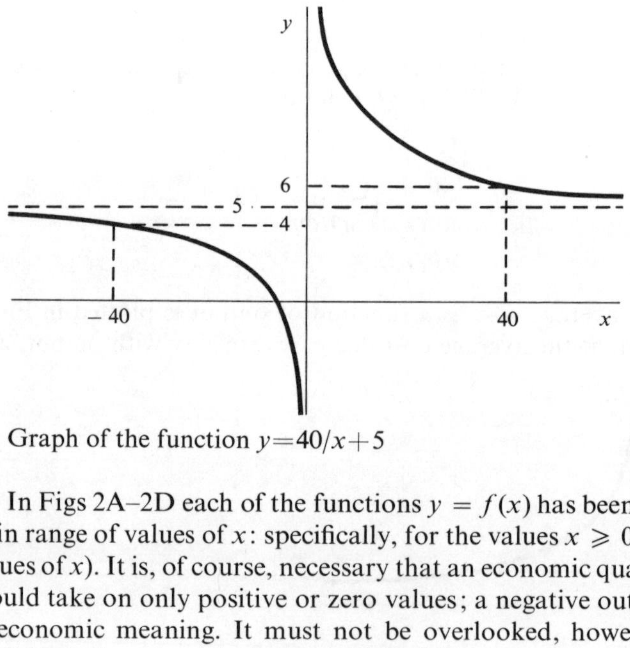

Fig. 2E Graph of the function $y=40/x+5$

In Figs 2A–2D each of the functions $y = f(x)$ has been plotted only for a certain range of values of x: specifically, for the values $x \geqslant 0$ (i.e. positive or zero values of x). It is, of course, necessary that an economic quantity such as output should take on only positive or zero values; a negative output does not have any economic meaning. It must not be overlooked, however, that the mathematical functions described above can be defined for almost any value of x. Figure 2E, for example, shows the values of the function $y = 40/x + 5$ for negative values of x. Notice, however, that when x approaches 0, the value of y becomes arbitrarily large, and it is not possible to define this function for the special case $x = 0$.

It is usually possible to sketch the graph of a function without having to plot a large number of points and then connect them up. The secret is to inspect the function to see if it belongs to a recognizable class of functions: if it does, the properties of this class of functions can often be used to fix the graph by plotting only a very few points. For example, since the graph of a linear function is a straight line, once any two points on the graph have been plotted, the rest of the graph can be plotted by ruling a straight line through the two points. The graph of every quadratic function is a parabola: for any particular quadratic the exact position and scale of the parabola is uniquely determined by plotting just three points.

A linear function and a quadratic function are special cases of a 'polynomial function'. A polynomial function of degree n has the form

$$y = a_0 + a_1x + a_2x^2 + \cdots + a_nx^n$$

where the coefficients $a_0, a_1, \ldots, a_{n-1}$ may take on any value, and the coefficient a_n may take on any nonzero value. An example of a polynomial function of degree 4 is

$$y = 8 - 22x + 21x^2 - 8x^3 + x^4$$

The degree, n, of the polynomial is usually a positive integer, though sometimes the constant function, $y = a_0$, is referred to as a polynomial of degree zero. The graph of a polynomial is always smooth, sometimes oscillatory, and tends to infinitely large (positive or negative) values for large values of the argument; the graph of a typical polynomial is shown in Fig. 2F.

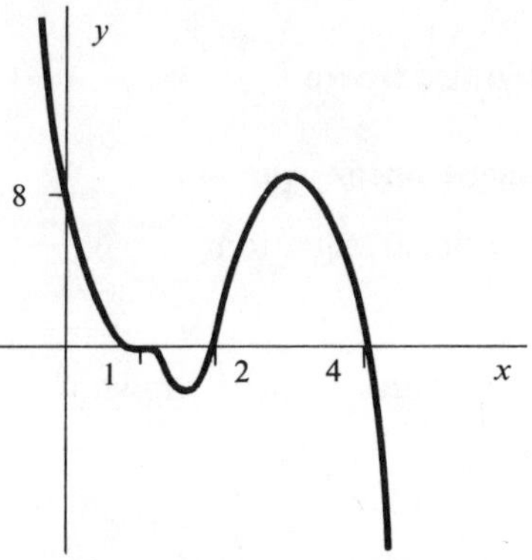

Fig. 2F Graph of the function $y = 8 - 22x + 21x^2 - 8x^3 + x^4$

All the functions discussed in this chapter are examples of 'rational functions'. A rational function is a function which is the ratio of two polynomials—hence the terminology '*ratio*nal function'. The general form of a rational function is

$$y = \frac{b_0 + b_1x + b_2x^2 + \cdots + b_px^p}{c_0 + c_1x + c_2x^2 + \cdots + c_qx^q}$$

where $p, q = 0, 1, 2, 3, \ldots$, and so on. Rational functions have many convenient properties, and are generally adequate to represent simple economic relationships between two variables, y and x. If a rational function is not a polynomial then its graph is not completely smooth: the graph will have one or more kinks or discontinuities (and possibly both); for example, see Fig. 2E, where there is a discontinuity at $x = 0$.

2.6 Continuity

A continuous function $y = f(x)$ is one for which an arbitrarily small change in the value of x always induces an arbitrarily small change in the value of y, i.e. the value of the function never jumps from one value to another very different value due to a small change in the value of the variable x. Formally, a function $y = f(x)$ is continuous at x if for any δ there is an ε such that $|f(x + h) - f(x)| < \delta$ for any h, $|h| < \varepsilon$. The graph of a continuous function is—roughly speaking—a continuous line with no sudden jumps or rapid oscillations. Figure 2E shows the graph of a function which is continuous everywhere except at $x = 0$. At $x = 0$ there is a discontinuity of infinitely large magnitude.

A smooth function is a continuous function for which an arbitrarily small change in the value of x always induces an arbitrarily small change in the slope of the graph. It is usual to measure the slope of the graph by the derivative of the function (see Section 4.3). If the slope is measured in this way, a smooth function may be defined as a continuous function whose derivative is also a continuous function of x. A function which is not smooth has a graph with one or more kinks or discontinuities.

2.7 Solution of equations

(a) Solution of a single linear equation

The general solution of the linear equation

$$y = a + bx$$

where a, b and y are known values is easily shown to be

$$x = (y - a)/b$$

provided that $b \neq 0$.

Example Suppose that the growth of car ownership (in millions of vehicles) since 1960 can be described by the equation

$$C = 5 + 0{\cdot}08t$$

where C is the number of cars and t is an index of time: $t = 0$ in 1960, $t = 1$ in 1961, and so on. At what date will car ownership reach 7 million?

Setting $C = 7$ gives the equation

$$7 = 5 + 0{\cdot}08t$$

Putting $a = 5$, $b = 0{\cdot}08$, $y = 7$ and $x = t$ into the formula above we find

$$t = (7 - 5)/0{\cdot}08 = 25$$

We conclude that car ownership will reach 7 million in 1985.

(b) Roots of a quadratic equation

The solutions of a quadratic equation are known as its roots. To find the roots of a quadratic equation

$$y = ax^2 + bx + k$$

where y, a, b, k are known values it is convenient to first of all subtract y from both sides, to get

$$0 = ax^2 + bx + k - y$$

Make the substitution $c = k - y$. The resulting equation

$$0 = ax^2 + bx + c$$

is solved by setting

$$x = \frac{-b + \sqrt{(b^2 - 4ac)}}{2a} \quad \text{and} \quad x = \frac{-b - \sqrt{(b^2 - 4ac)}}{2a}$$

Since a negative number does not have a square root, the roots of the quadratic exist only if $b^2 - 4ac \geqslant 0$. The formulae may be derived by the method of completing the square (described in all good school mathematics books). Discussion of what happens when $b^2 < 4ac$ is deferred until Chapter 19.

Example A car sells for £1,200. It can be purchased on H.P. by paying one-third down and two yearly instalments of £500 payable at the end of each year. What is the rate of interest charged by the hire purchase company?

Let $100r\%$ per annum be the unknown rate of interest. By using H.P. the customer receives a loan of $\frac{2}{3} \times$ £1,200 = £800 for the first year, which means that at the end of the year his indebtedness is £$800(1 + r)$. By paying the first instalment his indebtedness for the second year is reduced to £$800(1 + r) - 500$. At the end of the second year the customer owes £$(1 + r)[800(1 + r) - 500]$ and, by assumption, these debts are liquidated by the second instalment of £500; consequently

$$500 = (1 + r)[800(1 + r) - 500]$$

Dividing both sides by 100, multiplying out and rearranging terms gives

$$-2 + 11r + 8r^2 = 0$$

The formulae for the solutions of a quadratic equation give

$$r = \frac{-11 + \sqrt{(121 + 64)}}{16} \quad \text{and} \quad r = \frac{-11 - \sqrt{(121 + 64)}}{16}$$

The second root is negative and so is not the solution required. Evaluating the first root using square-root tables gives $r = 0{\cdot}16$ to two decimal places. We conclude that the rate of interest charged by the hire purchase company is 16% per annum.

(c) Solution of simultaneous linear equations

A typical set of simultaneous linear equations is shown below; the three linear equations (1)–(3) are to be solved for the three unknowns x_1, x_2, x_3:

$$\begin{array}{ll} (1) & 3x_1 + x_2 - 4x_3 = -3 \\ (2) & x_1 + 2x_2 + 6x_3 = 7 \\ (3) & -x_1 - x_2 + 2x_3 = 5 \end{array}$$

The method most commonly used for the numerical solution of simultaneous linear equations is to reduce the equations by algebraic manipulation to a single equation in a single unknown. The method works provided that a solution exists and is unique (what happens if there is no unique solution is described in Chapter 12). A systematic procedure based on this method is used to solve simultaneous equations on a computer. In the case where the number of equations is equal to the number of unknowns the method works as follows. By multiplying through all but one of the equations with suitable numbers and then either adding or subtracting them from the remaining equation it is possible to eliminate one of the unknowns and at the same time reduce the number of equations by one. Repeated application of this procedure reduces both the number of equations and the number of unknowns by one each time, until finally there is just one equation in one unknown. If the original equations were linear then the final equation is also linear, and so it can be solved using the formula in paragraph (a) above. Having evaluated one of the unknowns, the values of the other unknowns can be found by back substitution.

Applying this method to the solution of the equations above, the first step is to decide which variables are to be eliminated. One way of proceeding (though not the best) is to begin by eliminating x_1. Multiplying the second equation throughout by 3 gives

$$(4) = (2) \times 3 \qquad 3x_1 + 6x_2 + 18x_3 = 21$$

The expression on the left is a mnemonic indicating that equation (4) is equal to equation (2) multiplied through by 3. Such mnemonics are a useful way of keeping track of the calculations.

Subtracting (4) from (1) gives

$$(5) = (1) - (4) \qquad -5x_2 - 22x_3 = -24$$

Multiplying the third equation throughout by 3 gives

$$(6) = (3) \times 3 \qquad -3x_1 - 3x_2 + 6x_2 = 15$$

Adding (6) to (1) gives

$$(7) = (1) + (6) \qquad -2x_2 + 2x_3 = 12$$

Equations (5) and (7) constitute a set of two simultaneous linear equations in the two unknowns x_2, x_3. The two equations may be reduced to just one equation in one unknown by repeating the same procedure.

Multiplying equation (7) by 11 gives

(8) $= (7) \times 11 \qquad -22x_2 + 22x_3 = 132$

Adding (8) to (5) gives

(9) $= (5) + (8) \qquad -27x_2 = 108$

whence

(10) $\qquad x_2 = -4$

Substituting (10) into (7) gives

(11) $\qquad x_3 = 2$

and substituting (10) and (11) into (3) gives

(12) $\qquad x_1 = 3$

The solution of equations (1)–(3) is therefore $x_1 = 3$, $x_2 = -4$, $x_3 = 2$. It should be appreciated that the method described above does not give a simple algebraic formula for the solution of simultaneous linear equations; formulae do exist, but they are useful mainly for analysing the general properties of the solution rather than for solving numerical examples (see Chapter 11). An example of the economic application of simultaneous equations has already been described in Section 1.4. Another example is given below.

Example An economist believes that over the past two years there has been an inverse relationship between unemployment U (the number of unemployed as a percentage of the work force) and the rate of inflation I (the percentage increase in prices each year). He has just two sets of annual observations: $I = 7$ when $U = 1$ and $I = 3$ when $U = 1{\cdot}8$. The precise form of the relationship is believed to be

$$I = a + b/U$$

If the hypothesis is correct, what are the values of a and b? If unemployment is reduced to 0·5% what will be the rate of inflation?

Substituting the first set of observations into the equation gives

$$7 = a + b$$

and substituting in the second set gives

$$3 = a + (\tfrac{10}{18})b$$

This is a set of two simultaneous linear equations in the two unknowns a, b. Subtracting the second equation from the first gives

$$4 = (\tfrac{8}{18})b$$

whence

$$b = 9$$

Substituting this result into either the first or the second equation gives

$$a = -2$$

Since $I = -2 + 9/U$ it follows that if $U = 0{\cdot}5$ then $I = 16$, i.e. when unemployment is 0·5% the rate of inflation will be 16% per annum.

2.8 Geometric series

Geometric series have many applications in economics, the most important being the dynamic analysis of markets discussed in Chapter 3.

A geometric series of N terms is a sequence

$$a, ac, ac^2, \ldots, ac^{N-1}$$

where a and c are any real numbers. Most applications require a knowledge of the sum of the series, for which there is a very simple formula (see below). A geometric series may continue indefinitely, namely

$$a, ac, ac^2, \ldots$$

When a series continues indefinitely every term has another term after it, so that there is no 'last term'. A series which continues indefinitely is known as an infinite series.[3] Despite the fact that an infinite series has no 'last term' it is still possible for the sum of the series to have a definite value, as the following example shows.

Example When $a = 1$, $c = \frac{1}{2}$ the sum of the infinite geometric series $a, ac, ac^2, \ldots$, is

$$1 + \tfrac{1}{2} + (\tfrac{1}{2})^2 + \cdots = 2$$

PROOF Consider the process of subdividing a line AA′ of length 2.

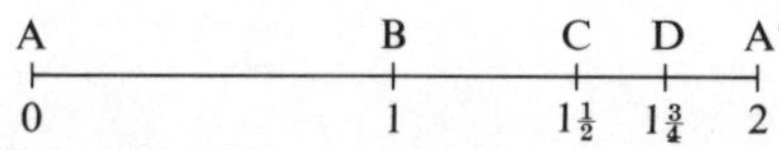

Step 1 Take the left-hand half of AA′: the length of AB is 1.
The length of the remainder BA′ is 1.
Step 2 Take the left-hand half of BA′: the length of BC is $\frac{1}{2}$.
The length of the remainder CA′ is $\frac{1}{2}$.
Step 3 Take the left-hand half of CA′: the length of CD is $\frac{1}{4}$.
The length of the remainder DA′ is $\frac{1}{4}$.

As we continue this process step by step the lengths of the left-hand segments are respectively $1, \frac{1}{2}, (\frac{1}{2})^2, \ldots$.

After N steps the total length of the left-hand segments is

$$1 + \tfrac{1}{2} + (\tfrac{1}{2})^2 + \cdots + (\tfrac{1}{2})^{N-1}$$

3 Great care is needed with the term 'infinite'. In mathematics a quantity is defined to be infinite if it is greater than any number, however large. In this sense the number of terms in a series which continues indefinitely is infinite, hence the terminology 'infinite series'.

and the length of the remainder is $(\frac{1}{2})^N \times 2$. Clearly, the more terms that are added into the series the closer the length of the left-hand segments becomes to the total length of the line. By continuing the process it is possible to make the difference between the length of the left-hand segments and the length of the line as small as we like; i.e. the sum of the infinite series $1 + \frac{1}{2} + (\frac{1}{2})^2 + \cdots$ is equal to 2. More precisely,

$$\begin{aligned} & 1 + \tfrac{1}{2} + (\tfrac{1}{2})^2 + \cdots + (\tfrac{1}{2})^{N-1} \\ &= \text{The length of the left-hand segments} \\ &= \text{The length of AA}' - \text{The length of the remainder} \\ &= 2 - (\tfrac{1}{2})^N \times 2 \\ &= 2(1 - (\tfrac{1}{2})^N) \end{aligned}$$

As N becomes very large, $(\frac{1}{2})^N$ becomes very small. Hence we may write

$$\lim_{N \to \infty} 2(1 - (\tfrac{1}{2})^N) = 2$$

This example illustrates a special case of two important theorems.

Theorem 2.1 The sum of the first N terms of the geometric series $a, ac, ac^2, \ldots$ is

$$\sum_{i=0}^{N-1} ac^i = a + ac + ac^2 + \cdots + ac^{N-1} = a(1 - c^N)/(1 - c)$$

provided that $c \neq 1$. If $c = 1$ then the sum of the first N terms is aN.

PROOF The proof for $c \neq 1$ is a matter of elementary algebra.[4] When $0 < c < 1$ the proof can be based on the proof of the example, by drawing a line of length $1/(1 - c)$ and performing N successive divisions in the ratio $1 - c{:}c$. The proof for $c = 1$ is trivial.

Theorem 2.2 The sum of the infinite geometric series $a, ac, ac^2, \ldots,$ is

$$\sum_{i=0}^{\infty} ac^i = a + ac + ac^2 + \cdots = a/(1 - c)$$

provided that $-1 < c < 1$.

4 Simple algebraic manipulation shows that

$$\frac{1}{1-c} = \frac{1-c+c}{1-c} = \frac{1-c}{1-c} + \frac{c}{1-c} = 1 + \frac{c}{1-c} = 1 + c\left(\frac{1}{1-c}\right)$$

Repeating this algebraic manipulation on the term in brackets gives

$$1 + c\left(\frac{1}{1-c}\right) = 1 + c\left(1 + c\frac{1}{1-c}\right) = 1 + c + c^2\left(\frac{1}{1-c}\right)$$

Successive application of this procedure shows that

$$\frac{1}{1-c} = 1 + c + c^2 + \cdots c^{N-1} + c^N\left(\frac{1}{1-c}\right)$$

for any N. Grouping the terms in $1/(1 - c)$ gives

$$1 + c + c^2 + \cdots + c^{N-1} = (1 - c^N)/(1 - c)$$

Multiplying both sides by a establishes Theorem 2.1.

PROOF The proof follows from Theorem 2.1 provided that the term c^N becomes negligible as the number of terms N increases indefinitely; it is easily verified that c^N tends to zero as N becomes large provided that $-1 < c < 1$.

2.9 Limits

The intuitive concept of a limit was introduced in the discussion of geometric series. It is essential to understand the more rigorous mathematical concept of a limit before embarking on a study of differential calculus.

Consider an infinite sequence of real numbers

$$a_0, a_1, a_2, \ldots$$

The sequence is said to converge to a limiting value A if the values of all the terms beyond some particular term a_N are arbitrarily close to A. Two numbers are close to one another when the difference between them is very small and they are *arbitrarily* close when the difference does not exceed some specified value, however small. These ideas are summarized in the formal definition of a limit given below.

Definition of a limit

The infinite sequence of real numbers

$$a_0, a_1, a_2, \ldots$$

converges to the limiting value A if for any value δ, however small, the sequence contains a term a_N such that all terms following a_N satisfy the inequality

$$|a_k - A| < \delta \qquad (k > N)$$

Generally speaking, the value of N will be greater the smaller the required value of δ.

If a sequence $a_0, a_1, a_2, \ldots,$ converges to A we write

$$\lim_{N \to \infty} a_N = A$$

Example Find the limit of the sequence

$$\tfrac{2}{1}, \tfrac{3}{2}, \tfrac{4}{3}, \tfrac{5}{4}, \ldots.$$

The Nth term of the sequence is $(N + 1)/N = 1 + (1/N)$ so that as N becomes very large the limit of the sequence is

$$\lim_{N \to \infty} \left(1 + \frac{1}{N}\right) = 1 + \lim_{N \to \infty} \frac{1}{N}$$

Now for any value $\delta > 0$ we can find a value of N such that $(1/N) < \delta$, in which case any number $k > N$ will satisfy $(1/k) < \delta$. It follows from the definition of a limit that

$$\lim_{N \to \infty} \frac{1}{N} = 0$$

Consequently

$$\lim_{N\to\infty}\left(1+\frac{1}{N}\right) = 1 + \lim_{N\to\infty}\frac{1}{N} = 1 + 0 = 1$$

We conclude that the sequence converges to unity.

An important property of limits is that the limit of a product is equal to the product of the limits. Consider two sequences $a_0, a_1, a_2, \cdots$, and $b_0, b_1, b_2, \ldots$, each of which converges to a limit,

$$\lim_{N\to\infty} a_N = A, \qquad \lim_{N\to\infty} b_N = B$$

By simple algebra

$$a_k b_k - AB = (a_k - A)b_k + (b_k - B)A$$

and from the rules of absolute values

$$|a_k b_k - AB| \leqslant |a_k - A||b_k| + |b_k - B||A|$$

It is a consequence of the definition of a limit that for any arbitrarily small value $\delta > 0$ there are numbers N_a, N_b such that

$$|a_k - A| < \delta \qquad (k > N_a)$$

$$|b_k - B| < \delta \qquad (k > N_b)$$

Taking M to be the larger of N_a, N_b, we find that for $k > M$,

$$|a_k - A| < \delta, \qquad |b_k - B| < \delta \qquad (k > M)$$

whence

$$\begin{aligned} |a_k b_k - AB| &\leqslant |\delta|(|B| + |\delta|) + |\delta||A| \qquad (k > M) \\ &= (|A| + |B|)|\delta| + |\delta|^2 \end{aligned}$$

Consequently by choosing δ sufficiently small we can make all terms $|a_k b_k - AB|$ for $k > M$ as small as we like, which proves that

$$\lim_{M\to\infty} a_M b_M = AB$$

Notes and references

Students who have difficulty with this chapter should consult Allen,[6] Ch. 1–5, Lewis,[79] Ch. 1, 2, Yamane,[126] Ch. 1, 2 and Meier and Archer,[83] Ch. 1–5.

Problems

2.1 Which of the following numbers are (a) integers, (b) rational numbers, (c) irrational numbers, (d) real numbers?

13, −8·4, 1/7, $\sqrt{2}$, 0

2.2 Express the following statements in the notation of Section 2.2.

(a) More than one million men are unemployed.
(b) At least 150,000 new cars are demanded this year.
(c) The price of butter exceeds the price of margarine.
(d) No more than ten ships are required to handle the traffic.
(e) The number of new jobs created this year will not exceed 25,000.

(f) The liquidity ratio is normally between 30 and 35% (exclusive).

(g) The number of machines required is usually not less than ten and no more than twenty.

2.3.1 Find the absolute values of (a) -3, (b) $(-2) \times (-4) \times (-1)$, (c) $(-\frac{3}{4}) \times (-\frac{1}{2})$.

2.3.2 Rewrite the following expressions using the Σ notation.

(a) $(x_1/N) + (x_2/N) + (x_3/N) + (x_4/N)$

(b) $x_1y_1 + x_2y_2 + x_3y_3 + x_4y_4 + x_5y_5$

(c) $x_1^2x_3 + x_2^2x_4 + x_3^2x_5 + x_4^2x_6$

2.3.3 Given that $x^2 = 16$ and $x^3 = 64$, evaluate (a) x^5, (b) x^{-1}, (c) $\sqrt{x^6}$.

2.3.4 A firm's rate of output, Q, depends upon the number of men employed, L, and the number of machines in use, K. If the functional relationship is

$$Q = AL^{1/2}K^{1/2}$$

where A is a constant of proportionality, show that the productivities of labour and machinery depend only on the ratio of the number of men employed to the number of machines in use.

2.4.1 The following table shows the relation between cost and output in a hypothetical firm. Show that the figures in the table can be summarized by the equation $C = 40 + 20Q + 4Q^2$ where C is the cost and Q is the output.

Output (*number of units*)	*Cost* (£)
0	40
1	64
2	96
3	136
4	184
5	240

From the table above derive a table showing how the cost of an additional unit of output depends upon the level of output. Show that the figures in the table can be summarized by the equation $\Delta C = 24 + 8Q$ where ΔC is the cost of an additional unit of output and Q is the level of output. Show how this equation can be derived directly from the equation $C = 40 + 20Q + 4Q^2$. (*Hint:* compare the cost of producing an output Q with the cost of producing an output $Q + 1$.)

2.4.2 One of the features which distinguishes the labour market from a typical commodity market is the way in which the supply of labour (measured in man-hours of work) depends upon the price of labour (measured by the wage rate). When the price paid for labour is high *an increase in price may decrease* (*rather than increase*) *the supply*. (The explanation is that when wage rates are high, wage earners' incomes are high and so wage earners become very willing to sacrifice additional income in order to enjoy more leisure; consequently, although an increase in the wage rate has some tendency to increase the desired hours of work because of the higher reward, it has an even greater tendency to reduce the desired hours of work because of the opportunity provided to workers of enjoying more leisure without reducing earnings.) At lower wage rates the supply of labour is more normal, in that an increase in the wage rate increases the desired number of hours work. The demand for labour is similar to the demand for most other commodities: an increase in the wage rate tends to decrease the demand.

(a) Graph typical demand and supply curves of labour, plotting the wage rate vertically and the quantity of labour demanded and the quantity of labour supplied horizontally.

(b) Show graphically that it is possible that there is no wage rate at which the demand for labour is equal to the supply.

(c) Show graphically that it is possible that there is more than one wage rate at which demand is equal to supply.

(d) Given the demand and supply curves of labour, outline how mathematical methods could be used to determine whether there is a unique wage rate at which the supply of labour is equal to the demand.

2.4.3 Two countries A and B trade only with one another. The value of A's imports (= the value of B's exports) is equal to $\frac{1}{4}$ of the value of A's national income; the value of B's imports (= the value of A's exports) is equal to $\frac{1}{5}$ of the value of B's national income. The aim of government policy in country A is to achieve a £2m surplus in the balance of trade (i.e. for the value of A's exports to exceed the value of A's imports by £2m). (i) If B's national income is £40m what should be the target value of A's national income? (ii) If the aim of government policy in country A were to achieve a £3m surplus in the balance of trade, would the target value of A's income be higher or lower than before? (iii) In the light of your answer to part (ii), do you think that, for country A, a policy of a large surplus in the balance of trade is compatible with a policy of full employment? Give reasons for your answer.

2.5.1 Graph the following functions, paying particular attention to their behaviour when x is very small, very large and positive and very large and negative.

(a) $y = 100 + x$
(b) $y = 50 + x^2$
(c) $y = x^3$
(d) $y = 1/x$
(e) $y = 1/(x - 4)$
(f) $y = 200x - x^2$

Which of these functions do you think would best represent (a) the relationship between the output of a firm, y, and the number of men employed, x, (b) the supply curve of a commodity which is easy to produce in small amounts but is very difficult to produce in large amounts (the supply curve relates the amount supplied, y, to the market price, x)? For what range of values of x are the above representations valid?

2.5.2 The expenditure of a household on consumer goods, C, is related to the household's income, Y, in the following way. When household income is £1,000 the expenditure on consumer goods is £900, and whenever income is increased by £100 the expenditure on consumer goods is increased by £80. Express the expenditure on consumer goods as a mathematical function of income.

2.5.3 The demand for a firm's product is $D = 120 - P$ where D is the quantity demanded and P is the price of the product. The firm's total costs are given by $C = 400 + 0{\cdot}5Q^2$ where Q is the quantity produced. If the firm only produces what it can sell, and no more, write down the revenue of the firm as a function of the quantity produced. What is the firm's profit when output is 50 units? Determine graphically the output at which profit is a maximum.

2.6 By graphing the following functions determine whether they are (a) continuous and (b) smooth:

(i) $y = \begin{cases} 40 + 4x & \text{for } 0 \leqslant x \leqslant 5 \\ 50 + 4x & \text{for } x > 5 \end{cases}$

(ii) $y = \begin{cases} 40 + 4x & \text{for } 0 \leqslant x \leqslant 10 \\ 8x & \text{for } x > 10 \end{cases}$

(iii) $y = x^3$
(iv) $y = 1/x^3$

2.7.1 Solve each of the following equations for x.

(a) $10 = 2 + 4x$
(b) $5 = 9 - 8x$

2.7.2 The quantity of a product demanded, D, depends upon price, P, in the following way:

$$D = 10 + (10/P)$$

If 15 units are sold, what is the price?

2.7.3 Solve the following quadratic equations

(a) $2x^2 + 6x - 56 = 0$
(b) $x^2 + 6x + 9 = 0$
(c) $x^2 - 15x - 34 = 0$
(d) $3x^2 - 7x + 2 = 0$

2.7.4 A man borrows £220 on personal credit. If he arranges to make two repayments of £144 one year and two years hence, what is the rate of interest on the loan?

2.7.5 Solve the following sets of simultaneous equations.

(a) $2x_1 + 3x_2 = 8$
$3x_1 - x_2 = 1$

(b) $3x_1 + 2x_2 = 18$
$2x_1 + x_2 = 11$

2.7.6 If two pounds of sugar and a bottle of milk cost 25p, and a pound of sugar and two bottles of milk cost 20p, what are the prices of sugar and milk?

2.7.7 There is a linear relationship between imports and national income. In two previous years imports, M, and national income, Y, were (in £1,000m) $M = 19$, $Y = 36$ and $M = 20$, $Y = 40$. Predict the value of imports if national income is expected to be £42,000m next year.

2.8.1 Use the formula for the sum of a geometric series to evaluate
(a) $1 + \frac{1}{4} + (\frac{1}{4})^2$
(b) $1 + (\frac{2}{3}) + (\frac{4}{9}) + (\frac{8}{27})$
(c) $1 + 2 + 4 + 8 + 16$

Check your answers by direct calculation.

2.8.2 Use the formula for the sum of an infinite geometric series to evaluate
(a) $1 + \frac{1}{5} + (\frac{1}{5})^2 + \cdots$
(b) $5 + 2\frac{1}{2} + 1\frac{1}{4} + \frac{5}{8} + \cdots$

2.9 Find the limits of the following sequences.
(a) $\frac{1}{2}, \frac{2}{3}, \frac{3}{4}, \frac{4}{5}, \ldots$
(b) $2^2/1^2, 3^2/2^2, 4^2/3^2, 5^2/4^2, \ldots$

Chapter 3

Elementary mathematics applied to macro and microeconomics

3.1 Introduction

Macroeconomics is the study of economic aggregates, e.g. national income, total employment, the balance of payments. It is contrasted with microeconomics which studies individual behaviour rather than aggregate behaviour.

In economics it is important to distinguish not only *fields* of study but also *methods* of study. A fundamental distinction is between static analysis and dynamic analysis. Static analysis looks at the economy at an instant of time, whereas dynamic analysis studies the evolution of the economy over time. *Economic analysis is dynamic or static depending on whether time is or is not allowed to vary.*

Not only is it necessary to distinguish dynamic analysis from static analysis; it is also necessary to distinguish dynamic models from static models. By a model is meant a set of one or more functional relations involving one or more variables. *A model is static if all the variables in the model are measured at the same time, t. A model is dynamic if it involves one or more variables measured at the different times t_1, t_2.*

These concepts may be clarified by a simple analogy. A static analysis may be likened to the study of a snapshot taken at an instant of time. A dynamic analysis may be likened to the study of a film taken over a period. A model accounts for what is seen in each frame of such a film. If the model is static, what is seen in any particular frame is independent of what is seen in the other frames; if the model is dynamic, what is seen in one frame influences what will be seen in subsequent frames, so that the film acquires some kind of continuity because of the relation between one frame and the next.

3.2 Static and dynamic models

(a) An elementary static macroeconomic model

The simplest macroeconomic model of the economy is concerned with the interaction of the aggregate demand and aggregate supply of goods. In a simple model it is usual to ignore foreign trade and government spending and taxation.

As a result, the aggregate demand for goods is assumed to have only two components: the demand of households for consumer goods and the demand of businesses for investment goods.

The demand of households for consumer goods depends on the income of the households. As a rule, households spend only a fraction of the income they receive; at lower levels of income this fraction tends to be larger than at higher levels of income. It has been found that, in the aggregate, the demand for consumer goods is adequately explained by a simple linear relation between households' demand for consumer goods, C, and income, Y. This linear relation is written

$$C = b + cY$$

where $b > 0$. According to this equation the effect of a marginal unit increase in aggregate income is to increase consumer demand by c units. For this reason the parameter c is called 'the marginal propensity to consume'.

So far as business investment is concerned, it is assumed that the demand for investment goods is independent of income; indeed, it is widely accepted that rather than being determined by the state of the economy business investment itself is one of the most important determinants of the state of the economy.[1] The aggregate demand in the economy may be expressed mathematically in the following way:

$$\begin{aligned} \text{Aggregate demand} &= \text{Consumer demand} + \text{Investment demand} \\ &= C + I \\ &= b + cY + I \end{aligned}$$

In order to complete this simple model of the economy it is necessary to describe the aggregate supply of goods. Now the aggregate supply may be measured by the value of the goods produced in the economy, and the value of these goods is equal to the value of the factor services used up in their production. In the simple economy which we are discussing the income of households is derived solely from the ownership of factor services used up in domestic production—rent from land, interest from capital, profit from risk taking, wages from labour, and so on. It follows that in this simple economy the aggregate supply of goods is equal to the income of the households, Y, i.e.

$$\text{Aggregate supply} = Y$$

(b) An elementary dynamic macroeconomic model

According to the definition given at the beginning of this chapter, a model is dynamic if it involves a functional relationship between variables measured at different times. In order to describe a dynamic model it is therefore convenient to write all the variables as functions of time, t.

Let us consider again the simple economy described in (a) above.

1 This is not to say that business investment is independent of the expected state of the economy at some future time.

The aggregate demand in period t has two components: consumer demand in period t, $C(t)$, and investment demand in period t, $I(t)$.

Suppose that there is a lag in consumption out of income: to be specific, suppose that one period elapses between the time the households receive their factor income and the time at which they spend this income on consumer goods. If there is a linear relation between consumption and income then consumption in period t is a linear function of income in period $t - 1$, i.e.

$$C(t) = b + cY(t - 1)$$

As before, investment in any period, $I(t)$ is independent of either current or previous values of income. It follows that aggregate demand in any period t may be expressed mathematically as follows:

$$\text{Aggregate demand in period } t = C(t) + I(t)$$
$$= b + cY(t - 1) + I(t)$$

Suppose that the aggregate supply in period t is always adjusted to meet the aggregate demand in period t, i.e. in the short run, businessmen always hire sufficient factors to produce the output which will satisfy aggregate demand.[2] Since total factor income in any one period is equal to the aggregate supply in that period, and since aggregate supply is adjusted to equal aggregate demand in the same period, it follows that the total factor income is equal to the aggregate demand, i.e.

$$\text{Aggregate demand in period } t = Y(t)$$

This is the second of two equations for aggregate demand in period t. On comparing the right-hand sides of the two equations it is seen that

$$Y(t) = b + cY(t - 1) + I(t)$$

This equation expresses income in any period as a function of income in the previous period and investment in the current period. The model described by this equation is dynamic because it establishes a relationship between the value of income at two different times. A relationship of this kind arises because of the lag in consumption out of income. If there were no such lag, so that consumption depended on income in the current period, then income at any time would be independent of income previously and the model would be static.

(c) An elementary static microeconomic model

Consider a competitive market for a consumer good such as packaged frozen food. When firms in an industry follow a profit-maximizing policy, their planned output depends on the price they believe the product will sell for. If the expectations of managers are based on the ruling market price then the total amount of the consumer good supplied, S, is a function of the market price, P:

$$S = f(P)$$

2 The possibility that demand may be met by running down inventories is ignored.

Consumer demand for the good depends on aggregate consumer income and the price of substitutes and complements (substitutes for frozen foods are fresh food, freeze-dried food, etc.; an important complement is a refrigerator). Let D be consumer demand, Y be income and $P_1, \ldots, P_m$ be the prices of substitutes and complements; then

$$D = f(P, P_1, \ldots, P_m, Y)$$

The precise form of the function $f(\ )$ depends on consumer tastes. In order to simplify the model we assume that both the demand and supply schedules are linear, and that the prices of substitutes and complements have a negligible influence on demand. The demand and supply equations then become

$$S = a + bP$$

$$D = c - dP + eY$$

where a, b, c, d, e are fixed parameters. (There is a negative sign in front of d because demand diminishes as price rises.)

(d) An elementary dynamic microeconomic model

Let us consider specifically the market for frozen vegetables. The supply of frozen vegetables each year is determined by the quantity frozen in the summer months. The quantity frozen will depend on the amount firms are willing to supply at the price anticipated in the forthcoming year. For want of better information, expected price will be based on ruling market price, i.e. the price at which vegetables frozen the previous year are selling. Consequently, if t is an index of time

$$S(t) = a + bP(t - 1)$$

Provided consumers behave rationally, the demand for frozen vegetables will depend on the *current* market price. It is difficult to say whether the effect of income on demand will be lagged; to be consistent with (b) we suppose there is a lag. The demand equation then becomes

$$D(t) = c - dP(t) + eY(t - 1)$$

It is usually undesirable for frozen food to be kept in storage a long time. Suppose that for this reason firms do not carry over stocks from one year to the next. In this case each year's total supply of frozen vegetables will be sold on the market within twelve months. The price obtained will be the price which equates supply and demand. Consequently, each year

$$S(t) = D(t)$$

Substituting in the equations of supply and demand gives

$$a + bP(t - 1) = c - dP(t) + eY(t - 1)$$

Rearranging terms we get

$$dP(t) = (c - a) - bP(t - 1) + eY(t - 1)$$

Dividing throughout by d gives

$$P(t) = (c - a)/d - (b/d)P(t - 1) + (e/d)Y(t - 1)$$

This equation shows how the market price each year is determined by price and income in the previous year. Because there is a definite relationship between prices in successive years the model is a dynamic one.

3.3 Equilibrium

The concept of equilibrium is fundamental in any study in which simple models of reality are constructed. Although it is a familiar concept, it is rarely given an exact definition in economics textbooks. Equilibrium is sometimes said to be a situation in which there are no forces tending to produce a change. For example, a market is said to be in equilibrium when supply is equal to demand; this is usually taken to mean that both buyers and sellers are satisfied and there is no tendency for either to make any change in their plans. As it stands, this idea is rather vague; to make it precise we need an exact definition. There are a number of possible definitions, each different and each suitable for certain purposes. The following definition is particularly suitable for dynamic analysis.

A market is in equilibrium when planned supply equals planned demand. In order to use this definition it is necessary to specify the plans of the traders involved in the market. By means of such information it is possible to deduce necessary and sufficient conditions for equilibrium.

(I) Macroeconomic equilibrium

Consider again the simple dynamic model of the economy described in Section 3.2(b). This model is based on four key assumptions:

(i) aggregate demand has two components, consumer demand and investment demand;

(ii) consumer demand reflects the plans of consumers for spending the last period's income: these plans are described by the equation

$$C(t) = b + cY(t - 1)$$

(iii) investment demand reflects the plans of businessmen for adding to productive capacity, and is independent of the present state of the economy;

(iv) aggregate supply adjusts in the short run to meet aggregate demand.

Assumptions (i)–(iii) describe planned aggregate demand, but assumption (iv) describes only the short run reaction of suppliers to changes in demand. To describe the plans of suppliers we need an additional assumption:

(v) Producers plan the supply to be equal to the amount supplied in the previous period.

From assumptions (i)–(v) we are able to deduce an equilibrium condition for the economy.

Theorem 3.1 For the economy to be in equilibrium in period t it is necessary and sufficient that

$$Y(t) = (b + I(t))/(1 - c)$$

provided $c \neq 1$.

PROOF Since in the short run supply is adjusted to demand, it follows that in each period planned demand is measured by actual supply, so that in period t planned aggregate demand is equal to $Y(t)$. Planned aggregate supply is equal to actual supply the previous period, $Y(t - 1)$. Consequently planned demand equals planned supply if and only if

$$Y(t) = Y(t - 1)$$

From Section 3.2(b) we know that successive values of income satisfy the equation $Y(t) = b + cY(t - 1) + I(t)$. Substituting the equilibrium condition $Y(t) = Y(t - 1)$ on the right-hand side shows that there is equilibrium if and only if

$$Y(t) = b + cY(t) + I(t)$$

Grouping terms in $Y(t)$ and applying the formula for the solution of a linear equation (see Section 2.7(a)) proves the theorem.

(II) Microeconomic equilibrium

The model in Section 3.2(d) is based on three important assumptions; the first is

(i) planned demand depends linearly on current price and previous income,

$$D(t) = c - dP(t) + eY(t - 1)$$

The two other assumptions concern supply. In the short run, the supply is fixed; because harvests are annual, the supply of frozen vegetables has to be decided upon the previous year in the light of the price then ruling in the market. It follows that each year

(ii) *actual* supply, $S(t)$, is equal to *planned* supply in the *previous* year, $S^*(t - 1)$,

$$S(t) = S^*(t - 1)$$

(iii) *planned* supply is determined by price in the *current* year,

$$S^*(t) = a + bP(t)$$

Because of the impossibility of short-run adjustments in supply, planned supply and actual supply normally differ in the same year.

Theorem 3.2 For the market to be in equilibrium in period t, it is necessary and sufficient that

$$P(t) = (c - a)/(b + d) + [e/(b + d)]Y(t - 1)$$

provided $b \neq -d$.

PROOF The plans for period t are

Planned demand $= c - dP(t) + eY(t-1)$

Planned supply $= S^*(t) = a + bP(t)$

In equilibrium, therefore, it is necessary and sufficient that

$$a + bP(t) = c - dP(t) + eY(t-1)$$

Grouping terms in $P(t)$ and applying the formula for the solution of a linear equation proves the theorem.

3.4 Stationary states

In many circumstances an equilibrium is also a *stationary state*. An economy is said to be in a stationary state if the values of all variables remain unchanged in the future. When an equilibrium is also a stationary state it is said to be a *steady-state equilibrium*.

Theorem 3.3 If investment is constant then for the economy as a whole to be in a stationary state in period t it is necessary and sufficient that the economy is in equilibrium in period $t+1$; this implies that if investment is constant then every equilibrium is a steady-state equilibrium.

PROOF The first part of the proof of Theorem 3.1 shows that there is equilibrium in period $t+1$ if and only if

(1) $\quad Y(t+1) = Y(t)$

But equation (1) must be satisfied if the economy is to be in a stationary state in period t. Consequently equilibrium in period $t+1$ is a necessary condition for a stationary state in period t.

We now prove that if investment is constant then equilibrium is *sufficient* for a stationary state. The proof is by 'induction'. Since investment is constant from period t onwards,

(2) $\quad I(T) = I(t) \quad \text{for all } T > t$

a necessary and sufficient condition for a stationary state in period t is that

(3) $\quad Y(T) = Y(t) \quad \text{for all } T > t$

It is easily shown using (2) that if for some value of $T \geqslant t$

(4) $\quad Y(T+1) = Y(T)$

then

(5) $\quad Y(T+2) = Y(T+1)$

[Substituting (2) and (4) into an equation for $Y(T+2)$ gives

$$\begin{aligned} Y(T+2) &= b + cY(T+1) + I(T+2) \\ &= b + cY(T) + I(T+1) \\ &= Y(T+1) \end{aligned}$$

which proves (5).] If there is equilibrium in period $t + 1$ then (1) is satisfied. Consequently, when there is equilibrium under conditions of constant investment not only does $Y(t + 1) = Y(t)$ but also $Y(T + 1) = Y(T)$ implies $Y(T + 2) = Y(T + 1)$ for any $T \geqslant t$. The principle of induction assures us that as a result equation (3) is satisfied. We conclude that equilibrium is sufficient for a stationary state, and hence that every equilibrium is a steady state equilibrium.

The arguments used to demonstrate Theorem 3.3 can be used to establish a similar result for the market in frozen vegetables.

Theorem 3.4 If consumer income is constant over time, then in the market for frozen vegetables every equilibrium is a steady state equilibrium.

3.5 Comparative static analysis

Comparative statics is concerned with the comparison of steady-state equilibria.

In comparative static analysis, it is important to distinguish *endogenous* and *exogenous* variables. The value of an endogenous variable is determined within the model, whereas the value of an exogenous variable is determined by forces outside the model. For example, in the macroeconomic models 3.2(a) and (b), income is endogenous because it is determined by the forces of aggregate demand and supply described in the model, whereas investment is exogenous because its value is fixed by forces outside the model. Similar reasoning shows that in the microeconomic models 3.2(c) and (d) the price level is endogenous and consumers' income is exogenous. All the variables within a model can be classified as either endogenous or exogenous. The classification is determined only by the structure of the model: the same variable may be endogenous in one model and exogenous in another, or vice versa.

A comparative static analysis may be defined as an analysis of the effect of changes in the values of the exogenous variables on the steady-state equilibrium values of the endogenous variables.

A useful concept in comparative static analysis is the multiplier. A multiplier measures the impact of a change in the value of an exogenous variable on the steady-state equilibrium value of an endogenous variable: it is defined by the ratio

$$\begin{array}{l}\text{Multiplier relating}\\ \text{exogenous variable } A\\ \text{to endogenous variable } B\end{array} = \frac{\left(\begin{array}{c}\text{Induced change in steady-state}\\ \text{equilibrium value of } B\end{array}\right)}{(\text{Initiating change in value of } A)}$$

Theorem 3.5 In the macroeconomic model the multiplier relating investment to income is equal to $1/(1 - c)$ where c is the marginal propensity to consume ($c \neq 1$).

PROOF Consider a hypothetical increase ΔI in the stationary-state value of investment, I. Theorems 3.1 and 3.3 together show that before the increase in investment the steady-state equilibrium income is equal to

$$(b + I)/(1 - c)$$

The effect of the increase in investment is to transform I to $I + \Delta I$, so that the steady-state equilibrium income becomes

$$(b + I + \Delta I)/(1 - c)$$

The induced change in the steady-state equilibrium income is therefore

$$[(b + I + \Delta I)/(1 - c)] - [(b + I)/(1 - c)] = \Delta I/(1 - c)$$

The initiating change in investment is ΔI. Consequently the multiplier is

$$[\Delta I/(1 - c)]/\Delta I = 1/(1 - c)$$

Similar reasoning establishes

Theorem 3.6 In the microeconomic model the multiplier effect of consumers' income on price is equal to $e/(b + d)$ provided that $b \neq -d$.

Examples

(i) If the marginal propensity to consume is $\frac{1}{2}$ then the multiplier relating investment and income is equal to $1/(1 - \frac{1}{2}) = 2$. If there is no autonomous component of consumption ($b = 0$) then when investment is equal to £10m the steady-state equilibrium income is £20m. If investment is increased by £1m then the steady-state equilibrium income is increased by £2m to £22m.

(ii) Suppose that the demand for frozen vegetables in year t is $D(t) = 30 - 2P(t) + 1{\cdot}5Y(t - 1)$ and that the amount supplied in year t is $S(t) = 5 + 2{\cdot}5P(t - 1)$; P is measured in £ and Y in £ million. The multiplier relating consumers' income and price is equal to $1{\cdot}5/(2{\cdot}5 + 2{\cdot}0) = \frac{1}{3}$. The effect of an increase of £6m in consumers' income is to increase the steady-state equilibrium price by £2.

3.6 Dynamic analysis

Dynamics analyses the evolution of the economy over time. By applying dynamic analysis to the macroeconomic model described in Section 3.2(b) we can solve the following problem: if investment is increased permanently by £1m what will be the effect on income (a) immediately, (b) after one period, (c) after two periods, (d) ultimately?

To begin with, let us answer this question as economists rather than as mathematicians. An increase in investment of £1m will immediately increase aggregate demand by £1m. Production will be increased in order to meet the increase in demand and, as a result, factor incomes will increase immediately by £1m. This answers part (a). The increase in factor incomes will lead to an increase in consumption in the following period; the increase in factor incomes is £1m and the marginal propensity to consume is c, so that consumption will increase by £c million in the following period. Investment will still be £1m higher than to begin with, so that aggregate demand after one period will have increased by a total of £$(1 + c)$ million. Production will be adjusted to meet demand and, as a result, factor incomes will also rise by £$(1 + c)$ million. This answers part (b). The calculations are illustrated in Table 3.1. After two periods

Table 3.1 The behaviour of consumption, investment and income following a permanent exogenous increase in investment of £1m.

	Increase (£m) *in*		
	Consumption C	*Investment* I	*Income* $Y = C + I$
(a) initially	0	1	1
(b) after one period	c	1	$1 + c$
(c) after two periods	$c(1 + c)$	1	$1 + c + c^2$
(d) ultimately*	$c/(1 - c)$	1	$1/(1 - c)$

* Provided that $-1 < c < 1$.

investment is still £1m higher than before. Consumption depends on income the previous period, and the previous period income was £$(1 + c)$million higher than before. Because the marginal propensity to consume is c, consumption after two periods will have increased by £$c(1 + c)$ million. The total increase in aggregate demand, and hence in income, after two periods is therefore £$(1 + c(1 + c))$ million $=$ £$(1 + c + c^2)$ million.

Continuing this argument it is seen that after N periods the increase in income is £$(1 + c + c^2 + \cdots + c^N)$ million. Ultimately, therefore, the increase in income is

$$\lim_{N \to \infty} £(1 + c + c^2 + \cdots + c^N) \text{ million}$$

This result can also be arrived at by mathematical reasoning. Suppose that the economy is in equilibrium in period 0 and that in period 1 there is a permanent increase in investment from £I million to £$(I + \Delta I)$ million. Since the economy is in equilibrium in period 0 it follows from Theorem 3.1 that

$$Y(0) = b + cY(0) + I$$

Substituting successively $t = 1, t = 2, \ldots, t = N + 1$ into the equation of the dynamic model and simplifying by using the equation for $Y(0)$,

$$Y(1) = Y(0) + \Delta I$$

$$Y(2) = Y(0) + (1 + c)\Delta I$$

and, in general,

$$Y(N + 1) = Y(0) + (1 + c + \cdots + c^N)\Delta I$$

Let $\Delta Y(N + 1) = Y(N + 1) - Y(0)$ denote the overall change in income N periods after the change in investment; then

$$\Delta Y(N + 1) = (1 + c + \cdots + c^N)\Delta I$$

Setting $\Delta I = 1$ shows that the effect of a permanent increase of £1m in investment is to increase income after N periods by

$$£(1 + c + \cdots + c^N) \text{ million}$$

Ultimately, therefore, the increase in income will be

$$\lim_{N \to \infty} £(1 + c + \cdots + c^N) \text{ million}$$

which is the same as the result obtained by the economic reasoning above. By using the theory of geometric series (see Section 2.8) it can be shown that under certain circumstances the ultimate increase in income will be £$1/(1 - c)$ million. This will certainly be the case if the absolute value of the marginal propensity to consume, c, is less than one. It can therefore be said that as a consequence of a permanent increase in investment of £1m the income in the economy will increase by £$1/(1 - c)$ million, provided that the absolute value of the marginal propensity to consume is less than one. This answers part (d) of the question.

It is interesting to compare the dynamic analysis with the comparative static analysis in the previous section. According to Theorem 3.5, the effect of an increase in investment of £1m is to increase the steady-state equilibrium income by £$1/(1 - c)$ million. According to the dynamic analysis the effect of a £1m increase in investment is to increase income by an amount ultimately equal to £$1/(1 - c)$ million. The results of the static and dynamic analyses together demonstrate that under certain circumstances the actual effect of an increase in investment is to alter the level of income by an amount just sufficient to adjust the economy from one equilibrium to another. Comparing the static analysis with the dynamic analysis shows that while the static analysis describes the change in the equilibrium income, the dynamic analysis describes the actual time path of income. Under certain conditions the time path of income will adjust the economy from one equilibrium to another; the conditions under which this happens can be deduced from the dynamic analysis.

3.7 Stability

An equilibrium is usually said to be stable if a disturbance of any kind sets up forces tending to restore the system to the equilibrium state. For example, a market equilibrium is stable if a sudden increase in demand raises price and thereby induces a compensating reduction in demand. A more precise definition of stability is given below.

A steady-state equilibrium is stable if the market adjusts to it from any initial state when all exogenous variables are stationary. An equilibrium which is not stable is said to be unstable. In order to appreciate the significance of this definition it is helpful to consider two special cases of the 'initial state'. The first case is when the market has been displaced from steady-state equilibrium by a *temporary* change in the values of one or more of the exogenous variables. In this case the definition implies that the equilibrium is stable if the market eventually returns to its original state. The second case is when the market has been displaced from steady-state equilibrium by a *permanent* change in the values of the exogenous variables. In this case there is a new steady-state equilibrium consistent with the new values of the exogenous variables; if the equilibrium is stable the market will adjust to it.

The concept of stability may be illustrated by reference to the dynamic macroeconomic model.

Theorem 3.7 The steady-state equilibrium of the economy as a whole is stable provided that the absolute value of the marginal propensity to consume is less than unity, $-1 < c < 1$. If the marginal propensity to consume exceeds unity, $c > 1$, then the equilibrium is unstable.

PROOF Consider the steady-state equilibrium situations both before and after an exogenous increase in investment of £1m. Comparing the equilibrium situations by using Theorem 3.5 shows that in the two cases income differs by £$1/(1 - c)$ million.

Dynamic analysis indicates that N periods after a £1m increase in investment income will have increased by

$$£(1 + c + c^2 + \cdots + c^N) \text{ million}$$

From Theorem 2.2 it follows that if $-1 < c < 1$ then ultimately, as N becomes very large, the increase in income will be £$1/(1 - c)$ million. We conclude that if $-1 < c < 1$ then after an exogenous increase in investment the economy will adjust from one equilibrium to another, and the economy is therefore stable.

Suppose that $c > 1$; then

$$c^N > \cdots > c^2 > c > 1$$

so that

$$1 + c + c^2 + \cdots + c^N > N + 1$$

since $N + 1$ is the number of terms in the series. Hence

$$\lim_{N \to \infty} 1 + c + c^2 + \cdots + c^N = \infty$$

so that income increases ultimately by an infinite amount. But for the economy to adjust from one equilibrium to another income must change by £$1/(1 - c)$ million, which is a finite amount. Hence if $c > 1$ the economy is unstable.

Graphical illustration

The mathematical proof is somewhat dry. A graphical illustration shows more clearly what is going on. Figure 3A shows the schedules of planned aggregate demand and planned aggregate supply in a stable economy. Planned demand depends on the income last period because of the lag in consumption out of income; planned supply depends on the income last period because producers plan current output to be equal to last year's output. The equilibrium income equates planned demand and planned supply. (It should be clear to the reader that the only essential difference between this analysis and the microeconomic analysis of a market is that in this case demand and supply depend on income and not on price.)

Suppose that the marginal propensity to consume is $\frac{1}{2}$ and that the economy is in equilibrium in period 0; income, as shown, is £20m. Suppose that government expenditure is planned to increase by £1m in period 1. On examining the figure it is seen that in period 1 planned demand will be £21m and planned supply will be equal to last year's output of £20m. The economy will not be in

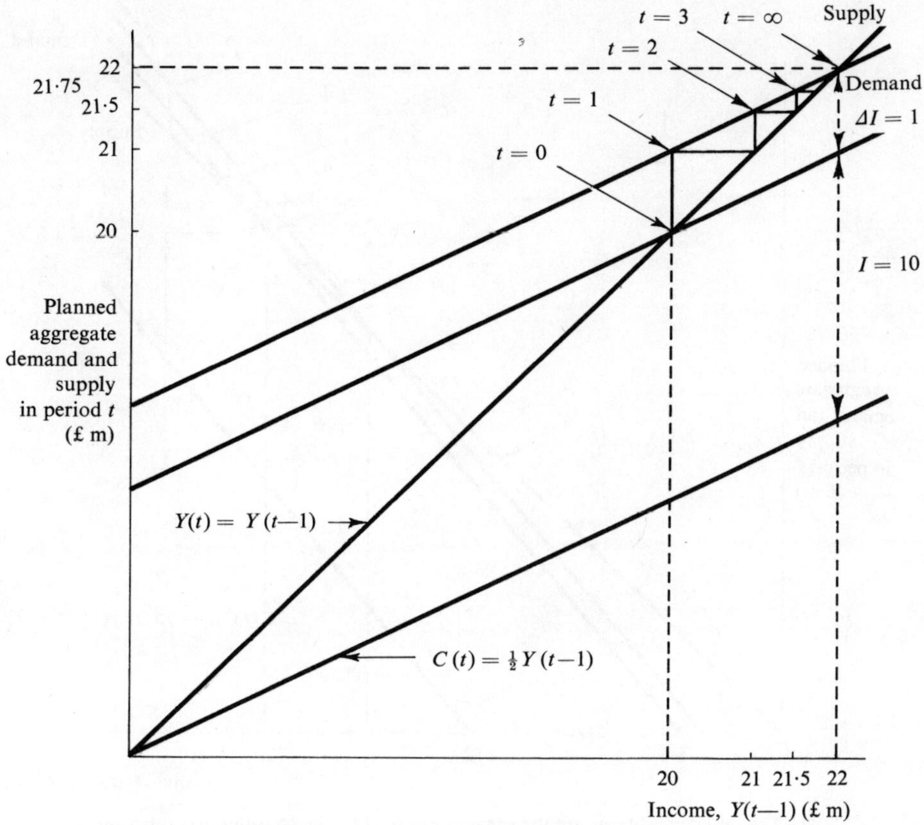

It is assumed that in period 0 the economy is in equilibrium with investment equal to £10 m. In period 1 investment is increased permanently to £11 m. The consumption function is

$$C(t) = \tfrac{1}{2}\, Y(t-1)$$

The time paths of aggregate demand and income can be read off from the coordinates of the points marked $t = 0$, $t = 1$, etc.

Fig. 3A Stable economy

equilibrium, but production will be increased to meet the aggregate demand of £21m. As a result, in the following period ($t = 2$) the planned supply will be £21m. According to the schedule of planned demand, the following period demand will be £21·5m. The economy will not be in equilibrium, but production will be increased to meet aggregate demand. The following period planned supply will be £21·5m and planned demand will be £21·75m. The figure shows that the process of adjustment continues until planned demand = planned supply = £22m.

Figure 3B shows the schedules of planned aggregate demand and planned aggregate supply in an unstable economy. As shown, the economy is in equilibrium in period 0 with an income of £20m. The result of an *increase* in government expenditure is a *decrease* in the equilibrium income. The dynamic

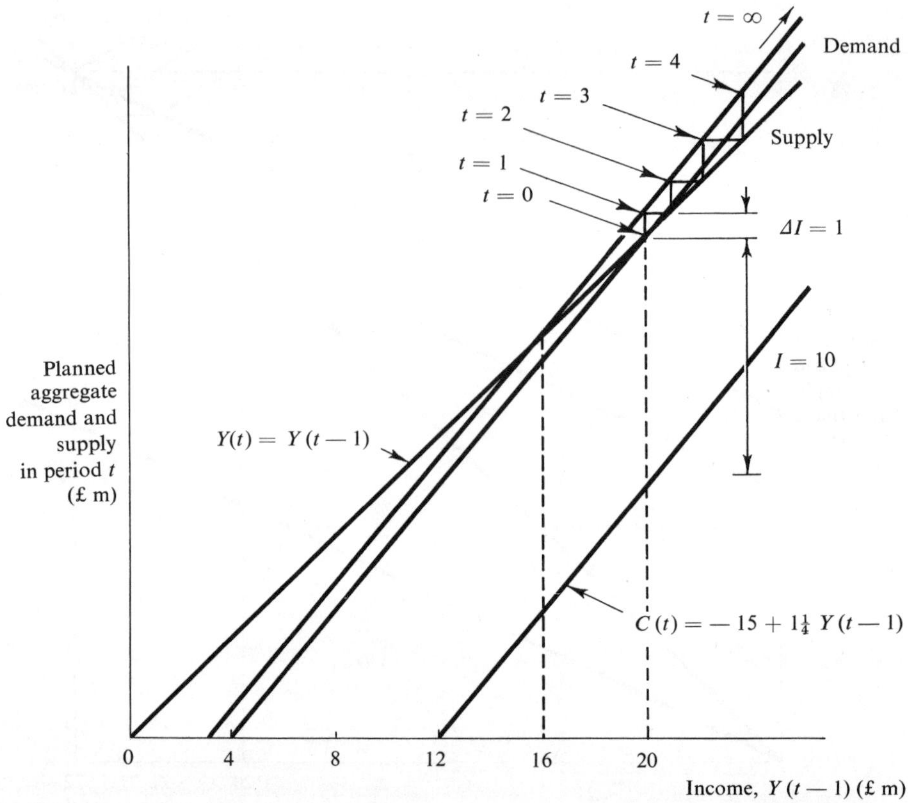

The initial conditions are the same as in Fig. 3A. The consumption function is $C(t) = -15 + 1{\cdot}25\, Y(t-1)$

Fig. 3B Unstable economy

analysis reveals, however, that as a result of the increase in government expenditure planned demand, planned supply and income all increase steadily over time, and that planned demand and planned supply grow steadily further apart. Clearly the economy diverges from equilibrium and hence is unstable.

In practice, of course, income cannot increase indefinitely; when unemployment has been eliminated it will no longer be possible in the short run for producers to meet a steadily increasing aggregate demand. Consequently, if there is an increase in exogenous demand in an unstable economy, sooner or later aggregate demand will exceed aggregate supply, supply will be fixed, and so prices will be competed up, i.e. inflation will result.

An application of stability analysis to microeconomics is called for in the problems at the end of the chapter.

3.8 Use of economic models for rational policy making: an example

The macroeconomic model described in Section 3.2(d) is very naive. It is possible to make this model much more realistic without complicating it to any great extent. The most important omission from the model is the government sector. The role of the government is twofold: it raises funds, mainly by taxing income, and it spends these funds, mainly by demanding goods and services. These activities of the government may be incorporated into the model in the following way. Aggregate demand has a component of government expenditure, G,

$$\text{Aggregate demand in period } t = C(t) + I(t) + G(t)$$

The effect of income taxation is to reduce disposable income to a proportion $(1 - t)$ of pre-tax income, where t is the rate of income tax; if consumers spend a proportion, c^*, of their post-tax income, then consumption in period t is equal to

$$C(t) = b + cY(t - 1)$$

where $c = c^*(1 - t)$. We neglect the fact that income tax is progressive, i.e. that the rate of tax increases with the level of income. However, it is easy to allow for the existence of social security payments, interest payments on the national debt, etc., for these constitute an autonomous component of post-tax income; the consumption out of this income constitutes an addition to the autonomous component of consumption, which may be allowed for by adjusting the value of the parameter b.

The model outlined in the preceding paragraph may be used to answer important questions of social policy. A model of this kind was originally developed by the Cambridge economist, Lord Kahn, on the suggestion of Keynes, to examine the role of fiscal policy in relieving unemployment.

Suppose that government expenditure can be determined exogenously by policy considerations, and that the object of policy is full employment. Let the target level of income (corresponding to full employment) be Y^*, and let the existing equilibrium level of income be Y. Income is determined by the equation

$$Y(t) = b + cY(t - 1) + I(t) + G(t)$$

If investment and government expenditure remain constant, $I(t) = I$, $G(t) = G$, then the steady-state equilibrium income is

$$Y = (b + I + G)/(1 - c)$$

Now the target level of government expenditure, G^*, necessarily satisfies the equation

$$Y^* = (b + I + G^*)/(1 - c)$$

Subtracting the first of these equations from the second shows that

$$Y^* - Y = (G^* - G)/(1 - c)$$

This equation tells us that the result of increasing government expenditure by $G^* - G$ is to increase the equilibrium income by a multiple $1/(1 - c)$. Rewriting the equation as

$$G^* - G = (1 - c)(Y^* - Y)$$

shows that if $Y^* > Y$ then to restore full employment to the economy it is necessary to increase government expenditure by a fraction $(1 - c)$ of the loss of income due to unemployment. The reader can easily verify that changes in investment and changes in government expenditure are equally effective in inducing full employment, i.e. if the government chooses to adjust business investment (by changes in company taxation, investment allowances, etc.) rather than its own expenditure then to restore full employment additional investment must be induced equal to a fraction $(1 - c)$ of the loss of income due to unemployment.

A dynamic analysis gives greater insight into these results, for it shows the manner in which the economy adjusts to full employment. Firstly it should be noted that the economy will only adjust to a full employment equilibrium if it is stable, and the economy is stable if and only if $-1 < c < 1$.

If the economy is stable, the adjustment proceeds in the following way. To begin with, the increase in government expenditure, $G^* - G$, induces an increase in aggregate demand of this same amount; this leads to the employment of men and materials to produce the additional output, and this in turn leads to additional factor income equal to $G^* - G$. The government takes a proportion t in income taxation, leaving an amount $(1 - t)(G^* - G)$ for the consumers' pockets. Out of this the consumers spend a proportion c^*, so that consumer demand increases by $c^*(1 - t)(G^* - G) = c(G^* - G)$. Investment is exogenous and remains unaltered by the change in income. The additional consumer demand leads to the employment of even more men and materials, and leads eventually to a further increase in factor incomes. This increase in factor incomes leads to a further increase in consumer demand, and so on. Eventually, the repercussions will tail off when income has increased by $(G^* - G)/(1 - c)$; by design, this is equal to $Y^* - Y$, which is the adjustment required to bring income to its full employment level.

Further developments of this model are discussed in the chapters on matrix algebra and difference equations.

Example Consumers spend $\frac{3}{4}$ of their post-tax income. The rate of income tax is $33\frac{1}{3}\%$. What is the multiplier relating government expenditure to income? At full employment the national income is equal to £80m. If the existing level of government expenditure is £30m by how much must government expenditure be increased to bring the economy to a full employment equilibrium? (Assume investment and autonomous consumption are zero.)

The multiplier is equal to $1/(1 - c)$ where $c = c^*(1 - t)$. Since $c^* = \frac{3}{4}$, $t = \frac{1}{3}$, it follows that $c = \frac{1}{2}$ and that $1/(1 - c) = 2$. Hence the multiplier is 2.

Since the existing level of government expenditure is £30m and the multiplier is 2, it follows that at present the equilibrium income is £60m. To bring the economy to a full employment equilibrium it is necessary to increase the equilibrium income by £20m. Since the multiplier is 2 this is effected by an increase in government expenditure of £10m. Thus to bring the economy to full employment government expenditure must be increased by £10m. Since the economy is stable ($-1 < c = \frac{1}{2} < 1$) the economy will adjust to a full employment equilibrium when this policy is implemented.

Further applications of the multiplier analysis are indicated in the problems.

Notes and references

Elementary macroeconomic models are discussed in Lipsey,[81] Ch. 40, 41 and Samuelson,[113] Ch. 11. More detailed discussions are given in Dernburg and McDougall,[34] Ch. 5 and Kurihara,[72] Ch. 1, 2. Alternative specifications of macroeconomic models are discussed by Metzler.[87] For a more advanced discussion of economic dynamics see Allen,[8] Ch. 1.

The economic background to Section 3.8 is well explained in Brooman,[21] Ch. 5, 6, Dernburg and McDougall,[34] Ch. 6, Kurihara,[72] Ch. 7, Lipsey,[81] Ch. 42–45, 47, and Samuelson,[113] Ch. 12, 13, 19. The functional relation between consumption and income (known as the consumption function) is lucidly discussed by Duesenberry[36] and the statistical evidence is comprehensively reviewed in Ackley,[1] Ch. 10.

There is a wealth of stimulating reading on the multiplier. Many of the best references are to be found in Hansen[49]; there is a discussion by Samuelson[111] of a famous special case of the multiplier analysis, known as 'the balanced budget theorem' (see also Problem 3.8.2) and there are discussions of the implications of this theorem by Alexander,[5] Bishop[18] and Lerner.[87] The subject of fiscal policy is comprehensively reviewed in Musgrave,[94] Ch. 18. The original article on the subject is by Kahn.[69] The use of economic models for policy purposes is discussed by Tinbergen[119] and is illustrated by many and various economic models: see especially Ch. 1–3 and Appendices 1–3. For a review of the work of Tinbergen and others see Evans,[37] Dasgupta and Hagger[33] and Peacock and Shaw.[99]

Problems

3.1.1 The quantity theory of money states that $MV = PQ$ where M is the stock of money, P is the price level, V is the speed with which money circulates from one person to another (V is known as the velocity of circulation of money) and Q is the rate of output of the economy. Is the quantity theory of money a static or dynamic model?

3.1.2 It is sometimes alleged that there are persistent cycles in the level of employment in an economy. If it is postulated that four years after a peak rate of employment the economy will have a peak rate of unemployment, is this model static or dynamic?

3.2 The supply of flats in a university town depends on the market rent six months ago. The demand for flats depends on the market rent at present and on the number of students at the university. Provide a mathematical model of the market for flats. Is the model static or dynamic?

3.3.1 Discuss what is meant by 'the *equilibrium* growth rate of the population'.

3.3.2 The demand and supply of lecturers may be analysed in the following way. The total number of lecturers required is proportional to the number of students in their final year: the staff–student ratio is a. A small, but constant, proportion, b, of all lecturers leaves the profession each year. At any one time the number of new lecturers available is equal to the number of students concluding postgraduate courses, and these are a proportion, c, of all students graduating three years ago. If the number of students increases each year by $100r\%$, under what conditions will the demand for lecturers equal the supply?

3.4.1 (3.2 continued) Whatever the initial level of rent, an increase of £1 per week in the market rent increases the number of available flats by 500 and reduces the demand for flats by 200. When the rent is £10 per week there is no demand for flats at all, and when the rent is £3 per week there are no flats available. The market rent equates demand and supply; the number of students at the university is fixed.

Express the market rent as a function of the market rent six months ago. (*Hint*: use the fact that both demand and supply are linear functions of rent.) At what value will the market rent remain constant over time? How many flats will be available at this rent?

3.5.1 It is postulated that the rate of growth of the population depends on real income per head and that real income per head depends on the productivity of the labour force and on the proportion of the population which is of working age. The proportion of the population which is of working age depends on the rate of growth of the population. In this model of population growth which variables are exogenous and which endogenous?

3.5.2 Suppose that each year households receive £A million in income from foreign countries (e.g. gifts, interest on investments in foreign companies, etc.). How does this alter the specification of the model in 3.2(b)? If income from foreign sources increases by £1m how does this affect (a) the equilibrium income (b) the equilibrium value of output? How does the effect of an increase in income from foreign countries compare with the effect of an increase in investment?

3.5.3 (3.5.2 continued) Suppose that a domestically owned company decides to stop investing at home and to build a large plant abroad instead. If the net effect is to reduce domestic investment permanently by £5m per annum and to increase profits from foreign sources by £5m per annum, is there any effect on (a) the equilibrium income in the home country (b) the equilibrium value of output in the home country? What effect, if any, do you think there would be on the distribution of income?

3.6.1 Verify that if investment increases permanently by £1 million then, provided that the marginal propensity to consume is less than one, consumption will increase ultimately by £$c/(1 - c)$ million.

3.6.2 Suppose that there is an increase in investment of £ΔI million which lasts for one period only, after which investment returns to its normal level. Show that after N periods the resulting increase in income is c^N times the temporary increase in investment, where c is the marginal propensity to consume. Under what conditions will the repercussions on income die out?

3.6.3 (3.6.2 continued) What is the total of the increments in income up to and including period N? If the repercussions on income die out what is the sum total of all the increments? Provide numerical answers for the case ΔI = £32m, $c = \frac{1}{2}$, $N = 5$.

3.6.4 The dividend policy of large companies is reliably explained by the Lintner dividend hypothesis. It is asserted that businesses have a target pay-out ratio, b, which is the proportion of profits which businessmen desire, in the long run, to pay out as dividends. In the short run, however, businessmen are cautious and are reluctant to pay out an amount very different from the amount paid out previously. Consequently each year's dividend payment represents a partial adjustment from last year's dividend to the target payment computed from the pay-out ratio. This hypothesis is expressed mathematically as

$$D(t) = D(t - 1) + c(bP(t) - D(t - 1))$$

where D is the dividend, P is profit, b is the target pay-out ratio and $0 \leqslant c \leqslant 1$ is a parameter of the partial adjustment process, known as the 'reaction coefficient'.

Demonstrate that according to this hypothesis the dividend payment each year is a weighted sum of the current and all previous values of profit, where the weights are proportional to the successive terms in a geometric series. Show that the sum of the weights is equal to b.

3.7.1 (3.4.1 continued) As a result of an increase in the number of students, the demand for flats increases by 350 for each value of the market rent. If the market rent was stable before the increase, write down a formula for the market rent N years after this increase in student numbers. As N becomes large, to what value will the market rent tend? When this rent is attained will the market rent remain constant from year to year?

3.7.2 The demand and supply of frozen vegetables (in tons per week) is governed by the following equations.

$$S(t) = a + bP(t - 1)$$

$$D(t) = c - dP(t) + eY(t - 1)$$

where P is the price of frozen vegetables (in £ per lb), Y is consumers' income (in £m) and $t = 1, 2, \ldots$ denotes the year. Supply and demand are equated by changes in the price. Show that the market is stable if and only if $-1 < b/d < 1$. (*Hint*: express $P(t)$ as a function of $P(t - 1)$ and then consider the effect of an exogenous change in consumers' income.)

Suppose that $a = 15$, $b = 5$, $c = 10$, $d = 10$, $e = 1$ and consumers' income is £20m. Plot the supply and demand curves of meat. If the initial price of meat is £0·9, trace out the movements of price, quantity demanded and quantity supplied for the next three periods. Show mathematically that after N periods the price of meat is $1 - 0{\cdot}1(-0{\cdot}5)^N$ (£ per lb). How does the quantity supplied vary with time?

3.8.1 Profits comprise 40% of total factor income; the remaining 60% is wages. Firms use $12\frac{1}{2}$% of all profits to purchase investment goods, they distribute 50% as dividends to households and pay $37\frac{1}{2}$% in tax to the government. All investment is financed out of profits. The rate of tax on household income is 25% and the households' marginal propensity to consume out of post-tax income is 75%. What is the multiplier relating government expenditure to income?

3.8.2 Suppose that government expenditure is increased by £ΔG million and that it is financed entirely by an equal increase in income taxation. Using comparative static analysis, show that although the government's budget remains balanced the equilibrium value of output in the economy increases by £ΔG million. Hence show that the post-tax income of consumers remains unchanged. This is the 'balanced budget theorem': it shows that an active policy of relieving unemployment by public works is compatible with a 'sound' policy of fiscal finance.

3.8.3 Show that the increase in the tax rate necessary to implement the balanced budget policy is $(1 - t)\Delta G/(Y + \Delta G)$, where t is the initial rate of income tax and Y is the initial equilibrium income.

3.8.4 Show that in implementing a policy to increase income, the target equilibrium income will be approached more quickly when the policy is implemented by increasing government expenditure than when it is implemented by reducing the rate of income tax. Show that, conversely, when implementing a policy to reduce income (e.g. in order to improve the balance of payments) the target equilibrium income will be approached more quickly when taxation is increased than when government expenditure is reduced.

Part 2
Calculus

Chapter 4
Maxima and minima

4.1 Introduction

Economic problems often involve finding the maximum or minimum of something. Four examples will illustrate this. (1) In Section 2.5 we discussed an example in which the managers of a firm maximize profit. (2) In the 'classical' economic theory of consumer behaviour it is postulated that consumers are 'rational' and that they endeavour to maximize utility, or satisfaction. (3) Firms in a competitive industry will, in the long run, endeavour to minimize the average cost of the output they produce. (4) A firm which produces a variety of products may well arrange its stocks to minimize the probability that the stock of any one product is exhausted. The list of examples is endless. Problems which involve finding a maximum or minimum occur frequently in the natural sciences, in statistics and engineering, and in many other disciplines as well.

A problem which involves finding a maximum can always be converted into a problem which involves finding a minimum, and vice versa. A firm which maximizes its profit is necessarily also a firm which minimizes its loss: a consumer who maximizes utility, or satisfaction, is necessarily also a consumer who minimizes disutility or dissatisfaction. Quite generally, finding the maximum of some quantity is the same thing as finding the minimum of the negative of that quantity. Since the problems of finding maxima and minima are inextricably linked, we shall discuss the properties of maxima and minima together.

4.2 Necessary conditions for maxima and minima

The concepts of maxima and minima are familiar from everyday life. For example, the maximum height of students on an economics course is the height of the tallest student, the minimum height is the height of the shortest student. One way of finding the maximum and minimum heights of a group of students would be to measure each student in turn. If a record were kept at each stage of the highest and lowest measurements, the maximum and minimum heights would be known as soon as the last student was measured. Another method would be to ask the students to arrange themselves in a line in decreasing order of height, students to the left being smaller than students to the right. The maximum height would be obtained by measuring the student at the extreme right, the minimum height by measuring the student at the extreme left.

Both the methods of solution described above are relatively laborious. Fortunately, in a number of important cases the determination of maxima and minima can be accomplished very simply. One of these cases is the determination of the maxima and minima of a continuous function.

Consider a continuous function $y = f(x)$, defined for a range of values $a \leqslant x \leqslant b$, such that for each value of x there is a unique value of y. A necessary condition for this function to be at a maximum is readily deduced. At any particular value of x the graph of the function either slopes upwards from left to right, downwards from left to right, or else is strictly horizontal.[1] If the graph slopes upwards from left to right then the point x cannot be the point at which the function $y = f(x)$ is a maximum, since if the value of x is slightly increased (which involves a movement to the right on the x axis) then the value of y will also be slightly increased. Since the value of y is higher than before the original value cannot have been a maximum.

If the graph slopes downwards from left to right, the point x still cannot be a maximum, for if the value of x is slightly *decreased* (which involves a movement to the left on the x axis) then the value of y will be slightly *increased*. Since the value of y is higher than before the original value cannot have been a maximum. We are left with the possibility that the slope is strictly horizontal: if the slope is strictly horizontal then by a small movement either to the right or the left we do not move to a point any higher or any lower than before: consequently, we *may possibly* be at a maximum.

A necessary condition for a function to be at a minimum can be deduced in the same way; in fact it is the same condition as above: only if the slope is horizontal can the function possibly be at a minimum.

In order to find either the maximum or the minimum of a certain type of function, therefore, it is necessary to find the value or values of x at which the slope of the function is horizontal.

Suppose we define a measure of the slope of a function as follows. Increase the value of x by an amount Δx (by a horizontal movement along the x axis) and denote the resulting increase in the value of y by Δy (Δy is the resulting change in the height of the graph): then the slope of the function between the points x and $x + \Delta x$ is $\Delta y/\Delta x$. If the interval, Δx, is small enough, we may refer to $\Delta y/\Delta x$ as the slope of the function *at the point* x. This definition of the slope is illustrated in Fig. 4A. It is seen from the figure that if, at any point, the graph of the function is horizontal then the slope of the function, as defined above, is zero. This is because, if the graph is horizontal, a change, Δx, in the value of x will leave the height of the graph, y, unaltered, so that $\Delta y = 0$. As a result, $\Delta y/\Delta x = 0$ when the graph is horizontal. It should be noted that this definition of the slope is formally identical with the definition of a gradient given in Section 2.5; the only difference is that in Section 2.5 it was assumed that the gradient was the same at every point on the graph. In the present discussion no such assumption is made: in general, the slope of the graph will depend on the value of x about which the slope is measured. This suggests that we can regard the slope *as a function* of x, since there is a definite correspondence between the value of x and the slope of the function at that point. If the slope of the function is itself a function of x, and if to find a maximum or minimum

1 The case in which the graph is vertical is ruled out by the assumption that the function is continuous.

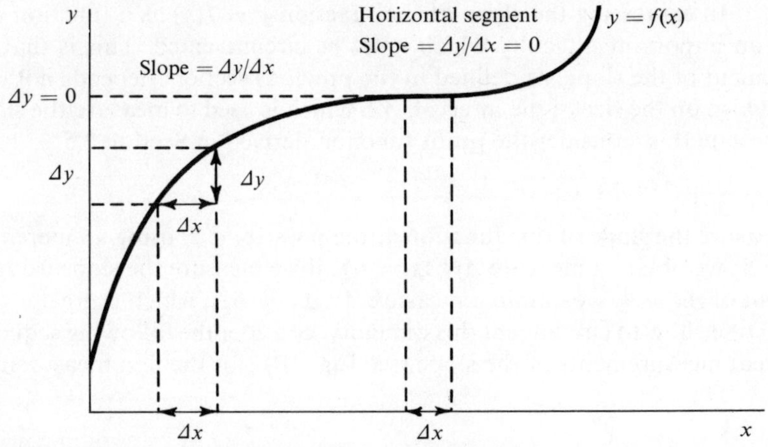

Fig. 4A Measurement of the slope of a function

we must find the values of x at which the slope is equal to zero, then to find a maximum (or minimum) it is necessary to find the value of x at which the slope, which is some function of x, is equal to zero: i.e. *to find a maximum (or minimum) it is necessary to solve an equation*

$$f'(x) = 0$$

where $f'(x)$ denotes the slope as a function of x.

4.3 Differentiation

We have now reduced the problem of finding the maximum and/or the minimum of some function to the problem of expressing the slope of the function as a function of x. If this can be done, so that the slope is some function, $f'(x)$, of x, then a necessary condition, both for a maximum and a minimum, is that the slope of the function is zero:

$$f'(x) = 0$$

This is an equation which can be solved for x. The solutions to this equation are the values of x at which the function may possibly be a maximum or a minimum.

The problem of expressing the slope of a function as a function of x is worth detailed examination in its own right. The slope of a function often has an important economic interpretation. In fact, when an economic relationship, $y = f(x)$, is postulated it is usual to specify that the slope of the function shall depend upon x in a certain way, i.e. we specify certain characteristics of the function $f'(x)$. We shall show later, for example, that if $y = f(x)$ is the cost schedule of a firm (where y is cost and x is output) then the function $f'(x)$ expresses the way in which the 'marginal cost' of output depends on the level of output. Economic considerations suggest that the graph of $f'(x)$—the graph of marginal cost against output—must lie above the x axis and, for large values of x, must be higher the higher is the value of x, i.e. for large values of x the graph of $f'(x)$ must slope upwards from left to right.

In expressing the slope of the function $y = f(x)$ as a function of x there is an important difficulty which must be circumvented. This is that the measurement of the slope, as defined in the previous section, depends not only on x but also on the size of the interval, Δx, which is used to measure the slope. To appreciate this, consider the profit function derived in Section 2.5,

$$y = -40 + 6\tfrac{2}{3}x - \tfrac{1}{12}x^2$$

If we measure the slope of this function at the point $x = 2$, using an increment of $\Delta x = 1$, we obtain a measure $\Delta y/\Delta x = 6\tfrac{1}{4}$; if we measure the slope using an increment of $\Delta x = \tfrac{1}{2}$, we obtain a measure $\Delta y/\Delta x = 6\tfrac{7}{24}$, which is greater than before. To see how to circumvent this difficulty, consider the following sequence of different measurements of the slope (see Fig. 4B): for the first measurement

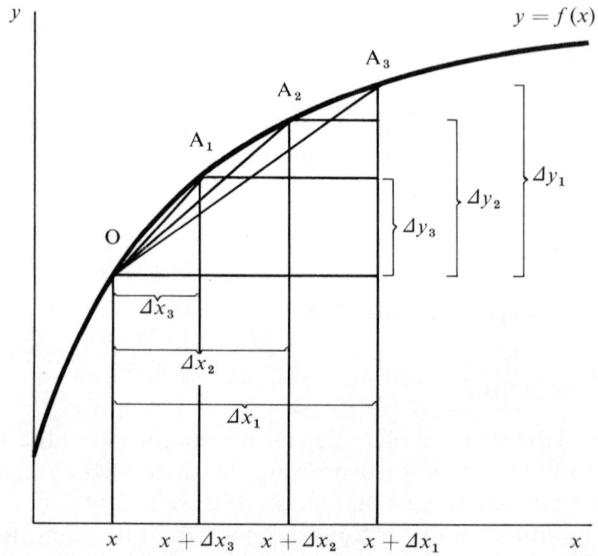

NOTE The sequence of measures of the slope, $\Delta y_1/\Delta x_1$, $\Delta y_2/\Delta x_2$, $\Delta y_3/\Delta x_3$, ... is obtained by measuring the gradients of smaller and smaller straight line segments OA_1, OA_2, OA_3, ... As they become smaller, the straight line segments approximate closer and closer to the form of the curve near the point x.

Fig. 4B A sequence of measurements of the slope of the function $y=f(x)$ at the point x

take a large interval, Δx_1, and measure the slope at the point x by the ratio $\Delta y_1/\Delta x_1$; for the second measurement of the slope, take a smaller interval, Δx_2, and measure $\Delta y_2/\Delta x_2$: the second measurement will, in a sense, be the more accurate measure of the slope at the point x, since the point $x + \Delta x_2$ is closer to x than is the point $x + \Delta x_1$. The third measurement of the slope $\Delta y_3/\Delta x_3$, is taken with an even smaller interval, Δx_3, and will be an even more accurate measure of the slope at x. It can be shown that, under certain reasonable conditions, as the intervals Δx_1, Δx_2, Δx_3, ... become smaller and smaller, and the measurements of the slope at x become more and more accurate, the sequence of measurements $\Delta y_1/\Delta x_1$, $\Delta y_2/\Delta x_2$, $\Delta y_3/\Delta x_3$, ... will tend to a definite limit which is independent of the particular values, Δx_1, Δx_2, Δx_3, used in the sequence.

The definite limit, which is a perfectly accurate measure of the slope at the point x, is denoted

$$\lim_{\Delta x \to 0} \Delta y/\Delta x$$

This limiting quantity is called 'the derivative of y with respect to x'.

We shall now demonstrate how this limiting quantity can be evaluated as a function of x. Consider the function

$$y = f(x) = x^2$$

The graph of this function is shown in Fig. 4C. How do we express the derivative of this function as a function of x? We consider the effect of increasing the value of x by an amount Δx, from x to $x + \Delta x$. The value of y to begin with is

$$y = x^2$$

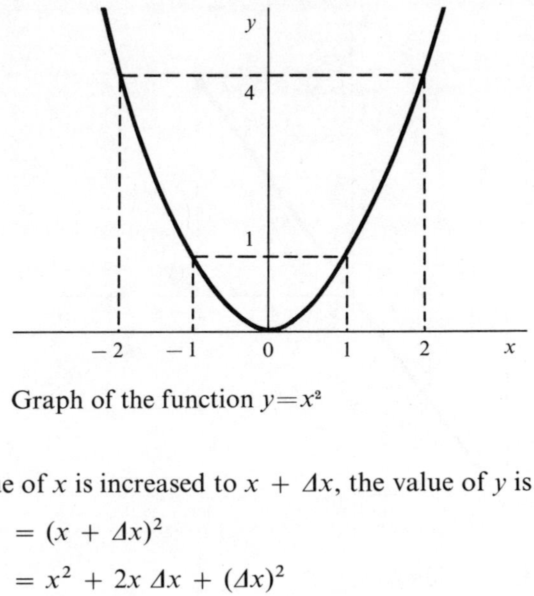

Fig. 4C Graph of the function $y=x^2$

If the value of x is increased to $x + \Delta x$, the value of y is increased to

$$\begin{aligned} y + \Delta y &= (x + \Delta x)^2 \\ &= x^2 + 2x\,\Delta x + (\Delta x)^2 \end{aligned}$$

The change in the value of y as a result of this change in the value of x, from x to $x + \Delta x$, is the difference between the new value $y + \Delta y = (x + \Delta x)^2$, and the old value $y = x^2$. This difference is Δy, and

$$\begin{aligned} \Delta y &= [x^2 + 2x\,\Delta x + (\Delta x)^2] - (x^2) \\ &= 2x\,\Delta x + (\Delta x)^2 \end{aligned}$$

The measure of the slope over the range x to $x + \Delta x$ is

$$\begin{aligned} \Delta y/\Delta x &= [2x\,\Delta x + (\Delta x)^2]/\Delta x \\ &= 2x + \Delta x \end{aligned}$$

As was remarked earlier, this measure of the slope depends both on the value of x and on the size of the interval, Δx. We are now in a position to evaluate the derivative,

$$\lim_{\Delta x \to 0} \Delta y/\Delta x$$

and thereby to obtain an accurate measure of the slope at the point x. We shall then be able to verify that this measure of the slope is indeed independent of Δx. It is readily seen that

$$\lim_{\Delta x \to 0} \Delta y/\Delta x = \lim_{\Delta x \to 0} (2x + \Delta x) = 2x$$

so that when the interval, Δx, used for the measurement of the slope, is arbitrarily small, the measure of the slope depends only on x. We have now expressed the slope of the function $y = x^2$ as a function of x; the notation we use to express this is

$$f'(x) = 2x$$

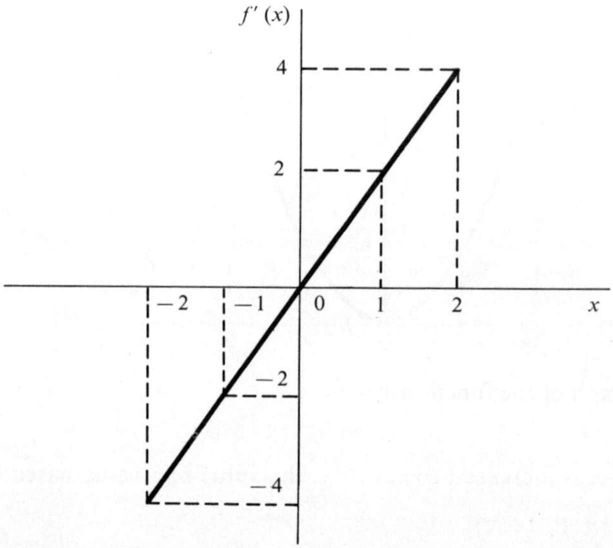

Fig. 4D Graph of the function $f'(x)=2x$

The graph of the function $f'(x)$ is plotted in Fig. 4D. It can be seen from this figure that the slope of the function $y = x^2$ is constantly increasing, and, furthermore, that the slope is a linear function $f'(x) = 2x$ of the variable x.

In case the reader feels that this evaluation of the function $f'(x)$ is a piece of algebraic sleight of hand, we give below another example of the evaluation of the derivative, together with a numerical illustration of the limiting process.

Consider the function

$$y = 4x^3$$

How does the slope of this function depend upon x, i.e. what is the form of the function $f'(x)$?

If the value of x is increased from x to $x + \Delta x$ then the value of y increases from

$$y = 4x^3$$

to

$$\begin{aligned} y + \Delta y &= 4(x + \Delta x)^3 \\ &= 4(x + \Delta x)^2(x + \Delta x) \\ &= 4(x^2 + 2x\,\Delta x + \Delta x^2)(x + \Delta x) \\ &= 4(x^3 + 3x^2\,\Delta x + 3x\,\Delta x^2 + \Delta x^3) \\ &= 4x^3 + 12x^2\,\Delta x + 12x\,\Delta x^2 + 4\Delta x^3 \end{aligned}$$

Subtracting y from $y + \Delta y$ gives

$$\Delta y = 12x^2\,\Delta x + 12x\,\Delta x^2 + 4\Delta x^3$$

The slope of the function y between x and $x + \Delta x$ is

$$\Delta y/\Delta x = 12x^2 + 12x\,\Delta x + 4\Delta x^2$$

and the slope at the point x is

$$\lim_{\Delta x \to 0} \Delta y/\Delta x = \lim_{\Delta x \to 0} (12x^2 + 12x\,\Delta x + 4\Delta x^2)$$

Now as Δx tends to zero, the term $12x^2$ remains the same because it is independent of Δx and the term $12x\,\Delta x$ is equal to something arbitrarily small (Δx) multiplied into something independent of Δx, and so this term tends to zero as Δx tends to zero.

The question of interest is: what happens to Δx^2 as Δx tends to zero? The answer is that Δx^2 tends to zero as Δx tends to zero, because, when Δx lies between -1 and $+1$, Δx^2 is always closer to zero than is Δx (see Table 4.1).

Table 4.1 Table of Δx and Δx^2 for $-1 \leqslant \Delta x \leqslant 1$

Δx	Δx^2	Δx	Δx^2
-1	1	1	1
$-1/2$	1/4	1/2	1/4
$-1/4$	1/16	1/4	1/16
$-1/8$	1/64	1/8	1/64
⋮	⋮	⋮	⋮
$-1/1,000$	1/1,000,000	1/1,000	1/1,000,000

When Δx becomes very close to zero it must of necessity lie between -1 and $+1$, and so as Δx tends to zero Δx^2, which is under these circumstances even closer to zero, must tend to zero as well.

We conclude that in the expression for the derivative all the terms except $12x^2$ tend to zero as x tends to zero. Consequently

$$\lim_{\Delta x \to 0} \Delta y/\Delta x = 12x^2$$

We express the fact that the derivative, that is, the slope of the function, depends on x by writing, in functional notation,

$$f'(x) = 12x^2$$

The process of evaluating the derivative of a function is known as 'differentiation'.

To emphasize the simplicity of this limiting argument, Table 4.2 illustrates the evaluation of the slope of the function $y = 4x^3$ at the point $x = 1$, as x tends to zero through the values 0·5, 0·2, 0·1, 0·05, 0·02, 0·01. The calculations shown in the table are for illustration only; in practice the slope of the function $y = 4x^3$ at $x = 1$ is evaluated simply by substituting $x = 1$ into the formula for the derivative, $f'(x) = 12x^2$: this shows immediately that when $x = 1$ the slope is equal to 12.

Table 4.2 Evaluation of the derivative of the function $y = 4x^3$ at the point $x = 1$

Δx	$x + \Delta x$	$y + \Delta y = 4(x + \Delta x)^3$	$y = 4x^3$	Δy	$\Delta y/\Delta x$
0·5	1·5	13·5	4	9·5	19·0
0·2	1·2	6·912	4	2·912	14·56
0·1	1·1	5·324	4	1·324	13·24
0·05	1·05	4·6305	4	0·6305	12·61
0·02	1·02	4·244832	4	0·244832	12·2416
0·01	1·01	4·121204	4	0·121204	12·1204
Limiting case					
0·0	1·0	4·0	4	0·0	12·0

4.4 Economic interpretation of the derivative

At this stage it may be helpful to see what the economic interpretation of the derivative is. To fix our ideas, let us consider the cost function of an oil refinery, in which the costs, y (in £ per annum) depend on the level of output, x (gallons of refined oil per annum). Let us inquire: what is the marginal cost of refined oil when the annual output of oil is one million gallons? The answer to this question is: the marginal cost of refined oil is equal to the derivative of the cost function at the value of x which represents an output of one million gallons. Denote the cost function $y = f(x)$: if the output of refined oil is increased by Δx gallons, the costs of the refinery increase by £Δy. The cost of a marginal batch of Δx gallons is therefore £Δy, so that, by this reckoning, the marginal cost of *one* gallon of oil is £$\Delta y/\Delta x$. However, the marginal cost of each fraction of the Δx gallons will not necessarily be *exactly* the same. Consequently, we shall obtain a better measure of the marginal cost of oil at the level of output x if the increment in output is reduced to one-half, one-quarter, one-eighth or, ideally, some infinitely small fraction of the increment originally considered. When the incremental output is infinitely small the increase in costs will be infinitely small as well, but the ratio of these two infinitely small amounts, $\Delta y/\Delta x$, will be an accurate measure of the marginal cost of oil at the exact output x: i.e. when Δy and Δx are infinitely small amounts, their ratio

$$\lim_{\Delta x \to 0} \Delta y/\Delta x$$

is an accurate measure of the marginal cost of oil at the output x. Consequently, the derivative of the cost function, $y = f(x)$, at the point x is the marginal cost of oil at the output x. If the derivative is a function, $f'(x)$, of x, then *the function $f'(x)$ expresses the marginal cost as a function of the level of output*.

Table 4.3 shows the interpretation of the derivative for a variety of other economic relationships.

Table 4.3 The interpretation of the derivative of certain functional relationships in economics

$y = f(x)$	x	*Derivative*, $\lim_{\Delta x \to 0} \Delta y/\Delta x$
Cost	Output	Marginal cost
Revenue	Output	Marginal revenue
Consumption	National Income	Marginal propensity to consume
Imports	National Income	Marginal propensity to import
Output	Labour employed	Marginal productivity of labour
Wealth	Time	Income
Capital	Time	Investment
Output	Time	Absolute rate of growth of output

4.5 Determination of maxima and minima by differentiation

In Section 4.2 it was shown that a necessary condition for a maximum or a minimum of $y = f(x)$ is that the slope of the function is horizontal. In Section 4.3 we demonstrated that the slope at a point can be measured by the limiting quantity, $\lim_{\Delta x \to 0} \Delta y/\Delta x$. When the slope is horizontal this limiting quantity, known as the derivative, is equal to zero.

The derivative at a particular value of x can often be expressed as a simple mathematical function of x,

$$\lim_{\Delta x \to 0} \Delta y/\Delta x = f'(x)$$

In this case the value of x at which the slope of the function is horizontal can be found by solving the equation

$$f'(x) = 0$$

The solutions are the values of x at which y may be either a maximum or a minimum.

Example 1 Find the maxima and minima of $y = 3x^2 - 6x + 5$. First of all, evaluate $f'(x)$. Since

$$y = 3x^2 - 6x + 5$$

if x increases to $x + \Delta x$ then y increases to

$$y + \Delta y = 3(x + \Delta x)^2 - 6(x + \Delta x) + 5$$
$$= 3x^2 + 6x\,\Delta x + 3\Delta x^2 - 6x - 6\Delta x + 5$$

It follows that an increase Δx in the value of x increases the value of y by

$$\Delta y = 6x\,\Delta x + 3\Delta x^2 - 6\Delta x$$

whence

$$\Delta y/\Delta x = 6x + 3\Delta x - 6$$

and so

$$\lim_{\Delta x \to 0} \Delta y/\Delta x = 6x - 6$$

The derivative expressed as a function of x is $f'(x) = 6x - 6$; the solution of the equation

$$6x - 6 = 0$$

is

$$x = 1$$

When $x = 1$, $y = 3 - 6 + 5 = 2$. Thus only at the point $x = 1$, $y = 2$ can y be either a maximum or a minimum. Sketching the graph of the function for values of x close to unity shows that the value $y = 2$ is in fact a minimum.

Example 2 Let us return to the example of Section 2.5 in which a firm chooses the output which will maximize profit, given the demand curve $D = 140 - 12P$ and the cost curve $C = 40 + 5Q$. It was shown that profit as a function of output is

$$y = -40 + 6\tfrac{2}{3}x - \tfrac{1}{12}x^2$$

where y is profit and x is output. A necessary condition that profit is a maximum is that the derivative of profit with respect to output is zero, i.e. profit cannot be increased by a small variation in the amount of output (this condition follows from Section 4.2). We can find the derivative of profit with respect to output in the usual way, by considering the effect of a small increase, Δx, in the amount of output: before the increase

$$y = -40 + 6\tfrac{2}{3}x - \tfrac{1}{12}x^2$$

and after the increase

$$\begin{aligned} y + \Delta y &= -40 + 6\tfrac{2}{3}(x + \Delta x) - \tfrac{1}{12}(x + \Delta x)^2 \\ &= -40 + 6\tfrac{2}{3}(x + \Delta x) - \tfrac{1}{12}(x^2 + 2x\,\Delta x + \Delta x^2) \\ &= -40 + 6\tfrac{2}{3}x + 6\tfrac{2}{3}\Delta x - \tfrac{1}{12}x^2 - \tfrac{1}{6}x\,\Delta x - \tfrac{1}{12}\Delta x^2 \end{aligned}$$

so that

$$\Delta y = (y + \Delta y) - y = 6\tfrac{2}{3}\Delta x - \tfrac{1}{6}x\,\Delta x - \tfrac{1}{12}\Delta x^2$$

Dividing throughout by Δx,

$$\Delta y/\Delta x = 6\tfrac{2}{3} - \tfrac{1}{6}x - \tfrac{1}{12}\Delta x$$

whence the derivative is

$$\lim_{\Delta x \to 0} \Delta y/\Delta x = 6\tfrac{2}{3} - \tfrac{1}{6}x$$

For a maximum it is necessary that the derivative is equal to zero, i.e. that

$$6\tfrac{2}{3} - \tfrac{1}{6}x = 0$$

which means that there is a maximum only if

$$x = 6\tfrac{2}{3} \times 6 = 40$$

We conclude that profit is at a maximum only if output is 40 units. This agrees with the result shown graphically in Fig. 2C.

4.6 Higher derivatives

We have seen in previous sections of this chapter how the slope of a function can be measured and how the measurement of the slope can be expressed as a function of x. If we plot the graph of something which is a function of x then the slope of the graph is obtained by differentiating the 'something' with respect to x. But the slope of a function of x is itself a 'something' which is a function of x. Consequently, if we plot the graph of the slope of a function, then the slope of the graph of the slope is obtained by differentiating the formula for the slope, $f'(x)$, with respect to x. But the formula for $f'(x)$ is obtained by differentiating $y = f(x)$ with respect to x. Consequently, if we differentiate $y = f(x)$ *twice* in succession with respect to x [once to get the derivative $f'(x)$, and once to differentiate $f'(x)$], the result is a measure of the slope of the graph of the slope of the function $y = f(x)$. The result of differentiating $f'(x)$ is denoted $f''(x)$ and is known as the 'second derivative' of $y = f(x)$; in graphical terms $f''(x)$ is a measure of 'the slope of the slope' of $y = f(x)$. By regarding $f''(x)$ as a 'something' which is a function of x we can obtain by differentiation the third derivative, $f'''(x)$, which is the derivative of $f''(x)$ and is obtained by differentiating $f(x)$ three times in succession. In general, the nth derivative, $f^{(n)}(x)$, of the function $y = f(x)$ is the derivative of the derivative of the derivative ... (n times) ... of $f(x)$, i.e. the nth derivative is the result of differentiating the function n times in succession.

Example The reader can easily verify that if $y = 3x^3 + 6x^2 + 2$ then $f'(x) = 9x^2 + 12x$, $f''(x) = 18x + 12$, $f'''(x) = 18$ and $f''''(x) = 0$.

A useful concept which is defined in terms of higher derivatives (i.e. in terms of derivatives other than the first) is the 'point of inflection'. When sketching the graph of a function it is often useful to locate the points of inflection; these are the points at which the graph 'straightens out' momentarily (see Figs 4E, 4F). Mathematically, a point of inflection of $y = f(x)$ is located at any value of x at which $f''(x) = 0$ and y is neither a maximum nor a minimum.

4.7 Sufficient conditions for maxima and minima

It is important to appreciate that although the condition that the derivative of a function is equal to zero is necessary both for a maximum and a minimum, it is neither sufficient to ensure a maximum, nor sufficient to ensure a minimum, nor sufficient to ensure *either* a maximum or a minimum. Figure 4E shows the

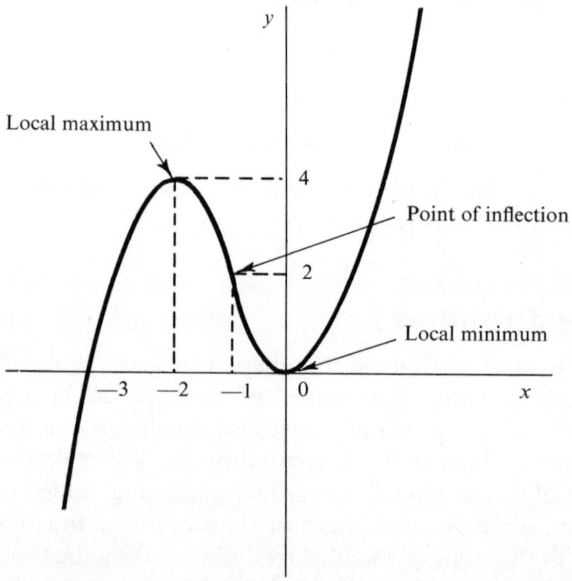

Fig. 4E Graph of the function $y=x^3+3x^2$

graph of the function $y = x^3 + 3x^2$; this function has a zero derivative (i.e. a horizontal slope) at $x = -2$ and $x = 0$; however, in neither of these cases is the function at a maximum or a minimum. The graph shows that for large positive values of x the value of y is much greater than it is when $x = -2$ and for large negative values of x the value of y is much less than it is when $x = 0$. It is nevertheless true that when $x = -2$ the value of y is higher than it is at any other point on the graph nearby, and similarly, when $x = 0$ the value of y is lower than it is at any other point on the graph nearby. For this reason we refer to the value of y when $x = -2$ as a 'local maximum' and to the value of y when $x = 0$ as a 'local minimum'. 'Local' maxima and minima are contrasted with ‘global’ maxima and minima. A function $y = f(x)$ defined over the range $a \leqslant x \leqslant b$ has a ‘global’ maximum (minimum) when the value of y is greater (less) than it is at any other value of x in the range $a \leqslant x \leqslant b$; the function has a ‘local’ maximum (minimum) at $x = \bar{x}$ when there is some small interval $c < \bar{x} < d$ (where $a \leqslant c, d \leqslant b$) within which the value of y is greater (less) at $x = \bar{x}$ than it is at any other value of x within the interval.

Not only is it necessary to distinguish between ‘local’ and ‘global’ maxima and minima, it is also necessary to distinguish between maxima and minima on the one hand and stationary values on the other. A stationary value of a function is defined to be any value of y at which the slope is zero. It follows that a stationary value is a value of y at which the necessary condition for a maximum or minimum is satisfied. It is by no means the case that all stationary values are maxima and minima, as a glance at Fig. 4F will confirm. Figure 4F shows the graph of the function $y = x^3 + 3x^2 + 3x$; although the function has a zero derivative at $x = -1$, this point is neither a local maximum nor a

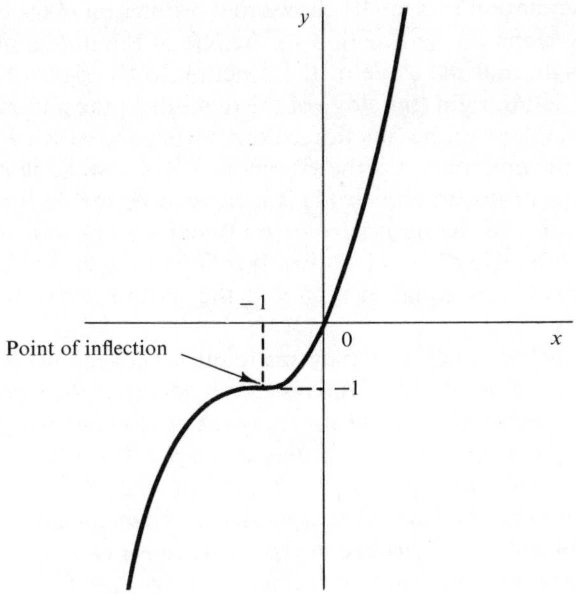

Fig. 4F Graph of the function $y=x^3+3x^2+3x$

local minimum, since as x decreases marginally the value of y decreases and as x increases marginally the value of y increases. The value of $y = -1$ when $x = -1$ is an example of a stationary value which is neither a maximum nor a minimum. If a stationary value is neither a maximum nor a minimum then it must be a point of inflection.

The question naturally arises: how is it possible to distinguish between a maximum, a minimum and a point of inflection? The following result provides a partial answer to this question. *A sufficient condition for, respectively, a maximum (minimum) is that the derivative of the function is zero and that the second derivative of the function is, respectively, negative (positive).*

This result can be appreciated by studying Fig. 4E. A function is at a local maximum when the slope of the function to the left of the maximum is upward from left to right and the slope of the function to the right of the maximum is downward from left to right (the slope of the function at the maximum being horizontal). In other words the function is at a maximum if the slope of the function changes from a positive value to a negative value about the maximum. The slope of the function $f(x)$ is measured by the derivative, $f'(x)$. The derivative $f'(x)$ will change from a positive value to a negative value about the maximum if the graph of $f'(x)$ is downward sloping and passes through zero at the point x for which $f(x)$ is a maximum. Now the slope of the graph of $f'(x)$ is measured by the derivative of $f'(x)$, which may be said to be the derivative of the derivative of the function $f(x)$. If the function $f'(x)$ is downward sloping from left to right then the derivative of $f'(x)$ is negative, i.e. the derivative of the derivative of $f(x)$ is negative. It follows that the derivative of a function $f(x)$ changes from a positive value to a negative value (i.e. the function is at a maximum) if the derivative $f'(x)$ is zero and the second derivative $f''(x)$ is negative.

A further examination of Fig. 4E shows that a function takes on a local minimum when the slope of the function to the left of the minimum is downward from left to right and the slope of the function to the right of the minimum is upward from left to right (the slope of the function at the minimum being zero). In this case the slope of the function changes from a negative value to a positive value about the minimum, i.e. the graph of $f'(x)$ is upward sloping at the minimum. The slope of the graph of $f'(x)$ is measured by the derivative of $f'(x)$ (i.e. by the derivative of the derivative of $f(x)$) and if $f'(x)$ is upward sloping then the second derivative $f''(x)$ is positive. It follows that a function is at a minimum if the derivative is equal to zero and the second derivative is positive.

The general rule by which one may distinguish between maxima, minima and points of inflection involves derivatives even higher than the second.

(i) *A necessary and sufficient condition for $f(x)$ to be at a maximum is that $f'(x) = 0$ and that the first nonzero derivative in the sequence $f''(x), f'''(x), \ldots, f^{(n)}(x), \ldots$ is negative and occurs for some even value of n ($n = 2, 4, 6, 8, \ldots$);*

(ii) *a necessary and sufficient condition for $f(x)$ to be at a minimum is that $f'(x) = 0$ and that the first nonzero derivative in the sequence $f''(x), f'''(x), \ldots, f^{(n)}(x), \ldots$ is positive and occurs for some even value of n ($n = 2, 4, 6, 8, \ldots$);*

(iii) *a necessary and sufficient condition for a stationary value to be point of inflection is that it is neither a maximum nor a minimum.*

This result is illustrated by the following examples.

Example 1 In Section 4.5 it was shown that a necessary condition for the function $y = -40 + 6\frac{2}{3}x - \frac{1}{12}x^2$ to be a maximum is that $x = 40$. To show that at this value y is indeed a maximum it is necessary to verify that the first nonzero derivative in the sequence $f''(x), f'''(x), \ldots, f^{(n)}(x), \ldots$ is negative and occurs for an even value of n. The sequence of derivatives is obtained by successive differentiation. We know from Section 4.5 that $f'(x) = 6\frac{2}{3} - \frac{1}{6}x$. To find the derivative of $f'(x)$ we examine the change in $f'(x)$ due to a small change, Δx, in x: before the change

$$f'(x) = 6\tfrac{2}{3} - \tfrac{1}{6}x$$

and after the change

$$\begin{aligned} f'(x + \Delta x) &= 6\tfrac{2}{3} - \tfrac{1}{6}(x + \Delta x) \\ &= 6\tfrac{2}{3} - \tfrac{1}{6}x - \tfrac{1}{6}\Delta x \end{aligned}$$

Hence

$$f'(x + \Delta x) - f'(x) = -\tfrac{1}{6}\Delta x$$

and so the derivative of $f'(x)$ is

$$f''(x) = \lim_{\Delta x \to 0} \frac{f'(x + \Delta x) - f'(x)}{\Delta x} = \frac{-\tfrac{1}{6}\Delta x}{\Delta x} = -\tfrac{1}{6}$$

Since $f''(x) = -\tfrac{1}{6}$ it follows that the first nonzero derivative in the sequence is negative and occurs for an even value of n, $n = 2$. It follows that the function does indeed attain a maximum.

Example 2 Find the maxima, minima and points of inflection of the function $y = x^3 + 3x^2$.

For the function to be either at a maximum, a minimum or a point of inflection it is necessary that $f'(x) = 0$. (When $f'(x) = 0$ the value x is said to be a 'stationary value' of the function $f(x)$.) By elementary algebra the slope of $y = x^3 + 3x^2$ is

$$\Delta y/\Delta x = [(3x^2 + 6x)\Delta x + (3x + 3)\Delta x^2 + \Delta x^3]/\Delta x$$

so that the derivative is

$$f'(x) = \lim_{\Delta x \to 0} \frac{\Delta y}{\Delta x} = 3x^2 + 6x$$

The conditions under which $f'(x) = 0$ are easily found. Writing $f'(x) = 3x^2 + 6x = 3x(x + 2)$ it is seen that $f'(x) = 0$ if either $x = 0$ or $x = -2$. These values $x = 0, -2$ are the only two values for which the function can be at either a maximum, a minimum or a point of inflection.

To distinguish between the three possibilities we first of all evaluate the second derivative. The algebra is straightforward. Since

$$f'(x) = 3x^2 + 6$$

it follows that

$$\begin{aligned} f'(x + \Delta x) &= 3(x + \Delta x)^2 + 6(x + \Delta x) \\ &= 3x^2 + 6x\,\Delta x + 3\Delta x^2 + 6x + 6\Delta x \end{aligned}$$

so that

$$\begin{aligned} [f'(x + \Delta x) - f'(x)]/\Delta x &= [6x\,\Delta x + 6\Delta x + 3\Delta x^2]/\Delta x \\ &= 6x + 6 + 3\Delta x \end{aligned}$$

and the second derivative is

$$f''(x) = \lim_{\Delta x \to 0} \frac{f'(x + \Delta x) - f'(x)}{\Delta x} = 6x + 6$$

When $x = 0, f''(x) = 6$; hence $f^{(n)}(x)$ is positive for $n = 2$, so that when $x = 0$ the function is at a minimum. When $x = -2, f''(x) = -6$; thus $f^{(n)}(x)$ is negative for $n = 2$, so that when $x = -2$ the function is at a maximum. Since $f''(x) = 0$ when $x = -1$ there is a point of inflection at $x = -1$. We conclude that the function $y = x^3 + 3x^2$ has a local minimum at $x = 0$, a local maximum at $x = -2$ and a point of inflection at $x = -1$ (see Fig. 4E).

Notes and references

Most introductory mathematics textbooks cover the material in this chapter. Students requiring parallel reading might consult Allen,[6] Ch. 6–8, Yamane,[126] Ch. 2, 3, Lewis,[79] Ch. 7–10, Tintner,[120] Ch. 9, 10 and Meier and Archer,[93] Ch. 7. Baumol,[13] Ch. 3, 4 contains a summary of the material together with many applications. Stephenson,[116] Ch. 3, collects a number of useful results in an easily accessible form. The standard text is Courant,[30] Ch. 2.

Problems

4.3 Evaluate the derivatives of the following functions:

(a) $y = 3x^2$
(b) $y = 6x^2 + 4x$
(c) $y = (3x^2 + 1)(x + 2)$
(d) $y = -1/(2x)$

4.4.1 The total costs of a firm, y, depends on output, x, in the following way:

$$y = 3x^3 + 6x^2 + x + 2$$

How does marginal cost depend on output?

4.4.2 The growth of a country's capital stock, K, is described by the equation

$$K = 40{,}000 + 5{,}400t + 400t^2 - 10t^3$$

where t is time (in number of years elapsed since some base date). Find how the rate of investment varies with time.

4.4.3 A firm has a demand curve $D = 200 - P$ where D is the quantity demanded and P is the price of the product. The firm's total costs are $C = 100 + Q^2$ where Q is the quantity produced.

(a) If the firm only produces what it can sell, and no more, write down the revenue as a function of the quantity produced.

(b) Express marginal revenue as a function of output.

(c) Express marginal cost as a function of output.

(d) Assume that the firm wishes to produce an amount such that marginal revenue = marginal cost. How much should it produce?

(e) What will be its profits when it produces this amount?

(f) Illustrate your solution graphically.

4.5.1 Referring to Problem 4.4.3 above, express profit as a function of output. At what output is profit a maximum? Confirm your answer by sketching the graph of profit against output. Explain graphically why the output which maximizes profit is also the output at which marginal revenue = marginal cost (refer to 4.4.3 (b)–(d) above).

4.5.2 For each of the functions in Problem 4.3, find the values of x at which y may possibly be a maximum or minimum.

4.6 Evaluate the second and third derivatives of

(a) $y = 3x^2 + 2$
(b) $y = 1/(2x)$
(c) $y = (x - 1)/(x - 2)$

4.7.1 Find the maxima and minima of

(a) $y = x^2 - 270x + 18{,}400$
(b) $y = x^3 - 24x^2 + 48x - 17$
(c) $y = x^4 + 4x^3 - 20x^2 + 36$

4.7.2 A university planning committee is considering a new hall of residence. The committee estimates the annual running costs of the hall (in £) to be

$$C = 12{,}100 + N^2$$

where N is the number of students in residence. The university receives a subsidy of £40 per annum for each student accommodated in hall. If the committee wants to minimize the net cost to the university per head, and intends to price accommodation to cover net costs exactly, what should be the size of the hall and what should be the fee charged to students? What difference would it make if the subsidy were reduced to £20 per head per annum?

4.7.3 A chemical firm has decided that it needs new productive capacity. A plant producing in the output range 250 to 600 tons per month is required. Technology determines that within this range the relationship between cost and output can be approximated by

$$C = 10Q^4 - 120Q^3 + 450Q^2$$

where C is annual cost (in £) and Q is output (in units of 100 tons per month). What size of plant minimizes average cost?

4.7.4 Jon is an economics student and runs a disco on Friday nights at the union. Jon wishes to maximize the profit from the disco. On two previous Fridays he charged 25p for admission and 50 people came, and 10p for admission and 200 people came. Jon is prepared to assume that (a) all Friday night discos have the same demand curve, and (b) this demand curve is linear. If the costs of the disco are independent of the attendance, what price should be charged for admission?

Chapter 5

Rules for differentiation

5.1 Notation for the derivative

In Section 4.3 we introduced the derivative, $f'(x)$, as a measure of the slope of the function $y = f(x)$ at the point x. The notation $f'(x)$ emphasizes that the derivative of $f(x)$ is itself a function of x. There is another notation for the derivative which is sometimes more convenient to use: the derivative of the function $y = f(x)$ is written dy/dx. This notation emphasizes that the derivative is a limiting value of the ratio of the increment in y to the increment in x

$$\frac{dy}{dx} = \lim_{\Delta x \to 0} \frac{\Delta y}{\Delta x}$$

This notation is extended to the second derivative, third derivative, etc., in the following way.

$$\frac{d^2y}{dx^2} = f''(x)$$

$$\frac{d^3f}{dx^3} = f'''(x)$$

In general,

$$\frac{d^nf}{dx^n} = f^{(n)}(x)$$

It is important to appreciate that not all functions have derivatives, in the sense that there are functions for which the ratio $\Delta y/\Delta x$ does not tend to a definite finite-valued limit as Δx tends to zero. However, functions which are widely used in economics almost always have derivatives; for example, a rational function (see Section 2.5) has a derivative at all points at which the function itself is not infinite. A necessary condition for a function to have a derivative is that it is continuous. As a rule, an arbitrary function $y = f(x)$ has a derivative provided that its value does not change quickly for a very small variation in x. A function which has a derivative is said to be *differentiable*.

5.2 Properties of the derivative

The derivative of a function has a number of important properties which make its evaluation very easy.

(1) *If a function is scaled by a constant factor, λ, then the derivative is scaled by the same constant factor, λ*, i.e. if $y = f(x) = \lambda g(x)$ then $f'(x) = \lambda g'(x)$.

To see this, note that by definition

$$f'(x) = \lim_{\Delta x \to 0} \frac{f(x + \Delta x) - f(x)}{\Delta x}$$

and since $f(x) = \lambda g(x)$,

$$\frac{f(x + \Delta x) - f(x)}{\Delta x} = \frac{\lambda g(x + \Delta x) - \lambda g(x)}{\Delta x}$$

$$= \lambda \left[\frac{g(x + \Delta x) - g(x)}{\Delta x} \right]$$

so that

$$f'(x) = \lim_{\Delta x \to 0} \lambda \left[\frac{g(x + \Delta x) - g(x)}{\Delta x} \right]$$

$$= \lambda \lim_{\Delta x \to 0} \frac{g(x + \Delta x) - g(x)}{\Delta x}$$

$$= \lambda g'(x)$$

(2) *The derivative is unchanged if the function is increased by a constant amount a*, i.e. if $y = f(x) = g(x) + a$ then $f'(x) = g'(x)$.

To see this, note that

$$f'(x) = \lim_{\Delta x \to 0} \frac{f(x + \Delta x) - f(x)}{\Delta x}$$

$$= \lim_{\Delta x \to 0} \frac{[g(x + \Delta x) + a] - [g(x) + a]}{\Delta x}$$

and cancelling the *a*s gives

$$\lim_{\Delta x \to 0} \frac{g(x + \Delta x) - g(x)}{\Delta x} = g'(x)$$

(3) *The derivative of the sum of two functions is equal to the sum of the derivatives*, i.e. if $y = f(x) = g(x) + h(x)$ then $f'(x) = g'(x) + h'(x)$

The proof is that

$$f'(x) = \lim_{\Delta x \to 0} \frac{f(x + \Delta x) - f(x)}{\Delta x}$$

$$= \lim_{\Delta x \to 0} \frac{[g(x + \Delta x) + h(x + \Delta x)] - [g(x) + h(x)]}{\Delta x}$$

and rearranging terms in the numerator gives

$$\lim_{\Delta x \to 0} \frac{[g(x + \Delta x) - g(x)] + [h(x + \Delta x) - h(x)]}{\Delta x}$$

$$= \lim_{\Delta x \to 0} \frac{g(x + \Delta x) - g(x)}{\Delta x} + \lim_{\Delta x \to 0} \frac{h(x + \Delta x) - h(x)}{\Delta x}$$

$$= g'(x) + h'(x)$$

Note that putting $h(x) = a$ gives property 2.

An obvious corollary is that the derivative of the difference between two functions is the difference between the derivatives.

An immediate consequence of properties 1, 2 and 3 is that for any sequence of functions $g(x)$, $h(x)$, ... and corresponding sequence of constants, α, β, γ, ... the derivative of

$$f(x) = \alpha + \beta g(x) + \gamma h(x) + \cdots$$

is

$$f'(x) = \beta g'(x) + \gamma h'(x) + \cdots$$

(**4**) (Product rule) *The derivative of the product of two functions,* $y = f(x) = g(x)h(x)$ *is equal to*

$$f'(x) = g(x)h'(x) + g'(x)h(x)$$

The proof is as follows. Let the increases in $g(x)$ and $h(x)$ when x is increased by Δx be Δg, Δh respectively. Then

$$f'(x) = \lim_{\Delta x \to 0} \frac{f(x + \Delta x) - f(x)}{\Delta x}$$

$$= \lim_{\Delta x \to 0} \frac{[g(x) + \Delta g][h(x) + \Delta h] - g(x)h(x)}{\Delta x}$$

$$= \lim_{\Delta x \to 0} \frac{g(x)h(x) + g(x)\,\Delta h + h(x)\,\Delta g + \Delta g\,\Delta h - g(x)h(x)}{\Delta x}$$

and cancelling the terms in $g(x)h(x)$ gives

$$\lim_{\Delta x \to 0} \frac{g(x)\,\Delta h + h(x)\,\Delta g + \Delta g\,\Delta h}{\Delta x}$$

Because we are considering the derivative at a specified value of x only the terms Δg, Δh depend on Δx, so that this expression may be written

$$g(x) \lim_{\Delta x \to 0} \frac{\Delta h}{\Delta x} + h(x) \lim_{\Delta x \to 0} \frac{\Delta g}{\Delta x} + \lim_{\Delta x \to 0} \frac{\Delta g\,\Delta h}{\Delta x}$$

$$= g(x)h'(x) + h(x)g'(x) + \lim_{\Delta x \to 0} \frac{\Delta g\,\Delta h}{\Delta x}$$

Consider the last term in this expression. If the derivatives $g'(x)$, $h'(x)$ have finite values then it must be true that as $\Delta x \to 0$ both $\Delta g \to 0$ and $\Delta h \to 0$ (otherwise one or other of the derivatives would be infinitely large). On using the result (proved in Section 2.9) that the limit of a product is equal to the product of the limits, we have

$$\lim_{\Delta x \to 0} \frac{\Delta g \, \Delta h}{\Delta x} = \lim_{\Delta x \to 0} \frac{\Delta g}{\Delta x} \lim_{\Delta x \to 0} \Delta h$$

$$= g'(x).0 = 0$$

Having established that if $g'(x)$ and $h'(x)$ exist then

$$\lim_{\Delta x \to 0} \frac{\Delta g \, \Delta h}{\Delta x} = 0$$

it follows that $f'(x) = g(x)h'(x) + g'(x)h(x)$.

(5) (Function of a function rule). *If $y = f(u)$ is a function of the variable u, and u is a function of the variable x, then the derivative of y with respect to x is equal to the derivative of y with respect to u multiplied by the derivative of u with respect to x*, i.e. if u is a function of x then y may be written as a function, $w(x)$ of x and

$$w'(x) = f'(u).u'(x)$$

This rule is easier to remember in the alternative notation

$$\frac{dy}{dx} = \frac{dy}{du} \cdot \frac{du}{dx}$$

The left-hand side of the equation can be thought of as the result of 'cancelling out' the *du*s on the right-hand side; this cancellation is not a legitimate mathematical operation—merely a convenient mnemonic.

Suppose that the effect of an increase, Δx, in x is to increase u by an amount Δu, and hence to increase y by an amount Δy. By definition

$$\frac{dy}{dx} = \lim_{\Delta x \to 0} \frac{\Delta y}{\Delta x}$$

and multiplying both the numerator and denominator by Δu gives

$$\lim_{\Delta x \to 0} \frac{\Delta y}{\Delta u} \cdot \frac{\Delta u}{\Delta x}$$

It is a consequence of the product rule for limits (Section 2.9) that if both the derivatives $f'(u)$ and $u'(x)$ are finite-valued then this expression is equal to

$$\lim_{\Delta x \to 0} \frac{\Delta y}{\Delta u} \cdot \lim_{\Delta x \to 0} \frac{\Delta u}{\Delta x}$$

Now if the derivative $u'(x)$ is finite, it must be true that $\Delta u \to 0$ as $\Delta x \to 0$, and hence the expression dy/dx may be written

$$\lim_{\Delta u \to 0} \frac{\Delta y}{\Delta u} \cdot \lim_{\Delta x \to 0} \frac{\Delta u}{\Delta x} = f'(u).u'(x)$$

(6) *The derivative of the function* $f(x) = x^\alpha$ *is equal to* $\alpha x^{\alpha - 1}$ *where* $\alpha \neq 0$ *is any real number.*

We shall prove this rule for the special case in which α is an integer. In principle there is no difficulty in generalizing the proof to the case where α is a rational number (i.e. where α can be expressed as a simple fraction with integers in both numerator and denominator). Unfortunately the same proof cannot be used when α is an irrational number, e.g. $\alpha = \pi = 3{\cdot}1412\ldots$; in this case there is a basic difficulty in defining what is meant by x raised to the power α. However, if x^α is suitably defined when x is irrational then property 6 is valid: the suitable definition is $x^\alpha = \exp(\alpha \log(x))$ (see Chapter 18).

To prove the rule for the case where n is a positive integer we first of all show that if $f(x) = x$ then $f'(x) = 1$. This is straightforward, since

$$f'(x) = \lim_{\Delta x \to 0} \frac{(x + \Delta x) - x}{\Delta x} = \lim_{\Delta x \to 0} \frac{\Delta x}{\Delta x} = 1$$

It follows from the 'product rule' (property 4) that if $f(x) = x^2 = x.x$ then $f'(x) = x + x = 2x$; furthermore if $f(x) = x^3 = x^2.x$ then $f'(x) = x^2 + 2x.x = 3x^2$; in general; if $f(x) = x^n = x^{n-1}.x$ then $f'(x) = x^{n-1} + (n-1)x^{n-2}.x = nx^{n-1}$. To prove the rule for negative integers we first of all show that if $f(x) = 1/x$ then $f'(x) = -1/x^2$. This is again straightforward, since

$$\begin{aligned} f'(x) &= \lim_{\Delta x \to 0} \left(\frac{1}{x + \Delta x} - \frac{1}{x}\right) \Big/ \Delta x \\ &= \lim_{\Delta x \to 0} \left[\frac{x - (x + \Delta x)}{(x + \Delta x)x}\right] \Big/ \Delta x \\ &= \lim_{\Delta x \to 0} \left[\frac{-\Delta x}{(x + \Delta x)x}\right] \Big/ \Delta x \\ &= \lim_{\Delta x \to 0} \frac{-1}{(x + \Delta x)x} \\ &= \frac{-1}{x^2} \end{aligned}$$

It follows from the product rule that if $f(x) = x^{-2} = 1/x^2 = (1/x).(1/x)$ then $f'(x) = (1/x)(-1/x^2) + (-1/x^2)(1/x) = -2/x^3 = -2x^{-3}$; in general, if $f(x) = x^{-n} = 1/x^n = (1/x^{n-1}).(1/x)$ then $f'(x) = (1/x^{n-1})(-1/x^2) + [-(n-1)/x^n](1/x) = -n/x^{n+1} = -nx^{-n-1}$.

(7) (Quotient rule) *The derivative of the quotient of two functions,* $y = f(x) = g(x)/h(x)$ *is equal to*

$$f'(x) = \frac{h(x)g'(x) - g(x)h'(x)}{[h(x)]^2}$$

The proof follows from the product rule (property 4) together with the function of a function rule (property 5). Putting $f(x) = g(x)w(x)$ where $w(x) = 1/h(x)$ and using the product rule gives $f'(x) = g(x)w'(x) + g'(x)w(x) = g(x)w'(x) + g'(x)/h(x)$. Put $h(x) = u$ so that $w = 1/u$ and use the function of a function rule to evaluate

$$\frac{dw}{dx} = \frac{dw}{du}\cdot\frac{du}{dx} = -\frac{1}{u^2}\cdot\frac{du}{dx} = -\frac{h'(x)}{[h(x)]^2}$$

Substituting this into the formula for $f'(x)$ and rearranging the terms over a common denominator gives

$$f'(x) = [h(x)g'(x) - g(x)h'(x)]/[h(x)]^2$$

Examples Differentiate with respect to x:

(i) $y = 3x^2$. From property 1 the derivative of $3x^2$ is 3 times the derivative of x^2 and from property 6 the derivative of x^2 is $2x$. Substituting $g(x) = x^2$, $\lambda = 3$ into property 1 shows that $dy/dx = 3(2x) = 6x$.

(ii) $y = 3x^2 + 6x$. From property 3 the derivative of $3x^2 + 6x$ is the sum of the derivative of $3x^2$ and the derivative of $6x$; from properties 1 and 6 the derivative of $3x^2$ is $6x$ and the derivative of $6x$ is 6. Substituting $g(x) = 3x^2$, $h(x) = 6x$ into property 3 shows that $dy/dx = 6x + 6$.

(iii) $y = (3x^2 + 6x)5x^3$. Substituting $g(x) = 3x^2 + 6x$ and $h(x) = 5x^3$, it follows from property 4 that

$$dy/dx = g(x)h'(x) + g'(x)h(x)$$

From properties 1, 3 and 6 the derivative of $3x^2 + 6x$ is $6x + 6$ and from properties 1 and 6 the derivative of $5x^3$ is $15x^2$. Hence

$$\begin{aligned} dy/dx &= (3x^2 + 6x)(15x^2) + (6x + 6)5x^3 \\ &= 45x^4 + 90x^3 + 30x^4 + 30x^3 \\ &= 75x^4 + 120x^3 \\ &= 15x^3(5x + 8) \end{aligned}$$

(iv) $y = (3x^2 + 6x)^3$. Substituting $u = 3x^2 + 6x$ we may write $y = u^3$; from property 5 we know that

$$\frac{dy}{dx} = \frac{dy}{du}\cdot\frac{du}{dx}$$

From properties 1 and 6 $dy/du = 3u^2$ and from properties 1, 3 and 6 $du/dx = 6x + 6$. Hence

$$dy/dx = 3u^2(6x + 6)$$

Substituting back $u = (3x^2 + 6x)$ into this expression gives

$$dy/dx = 162x^2(x + 2)^2(x + 1)$$

(v) $y = (2x + 5)/(3x^2 + 6x)$. By substituting $g(x) = 2x + 5$ and $h(x) = 3x^2 + 6x$ it follows from property 7 that

$$\frac{dy}{dx} = \frac{h(x)g'(x) - g(x)h'(x)}{[h(x)]^2}$$

From properties 1, 3 and 6 it follows that $f'(x) = 2$, $g'(x) = 6x + 6$. Hence

$$\frac{dy}{dx} = \frac{(3x^2 + 6x)2 - (2x + 5)(6x + 6)}{(3x^2 + 6x)^2}$$

$$= \frac{6x^2 + 12x - (12x^2 + 12x + 30x + 30)}{(3x^2 + 6x)^2}$$

$$= \frac{-6x^2 - 30x - 30}{(3x^2 + 6x)^2}$$

$$= \frac{-2(x^2 + 5x + 5)}{3x^2(x + 2)^2}$$

(vi) Find the second derivative of $y = 4x^3 + 7x$.

The second derivative is the derivative of the first derivative; the first derivative is (from properties 1, 3 and 6)

$$dy/dx = 12x^2 + 7$$

and so the second derivative is the derivative of $12x^2 + 7$ which is

$$d^2y/dx^2 = 24x$$

(using properties 1, 2 and 6).

5.3 Marginal analysis in economics

If the functional dependence of the variable y on the variable x can be represented in the form $y = f(x)$ then the derivative of y with respect to x, dy/dx, measures the rate at which y changes with respect to an infinitely small change in x. If y represents sales revenue and x represents output then dy/dx is the rate at which revenue changes with respect to an infinitely small change in output, i.e. dy/dx is equal to marginal revenue. If y represents cost and x represents output then dy/dx is the rate at which cost changes with respect to an infinitely small change in output, i.e. dy/dx is a measure of marginal cost.

Using these economic interpretations of the derivative, together with the properties of the derivative described in the previous section it is possible to give a simple demonstration of certain well-known economic theorems.

(i) *For the profits of a firm to be maximized it is necessary* (*but not sufficient*) *that marginal revenue is equal to marginal cost.*

For any firm, both revenue, R, and cost, C, are functions of output, Q, i.e. $R = R(Q)$ and $C = C(Q)$. Profit, P, is the excess of revenue over cost, $P = R - C$. Since profit is equal to the difference between two variables which are functions of output, profit itself is a function of output, i.e.

$$P = P(Q) = R(Q) - C(Q)$$

Profit is at a maximum with respect to output when $P(Q)$ is at a maximum with respect to Q, and a necessary condition for this (see Section 4.2) is that $P'(Q) = 0$. From property 3 it is seen that

$$P'(Q) = R'(Q) - C'(Q)$$

so that $P'(Q) = 0$ if and only if $R'(Q) = C'(Q)$. But $R'(Q)$ is the derivative of revenue with respect to output and is therefore a measure of marginal revenue. $C'(Q)$ is the derivative of cost with respect to output and is a measure of marginal cost. It follows that for profit to be at a maximum it is necessary for marginal revenue to equal marginal cost.

(ii) *A marginal change in the price of a commodity leaves the sales revenue of a firm unchanged if and only if the firm's demand curve $D = f(P)$ is such that when $D = Q$ then*

$$-\frac{dQ}{dP}\cdot\frac{P}{Q} = 1$$

where Q is the output of the firm. The quantity $-(dQ/dP)(P/Q)$ is known as the elasticity of demand.[1]

The proposition can be proved by using property 4 in the previous section. Revenue, R, is equal to price, P, times the quantity sold, Q. The quantity that is sold, Q, is equal to the demand for the commodity, D, which is a function, $D(P)$, of the price; it follows that the quantity sold is a function, $Q(P)$, of the price. Hence

$$R = P.Q = P.Q(P)$$

The change in revenue induced by a marginal unit change in price is zero if and only if $dR/dP = 0$. Substituting $y = R$, $g = P$, $h = Q(P)$ in property 4 it follows that

$$\frac{dR}{dP} = P\frac{dQ}{dP} + Q$$

1 The elasticity of demand is the ratio of the proportional change in the quantity sold to the proportional change in the price, when the change in the price is infinitely small. To see this note that

$$-\frac{dQ}{dP}\cdot\frac{P}{Q} = -\frac{P}{Q}\lim_{\Delta P\to 0}\frac{\Delta Q}{\Delta P} = -\lim_{\Delta P\to 0}\frac{P}{Q}\cdot\frac{\Delta Q}{\Delta P} = -\lim_{\Delta P\to 0}\frac{P}{\Delta P}\cdot\frac{\Delta Q}{Q}$$

$$= \lim_{\Delta P\to 0}\left(\frac{\Delta Q/Q}{\Delta P/P}\right)$$

Since demand usually falls as price increases the negative sign ensures that the measure of elasticity is normally positive.

Hence $dR/dP = 0$ if and only if $Q = -P.dQ/dP$, or, dividing by Q, if and only if $-(P/Q)(dQ/dP) = 1$.

(iii) *A firm's average cost is at a minimum only if marginal cost is equal to average cost.*

The average cost of the firm, $A(Q)$, is the total cost, $C = C(Q)$, divided by the number of units of output, Q. For average cost to be at a minimum it is necessary that the derivative of average cost with respect to output is zero; on substituting $y = A(Q)$, $g = C(Q)$, $h = Q$ it follows from property 7 that

$$\frac{dA}{dQ} = \frac{Q.dC/dQ - C}{Q^2}$$

When $Q > 0$, $Q^2 > 0$ so that when $Q > 0$, $dA/dQ = 0$ if and only if $Q.dC/dQ = C$; i.e. if and only if $dC/dQ = C/Q$: this condition shows that for average cost to be a minimum, marginal cost must be equal to average cost. By evaluating d^2A/dQ^2 and using the results of Section 4.7 the reader can verify that if cost is a steadily increasing function of output (i.e. $dC/dQ > 0$, $d^2C/dQ^2 > 0$) then the condition that marginal cost is equal to average cost is not only necessary but is also sufficient to ensure that average cost is at a minimum.

(iv) *Suppose that a firm's total cost has two components, fixed cost and variable cost: variable costs vary with the level of output whereas fixed costs do not.* (*a*) *The firm's marginal cost is independent of its fixed cost.* (*b*) *The firm's average variable cost is at a minimum when marginal cost equals average variable cost.* (*c*) *The firm's average total cost is at a minimum when marginal cost equals average total cost.*

Let variable cost be $V(Q)$ and let fixed cost be F; then total cost is $C(Q) = V(Q) + F$ where F is a constant. Setting $y = C(Q)$, $f = V(Q)$, $a = F$ in property 2 shows that

$$C'(Q) = V'(Q)$$

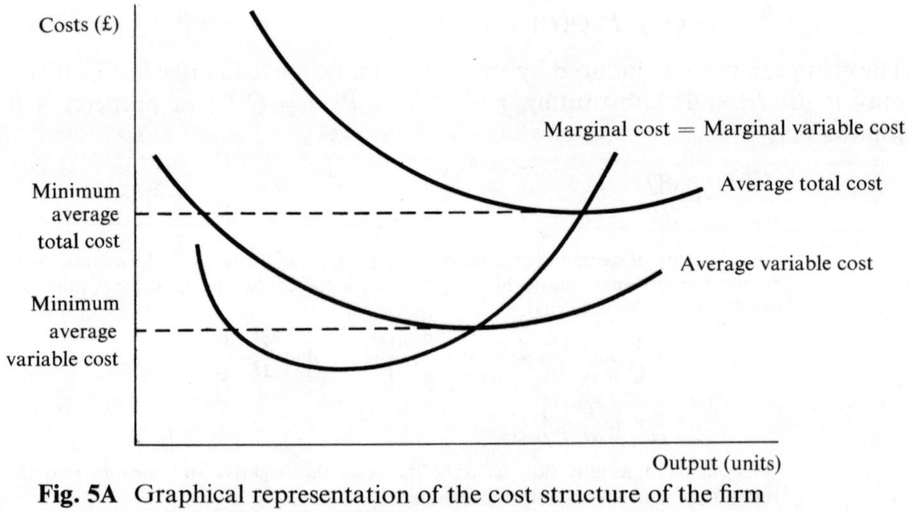

Fig. 5A Graphical representation of the cost structure of the firm

i.e. marginal total cost, $C'(Q)$, is equal to marginal variable cost, $V'(Q)$, and is independent of the fixed cost, F.

Part (b) is an immediate corollary of the discussion of average variable cost above; it is proved by setting $A(Q)$ equal to $V(Q)/Q$ and using the fact that $V'(Q) = C'(Q)$. Part (c) has already been proved.

The cost structure of the firm is often represented in the way shown in Fig. 5A; note how the graphs illustrate the various properties described in the text.

(v) *When a firm's demand curve is linear the average revenue at an output $2Q$ is equal to the marginal revenue at an output Q.*

The average revenue of the firm is equal to the price at which the commodity is sold, since

$$\text{Average revenue} = R/Q = (PQ)/Q = P$$

If the demand curve is linear, $D = a - bP$, then the quantity that can be sold, Q, which equals the quantity demanded, D, is a linear function of price, $Q = a - bP$. Since $Q = a - bP$ it follows that $P = (a - Q)/b$ and so when the output is $2Q$ the average revenue is $P = (a - 2Q)/b$.

The marginal revenue of the firm is $R'(Q)$ where $R = PQ = [(a - Q)/b]Q = (aQ - Q^2)/b$. It follows from properties 1 and 6 that

$$R'(Q) = (a - 2Q)/b$$

Hence the marginal revenue at an output Q is equal to the average revenue at an output $2Q$. This result is illustrated graphically in Fig. 5B.

By combining the graphical representation of costs (Fig. 5A) with the graphical representation of revenue (Fig. 5B) it is possible to illustrate the

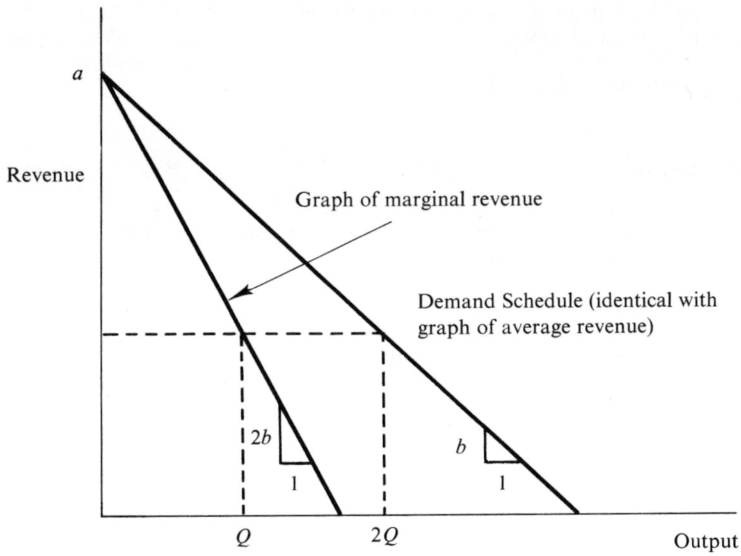

Fig. 5B Variation of revenue with output

short-run equilibrium of the firm in the way shown in Fig. 5C: the firm is in equilibrium when profit is maximized, and for profit to be maximized it is necessary for marginal revenue to equal marginal cost. It is this condition which establishes the connection between cost and revenue in the equilibrium of the firm.

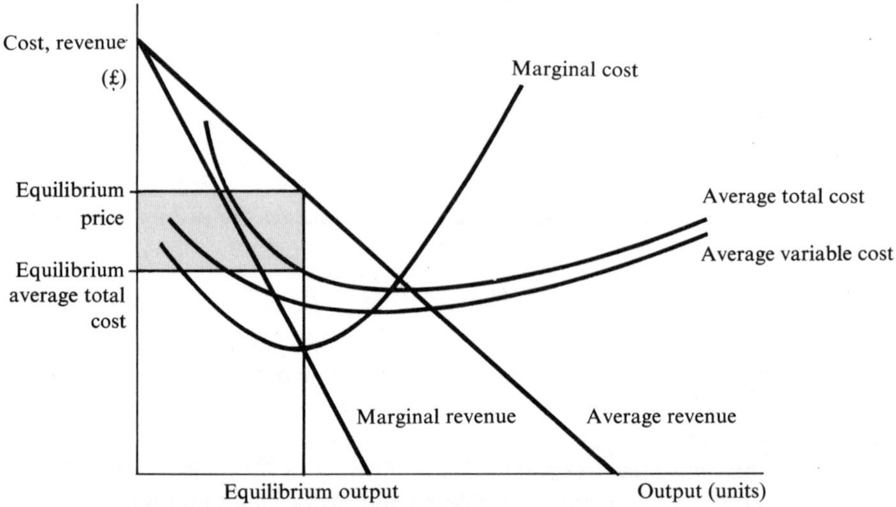

NOTE Shaded area is a measure of profit

Fig. 5C Equilibrium of the firm

Notes and references

On mathematical aspects see the references to the previous chapter. The technique of differentiation is widely used in economics, particularly in the application of marginal analysis to microeconomic problems. Baumol,[13] Henderson and Quandt[56] and Cohen and Cyert[28] all make extensive use of differentiation as a technique of marginal analysis. For students interested in applications to inventory analysis Baumol,[13] Ch. 1 presents a simple inventory model while Lesbourne,[78] Ch. 11 considers more sophisticated models.

Problems

5.1 Show from first principles that the derivative of $y = 1/(x - 2)$ exists for all values of x except $x = 2$, and that when $x = 2$ both the derivative and the function itself are infinite.

5.2.1 Differentiate with respect to x

(a) $y = 5x^6 - 4x^3 + 2x + 9$
(b) $y = (2x + 4)(6x - 5)$ (use product rule)
(c) $y = (5x + 4)^3$ (use function of a function rule)
(d) $y = x^2/(3x + 4)$ (use quotient rule)

5.2.2 Differentiate with respect to x

(a) $y = 1/(3x - 2)^2$
(b) $y = (7x^2 + 1)/(x - 3)^3$
(c) $y = 1/\sqrt{x}$
(d) $y = x^2\sqrt{x}$
(e) $y = x^4\sqrt[3]{x}$
(f) $y = (\sqrt[4]{x})^5$
(g) $y = (6x + 1)/\sqrt{(x - 2)^3}$

5.2.3 Evaluate the first, second, third, fourth and fifth derivatives of $y = (5x^2 + 4)^2$.

5.2.4 Show that if $f(x) \neq 0$ the product rule and the quotient rule may be written respectively as

$$\frac{f'(x)}{f(x)} = \frac{g'(x)}{g(x)} + \frac{h'(x)}{h(x)}$$

$$\frac{f'(x)}{f(x)} = \frac{g'(x)}{g(x)} - \frac{h'(x)}{h(x)}$$

Express these rules verbally in terms of 'percentage rate of change'.

5.2.5 Find the values of x at which $y = 2x^3 - 15x^2 + 36x + 12$ may possibly be a maximum or minimum.

5.3.1 Assume that in Problem 4.7.2 an economist is now drafted onto the university planning committee. He suggests that a more scientific pricing policy for accommodation in the new hall would be to price at the marginal cost to the university, rather than at the average cost. What effect does this new pricing policy have—for example, does the hall now make a profit?

5.3.2 It is often reasonable to describe the demand for a commodity by an equation

$$D = AP^{-\alpha}$$

where D is demand, P is price and A, α are suitably chosen positive constants. Show that the elasticity of demand is independent of both the price and the quantity demanded. Does the elasticity of demand depend on the constant A?

5.3.3 The income elasticity of consumer expenditure is defined to be $\xi = (dC/dY)Y/C$ where C is consumer expenditure and Y is income. If $C = a + bY$, where a and b are fixed values, show that $\xi = 1/[1 + a/(bY)]$. Show that ξ is independent of both C and Y if and only if $a = 0$.

5.3.4 Assuming that demand is a function of price, and that output is adjusted to meet demand, derive a relationship between marginal revenue and elasticity of demand.

5.3.5 The cost curve of a firm is $C = 500 + 20Q + Q^2/5$ where C is cost (in £) and Q is output.

(a) Sketch the graphs of marginal total cost, marginal variable cost, average total cost and average variable cost. Pay particular attention to the shape of the graphs where output is small and where average costs are a minimum.

The demand curve of the same firm is $D = 250 - (\frac{5}{4})P$.

(b) Sketch the graphs of marginal revenue and average revenue.

(c) Find the values of output and profit at which profit is a maximum, and illustrate your solution graphically.

5.3.6 A businessman wishes to minimize his raw material costs. These costs are the purchase price of the raw material, the cost of ordering new stocks of the raw material, and the storage costs required to maintain the stock in good condition. If the raw material is used at a steady rate of 20,000 lb per annum and costs 20p a lb, the fixed cost of ordering stock is £4 per order, and the cost of storage is 10% per year of the average value of stock on hand, find the least cost size of each order (i.e. the size of order which minimizes costs over the year).

5.3.7 Derive a general relationship for the businessman in Problem 5.3.6 relating optimum order size (S) to the annual quantity sold (Q), the unit purchase price (P), the ordering costs (K) and the annual storage costs as a proportion of the price of a unit of raw material (r).

5.3.8 It is sometimes argued that if a few firms of similar size are competing to increase their market share, each firm has a demand curve which is 'kinked' at a price corresponding to the ruling market price. (The reason is that if one firm reduces its price, other firms will follow suit to prevent the firm increasing its market share at their expense; on the other hand, if the firm increases its price then other firms will leave their prices unchanged in order to increase their own market share. For this reason an increase in price by any firm will, as a result of the competitor's reaction, lead to a relatively large fall in demand whereas a decrease in price will, in the same way, lead to only a small increase in demand. This implies that there is a kink in each firm's demand curve at the point corresponding to the ruling market price.)

Consider a firm with the following kinked demand curve:

$$D = 400 - 5P \qquad P > 50$$

$$D = 200 - P \qquad 50 \geqslant P \geqslant 0$$

where D is demand (in units of output) and P is price (in £); the ruling market price is £50.

(a) Graph the demand curve, plotting demand horizontally and price vertically.

(b) If the firm produces only what it can sell, and no more, how does revenue depend upon output?

(c) How does marginal revenue depend upon output?

(d) Show that when the output is just below 150 units the marginal revenue is £20 and when the output becomes 150 units the marginal revenue is −£100.

(e) Suppose that the cost function of the firm is $C = 50 + 10Q$ where C is cost (in £) and Q is output. Show that although there is no output at which marginal revenue equals marginal cost there is nevertheless an output at which profit is a maximum and this output is 150 units.

(f) Show that if the costs of the firm change to $C = 150 + 15Q$ the profit-maximizing output remains unchanged.

(g) Why do the usual conditions for a maximum of profit not apply in parts (e) and (f) above?

Chapter 6

Functions of several variables

6.1 Introduction

The case in which an economic variable, y, is dependent on just one economic variable, x, is of limited interest. As a general rule, this case is a reasonable description of economic behaviour in the short run; however, in the long run an economic variable typically depends on several variables. It is often convenient to distinguish between economic variables which change relatively slowly (e.g. the capital stock of the economy, population, available natural resources) and those which change relatively quickly (e.g. employment, inventories, the balance of payments). In the short run it is reasonable to regard the slowly changing variables as fixed, i.e. as taking on definite values and not varying at all. If an economic variable is a function of one quickly changing variable and several slowly changing variables—e.g. output depends on employment (quickly varying) and the stock of capital and available natural resources (slowly varying)—then in the short run it is legitimate to regard the variable as a function only of the quickly changing variable; for example, in the short run output depends only on employment because the capital stock and the available natural resources are fixed. The mathematical analysis in this chapter can be used to analyse the relationship between short-run behaviour in which the variable y depends on only one variable, x_1, and long-run behaviour in which y depends on the several variables $x_1, \ldots, x_n$.

6.2 Functions of several variables—two examples

To begin with, we give two examples of functions of several variables which frequently occur in economics.

(1) The production function

A production function describes the technology of a productive process; it relates the quantity of the output of a commodity to the factor inputs (land, labour, capital, raw materials, etc.) used up in production.

A simple example of the production function of a plant is

$$Y = f(L, K)$$

where Y is the rate of output (number of units per unit time), L is the labour force (number of men employed) and K is the capital stock (number of machines in use). Evidently, Y is a function of both the labour employed, L, and the capital stock, K. If the capital stock is fixed and the employment of labour is varied then the output, Y, becomes a function only of L, $Y = g(L)$, though the precise form of the function g depends on the value of K. For example, if the production function is of the form

$$Y = 10\sqrt{(LK)}$$

and the capital stock is fixed at 100 units then, with $K = 100$,

$$Y = 10\sqrt{(100L)} = 100\sqrt{L}$$

so that output, Y, is a function only of labour employed, L. (How does Y depend on L when K is fixed at 400 units?) In the long run it is unreasonable to assume that the capital stock is fixed, but in the short run it is a justifiable approximation.

(2) The utility function

A utility function is a simple way of describing consumers' preferences. A consumer is supposed to derive utility from the consumption of goods and services, and in simple theories of consumer behaviour utility is derived *only* from the consumer's own consumption of goods and services. Let x_1 be the consumption of food, x_2 the consumption of clothing and footwear, x_3 the consumption of housing services, x_4 the consumption of power (coal, electricity, gas, etc.) and x_5 the consumption of consumer durables. The consumer's utility is expressed mathematically as

$$U = f(x_1, x_2, x_3, x_4, x_5)$$

Suppose we are asked: (a) How does the consumer's utility vary with his consumption of food when his consumption of clothing is fixed at 5 units per week, his consumption of housing is fixed at 10 units per week, his consumption of power is fixed at 10 units per week and his consumption of durables is fixed at $2\frac{1}{2}$ units per week? (b) Does the consumer's utility vary in the same way if his consumption of clothing is increased to 10 units per week?

To answer these questions we require a specific form for the utility function, such as

$$\begin{aligned} U = {} & 10x_1 + 20x_2 + 20x_3 + 20x_4 + 10x_5 \\ & - x_1^2 - x_2^2 - x_3^2 - x_4^2 - 4x_4^2 \\ & + 15x_1x_2 + 15x_2x_3 + 25x_1x_3 + 5x_3x_4 \end{aligned}$$

The general form of this utility function is suggested by the view that the additional utility derived from a small increase in the consumption of one particular good diminishes as the total consumption of the good increases, the consumption of other goods remaining constant, and that the additional utility derived from a small increase in the consumption of all goods also diminishes as the total of all goods increases, but not so fast as in the case where all the increase is in the consumption of one particular good. The precise numbers used in the utility function are purely hypothetical.

Substituting the values $x_2 = 5$, $x_3 = 10$, $x_4 = 10$, $x_5 = 2\frac{1}{2}$ shows that

$$U = 1525 + 325x_1 - x_1^2$$

This equation expresses the consumer's utility as a function only of the amount of food consumed: the equation is derived by assuming that his consumption of other goods is fixed. If the value of x_2 is increased to 10 units then substituting the values $x_2 = 10$, $x_3 = 10$, $x_4 = 10$, $x_5 = 2\frac{1}{2}$ shows that

$$U = 2200 + 400x_1 - x_1^2$$

This equation describes the variation of utility with the consumption of food when the fixed consumption of clothing is increased to 10 units. We conclude that with this specification of the utility function the way in which the consumer's utility varies with his consumption of food depends on the amount of clothing which is consumed.

It was remarked in Section 4.3 that in specifying the form of a function it is often necessary to impose restrictions on the derivative of the function. This applies particularly to the production function and the utility function. The restriction on the production function arises from the law of diminishing returns; this law states that, for fixed employment of factors 2, 3, 4, . . ., the greater the amount of factor 1 that is used (above a certain minimum amount) the smaller is the addition to output due to a marginal increase in the employment of factor 1. The rate at which output increases as a result of a marginal increase in the employment of factor 1 is measured by the derivative of output with respect to the employment of factor 1. The law of diminishing returns states that, beyond a certain point, this derivative will be a declining function of the amount of factor 1 employed.

It is readily verified that the production function $Y = f(L, K) = 10\sqrt{(LK)}$, described above, satisfies the law of diminishing returns. To show this, we must establish that (i) when the amount of capital is fixed the derivative of output with respect to labour is a declining function of the amount of labour employed (above a certain minimum level of employment) and (ii) when the amount of labour is fixed the derivative of output with respect to capital is a declining function of the amount of capital employed (above a certain minimum level of capital).

(i) When the amount of capital is fixed, K (the number of units of capital) is a constant. Hence output is a function only of labour, $Y = 10\sqrt{(LK)} = 10\sqrt{K}\sqrt{L}$ where $10\sqrt{K}$ is a constant and L is a variable. Now the derivative of $\sqrt{L}$ is $1/(2\sqrt{L})$[1] and so the derivative of a constant times $\sqrt{L}$ is simply a

1 The derivative of $\sqrt{L}$ is

$$\lim_{\Delta L \to 0} \frac{\sqrt{(L + \Delta L)} - \sqrt{L}}{L} = \lim_{\Delta L \to 0} \frac{\sqrt{(L + \Delta L)} - \sqrt{L}}{\Delta L}\left(\frac{\sqrt{(L + \Delta L)} + \sqrt{L}}{\sqrt{(L + \Delta L)} + \sqrt{L}}\right)$$

$$= \lim_{\Delta L \to 0} \frac{\Delta L}{\Delta L[\sqrt{(L + \Delta L)} + \sqrt{L}]}$$

$$= \lim_{\Delta L \to 0} \frac{1}{\sqrt{(L + \Delta L)} + \sqrt{L}} = \frac{1}{2\sqrt{L}}$$

The same result can be obtained using property 6 of Section 5.2.

constant times $1/(2\sqrt{L})$, i.e. the derivative of $10\sqrt{K}\sqrt{L}$ is $10\sqrt{K}[1/(2\sqrt{L})] = 5\sqrt{(K/L)}$. We conclude that when K is a constant the derivative of $Y = 10\sqrt{(LK)}$ is $5\sqrt{(K/L)}$. This derivative is written

$$\frac{\partial Y}{\partial L} = 5\sqrt{\left(\frac{K}{L}\right)}$$

(the notation is explained in Section 6.3). Since the variable L occurs only in the denominator of the expression for the derivative it follows that when the amount of capital is fixed the derivative of output with respect to labour is a declining function of the amount of labour employed.

(ii) When the amount of labour is fixed, L, the number of men employed, is a constant. Hence output is a function only of capital, $Y = 10\sqrt{(LK)} = 10\sqrt{L}\sqrt{K}$ where $10\sqrt{L}$ is a constant and K is a variable. Since the derivative of $\sqrt{K}$ is $1/(2\sqrt{K})$, the derivative of $Y = 10\sqrt{L}\sqrt{K}$ is $10\sqrt{L}[1/(2\sqrt{K})] = 5\sqrt{(L/K)}$ i.e. the derivative of Y with respect to K when L is fixed is

$$\frac{\partial Y}{\partial K} = 5\sqrt{\left(\frac{L}{K}\right)}$$

Since the variable K occurs only in the denominator it follows that the derivative of output with respect to capital (for a fixed amount of labour) is a declining function of the amount of capital employed. This completes our demonstration that the production function $Y = 10\sqrt{(LK)}$ satisfies the law of diminishing returns.

A consumer's utility function is restricted by the law of diminishing marginal utility; this law states that, for a fixed consumption of commodities 2, 3, 4, . . ., the greater the amount of commodity 1 that is consumed the smaller is the additional utility derived from a marginal increase in the consumption of commodity 1: in other words, the more one has of a commodity, the less one appreciates a bit extra. The law of diminishing marginal utility was at one time interpreted very literally as describing the consumer's state of mind; nowadays it is interpreted as an axiom from which a simple theory of consumer behaviour can be deduced. Let x_1 and x_2 measure the consumption of two categories of commodities. We shall demonstrate that the utility function

$$U = 10x_1 + 20x_2 - x_1^2 - x_2^2 + 2x_1x_2$$

satisfies the law of diminishing marginal utility.

(i) The change in utility due to a marginal change in the consumption of commodity 1 is measured by the derivative of utility with respect to the consumption of commodity 1 when the consumption of commodity 2 is constant. Writing

$$U = (20x_2 - x_2^2) + (10 + 2x_2)x_1 - x_1^2$$

where the terms $20x_2 - x_2^2$, $10 + 2x_2$ are terms in x_2 and are therefore constant, it follows that the derivative of utility with respect to the consumption of commodity 1 is, by the ordinary rules of differentiation,

$$\frac{\partial U}{\partial x_1} = (10 + 2x_2) - 2x_1$$

This equation indicates that as the consumption of commodity 1, x_1, increases the additional utility derived from a marginal increase in x_1, measured by $\partial U/\partial x_1$, decreases.

(ii) The change in utility due to a marginal change in the consumption of commodity 2 is measured by the derivative of utility with respect to the consumption of commodity 2 when the consumption of commodity 1 is constant. Writing

$$U = (10x_1 - x_1^2) + (20 + 2x_1)x_2 - x_2^2$$

where the terms $10x_1 - x_1^2$, $20 + 2x_1$ are terms in x_1 and are therefore constant, it follows that the derivative of utility with respect to the consumption of commodity 2 is, by the ordinary rules of differentiation,

$$\frac{\partial U}{\partial x_2} = (20 + 2x_1) - 2x_2$$

This equation indicates that as the consumption of commodity 2, x_2, increases the additional utility derived from a marginal increase is x_2, measured by $\partial U/\partial x_2$, decreases.

We have demonstrated that (i) when the consumption of commodity 2 is fixed and the consumption of commodity 1 increases then consumer utility increases less the greater the consumption of commodity 1 and (ii) when the consumption of commodity 1 is fixed and the consumption of commodity 2 increases then utility increases less the greater the consumption of commodity 2. This shows that the utility function specified above satisfies the law of diminishing marginal utility.

6.3 Partial derivatives

Any function of the form

$$y = f(x_1, \ldots, x_n) \qquad n > 1$$

is an example of a function of several variables. If any variable, x_j, is set equal to some constant value, $\bar{x}_j$, then y becomes a function of the remaining $n - 1$ variables

$$y = g_j(x_1, \ldots, x_{j-1}, x_{j+1}, \ldots, x_n)$$

where the form of the function g_j depends on the constant value $\bar{x}_j$. The most usual way to analyse a function of several variables is to take each variable in turn, set the other $n - 1$ variables equal to fixed values, and examine how y varies with the variation in the one remaining variable, i.e. to examine in succession the functions

$$\begin{aligned} y &= f(x_1, \bar{x}_2, \ldots, \bar{x}_n) &&= h_1(x_1) \\ y &= f(\bar{x}_1, x_2, \bar{x}_3, \ldots, \bar{x}_n) &&= h_2(x_2) \\ &\vdots && \vdots \\ y &= f(\bar{x}_1, \ldots, \bar{x}_{n-1}, x_n) &&= h_n(x_n) \end{aligned}$$

Each of the functions $h_j(x_j)$ $(j = 1, \ldots, n)$ has a sequence of derivatives $h_j'(x_j)$, $h_j''(x_j), \ldots$; these derivatives are the 'partial derivatives' of the function $y = f(x_1, \ldots, x_n)$. The nth order partial derivative of y with respect to x_j is the nth derivative of the function h_j obtained from y by setting all the other variables $x_1, \ldots, x_{j-1}, x_{j+1}, \ldots, x_n$ equal to the fixed values $\bar{x}_1, \ldots, \bar{x}_{j-1}, \bar{x}_{j+1}, \ldots, \bar{x}_n$. In the standard notation for partial derivatives we write

$$\frac{\partial^n y}{\partial x_j^n} = h^{(n)}(x_j)$$

where $\partial^n y/\partial x_j^n$ represents the nth order partial derivative of y with respect to x. The nth order partial derivative $\partial^n y/\partial x_j^n$ is the nth derivative of the function $y = f(x_1, \ldots, x_n)$ when all the variables except x_j are maintained at fixed values.

In general, a partial derivative of y with respect to x_j depends not only on the value of the variable x_j but also on the fixed values of the other variables $x_1, \ldots, x_{j-1}, x_{j+1}, \ldots, x_n$. Having evaluated a partial derivative it is possible to examine how this partial derivative varies with the different fixed values of any one other variable by regarding the partial derivative as a function of this other variable; for example, we may regard the partial derivative $\partial^n y/\partial x_j^n$ as a function of the variable x_k $(k = 1, \ldots, n)$. To examine how this partial derivative varies with x_k we may differentiate the partial derivative any number of times with respect to x_k. If the partial derivative $\partial^n y/\partial x_j^n$ is differentiated m times with respect to x_k then the resulting derivative is denoted

$$\frac{\partial^m}{\partial x_k^m}\frac{(\partial^n y)}{(\partial x_j^n)} \quad \text{or, more compactly,} \quad \frac{\partial^{m+n} y}{\partial x_k^m\, \partial x_j^n}$$

Any derivative of this form, with $k \neq j$ and $m, n \geqslant 1$, is known as a 'cross partial derivative' of the function y. It is easily verified that in a cross partial derivative the order of differentiation is irrelevant, i.e. that

$$\frac{\partial^{m+n} y}{\partial x_j^n\, \partial x_k^m} = \frac{\partial^{m+n} y}{\partial x_k^m x_j^n}$$

provided that both partial derivatives exist.

Example 1 Evaluate all the first- and second-order partial derivatives of the production function

$$Y = 10\sqrt{(LK)}$$

To evaluate the first partial derivative of Y with respect to L, consider K as a constant and apply the normal rules of differentiation to get

$$\frac{\partial Y}{\partial L} = 10\sqrt{K}\frac{\partial}{\partial L}(\sqrt{L}) = 10\sqrt{K}\frac{1}{2\sqrt{L}} = 5\sqrt{\left(\frac{K}{L}\right)}$$

Similarly, the first partial derivative of Y with respect to K is obtained by taking L as a constant and differentiating in the usual way:

$$\frac{\partial Y}{\partial K} = 10\sqrt{L}\frac{\partial}{\partial K}\sqrt{K} = 10\sqrt{L}\frac{1}{2\sqrt{K}} = 5\sqrt{\left(\frac{L}{K}\right)}$$

The second derivative of Y with respect to L is evaluated by maintaining K constant and differentiating the first derivative with respect to L:

$$\frac{\partial^2 Y}{\partial L^2} = \frac{\partial}{\partial L}\cdot\frac{\partial Y}{\partial L} = \frac{\partial}{\partial L}5\sqrt{\left(\frac{K}{L}\right)} = 5\sqrt{K}\frac{\partial}{\partial L}\cdot\frac{1}{\sqrt{L}}$$

$$= 5\sqrt{K}\frac{-1}{2L\sqrt{L}} = \frac{-5}{2L}\sqrt{\left(\frac{K}{L}\right)}$$

The second derivative of Y with respect to K is evaluated by maintaining L constant and differentiating the first derivative with respect to K:

$$\frac{\partial^2 Y}{\partial K^2} = \frac{\partial}{\partial K}\cdot\frac{\partial Y}{\partial K} = \frac{\partial}{\partial K}5\sqrt{\left(\frac{L}{K}\right)} = 5\sqrt{L}\frac{\partial}{\partial K}\cdot\frac{1}{\sqrt{K}}$$

$$= 5\sqrt{L}\frac{-1}{2K\sqrt{K}} = \frac{-5}{2K}\sqrt{\left(\frac{L}{K}\right)}$$

The function $Y = f(L, K)$ has two cross partial derivatives, one measuring the change in the partial derivative of Y with respect to L due to a marginal change in the fixed value of K, and the other measuring the change in the partial derivative of Y with respect to K due to a marginal change in the fixed value of L. These cross partial derivatives are, respectively,

$$\frac{\partial^2 Y}{\partial K\,\partial L} = \frac{\partial}{\partial K}\cdot\frac{\partial Y}{\partial L} = \frac{\partial}{\partial K}5\sqrt{\left(\frac{K}{L}\right)} = \frac{5}{\sqrt{L}}\cdot\frac{\partial}{\partial K}\sqrt{K}$$

$$= \frac{5}{\sqrt{L}}\cdot\frac{1}{2\sqrt{K}} = \frac{5}{2\sqrt{(LK)}}$$

$$\frac{\partial^2 Y}{\partial L\,\partial K} = \frac{\partial}{\partial L}\cdot\frac{\partial Y}{\partial K} = \frac{\partial}{\partial L}5\sqrt{\left(\frac{L}{K}\right)} = \frac{5}{\sqrt{K}}\cdot\frac{\partial}{\partial L}\sqrt{L}$$

$$= \frac{5}{\sqrt{K}}\cdot\frac{1}{2\sqrt{L}} = \frac{5}{2\sqrt{(LK)}}$$

Example 2 Evaluate all the first- and second-order partial derivatives and cross partial derivatives of the utility function

$$U = 10x_1 + 20x_2 - x_1^2 - x_2^2 + 2x_1x_2$$

The reader should verify for himself that

$$\frac{\partial U}{\partial x_1} = 10 - 2x_1 + 2x_2$$

$$\frac{\partial U}{\partial x_2} = 20 - 2x_2 + 2x_1$$

$$\frac{\partial^2 U}{\partial x_1^2} = -2$$

$$\frac{\partial^2 U}{\partial x_2^2} = -2$$

$$\frac{\partial^2 U}{\partial x_1\, \partial x_2} = 2$$

$$\frac{\partial^2 U}{\partial x_2\, \partial x_1} = 2$$

6.4 The differential

So far we have studied the behaviour of a function of several variables by examining those cases when only one variable at a time is allowed to vary and all the other variables take on fixed values. It was suggested at the beginning of the chapter that this approach might be legitimate in studies of short-run behaviour. However, long-run studies of economic behaviour require the analysis of situations in which all the variables are free to vary. We state below a result which is quite fundamental for functions of several variables when there is simultaneous variation in all the variables.

The effect on $y = f(x_1, \ldots, x_n)$ of simultaneous increments $dx_1, \ldots, dx_n$ in $x_1, \ldots, x_n$ is to change the value of y by an amount approximately equal to the differential of y; where the differential, dy, of y is defined by the formula

$$dx = \frac{\partial y}{\partial x_1}\, dx_1 + \frac{\partial y}{\partial x_2}\, dx_2 + \cdots + \frac{\partial y}{\partial x_n}\, dx_n$$

This is true provided that each partial derivative, $\partial y/\partial x_i$, is a continuous function of the variables $x_1, \ldots, x_n$.(2)

The proof is given in the appendix to this chapter (Theorem 6.1).

The fact that the differential is an approximate measure of the change in y induced by simultaneous variations in $x_1, \ldots, x_n$ shows that the effect on y of such simultaneous variation is approximately equal to the sum of the effects on y of partial variations in the x_i (provided that all the variations are small).

2 A continuous function of a variable is one for which an arbitrarily small change in the variable always induces an arbitrarily small change in the value of the function, i.e. the function never jumps from one value to another very different value due to a small change in the variable. Formally, a function $f(x)$ is continuous at x if for any δ there is an ε such that $|f(x + h) - f(x)| < \delta$ for any h, $|h| < \varepsilon$.

Example 1 The differential associated with the production function $Y = 10\sqrt{(LK)}$ is

$$dY = \frac{\partial Y}{\partial L}dL + \frac{\partial Y}{\partial K}dK$$

where $\partial Y/\partial L = 5\sqrt{(K/L)}$ and $\partial Y/\partial K = 5\sqrt{(L/K)}$; it follows that

$$dY = 5\sqrt{(K/L)}\,dL + 5\sqrt{(L/K)}\,dK$$

The effect of a simultaneous increment of dL in the labour force and dK in the capital stock is to increase output by an amount approximately equal to dY.

Example 2 The differential associated with the utility function $U = 10x_1 + 20x_2 - x_1^2 - x_2^2 + 2x_1x_2$ is

$$dU = \frac{\partial Y}{\partial x_1}dx_1 + \frac{\partial Y}{\partial x_2}dx_2$$

where $\partial Y/\partial x_1 = 10 - 2x_1 + 2x_2$ and $\partial Y/\partial x_2 = 20 - 2x_2 + 2x_1$; it follows that

$$dU = (10 - 2x_1 + 2x_2)\,dx_1 + (20 - 2x_2 + 2x_1)\,dx_2$$

The effect of a simultaneous increment of dx_1 in the consumption of commodity 1 and of dx_2 in the consumption of commodity 2 is to increase utility by an amount approximately equal to dU.

6.5 The total derivative

The concept of the total derivative is closely allied to the concept of the differential discussed in the previous section. Suppose that the variables $x_1, \ldots, x_n$ are themselves functions of a single variable, t; in this case the increments $dx_1, \ldots, dx_n$ in $x_1, \ldots, x_n$ are themselves the result of an increment dt in the variable t. The effect of an increment dt on the value of $y = f(x_1, \ldots, x_n)$ is measured by the total derivative of y with respect to t, dy/dt, which is defined as

$$\frac{dy}{dt} = \lim_{\Delta t \to 0} \frac{\Delta y}{\Delta t}$$

The total derivative may be evaluated by using the following rule.

If $y = f(x_1, \ldots, x_n)$ is a function with continuous partial derivatives and $x_1, \ldots, x_n$ are differentiable functions of the variable t then the total derivative of y with respect to t is

$$\frac{dy}{dt} = \frac{\partial y}{\partial x_1}\cdot\frac{dx_1}{dt} + \frac{\partial y}{\partial x_2}\cdot\frac{dx_2}{dt} + \cdots + \frac{\partial y}{\partial x_n}\cdot\frac{dx_n}{dt}$$

(Note that this rule may be obtained by 'dividing through' the definition of the differential by dt: this, however, is only a way of remembering the formula—it is not a proof.) The proof is given in the appendix (Theorem 6.2).

Example 1 The production function of a firm is $Y = 10\sqrt{(LK)}$. The capital stock increases at a steady rate $K = 0{\cdot}09t$ where t denotes time and the labour force also increases but more slowly, $L = 0{\cdot}04t$. At what rate does output increase?

The rate of increase of output is measured by the derivative of output with respect to time, dY/dt. Since the production function relates output to both labour and capital, and both labour and capital are functions of time, the derivative of output with respect to time is the total derivative of the production function,

$$\frac{dY}{dt} = \frac{\partial Y}{\partial L}\cdot\frac{dL}{dt} + \frac{\partial Y}{\partial K}\cdot\frac{dK}{dt}$$

where $\partial Y/\partial L = 5\sqrt{(K/L)}$, $dL/dt = 0{\cdot}04$, $\partial Y/\partial K = 5\sqrt{(L/K)}$, $dK/dt = 0{\cdot}09$. Now we know that $K = 0{\cdot}09t$, $L = 0{\cdot}04t$, so that $\sqrt{(K/L)} = \frac{9}{4} = \frac{3}{2}$ and similarly $\sqrt{(L/K)} = \frac{2}{3}$. Hence

$$\frac{dY}{dt} = 5 \times \tfrac{3}{2} \times 0{\cdot}04 + 5 \times \tfrac{2}{3} \times 0{\cdot}09$$

$$= 0{\cdot}60$$

Because of the simplicity of this example, the result could easily have been obtained directly by substituting $K = 0{\cdot}09t$, $L = 0{\cdot}04t$ into the production function $Y = 10\sqrt{(LK)}$ to get $Y = 10\sqrt{(0{\cdot}0036t^2)} = 10 \times 0{\cdot}06t = 0{\cdot}60t$ and then differentiating to get $dY/dt = 0{\cdot}60$.

Example 2 A consumer's utility depends on his consumption of two commodities; if x_1 and x_2 are the amounts consumed then utility, U, is

$$U = 200x_1 + 200x_2 + x_1x_2 - x_1^2 - x_2^2$$

Suppose that the first commodity is leisure (in hours per week), the second commodity is income (in £ per week) and that the consumption of both leisure and income depends on the number of hours worked per week, w:

$$x_1 = 168 - w; \qquad x_2 = 1{\cdot}5w$$

What is the effect on utility of a marginal change in the number of hours worked?

The effect on utility is measured by the derivative of utility with respect to the number of hours worked. Since the utility function relates utility to the consumption of both leisure and income, and both leisure and income depend on the number of hours worked, the derivative of utility with respect to the number of hours worked is the total derivative of the utility function,

$$\frac{dU}{dw} = \frac{\partial U}{\partial x_1}\cdot\frac{dx_1}{dw} + \frac{\partial U}{\partial x_2}\cdot\frac{dx_2}{dw}$$

where $\partial U/x_1 = 200 + x_2 - 2x_1$, $dx_1/dw = -1$, $\partial U/\partial x_2 = 200 + x_1 - 2x_2$, $dx_2/dw = 1{\cdot}5$. Hence

$$\frac{dU}{dw} = -(200 + x_2 - 2x_1) + 1{\cdot}5(200 + x_1 - 2x_2)$$

$$= 100 + 3{\cdot}5x_1 - 4x_2$$

It follows that the increase in utility due to a marginal increase in the number of hours worked is greater, the greater is the amount of leisure that is enjoyed, and is less, the greater the amount of income that is already earned.

6.6 Implicit functions

It has already been noted (see Section 6.3) that a convenient way to study functions of several variables is to set one or more of the variables equal to some constant value. For example, to study the function $y = f(x_1, x_2)$ one may begin by setting $x_2 = \bar{x}_2$, and examine the functional relationship $y = f(x_1, \bar{x}_2) = h_1(x_1)$ between y and x_1; then one may set $x_1 = \bar{x}_1$ and examine the functional relationship $y = f(\bar{x}_1, x_2) = h_2(x_2)$ between y and x_2. It would seem reasonable to complete this investigation of the function $y = f(x_1, x_2)$ by setting $y = \bar{y}$ and examining the relationship $f(x_1, x_2) = \bar{y}$ between x_1 and x_2. A functional relationship of the kind $f(x_1, x_2) = \bar{y}$ is an example of an *implicit function* of x_1 and x_2. x_1 is not given as an explicit function of x_2—with x_1 on the left and x_2 on the right of the equation—nor is x_2 an explicit function of x_1, but a relationship between x_1 and x_2 is implicit in the solution of the equation. In general, any equation is of the form

$$f(x_1, \ldots, x_n) = \bar{y}$$

can be written

$$f(x_1, \ldots, x_n) - \bar{y} = 0$$

or, more generally, as

$$g(x_1, \ldots, x_n) = 0$$

This last equation is the general form of an implicit function. It is an immediate consequence of this equation that the value of the implicit function never changes with changes in $x_1, \ldots, x_n$. Because of this it is possible to find the partial derivative of any one variable x_1, with respect to any other variable, x_j, $(i \neq j,\ i, j = 1, \ldots, n)$ in the following way. Firstly, set all the variables except x_i and x_j equal to constant values; the implicit function then establishes a relationship between x_i and x_j, $x_i = h(x_j)$. We assume that this functional relationship is differentiable. It follows that g is a function of just x_i and x_j, and because of the relationship established by the implicit function both x_i and x_j are functions of x_j. Hence we may evaluate the total derivative of g with respect to x_j,

$$\frac{dg}{dx_j} = \frac{\partial g}{\partial x_j} \cdot \frac{dx_j}{dx_j} + \frac{\partial g}{\partial x_i} \cdot \frac{dx_i}{dx_j}$$

and since $dx_j/dx_j = 1$,

$$\frac{dg}{dx_j} = \frac{\partial g}{\partial x_j} + \frac{\partial g}{\partial x_i} \cdot \frac{dx_i}{dx_j}$$

But because g is constant, $dg/dx_j = 0$ so that

$$0 = \frac{\partial g}{\partial x_j} + \frac{\partial g}{\partial x_i} \cdot \frac{dx_i}{dx_j}$$

and hence

$$\frac{dx_i}{dx_j} = -\frac{\partial g/\partial x_j}{\partial g/\partial x_i}$$

This result is known as the implicit function rule.

Example 1 Given the production function $Y = 10\sqrt{(LK)}$ what alternative combinations of labour and capital will produce an output of 40 units?

The amounts of labour and capital used must satisfy the equation

$$40 = 10\sqrt{(LK)}$$

which may be written

$$10\sqrt{(LK)} - 40 = 0$$

This is an implicit function of L and K. The values of L and K which satisfy this equation indicate those combinations of labour and capital which will produce 40 units of output. Because the implicit function is associated with a fixed quantity of output the graph of the implicit function is an *isoquant*. Dividing through the first equation by 10, squaring both sides and dividing by K shows that $L = 16/K$. The graph of this equation is shown in Fig. 6A. It can be seen

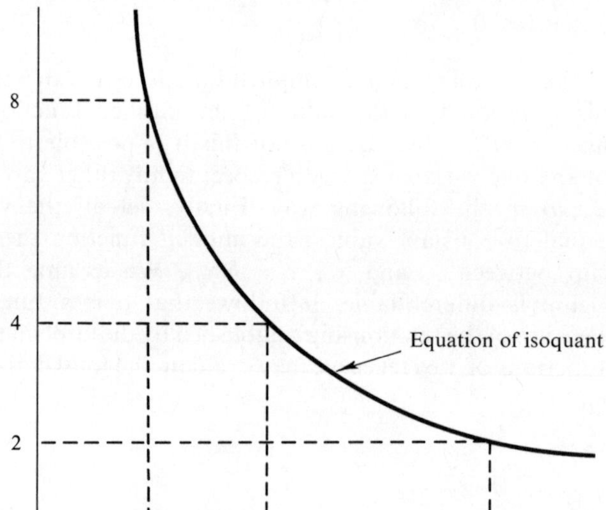

Fig. 6A Graph of an isoquant of the production function $Y = 10\sqrt{(LK)}$ corresponding to an output of 40 units

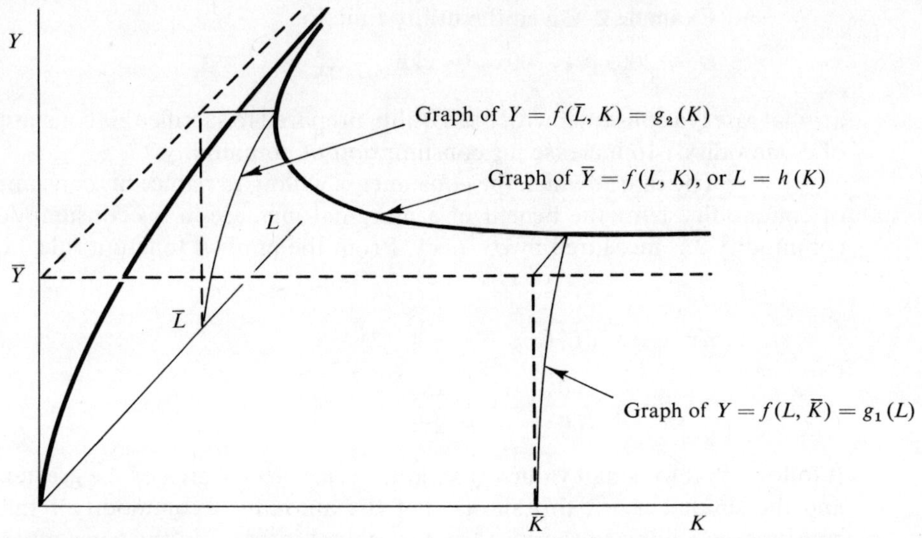

Fig. 6B Three dimensional illustration of the production function $Y=f(L,K)$

that to produce a given quantity of output, the greater is the amount of capital used the less is the amount of labour required (and vice versa).

The marginal rate at which labour may be substituted for capital (in order to produce the same output) may be evaluated by using the implicit function rule. The rate of change of labour with respect to a small change in capital when output is constant is

$$\frac{dL}{dK} = -\frac{\partial g/\partial K}{\partial g/\partial L}$$

where $g = 10\sqrt{(LK)} - 40$. Hence

$$\frac{dL}{dK} = -\frac{5\sqrt{(L/K)}}{5\sqrt{(K/L)}} = -\frac{L}{K}$$

and since $L = 16/K$ we have the alternative expression

$$\frac{dL}{dK} = -\frac{16}{K^2}$$

This result could also have been obtained directly by differentiating $L = 16/K$ with respect to K. It can be seen that it is easy to substitute labour for capital (dL/dK is small) when the amount of capital employed is relatively high and the amount of labour employed is relatively low, i.e. it is easy to substitute labour for capital when production is capital-intensive.

Example 2 Given the utility function

$$U = 200x_1 + 200x_2 + x_1x_2 - x_1^2 - x_2^2$$

at what rate is a consumer with fixed utility prepared to sacrifice his consumption of commodity 1 to increase his consumption of commodity 2?

The rate at which the consumer is willing to reduce his consumption of commodity 1 for the benefit of a marginal increase in his consumption of commodity 2 is measured by dx_1/dx_2. From the implicit function rule

$$\frac{dx_1}{dx_2} = -\frac{\partial U/\partial x_2}{\partial U/\partial x_1}$$

$$= -\frac{200 + x_1 - 2x_2}{200 + x_2 - 2x_1}$$

It follows that for small values of x_1 and x_2, dx_1/dx_2 is greater the greater is x_1 and the smaller is x_2; this shows that the amount of commodity 1 that the consumer is willing to sacrifice for a marginal increase in the consumption of commodity 2 is greater, the greater is the existing consumption of commodity 1 and the smaller is the existing consumption of commodity 2.

6.7 Homogeneous functions

The concept of homogeneity is an important one in economics. A function $y = f(x_1, \ldots, x_n)$ is said to be homogeneous of degree m if for any constant, λ,

$$f(\lambda x_1, \ldots, \lambda x_n) = \lambda^m . f(x_1, \ldots, x_n) = \lambda^m y$$

Example 1 The production function $Y = 10\sqrt{(LK)}$ is homogeneous of degree one because $10\sqrt{[(\lambda L)(\lambda K)]} = 10\sqrt{(\lambda . \lambda)}\sqrt{(LK)} = 10\lambda\sqrt{(LK)} = \lambda Y$.

Example 2 Let D be the demand for a commodity, P the price of the commodity and let Y be the consumers' income. The demand function $D = 25Y/P$ is homogeneous of degree zero since $25(\lambda Y)/(\lambda P) = 25Y/P = D = \lambda^0 D$ (since $\lambda^0 = 1$).

The homogeneity of the function $y = f(x_1, \ldots, x_n)$ concerns what happens to the value of the function when all the variables $x_1, \ldots, x_n$ are scaled by the same arbitrary amount. If the value of the function remains unchanged then the function is homogeneous of degree zero. If the value of the function increases in the same proportion as do the variables $x_1, \ldots, x_n$ then the function is homogeneous of degree 1. If the value of the function increases as the square of the proportion by which the variables $x_1, \ldots, x_n$ increase then the function is homogeneous of degree 2. The concept of homogeneity often appears in economics by some other name: a production function which is homogeneous of degree 1 is said to exhibit 'constant returns to scale'; a demand function in which income and prices influence demand and which is homogeneous of degree zero is said to exhibit the absence of 'money illusion'. A production function exhibits constant returns to scale when an increase in the labour force from L

to λL together with an equi-proportional increase in the capital stock from K to λK results in output changing by this same proportion, i.e. when

$$f(\lambda L, \lambda K) = \lambda f(L, K) = \lambda y$$

which is the case when the production function is homogeneous of degree one. A demand function $D = f(P, Y)$ exhibits the absence of money illusion when a change in price from P to λP together with an equi-proportional change in money income from Y to λY leaves the demand for the commodity unchanged—this means that the demand for the commodity is invariant with respect to a general inflation of money values. If the demand is invariant under a change in money values then

$$f(\lambda P, \lambda Y) = f(P, Y) = D = \lambda^0 D$$

so that the demand function is homogeneous of degree zero.

Homogeneous functions have the following very important property.

Euler's theorem

Let $y = f(x_1, \ldots, x_n)$ be homogeneous of degree m; then the partial derivatives of y satisfy the equation

$$\frac{\partial y}{\partial x_1} x_1 + \frac{\partial y}{\partial x_2} x_2 + \cdots + \frac{\partial y}{\partial x_n} x_n = my$$

The proof of this result is given in the appendix (Theorem 6.3).

Euler's theorem is very important in the theory of the factor distribution of income. Suppose that $y = f(x_1, \ldots, x_n)$ is a production function showing how output y depends on the quantities of the factors employed. It can be shown that a profit maximizing firm in a competitive economy will employ a combination of factors which equates the marginal product of each factor to the real cost of hiring the factor (see Chapter 7). Since the marginal product of the ith factor is measured by $\partial y/\partial x_i$ it follows that for a profit maximizing firm the product $(\partial y/\partial x_i)x_i$ is equal to the product of the cost per unit of the factor and the quantity of the factor employed, and is therefore a measure of the firm's total payment to the ith factor. The sum $\Sigma_{i=1}^{n} (\partial y/\partial x_i)x_i$ taken over all factors is therefore a measure of total factor payments. It follows that the total factor payments will be less than, equal to, or in excess of the total output depending on whether

$$\frac{\partial y}{\partial x_1} x_1 + \frac{\partial y}{\partial x_2} x_2 + \cdots + \frac{\partial y}{\partial x_n} x_n \lesseqgtr y$$

Euler's theorem tells us that if the production function is homogeneous of degree m then factor payments exceed the total output if $m > 1$, just exhaust total output if $m = 1$ and fail to exhaust output if $m < 1$; this result establishes an important connection between the technology of production and the factor distribution of income.

6.8 A necessary condition for maxima and minima

It is easy to deduce a necessary condition for a function of several variables $y = f(x_1, \ldots, x_n)$ to have either a maximum or a minimum at some particular set of values $\bar{x}_1, \ldots, \bar{x}_n$. The simple logic by which a condition can be derived is as follows.

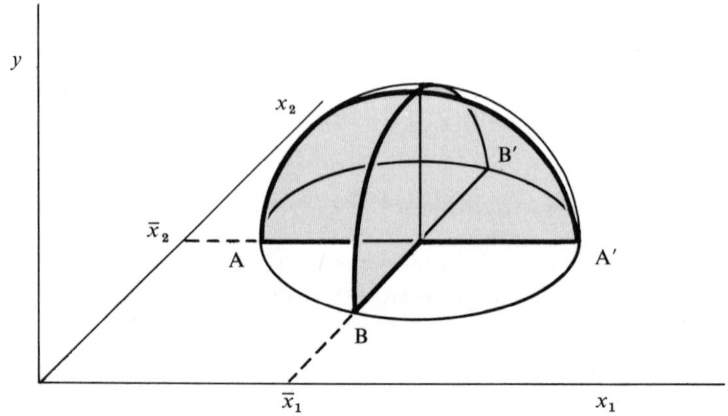

Fig. 6C Maximum of a function of two variables

For there to be a maximum of a function of several variables at the particular set of values $\bar{x}_1, \ldots, \bar{x}_n$ it is necessary that for each variable, x_i $(i = 1, \ldots, n)$, a small variation in the value of that variable, from $\bar{x}_i$ to $\bar{x}_i + \Delta x_i$, should not increase the value of y: for if such a variation were to increase the value of y then the value of y at $\bar{x}_1, \ldots, \bar{x}_n$ could not have been a maximum. In a similar way, for a minimum at $\bar{x}_1, \ldots, \bar{x}_n$ it is necessary that a small variation, from $\bar{x}_i$ to $\bar{x}_i + \Delta x_i$, in the value of any one variable should not decrease the value of y: for if such variation were to decrease the value of y, the value of y at $\bar{x}_1, \ldots, \bar{x}_n$ could not have been a minimum. Now the effect on y of a small change in just one variable x_i is measured by the ratio $\Delta y/\Delta x_i$, which is the ratio of the change in y, Δy, to the small change, Δx_i, which induces it (when all the variables except x_i take on fixed values). For a maximum it is necessary that the change in y should be zero, for if it were not zero an appropriate marginal increase (or decrease) in the value of x_i (depending on whether the ratio $\Delta_y/\Delta x_i$ is positive or negative) would be sufficient to increase the value of y and thereby make it impossible that the values $\bar{x}_1, \ldots, \bar{x}_n$ represent a maximum. For a minimum it is also necessary that the change in y should be zero, for if it were not zero an appropriate marginal increase (or decrease) in the value of x_i (depending on whether the ratio $\Delta y/\Delta x_i$ is respectively, negative or positive) would be sufficient to decrease the value of y and thereby make it impossible that the values $\bar{x}_1, \ldots, \bar{x}_n$ represent a minimum. If and only if the change in y is zero then the ratio $\Delta y/\Delta x_i$ is zero as well. It follows that $\Delta y/\Delta x_i = 0$ for $i = 1, \ldots, n$ is a necessary condition that the function is at a maximum or a minimum in the range $\bar{x}_i, \ldots, \bar{x}_n$ to $\bar{x}_n + \Delta x_1, \ldots, \bar{x}_n + \Delta x_n$. As each Δx_i tends to zero the ratio $\Delta y/\Delta x_i$ tends to $\partial y/\partial x_i$, the partial derivative of y with respect to x_i, and the range $\bar{x}_1, \ldots, \bar{x}_n$ to $\bar{x}_1 + \Delta x_1, \ldots, \bar{x}_n + \Delta x_n$ tends to the point $\bar{x}_1, \ldots, \bar{x}_n$. Consequently it is necessary for there to be either a maximum or a minimum at the particular set of values $\bar{x}_1, \ldots, \bar{x}_n$ that each partial derivative $\partial y/\partial x_i$ is zero. We have established that *a necessary condition for there to be either a maximum or a minimum of the function of several variables* $y = f(x_1, \ldots, x_n)$ *at some particular set of values* $\bar{x}_1, \ldots, \bar{x}_n$ *is that at this set of values all the partial derivatives of y are zero,* $\partial y/\partial x_1, \ldots, \partial y/\partial x_n = 0$.

For a function of two variables this result can be illustrated diagrammatically. Figure 6C shows a function $y = f(x_1, x_2)$ which has a maximum at the particular values $\bar{x}_1, \bar{x}_2$. The values of x_1 and x_2 are plotted in the 'base plane' of the figure and the value of y is read off along the vertical axis; the shape of the graph of y could be described as an inverted basin. When $x_2 = \bar{x}_2$ the variation of y with respect to x_1 is shown by the height of the shaded surface AA′: the height of the shaded surface represents the graph of y as a function of x_1 when the value of x_2 is fixed at $\bar{x}_2$. For y to be at a maximum with respect to x_1 it is necessary that the height of the shaded area should be a constant—otherwise by marginally increasing or decreasing the value of x_1 the height (which is the value of y) could be increased and so the original position could not represent a maximum. The rate of change of the height is determined by the slope of the edge of the area, and this is measured by the derivative of y with respect to x_1 when x_2 is fixed at $\bar{x}_2$: i.e. it is measured by the partial derivative of y with respect to x_1 evaluated when $x_2 = \bar{x}_2$. For y to be at a maximum the height of the shaded area must be constant, which means that the slope must be horizontal and hence the partial derivative of y with respect of x_1 must be zero; as shown in the figure, this is the case only when $x_1 = \bar{x}_1$.

Suppose now that x_1 is fixed at the value $\bar{x}_1$ and that x_2 is allowed to vary: the variation of y with respect to x_2 is shown by the height of the shaded area BB′ in the figure. For y to be at a maximum with respect to x_2 it is necessary that the height of the shaded area should be a constant; otherwise by marginally increasing or decreasing the value of x_2 the height (the value of y) could be increased, and the original position would not represent a maximum. The rate of change of the height of BB′ is determined by the slope of the edge, and this is measured by the partial derivative of y with respect of x_2, evaluated when $x_1 = \bar{x}_1$. For y to be at a maximum the height must be constant, so that the slope must be horizontal and so the partial derivative of y with respect to x_2 must be zero; as shown in the figure, this is the case only when $x_2 = \bar{x}_2$. This demonstrates that for y to be at a maximum it is necessary that $x_1 = \bar{x}_1$ and $x_2 = \bar{x}_2$.

Example What are the necessary conditions for a maximum or minimum of the function

$$y = 2x_1 + 4x_2 - x_1^2 - 2x_2^2 + x_1 x_2$$

The conditions are readily deduced to be

$$\partial y/\partial x_1 = 2 - 2x_1 + x_2 = 0$$

$$\partial y/\partial x_2 = 4 - 4x_2 + x_1 = 0$$

These conditions constitute a pair of linear equations which can be solved for the exact values of x_1 and x_2. Multiplying the second of the equations through by two gives

$$8 - 8x_2 + 2x_1 = 0$$

Adding this equation to the first equation gives

$$10 - 7x_2 = 0$$

(since the terms in x_1 cancel out). It follows that

$$7x_2 = 10$$

so that $x_2 = 10/7 = 1\frac{3}{7}$. Substituting the result $x_2 = 1\frac{3}{7}$ into the first equation gives

$$2 - 2x_1 + 1\tfrac{3}{7} = 0$$

so that

$$2x_1 = 3\tfrac{3}{7}$$

and hence

$$x_1 = 1\tfrac{5}{7}$$

We conclude that the function y has either a maximum or a minimum only when $x_1 = 1\frac{5}{7}$ and $x_2 = 1\frac{3}{7}$.

6.9 A necessary and sufficient condition for maxima and minima

In Section 6.8 we have stated a necessary condition for there to be either a maximum or a minimum of the function $y = f(x_1, \ldots, x_n)$ at a particular set of values $\bar{x}_1, \ldots, \bar{x}_n$. In this section we state a criterion which will enable us to distinguish between a maximum and a minimum, and also to distinguish the case in which there is no maximum or minimum (although the necessary conditions of Section 6.8 are satisfied). A typical case in which there is no maximum or minimum is the case of a 'saddle point'; at a saddle point the function is at a maximum when looked at from one point of view (along the saddle) and at a minimum when looked at from another point of view (across the saddle). For a function of two variables the various possibilities can be illustrated graphically (see Fig. 6D).

A necessary and sufficient condition for a maximum at $\bar{x}_1, \ldots, \bar{x}_n$ is deduced on the following lines. In its most general form the condition is that for any set of incremental values $\Delta x_1, \ldots, \Delta x_n$, the value of $f(\bar{x}_1 + \Delta x_1, \ldots, \bar{x}_n + \Delta x_n)$ must be less than or equal to the value $f(\bar{x}_1, \ldots, \bar{x}_n)$; if this is the case then any incremental change in the values of $x_1, \ldots, x_n$ cannot increase the value of y, so that the value of y at $\bar{x}_1, \ldots, \bar{x}_n$ is a maximum. Let us now consider what happens to the function $f(\bar{x}_1 + k\,\Delta x_1, \ldots, \bar{x}_n + k\,\Delta x_n)$ as the variable k increases from -1 to $+1$. When $k = -1$ the value of the function is $f(\bar{x}_1 - \Delta x_1, \ldots, \bar{x}_n - \Delta x_n)$ which is the value of y at $\bar{x}_1 - \Delta x_1, \ldots, \bar{x}_n - \Delta x_n$

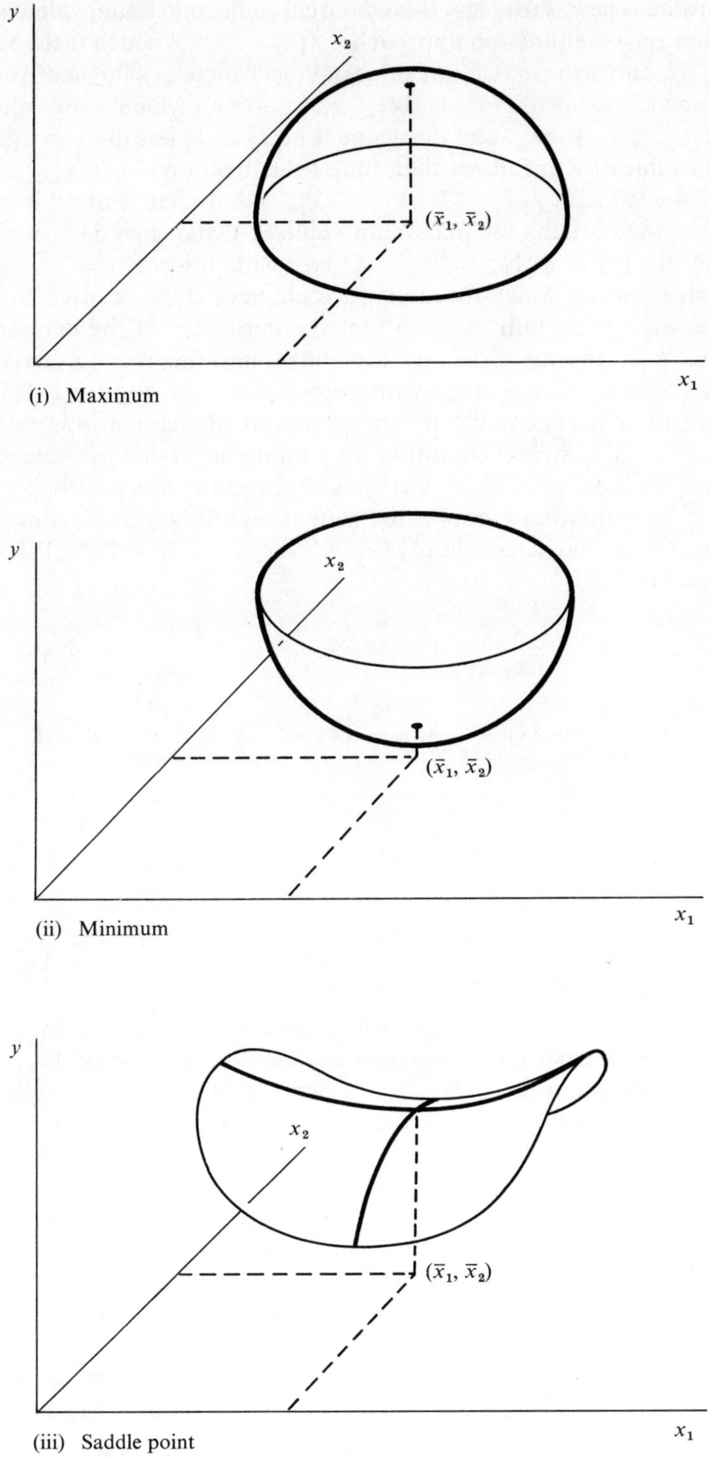

Fig. 6D Maximum, minimum, and saddle point of a function of two variables

and this value is necessarily less than or equal to the maximum value of y. As k approaches zero the function approaches $f(\bar{x}_1, \ldots, \bar{x}_n)$ which is the value of y at $\bar{x}_1, \ldots, \bar{x}_n$ and is the maximum value of y; as k increases further from zero to $+1$ the function tends to $f(\bar{x}_1 + \Delta x_1, \ldots, \bar{x}_n + \Delta x_n)$ which is the value of y at $\bar{x}_1 + \Delta x_1, \ldots, \bar{x}_n + \Delta x_n$, and this value is necessarily less than or equal to the maximum value of y. It follows that, unless the function $y = f(x_1, \ldots, x_n)$ is a constant, the value of $f(\bar{x}_1 + k\,\Delta x_1, \ldots, \bar{x}_n + k\,\Delta x_n)$ first of all increases as k increases then attains the maximum value of y and then decreases, i.e. the derivative of $f(\bar{x}_1 + k\,\Delta_1, \ldots, x_n + k\,\Delta x_n)$ with respect to k changes from positive to negative. Since the derivative changes from positive to negative it is a decreasing function of k, so that the derivative of the derivative with respect to k is negative: i.e. at the maximum the second derivative of $f(\bar{x}_1 + k\,\Delta x_1, \ldots, \bar{x}_n + k\,\Delta x_n)$ with respect to k is negative. This is the necessary and sufficient condition for a maximum. Similar reasoning shows that the necessary and sufficient condition for a minimum is that the second derivative of $f(\bar{x}_1 + k\,\Delta x_1, \ldots, \bar{x}_n + k\,\Delta x_n)$ with respect to k is positive.

By somewhat complicated (but straightforward) algebra it can be shown that the second derivative of $f(\bar{x}_1 + k\Delta x_1, \ldots, \bar{x}_n + k\,\Delta x_n)$ with respect to k is equal to[3]

$$
\begin{aligned}
&\frac{\partial^2 y}{\partial x_1^2}\,\Delta x_1^2 + \frac{\partial^2 y}{\partial x_2\,\partial x_1}\,\Delta x_2\,\Delta x_1 + \cdots + \frac{\partial^2 y}{\partial x_n\,\partial x_1}\,\Delta x_n\,\Delta x_1 \\
&+ \frac{\partial^2 y}{\partial x_1\,\partial x_2}\,\Delta x_1\,\Delta x_2 + \frac{\partial^2 y}{\partial x_2^2}\,\Delta x_2^2 + \cdots + \frac{\partial^2 y}{\partial x_n\,\partial x_2}\,\Delta x_n\,\Delta x_2 \\
&+ \cdots \\
&\vdots \\
&+ \cdots \\
&+ \frac{\partial^2 y}{\partial x_1\,\partial x_n}\,\Delta x_1\,\Delta x_n + \frac{\partial^2 y}{\partial x_2\,\partial x_n}\,\Delta x_2\,\Delta x_n + \cdots + \frac{\partial^2 y}{\partial x_n^2}\,\Delta x_n^2
\end{aligned}
$$

For a maximum, this expression is positive *whatever the values of* $\Delta x_1, \ldots, \Delta x_n$; for a minimum, the expression is negative *whatever the values of* $\Delta x_1, \ldots, \Delta x_n$; and for a saddle point the expression is positive or negative *depending on the values of* $\Delta x_1, \ldots, \Delta x_n$.

The expression above is always positive (or always negative) whatever the values of $\Delta x_1, \ldots, \Delta x_n$ if and only if the second-order partial derivatives $\partial^2 y/\partial x_i\,\partial x_j$ satisfy certain conditions. These conditions are stated here for reference, though their interpretation will not be clear to the reader until he has studied Chapter 11.

A necessary and sufficient condition for there to be a maximum (minimum) of the function of several variables $y = f(x_1, \ldots, x_n)$ *at* $\bar{x}_1, \ldots, \bar{x}_n$ *is that all the partial derivatives* $\partial y/\partial x_i$ *are zero and that the second derivative with respect to* k *of* $f(\bar{x}_1 + k\,\Delta x_1, \ldots, \bar{x}_n + k\,\Delta x_n)$ *is negative (positive) when*

3 Differentiate twice using the formula for the total derivative and then note that, by definition, the point at which y is a maximum is the point at which $k = 0$.

k = 0. This second derivative is negative (positive) if and only if the n × n matrix of second-order partial derivatives $\partial^2 y/\partial x_i\, \partial x_j$ (i, j = 1, ..., n) is negative definite (positive definite) i.e. if and only if all the leading principal minors of the matrix are alternately negative and positive (all positive).

In the special case of a function of two variables these conditions become:

for a maximum

$$\partial y/\partial x_1 = \partial y/\partial x_2 = 0, \qquad \partial^2 y/\partial x_1^2 < 0,$$
$$(\partial^2 y/\partial x_1^2)(\partial^2 y/\partial x_2^2) - (\partial^2 y/\partial x_1\, \partial x_2)^2 > 0$$

for a minimum

$$\partial y/\partial x_1 = \partial y/\partial x_2 = 0, \qquad \partial^2 y/\partial x_1^2 > 0,$$
$$(\partial^2 y/\partial x_1^2)(\partial^2 y/\partial x_2^2) - (\partial^2 y/\partial x_1\, \partial x_2)^2 > 0.$$

(the derivatives are evaluated with $x_1 = \bar{x}_1, x_2 = \bar{x}_2$).

Example In the example in Section 6.8, is the function at a maximum, a minimum, or a saddle point when $x_1 = 1\frac{5}{12}, x_2 = \frac{5}{6}$?

Since $\partial y/\partial x_1 = 2 - 2x_1 + x_2$ and $\partial y/\partial x_2 = 4 - 4x_2 + x_1$ it follows that

$$\partial^2 y/\partial x_1^2 = -2 < 0$$

and that

$$(\partial^2 y/\partial x_1^2)(\partial^2 y/\partial x_2^2) - (\partial^2 y/\partial x_1 \partial x_2)^2$$
$$= (-2)(-4) - (1)^2 = >0$$

so that the function is at a maximum.

Appendix

This appendix contains the proofs of the major results of Chapter 6. The proof of Theorem 6.1 below is based on the 'mean value' theorem.

Mean value theorem

If a function $y = f(x)$ has a derivative $f'(x)$ which is a continuous function of x then for some k, $0 \leqslant k \leqslant 1$,

$$f(x + dx) - f(x) = f'(x + k\, dx).dx$$

In graphical terms the mean value theorem states that if a function has a continuous derivative then the change in the value of the function between two points x and $x + dx$ can always be expressed as the product of the length of the interval, dx, and the slope of the function at some point within the range x to $x + dx$. Another way of putting this is to say that the change in the value of the function is the same as the change in the height of a straight line drawn tangent to the graph at some point within the range x to $x + dx$. The two statements are equivalent because the slope of a graph at a point of tangency is necessarily the same as the slope of the tangent (see Fig. 6E).

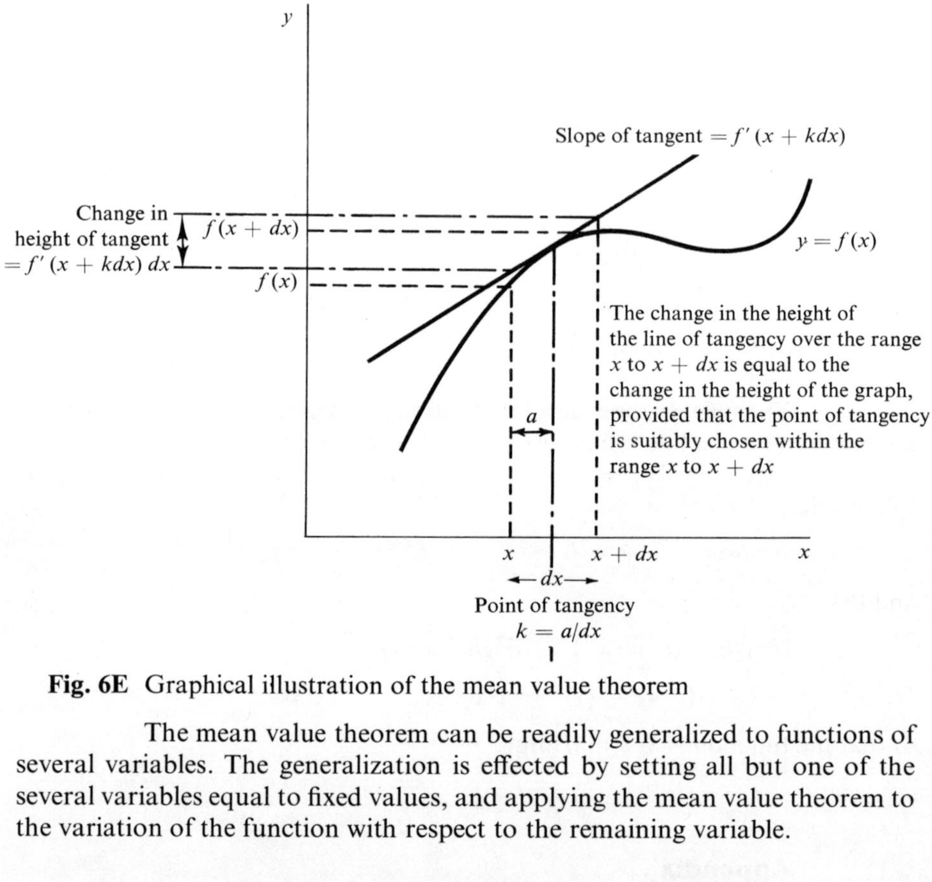

Fig. 6E Graphical illustration of the mean value theorem

The mean value theorem can be readily generalized to functions of several variables. The generalization is effected by setting all but one of the several variables equal to fixed values, and applying the mean value theorem to the variation of the function with respect to the remaining variable.

Mean value theorem for functions of several variables

If a function $y = f(x_1, \ldots, x_n)$ has a partial derivative $\partial y/\partial x_i = f_i'(x_1, \ldots, x_n)$ which is a continuous function of x_i then for some k_i, $0 \leqslant k_i \leqslant 1$,

$$f(x_1, \ldots, x_{i-1}, x_i + dx_i, x_{i+1}, \ldots, x_n) - f(x_1, \ldots, x_{i-1}, x_i, x_{i+1}, \ldots, x_n)$$
$$= f'(x_1, \ldots, x_{i-1}, x_i + k_i\, dx_i, x_{i+1}, \ldots, x_n)\, dx_i$$

Theorem 6.1 The effect on $y = f(x_1, \ldots, x_n)$ of simultaneous increments $dx_1, \ldots, dx_n$ in $x_1, \ldots, x_n$ is to change the value of y by approximately

$$dy = \frac{\partial y}{\partial x_1} dx_1 + \frac{\partial y}{\partial x_2} dx_2 + \cdots + \frac{\partial y}{\partial x_n} dx_n$$

provided that each partial derivative, $\partial y/\partial x_i$, is a continuous function of $x_1, \ldots, x_n$.

PROOF Let Δy be the increase in y as a result of simultaneous increments $dx_1, \ldots, dx_n$ in $x_1, \ldots, x_n$; then

$$\Delta y = f(x_1 + dx_1, x_2 + dx_2, \ldots, x_n + dx_n) - f(x_1, x_2, \ldots, x_n)$$

which may be expanded as

$$\begin{aligned}\Delta y = {} & [f(x_1 + dx_1, x_2 + dx_2, \ldots, x_n + dx_n) \\ & - f(x_1, x_2 + dx_2, \ldots, x_n + dx_n)] \\ & + [f(x_1, x_2 + dx_2, \ldots, x_n + dx_n) - f(x_1, x_2, x_3 + dx_3, \ldots, x_n + dx_n)] \\ & + \cdots \\ & + [f(x_1, x_2, \ldots, x_{n-1}, x_n + dx_n) - f(x_1, x_2, \ldots, x_n)]\end{aligned}$$

It is a consequence of the mean value theorem that when dx_i is very small

$$\begin{aligned}& f(x_1, \ldots, x_{i-1}, x_i + dx_i, \ldots, x_n + dx_n) \\ & - f(x_1, \ldots, x_i, x_{i+1} + dx_{i+1}, \ldots, x_n + dx_n) \\ & = f'(x_1, \ldots, x_{i-1}, x_i + k_i\, dx_i, x_{i+1} + dx_{i+1}, \ldots, x_n + dx_n)\, dx_i\end{aligned}$$

where $0 \leqslant k_i \leqslant 1$ $(i = 1, \ldots, n)$. Hence, when the increments $dx_1, \ldots, dx_n$ are very small,

$$\begin{aligned}\Delta y = {} & f_1'(x_1 + k_1\, dx_1, x_2 + dx_2, \ldots, x_n + dx_n)\, dx_1 \\ & + f_2'(x_1, x_2 + k_2 dx_2, x_3 + dx_3, \ldots, x_n + dx_n)\, dx_2 \\ & \vdots \\ & + f_n'(x_1, x_2, \ldots, x_{n-1}, x_n + k_n\, dx_n)\, dx_n\end{aligned}$$

where $0 \leqslant k_i \leqslant 1$. Since the partial derivative $f_i'(x_1, \ldots, x_n)$ is a continuous function of $x_1, \ldots, x_n$ it follows that when dx_i is very small, $f_i'(x_1, \ldots, x_{i-1}, x_1 + k_i\, dx_i, x_{i+1} + dx_{i+1}, \ldots, x_n + dx_n)$ is very nearly equal to $f_i'(x_1, \ldots, x_n)$, i.e.

$$\begin{aligned}& f_i'(x_1, \ldots, x_{i-1}, x_i + k_i\, dx_i, x_{i+1} + dx_{i+1}, \ldots, x_n + dx_n) \\ & = f_i'(x_1, \ldots, x_n) + df_i'\end{aligned}$$

where df_i' is small when $dx_1, \ldots, dx_n$ are small. Hence

$$\begin{aligned}\Delta y = {} & f_1'(x_1, \ldots, x_n)\, dx_1 + f_2'(x_1, \ldots, x_n)\, dx_2 + \cdots \\ & \cdots + f_n'(x_1, \ldots, x_n)\, dx_n + df_1'\, dx_1 + df_2'\, dx_2 + \cdots + df_n'\, dx_n.\end{aligned}$$

where the terms $df_i'\, dx_i$ are very small indeed. It follows that a good approximation to Δy is given by

$$\begin{aligned}& f_1'(x_1, \ldots, x_n)\, dx_1 + f_2'(x_1, \ldots, x_n)\, dx_2 + \cdots + f_n'(x_1, \ldots, x_n)\, dx_n \\ & = \frac{\partial y}{dx_1}\, dx_1 + \frac{\partial y}{dx_2}\, dx_2 + \cdots + \frac{\partial y}{dx_n}\, dx_n\end{aligned}$$

which is, by definition, the differential of y.

Theorem 6.2 If $y = f(x_1, \ldots, x_n)$ has continuous partial first derivatives and if $x_1, \ldots, x_n$ are differentiable functions of t then y is differentiable with respect to t and

$$\frac{dy}{dt} = \frac{\partial y}{\partial x_1} \cdot \frac{dx_1}{dt} + \frac{\partial y}{\partial x_2} \cdot \frac{dx_2}{dt} + \cdots + \frac{\partial y}{\partial x_n} \cdot \frac{dx_n}{dt}$$

PROOF Let the effect of an increase, Δt, in t be to increase $x_1, \ldots, x_n$ by the amounts $\Delta x_1, \ldots, \Delta x_n$, and hence to increase y by an amount Δy. Now

$$\frac{\Delta y}{\Delta t} = \frac{f(x_1 + \Delta x_1, \ldots, x_n + \Delta x_n) - f(x_1, \ldots, x_n)}{\Delta t}$$

and by elementary algebra[4]

$$\frac{\Delta y}{\Delta t} =$$

$$\frac{f(x_1 + \Delta x_1, x_2 + \Delta x_2, \ldots, x_n + \Delta x_n) - f(x_1, x_2 + \Delta x_2, \ldots, x_n + \Delta x_n)}{\Delta x_1} \cdot \frac{\Delta x}{\Delta t}$$

$$+ \frac{f(x_1, x_2 + \Delta x_2, \ldots, x_n + \Delta x_n) - f(x_1, x_2, x_3 + \Delta x_3, \ldots, x_n + \Delta x_n)}{\Delta x_2} \cdot \frac{\Delta x_2}{\Delta t}$$

$$+ \cdots$$

$$+ \frac{f(x_1, \ldots, x_{n-1}, x_n + \Delta x_n) - f(x_1, \ldots, x_n)}{\Delta x_n} \cdot \frac{\Delta x_n}{\Delta t}$$

From the ordinary definition of a partial derivative,

$$\lim_{\Delta x_i \to 0} \frac{\begin{array}{l} f(x_1, \ldots, x_{i-1}, x_i + \Delta x_i, \ldots, x_n + \Delta x_n) \\ - f(x_1, \ldots, x_i, x_{i+1} + \Delta x_{i+1}, \ldots, x_n + \Delta x_n) \end{array}}{\Delta x_i}$$

$$= f_i'(x_1, \ldots, x_i, x_{i+1} + \Delta x_{i+1}, \ldots, x_n + \Delta x_n)$$

Since all the derivatives are continuous functions of $x_1, \ldots, x_n$,

$$\lim_{\Delta x_1, \ldots, \Delta x_n \to 0} f_i'(x_1, \ldots, x_i, x_{i+1} + \Delta x_{i+1}, \ldots, x_n + \Delta x_n) = f_i'(x_1, \ldots, x_n)$$

If all the x_i are differentiable with respect to t then as t tends to zero, $\Delta x_1, \ldots, \Delta x_n$ tend to zero and

$$\lim_{\Delta t \to 0} \frac{\Delta x_i}{\Delta t} = \frac{dx_i}{dt}$$

4 This proof assumes that $\Delta x_1, \ldots, \Delta x_n \neq 0$, although the result is still valid if some or all $\Delta x_i = 0$.

Hence as t tends to zero, $\Delta x_1, \ldots, \Delta x_n$ tend to zero and

$$\lim_{\Delta t \to 0} \frac{\Delta y}{\Delta t} = f_1'(x_1, \ldots, x_n) \frac{dx_1}{dt} + f_2'(x_1, \ldots, x_n) \frac{dx_2}{dt} + \cdots$$

$$\cdots + f_n'(x_1, \ldots, x_n) \frac{dx_n}{dt}$$

$$= \frac{\partial y}{\partial x_1} \cdot \frac{dx_1}{dt} + \frac{\partial y}{\partial x_2} \cdot \frac{dx_2}{dt} + \cdots + \frac{\partial y}{\partial x_n} \cdot \frac{dx_n}{dt}$$

Theorem 6.3 (Euler's theorem). If $y = f(x_1, \ldots, x_n)$ is homogeneous of degree m then

$$\frac{\partial y}{\partial x_1} x_1 + \frac{\partial y}{\partial x_2} x_2 + \cdots + \frac{\partial y}{\partial x_n} x_n = my$$

PROOF Let $y(\lambda) = f(\lambda x_1, \ldots, \lambda x_n)$ and set $w_i = \lambda x_i$ $(i = 1, \ldots, n)$. The proof is simply to evaluate $\partial y(\lambda)/\partial \lambda$ in two different ways and equate the results in the special case $\lambda = 1$. Expressing $y(\lambda)$ as a function of the w_i and using the formula for the total derivative we get

(1) $$\frac{\partial y(\lambda)}{\partial \lambda} = \frac{\partial y}{\partial w_1} \cdot \frac{dw_1}{d\lambda} + \frac{\partial y}{\partial w_2} \frac{dw_2}{d\lambda} + \cdots + \frac{\partial y}{\partial w_n} \cdot \frac{dw_n}{d\lambda}$$

$$= \frac{\partial y}{\partial w_1} x_1 + \frac{\partial y}{\partial w_2} x_2 + \cdots + \frac{\partial y}{\partial w_n} x_n$$

But since y is homogeneous of degree m, $y(\lambda) = \lambda^m f(x_1, \ldots, x_m)$ so that we have the alternative formula

(2) $$\partial y(\lambda)/\partial \lambda = m\lambda^{m-1} f(x_1, \ldots, x_m)$$

When $\lambda = 1$, $w_i = x_i$ and so the right-hand side of (1) becomes

(3) $$\frac{\partial y}{\partial x_1} x_1 + \frac{\partial y}{\partial x_2} x_2 + \cdots + \frac{\partial y}{\partial x_n} x_n$$

and the right-hand side of (2) becomes

(4) $$mf(x_1, \ldots, x_n) = my$$

Since (1) and (2) are just different formulae for the same derivative, (3) is equal to (4) and so the theorem is proved.

Notes and references

For parallel reading consult Allen,[6] Ch. 11–14, Yamane,[126] Ch. 4, Lewis,[79] Ch. 18, 19, Tintner,[120] Ch. 16 and Courant,[30] Ch. 10. Baumol,[13] Henderson and Quandt[56] and Cohen and Cyert[28] make use of partial differentiation techniques throughout their books. For the applications to production functions in particular see Brown[22] and Heathfield.[55] Johnston[65] makes use of the theory of production functions in a well known empirical study. A good source for applications to consumer theory is Green.[44]

Problems

6.2 A firm has the production function $Y = 1{\cdot}5K^{3/4}L^{1/4}$. If the capital stock, K, is fixed at 256 units how does output, Y, vary with the amount of labour employed, L?

6.3.1 Evaluate the partial derivative $\partial y/\partial x_1$ for each of the functions below:

(a) $y = x_1x_2 + 5$
(b) $y = 3x_1^2x_2^2 + x_1 + 2$
(c) $y = x_1^{3/4}x_2^{1/4}$

6.3.2 Evaluate all the first- and second-order partial derivatives and the cross partial derivatives of the following functions:

(i) $y = x_1^2x_2 + x_2^2 + 6$
(ii) $y = 20x_1^{1/2}x_2$
(iii) $y = 2x_1^{2/3}x_2^{2/3} + x_1^2x_2 + 2$

6.4 Find the differential associated with the production function in Problem 6.2.

6.5.1 Evaluate the total derivative of y with respect to x where $y = \sqrt{(uv)}$ and $u = (x + 2)^2$, $v = 3x + 1$.

6.5.2 An individual has a utility function defined solely in terms of daily income (in £), x_1, and daily hours of leisure, x_2:

$$U = x_2\sqrt{x_1}$$

If the individual is rational how many hours a day will he choose to work when his wage is £2 per hour? How would an increase in the wage rate to £5 per hour affect his hours of work?

6.6 Given the production function in 6.2 what alternative combinations of labour and capital will produce an output of 121·5 units?

6.7.1 Suppose that the demand for frozen foods is given by

$$D = AY^{\alpha}F^{\beta}/P^{\gamma}$$

where A is a constant, Y is consumers' money income, F is the ownership of refrigerators and P is the price level of frozen food. What is the degree of homogeneity of the demand function? Under what conditions do consumers display money illusion?

6.7.2 Given a production function of the form

$$y = L^{3/4}K^{1/4}$$

(i) find the marginal product of labour in terms of L and K;
(ii) find the marginal product of capital in terms of L and K;
(iii) show that, if factors are paid their marginal product, the wage bill is three times the capital rental bill;
(iv) show that the total factor payments equal the value of output.

6.7.3 Given a production function of the general form

$$y = L^{\alpha}K^{\beta}S^{\gamma}$$

where L is labour, K is capital machinery and S is stocks (we assume that stocks assist in the smooth running of the productive process);

(i) Show that if factors are paid their marginal products then the wage bill is αy, the owners of capital are paid an amount βy, and the owners of stocks are paid an amount γy

(ii) Show that the total factor payments equal the value of output only if $\alpha + \beta + \gamma = 1$ (trivial, using (i))

(iii) Show that if $\alpha + \beta + \gamma < 1$ then there will be decreasing returns to scale. (*Hint:* examine the effect of doubling the scale of production by doubling the amount of each of the inputs.)

6.8.1 Find the possible maxima and minima of the functions

(a) $y = 3x_1 + 4x_2 + 6x_1x_2 - x_1^2 - 2x_2^2$
(b) $y = (x_1 - 2)^2 + (x_2 - 3)^2 + x_1x_2$

6.8.2 A car manufacturer produces the same model in two different plants. He has two cost functions thus:

$$\text{Total costs in plant 1 (£ per week)} = 500x_1 + 2x_1^2$$
$$\text{Total costs in plant 2 (£ per week)} = 100x_2 + x_2^2$$

where x_1, x_2 are the respective outputs of cars (numbers of cars per week). If the cars can be sold in unlimited quantities at £1,000 each how many cars should be produced in each plant to maximize profit? What is maximum profit? Suppose the car firm acquires a monopoly and the demand for the firm's cars becomes a function of price:

$$D = 1575 - P$$

where D is demand (cars per week) and P is price (£). How many cars should be produced and what is the profit?

6.8.3 An international company has two factories, one at home and one in a foreign country and it sells its products in both countries. The cost structure of the foreign factory differs from that of the home factory and the demand conditions in the foreign country differ from those in the home country.

(a) Show that if the company transports some of its product from the home country to the foreign country then to maximize profit it is necessary that production is organized so that the marginal cost of production in the foreign country is equal to the marginal cost of production in the home country plus the marginal cost of transport.

(b) Suppose that it is possible for the company to transport the product from one country to another without cost. Show that for the company to maximize profit it is necessary that production is organized so that the marginal revenue is the same in each country and the marginal cost of production is the same in each country.

6.8.4 A theatre and a restaurant are adjacent to one another. The demand for theatre seats and the demand for restaurant meals have both two components: the demand by people with high incomes (for whom theatre-going and dining out are complementary activities) and the demand by people with lower incomes (for whom theatre-going and dining out are substitute activities). Let £p_1 be the average price of theatre tickets and £p_2 be the average price of restaurant meals. The average number of theatre tickets demanded per week by the high income group is $a_1/[p_1\sqrt{(p_1p_2)}]$ and by the lower income group is $b_1\sqrt{(p_2/p_1)}$. The average number of meals demanded per week by the high income group is $a_2/[p_2\sqrt{(p_1/p_2)}]$ and by the lower income group is $b_2\sqrt{(p_1/p_2)}$. The costs of the theatre are £c_1 per week (independent of the size of the audience) and the costs of the restaurant are £c_2 per week (independent of the number of meals served).

(a) Express the profits of the theatre and the restaurant as a function of the prices of theatre tickets and restaurant meals.

(b) If the restaurant is to maximize profit how must the price of meals be fixed to the price of theatre tickets?

(c) If the theatre is to maximize profit how must the price of theatre tickets be fixed relative to the price of restaurant meals?

(d) Show that the pricing policy of the theatre and the restaurant will agree only if $a_1a_2 = b_1b_2$.

(e) Suppose that the theatre announces its prices in advance of the restaurant and that the restaurant follows a profit maximizing pricing policy once it knows the theatre prices. Show that in this case the profit of the theatre is independent of its own pricing policy.

(f) Suppose that, on the other hand, the restaurant announces its prices in advance of the theatre and that the theatre follows a profit maximizing pricing policy once it knows the restaurant's prices. Show that, provided $a_1a_2 \neq b_1b_2$ this policy will be less profitable to the restaurant than the policy of waiting until the theatre prices have been announced before deciding its own prices.

6.8.5 Two firms share a market of constant size equal to k units per annum. Their market shares depend upon their advertising expenditures, which are £A_1, £A_2 respectively. The market share of firm 1 is $1/[1 + (A_2/A_1)]$. Each firm charges the same constant price for the product (£1 per unit) so that the firms compete only by varying their advertising expenditures. The objective of each firm is to maximize the excess of sales revenue over advertising expenditure.

(a) Show that the policy of firm 1 will be to fix its advertising expenditure so that $A_1 = \sqrt{(kA_2)} - A_2$ and that the policy of firm 2 will be to fix its advertising expenditure so that $A_2 = (\sqrt{k} - 1)A_1$ (£ units).

(b) Show that the policies of the two firms are compatible if and only if the advertising expenditures are $A_1 = \sqrt{k} - 1$, $A_2 = (\sqrt{k} - 1)^2$ (£ units).

6.9 Distinguish between the maxima and the minima of the functions in Problem 6.8.1.

Chapter 7

Maximization and minimization subject to constraints

7.1 Introduction

Economic problems often involve the maximization or minimization of something, but usually there are constraints which limit the alternatives from which the maximum or minimum is chosen.

Example 1 The aim of a consumer is to maximize utility, but he is subject to the constraint that he can purchase commodities only up to the limit imposed by his income.

Suppose that the consumer derives utility from the consumption of two goods, 1 and 2. Let the prices of the two goods be p_1 and p_2 respectively, let the amounts consumed be x_1, x_2 and let the consumer's income be y. Utility depends on the amounts consumed, $U = f(x_1, x_2)$ and the amounts consumed are constrained by the fact that the consumer's expenditure must be equal to his income, $p_1x_1 + p_2x_2 = y$. For the consumer to maximize utility he must maximize

$$U = f(x_1, x_2) \quad \text{subject to} \quad p_1x_1 + p_2x_2 = y$$

Example 2 An efficient producer is one who maximizes his output for a given expenditure on factor inputs.

Suppose that output depends on the factor inputs of land, labour and capital. Let Y be the output, L be the amount of labour employed, K the amount of capital employed and M the amount of land used. The production function is of the form $Y = f(L, K, M)$. Let Z be the fixed expenditure on factor inputs; if p_L, p_K, p_M are the respective prices of the factor inputs then $Z = p_LL + p_KK + p_MM$. Consequently the efficient producer maximizes

$$Y = f(L, K, M) \quad \text{subject to} \quad p_LL + p_KK + p_MM = Z$$

Example 3 A criterion for a good policy decision taken under conditions of imperfect information is that the decision minimizes the probability of mistakenly adopting the policy while constraining to some fixed value the probability that the policy is not adopted when it is appropriate.

Suppose that the government adopts either policy A (to stimulate investment) or policy B (to discourage investment) depending on whether it believes the economy to be in state I (recession) or state II (inflation). The government has imperfect knowledge of the state of the economy; what knowledge it has is based on official statistics, denoted by Z. The policy decision is based on the government's interpretation of the evidence, Z. The aim of the government is to minimize the probability that policy A is adopted when the economy is in state II (i.e. investment is stimulated in an inflationary situation) subject to the constraint that the probability that policy B is adopted when the economy is in state I (i.e. investment is discouraged in a recession) is equal to some small fixed amount, k. It can be shown, by using the laws of probability, that the smaller the probability of the first type of error, the greater the probability of the second type of error, but that the exact trade-off between the two depends on the way in which the decision is based on the evidence Z. A good decision procedure is that which minimizes

Prob (adopt policy A on evidence Z when the economy is in state II)

subject to the constraint that

Prob (adopt policy B on evidence Z when the economy is in state I) $= k$

In the first part of this chapter we shall concentrate on the type of problem exemplified above, in which the constraints are represented by a single equation. In the final section we discuss problems in which the constraints involve a mixture of equations and inequalities. The latter case is by far the most common in applied economics.

7.2 First method of solution

There is a very elegant method of maximizing or minimizing a function subject to constraints which is due to the eighteenth-century French-Italian mathematician Lagrange. To emphasize the elegance of Lagrange's approach we shall first of all describe a more pedestrian method of solution. The reader interested only in results is advised to skip to Section 7.3.

Consider the problem of finding the maximum or minimum of the function $y = f(x_1, \ldots, x_n)$ subject to the constraint that $g(x_1, \ldots, x_n) = k$. (Economic theory usually gives the constraint in the form of an implicit function.) The obvious method of solving this problem is to use the equation $g(x_1, \ldots, x_n) = k$ in order to write x_1 as an explicit function of $x_2, \ldots, x_n$,[1] say $x_1 = h(x_2, \ldots, x_n)$. Substituting this expression for x_1 into the expression for y gives

$$y = f[x_2, \ldots, x_n, h(x_2, \ldots, x_n)]$$

which expresses y as a function only of $x_2, \ldots, x_n$,

$$y = q(x_2, \ldots, x_n)$$

The function $q(x_2, \ldots, x_n)$ describes how y varies with respect to $x_2, \ldots, x_n$ *when the constraint is binding*, whereas $f(x_1, \ldots, x_n)$ describes how y varies with

1 This is not always possible but we shall assume it can be done.

respect to $x_1, \ldots, x_n$ *when there is no constraint*. It is essential to keep this distinction in mind throughout the following discussion.

To find the maximum or minimum of $y = q(x_2, \ldots, x_n)$ one need only apply the results of Section 6.9. The necessary condition for a maximum or minimum of $y = q(x_2, \ldots, x_n)$ is that all the partial derivatives of q are zero, i.e. that

$$(1) \qquad \begin{aligned} \partial q/\partial x_2 &= 0 \\ \partial q/\partial x_3 &= 0 \\ &\vdots \\ \partial q/\partial x_n &= 0 \end{aligned}$$

Equations (1) are $(n - 1)$ equations in $(n - 1)$ unknowns; normally they can be solved for the values of $x_2, \ldots, x_n$. The value of x_1 can then be found from the equation $x_1 = h(x_2, \ldots, x_n)$.

In order to find maxima and minima by this method it is necessary to determine both the functions h and q. It is interesting to enquire whether $\partial q/\partial x_i$ $(i = 1, \ldots, n)$ can be expressed in terms of the original functions f and g; if this is possible then the necessary conditions can be written down directly without evaluating h and q. Fortunately this can be done, simply by noting that because $q(x_2, \ldots, x_n) = f(h(x_2, \ldots, x_n), x_2, \ldots, x_n)$ the partial derivative of q with respect to x_i $(i = 1, \ldots, n)$ is equal to the *total* derivative of f with respect to x_i when all variables except x_1, x_i are fixed, i.e.

$$(2) \qquad \frac{\partial q}{\partial x_i} = \frac{df}{dx_i} \qquad \text{(all } x\text{s fixed except } x_1, x_i)$$

Applying the formula for the total derivative (see Section 6.5) shows that

$$(3) \qquad \frac{df}{dx_i} = \frac{\partial f}{\partial x_1} \cdot \frac{dx_1}{dx_i} + \frac{\partial f}{\partial x_i} \cdot \frac{dx_i}{dx_i}$$

where $\partial f/\partial x_i$ is the partial derivative of f with respect to x_i. Substituting $dx_i/dx_i = 1$ on the right-hand side of equation (3) and applying equation (2) to the left-hand side of (3) shows that

$$(4) \qquad \frac{\partial q}{\partial x_i} = \frac{\partial f}{\partial x_1} \cdot \frac{dx_1}{dx_i} + \frac{\partial f}{\partial x_i}.$$

The implicit function rule applied to the constraint $g(x_1, \ldots, x_n) = k$ gives

$$(5) \qquad \frac{dx_1}{dx_i} = -\frac{\partial g/\partial x_i}{\partial g/\partial x_1}$$

Substituting (5) into (4) and equating $\partial q/\partial x_i$ to zero ($i = 2, \ldots, n$) shows that the necessary conditions (1) can be written in the form

$$\begin{aligned}
&\frac{\partial f}{\partial x_2} - \frac{\partial f/\partial x_1}{\partial g/\partial x_1}\frac{\partial g}{\partial x_2} = 0 \\
(6)\quad &\frac{\partial f}{\partial x_3} - \frac{\partial f/\partial x_1}{\partial g/\partial x_1}\frac{\partial g}{\partial x_3} = 0 \\
&\vdots \qquad\quad \vdots \qquad\quad \vdots \qquad \vdots \\
&\frac{\partial f}{\partial x_n} - \frac{\partial f/\partial x_1}{\partial g/\partial x_1}\frac{\partial g}{\partial x_n} = 0
\end{aligned}$$

Equations (6) contain only the partial derivatives of the original functions f and g. It is interesting to compare equations (6) with the necessary conditions for unconstrained maxima and minima of $y = f(x_1, \ldots, x_n)$ with respect to $x_2, \ldots, x_n$, which are

$$\begin{aligned}
&\partial f/\partial x_2 = 0 \\
&\partial f/\partial x_3 = 0 \\
(7)\quad &\vdots \qquad\quad \vdots \\
&\partial f/\partial x_n = 0
\end{aligned}$$

It can be seen that equations (6) differ from (7) by the addition of the terms $[(\partial f/\partial x_1)/(\partial g/\partial x_1)]\ \partial g/\partial x_i$. The additional terms are attributable to the presence of the constraint: intuitively, each term measures the change in the sensitivity of y to x_i due to the fact that the constraint requires changes in x_i to be accompanied by compensating changes in x_1 which induce a 'feed-back' effect on y.

A disadvantage of the conditions (6) above is that they are not symmetrical in the variables $x_1, \ldots, x_n$; the variable x_1 appears to have a different role from the other variables $x_2, \ldots, x_n$. This is simply because we have chosen to express x_1 in terms of other variables in order to solve the problem; there is no lack of symmetry as the problem is formulated. It is quite easy to restore symmetry to the solution. Firstly, note that the following equation is tautologically true

$$(8)\qquad \frac{\partial f}{\partial x_1} - \frac{\partial f/\partial x_1}{\partial g/\partial x_1}\cdot\frac{\partial g}{\partial x_1} = 0$$

Equation (8) may be regarded as a 'dummy' necessary condition. If equation (8) is added to the other necessary conditions, the only lack of symmetry in the necessary conditions will be that due to the variable $(\partial f/\partial x_1)/(\partial g/\partial x_1)$. If we make the substitution $(\partial f/\partial x_1)/(\partial g/\partial x_1) = \lambda$ in the necessary conditions then the n equations become perfectly symmetrical in the variables $x_1, \ldots, x_n$. However, these equations now involve an additional variable, λ. In order to have sufficient equations to solve for the variables we must find another equation—an equation which should also be symmetrical in the variables $x_1, \ldots, x_n$: such an equation is the constraint itself, $g(x_1, \ldots, x_n) =$

k. It follows that the necessary conditions may be written in the form of the $n + 1$ equations

$$\begin{aligned}
\partial y/\partial x_1 - \lambda\, \partial g/\partial x_1 &= 0 \\
\partial y/\partial x_2 - \lambda\, \partial g/\partial x_2 &= 0 \\
\vdots \qquad\qquad \vdots \qquad &\quad \vdots \\
\partial y/\partial x_n - \lambda\, \partial g/\partial x_n &= 0 \\
g(x_1, \ldots, x_n) \qquad\quad &= k
\end{aligned} \tag{9}$$

in the $n + 1$ unknowns $x_1, \ldots, x_n, \lambda$.

An interesting point about equations (9) is that not only are they the necessary conditions for a constrained maximum or minimum of $y = f(x_1, \ldots, x_n)$ but that *they are also the necessary conditions for an unconditional maximum or minimum of the function*

$$v = f(x_1, \ldots, x_n) + \lambda[k - g(x_1, \ldots, x_n)$$

(as the reader may verify by differentiating v partially with respect to the $n + 1$ variables $x_1, \ldots, x_n, \lambda$ and equating the partial derivatives to zero). At this stage it is appropriate to introduce the second method of solution, due to Lagrange.

7.3 The method of Lagrange

The fundamental theorem of Lagrange may be stated as follows.

A maximum (minimum) of a function of n variables $y = f(x_1, \ldots, x_n)$ subject to the constraint $g(x_1, \ldots, x_n) = k$ is also an unconditional maximum (minimum) of $v = f(x_1, \ldots, x_n) + \lambda[k - g(x_1, \ldots, x_n)]$ with respect to the $(n + 1)$ variables $x_1, \ldots, x_n, \lambda$. The converse is also true.

It is usual to refer to the function v as the 'Lagrangian' and to λ as the 'Lagrange multiplier'. It is a consequence of Lagrange's theorem that a necessary and sufficient condition for an unconstrained maximum (minimum) of v is also a necessary and sufficient condition for a constrained maximum (minimum) of y. Now it follows from Section 6.8 that the necessary conditions for an unconstrained maximum or minimum of v with respect to $x_1, \ldots, x_n, \lambda$ are

$$\begin{aligned}
\frac{\partial v}{\partial x_1} &= \frac{\partial f}{\partial x_1} - \lambda \frac{\partial g}{\partial x_1} = 0 \\
\frac{\partial v}{\partial x_2} &= \frac{\partial f}{\partial x_2} - \lambda \frac{\partial g}{\partial x_2} = 0 \\
\vdots \quad &\quad \vdots \qquad\quad \vdots \quad\;\; \vdots \\
\frac{\partial v}{\partial x_n} &= \frac{\partial f}{\partial x_n} - \lambda \frac{\partial g}{\partial x_n} = 0 \\
\frac{\partial v}{\partial \lambda} &= k - g(x_1, \ldots, x_n) = 0
\end{aligned}$$

These are $(n + 1)$ equations in $(n + 1)$ unknowns and their solution determines the values $x_1, \ldots, x_n$ at which y may be either a constrained maximum or a constrained minimum. It is possible to distinguish constrained maxima from constrained minima by applying the necessary and sufficient conditions of Section 6.9 to the Lagrangian v.

The theorem of Lagrange is something of a mathematical oddity: to explore all of its ramifications would take us well beyond the scope of this book. However, it is easy to explain why the $(n + 1)$ equations in the $(n + 1)$ unknowns are the necessary conditions for a constrained maximum or minimum of a function of n variables (it is explaining the sufficiency of the conditions that is difficult). A formal mathematical explanation was given in Section 7.2; the key to an intuitive understanding of the result is to consider the effect of a small variation in the value of the constraint, k.

Consider some of the different ways in which a variation, Δk, in the constraint may influence the value of y. Firstly, suppose that as a result of the variation in k only the value of x_1 is changed and the values of the variables $x_2, \ldots, x_n$ remain fixed at their initial levels. The effect of the resulting change, Δx_1, in the value of x_1 is to change y by an amount Δy_1 where $\Delta y_1 = y(x_1 + \Delta x_1, x_2, \ldots, x_n) - y(x_1, x_2, \ldots, x_n)$. The ratio $\Delta y_1/\Delta k$ measures the rate at which y changes as a result of a small change in the constraint, *when the effect on y of the change in the constraint is channelled entirely through a variation in x_1.*

Secondly, consider what happens when a change in the constraint is accommodated by a change in x_2. The result of the variation Δk is to change the value of x_2 by an amount Δx_2, the values of $x_1, x_3, \ldots, x_n$ remaining fixed. The effect of the variation in x_2 is to change y by an amount $\Delta y_2 = y(x_1, x_2 + \Delta x_2, x_3, \ldots, x_n) - y(x_1, x_2, x_3, \ldots, x_n)$. The ratio $\Delta y_2/\Delta k$ measures the rate at which y changes when the effect of the change in the constraint is channelled entirely through a variation in x_2.

If we consider successively the effect on y of channelling the variation in the constraint through each one of the variables $x_1, \ldots, x_n$, taken one at a time, then we shall obtain n different ratios $\Delta y_1/\Delta k, \Delta y_2/\Delta k, \ldots, \Delta y_n/\Delta k$ and each of these ratios will measure the rate of change of y when the variation in k is channelled through just one of the variables $x_1, \ldots, x_n$.

Now it is necessary for either a maximum or minimum of y that $\Delta y_1 = \Delta y_2 = \cdots = \Delta y_n$. For suppose the contrary to be the case: then there are two variables x_i, x_j such that the effect on y (measured by Δy_i, Δy_j respectively) of channelling the variation through one variable rather than another is different (i.e. $\Delta y_i \neq \Delta y_j$). Assume a reasonable degree of continuity in the variation of y, and suppose that x_i is varied by an amount Δx_i which, other things being equal, reduces $g(x_1, \ldots, x_n)$ by Δk and that x_j is simultaneously varied by an amount Δx_j which, other things being equal, increases $g(x_1, \ldots, x_n)$ by Δk; then the effect of a simultaneous variation in x_i, x_j of $\Delta x_i, \Delta x_j$ respectively is to leave the value of the constraint, k, unchanged i.e. x_i and x_j are varied simultaneously but subject to the constraint $g(x_1, \ldots, x_n) = k$. However, this simultaneous variation in x_i and x_j does not leave the value of y unchanged, for the effect of the variation in x_i is to reduce the value of y by Δy_i and the effect of the variation in x_j is to increase the value of y by Δy_j. Thus the total effect on y of the simultaneous variation in x_i and x_j is to change the value of y by an amount $\Delta y = \Delta y_j - \Delta y_i$ where $\Delta y \neq 0$ since $\Delta y_i \neq \Delta y_j$. If the signs of the variations in x_i and x_j are reversed then the sign of the variation in y due to the simultaneous variation in x_i and x_j is also reversed. It follows that if $\Delta y_i \neq \Delta y_j$ for some i, j then there is some simultaneous variation subject to the constraint which will increase the value of y, and some other variation subject to the constraint which will reduce the value of y. But if the value of y can be increased or decreased by a variation subject to the constraint, the original value of y cannot be either a maximum or a minimum. Hence for either a constrained maximum or constrained minimum of y it is necessary that $\Delta y_1 = \Delta y_2 = \cdots = \Delta y_n$.

The necessary condition for a maximum or minimum of y, as established above, may be written in the form

$$\Delta y_1/\Delta k = \Delta y_2/\Delta k = \cdots = \Delta y_n/\Delta k = \lambda$$

where λ is an appropriate constant. Assuming that $\Delta x_1, \ldots, \Delta x_n$ are nonzero and finite, this condition may also be written as

$$\frac{\Delta y_1}{\Delta x_1}\cdot\frac{\Delta x_1}{\Delta k} = \frac{\Delta y_2}{\Delta x_2}\cdot\frac{\Delta x_2}{\Delta k} = \cdots = \frac{\Delta y_n}{\Delta x_n}\cdot\frac{\Delta x_n}{\Delta k} = \lambda$$

Changing the notation by setting $\Delta k = \Delta g$ and rearranging terms gives the n equations

$$\frac{\Delta y_1}{\Delta x_1} = \lambda\frac{\Delta g}{\Delta x_1}$$

$$\frac{\Delta y_2}{\Delta x_2} = \lambda\frac{\Delta g}{\Delta x_2}$$

$$\vdots$$

$$\frac{\Delta y_n}{\Delta x_n} = \lambda\frac{\Delta g}{\Delta x_n}$$

If y and g are differentiable functions then, letting k tend to zero, it follows that $\Delta g, \Delta x_1, \ldots, \Delta x_n, \Delta y_1, \ldots, \Delta y_n$ tend to zero as well, and that these equations become, respectively,

$$\frac{\partial f}{\partial x_1} - \lambda\frac{\partial g}{\partial x_1} = 0$$

$$\frac{\partial f}{\partial x_2} - \lambda\frac{\partial g}{\partial x_2} = 0$$

$$\vdots \qquad \vdots$$

$$\frac{\partial f}{\partial x_n} - \lambda\frac{\partial g}{\partial x_n} = 0$$

where $\partial f/\partial x_i$ denotes the partial derivative of $y = f(x_1, \ldots, x_n)$ with respect to x_i. Furthermore, from the equation defining λ,

$$\lambda = \frac{dy}{dk}$$

so that λ measures the rate at which a small variation in the constraint changes the value of y when y is at either a constrained maximum or a constrained minimum. A summary of the argument above is given in Fig. 7A.

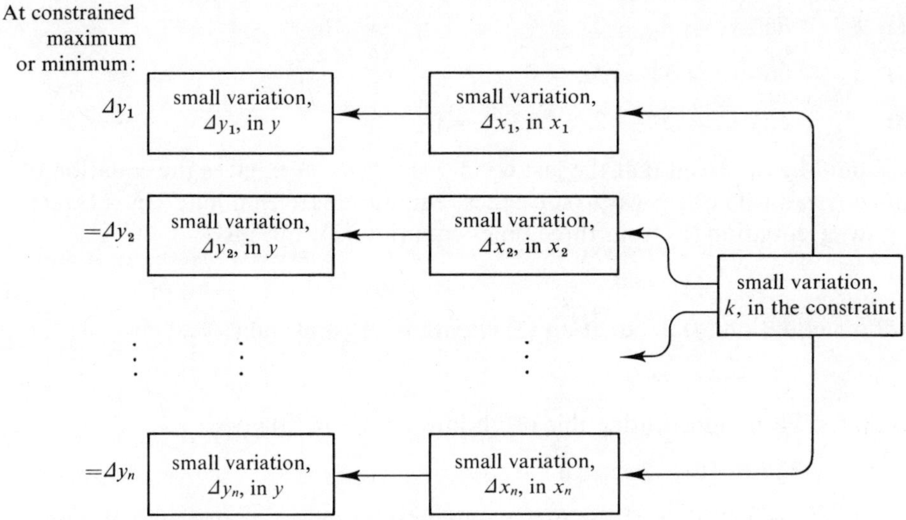

Fig. 7A Effect of a variation in the constraint on the value of the function $y=f(x_1, \ldots, x_n)$ at a constrained maximum or minimum of y

The rate at which the variation of the constraint induces variation in x_i when the other variables take on fixed values is measured by $1/(\partial g/\partial x_i)$. The rate at which the variation of x_i induces variation in y is measured by $\partial y/\partial x_i$. When each of the n channels of variation (as shown in the figure) lead to the same effect on y then the net effect of the variation of the constraint on the value of y is measured by

$$\lambda = \frac{dy}{dk} = \frac{dy}{dg} = \frac{\partial f/\partial x_1}{\partial g/\partial x_1} = \frac{\partial f/\partial x_2}{\partial g/\partial x_2} = \cdots = \frac{\partial f/\partial x_n}{\partial g/\partial x_n}$$

and from this equation the necessary conditions for a maximum or a minimum can be derived immediately.

These ideas are perhaps best explained by an example.

Example 1 A consumer's utility depends on his consumption of two goods. If x_1 and x_2 are the respective amounts of goods 1 and 2 consumed then utility is $U = 2x_1x_2$. The price of good 1 is £2 and the price of good 2 is £3; the consumer's income is £24. With what consumption of goods 1 and 2 does the consumer maximize utility?

Utility must be maximized subject to a budget constraint which expresses the fact that the consumer's total expenditure (in £), $2x_1 + 3x_2$, must be equal to his income, 24, i.e. the consumer maximizes $U = x_1x_2$ subject to $2x_1 + 3x_2 = 24$. From the theorem of Lagrange we know that an equivalent procedure is to maximize the function

$$v = x_1x_2 + \lambda(24 - 2x_1 - 3x_2)$$

with respect to x_1, x_2 and λ. The necessary conditions for either a maximum or minimum are

(1) $\partial v/\partial x_1 = x_2 - 2\lambda = 0$

(2) $\partial v/\partial x_2 = x_1 - 3\lambda = 0$

(3) $\partial v/\partial \lambda = 24 - 2x_1 - 3x_2 = 0$

It should be observed that the last condition, $\partial v/\partial \lambda = 0$, gives the equation of the constraint. The best way to solve these equations is to eliminate λ by subtracting twice equation (2) from three times equation (1); this gives

(4) $3x_2 - 2x_1 = 0$

Adding equation (4) to equation (3) eliminates x_2 and shows that

$$24 - 4x_1 = 0$$

so that $x_1 = 6$. Substituting this result into equation (3) gives

$$24 - 12 - 3x_2 = 0$$

so that $x_2 = 4$. Either of the first two equations shows that $\lambda = 2$. We have established that for the consumer to maximize utility it is necessary that he consumes 6 units (or £12 worth) of commodity 1 and 4 units (or £12 worth) of commodity 2, i.e. the consumer should spend equal amounts of his income on commodities 1 and 2. That the consumer should spend the same amount of his income on each commodity will be found to be a necessary implication of the utility function $U = x_1x_2$. The value of the Lagrange multiplier, $\lambda = 2$, shows that a marginal increase in income, Δk, will lead to a marginal increase in utility of twice that amount, $\Delta U = 2\Delta k$ (since $\lambda = dU/dk = 2$). In this example the Lagrange multiplier, λ, measures the marginal rate at which income is transformed into utility by an optimal policy of consumer expenditure, i.e. λ measures the price of income in terms of utility.

It is easy to see that with any other consumption pattern the consumer cannot be maximizing utility. Suppose, for example, that the consumer spends his income by purchasing 3 units (or £6 worth) of commodity 1 and 6 units (or £18 worth) of commodity 2. It is readily established that a small rearrangement of his consumption pattern will increase his utility. If the consumer were to marginally reduce his consumption of commodity 2 (by an amount Δx_2) then, other things being equal, he would save out of his income at a rate equal to, in £, three times his reduction in consumption of commodity 2, i.e. since the price of commodity 2 is £3 he would save an amount £$3\Delta x_2$. If these savings were all spent on increased consumption of commodity 1 then, since the price of commodity 1 is £2, the additional amount of commodity 1 that could be bought out of £3Δx_2 is $\Delta x_1 = \frac{3}{2}\Delta x_2$. Thus while maintaining his income at £24 the consumer may adjust his consumption pattern by marginally reducing his consumption of commodity 2 and increasing his consumption of commodity 1 by $\frac{3}{2}$ times his reduction in consumption of commodity 2. However, the effect of this adjustment will be to increase utility, as the following calculations show. When $x_1 = 3$, $x_2 = 6$ the marginal utility of commodity 1 is $\partial U/\partial x_1 = 6$ and the marginal utility of commodity 2 is $\partial U/\partial x_2 = 3$; it follows from these figures that the effect of a marginal reduction of Δx_2 in the consumption of commodity 2 is to reduce utility by $3\Delta x_2$ while the effect of a marginal increase of $\Delta x_1 = \frac{3}{2}\Delta x_2$ in the consumption of commodity 1 is to increase utility by $6\Delta x_1 = 9\Delta x_2$ whence the effect of the adjustment in the consumption pattern is to increase utility by $9\Delta x_2 - 3\Delta x_2 = 6\Delta x_2 > 0$. Since utility can be increased by a small rearrangement in the consumption pattern it follows that the consumption pattern $x_1 = 3$ units, $x_2 = 6$ units does not maximize utility.

Example 2 An efficient producer obtains the greatest possible output at a given factor cost. What quantities of land, labour and capital will be used by an efficient producer whose production function is $Y = AL^\alpha K^\beta M^\gamma$ (where L is labour, K is capital, M is land and A, α, β, γ are parameters) and whose total cost of production is Z (£)?

Let the prices of the factors of production be respectively p_L, p_K, p_M. The efficient producer maximizes $Y = AL^\alpha K^\beta M^\gamma$ subject to the constraint $p_L L + p_K K + p_M M = Z$, which is equivalent to maximizing the function

$$v = AL^\alpha K^\beta M^\gamma + \lambda(Z - p_L L - p_K K - p_M M)$$

The necessary conditions for either a maximum or minimum of v are, when simplified,

(1) $\partial v/\partial L = \alpha Y/L - p_L\lambda = 0$

(2) $\partial v/\partial K = \beta Y/K - p_K\lambda = 0$

(3) $\partial v/\partial M = \gamma Y/M - p_M\lambda = 0$

(4) $\partial v/\partial \lambda = Z - p_L L - p_K K - p_M M = 0$

Eliminating λ from equations (1) and (2) gives

(5) $p_K\alpha Y/L - p_L\beta Y/K = 0$

and eliminating λ from equations (2) and (3) gives

(6) $p_K\alpha Y/M - p_M\gamma Y/K = 0$

Dividing equations (5) and (6) throughout by Y and rearranging terms gives

(7) $$(p_L L)/(p_K K) = \alpha/\beta$$
$$(p_K K)/(p_M M) = \beta/\gamma$$

Now the factor payments for land, labour and capital are respectively $p_L L$, $p_K K$ and $p_M M$; equations (7) above show that the factor payments are in the ratio

$p_L L : p_K K : p_M M = \alpha : \beta : \gamma$. It follows from the fourth of the necessary conditions that the wage bill is $\alpha Z/(\alpha + \beta + \gamma)$, the capital payments are $\beta Z/(\alpha + \beta + \gamma)$ and the rent bill is $\gamma Z/(\alpha + \beta + \gamma)$. It follows that the employments of labour, capital and land are respectively $\alpha Z/p_L(\alpha + \beta + \gamma)$, $\beta Z/p_K(\alpha + \beta + \gamma)$, $\gamma Z/p_M(\alpha + \beta + \gamma)$. This describes the behaviour of an efficient producer.

7.4 Several constraints

In the previous section the discussion was confined to the case in which there is just one constraint. However, the method of Lagrange is readily generalized to the maximization or minimization of a function subject to several constraints. This generalization is stated below.

To maximize (minimize) the function $y = f(x_1, \ldots, x_n)$ *subject to the* $m < n$ *constraints* $g_1(x_1, \ldots, x_n) = k_1, \ldots, g_m(x_1, \ldots, x_n) = k_m$ *it is necessary and sufficient to maximize (minimize) unconditionally the function*

$$\begin{aligned} v &= f(x_1, \ldots, x_n) + \lambda_1[k_1 - g_1(x_1, \ldots, x_n)] \\ &\quad + \lambda_2[k_2 - g_2(x_1, \ldots, x_n)] + \cdots + \lambda_m[k_m - g_m(x_1, \ldots, x_n)] \end{aligned}$$

with respect to the $(n + m)$ *variables* $x_1, \ldots, x_n, \lambda_1, \ldots, \lambda_m$.

Example A consumer's utility function is $U = x_1 x_2$, where x_1 and x_2 are the respective consumptions of goods 1 and 2. The goods are available both in the open market (at £3 and £4 respectively) and also through a government rationing scheme in which good 1 costs 2 coupons and good 2 costs 6 coupons. If a consumer's income is £24 and he has 60 coupons available, how much of each good should he consume?

Let the subscript a denote the quantity of a good bought in the open market and the subscript b denote the quantity bought using coupons. The consumer maximizes utility, $U = (x_{1a} + x_{1b})(x_{2a} + x_{2b})$ subject to the two constraints $3x_{1a} + 4x_{2a} = 24$ and $2x_{1b} + 6x_{2b} = 60$. A casual look at these two constraints suggests that we do not yet have a well-defined problem. On comparing the two constraints it is seen that the price of good 1 relative to good 2 is higher in money terms than it is in terms of coupons; hence to purchase good 1 it is always better to use coupons (if they are available) and to purchase good 2 it is always better to use money (if available). Unless there are constraints on the selling of goods for coupons, the solution of the constrained maximization problem will indicate that the consumer should conduct unlimited arbitrage, purchasing good 1 with coupons, selling it for money and using the money to purchase good 2, redeeming good 2 for coupons and then purchasing more good 1 etc. In this way the consumer can augment his income, and thereby his consumption and utility, indefinitely. To obtain a solution it is convenient to assume that there is no black market in coupons or, which is the same thing, that goods cannot be sold in exchange for coupons. If goods cannot be sold in exchange for coupons, arbitrage of the kind described above is not possible. If arbitrage is not possible, it will never be optimal for the consumer to purchase both good 1 with money and good 2 with coupons, since more of both goods could be obtained by using the coupons to purchase good 1 and the money to purchase good 2. It follows that the optimal behaviour is such that either $x_{1a} = 0$ or $x_{2b} = 0$.

If $x_{1a} = 0$, maximizing utility is equivalent to maximizing unconditionally

$$v = x_{1b}(x_{2a} + x_{2b}) + \lambda_1(24 - 4x_{2a}) + \lambda_2(60 - 2x_{1b} - 6x_{2b})$$

The necessary conditions for a maximum are

$$\begin{aligned}
\partial v/\partial x_{1b} &= x_{2a} + x_{2b} - 2\lambda_2 &&= 0\\
\partial v/\partial x_{2a} &= x_{1b} - 4\lambda_1 &&= 0\\
\partial v/\partial x_{2b} &= x_{1b} - 6\lambda_2 &&= 0\\
\partial v/\partial \lambda_1 &= 24 - 4x_{2a} &&= 0\\
\partial v/\partial \lambda_2 &= 60 - 2x_{1b} - 6x_{2b} &&= 0
\end{aligned}$$

The solution of these equations is $x_{1a} = 0, x_{1b} = 24, x_{2a} = 6, x_{2b} = 2, \lambda_1 = 6, \lambda_2 = 4$, so that $x_1 = 24$, $x_2 = 8$ and $U = 192$. If $x_{2b} = 0$, maximizing utility is equivalent to maximizing unconditionally

$$v = x_{2a}(x_{1a} + x_{1b}) + \lambda_1(24 - 3x_{1a} - 4x_{2a}) + \lambda_2(60 - 2x_{1b})$$

The necessary conditions for a maximum are

$$\begin{aligned}
\partial v/\partial x_{1a} &= x_{2a} - 3\lambda_1 &&= 0\\
\partial v/\partial x_{1b} &= x_{2a} - 2\lambda_2 &&= 0\\
\partial v/\partial x_{2a} &= x_{1a} + x_{1b} - 4\lambda_1 &&= 0\\
\partial v/\partial \lambda_1 &= 24 - 3x_{1a} - 4x_{2a} &&= 0\\
\partial v/\partial \lambda_2 &= 60 - 2x_{1b} &&= 0
\end{aligned}$$

The solution of these equations implies that the amount of good 1 purchased with money should be a negative quantity, i.e. that some of the good 1 purchased with coupons should be sold on the open market and the augmented money income spent entirely on purchases of good 2. If this policy is adopted then $x_{1a} = -11, x_{1b} = 30, x_{2a} = 14\frac{1}{4}, x_{2b} = 0, \lambda_1 = 4\frac{3}{4}, \lambda_2 = 8\frac{1}{8}$ and so $x_1 = 19$, $x_2 = 14\frac{1}{4}$ and $U = 270\frac{3}{4}$. Under this policy the utility is higher than under the policy considered before. We conclude that the consumer's optimal consumption pattern is to consume 19 units of good 1 and $14\frac{1}{4}$ units of good 2, and to do this he must sell 11 units of good 1 on the open market.

In the example above it was assumed that neither good 1 nor good 2 can be exchanged for coupons. It was deduced that in this case either $x_{1a} = 0$ or $x_{2b} = 0$; these two cases were then examined separately. It is possible to give a more unified treatment of the problem by expressing mathematically the constraint that neither good 1 nor good 2 can be exchanged for coupons. This constraint may be written $x_{1b} \geqslant 0, x_{2b} \geqslant 0$, where the non-negativity shows that no sales in exchange for coupons are possible. It should be noted that this additional constraint is not an equation, but a pair of inequalities. The method of Lagrange becomes much less elegant when it is applied to the solution of problems involving inequalities.

To maximize (minimize) the function $y = f(x_1, \ldots, x_n)$ *subject to* $m < n$ *equations,* $g_1(x_1, \ldots, x_n) = k_1, \ldots, g_m(x_1, \ldots, x_n) = k_m$ *and also to p inequalities* $g_{m+1}(x_1, \ldots, x_n) \geqslant k_{m+1}, \ldots, g_{m+p}(x_1, \ldots, x_n) \geqslant k_{m+p}$ *it is sufficient to maximize (minimize) in turn all the Lagrangians of the form*

$$v = f(x_1, \ldots, x_n) + \sum_{i=1}^{m+p} \lambda_i[k_i - g_i(x_1, \ldots, x_n)]$$

generated by setting, in turn, each possible set of $\lambda_{m+1}, \ldots, \lambda_{m+p}$ *equal to zero, and then to choose the maximum (minimum) value of v from among the maxima (minima) of v which represent a solution satisfying the inequalities.*

Example continued It is assumed that the consumer is unable to sell goods in exchange for coupons, i.e. that $x_{1b} \geqslant 0$ and $x_{2b} \geqslant 0$. To apply the result given above we first of all form the Lagrangian

$$v = (x_{1a} + x_{1b})(x_{2a} + x_{2b}) + \lambda_1(24 - 3x_{1a} - 4x_{2a}) + \lambda_2(60 - 2x_{1b} - 6x_{2b}) + \lambda_3(-x_{1b}) + \lambda_4(-x_{2b})$$

There are four possible ways in which the Lagrange multipliers λ_3, λ_4 may be equal to zero, viz: (i) $\lambda_3 = \lambda_4 = 0$, (ii) $\lambda_4 = 0$, (iii) $\lambda_3 = 0$ and (iv) $\lambda_3, \lambda_4 \neq 0$. We consider each of these cases in turn.

(i) If $\lambda_3 = \lambda_4 = 0$ then

$$v = (x_{1a} + x_{1b})(x_{2a} + x_{2b}) + \lambda_1(24 - 3x_{1a} - 4x_{2a}) + \lambda_2(60 - 2x_{1b} - 6x_{2b})$$

and the necessary conditions for a maximum are

$$\partial v/\partial x_{1a} = x_{2a} + x_{2b} - 3\lambda_1 = 0$$

$$\partial v/\partial x_{1b} = x_{2a} + x_{2b} - 2\lambda_2 = 0$$

$$\partial v/\partial x_{2a} = x_{1a} + x_{1b} - 4\lambda_1 = 0$$

$$\partial v/\partial x_{2b} = x_{1a} + x_{1b} - 6\lambda_2 = 0$$

$$\partial v/\partial \lambda_1 = 24 - 3x_{1a} - 4x_{2a} = 0$$

$$\partial v/\partial \lambda_2 = 60 - 2x_{1b} - 6x_{2b} = 0$$

Comparing the first two equations shows that $\lambda_1 = \frac{2}{3}\lambda_2$ and comparing the third and fourth equations shows that $\lambda_1 = \frac{3}{2}\lambda_2$, so that $\lambda_1 = \lambda_2 = 0$. It follows from the first and third (or second and fourth) equations that $x_{1a} = -x_{1b}$ and $x_{2a} = -x_{2b}$. Substituting these two results into the last equation gives $60 + 2x_{1a} + 6x_{2a} = 0$ and comparing this with the fifth equation gives $x_{1a} = -x_{1b} = 38{\cdot}4$, $x_{2a} = -x_{2b} = -22{\cdot}8$ whence $x_1 = 0$, $x_2 = 0$ and $U = 0$. The apparent absurdity of this result is due to the fact that we have found a minimum, and not a maximum, of utility. The reason for this is that there is no well-defined maximum of utility because unlimited arbitrage is possible when the selling of goods in return for coupons is permitted (since the non-negativity requirements have been omitted).

(ii) If $\lambda_4 = 0$, $v = (x_{1a} + x_{1b})(x_{2a} + x_{2b}) + \lambda_1(24 - 3x_{1a} - 4x_{2a}) + \lambda_2(60 - 2x_{1b} - 6x_{2b}) + \lambda_3(-x_{1b})$ and the necessary conditions for a maximum are

$$\begin{aligned}
\partial v/\partial x_{1a} &= x_{2a} + x_{2b} - 3\lambda_1 &&= 0\\
\partial v/\partial x_{1b} &= x_{2a} + x_{2b} - 2\lambda_2 - \lambda_3 &&= 0\\
\partial v/\partial x_{2a} &= x_{1a} + x_{1b} - 4\lambda_1 &&= 0\\
\partial v/\partial x_{2b} &= x_{1a} + x_{1b} - 6\lambda_2 &&= 0\\
\partial v/\partial \lambda_1 &= 24 - 3x_{1a} - 4x_{2a} &&= 0\\
\partial v/\partial \lambda_2 &= 60 - 2x_{1b} - 6x_{2b} &&= 0\\
\partial v/\partial \lambda_3 &= -x_{1b} &&= 0
\end{aligned}$$

The solution of these equations is $x_{1a} = 10\frac{2}{3}$, $x_{1b} = 0$, $x_{2a} = -2$, $x_{2b} = 10$, $\lambda_1 = \frac{8}{3}$, $\lambda_2 = \frac{16}{9}$, $\lambda_3 = \frac{40}{9}$ and so $x_1 = 10\frac{2}{3}$, $x_2 = 8$ and $U = 82\frac{2}{3}$.

(iii) If $\lambda_3 = 0$, $v = (x_{1a} + x_{1b})(x_{2a} + x_{2b}) + \lambda_1(24 - 3x_{1a} - 4x_{2a}) + \lambda_2(60 - 2x_{1b} - 6x_{2b}) + \lambda_4(-x_{2b})$ and the necessary conditions for a maximum are

$$\begin{aligned}
\partial v/\partial x_{1a} &= x_{2a} + x_{2b} - 3\lambda_1 &&= 0\\
\partial v/\partial x_{1b} &= x_{2a} + x_{2b} - 2\lambda_2 &&= 0\\
\partial v/\partial x_{2a} &= x_{1a} + x_{1b} - 4\lambda_1 &&= 0\\
\partial v/\partial x_{2b} &= x_{1a} + x_{1b} - 6\lambda_2 - \lambda_4 &&= 0\\
\partial v/\partial \lambda_1 &= 24 - 3x_{1a} - 4x_{2a} &&= 0\\
\partial v/\partial \lambda_2 &= 60 - 2x_{1b} - 6x_{2b} &&= 0\\
\partial v/\partial \lambda_4 &= -x_{2b} &&= 0
\end{aligned}$$

The solution of these equations is $x_{1a} = -11$, $x_{1b} = 30$, $x_{2a} = 14\frac{1}{4}$, $x_{2b} = 0$, $\lambda_1 = 4\frac{3}{4}$, $\lambda_2 = 7\frac{1}{8}$ and so $x_1 = 19$, $x_2 = 14\frac{1}{4}$ and $U = 270\frac{3}{4}$.

(iv) If $\lambda_3, \lambda_4 \neq 0$, $v = (x_{1a} + x_{1b})(x_{2a} + x_{2b}) + \lambda_1(24 - 3x_{1a} - 4x_{2a}) + \lambda_2(60 - 2x_{1b} - 6x_{2b}) + \lambda_3(-x_{1b}) + \lambda_4(-x_{2b})$ and the necessary conditions for a maximum are

$$\begin{aligned}
\partial v/\partial x_{1a} &= x_{2a} + x_{2b} - 3\lambda_1 &&= 0\\
\partial v/\partial x_{1b} &= x_{2a} + x_{2b} - 2\lambda_2 - \lambda_3 &&= 0\\
\partial v/\partial x_{2a} &= x_{1a} + x_{1b} - 4\lambda_1 &&= 0\\
\partial v/\partial x_{2b} &= x_{1a} + x_{1b} - 6\lambda_2 - \lambda_4 &&= 0\\
\partial v/\partial \lambda_1 &= 24 - 3x_{1a} - 4x_{2a} &&= 0\\
\partial v/\partial \lambda_2 &= 60 - 2x_{1b} - 6x_{2b} &&= 0\\
\partial v/\partial \lambda_3 &= -x_{1b} &&= 0\\
\partial v/\partial \lambda_4 &= -x_{2b} &&= 0
\end{aligned}$$

The last two equations are inconsistent with the sixth equation and so there is no solution, i.e. there is no way of simultaneously satisfying the three constraints $x_{1b} = 0, x_{2b} = 0, 60 - 2x_{1b} - 6x_{2b} = 0$.

On reviewing the four cases above it is seen that the maximum value of v is $270\frac{3}{4}$ and that the solution associated with this value of v satisfies all the constraints. This solution is therefore the optimal one. As regards case (ii), it is seen that we have arrived at the same result as before, but by using a method of general applicability.

This example illustrates that the method of the Lagrange multiplier becomes very cumbersome when some of the constraints are inequalities. For this reason special computational methods have been devised for solving constrained maximization and minimization problems involving inequalities. Some of these methods are referred to in Chapter 9.

Notes and references

Constrained maximum and minimum problems are very common in economics. The standard microeconomic texts referred to in the notes to Chapter 6 contain many such problems. Baumol,[13] Ch. 6 also contains a section relating Lagrange multipliers to the dual problem in linear programming. A number of examples of the use of Lagrange multipliers in solving operational research problems may be found in Lesbourne[78] and in Sasieni, Yaspan and Friedman.[114]

Standard mathematical treatments may be found in Yamane,[126] Ch. 5, Lewis,[79] Ch. 21, Tintner,[120] Ch. 18 and Courant,[30] Ch. 3.

Problems

7.1 A peasant farmer can produce either maize or sweet potato. The production of each crop depends on the number of hours spent sowing and harvesting the crop. If x_1, x_2 are the number of hours devoted to the growing of maize and sweet potato, the production of these crops is respectively $\sqrt{x_1}$ (bushels), $(\sqrt{x_2})/4$ (tons). The total number of hours worked in a year is limited to 1,600. The price of sweet potatoes per ton is twice the price of maize per bushel.

(a) If y_1, y_2 denote the respective outputs of maize and sweet potato, express mathematically the constraint on the production of maize and sweet potato.

(b) The constraint deduced in (a) is an implicit function of y_1 and y_2; it is sometimes known as the 'production possibility schedule' for maize and sweet potato. Graph the production possibility schedule, plotting y_1 horizontally and y_2 vertically. Comment on the economic implications of the shape of the graph.

(c) The farmer's objective is to maximize his income. Express the economic problem facing the farmer as a mathematical problem of constrained maximization.

7.2 The owner of a small art gallery is offered some floor space on a large indoor shopping market. His expected revenue from such a project depends on the wall area for exhibits and the area of floor space. If his booth has floor dimensions $x$ft by $y$ft and a wall height of 10ft, his expected revenue is $R = 20(x + y) + 2xy - x^2 - y^2$.

If rents are £2 per square foot and he can afford £800 for the first year's rent (payable in advance) what size lot should he ask for? (Solve this problem by substitution.)

7.3.1 Minimize $y = 20 + x_1^2 + x_2^2$ subject to the constraint $x_1 + x_2 = 4$. Give the values of x_1, x_2, λ and y at the minimum and explain the significance of λ.

7.3.2 Maximize $y = 5x_1x_2$ subject to the constraint $10x_1 + 15x_2 = 260$. Give the values of x_1x_2, λ and y at the minimum and explain the significance of λ.

7.3.3 The manager of a company's vehicle pool has asked for a storage tank for diesel fuel. He has been allocated £44,000 to build one. If materials cost £10 per square foot of tank surface area, what dimensions should the tank have to maximize its volume if for technical reasons the tank has to be cylindrical in shape? (Take $\pi = \frac{22}{7}$.)

7.3.4 Find the income-maximizing outputs of maize and sweet potato in Problem 7.1.

7.3.5 A firm allocates a budget of £145,200 for the building of a new warehouse. There are three components of cost: the cost of flooring is £1 per square yard, the cost of roofing is £3 per square yard and the cost of the walls is £2 per square yard. What dimensions of the warehouse will maximize its cubic capacity?

7.3.6 A student has £6 a week to spend on luxuries; the money can be spent either on clothes, which cost £1 per item, or on visits to the cinema, which cost 50p.

If x_1 is the number of items of clothing bought, and x_2 is the number of visits to the cinema, then the student's utility is

$$U = x_1 x_2$$

(i) Find his optimal expenditure on clothing and his optimal expenditure on the cinema.

(ii) Now consider the general case where the price of clothing is £p_1 and the price of visits to the cinema is £p_2.

By using the 3 equations obtained from differentiating the Lagrangian v, show that the equation of the student's demand curve

$$x_1 = \text{function of } p_1 \text{ and } p_2$$

is just

$$x_1 = 3/p_1$$

and that the demand curve

$$x_2 = \text{function of } p_1 \text{ and } p_2$$

is just

$$x_2 = 3/p_2$$

Check your answer to (i) using the demand curve equations.

7.3.7 A firm producing cars has a production function $Q = 4L^{1/4}K^{1/4}S^{1/4}$ where Q is the number of cars produced per year, L is the number of men employed (each is paid a wage of £1,000 per year), K is the number of machines employed (each is rented at £500 per year) and S is the value of stocks in units of £1,000; stocks are valued at cost price and are financed by a loan at a rate of interest of 10%. The firm has an annual budget of £60,000.

(a) Find the amounts of labour, machinery and stocks which should be employed in order to maximize output.

(b) Show that the output of cars when the factors are employed most efficiently is 80 per annum.

(c) If the firm were to increase its budget by £1, how many more cars could be produced? (*Hint:* use the value of the Lagrange multiplier.)

(d) If the firm maximizes its profit in the long run by operating at the scale where costs are £60,000, what must be the market price of a car?

(e) What will be the profit of the firm?

(*Note:* to assist your working, simplify as many expressions as possible as you go along.)

7.3.8 Show that a producer who is efficient in the sense of maximizing the output produced at a given factor cost, is also efficient in the sense of minimizing the factor cost of producing a given output. Does such a producer also produce at minimum average cost?

7.3.9 It is sometimes suggested that the aim of the managements of large companies is to maximize the sales revenue of the firm, subject to a constraint that the profit of the firm must not fall below a minimum value. Suppose that the demand for a firm's output is $D = 100 - P$, where £P is the price, and the costs of the firm (in £) are $C = 50 + 20Q + Q^2$, where Q is the output. What is the output at which sales revenue is maximized subject to the constraints that profit is not less than £250? Is this output greater than or less than the profit-maximizing output? (*Hint:* to distinguish a maximum of the Lagrangian from a minimum use the necessary and sufficient conditions given in Section 6.9.)

7.3.10 A farmer has 2,500 acres on which he wishes to plant wheat, oats, and barley. He appreciates that extreme specialization in any one crop may be detrimental to his profits due to the possibility of a glut of that crop. Thus he estimates his profit function as:

$$P = 200x_1x_2x_3 - 100x_1^2 - 50x_2^2 - 50x_3^2$$

where

x_1 is the acreage of wheat
x_2 is the acreage of oats
x_3 is the acreage of barley.

If he wants to maximize his profits how many acres should he devote to each crop?

7.3.11 The owner of an electrical goods shop believes that his sales depend on the quality of after sales service, the number of salesmen on the shop floor and the efficiency of the shop's administration in dealing with orders, complaints, repair calls etc. If his sales function is

$$S = 500x_1x_2x_3 - x_1^2 - x_2^2 - x_3^2 - 2x_1x_2 - 8x_3$$

where

x_1 is the number of salesmen
x_2 is the number of clerical staff
x_3 is the number of maintenance and repair men

determine how many of each type of employee he should take on if he is limited to a total staff of 12.

7.4.1 The distribution of goods in an economy is said to be 'Pareto optimal' if no consumer can be made better off without some other consumer being made worse off; in a Pareto optimal situation, the utility of each consumer is maximized subject to the constraint that the other consumers enjoy certain fixed utilities. Consider a simple economy in which there are just two consumers, and each consumer derives utility from the consumption of two commodities, commodity 1 and commodity 2. There are fixed stocks of each of these commodities, and the stock of each commodity is exhausted by the demands of the two consumers.

(a) Show that the condition for the distribution of goods to be Pareto optimal can be expressed as a constrained maximization problem involving three constraints. (*Hint:* use the fact that in a Pareto optimal situation the utility of the first consumer is maximized subject to the constraint that the second consumer enjoys a fixed utility.)

(b) Show that if the distribution of goods is Pareto optimal the ratio of the marginal utilities of the two goods must be the same for each consumer.

7.4.2 A multinational enterprise has two factories in different countries. The output of each factory depends on the amount of labour and capital employed; the technology of production is different in each country. Suppose that the flow of funds between the two countries is blocked, so that there are two budget constraints, one for each country: in the first country the total factor payments are limited to £Z_1 and in the second country to \$$Z_2$.

(a) Show that for the firm to maximize output it is necessary that in each country the ratio of the marginal product to the factor price is the same for each factor, labour and capital.

(b) Explain the economic significance of the values of the two Lagrange multipliers. What significance attaches to the ratio of the two Lagrange multipliers?

(c) Suppose that when output is maximized the value of the first Lagrange multiplier is £3 and the value of the second Lagrange multiplier is \$7. If the restrictions on the international flow of funds are removed, and dollars and sterling can be exchanged at a rate of \$2·4 to £1, should the firm (a) sell dollars and buy sterling, (b) buy dollars and sell sterling, (c) do neither?

7.4.3 An architect is designing the kitchens for a developer's housing estate. The value of the house attributable to the kitchen is

$$v = 6xy$$

where y is the number of square feet of working surface and x is the number of cubic feet of cupboard space. The architect wishes to maximize this value within his budget. One square foot of working surface requires £1's worth of materials; one cubic foot of cupboard space requires £2 of materials; the architect is given a budget of £80 for materials. A carpenter can produce 2 square feet of working surface per hour and 4 cubic feet of cupboard space. Carpenters are paid £1 an hour and the architect is allowed a budget of £25 for labour. How many square feet of working surface and how much cupboard space should the architect design for?

Chapter 8
Integration

8.1 Integration and differentiation

Integration is the inverse operation to differentiation. The integral of the function $y = f(x)$ is the function which, when differentiated, is equal to $f(x)$. The integral of a function $f(x)$ is written $\int f(x)\,dx$; since the integral of $f(x)$ is the function which when differentiated is equal to $f(x)$, it follows that if $f(x) = dF/dx$ then $\int f(x)\,dx = F(x)$.

Example Find the integral of the function $y = x^2$. Putting $f(x) = x^2$, we see that we must find the function $F(x)$ such that $dF/dx = x^2$. Now it is easily verified from the rules of differentiation that if $F(x) = x^3/3$ then $dF/dx = x^2$. However, any function of the form $F(x) = x^3/3 + K$, where K is an arbitrary constant, will also have a derivative $dF/dx = x^2$. Consequently the general formula for the function $F(x)$ is $x^3/3 + K$. It follows that the integral of $y = x^2$ is $\int x^2\,dx = x^3/3 + K$.

An obvious case where the need for integration arises is when one is given the derivative of a function and asked to find the function itself; in this case the function is found by integrating the derivative.

Example The marginal cost of a firm is a function, $f(x) = 10 + 2x$, of the output, x. How does total cost vary with the output of the firm?

The marginal cost is the derivative of total cost with respect to output. To find total cost from marginal cost it is therefore necessary to integrate the function $f(x) = 10 + 2x$. Now if $\int (10 + 2x)\,dx = F(x)$ then $F(x)$ is the function whose derivative is $10 + 2x$; it follows from the rules of differentiation that $F(x)$ is of the form $K + 10x + x^2$, i.e. the total cost of the firm is $\int (10 + 2x)\,dx = K + 10x + x^2$.

It can be seen that the formula for the integral always involves an arbitrary constant, K. This is simply a consequence of property 2 of the derivative (see Chapter 5): the derivative of any function is unchanged if an arbitrary constant is added to the function. Consequently, given the derivative and asked to find the original function, one can only pin down the original function to some function involving an arbitrary constant.

8.2 Properties of the integral

Using the properties of the derivative, and the fact that integration is the inverse of differentiation, it is easy to prove the following rules of integration.

1 *For any real number*, α, $\int x^\alpha \, dx = x^{\alpha+1}/(\alpha + 1) + K$. (The proof follows immediately from property 4 of the derivative.)

2 *For any continuous function*, $f(x)$, *and any real number*, λ, $\int \lambda f(x) \, dx = \lambda \int f(x) \, dx$. (The proof follows from property 1 of the derivative.)

3 *For any two continuous functions*, $u(x)$, $v(x)$, $\int [u(x) + v(x)] \, dx = \int u(x) \, dx + \int v(x) \, dx$. (The proof follows from property 3 of the derivative.)

4 (Integration by parts) *For any two continuous functions*, $u(x)$, $v(x)$,

$$\int u(x) \, v(x) \, dx = u(x) \int v(x) \, dx - \int \left(\int v(x) \, dx \right) (du/dx) \, dx + K$$

When one uses this formula, the arbitrary constant of integration is introduced only in the final step of the calculation. The proof follows from the product rule (property 5 of the derivative). Substituting $g(x) = u(x)$, $h(x) = \int v(x) \, dx$ into the formula for the product rule, it follows that

$$\frac{d}{dx}\left[u(x) \int v(x) \, dx \right] = u(x) \frac{d}{dx}\left[\int v(x) \, dx \right] + \frac{du}{dx} \int v(x) \, dx$$

Now since differentiation and integration are operations inverse to one another it follows that

$$\frac{d}{dx}\left[\int v(x) \, dx \right] = v(x)$$

Substituting this result into the equation above and subtracting $(du/dx) \int v(x) \, dx$ from both sides gives

$$\frac{d}{dx}\left[u(x) \int v(x) \, dx \right] - \frac{du}{dx} \int v(x) \, dx = u(x) \, v(x)$$

Finally, integrating both sides of this equation with respect to x gives the equation

$$u(x) \int v(x) \, dx - \int \frac{du}{dx} \left[\int v(x) \, dx \right] dx + C_1 = \int u(x) \, v(x) \, dx + C_2$$

where C_1 and C_2 are arbitrary constants. Subtracting C_2 from both sides of this equation and setting $K = C_1 - C_2$ gives the result which was to be proved.

Examples

(i) $\int (3x^2 + 6x) \, dx = x^3 + 3x^2 + K$ (using properties 1, 2 and 3).

(ii) $\int \sqrt{(x)} \, dx = 2x\sqrt{(x)}/3$ (writing $\sqrt{x} = x^{1/2}$ and using property 1).

(iii) Substituting $u(x) = 6x + 5$, $v(x) = 4x^3 - 2$ into the formula for integration by parts (property 4) it follows that

$$\int (6x + 5)(4x^3 - 2) \, dx$$

$$= (6x + 5)(x^4 - 2x) - \int (x^4 - 2x)(6) \, dx + K$$

and since

$$\int (x^4 - 2x)(6)\,dx = \int (6x^4 - 12x)\,dx = (24x^5/5) - 6x^2$$

the right-hand side simplifies to

$$K - 10x - 6x^2 + 5x^4 + 24x^5/5$$

8.3 The integral as the area under a curve

The graph of an arbitrary function $y = f(x)$ can be plotted as in Fig. 8A. By using this figure the quantity 'the area under the graph up to x' can be defined as the area lying below the graph and above the x axis and extending from a point indefinitely far to the left along the x axis up to a point located at x (if a portion of the graph lies below the x axis then the area so enclosed is measured as a negative quantity). The integral of the arbitrary function $y = f(x)$ can be interpreted as a measure of this area under the graph of the function $f(x)$. In Fig. 8A the area ABCD under the graph is measured from a point located at $\bar{x}$ on the x axis. The area ABCD is measured in square units. It is easy to demonstrate that the integral $f(x)$ is a measure of this area under the graph.

Quite clearly, the area under the graph from $\bar{x}$ up to a point located at x is a function, $A(x)$, of the value of x. If the point is displaced through a small distance Δx then the area up to the point is increased by an amount $A(x + \Delta x) - A(x)$ and the rate at which the area increases with respect to an increase in the value of x is measured by the ratio $[A(x + \Delta x) - A(x)]/\Delta x$. As

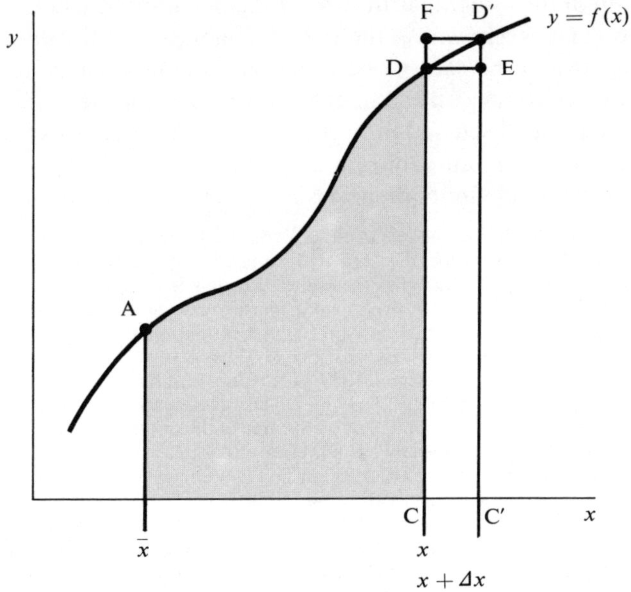

Fig. 8A Graphical representation of the integral as a measure of the area under a curve

the increment Δx becomes very small we obtain a measure of the rate of increase of the area with respect to x at a particular value of x and this measure is equal to

$$\lim_{\Delta x \to 0} \frac{A(x + \Delta x) - A(x)}{\Delta x} = A'(x)$$

where $A'(x)$ is the derivative of $A(x)$ with respect to x. But, looking at the figure, it can be seen that the derivative $A'(x)$ is measured simply by $f(x)$, the height of the graph. The figure shows that the increase in the area due to an increment Δx in the value of x is approximately equal to $f(x)\ \Delta x$ (the approximation becoming better the smaller is Δx). It follows by geometry that the rate of the increase of the area at the point x is $f(x)$.[1] Since the rate of increase of the area is measured by the derivative $A'(x)$, it follows that $A'(x) = f(x)$. Since the derivative of $A(x)$ is equal to $f(x)$ it follows that the integral of $f(x)$ is $A(x)$, i.e. the integral of the function $y = f(x)$ is a measure of the area under the graph of $f(x)$.

The interpretation of the integral of $f(x)$ as the area under the graph of $f(x)$ up to the point x gives an alternative explanation of why the formula for the integral always contains an arbitrary constant. The reason is quite simply that the area under the graph can be measured from any point lying to the left of the point x; since the point from which the area is measured is quite arbitrary, the area itself is quite arbitrary, but the way in which the area varies with changes in the value of x is completely determined. Thus the variation of the area under the graph of x is a function of x which is determined completely apart from an arbitrary constant.

8.4 The definite integral

The interpretation of the integral as the area under a curve is particularly useful when discussing what is known as the definite integral. Intuitively speaking, the definite integral may be said to be a measure of the area under a graph between two fixed points. A definite integral always has an exact value, unlike an indefinite integral (as discussed in Sections 8.1–8.3) which is expressed as a general formula containing an arbitrary constant. The distinction between a definite integral and an indefinite integral is not so trivial as it may seem, as it is

1 As shown in the figure, the result of an increase, Δx, in the value of x is to include the region CDD′C′ within the area under the graph. The region CDD′C′ may be split into the region CDEC′ and the region DD′E. The region CDEC′ is rectangular so that its area is equal to the product of its base and its height: the length of the base is Δx and its height is the height of the graph at the point x, which is $f(x)$, so that the area of the rectangle CDEC′ is $f(x)\ \Delta x$. The area of the region DD′E cannot exceed the area of the rectangle DFD′E. If the function $f(x)$ is a continuous function then as Δx (the length of the base of DFD′E) becomes very small the height of DFD′E also becomes very small, and so the area of the rectangle DFD′E is the product of two very small quantities and is therefore small relative to Δx. It follows that as Δx becomes small the area of the region DD′E becomes arbitrarily small compared with Δx. We conclude that as Δx tends to zero the area of the region CDD′C′ is equal to the sum of two areas, one of which remains proportional to Δx [with a constant of proportionality $f(x)$] and the other of which becomes arbitrarily small compared with Δx. It follows that as Δx tends to zero the ratio of the area of CDD′C′ to the increment Δx tends to $f(x)$, the height of the graph at the point x. This demonstrates that the rate of increase of the area under the graph up to the point x is equal to the height of the graph at the point x, which is $f(x)$.

possible for a definite integral to exist when an indefinite integral of the same function does not exist. However, we shall only discuss functions for which both a definite integral and an indefinite integral exist.

The definite integral of the function $f(x)$ between $x = a$ and $x = b$ is equal to the difference between the indefinite integral of $f(x)$ evaluated at $x = b$ and the indefinite integral of $f(x)$ evaluated at $x = a$. Using the notation $F(x)$ for the indefinite integral and the notation $\int_a^b f(x)\,dx$ for the definite integral wc may write

$$\int_a^b f(x)\,dx = F(b) - F(a)$$

It is easily established that the area under the graph of the function $f(x)$ between the points $x = a$ and $x = b$ is measured by the definite integral $\int_a^b f(x)\,dx$. By convention let $b > a$; then the area between a and b is equal to the area to the left of b less the area to the left of a. The area under the graph to the left of b is measured by the indefinite integral of $f(x)$ evaluated with $x = b$, $F(b)$, and the area under the graph to the left of a is measured by the indefinite integral of $f(x)$ evaluated with $x = a$, $F(a)$. It follows that the area under the graph between a and b is measured by $F(b) - F(a)$ which, by definition, is equal to $\int_a^b f(x)\,dx$.

Example What is the area under the graph of $y = x^2$ between $x = 1$ and $x = 2$? The required area is equal to the difference between the area to the left of the point $x = 2$ and the area to the left of the point $x = 1$. The area to the left of the point $x = 2$ is measured by the indefinite integral of $y = x^2$ evaluated with $x = 2$; now $\int x^2\,dx = x^3/3 + K$ so that the area to the left of the point $x = 2$ is $F(2) = \frac{8}{3} + K$. The area to the left of the point $x = 1$ is measured by the indefinite integral of $y = x^2$ evaluated with $x = 1$, which is $F(1) = \frac{1}{3} + K$. The area between the points $x = 1$ and $x = 2$ is equal to the difference of these two areas, which is $F(2) - F(1) = (\frac{8}{3} + K) - (\frac{1}{3} + K) = \frac{7}{3}$. This is the definite integral of the function $y = x^2$ between $x = 1$ and $x = 2$ and is a measure of the area under the graph of $y = x^2$ between $x = 1$ and $x = 2$. The area is shown diagrammatically in Fig. 8B.

The definite integral never contains an arbitrary constant because in evaluating the definite integral as the difference between two indefinite integrals the arbitrary constants in the indefinite integrals cancel out. For this reason it is legitimate to omit the arbitrary constants altogether when working out a definite integral.

Example Evaluate $\int_2^4 (3x^2 + 6x)\,dx$. The indefinite integral of the function $y = (3x^2 + 6x)$ is $F(x) = x^3 + 3x^2 + K$; hence $\int_2^4 (3x^2 + 6x)\,dx = F(4) - F(2) = [64 + 3 \times 16] - [8 + 3 \times 4] = 92$.

8.5 The definite integral as a sum

The interpretation of the definite integral as the area under a curve between two points suggests a further interpretation—the definite integral may be regarded

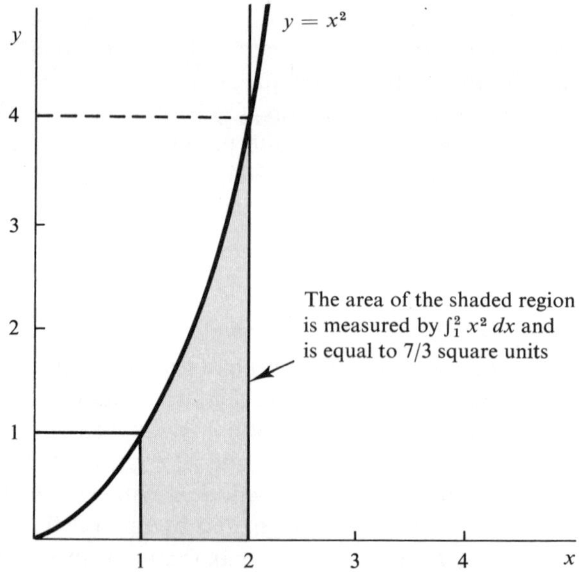

Fig. 8B Graphical representation of the definite integral $\int_1^2 x^2\,dx$ as a measure of the area under the graph of $y=x^2$ between $x=1$ and $x=2$

as the continuous analogue of a sum. Figure 8C shows that the area under a curve between two points may be approximated by the sum of the areas of a number of narrow strips. The width of each strip is arbitrary. The height of each strip is set equal to the height of the graph at some value of x within the range fixed by the width of the strip. If the width of each strip is reduced and the number of strips increased, the approximation becomes even better. It can be shown that if the function is continuous, then as the number of strips is increased indefinitely, and the width of each strip tends to zero, the sum of the areas of the strips converges to a limit which is equal to the area under the curve. This limit is independent of the particular strips used in the sequence of approximations.

A formal statement of the above argument may be given as follows. Consider the kth approximation to the area under the graph of the function $f(x)$ between $x = a$ and $x = b$. Suppose that the range $a \leqslant x \leqslant b$ is divided into $N(k)$ intervals, the width of the ith interval being $\Delta x(i, k)$ $[i = 1, \ldots, N(k)]$. Let $x(i, k)$ be an arbitrarily chosen value of x within the ith interval and let $f(x(i, k))$ be the corresponding value of the function. If $\Delta x(i, k)$ is the width of the ith strip and $f(x(i, k))$ its height then the area of the ith strip is

$$f(x(i, k))\,\Delta x(i, k)$$

The total area of all the strips used in the kth approximation is therefore

$$\sum_{i=1}^{N(k)} f(x(i, k))\,\Delta x(i, k)$$

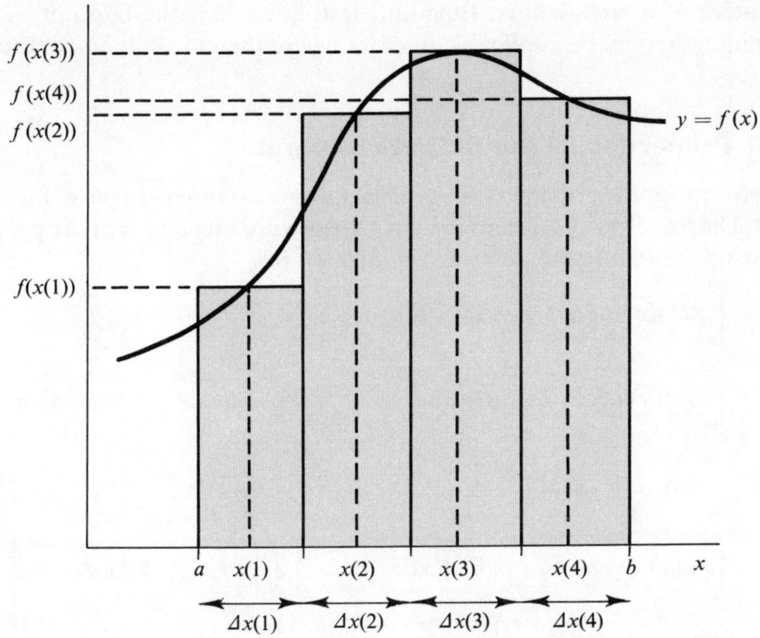

Fig. 8C Approximation to the area under a curve by the sum of the areas of a number of narrow strips

Consider a process of successive approximation in which the number of strips used becomes infinitely large,

$$\lim_{k \to \infty} N(k) = \infty$$

and the width of each strip becomes infinitely small,

$$\lim_{k \to \infty} \Delta x(i, k) = 0 \qquad (i = 1, \ldots, N(k))$$

It is a consequence of the continuity of $f(x)$ within the range $a \leqslant x \leqslant b$ that

$$\lim_{k \to \infty} \sum_{i=1}^{N(k)} f(x(i, k))\, \Delta x(i, k)$$

$$= \text{Area under the curve between } x = a \text{ and } x = b$$

$$= \int_a^b f(x)\, dx$$

The proof of this result is given in more advanced texts. The limiting value of the sum is known as the *Riemann integral* of $f(x)$.

It is important to note that the definition of the Riemann integral assumes only the continuity of $f(x)$ in the range $a \leqslant x \leqslant b$. On the other hand, the definition of a definite integral as the difference between two specific values of the indefinite integral assumes the existence of a well-defined function whose derivative is $f(x)$. It is quite possible that $f(x)$ is continuous without its being the derivative of a well-defined function. It follows that the concept of the Riemann integral may be applicable in cases where the indefinite integral does not exist.

8.6 Properties of the definite integral

Some useful properties of the definite integral are catalogued below for easy reference. The first four properties are straightforward analogues of the properties of the indefinite integral described in Section 8.2.

1 $$\int_a^b x^\alpha\,dx = [b^{\alpha+1} - a^{\alpha+1}]/(\alpha+1)$$

2 $$\int_a^b \lambda f(x)\,dx = \lambda \int_a^b f(x)\,dx$$

3 $$\int_a^b [u(x) + v(x)]\,dx = \int_a^b u(x)\,dx + \int_a^b v(x)\,dx$$

4 $$\int_a^b u(x)v(x)\,dx = \left[u(x)\int v(x)\,dx - \int\left(\int v(x)\,dx\right)(du/dx)\,dx\right]_{x=b} - \left[u(x)\int v(x)\,dx - \int\left(\int v(x)\,dx\right)(du/dx)\,dx\right]_{x=a}$$

5 $$\int_a^b f(x)\,dx = \int_a^c f(x)\,dx + \int_c^b f(x)\,dx$$

6 $$\left|\int_a^b f(x)\,dx\right| \leqslant \int_a^b |f(x)|\,dx$$

7 $$\int_a^b f(x)\,dx \leqslant \int_a^b g(x)\,dx \quad \text{if} \quad f(x) \leqslant g(x) \text{ and } a < b$$

These results also apply when the limits of integration are infinite (provided that the value of the integral itself remains finite). Definite integrals with infinite limits are defined in the following way:

$$\int_a^\infty f(x)\,dx = \lim_{b\to\infty} \int_a^b f(x)\,dx$$

$$\int_{-\infty}^b f(x)\,dx = \lim_{a\to-\infty} \int_a^b f(x)\,dx$$

$$\int_{-\infty}^\infty f(x)\,dx = \lim_{a\to-\infty,\, b\to\infty} \int_a^b f(x)\,dx$$

It is possible for an integral over a range $a \leqslant x \leqslant b$ to have a finite value even though the value of the function is infinite at some point, say $x = c$, within the range. In such cases, the integral is defined as

$$\int_a^b f(x)\,dx = \lim_{\varepsilon\to 0} \int_a^{c-\varepsilon} f(x)\,dx + \lim_{\varepsilon\to 0} \int_{c+\varepsilon}^b f(x)\,dx$$

8.7 Economic application of the integral

The economic application of the integral is illustrated by the following worked examples.

Example 1 The marginal cost of a firm (in £) is an increasing function, $y = 50 + 4x$, of the output x. What will be the increase in total cost if output is increased from 5 units to 10 units?

The marginal cost of the firm is the derivative of total cost, so that the total cost of the firm is the integral of marginal cost, i.e. the indefinite integral of marginal cost expresses the total cost of the firm as a function of output. The increase in cost when output is increased from 5 units to 10 units is equal to the difference between total cost when output is 10 units and total cost when output is 5 units. Since total cost is the integral of marginal cost it follows that the increase in cost is measured by the definite integral of the marginal cost between 5 units and 10 units. To evaluate the definite integral of marginal cost, first of all note that the relevant indefinite integral is $F(x) = \int (50 + 4x)\,dx = 50x + 2x^2 + K$ and then use the fact that $\int_5^{10} (50 + 4x)\,dx = F(10) - F(5) = [50 \times 10 + 2 \times 100] - [50 \times 5 + 2 \times 25] = 400$. This shows that when output increases from 5 units to 10 units total cost increases by £400.

Example 2 Beginning at a date $t = 0$, an economy invests at a net rate of $5 + 0{\cdot}5t + 0{\cdot}015t^2$ (measured in £m per annum). By how much will the capital stock of the economy have increased at the end of 5 years?

The rate of investment is the rate of change of the capital stock with respect to time. If the capital stock is expressed as a function of time then the rate of investment is the derivative of the capital stock with respect to time; it follows that the capital stock is the integral of the rate of investment. The increase in the capital stock at the end of 5 years is the difference between the capital stock at the date $t = 5$ and the capital stock at the date $t = 0$. Since the capital stock is the integral of the rate of investment, it follows that the increase in the capital stock is measured by the definite integral of the rate of investment between $t = 0$ and $t = 5$. Now the indefinite integral of the rate of investment is $F(t) = \int (5 + 0{\cdot}5t + 0{\cdot}015t^2)\,dt = 5t + 0{\cdot}25t^2 + 0{\cdot}005t^3 + K$ so that the required definite integral is $\int_0^5 (5 + 0{\cdot}5t + 0{\cdot}015t^2)\,dt = F(5) - F(0) = [25 + 0{\cdot}25 \times 25 + 0{\cdot}005 \times 125] - [5] = 26{\cdot}875$. We conclude that after 5 years the capital stock of the economy has increased by £26·875m.

Example 3 The 'consumers' surplus' is defined to be the difference between the maximum amount that consumers as a whole are willing to pay for a given total output of a commodity and the amount that they would have to pay in a perfectly competitive market. If the demand for a commodity is $D = 16/P^2$ where P is the price (in £), what is the consumers' surplus when output is 25 units?

It is readily deduced that the rate of change with respect to output of the maximum amount that consumers are willing to pay is equal to the maximum price per unit the consumers are willing to pay for the marginal output. In other words, the derivative with respect to output of the maximum amount that consumers are willing to pay is equal to the maximum price at which marginal output can be sold, so that the maximum amount that consumers are willing to pay for a given output is equal to the integral with respect to output of the maximum price of the marginal output. Now the maximum price at which marginal output can be sold is found from the demand curve;[2] since $D = 16/P^2$ it follows that the price at which an output Q just satisfies demand is such that $Q = 16/P^2$, so that $P = 4/\sqrt{Q}$ which is the maximum price at which marginal output can be sold when the total output is Q. It follows that the maximum amount that consumers are willing to pay for an output of 25 units is given by the definite integral $\int_0^{25} P(Q)\, dQ = \int_0^{25} 4/\sqrt{Q}\, dQ = F(25) - F(0)$ where $F(Q) = 8\sqrt{(Q)} + K$, so that the definite integral is equal to $[8 \times 5] - [8 \times 0] = 40$, i.e. the maximum amount that the consumers will pay for an output of 25 units is £40.

To evaluate consumers' surplus it is necessary to deduct from this figure the amount that consumers will have to pay in a perfectly competitive market. In a perfectly competitive market all the output is sold at the same price, which is the maximum price at which the last unit of output can be sold. This price is found from the demand curve to be $P = 4/\sqrt{Q}$, where Q is the total output, so that when the output is 25 units the price in a competitive market is £$\frac{4}{5}$; it follows that the amount that consumers must pay in a competitive market is £$(\frac{4}{5}) \times 25 =$ £20. The consumers' surplus is equal to the difference between the maximum amount that consumers are willing to pay, which is £40, and the amount that they must pay in a perfectly competitive market, which is £20, i.e. consumers' surplus is £$(40 - 20) =$ £20.

Using the interpretation of the integral as a measure of the area under a graph it can be deduced that the consumers' surplus is equal to the area of the shaded region shown in Fig. 8D.

8.8 Integration of functions of several variables

To integrate a function of several variables, $y = f(x_1, \ldots, x_n)$ with respect to just one variable, x_j, is the same as finding the function whose partial derivative with respect to x_j is equal to y, i.e. the integral of y with respect to x_j is

$$\int f(x_1, \ldots, x_n)\, dx_j = F(x_1, \ldots, x_n)$$

where

$$\partial F/\partial x_j = f(x_1, \ldots, x_n)$$

It is easy to see that to integrate a function of several variables with respect to just one variable it is sufficient to regard all the other variables as constants and apply the standard rules of integration.

Example 1 Evaluate $\int x_1 x_2\, dx_2$. Regarding $y = x_1 x_2$ as a function of the variable x_2 (with x_1 a constant) the indefinite integral of y with respect to

2 It is assumed that each consumer's expenditure on the commodity is a negligible proportion of his total expenditure; otherwise 'income effects' may be important.

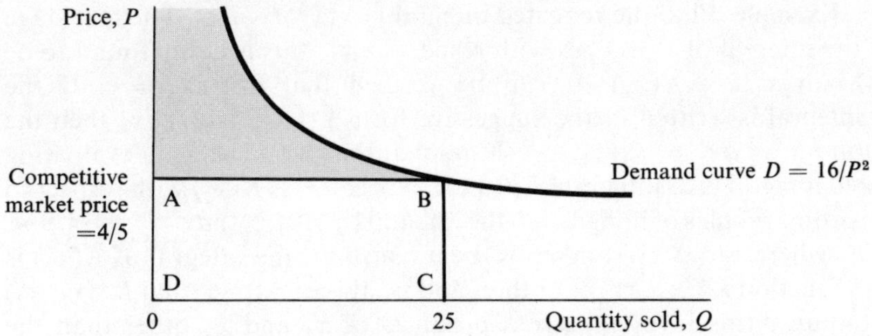

NOTE The maximum amount that consumers are willing to pay for 25 units of output is equal to the area under the demand curve from $Q = 0$ to $Q = 25$. The amount that consumers will have to pay in a perfectly competitive market is equal to the area of the rectangle ABCD, which is $(\frac{4}{5}) \times 25 = 20$ square units. The consumers' surplus is the difference between the maximum amount that consumers are willing to pay and the amount that they will have to pay in a perfectly competitive market; in terms of the areas it is equal to the difference between the area under the graph and the area of the rectangle ABCD, i.e. it is equal to the area of the shaded region shown in the figure.

Fig. 8D Graphical representation of consumers' surplus

x_2 is found by rules 1 and 2 of Section 8.2 to be $F_2(x_1, x_2) = x_1x_2^2/2 + K$ where K is an arbitrary constant. However, since x_1 is taken to be a constant it is possible that the arbitrary constant, K, may be a function, $K(x_1)$, of c_1, so that the general form of the indefinite integral is $F_2(x_1, x_2) = x_1x^2/2 + K(x_1)$. It is easily verified that $\partial F_2/\partial x_2 = x_1x_2$.

Example 2 Evaluate $\int x_1^2 + (x_2/x_1)\,dx_1$. Regarding $y = x_1^2 + (x_2/x_1)$ as a function of x_1 (with x_2 a constant), the indefinite integral of y with respect to x_1 is found by rules 1, 2 and 3 of Section 8.2 to be $F_1(x_1, x_2) = (x_1^3/3) - (x_2/2x_1^2) + K(x_2)$ where $K(x_2)$ is an arbitrary function of x_2. It is readily verified that $\partial F_1/\partial x_1 = x_1^2 + (x_2/x_1)$.

It is often useful to be able to integrate a function of several variables with respect to each of the variables in turn; the result is known as a 'repeated integral'.[3] To find the repeated integral of a function of several variables is the same thing as to find the function which, when partially differentiated with respect to each of the variables in turn, is equal to the given function, i.e. the repeated integral of $y = f(x_1, \ldots, x_n)$ is

$$\underbrace{\int\int\cdots\int}_{n\text{ times}} f(x_1, \ldots, x_n)\,dx_1 \ldots dx_n = F(x_1, \ldots, x_n)$$

.where

$$\frac{\partial}{\partial x_n}\left(\frac{\partial}{\partial x_{n-1}}\right)\cdots\left(\frac{\partial F}{\partial x_1}\right) = f(x_1, \ldots, x_n)$$

3 More generally, a repeated integral is the result of integrating a function of several variables with respect to two or more of the variables.

Example Find the repeated integral $\iint x_1^2 x_2^2 \, dx_1 \, dx_2$. The first stage is to find the integral of $y = x_1^2 x_2^2$ with respect to x_1; this is easily found to be $F_1(x_1, x_2) = x_2^2 x_1^3/3 + K(x_2)$. It can be verified that $\partial F_1/\partial x_1 = y$. If the repeated integral is written in the suggestive form $\int (\int x_1^2 x_2^2 \, dx_1) \, dx_2$ then the substitution $\int x_1^2 x_2^2 \, dx_1 = F_1(x_1, x_2)$ shows that the second stage in evaluating the repeated integral is to integrate $F_1(x_1 x_2) = x_2^2 x_1^3/3 + K(x_2)$ with respect to x_2. By the ordinary rules of integration the integral $\int F_1(x_1, x_2) \, dx_2 = x_1^3 x_2^3/9 + \int K(x_2) \, dx_2$ where, since x_1 is taken to be a constant, the integral of $K(x_2)$ is generally a function $K^*(x_1, x_2)$ of both x_1 and x_2. It is easy to see that $K^*(x_1, x_2)$ cannot contain terms involving cross products of x_1 and x_2 other than the simple cross product $x_1 x_2$. We conclude that $\iint x_1^2 x_2^2 \, dx_1 \, dx_2 = F(x_1, x_2) = x_1^3 x_2^3/9 + K^*(x_1, x_2)$ where K^* is a relatively simple function of x_1 and x_2. The reader may easily verify that the function $K^*(x_1, x_2)$ is such that $\partial^2 K/\partial x_1 \, \partial x_2 = 0$ and that therefore $\partial^2 F/\partial x_1 \, \partial x_2 = x_1^2 x_2^2 = f(x_1, x_2)$.

When evaluating a repeated integral it is legitimate to interchange the order of integration—provided that the integral of the function can be defined in the way described in this chapter. For a function of two variables this may be written symbolically as

$$\iint f(x_1, x_2) \, dx_1 \, dx_2 = \int \left[\int f(x_1, x_2) \, dx_1 \right] dx_2$$

$$= \int \left[\int f(x_1, x_2) \, dx_2 \right] dx_1$$

Example Find the repeated integral $\iint x_1^2 x_2^2 \, dx_1 \, dx_2$ by interchanging the order of integration. The first stage is now to find the integral of $y = x_1^2 x_2^2$ with respect to x_2 (not x_1). By the ordinary rules of integration the integral is $F_2(x_1, x_2) = x_1^2 x_2^3/3 + K(x_1)$. The second stage is to evaluate the integral of $F_2(x_1, x_2)$ with respect to x_1, which is

$$\int F_2(x_1, x_2) \, dx_1 = x_2^3 x_1^3/9 + \int K(x_1) \, dx_1 = x_2^3 x_1^3/9 + K^*(x_1, x_2)$$

The repeated integral evaluated in this way is exactly the same as before.

It can be demonstrated that the repeated integral of a function of two variables is a measure of the volume lying below the surface representing the graph of the function (see Fig. 8E).

A useful result on integrals of functions of several variables concerns differentiation under the integral sign. If $f(x_1, x_2)$ is twice differentiable with respect to x_1 and x_2 then it is legitimate to interchange the order of differentiation and integration, viz.:

$$\frac{d}{dx_2} \int f(x_1, x_2) \, dx_1 = \int \frac{\partial f(x_1, x_2)}{\partial x_2} \, dx_1 - K$$

where K is an arbitrary constant.

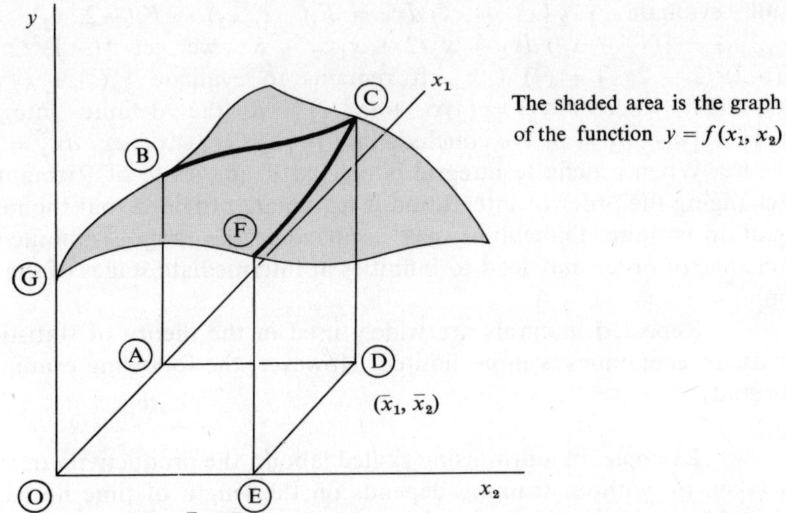

The integral $\int_0^{\bar{x}_2} \int_0^{\bar{x}_1} f(x_1, x_2)\, dx_1\, dx_2$ is a measure of the volume OABCDEFG

Fig. 8E Graphical representation of the repeated integral of a function of two variables as a measure of the volume under the graph of the function

Example Given $f(x_1, x_2) = x_1^2 x_2^4$ we may evaluate directly $\int f(x_1, x_2)\, dx_1 = x_1^3 x_2^4/3 + C$ to get

$$\frac{d}{dx_2} \int f(x_1, x_2)\, dx_1 = \frac{d}{dx_2} [x_1^3 x_2^4/3 + C] = (\tfrac{4}{3})(x_1 x_2)^3$$

An alternative method is to evaluate $\partial f(x_1, x_2)/\partial x_2 = 4x_1^2 x_2^3$ and then to find

$$\int \frac{\partial f(x_1, x_2)}{\partial x_2}\, dx_1 = \int 4x_1^2 x_2^3\, dx_1 = (\tfrac{4}{3})(x_1 x_2)^3 + K$$

Setting

$$\frac{d}{dx_2} \int f(x_1, x_2)\, dx_1 = \int \frac{\partial f(x_1, x_2)}{\partial x_2}\, dx_1 - K$$

we get

$$\frac{d}{dx_2} \int f(x_1, x_2)\, dx_1 = (\tfrac{4}{3})(x_1 x_2)^3$$

which agrees with the previous result.

So far, the discussion has been confined to the indefinite integral of a function of several variables; however, the definite integral of a function of several variables can be defined simply by providing fixed upper and lower limits of integration.

Example Evaluate the definite integral $\int_0^1 \int_{-2}^{-1} (x_1 + x_2)\, dx_1\, dx_2$. We write the integral in the suggestive form $\int_0^1 (\int_{-2}^{-1} (x_1 + x_2)\, dx_1)\, dx_2$ and first of all evaluate $\int_{-2}^{-1} (x_1 + x_2)\, dx_1 = F_1(-1, x_2) - F_1(-2, x_2)$, where $F_1(x_1, x_2) = \int (x_1 + x_2)\, dx_1 = x_1^2/2 + x_1x_2 + K$; we get $[(-1)^2/2 - x_2] - [(-2)^2/2 - 2x_2] = (\frac{5}{2}) + x_2$. It remains to evaluate $\int_0^1 (\frac{5}{2}) + x_2\, dx_2 = F(1) - F(0)$; since $F(x_2) = (\frac{5}{2})x_2 + (x_2^2/2) + K$ the definite integral is $[\frac{5}{2} + \frac{1}{2}] - [0 + 0] = 3$. We conclude that $\int_0^1 \int_{-2}^{-1} (x_1 + x_2)\, dx_1\, dx_2 = 3$.

When a definite integral is defined in the sense of Riemann then interchanging the order of integration is legitimate provided that the range of integration is finite. Difficulties may occur when the range is infinite as the interchange of order may lead to infinities at intermediate stages of the calculation.

Repeated integrals are widely used in the theory of statistics but their use in economics is more limited. However, the following example will repay study.

Example In a firm using skilled labour, the productivity of a workman taken on without training depends on the length of time he has been employed by the firm. If a firm takes on men at a rate of $f(t)$ per year at time t, how much output will be produced in the first M years?

Let productivity be a function $g(l)$ of the length of training, l. Consider an arbitrary time T. Men taken on in a small time interval dt at about date t will have $T - t$ years training at time T, so that the number of men with a productivity $g(T - t)$ is measured by $f(t)\, dt$. It follows that the rate of output at time T due to men taken on at time t is $g(T - t)f(t)\, dt$, and so the total rate of output at time T is $\int_0^T f(t)g(T - t)\, dt$. Since the rate of output at time T is the derivative with respect to T of the total output up to and including time T, it follows that the total output up to time T is the integral of the rate of output at time T. It follows that the total output produced in the first M years is $\int_0^M \int_0^T f(t)\, g(T - t)\, dt\, dT$. This expression is a repeated integral; in this particular case the upper limit, T, of one of the integrals is the variable with respect to which the other integral is evaluated.

Notes and references

There are few direct uses of integration in elementary economics; one exception is the problem of optimization over time, see Henderson and Quandt,[56] Ch. 8. Interesting economic examples are given by Yamane,[126] Ch. 6. Any standard statistics text makes use of integration; for example see Merrill and Fox.[84] Courant,[30] Ch. 2–4 gives a rigorous treatment of elementary integration.

Problems

8.2.1 Evaluate the indefinite integrals

(a) $\displaystyle\int 3x^2\, dx$

(b) $\displaystyle\int x + 2x^2 + x^5/5\, dx$

(c) $\displaystyle\int (x + 5)(x - 1)\, dx$

(d) $\displaystyle\int (2x + 5)(x^3 - 5x)\, dx$

8.2.2 A firm's marginal cost function is

$$MC = 4 + 6Q + 30Q^2$$

where Q is the number of units of output and cost is measured in £. Find the firm's total cost function given that fixed costs are £100.

8.4 Evaluate the definite integrals

(a) $\int_0^4 3x + 5\,dx$

(b) $\int_0^3 2x^2 + 3x - 7\,dx$

(c) $\int_{-2}^2 2x^3\,dx$

(d) $\int_1^9 (x + 3)(x^2 - 6)\,dx$

8.5 Evaluate the area under the graph of $y = x^2 + 3x + 2$ between $x = 0$ and $x = 4$. Check your answer by an approximate calculation using four strips of unit width.

8.6.1 Show that $\int_{-1}^{1} |x^3 + x^2 - \frac{1}{2}|\,dx \geq \frac{1}{3}$.

8.6.2 Using the fact that $|x^3| = x^3$ when $x \geq 0$ and $|x^3| = -x^3$ when $x \leq 0$, evaluate $\int_{-2}^{3} |x^3|\,dx$.

8.7.1 The marginal cost of a firm (in £) is a function $MC = 6 + 2Q + 3Q^2$ of output Q. Find the increase in total cost when output is increased from 10 to 30 units.

8.7.2 A young man takes a job. The salary scale to which he is appointed may be approximated by

$$S = 1000(5x^2 - 1520)/x^2 \qquad (x \leq 60)$$

where S is annual salary and x is age in years (retiring age is 60).

(a) Find his salary when he starts at age 20 and when he retires.

(b) The rate of interest is 7% per annum and so is the rate of inflation; if he saves one-fifth of his income, find his total real wealth at retiring age (i.e. his wealth in terms of the value of money when he started the job).

(c) Suppose now that the proportion of income which he saves, λ, varies with his age thus:

$$\lambda = (\tfrac{3}{8}) - (x^2/9600)$$

Find his real total wealth at retiring age.

8.7.3 Given the demand curve $D = a - bP$ where D is quantity demanded, P is price and a, b are constants, find how consumers' surplus varies with the quantity purchased.

8.7.4 Given the demand curve $D = AP^{-\beta}$ where $\beta > 0$, find how consumers' surplus varies with the quantity purchased. Under what circumstances is consumers' surplus infinite?

8.8.1 Evaluate the definite integrals

(a) $\int_{-1}^{1} \int_{0}^{10} (x_1 - x_2)(x_1 + 2x_2)\,dx_1\,dx_2$

(b) $\int_{0}^{64} \int_{-64}^{0} \sqrt[3]{(x_1 x_2)}\,dx_1\,dx_2$

8.8.2 Verify that interchanging the order of differentiation and integration is valid for the function $y = \sqrt{(x_1^2 x_2^3)} + 5x_1$.

Chapter 9

Programming methods for the solution of optimization problems

9.1 Introduction

Optimization problems are problems which involve the maximization or minimization of a function, with or without constraints. The function to be maximized or minimized is known as the objective function. The following are typical optimization problems:

(i) (unconditional maximization) find the growth policy of the firm which maximizes the wealth of the equity shareholders;

(ii) (unconditional minimization) fit a straight line to a scatter of points by minimizing the sum of the squares of the distances of the points from the fitted line (this is the way many economic relationships are estimated from statistical data);

(iii) (constrained maximization) find the consumption pattern which maximizes a consumer's utility subject to a fixed income;

(iv) (constrained minimization) find the employment of factors of production which minimizes the cost of producing a given output.

Further examples of optimization problems will be discussed later.

In Section 7.4 we saw that optimization problems involving inequality constraints cannot be solved easily by the method of Lagrange. Essentially the difficulty is that to solve this type of problem by the Lagrangian method it is necessary to examine a whole range of possible solutions and then select from these solutions the one which is optimal. But this is not the only case in which it is necessary to examine in turn a whole range of possible solutions in order to find the optimal solution. It also happens when the necessary conditions for the maximum or minimum are so complicated that they cannot be solved. If the solution cannot be found from the necessary conditions then, in the absence of any other method, the optimal solution must be found by examining in turn all the possible solutions to the problem (or as many of them as is practicable).

The advantage of a programming approach[1] to the solution of an optimization problem is that it offers a short cut to selecting the optimum from the set of all possible solutions. Essentially, the idea of a programming method is to organize the search for the optimal solution in such a way that it is not

1 In this chapter the term 'programming' refers to a method of solution rather than to a type of problem. (Most writers take the term programming to mean simply optimization subject to constraints.)

necessary to examine in detail all the possible solutions; for by making use of special characteristics of the problem it is often possible after a few simple calculations to determine that certain types of solution cannot possibly be optimal. As the search for the optimal solution proceeds the number of solutions which must be considered can be progressively reduced until after a few stages in the calculations the optimal solution is arrived at. In a nutshell, a programming method exploits the special characteristics of a problem and narrows down step by step the 'field of search' so that the optimal solution is arrived at without examining in detail every possible solution. The principles of the programming method are illustrated by the example in the following section.

9.2 An example: dynamic programming

Suppose that there are several possible routes between two cities, A and L; the mileages between the intermediate towns on each route are shown in Fig. 9A. Find the shortest route between the two cities.

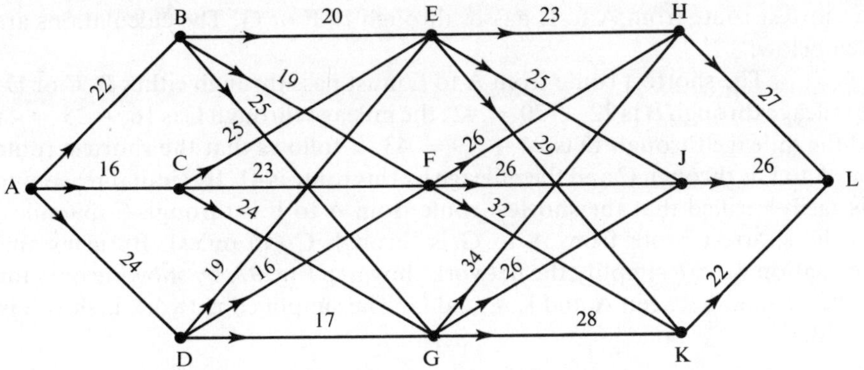

Fig. 9A The alternative routes between A and L

Formally, the problem is to find the route for which the mileage between the two cities is a minimum, subject to constraints which specify the mileage between the towns on each possible route. The nature of the problem is such that it is virtually impossible to find the solution by the method of Lagrange. The most obvious alternative method of solution is to evaluate the mileage of every possible route between the two cities and then select the route with the smallest mileage. However, in this example there are 27 possible routes, and each route passes through three intermediate towns; in order to find the mileage of all the routes it is necessary to perform $27 \times 3 = 81$ additions and to find the shortest of the 27 routes it is necessary to find the smallest of 27 numbers. These calculations are very tedious. By using a programming approach the calculations are significantly reduced; in the method of solution described below it is necessary to perform only 21 additions and to find the smallest number in each of seven sets of three numbers.

As noted in the previous section, the idea of a programming approach to a problem is to make use of some special characteristic of the problem in order to simplify the calculations. The programming method we shall adopt is based on the fact that the shortest route between any two cities necessarily follows the shortest route between any two towns on the route, for if the route between the cities does not follow the shortest route between any two towns on the route then it can be shortened by changing the route between the two towns. If we think of breaking up the route between A and L into the route between A and some intermediate town and the route between that intermediate town and L, then it is easy to deduce from the principle described above that the shortest route from A to L must follow the shortest route from A to any given town on the route and then the shortest route from that town to L. In this particular example, every route has to pass through either of the towns E, F or G; it follows that the shortest route between the two cities is composed of either the shortest route from A to E followed by the shortest route from E to L, or the shortest route from A to F followed by the shortest route from F to L, or the shortest route from A to G followed by the shortest route from G to L. It is relatively easy to determine the shortest of the routes from A to E, A to F, A to G, E to L, F to L and G to L; it is then a simple matter to determine whether the shortest route from A to L passes through E, F or G. The calculations are given below.

The shortest route from A to E must pass through either B, C or D; the mileage through B is 22 + 20 = 42; the mileage through C is 16 + 25 = 41 and the mileage through D is 24 + 19 = 43; it follows that the shortest route from A to E is through C and the mileage by this route is 41. By similar reasoning it is easily verified that the shortest route from A to F is through C (39 miles) and the shortest route from A to G is through C (40 miles). By using this information we can simplify the network shown in Fig. 9A by showing only the shortest routes between A and E, F and G. The simplified network is shown in Fig. 9B.

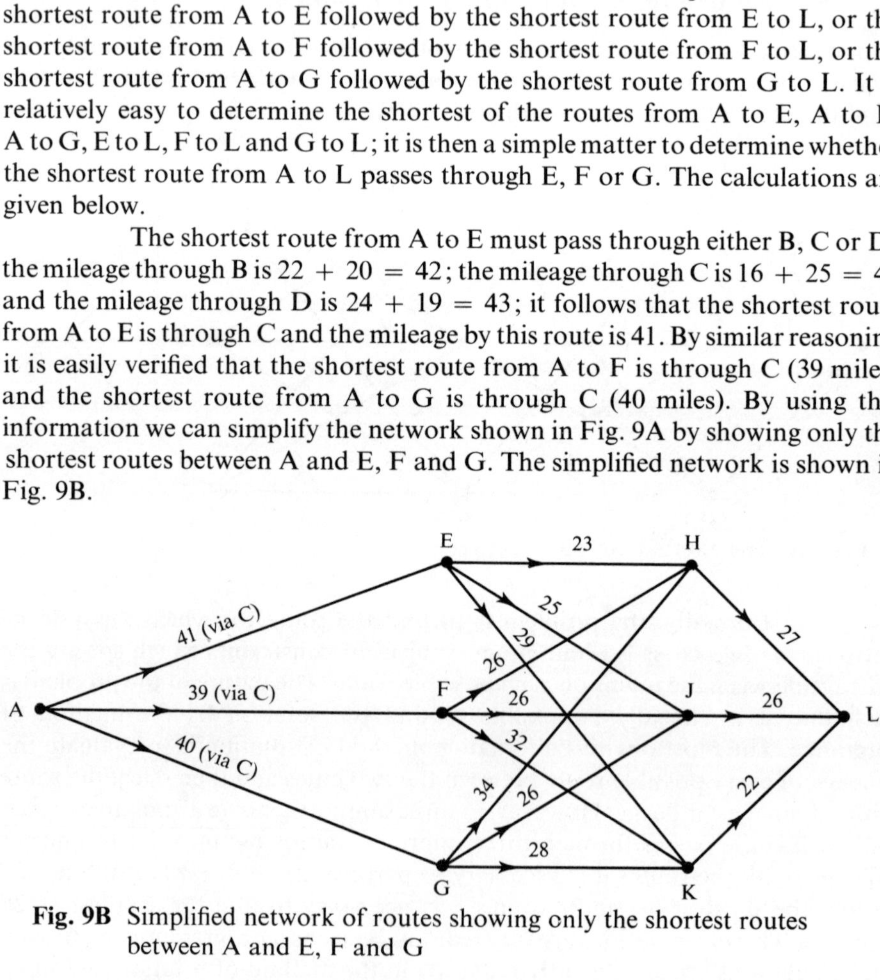

Fig. 9B Simplified network of routes showing only the shortest routes between A and E, F and G

The shortest routes from E to K, F to K and G to K are respectively through H (50 miles), J (52 miles) and K (50 miles). This result permits a further simplification of the network which is shown in Fig. 9C.

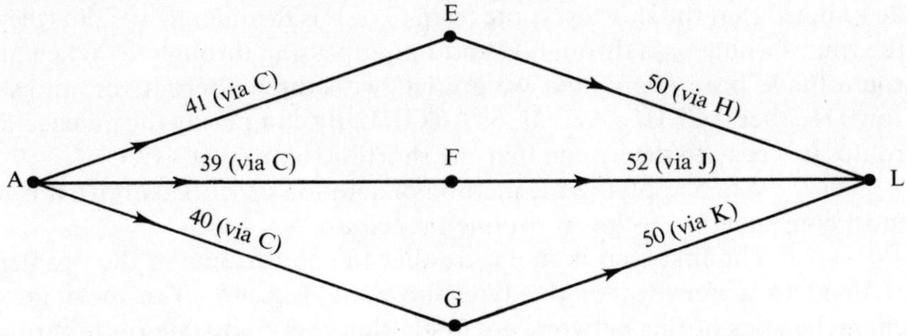

Fig. 9C Simplified network of routes showing only the shortest routes from A and E, F and G, and from E, F, and G to L

Now the shortest route from A to L is either the shortest route from A to E followed by the shortest route from E to L (a total distance of 41 + 50 = 91 miles) or the shortest route from A to F followed by the shortest route from F to L (a total distance of 39 + 52 = 91 miles) or the shortest route from A to G followed by the shortest route from G to L (a total distance of 40 + 50 = 90 miles). The shortest of these routes is the route through G. Since the shortest route from A to G is through C and the shortest route from G to L is through K, it follows that the shortest route from A to L is through C, G and K (see Fig. 9D). This is the solution to the problem obtained by the programming method.

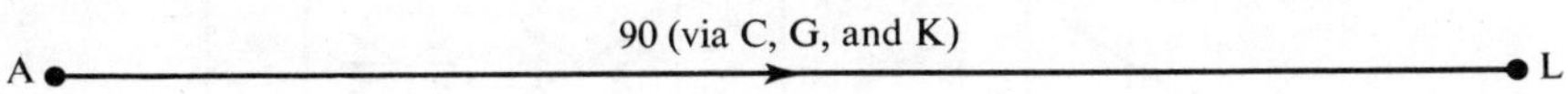

Fig. 9D The shortest route from A to L

The principle of the programming method described above can be elucidated in the following way. First of all, think of all the possible routes commencing from A, and passing eventually through E; when we have determined that the shortest route between A and E is through C, we can be sure that no other route passing through E which does not also pass through C can be the shortest route; this rules out all the routes which pass through B and D before passing through E, i.e. it rules out the routes ABEHL, ABEJL, ABEKL, ADEHL, ADEJL, ADEKL. Secondly think of all the possible routes from A which pass through F; when we have determined that the shortest route passing through F is through C then we can be sure that no route passing through F which does not also pass through C can be the shortest route; this rules out all the routes which pass through B and D before passing through F, i.e. it rules out the routes ABFHL, ABFJL, ABFKL, ADFHL, ADFJL, ADFKL. Similarly, when we have determined that the shortest route from A to G is through C we can rule out all the routes which pass through B and D before passing through G; having determined that the shortest route from E to L is through H, we can rule out all the routes which pass through J and K after passing through E; having determined that the shortest route from F to L is through J, we can rule out all the routes which pass through H and K after passing through F; and having determined that the shortest route from G to L is through K, we can rule out all the routes which pass through H and J after passing through G. When all these routes have been eliminated we are left with three alternatives: the shortest route is either ACEHL, ACFJL or ACGKL. By comparing the mileage of these routes it is easy to determine that the shortest route is ACGKL.

When applying the method of solution described above it is usually most convenient to follow a routine procedure.

The first step is to ensure that the constraints in the problem correspond to a network of the type shown in Fig. 9A. The most important characteristics of this network are firstly that every possible route through the network passes through the same number of intermediate points and secondly that each intermediate point occurs at the same stage (i.e. first stage, second stage, etc.) on every route passing through it. This second requirement rules out cyclical routes, i.e. routes which pass through the same point twice; it also rules out the possibility that any part of a route is traversed in more than one direction.

The second step is to draw the network and classify the intermediate points into first stage, second stage, etc. (see Fig. 9E). It is not necessary to have the same number of points at each stage, nor is it necessary that each point

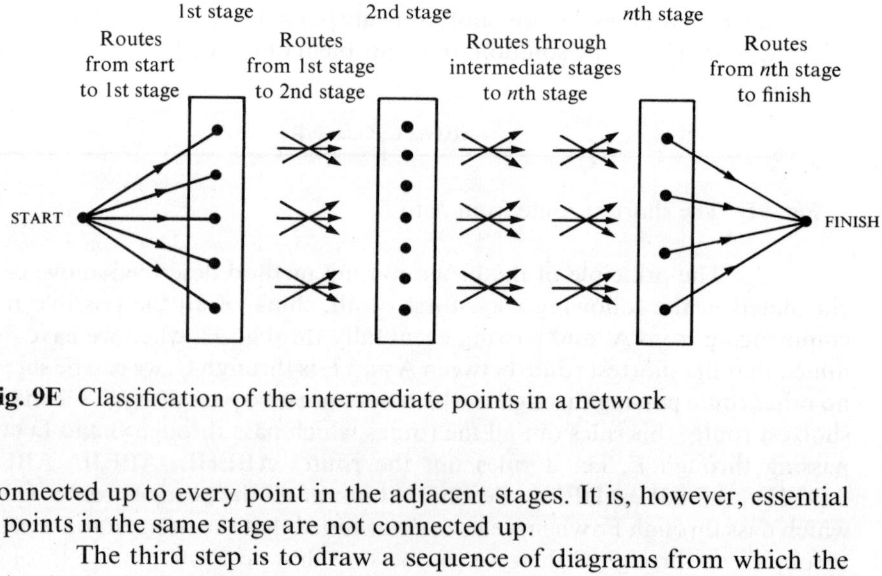

Fig. 9E Classification of the intermediate points in a network

be connected up to every point in the adjacent stages. It is, however, essential that points in the same stage are not connected up.

The third step is to draw a sequence of diagrams from which the solution is obtained. If there are n intermediate stages, n diagrams are required. The first diagram shows the simplification of the network effected by eliminating details of the nth stage—it shows only the shortest routes between each of the $(n - 1)$th stage points and the finish. The second diagram eliminates the details of the $(n - 1)$th stage and shows only the shortest distances between each of the $(n - 2)$th stage points and the finish. The final diagram in this sequence shows a single line connecting start to finish. This line describes the optimal route through the network. An example of this diagrammatic procedure is shown in Fig. 9F.

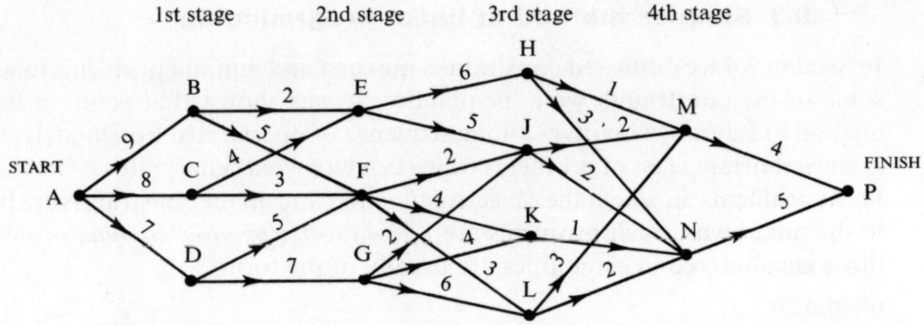

INITIAL DIAGRAM

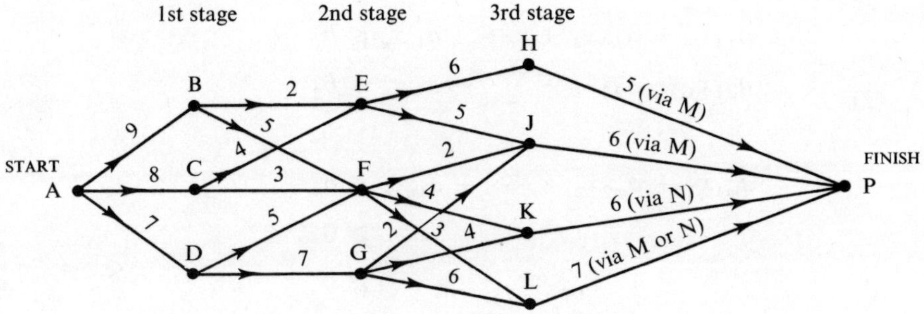

FIRST SOLUTION DIAGRAM ELIMINATES DETAILS OF FOURTH STAGE

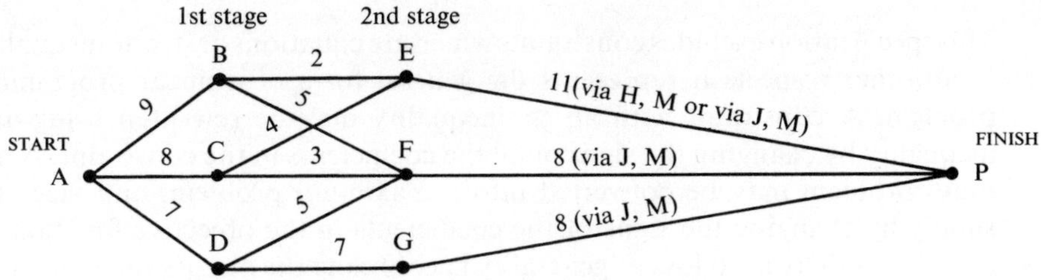

SECOND SOLUTION DIAGRAM ELIMINATES DETAILS OF THIRD STAGE

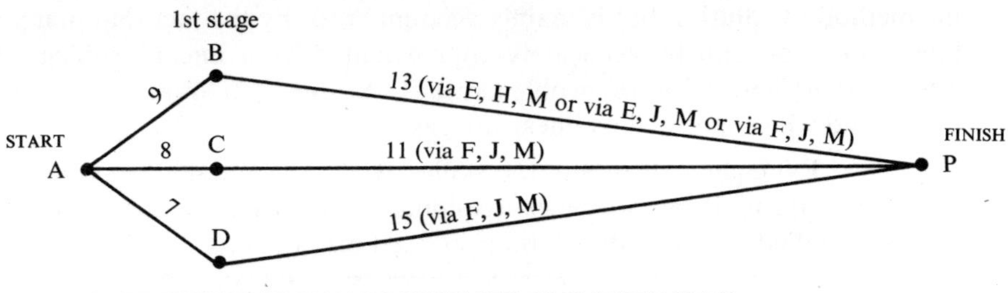

THIRD SOLUTION DIAGRAM ELIMINATES DETAILS OF SECOND STAGE

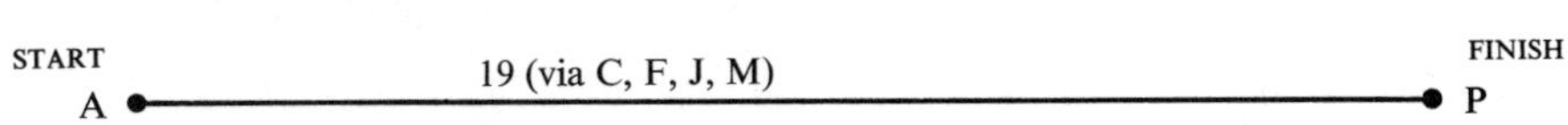

FOURTH SOLUTION DIAGRAM ELIMINATES DETAILS OF FIRST STAGE

Fig. 9F Diagrammatic solution of the shortest route through a network

9.3 Simplex method of linear programming

In Section 7.4 we discussed constrained maxima and minima problems in which some of the constraints were inequalities. It was shown that solution by the method of Lagrange involves a long sequence of operations. Fortunately, there is one important class of problems which can be solved simply; this is the class of linear problems, in which the objective function and all the constraints are linear in the unknowns. Such problems are known as *linear programming* problems; those encountered in economics are usually of the form

maximize

(1) $$z = c_1x_1 + c_2x_2 + \cdots + c_nx_n$$

subject to

(2) $$\begin{aligned} a_{11}x_1 + a_{12}x_2 + \cdots \quad a_{1n}x_n &\leqslant b_1 \\ a_{21}x_1 + a_{22}x_2 + \cdots + a_{2n}x_n &\leqslant b_2 \\ \vdots \qquad \vdots \qquad\quad \vdots \quad &\quad \vdots \\ a_{m1}x_1 + a_{m2}x_2 + \cdots + a_{mn}x_n &\leqslant b_m \\ x_1 \qquad\qquad\qquad\qquad &\geqslant 0 \\ x_2 \qquad\qquad\quad &\geqslant 0 \\ \ddots \qquad &\quad \vdots \\ x_n &\geqslant 0 \end{aligned}$$

This specification excludes constraints which are equations or strong inequalities; in all other respects it represents the general form of a linear programming problem. A constraint with an $\geqslant$ inequality may be rewritten using an $\leqslant$ inequality by changing the signs of all the coefficients in the constraint. A minimum problem may be converted into a maximum problem, and vice versa, simply by changing the signs of the coefficients in the objective function. For this reason there is no loss of generality in confining the discussion to maximum problems.

The importance of linear problems is due in part to the simplicity of the method of solution but is mainly accounted for by the fact that many non-linear problems can be accurately approximated by a linear problem. Thus although very few real world problems are *exactly* linear many are *approximately* linear, and when specified as linear are easily solved.

Example A firm has 160 skilled workmen and 400 unskilled workmen on its payroll. It can produce three commodities, each commodity requiring inputs of skilled and unskilled labour in fixed proportions.

Commodity	*Input of skilled labour per unit output*	*Input of unskilled labour per unit output*	*Price (£)*
1	2	12	2
2	2	8/3	1
3	8/3	20/9	1

Commodity 1 uses a very large amount of unskilled labour but sells for a high price. Commodity 3 uses the largest amount of skilled labour but the smallest amount of unskilled labour. Commodity 2 uses less skilled labour than 3, but more unskilled labour.

How much of each commodity should the firm produce in order to maximize profit?

Mathematical formulation

Because the number of workmen on the payroll is fixed, the wage bill is fixed, so that maximizing profit is equivalent to maximizing revenue. Let x_i be the amount of the ith commodity produced. Formally the problem is to

maximize

$$z = 2x_1 + x_2 + x_3$$

subject to

$$\begin{aligned} 2x_1 + 2x_2 + (\tfrac{8}{3})x_3 &\leqslant 160 \\ 12x_1 + (\tfrac{8}{3})x_2 + (\tfrac{20}{9})x_3 &\leqslant 400 \\ x_1 &\geqslant 0 \\ x_2 &\geqslant 0 \\ x_3 &\geqslant 0 \end{aligned}$$

The objective function z is equal to the total revenue from the sale of the three commodities. The first constraint indicates that the total use of skilled labour cannot exceed the amount of skilled labour available. The total use of skilled labour is shown on the left-hand side of the first inequality. It is the sum of three terms; each represents the use of skilled labour in the production of one of the commodities. The respective terms indicate that $2x_1$ skilled workmen are required for producing x_1 units of commodity 1, $2x_2$ are required for producing x_2 units of commodity 2 and $(\frac{8}{3})x_3$ for producing x_3 units of commodity 3. The term on the right-hand side of the inequality indicates that altogether 160 skilled workmen are available. The second constraint indicates that the total use of unskilled labour cannot exceed the amount of unskilled labour available. The last three constraints indicate that the output of a commodity cannot be negative.

Although the method of solution described below is purely algebraic, it can only be properly understood in geometrical terms. For this reason, it is helpful to begin by discussing the geometrical representation of a linear programming problem. It is appropriate to do this in terms of the example above.

Geometry of the individual constraints

Figure 9G shows the various commodity outputs which satisfy each constraint. For example, all points on or beneath the plane AA′A″ represent outputs which satisfy the first constraint. The points on the plane itself represent outputs which

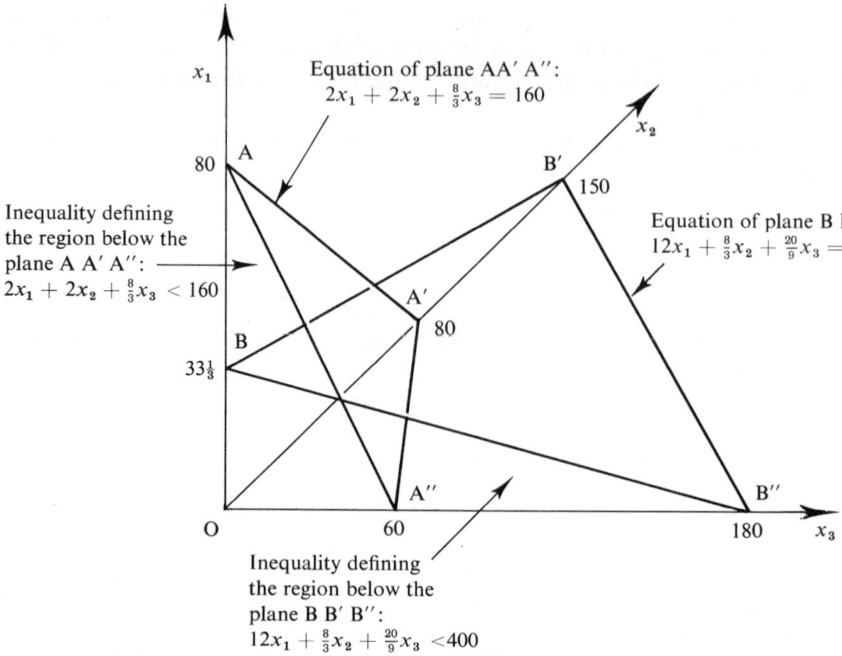

Fig. 9G Geometric representation of the constraints

just exhaust available stocks of skilled labour; the points beneath the plane represent outputs which leave some skilled labour surplus to requirements. All points on or beneath the plane BB′B″ represent outputs which satisfy the second constraint; points on the plane itself correspond to outputs which exhaust the supply of unskilled labour, while points beneath the plane correspond to outputs which leave surplus unskilled labour. Finally note that we have shown in the figure only the sections of the planes which represent outputs satisfying the non-negativity constraints $x_1 \geqslant 0$, $x_2 \geqslant 0$, $x_3 \geqslant 0$.

The feasible region

The solution to the problem must satisfy five constraints: the constraint on skilled labour, the constraint on unskilled labour and the three non-negativity constraints. It is *not* sufficient that *either* one or other of these constraints is satisfied—*all* of them must be satisfied. In terms of Fig. 9G this means that we can only consider points representing outputs which are (i) non-negative and (ii) lie on or beneath *both the plane* AA′A″ *and the plane* BB′B″. The only points open to consideration are therefore those within the region OBC′A′A″C (shown in Fig. 9H); these points represent commodity outputs which satisfy all the constraints. The region OBC′A′A″C is known as the 'feasible region'.

Geometry of the objective function

Having examined the geometry of the constraints we now turn our attention to the geometry of the objective function $z = 2x_1 + x_2 + x_3$. Suppose some

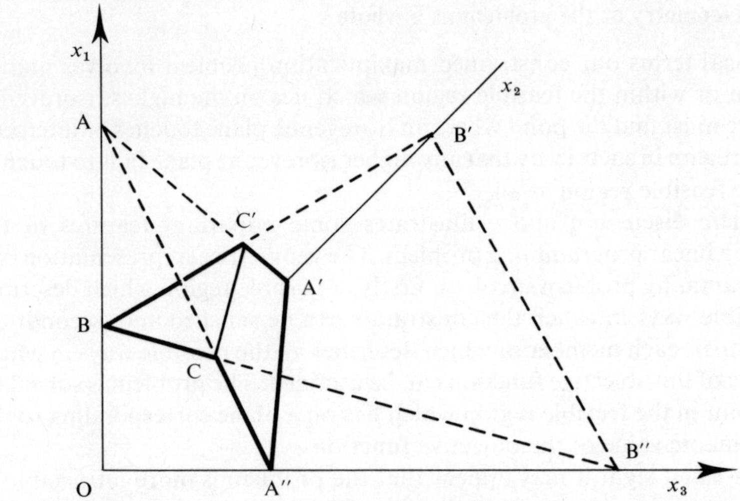

NOTE The region OAA′ A″ is the set of all points with coordinates x_1, x_2, x_3 satisfying the constraints $2x_1 + 2x_2 + \frac{8}{3}x_3 \leq 160$, $x_1 \geq 0, x_2 \geq 0, x_3 \geq 0$. The region OB B′ B″ is the set of all points with coordinates x_1, x_2, x_3 satisfying the constraints $12x_1 + \frac{8}{3}x_2 + \frac{20}{3}x_3 \leq 400$, $x_1 \geq 0, x_2 \geq 0, x_3 \geq 0$.

Fig. 9H The feasible region

particular value of z is chosen, say $z = 150$. The set of all points representing outputs for which $z = 150$ is shown in Fig. 9J. It can be seen that all the points lie on a plane. The *slope* of the plane is determined by the coefficients of x_1, x_2, x_3 in the function z. The *location* of the plane depends on the value of z chosen, for example, if the value of z is reduced to 120, the plane moves closer to the origin. In this particular example, the planes corresponding to the objective function are *isorevenue planes*, because each point on a given plane corresponds to a set of commodity outputs which earns the same revenue.

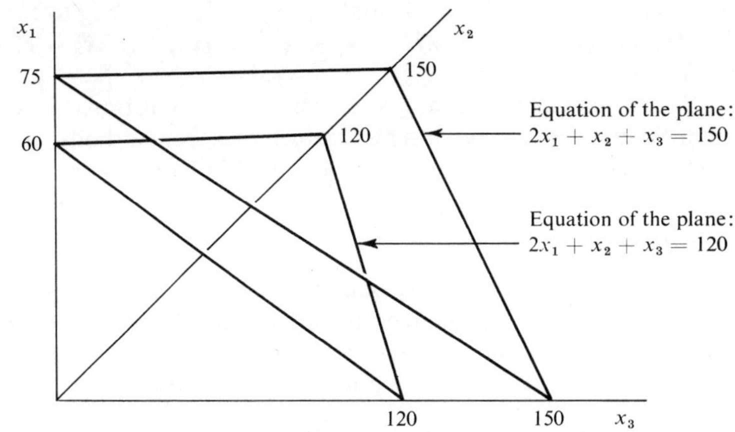

Fig. 9J Geometric representation of the objective function $z = 2x_1 + x_2 + x_3$ for the values $z = 120$, 150

Geometry of the problem as a whole

In geometrical terms our constrained maximization problem involves finding the point on or within the feasible region which lies on the highest isorevenue plane, i.e. we must find the point where an isorevenue plane touches or intersects the feasible region in such a way that any higher isorevenue plane fails to touch or intersect the feasible region at all.

The discussion above illustrates some important features of the geometry of a linear programming problem. The geometrical representation of a linear programming problem involves, firstly, a feasible region which describes all the possible ways in which the constraints can be satisfied and, secondly, a family of planes, each member of which describes all the possible ways in which a given value of the objective function can be attained. The problem is solved by finding a point in the feasible region which lies on a plane corresponding to the highest attainable value of the objective function.

At first sight it may appear that the problem is more intractable in geometrical terms than it is in algebraic terms. However, the shape of the feasible region of almost every economically meaningful linear programming problem has a characteristic form: it is convex and—not only that—it is also a 'simplex'. By exploiting the special features of the shape of the feasible region, together with the linearity of the objective function, it is possible to devise a very simple method of solution.

Convexity

A region is convex if for any two points within or on the boundary of the region, all points on a straight line connecting them also lie within or on the boundary of the region. Suppose that the coordinates of the two points are $\bar{x}_1, \bar{x}_2, \ldots, \bar{x}_n$ and $\bar{\bar{x}}_1, \bar{\bar{x}}_2, \ldots, \bar{\bar{x}}_n$ respectively; then all points on a straight line between them have coordinates of the form $\lambda\bar{x}_1 + (1 - \lambda)\bar{\bar{x}}_1$, $\lambda\bar{x}_2 + (1 - \lambda)\bar{\bar{x}}_2, \ldots,$ $\lambda\bar{x}_n + (1 - \lambda)\bar{\bar{x}}_n$ where $0 \leqslant \lambda \leqslant 1$. The straight line between the two points is traced out by allowing λ to vary continuously from zero to unity. The condition for convexity is that if $\bar{x}_1, \bar{x}_2, \ldots, \bar{x}_n$ and $\bar{\bar{x}}_1, \bar{\bar{x}}_2, \ldots, \bar{\bar{x}}_n$ belong to the region then so do all points $\lambda\bar{x}_1 + (1 - \lambda)\bar{\bar{x}}_1, \lambda\bar{x}_2 + (1 - \lambda)\bar{\bar{x}}_2, \ldots, \lambda\bar{x}_n + (1 - \lambda)\bar{\bar{x}}_n$ $(0 \leqslant \lambda \leqslant 1)$.

A two-dimensional example of convexity is illustrated in Fig. 9K. A three-dimensional convex region is also known as a 'convex body'. Potatoes, oranges and loaves of bread are normally convex, but bananas are not.

Simplex

A simplex is a convex region whose boundary consists of a series of 'flats'. Mathematically, a simplex is a convex region formed by one or more linear constraints. A *ridge* of a simplex is a line on the boundary along which two distinct flats touch one another. A *vertex* is a point at which two or more ridges of a simplex meet.

A solid cube and a pyramid are examples of a simplex in three dimensions, whereas a solid sphere is not. In Fig. 9H, the feasible region is a

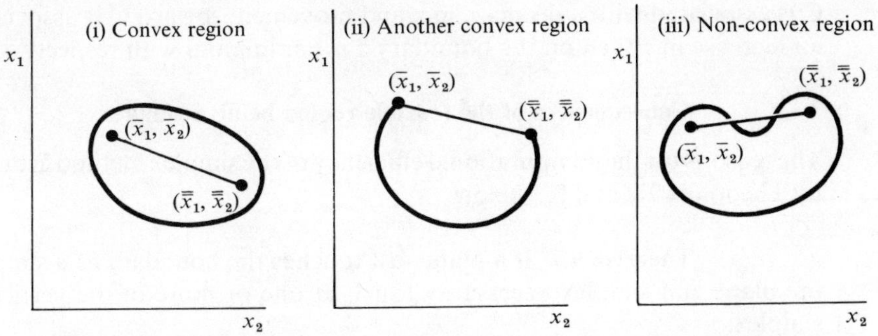

The straight line is the set of all points $[\lambda\bar{x}_1, + (1-\lambda)\bar{\bar{x}}_1, \lambda\bar{x}_2 + (1-\lambda)\bar{\bar{x}}_2], (0 \leqslant \lambda \leqslant 1)$. It lies entirely within the region.

The straight line $[\lambda\bar{x}_1 + (1-\lambda)\bar{\bar{x}}_1, \lambda\bar{x}_2 + (1-\lambda)\bar{\bar{x}}_2]$, $(0 \leqslant \lambda \leqslant 1)$, lies entirely on the boundary of the region.

The straight line lies partly outside the region.

Fig. 9K Illustration of convexity in two dimensions

simplex, with ridges BC, BC′, CC′, C′A′, A′A″, A″C, OA″, OB and vertices O, B, C′, A′, A″ and C.

Consequences of convexity

The reason why the convexity of the feasible region is so important is explained by Theorem 9.1 below.

Theorem 9.1 A maximum or minimum of a linear function $z = a_1x_1 + \cdots + a_nx_n$ over a convex region C occurs wherever one of the family of planes representing the objective function just touches the boundary of C.

PROOF The geometric representation of z is a family of planes in a space of n dimensions (the special case $n = 3$ is illustrated in Fig. 9J). If a plane intersects a region C then parts of C lie on both sides of the plane, so that a small shift of the plane corresponding to a small change in the value of z will still leave some point of contact between the plane and the region C. But a shift of the plane in one direction corresponds to an increase in the value of z and in the other direction corresponds to a reduction in z, so that the original value of z cannot have been either a maximum or a minimum. It follows that a point at which a plane intersects the region C cannot possibly correspond to either a maximum or a minimum of z. On the other hand, if a plane just touches the boundary of C then if C is convex a small shift of the plane in one direction will remove all contact between the plane and the region C, for if this were not so then there would exist a plane touching C at one point and intersecting it at another, which is impossible when C is convex. Recalling that shifts in the plane correspond to changes in the value of z, it follows that the section of the boundary at which the plane just touches C is associated with an extreme value of z over C. If a movement of the plane away from C is associated with an increase in z and a movement toward C is associated with a reduction in z then on the boundary z is a maximum with respect to C, whereas if a movement of the plane away from

C is associated with a decrease in z and movement toward C is associated with an increase in z then on the boundary z is a minimum with respect to C.

Consequences of the feasible region being a simplex

The reasons for the computational efficiency of the simplex method are explained by Theorems 9.2 and 9.3 below.

Theorem 9.2 If a plane just touches the boundary of a simplex then the plane and simplex necessarily touch at one or more of the vertices of the simplex.

PROOF The proof is elementary. Since the boundary of a simplex is a series of flats, either the plane touches the simplex over the entire surface of one of the flats, in which case it also touches the vertices at which the surrounding edges meet, or else it simply touches a vertex. In either case, the plane and simplex touch at a vertex.

Theorems 9.1 and 9.2 imply that to maximize or minimize z over a simplex it is sufficient to find a vertex at which a plane representing the objective function just touches the surface of the simplex. Any such point represents either a maximum or a minimum of z. By using this result it is possible to narrow down the field of search for the maximum to the vertices of a simplex. Indeed, it is possible to do even better than this, as the following theorem shows.

Theorem 9.3 Every path following the ridges of a simplex, and along which the value of z steadily increases leads eventually to a vertex at which z is a maximum. For each vertex there is at least one such path connecting it to a vertex at which z is a maximum.

Theorem 9.3 indicates that to find a vertex at which z is a maximum it is sufficient to begin the search at an arbitrary vertex and then to move along a sequence of ridges—the value of z increasing all the time—until a vertex is reached from which no ridge leads to a higher value of z. This vertex corresponds to a maximum of z.

The algebra of the simplex method: (i) slack variables

The search procedure outlined in Theorem 9.3 is the basis of the simplex method. The procedure can be reduced to a sequence of elementary algebraic operations which are ideal for programming on a computer. For this purpose it is convenient to introduce some additional variables known as *slack variables*. The ith slack variable, s_i, is equal to the difference between the left-hand side and the right-hand side of the ith inequality in (2). There is a slack variable corresponding to each of the first m inequalities:

$$\begin{aligned} s_1 &= b_1 - [a_{11}x_1 + a_{12}x_2 + \cdots + a_{1n}x_n] \\ s_2 &= b_2 - [a_{21}x_1 + a_{22}x_2 + \cdots + a_{2n}x_n] \\ &\vdots \\ s_m &= b_m - [a_{m1}x_1 + a_{m2}x_2 + \cdots + a_{mn}x_n] \end{aligned}$$

Slack variables are so called because they measure the extent to which the inequalities in (2) are satisfied with room to spare; if a slack value is large it means that the left-hand side of the inequality can be substantially increased without violating the constraint, i.e. there is a certain amount of slack to be taken up.

Since the inequalities require the right-hand side to exceed the left-hand side and a slack variable is defined to be the excess of the right-hand side over the left-hand side, it follows that each inequality can be expressed as a simple non-negativity constraint on the corresponding slack variable. Thus the first m constraints can be represented in the form

$$\begin{aligned} s_1 &\geqslant 0 \\ s_2 &\geqslant 0 \\ &\vdots \\ s_m &\geqslant 0 \end{aligned}$$

By using slack variables it is possible to express a linear programming problem as the maximization of an objective function subject to m equality constraints and $(m + n)$ non-negativity constraints, viz:

maximize

(3) $$z = c_1x_1 + c_2x_2 + \cdots + c_nx_n$$

subject to

(4) $$\begin{aligned} s_1 &= b_1 - a_{11}x_1 - a_{12}x_2 - \cdots - a_{1n}x_n \\ s_2 &= b_2 - a_{21}x_1 - a_{22}x_2 - \cdots - a_{2n}x_n \\ &\vdots \\ s_m &= b_m - a_{m1}x_1 - a_{m2}x_2 - \cdots - a_{mn}x_n \end{aligned}$$

and

(5) $$\begin{aligned} &x_1 \geqslant 0, x_2 \geqslant 0, \ldots, x_n \geqslant 0 \\ &s_1 \geqslant 0, s_2 \geqslant 0, \ldots, s_m \geqslant 0 \end{aligned}$$

The formulation of the problem in terms of slack variables is useful because there is a very simple result relating the signs of the slack variables to the geometry of the feasible region. *Except in certain pathological cases, every vertex of the feasible region is associated with strictly positive values of exactly m of the* $(m + n)$ *variables* $x_1, x_2, \ldots, x_n, s_1, s_2, \ldots, s_m$. The remaining n variables have zero values. It follows from this result that in algebraic terms a movement from one vertex of the feasible region to another involves the substitution of one set of m positive-valued variables for another set of m positive-valued variables. Some of the variables in the two sets may be the same. In particular, a movement from one vertex to a *neighbouring* vertex involves the dropping of just one variable from the set of m positive-valued variables and the introduction to the set of just one new variable.

The reason why these results are relevant to the algebra of the simplex method may be explained as follows. Since we know from Theorems 9.1, 9.2 that a solution of a linear programming problem is always to be found at one of the vertices, it follows from the first result above that an algebraic search for the solution can be confined to an examination of trial solutions associated with positive values for exactly m of the $(m + n)$ variables $x_1, x_2, \ldots, x_n, s_1, s_2, \ldots, s_m$. Theorem 9.3 tells us that a search for the solution can be conducted by following a path along the ridges of the simplex, i.e. by a succession of movements between *neighbouring* vertices. According to the second result above, a movement between neighbouring vertices involves dropping one old and introducing one new variable into the set of m positive-valued variables. It follows that a search for the solution proceeds algebraically by a succession of operations in which one variable is dropped from and another variable introduced to a set of m positive-valued variables. The only requirement imposed by Theorem 9.3 is that each of these operations should increase the value of the objective function. Consequently the algebraic solution by the simplex method will consist of a sequence of steps; each step will involve dropping one old variable and introducing one new variable—the new variable being chosen so that (if possible) its introduction increases the value of the objective function.

The algebra of the simplex method: (ii) the tableau

To solve by the simplex method, arrange equations (3) and (4) in the form of the tableau shown below.

		x_1	x_2	. . .	x_n
z	0	c_1	c_2	. . .	c_n
s_1	b_1	$-a_{11}$	$-a_{12}$	. . .	$-a_{1n}$
s_2	b_2	$-a_{21}$	$-a_{22}$	. . .	$-a_{2n}$
.	.	.	.		.
.	.	.	.		.
.	.	.	.		.
s_m	b_m	$-a_{m1}$	$-a_{m2}$	. . .	$-a_{mn}$

NOTE The tableau is formed from the equations by replacing the repeated x_is by a single x_i set at the top of the appropriate column. The addition signs and equals signs are removed. The coefficients in the first column are constant terms.

This tableau represents the first trial solution by the simplex method; the first trial solution is by convention taken (where possible) to be the point at the origin, i.e. it corresponds to the trial values $x_1 = 0$, $x_2 = 0, \ldots, x_n = 0$. It follows from equation (4) that the corresponding values of the slack variables are $s_1 = b_1, s_2 = b_2, \ldots, s_m = b_m$. This illustrates the first important feature of the tableau: the variables which appear along the top of the tableau always have a zero value and the variables which appear down the left-hand side of the tableau always have a value equal to the corresponding element in the first column. For example, it is readily deduced from equation (3) that the first trial value of z is zero, which is the element in the first row and first column of the tableau.

It has already been remarked that each step in the simplex method of solution involves a movement from one vertex of the feasible region to a neighbouring vertex corresponding to a higher value of z. Algebraically this involves dropping one of the variables from the set of m positive-valued variables and introducing a new variable. In the first trial solution the m positive-valued variables are $s_1, s_2, \ldots, s_m$. Consequently the first step in the simplex method of solution is to set one of the s_i equal to zero and to set one of the zero-valued variables $x_1, x_2, \ldots, x_n$ equal to a positive value. But which of the slack variables is to be dropped, and which x_i is to become positive? Since the aim is to maximize the value of the objective function, a very reasonable criterion is to make positive the x_i for which the increase in the value of the objective function per unit increase in the value of the x_i is greatest. The slack variable which becomes zero is chosen in the following way. To make the value of the objective function as large as possible the value of the newly introduced x_i should be as large as possible, which means that its value should be increased until one of the constraints becomes binding. When one of the constraints is binding the corresponding slack variable is equal to zero. Consequently we choose the slack variable to be the one associated with the first constraint to become binding as the value of the newly introduced variable is increased. The way in which these criteria are implemented is described by steps 1–4 below.

Step 1 Examine the top row of the tableau and identify the positive elements (ignoring the element in the first column). If the calculations are to be carried out in decimals choose the largest of the positive elements. If the calculations are to be carried out in fractions it may be advantageous to choose instead a positive element in a column with few complicated fractions. Note which column the element is in.

Step 2 Take in turn each negative element in the column selected in step 1 and divide it into the corresponding element in the first column. Note the row corresponding to the ratio of smallest absolute value.

Step 3 Change all the elements in the column selected in step 1 and the row selected in step 2 according to the following rules.

(a) The element common to both the row and column (known as the *pivot element*) is replaced by its reciprocal.

(b) Each of the other elements in the column is divided through by the pivot element.

(c) Each of the other elements in the row is divided through by the pivot element *and the sign of the result is reversed.*

Step 4 Change all the terms not so far altered in the following way.

Suppose that the pivot element is in the ith row and jth column. Change the value of the element in the kth row and lth column to

$$\text{New }(k, l)\text{th element} = \frac{\left\{\begin{array}{l}\text{Original }(k, l)\text{th element} \times \text{Original }(i, j)\text{th 'pivot' element} \\ -\text{ Original }(i, l)\text{th element} \times \text{Original }(k, j)\text{th element}\end{array}\right\}}{\text{Original }(i. j)\text{th 'pivot' element}}$$

Interchange the subscripted variable bordering the ith row and the subscripted variable at the top of the jth column.

We include here for easy reference the two further steps in the simplex method. These steps are discussed in the second paragraph below.

Step 5 Examine the new top row of the tableau. If all the elements except the first are negative or zero then proceed to step 6. If one or more of the elements is positive return to step 1 and repeat the process.

Step 6 Perform this step only when all the elements in the top row except the first are either negative or zero. Read off the elements in the first column. Each element is the optimal value of the variable opposite to it, bordering the tableau. Variables which appear at the top of a column rather than on the left-hand border all have an optimal value of zero.

Remarks on steps 1–4 By the time step 4 is completed the tableau has been transformed into the algebraic representation of the second trial solution. One of the variables originally appearing at the top of the tableau has been interchanged with one of the variables originally on the left-hand side of the tableau. This indicates that the set of m positive-valued variables has been changed by the introduction of one of the previously zero-valued variables (i.e. one of the x_i) and by the dropping of one of the other variables (i.e. one of the s_i). The variable to be introduced is selected in step 1. Other things being equal, the new variable is chosen to be the one which has the greatest positive effect on the value of the objective function. (Sometimes other things are *not* equal, as when the selection of a particular variable results in cumbersome fractions appearing throughout the calculations.) Each element in the top row of the tableau measures the effect on the value of the objective function of a unit increase in the value of the variable shown at the head of the column. If an element is positive it means that an increase in the value of the corresponding variable will increase (rather than decrease) the value of the objective function. By isolating the largest positive element in the top row of the tableau we fix on the corresponding variable as being the variable for which the increase in the value of the objective function per unit increase in the value of the variable is greatest. In step 2 we select the variable to be dropped. This variable is the slack variable associated with the constraint which is the first to become binding as the value of the newly introduced variable is increased. Each of the ratios evaluated in step 2 measures the maximum value of the newly introduced variable which is permitted when each particular one of the constraints is binding. By selecting the ratio which is smallest in absolute value we identify the slack variable associated with the constraint which first becomes binding when the value of the newly introduced variable is increased. This determines the slack variable which is to be dropped. Having chosen a new set of positive-valued variables for the second trial solution it is convenient to rewrite the objective function (3) and the constraints (4) by putting on the right-hand side of each equation the variables which now have zero values and bringing to the left-hand side those variables which now have positive values. In rewriting (3) and (4) in this way it is necessary to make appropriate changes in the numerical coefficients. Fortunately the requisite changes are determined by relatively simple rules; this means that when the changes are effected and the new equations are written in tableau form there is a simple relationship between the elements of the old (first trial) tableau and the elements of the new (second trial) tableau. The procedure for getting the elements of the new tableau from the elements of the old tableau is described in steps 3 and 4.

Remarks on steps 5 and 6 There are two important advantages in having the zero-valued variables always on the right-hand side (i.e. on top of the tableau) and the positive-valued variables on the left-hand side (i.e. down the side of the tableau). Firstly, the equation represented by the first row of the tableau expresses the objective z as a linear function of the zero-valued variables, so that each coefficient in the top line (apart from the constant term in the first column) measures the increase in the value of the objective function due to a unit increase in the value of the zero-valued variable shown at the head of the column. Because each variable has a zero value, the sign of each of the coefficients in the top line indicates whether making a particular variable positive would increase or decrease the value of the objective function. If one or more of these coefficients is positive it indicates that the trial solution cannot be optimal, since the value of the objective function would be increased by introducing the appropriate variable(s) into the set of positive-valued variables. On the other hand, if none of the coefficients is positive the trial solution must be optimal, because the value of the objective function cannot be increased by introducing any of these variables into the set of positive-valued variables. This test for the optimality of the trial solution is described in step 5. The second advantage of the arrangement of the tableau is illustrated by step 6. Because all the variables on the right-hand side of the equations represented by the tableau are zero, for every trial solution each variable shown on the left-hand side is equal to the constant term shown in the first column of the tableau. This means that as soon as the test in step 5 indicates that the solution is optimal, the optimal values of the positive variables can be read off directly from the first column of the tableau. Naturally, the variables whose optimal value is zero are indicated by their appearance at the top of the tableau.

Example Consider the profit-maximization problem above. By using the slack variables s_1, s_2 the problem may be formulated as follows:

maximize

(6) $$z = 2x_1 + x_2 + x_3$$

subject to

$$(7)\qquad \begin{aligned} s_1 &= 160 - 2x_1 - 2x_2 - (\tfrac{8}{3})x_3 \\ s_2 &= 400 - 12x_1 - (\tfrac{8}{3})x_2 - (\tfrac{20}{9})x_3 \end{aligned}$$

and

$$(8)\qquad \begin{aligned} &x_1 \geqslant 0, x_2 \geqslant 0, x_3 \geqslant 0 \\ &s_1 \geqslant 0, s_2 \geqslant 0 \end{aligned}$$

The initial form of the tableau is

		x_1	x_2	x_3
z	0	2	1	1
s_1	160	—2	—2	8/3
s_2	400	—12	—8/3	—20/9

This tableau represents the first trial solution. Each variable appearing at the top of the tableau has a zero value. Each variable appearing at the left-hand side of the tableau has a value equal to the element opposite to it in the first column. The reader can easily check the consistency of the tableau: if $x_1 = x_2 = x_3 = 0$ then it follows from equation (6) that $z = 0$, and from equations (7) that $s_1 = 160, s_2 = 400$. The first trial solution is indicated by the point O in Fig. 9L.

Step 1 All the elements in the top row (excluding the first) are positive. The largest element is the number 2, which occurs in a column contain-

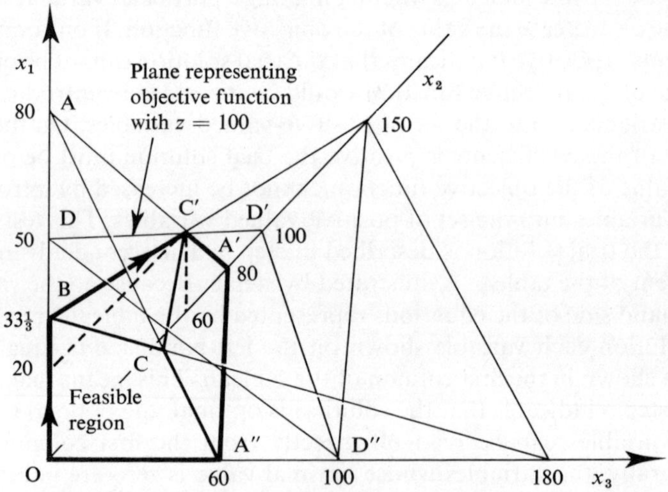

NOTE The arrows indicate the direction of movement along the ridges from the first trial solution at O to the second trial solution at B and the third trial solution (which is in fact the optimum) at C′. At C′ the plane D D′ D″ representing the objective function with $z = 100$ just touches the feasible region. If the value of z is increased then the plane is moved out of contact with the feasible region. It follows that at C′ z is a maximum with respect to the feasible region.

Fig. 9L Graphical representation of the simplex method of solution

ing no fractions, so whether working in decimals or fractions it is appropriate to select the element 2 in the second column.

Step 2 The results of dividing each negative element in the second column into the corresponding element in the first column are (reading downwards) $160/-2 = -80$ and $400/-12 = -33\frac{1}{3}$. The ratio of smallest absolute value is $-33\frac{1}{3}$ which is formed from the element in the third row.

Step 3 The pivot element is the number -12 in the second column and third row. Let us denote the *new* element in the kth row and lth column of the tableau by t_{kl}. Then

(a) the new pivot element is

$$t_{32} = 1/-12 = -\tfrac{1}{12}$$

(b) the new elements in the second column are

$$t_{12} = 2/-12 = -\tfrac{1}{6}$$
$$t_{22} = -2/-12 = \tfrac{1}{6}$$

(c) the new elements in the third row are

$$t_{31} = -[400/-12] = 33\tfrac{1}{3}$$
$$t_{33} = -[(-\tfrac{8}{3})/-12] = -\tfrac{2}{9}$$
$$t_{34} = -[(-\tfrac{20}{9})/-12] = -\tfrac{5}{27}$$

Step 4 The new elements in the rest of the tableau are

$$t_{11} = [0 \times -12 - 400 \times 2]/-12 = 66\tfrac{2}{3}$$
$$t_{13} = [1 \times -12 - (-\tfrac{8}{3}) \times 2]/-12 = \tfrac{5}{9}$$
$$t_{14} = [1 \times -12 - (-\tfrac{20}{9}) \times 2]/-12 = \tfrac{17}{27}$$
$$t_{21} = [160 \times -12 - 400 \times -2]/-12 = 93\tfrac{1}{3}$$
$$t_{23} = [-2 \times -12 - (-\tfrac{8}{3}) \times -2]/-12 = -\tfrac{14}{9}$$
$$t_{24} = [(-\tfrac{8}{3}) \times -12 - (-\tfrac{20}{9}) \times -2]/-12 = -\tfrac{62}{27}$$

Interchanging the subscripted variable bordering the third row, s_2, and the subscripted variable at the top of the second column, x_1, gives the new tableau:

		s_2	x_2	x_3
z	$66\frac{2}{3}$	$-1/6$	$5/9$	$17/27$
s_1	$93\frac{1}{3}$	$1/6$	$-14/9$	$-62/27$
x_1	$33\frac{1}{3}$	$-1/12$	$-2/9$	$-5/27$

This tableau represents the second trial solution. Each variable appearing at the top of the tableau has a zero value. Each variable appearing at the left-hand side of the tableau has a value equal to the element opposite to it in the first column. To check the consistency of the tableau note that when $x_1 = 33\frac{1}{3}, x_2 = 0$, equation (6) gives $z = 2 \times 33\frac{1}{3} = 66\frac{2}{3}$ and equations (7) give $s_1 = 160 - 2 \times 33\frac{1}{3} = 93\frac{1}{3}$, $s_2 = 400 - 12 \times 33\frac{1}{3} = 0$. The second trial solution is represented by the point B in Fig. 9L.

Step 5 Examination of the first row of the new tableau shows that some of the elements besides the first are positive. We must therefore repeat the process, beginning again at step 1.

Steps 1 and 2 indicate that when working in fractions the next pivot element should be the number $-\frac{14}{9}$ in the second row and third column. Steps 3 and 4 give a new tableau:

		s_2	s_1	x_3
z	100	—9/84	—5/14	— 4/21
x_2	60	9/84	—9/14	—31/21
x_1	20	—9/84	1/7	1/7

Step 5 shows that all the elements in the top row (except the first) are negative, so that we may now proceed to step 6. In step 6, reading down the first column of the tableau shows that the maximum value of z is 100, which is achieved when $x_2 = 60$ and $x_1 = 20$. Looking along the top of the tableau shows that the optimal values of the slack variables and the optimal value of x_3 are all zero: $s_2 = 0$, $s_1 = 0$, $x_3 = 0$. The optimal solution is represented by the point C′ in Fig. 9F.

The economic interpretation of this solution is that the maximum revenue is £100, which is attained when 20 units of commodity 1 and 60 units of commodity 2 are produced. Production of these amounts of the two commodities completely exhausts the supplies of skilled and unskilled labour. It is uneconomic to produce commodity 3.

Relation of the simplex method to the method of Lagrange

It is possible to solve a linear programming problem by a straightforward application of the method of Lagrange only when it is known (a) which constraints are binding at the optimum (i.e. which slack variables are zero) and (b) which of the unknowns $x_1, \ldots, x_n$ has an optimal value of zero. The simplex method provides this information as part of the solution whereas the method of Lagrange does not.

Example Solve the profit maximization problem by the method of Lagrange, using the fact that (a) both constraints are binding at the optimum and (b) the optimal value of x_3 is zero.

The Lagrangian is

$$V = 2x_1 + x_2 + x_3 + \lambda_1(160 - 2x_1 - 2x_2 - (\tfrac{8}{3})x_3) + \lambda_2(400 - 12x_1 - (\tfrac{8}{3})x_2 - (\tfrac{20}{9})x_3) \tag{9}$$

Since both constraints are binding, a small relaxation in either constraint will increase the value of profit. This implies that both λ_1 and λ_2 are positive. It follows that the only variable in equation (9) which is zero is x_3. Substituting $x_3 = 0$ into (9) gives

$$V = 2x_1 + x_2 + \lambda_1(160 - 2x_1 - 2x_2) + \lambda_2(400 - 12x_1 - (\tfrac{8}{3})x_2) \tag{10}$$

The necessary conditions for a maximum of (10) with respect to $x_1, x_2, \lambda_1, \lambda_2$ are

$$\begin{aligned}\partial V/\partial x_1 &= 2 - 2\lambda_1 - 12\lambda_2 = 0\\ \partial V/\partial x_2 &= 1 - 2\lambda_1 - (\tfrac{8}{3})\lambda_2 = 0\\ \partial V/\partial \lambda_1 &= 160 - 2x_1 - 2x_2 = 0\\ \partial V/\partial \lambda_2 &= 400 - 12x_1 - (\tfrac{8}{3})x_2 = 0.\end{aligned}$$

The first two equations show that $\lambda_1 = \frac{10}{28}$, $\lambda_2 = \frac{3}{28}$. The last two equations show that $x_1 = 20$, $x_2 = 60$.

It can be seen that the method of Lagrange offers a certain amount of additional information as compared with the simplex method; specifically, it gives the values of the Lagrange multiples λ_1, λ_2, which measure the rate of change of the objective function with respect to a small variation in the respective constraints. Fortunately, however, these values can be obtained directly from the solution of a 'dual' linear programming problem.

The 'dual' problem

Every linear programming problem of the form:

maximize

$$z = c_1x_1 + c_2x_2 + \cdots + c_nx_n$$

subject to

$$\begin{aligned}a_{11}x_1 + a_{12}x_2 + \cdots + a_{1n}x_n &\leqslant b_1\\ a_{21}x_1 + a_{22}x_2 + \cdots + a_{2n}x_n &\leqslant b_2\\ \vdots \qquad\qquad\qquad\quad \vdots\quad &\quad \vdots\\ a_{m1}x_1 + a_{m2}x_2 + \cdots + a_{mn}x_n &\leqslant b_m\end{aligned}$$

$$x, x_2, \ldots, x_n \geqslant 0$$

has a dual problem:

minimize

$$z = b_1\lambda_1 + b_2\lambda_2 + \cdots + b_m\lambda_m$$

subject to

$$\begin{aligned}a_{11}\lambda_1 + a_{21}\lambda_2 + \cdots + a_{m1}\lambda_m &\geqslant c_1\\ a_{12}\lambda_1 + a_{22}\lambda_2 + \cdots + a_{m2}\lambda_m &\geqslant c_2\\ \vdots \qquad\quad \vdots \qquad\qquad\quad \vdots\quad &\quad \vdots\\ a_{1n}\lambda_1 + a_{2n}\lambda_2 + \cdots + a_{mn}\lambda_m &\geqslant c_n\end{aligned}$$

$$\lambda_1, \lambda_2, \ldots, \lambda_m \geqslant 0$$

The general rules for forming the dual are

(i) replace $x_1, x_2, \ldots, x_n$ by $\lambda_1, \lambda_2, \ldots, \lambda_m$;
(ii) replace $c_1, c_2, \ldots, c_n$ by $b_1, b_2, \ldots, b_m$ and vice versa;
(iii) replace a_{ij} by a_{ji} ($i = 1, \ldots, m; j = 1, \ldots, n$);
(iv) reverse the inequalities.

The solution of the dual is a set of Lagrange multipliers; the ith Lagrange multiplier, λ_i ($i = 1, \ldots, m$), measures the sensitivity of the objective function z to a small change in the ith constraint in the original problem.

The relationship between the dual and the original problem is a very close one. The minimum of the objective function in the dual problem is equal to the maximum of the objective function in the original problem. It is easily verified that the dual of the dual is the original.

Example The dual of the profit-maximization problem is to:

minimize

$$z = 160\lambda_1 + 400\lambda_2$$

subject to

$$\begin{aligned} 2\lambda_1 + 12\lambda_2 &\geqslant 2 \\ 2\lambda_1 + (\tfrac{8}{3})\lambda_2 &\geqslant 1 \\ (\tfrac{8}{3})\lambda_1 + (\tfrac{20}{9})\lambda_2 &\geqslant 1 \\ \lambda_1 &\geqslant 0 \\ \lambda_2 &\geqslant 0 \end{aligned}$$

Solution by the simplex method shows that $\lambda_1 = \frac{10}{28}$, $\lambda_2 = \frac{3}{28}$, whence $z = 100$. Because there are only two unknowns, λ_1 and λ_2, it is also possible to solve

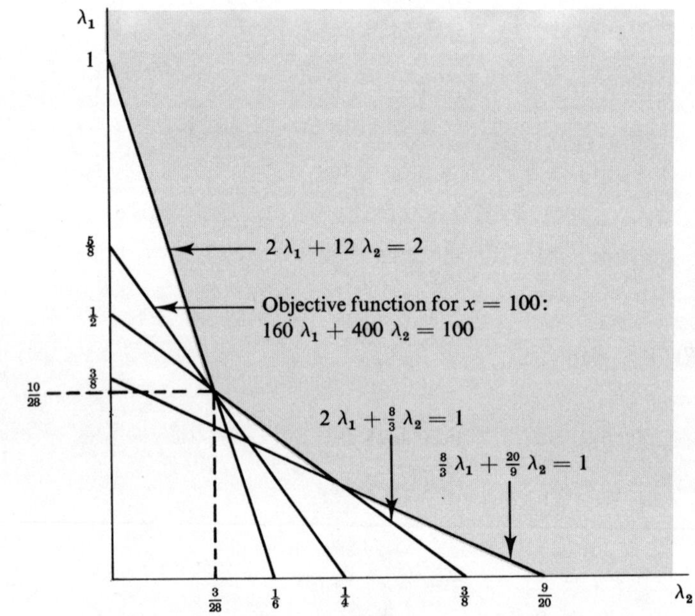

NOTE The shaded area is the feasible region. The minimum of z is at the point where the lowest of the planes $z = 160\lambda_1 + 400\lambda_2$ is just in contact with the feasible region. Notice the difference in the graphical representations of the original and the dual. In the original the feasible region is in the lower left-hand corner and its dimension (in cubic units) is finite, whereas in the dual the feasible region is in the upper right-hand corner and its dimension (in square units) is infinite.

Fig. 9M Graphical solution of the dual

graphically (see Fig. 9M). Indeed, in many practical cases, where there are few constraints but many unknowns, it is often much easier to solve the dual than to solve the original.

Relationship between the dual and the original

It is well beyond the scope of this book to explore in detail the causes and consequences of duality. It is nevertheless interesting to note that the Lagrangian for the dual problem is identical with the Lagrangian for the original problem. Given just the Lagrangian it is impossible to decide whether you are solving the original problem or the dual. The Lagrangian for the dual is

$$\begin{aligned} V = {} & b_1\lambda_1 + b_2\lambda_2 + \cdots + b_m\lambda_m \\ & + x_1(c_1 - a_{11}\lambda_1 - a_{21}\lambda_2 - \cdots - a_{m1}\lambda_m) \\ & + x_2(c_2 - a_{12}\lambda_1 - a_{22}\lambda_2 - \cdots - a_{m2}\lambda_m) \\ & \vdots \\ & + x_n(c_n - a_{1n}\lambda_1 - a_{2n}\lambda_2 - \cdots - a_{mn}\lambda_m) \end{aligned}$$

where $x_1, \ldots, x_n$ are the Lagrange multipliers of the dual. Multiplying out and regrouping terms shows that

$$\begin{aligned} V = {} & c_1x_1 + c_2x_2 + \cdots + c_mx_m \\ & + \lambda_1(b_1 - a_{11}x_1 - a_{12}x_2 - \cdots - a_{1n}x_n) \\ & + \lambda_2(b_2 - a_{21}x_1 - a_{22}x_2 - \cdots - a_{2n}x_n) \\ & \vdots \\ & + \lambda_m(b_m - a_{m1}x_1 - a_{m2}x_2 - \cdots - a_{mn}x_n) \end{aligned}$$

which is the Lagrangian for the original problem.

9.4 Other programming methods

We outline below the scope of some other programming methods of interest to the economist.

(i) Integer programming by the Gomory accelerated cutting plane method

This method is used to solve linear programming problems in which the unknowns $x_1, x_2, \ldots, x_n$ are integer-valued.

Example The transport planning problem discussed in Section 1.4 may be formulated as an integer programming problem. Suppose that the total distance covered on a return journey on each of the four routes is as follows:

	Route number	*Mileage*
1	London – Chatham – Ramsgate	155
2	London – Chatham – Canterbury – Dover	150
3	London – Tonbridge – Canterbury – Ramsgate	178
4	London – Tonbridge – Dover	154

If the objective of management is to minimize the total train-miles required to operate the services, subject to the constraints imposed by the market researcher, then the problem is to minimize

$$z = 155f_1 + 150f_2 + 178f_3 + 154f_4$$

subject to

$$\begin{aligned}
f_1 \quad + f_3 \quad &\geq 12 \\
f_2 \quad + f_4 &\geq 12 \\
f_2 + f_3 \quad &\geq 8 \\
f_1 + f_2 \quad &\geq 16 \\
f_3 + f_4 &\geq 8 \\
f_1 &\geq 0 \\
f_2 &\geq 0 \\
f_3 &\geq 0 \\
f_4 &\geq 0
\end{aligned}$$

where f_1, f_2, f_3, f_4 are integer values. The restriction to integer values is due simply to the fact that fractional trains cannot be operated.

(ii) Solution of a factory to warehouse transportation problem by the 'stepping stone' method

Suppose that a product is produced at m different factories and has to be distributed to n different warehouses. The transportation problem is to organize the system of distribution to minimize total transport costs.

The ith factory produces $q_i \geq 0$ units per week ($i = 1, \ldots, m$) and $s_j \geq 0$ units per week are delivered to the jth warehouse ($j = 1, \ldots, n$). Let c_{ij} be the cost of transporting a unit of the product from the ith factory to the jth warehouse, and let x_{ij} be the amount actually transported. The problem is to minimize

$$\begin{aligned}
z = \; & c_{11}x_{11} + c_{12}x_{12} + \cdots + c_{1n}x_{1n} \\
& + c_{21}x_{21} + c_{22}x_{22} + \cdots + c_{2n}x_{2n} \\
& \quad \vdots \qquad\qquad \vdots \qquad\qquad\qquad \vdots \\
& + c_{m1}x_{m1} + c_{m2}x_{m2} + \cdots + c_{mn}x_{mn}
\end{aligned}$$

subject to

$$\begin{aligned}
x_{11} + x_{12} + \cdots + x_{1n} &= q_1 \\
x_{21} + x_{22} + \cdots + x_{2n} &= q_2 \\
\vdots \qquad \vdots \qquad\qquad \vdots \quad & \quad \vdots \\
x_{m1} + x_{m2} + \cdots + x_{mn} &= q_m \\
x_{11} + x_{21} + \cdots + x_{m1} &= s_1 \\
x_{12} + x_{22} + \cdots + x_{m2} &= s_2 \\
\vdots \qquad \vdots \qquad\qquad \vdots \quad & \quad \vdots \\
x_{1n} + x_{2n} + \cdots + x_{mn} &= s_n \\
q_1 + q_2 + \cdots + q_m &= s_1 + s_2 + \cdots + s_n
\end{aligned}$$

It can be seen that each unknown x_{ij} appears once in the objective function, once in a q-constraint and once in an s-constraint; furthermore, every coefficient on the left-hand side of the constraints is equal to unity. By exploiting these and other special features of the problem it is possible to devise a number of very efficient methods of solution. The most straightforward of these is the 'stepping stone' method, which is essentially an adaptation of the simplex method.

(iii) Decomposition of a problem using the Dantzig–Wolfe method

Consider a linear programming problem in which the constraints form a sequence of distinct blocks, e.g.

maximize

$$z = c_1x_1 + c_2x_2 + \cdots + c_nx_n$$

subject to

$$\begin{array}{llllll}
a_{11}x_1 & + a_{12}x_2 & + \cdots & & \cdots + a_{1n}x_n & \leqslant b_1 \\
\vdots & & & & & \\
a_{j1}x_1 & + a_{j2}x_2 & + \cdots & & \cdots + a_{jn}x_n & \leqslant b_j \\
a_{j+1\,1}x_1 & + a_{j+1\,2}x_2 & + \cdots + a_{j+1\,k}x_k & & & \leqslant b_{j+1} \\
\vdots & & & & & \\
a_{l1}x_1 & + a_{l2}x_2 & + \cdots + a_{lk}x_k & & & \leqslant b_l \\
 & & & a_{l+1\,k+1}x_{k+1} & + \cdots + a_{l+1\,n}x_n & \leqslant b_{l+1} \\
 & & & \vdots & & \\
 & & & a_{mk+1}x_{k+1} & + \cdots + a_{mn}x_n & \leqslant b_m
\end{array}$$

$$x_1, x_2, \ldots, x_n \geqslant 0$$

If it were not for the first j constraints, this problem would decompose into two distinct problems:

(i) maximize

$$z = c_1x_1 + c_2x_2 + \cdots + c_kx_k$$

subject to

$$\begin{array}{l}
a_{j+1\,1}x_1 + a_{j+1\,2}x_2 + \cdots + a_{j+1\,k}x_k \leqslant b_{j+1} \\
\vdots \\
a_{l1}x_1 + a_{l2}x_2 + \cdots + a_{lk}x_k \leqslant b_l
\end{array}$$

and $\quad x_1, x_2, \ldots, x_k \geqslant 0$

(ii) maximize

$$z = c_{k+1}x_{k+1} + \cdots + c_nx_n$$

subject to

$$
\begin{aligned}
a_{l+1k+1}x_{k+1} + \cdots + a_{l+1n}x_n &\leqslant b_{l+1} \\
&\vdots \\
a_{mk+1}x_{k+1} + \cdots + a_{mn}x_n &\leqslant b_m \\
x_{k+1}, \ldots, x_n &\geqslant 0
\end{aligned}
$$

It is much easier to solve the two smaller problems than it is to solve the single larger problem. The principle of the Dantzig–Wolfe method is to remove the first j constraints from the original problem and formulate them in terms of a dual problem. The original problem then consists of two smaller problems with certain adjustments determined by the solution of the dual problem. The Dantzig–Wolfe method has an instructive economic interpretation in terms of decentralized decision-taking.

(iv) Quadratic programming by the Theil–van de Panne method

The Theil–van de Panne method can be used to solve all optimization problems in which the objective function is a quadratic function of the variables, and the constraints are linear functions of the variables, i.e. all problems of the kind:

maximize

$$
\begin{aligned}
z = c_{11}x_1^2 + c_{12}x_1x_2 + \cdots & + c_{1n}x_1x_n \\
+ c_{22}x_2^2 + c_{23}x_2x_3 + \cdots & + c_{2n}x_2x_n \\
\ddots \qquad \ddots \qquad & \vdots \\
+ c_{n-1n-1}x_{n-1}^2 & + c_{n-1n}x_{n-1}x_n \\
& + c_{nn}x_n^2
\end{aligned}
$$

subject to

$$
\begin{aligned}
a_{11}x_1 + a_{12}x_2 + \cdots + a_{1n}x_n &= b_1 \\
&\vdots \\
a_{j1}x_1 + a_{j2}x_2 + \cdots + a_{jn}x_n &= b_j \\
a_{j+11}x_1 + a_{j+12}x_2 + \cdots + a_{j+1n}x_n &\leqslant b_{j+1} \\
&\vdots \\
a_{m1}x_1 + a_{m2}x_2 + \cdots + a_{mn}x_n &\leqslant b_m \\
x_1, x_2, \ldots, x_n &\geqslant 0
\end{aligned}
$$

The method of solution is to first of all solve the problem without the constraints and then to progress from one trial solution to another by introducing at each stage one of the constraints which was violated by the previous trial solution. A procedure of this kind will eventually lead to an optimum.

Example Consider the choice of an efficient portfolio which is to consist of n different assets (ordinary shares, debentures, money, etc.). The financial return on each of these assets (except money) normally fluctuates over time. Suppose that the variation in the return on the ith asset is measured by v_{ii} and the covariation between the return on the ith asset and the return on the jth asset is measured by v_{ij}. It can be shown by using probability theory that if a portfolio consists of x_i units of the ith asset ($i = 1, \ldots, n$) then the variation in the total return on the portfolio is measured by

$$
(1) \quad \begin{aligned}
v = v_{11}x_1^2 &+ 2v_{12}x_1x_2 + \cdots && + 2v_{1n}x_1x_n \\
+ v_{22}x_2^2 & \quad + 2v_{23}x_2x_3 + \cdots && + 2v_{2n}x_2x_n \\
& \quad \ddots && \quad \vdots \\
& \quad + v_{n-1n}x_{n-1}x_n && + v_{n-1n-1}x_{n-1}^2 \\
& && + v_{nn}x_n^2
\end{aligned}
$$

Suppose that the average rate of return on the ith asset is μ_i and that its current price is p_i. If the holder of the portfolio has £y to invest and he requires an average overall return of μ at minimum risk, the optimal portfolio minimizes (1) subject to

$$
(2) \quad \begin{aligned}
p_1x_1 + p_2x_2 + \cdots + p_nx_n &= y \\
\mu_1x_1 + \mu_2x_2 + \cdots + \mu_nx_n &\geqslant \mu
\end{aligned}
$$

If the holder of the portfolio does not wish to incur debts there are additional constraints

$$
(3) \quad x_1, x_2, \ldots, x_n \geqslant 0
$$

The minimization of (1) subject to (2) and (3) is easily solved by using the Theil–van de Panne method.

(v) Separable programming by Miller's method

Separable programming is concerned with problems in which the objective function and most of the constraints are linear, but some of the constraints contain nonlinear terms. The method of solution is to approximate the graphs of the nonlinear terms by a sequence of connected linear segments.

(vi) Stochastic and chance-constrained programming

In stochastic and chance-constrained programming the unknowns are random variables and the problem is to choose the optimal values of their means, variances, etc. In stochastic programming the unknowns satisfy the constraints exactly, whereas in chance-constrained programming there is a certain probability that the constraints will be violated by a given margin.

Notes and references

There is an enormous technical literature on programming methods, but very few good textbooks. The best references for a general view of the subject are Baumol,[13] Beale,[14] Bellman,[16] Lange[74] and Vajda.[121,122] For a more abstract approach see Intriligator,[62] Ch. 1–5. A useful text on linear programming is Hadley[47]; the classic work by Dantzig[32] is still worth dipping into. For a description of the simplex method see Baumol,[13] Hadley[47] and Wolfe.[123] Applications of linear programming to advanced economic theory are described in Dorfman, Samuelson and Solow[35] and Gale.[39] Surveys of the technical literature have been prepared by Graves and Wolfe[43] and Vajda.[121] For a review of nonlinear programming see Hadley.[48] The basic text on quadratic programming is Boot.[20]

Problems

9.2 A transformer has to be moved by road from A to L. The journey times (in hours) over various routes are shown in the figure.

(a) Which route minimizes the journey time?

(b) Suppose that the transformer is prohibited from using the roads from A to C, F to J and K to L. How does this change the optimal route? [*Hint:* consider a prohibited route as one with an infinitely long journey time.]

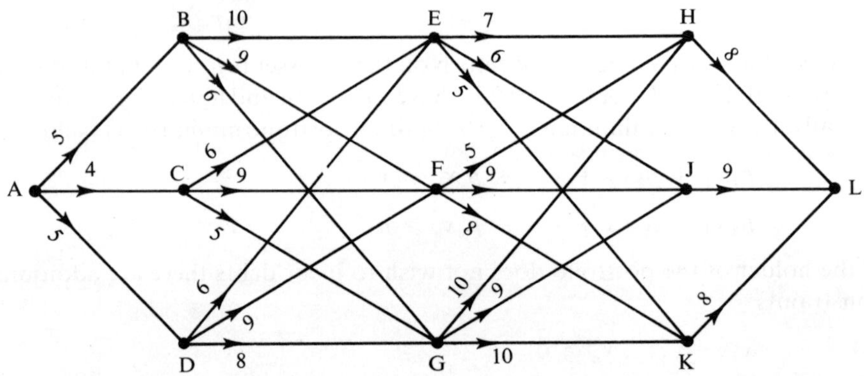

9.3.1 Here are some of the things you might see on a breakfast table: toast, a toast rack, a half pound packet of butter, sugar cubes, a sugar bowl, a boiled egg, a teacup, a saucer, a plate, a cork table mat, and a jar of marmalade. How many of these objects are convex?

9.3.2 Using the simplex method, maximize

$$R = 12x + 3y$$

subject to

$$2x + 4y \leqslant 10$$

$$8x + 8y \leqslant 13$$

$$x \geqslant 0, \quad y \geqslant 0$$

9.3.3 The manager of an electronic assembly shop can produce three products; radios, stereograms and television sets. The price of each radio is £20, of each stereogram is £60 and each television set is £60. He has two limits on his production. His labour force is restricted to 30 men, and the assembly area has only 200 square feet of working surfaces. Each radio needs one man and 20 square feet to produce, each stereo needs 2 men and 30 square feet, and each television set requires 2 men and 25 square feet. The manager wishes to maximize his profits. Formulate this problem in linear programming terms and solve by the simplex method.

9.3.4 Set up the dual problem to 9.3.3 and solve it graphically.

Part 3
Matrix algebra

Chapter 10
Equilibrium conditions for interacting markets

10.1 Introduction

In Chapter 3 dynamic analysis was used to examine the equilibrium and stability of single markets—the market for all finished goods and services, and also the market for frozen food. The analysis of Chapter 3 can be easily generalized to systems of interacting markets. The equilibrium conditions for a system of interacting markets are usually a set of simultaneous equations; the solution of these equations gives the equilibrium values of the endogenous economic variables. In this chapter we shall derive the equilibrium conditions for models of (i) international trade, (ii) monetary policy and (ii) inter-industry transactions.

Equilibrium conditions are not the only examples of simultaneous equations in economics (see for example Section 1.4). However, when simultaneous equations are equilibrium conditions they have a particular significance because general questions concerning the nature of their solution are important. For example, if the nature of the solution determines the nature of the equilibrium it is important to know whether a solution necessarily exists, whether it is always unique, and whether it is attainable in a 'real world' economic situation.

General questions about the properties of the solution of simultaneous linear equations can often be analysed very simply by the algebra of vectors and matrices. The great strength of matrix algebra lies not in deriving computational methods of solution but in bringing to light general principles which might otherwise remain undiscovered. It is because matrix algebra is so well adapted to analysing the general questions which arise in connection with the solution of equilibrium conditions that the discussion in this chapter provides a useful introduction for economists to the abstract results of matrix algebra presented in the chapters which follow.

It is important to emphasize that the methods of matrix algebra apply only to sets of simultaneous equations which are linear in the unknowns. The three models described in this chapter suggest that this restriction is not so serious as it may at first appear.

10.2 International trade

The model of the aggregate supply and demand for finished goods and services (see Section 3.8) can be generalized to an 'open economy', i.e. to an economy which trades with other countries. To be specific, let us suppose that there are two countries, 1 and 2, which trade with each other and with no one else. As before, let C denote consumption, I investment and G government expenditure; also let X denote exports, M imports, and let a subscript denote the country. As a result of trade, aggregate demand in each country is equal to aggregate domestic demand $C + I + G$ plus the balance of export demand over import demand, $X - M$. It follows that in period t

(1)
$$\begin{aligned}&\text{Aggregate demand in country 1}\\&= C_1(t) + I_1(t) + G_1(t) + X_1(t) - M_1(t)\\&\text{Aggregate demand in country 2}\\&= C_2(t) + I_2(t) + G_2(t) + X_2(t) - M_2(t)\end{aligned}$$

As before, we assume that in each country consumption is a linear function of lagged income,

(2)
$$\begin{aligned}C_1(t) &= b + c_1 Y_1(t - 1)\\C_2(t) &= b + c_2 Y_2(t - 1)\end{aligned}$$

where c_1, c_2 are marginal propensities to consume out of pre-tax income, and are functions of the rate of income tax in each country. Investment and government expenditure are exogenous. In the short run, aggregate supply is adjusted to meet aggregate demand, although planned supply each period is equal to the amount supplied previously. We specify trading relations by taking imports into each country to be a linear function of lagged domestic income:

(3)
$$\begin{aligned}M_1(t) &= l_1 + m_1 Y_1(t - 1)\\M_2(t) &= l_2 + m_2 Y_2(t - 1)\end{aligned}$$

The parameter m is the marginal propensity to import; it measures the rate of change of imports with respect to a marginal change in domestic income. This behavioural relation between imports and income is not as well established as the behavioural relation between consumption and income. However, by assuming such a relation one can analyse the processes of international trade very simply.

Since there are only two countries engaged in trade, the exports of country 1 are the imports of country 2 and vice versa:

(4)
$$\begin{aligned}X_1(t) &= M_2(t)\\X_2(t) &= M_1(t)\end{aligned}$$

Substituting equations (2)–(4) into equations (1) and grouping terms shows that aggregate demand in country 1 is

$$(c_1 - m_1)Y_1(t - 1) + m_2 Y_2(t - 1) + I_1(t) + G_1(t) + b_1 - l_1$$

and that aggregate demand in country 2 is

$$(c_2 - m_2)Y_2(t - 1) + m_1 Y_1(t - 1) + I_2(t) + G_2(t) + b_2 - l_2$$

These expressions may be simplified by noting that the last four terms on the right are components of total exogenous demand (denoted by E):

(5) Aggregate demand in country 1
$= (c_1 - m_1)Y_1(t - 1) + m_2 Y_2(t - 1) + E_1(t)$

Aggregate demand in country 2
$= (c_2 - m_2)Y_2(t - 1) + m_1 Y_1(t - 1) + E_2(t)$

10.3 Equilibrium in the world economy

We say that the world economy is in equilibrium if both the market for the products of country 1 and the market for the products of country 2 are in equilibrium; in this case planned supply equals planned demand in each country. Let the exogenous demands be constant in both countries and equal to E_1 and E_2 respectively.

Since in each country planned aggregate supply is equal to the amount actually supplied in the previous period, a consideration of the plans for period $t + 1$ shows that the equilibrium conditions are

$$Y_1(t) = (c_1 - m_1)Y_1(t) + m_2 Y_2(t) + E_1$$
$$Y_2(t) = (c_2 - m_2)Y_2(t) + m_1 Y_1(t) + E_2$$

By rearranging terms we obtain the simpler result

$$(6) \quad \begin{aligned} (1 - c_1 + m_1)Y_1(t) \qquad\qquad - m_2 Y_2(t) &= E_1 \\ - m_1 Y_1(t) + (1 - c_2 + m_2)Y_2(t) &= E_2 \end{aligned}$$

Equations (6) are simultaneous linear equations in the variables $Y_1(t)$, $Y_2(t)$. From these equations we may obtain the values that $Y_1(t)$, $Y_2(t)$ must take on for the two interacting product markets to be in equilibrium. It is easily shown that when exogenous demands are constant a state of equilibrium in both countries ensures a steady state equilibrium in the 'world' as a whole.

Example Find the equilibrium incomes in country 1 and country 2 when exogenous demand in each country is £10m and

$$c_1 = 0{\cdot}75 \qquad m_1 = 0{\cdot}25$$
$$c_2 = 1{\cdot}0 \qquad m_2 = 0{\cdot}5$$

SOLUTION The conditions for equilibrium are given by equations (6) above. Direct substitution gives

$$0{\cdot}5 Y_1(t) - 0{\cdot}5 Y_2(t) = 10$$
$$-0{\cdot}25 Y_1(t) + 0{\cdot}5 Y_2(t) = 10$$

On adding, we get

$$0{\cdot}25 Y_1(t) = 20$$

Therefore

$$Y_1(t) = 80$$

Substituting this result into the first equation gives

$$40 - 0{\cdot}5Y_2(t) = 10$$

Therefore

$$Y_2(t) = 60$$

When each product market is in equilibrium, the income in country 1 is £80m and the income in country 2 is £60m. Note that it is not necessarily the case that when the world economy is in equilibrium each country's balance of trade is zero. In the present case

$$X_2(t) = m_1 Y_1(t) = 0{\cdot}25 \times 80 = 20 \text{ (£m)}$$

$$M_2(t) = m_2 Y_2(t) = 0{\cdot}5 \times 60 = 30 \text{ (£m)}$$

so that country 2's balance of trade has a deficit of £10m. This is not surprising since country 2 has a higher marginal propensity to import than country 1.

10.4 The multiplier in an open economy

Suppose that there is an increase in government expenditure, or indeed in any component of exogenous demand, in one or other of the countries. Is there still a multiplier effect on equilibrium income in the home country even though the economy is open? If so, is the size of the multiplier the same when the economy is open as when the economy is closed? And does a change in exogenous demand in one country change the equilibrium income in the foreign country? A comprehensive answer to these questions requires the methods of matrix algebra developed in Chapters 11 and 12. However, it is instructive to consider the questions in terms of the example described above.

Suppose that there is an increase in exogenous demand of £1m in country 1. The conditions for equilibrium become

$$0{\cdot}5Y_1(t) - 0{\cdot}5Y_2(t) = 11$$

$$-0{\cdot}25Y_1(t) + 0{\cdot}5Y_2(t) = 10$$

The solution is obtained in the same way as before and is

$$Y_1(t) = 84 \qquad Y_2(t) = 62 \quad \text{(£m)}$$

The effect of an increase in exogenous demand of £1m in country 1 is to increase the equilibrium income in country 1 by £4m and to increase the equilibrium income in country 2 by £2m. Clearly, so far as this example is concerned, there is a multiplier effect not only on the income in the home country but on the income in the foreign country as well. The multiplier for income in the home country is 4 and the multiplier for income in the foreign country is 2. Let us investigate the relation between the multiplier in the open economy and the multiplier in the closed economy. The marginal propensity to consume in the home country, country 1, is 0·75. When the economy is closed the multiplier is therefore $1/1 - 0{\cdot}75 = 4$. Evidently in country 1 the multiplier effect on income at home is the same whether the economy is open or closed.

However, this is not usually the case. The reader may verify that in country 2 the multiplier effect on income at home is smaller when the economy is open than when the economy is closed.

Graphical illustration The simultaneous linear equations can be solved graphically. Each of the linear equations corresponds to a straight line in Fig. 10A. The line AA′ indicates all the points $[Y_1(t), Y_2(t)]$ for which planned supply equals planned demand in country 1 when exogenous demand is £10m. The line BB′ indicates all those points for which planned supply equals planned demand in country 2. The world economy is in equilibrium if and only if planned supply equals planned demand in each country. Consequently, when exogenous demand is £10m in each country the world economy can only be in equilibrium when the point $[Y_1(t), Y_2(t)]$ lies on both the lines AA′, BB′. As shown, there is only one point for which this is true; the coordinates of this point are the equilibrium values of income.

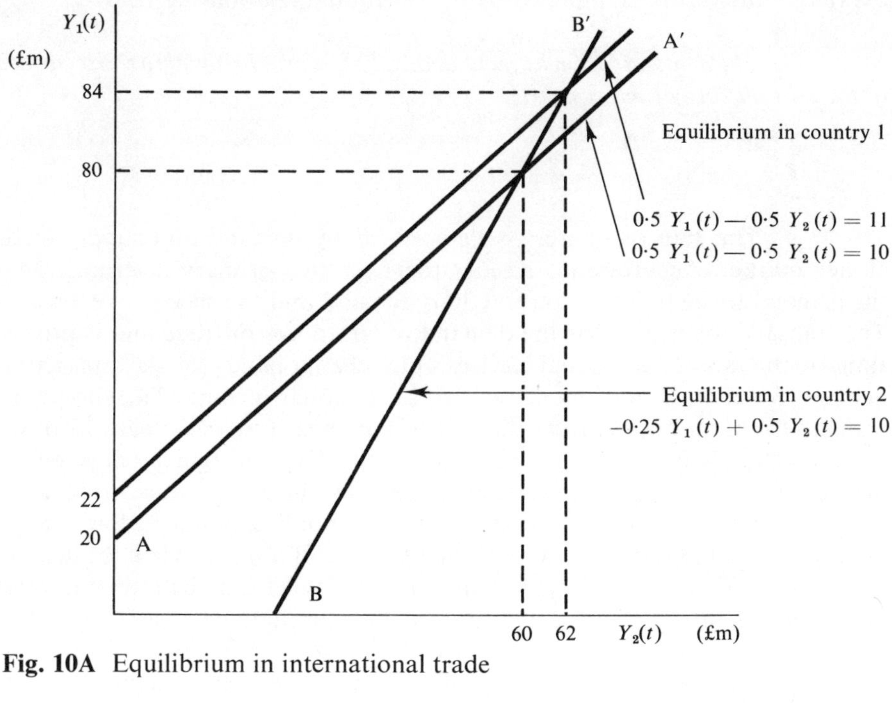

Fig. 10A Equilibrium in international trade

The effect of an increase in exogenous demand in country 1 is to shift the line AA′ upwards; a new point of intersection is obtained, which corresponds to a new equilibrium income in each country.

10.5 Monetary policy

So far in this book we have examined only the equilibrium of markets for goods and services. It has been implicitly assumed that monetary factors have no influence on either the demand or the supply of goods. This is often a reasonable assumption for capitalist economies in which there is severe unemployment. In most circumstances though, it is not a tenable assumption because the goods market and the money market interact with one another.

One of the most influential discussions of the interplay of the demand and supply of money and the demand and supply of goods is due to J. M. Keynes. Keynes assumed that the market for goods and services is adjusted to equilibrium by changes in the level of national income (as described in the simple macroeconomic model of Section 3.8) and that the money market is adjusted to equilibrium by changes in the rate of interest. The interaction between the money market and the goods market is due to the fact that the rate of interest not only equates the demand and supply of money but also measures the opportunity cost of investing in goods rather than in bonds or other financial assets. As a result, the higher is the rate of interest the greater is the investment in bonds and the lower is the investment in goods such as plant and machinery. The hypothesis that investment demand for goods and services varies inversely with the rate of interest is exemplified by the functional relationship below.

The demand for investment goods, $I(t)$, is proportional to the reciprocal of the current rate of interest, $r(t)$:

(1) $$I(t) = d/r(t)$$

where $d > 0$.

The rate of interest is determined by demand and supply in the money market. According to Keynes there are two primary determinants of the demand for money: the transactions demand and the speculative demand. The transactions demand is the demand for purposes of trade and is proportional to the value of goods and services which change hands, i.e. the transactions demand for money is proportional to the national income. The speculative demand for money arises from the role of money as low-risk asset which provides a hedge against a fall in the price of bonds. Keynes argued that if the rate of interest is low then an increase is very probable; since an increase in the rate of interest reduces the price of bonds the risk in holding bonds at low rates of interest is very high. It follows that when the rate of interest is low the demand for money will be large because of speculation concerning the rate of interest. On these grounds Keynes postulated that the speculative demand for money varies inversely with the rate of interest.

The demand for money may be described mathematically in the following way

The transactions demand for money in any period t, $L_1(t)$, is directly proportional to the national income in the same period,

(2) $$L_1(t) = eY(t)$$

where $e > 0$ is a constant of proportionality. If prices are constant then $1/e$ measures the number of times money changes hands each period: it is known as 'the velocity of circulation' of money.

The speculative demand for money in any period t, $L_2(t)$, varies as the reciprocal of the rate of interest, r(t),

$$(3) \qquad L_2(t) = f/r(t) \qquad r(t) > r_{\min} > 0$$

where $f > 0$. However, at some minimum rate of interest the speculative demand for money becomes indefinitely large,

$$r(t) = r_{\min} \quad \text{if} \quad L_2(t) \geqslant f/r_{\min}$$

When the rate of interest takes on its minimum value the economy is said to be 'in the liquidity trap'.

The aggregate supply of money, $M(t)$, is usually taken to be exogenously determined by government policy. This assumption is often unreasonable in situations in which a considerable amount of 'near money' is created by the financial sector of the economy: for example, in inflation.

10.6 Equilibrium in a Keynesian economy

For the economy as a whole to be in equilibrium it is necessary that both the goods market and the money market are in equilibrium.

There will be equilibrium in the money market in period t if and only if

Planned demand for money in period t = Planned supply of money in period t, i.e. if and only if

$$L_1(t) + L_2(t) = M(t)$$

which, by using equations (2) and (3), becomes

$$(4) \qquad eY(t) + f/r(t) = M(t) \qquad r(t) > r_{\min} > 0$$

This is the equation of the so-called '*LM* curve'.

There will be equilibrium in the goods market in period t if and only if

Planned aggregate demand for goods in period t
= Planned aggregate supply of goods in period t

Suppose that in the short run aggregate supply is adjusted to meet aggregate demand, so that planned aggregate demand in period t is measured by actual supply, $Y(t)$. If planned aggregate supply in period t is equal to the actual supply in the previous period, $Y(t - 1)$, then the equilibrium condition requires that

$$(5) \qquad Y(t) = Y(t - 1)$$

If foreign trade is ignored, planned aggregate demand in period t is

$$Y(t) = C(t) + I(t) + G(t)$$

which, by using equation (1) together with the consumption function

$$C(t) = b + cY(t - 1)$$

becomes

$$Y(t) = b + cY(t-1) + d/r(t) + G(t) \qquad r(t) > r_{\min} > 0$$

On substituting in the equilibrium condition (5) and rearranging terms we get

$$(6) \qquad (1-c)Y(t) - d/r(t) = G(t) + b \qquad r(t) > r_{\min} > 0$$

This is the equation of the so-called '*IS* curve'.

The economy is in equilibrium when the goods market and the money market are simultaneously in equilibrium. Consequently, the conditions for equilibrium are given by the simultaneous equations (4), (6),

$$(7) \qquad \begin{aligned} eY(t) + f[1/r(t)] &= M(t) \\ (1-c)Y(t) - d[1/r(t)] &= G(t) + b \end{aligned} \qquad r(t) > r_{\min} > 0$$

Although these equations are not linear in $Y(t)$ and $r(t)$, they are linear in the variables $Y(t)$ and $1/r(t)$. Because of this, it is possible to examine quite simply the general properties of economic equilibrium in the Keynesian model of the closed economy.

Example (see Fig. 10B). The marginal propensity to consume is $\frac{3}{4}$. The transactions demand for money equals $\frac{1}{2}$ the national income. The parameters determining the speculative demand for money and the investment demand for goods are respectively $f = 200$, $d = 100$. Income is measured in units of £m and the rate of interest is measured as a percentage per annum. The minimum rate of interest is $2\frac{1}{2}\%$.

If the stock of money is £140m, government expenditure is £20m and autonomous consumption is £10m, find the equilibrium income and the equilibrium rate of interest.

To begin with, assume that the economy is not in the liquidity trap. Direct substitution into equations (7) shows that

$$(8) \qquad 0{\cdot}5Y(t) + 200[1/r(t)] = 140$$

$$(9) \qquad 0{\cdot}25Y(t) - 100[1/r(t)] = 30$$

Subtracting twice equation (9) from equation (8) gives

$$400[1/r(t)] = 80$$

so that $1/r(t) = 0{\cdot}2$ and hence $r(t) = 5$. Since the rate of interest is $5\% > 2\frac{1}{2}\%$, the economy is not in the liquidity trap and the equation of equilibrium in the money market is correctly specified. Substituting the result $r = 5$ into the equation (8) gives

$$0{\cdot}5Y(t) + 40 = 140$$

so that $Y(t) = 200$. It follows that the equilibrium income is £200m and the equilibrium rate of interest is 5%.

The equations of equilibrium are plotted graphically in Fig. 10B. The *LM* curve shows the condition for equilibrium in the money market and the *IS* curve the condition for equilibrium in the goods market. The intersection of the curves determines the equilibrium income and the equilibrium rate of interest.

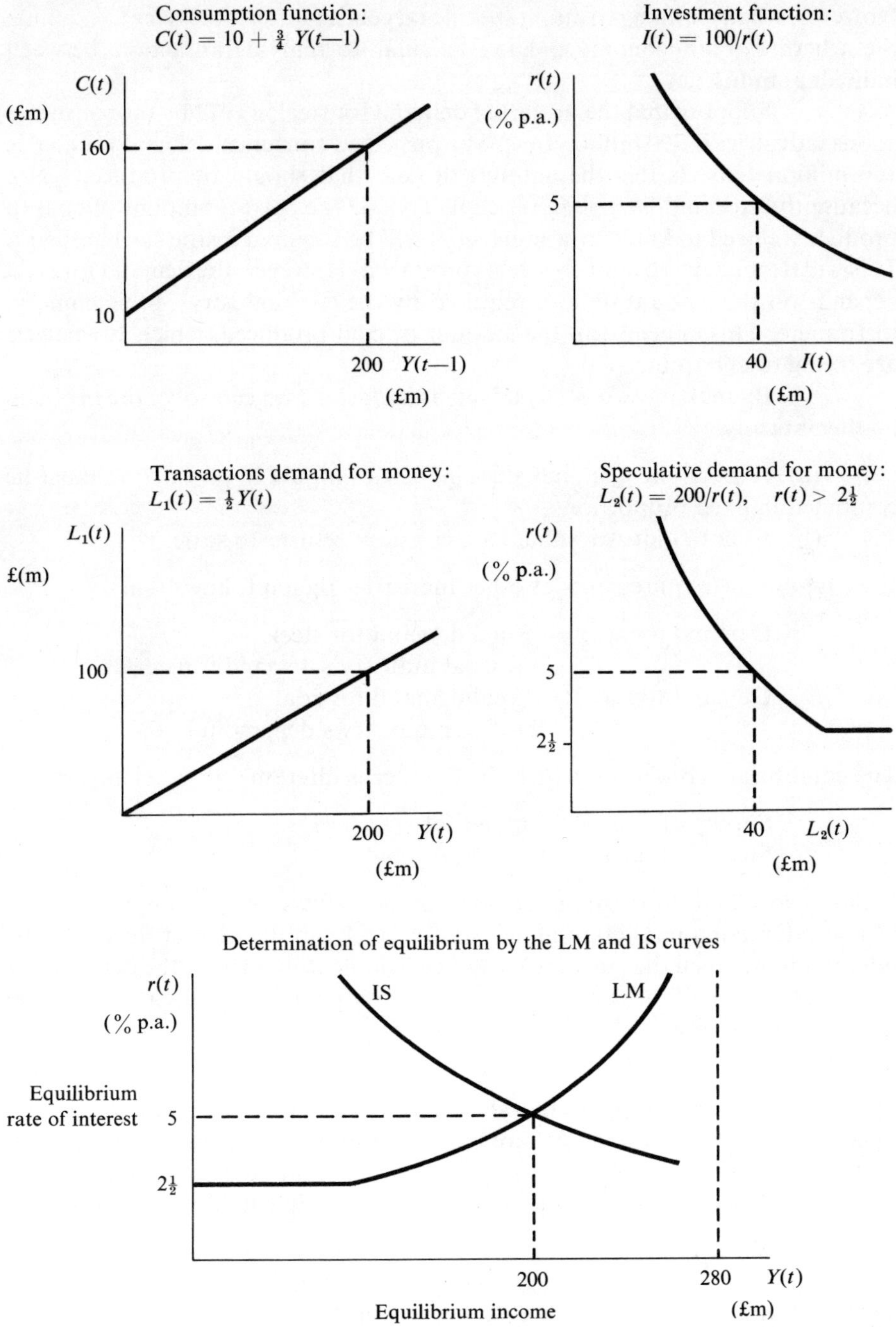

Fig. 10B Equilibrium of an economy with a goods market and a money market

10.7 Inter-industry transactions

So far the discussion in this chapter has been confined to the behaviour of economic aggregates such as national income, the balance of payments, etc. However, when planning to attain specific targets it is often necessary to examine the structure of the economy and, in particular, to analyse transactions between individual industries.

Suppose that the projected demand for steel in 1972 by the consumer goods industries is 200 million tons. The projected consumer demand for coal is 160 million tons. Is this the amount of coal that should be produced? No, because the steel industry requires coal. To find the correct amount of coal to produce we need to know how much coal will be required by the steel industry. This will depend on how much steel is produced. However, the demand for steel depends on the amount of steel required by the coal industry—in machinery, lorries, etc. This depends on the amount of coal produced, which is what we are trying to determine.

By making two quite strong assumptions we can solve the problem mathematically.

(a) In both the coal and steel industries inputs to production must be combined in fixed proportions.

(b) In both industries there are constant returns to scale.

If we ignore the requirements of other industries then it follows that

Demand for steel = Final demand for steel
+ Coal industry's demand for steel
Demand for coal = Final demand for coal
+ Steel industry's demand for coal

The equilibrium conditions which the planner is interested in satisfying are

Supply of steel = Demand for steel
Supply of coal = Demand for coal

It can be seen that the planning problem involves the simultaneous equilibrium of two interacting markets: the market for steel and the market for coal. The interaction between the markets arises because a component of the demand for steel is a function of the supply of coal and a component of the demand for coal is a function of supply of steel.

Example Suppose that 0·1 tons of steel are needed to produce 1 ton of coal and that 0·4 tons of coal are required to produce 1 ton of steel. Let the output of steel be X_1 and the output of coal be X_2 (in units of a million tons).

The condition for the steel market to be in equilibrium is that

$$X_1 = 200 + 0{\cdot}1X_2$$

The condition for the coal market to be in equilibrium is that

$$X_2 = 160 + 0{\cdot}4X_1$$

Consequently, both the steel market and the coal market will be in equilibrium when

$$X_1 - 0{\cdot}1X_2 = 200$$
$$-0{\cdot}4X_1 + X_2 = 160$$

These equations can be solved algebraically for X_1 and X_2, but it is more instructive to solve them graphically (see Fig. 10C).

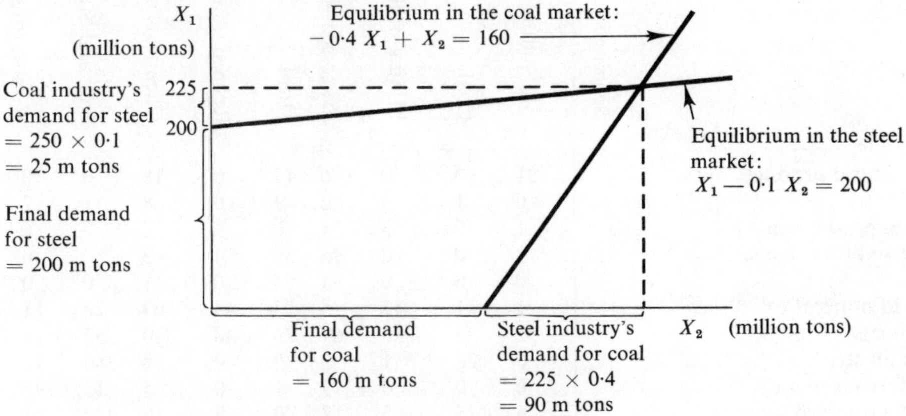

Fig. 10C Equilibrium of inter-industry transactions

The graphical solution indicates that 225m tons of steel should be produced, 200m tons for final demand and 25m tons for the coal industry; 250m tons of coal should be produced, 160m tons to meet final demand, and 90m tons to meet the requirements of the steel industry.

The solution can be represented in the form of Table 10.1.

Table 10.1 Tabular representation of the equilibrium of inter-industry transactions (units £m)

	Supply to			
Demand for	*Steel*	*Coal*	*Final demand*	*Total output*
Steel	—	25	200	225
Coal	90	—	160	250

The pattern of inter-industry transactions has been studied in detail for many countries. By estimating the input requirements of each industry and then forecasting the final demands for output it is possible to determine the equilibrium output for each industry in the economy, and thereby the equilibrium matrix of interindustry transactions.

Projections of the input requirements per unit output of industries in the United Kingdom are shown in Table 10.2. By combining these 'input-output coefficients' with projections of final demand to 1972 it is possible to determine

Table 10.2 Coefficients of input per unit output for 25 UK industries, projected to 1972

Supply to → / *Demand for* ↓	Agricultural products n.e.s.	Coal	Mining products n.e.s.	Processed foods n.e.s.	Drink	Refined mineral oil	Chemicals n.e.s.	Iron and Steel	Non-ferrous metals
Agricultural products n.e.s.	21	0	0	176	17	0	18	0	0
Coal	0	1	5	2	3	0	8	1	2
Mining products n.e.s.	1	0	3	1	0	4	12	0	6
Processed food n.e.s.	1	0	0	96	55	0	3	0	0
Drink	0	0	0	4	54	0	1	0	0
Refined mineral oil	21	1	42	5	23	44	9	26	11
Chemicals n.e.s.	52	21	36	67	25	40	320	37	11
Iron and steel	0	28	1	3	0	0	2	280	12
Non-ferrous metals	0	0	0	2	1	0	5	15	395
Engineering products	24	45	45	18	20	8	13	24	21
Metal goods n.e.s.	20	15	3	44	19	5	19	25	12
Textiles n.e.s.	1	5	0	3	1	0	3	1	1
Leather, clothing and footwear	1	3	0	0	0	0	1	1	0
Building materials	2	7	1	0	0	4	3	7	1
Timber, furniture etc.	1	11	5	4	4	0	5	3	1
Paper, printing and publishing n.e.s.	2	3	14	39	6	2	14	2	3
Rubber products	3	25	3	0	1	0	2	1	1
Manufactures n.e.s.	4	3	0	3	4	0	6	1	2
Construction	24	40	1	4	7	4	5	6	2
Gas	16	0	0	2	2	5	20	27	5
Electricity	14	26	41	8	14	13	20	30	18
Water	0	0	1	1	1	0	1	0	0
Transport and communications	43	24	118	33	20	6	33	46	21
Distribution	37	18	37	24	20	2	18	25	35
Services	28	22	25	40	25	9	39	30	45

SOURCE Adapted from *A Programme for Growth, No. 9: Exploring 1972*, Department of Applied Economics, University of Cambridge, and Chapman & Hall, London 1970, Appendix 2.

NOTE Inputs and outputs are measured in value terms. Each coefficient in the table measures the value of the input (in £) required per £1,000 of output (at 1960 prices). The coefficient in the *i*th row and *j*th column measures the value (in £) of the products of the *i*th industry that are required to produce £1,000 of output in the *j*th industry. The sum of the coefficients in each column is less than 1,000; this indicates that in each industry £1,000 of goods can be produced at a cost, in inputs from other industries, of less than £1,000. Thus production in each industry increases the value of the goods used up in production.

the equilibrium output of each industry in 1972. To evaluate the equilibrium output for each of the 25 industries which appear in Table 10.2 it is necessary to solve a set of 25 simultaneous linear equations in 25 unknowns. The set of equilibrium outputs is the target of a simple national economic plan.

Engineering products	Metal goods n.e.s.	Textiles n.e.s.	Leather, clothing & footwear	Building materials	Timber, furniture etc.	Paper, printing & publishing n.e.s.	Rubber products	Manufactures n.e.s.	Construction	Gas	Electricity	Water	Transport & communications	Distribution	Services n.e.s.
0	0	0	32	0	1	0	38	2	0	0	0	0	0	0	0
1	1	0	0	19	0	1	2	1	0	26	117	3	0	0	0
1	1	2	0	92	0	0	1	2	13	1	0	0	0	1	0
0	0	1	0	0	0	3	0	0	0	0	0	0	4	0	0
0	0	0	0	0	0	0	0	0	0	0	0	0	2	3	0
4	8	7	4	68	5	6	2	3	5	87	107	32	22	26	8
25	8	16	8	32	29	29	290	205	30	12	3	3	7	10	2
83	276	0	0	6	2	0	3	12	39	57	2	52	5	0	0
55	94	2	0	1	2	7	3	4	18	1	1	7	0	1	0
163	19	13	7	33	11	14	17	22	34	29	45	7	6	3	34
50	111	5	20	8	38	4	22	39	19	6	3	2	2	6	14
4	0	483	320	3	29	2	115	40	1	0	0	0	1	8	3
1	0	5	130	0	4	1	2	3	1	0	0	0	1	2	0
4	1	0	0	52	2	0	3	6	108	4	4	9	2	1	0
12	8	1	4	7	314	0	2	11	35	1	2	0	3	7	1
12	5	5	13	49	2	45	15	28	6	2	2	5	2	35	82
5	4	3	9	1	9	1	66	4	1	0	2	0	10	5	9
11	9	1	20	1	2	2	11	8	6	0	2	0	6	16	8
3	2	6	5	6	5	5	6	7	172	5	2	7	16	18	13
3	8	2	4	1	3	8	3	9	1	172	27	0	0	8	7
12	13	12	8	34	11	7	27	24	3	15	57	73	2	19	20
0	0	1	0	2	0	0	1	1	1	1	1	34	0	6	1
16	18	25	17	35	31	30	23	24	27	28	35	15	91	30	8
14	15	22	19	25	48	31	25	30	22	16	15	5	21	30	10
29	28	22	28	45	56	53	28	35	40	13	18	31	24	28	20

10.8 Equilibrium conditions where the number of equations exceeds the number of unknowns

So far we have only discussed cases in which the equilibrium conditions consist of the same number of equations as unknowns. Although such cases are very frequent in practice, the most challenging economic problems are usually cases in which the number of equations exceeds the number of unknowns. We give below two simple examples, one in the field of international trade, the other in national economic planning.

Example 1 Consider again the trading relations between countries 1 and 2, as described in Section 10.2. Suppose that the aim of economic policy in each country is not only to attain an equilibrium of aggregate demand and supply, but also to attain an equilibrium in the balance of payments, in the sense that the net payments abroad from each country are zero.

Let the annual payment on capital account from country 1 to country 2 be £Z million. We suppose this to be exogenously determined. On current account, the value of country 2's exports to country 1 is £$m_1 Y_1$ million, and the value of country 1's exports to country 2 is £$m_2 Y_2$ million. The net payment from country 1 to country 2 on current account is therefore £$(m_1 Y_1 - m_2 Y_2)$ million. If the balance of payments between the two countries is to be zero, it is necessary that the payments on current account balance the payments on capital account, i.e. it is necessary that

$$m_1 Y_1 - m_2 Y_2 = -Z$$

The first question which suggests itself is: is it possible for there to be an equilibrium of aggregate supply and demand in each country and, simultaneously, an equilibrium in the balance of payments? The conditions for an equilibrium of supply and demand in each country are given by equations (6) of Section 10.3; combining these equations with the balance of payments equation gives a new set of equilibrium conditions:

$$\begin{aligned} (1 - c_1 + m_1)Y_1 \qquad\qquad & - m_2 Y_2 = E_1 \\ - m_1 Y_1 + (1 - c_2 &+ m_2)Y_2 = E_2 \\ - m_1 Y_1 \qquad\qquad & + m_2 Y_2 = Z \end{aligned}$$

These conditions are three linear equations in two unknowns. If they have a solution, there exists an international equilibrium such that the balance of payments in each country is zero. If they have no solution then one country must necessarily run a balance of payments deficit. The mathematical results of Chapter 12 suggest that in almost every case a balance of payments equilibrium is impossible unless either prices or exchange rates are flexible.

Example 2 A reconsideration of the theory of inter-industry transactions shows that this theory can be used to plan for the full employment of labour. In our earlier discussion (see Section 10.7) we assumed that the only scarce inputs into the productive process in each industry were the goods and services produced by other industries. In most circumstances, however, labour is also a scarce input; furthermore, it is often reasonable to suppose that labour, like other inputs, must be combined in fixed proportions in the productive process.[(1)] If we retain the assumption of constant returns to scale in production, and assume that labour is a necessary input, then we can describe the productive process in a two-commodity economy in the following way. To produce one unit of commodity 1 requires m_{11} units of commodity 1, m_{21} units of commodity 2 and m_{31} units of labour (measured in, say, man-hours); to produce one unit of commodity 2 requires m_{12} units of commodity 1, m_{22} units of commodity 2 and m_{32} units of labour.

1 Sometimes it is assumed that labour and capital are substitutable.

Let the final demand for the commodities be y_1, y_2, and let y_3 be the number of man-hours worked at full employment. Let the outputs of commodities 1 and 2 be x_1, x_2. Equilibrium in the market for commodity 1 requires that

$$m_{11}x_1 + m_{12}x_2 + y_1 = x_1$$

Equilibrium in the market for commodity 2 requires that

$$m_{21}x_1 + m_{22}x_2 + y_2 = x_2$$

Equilibrium in the labour market, i.e. full employment without excess demand for labour, requires that

$$m_{31}x_1 + m_{32}x_2 = y_3$$

The conditions for there to be equilibrium in every market are three simultaneous linear equations in the two unknown outputs x_1, x_2:

$$\begin{aligned} (1 - m_{11})x_1 \quad & - m_{12}\,x_2 = y_1 \\ - m_{21}\,x_1 + & (1 - m_{22})x_2 = y_2 \\ m_{31}\,x_1 \quad & + m_{32}\,x_2 = y_3 \end{aligned}$$

Only if there is a solution to these equations is it possible both to have full employment and to meet the planned final demands.

Although this is only a very simple model, it has the following important implication: a government plan which specifies the target values of final demand for various commodities has definite implications for the demand for labour. It is possible that the plan may imply a socially unacceptable level of unemployment; it is also possible that the plan may not be feasible (if the demand for labour exceeds the supply). If the demand for labour is disaggregated into the demand for various skills, one can make a detailed assessment of the likely shortages (if any) of skilled labour and the shortages and surpluses (if any) of unskilled labour that may arise as a result of implementing the plan. By using this information it is possible to decide whether it will be necessary to retrain some workers whose skills are in excess supply, and whether such retraining will be adequate to meet the excess demand for other skills.

10.9 Generalization to many markets

The condition that a market is in equilibrium can often be expressed as a linear equation, as shown for example in Chapter 3. In this chapter we have examined economies with two or three interacting markets, and in every case the condition that all the interacting markets are in equilibrium has been expressed by a set of simultaneous linear equations in two unknowns.

It is possible to generalize the analysis of this chapter to economies with any number of interacting markets, e.g. to trade between any number of countries, to transactions between any number of industries. In such cases the condition that m interacting markets are simultaneously in equilibrium is expressed by a set of m simultaneous linear equations in n economic variables.

Consequently, to find the equilibrium values of economic variables it is necessary to solve a set of m simultaneous linear equations of the form

$$\begin{aligned} a_{11}x_1 + a_{12}x_2 + \cdots + a_{1n}x_n &= y_1 \\ a_{21}x_1 + a_{22}x_2 + \cdots + a_{2n}x_n &= y_2 \\ \vdots \qquad \vdots \qquad\qquad \vdots \quad &\quad \vdots \\ a_{m1}x_1 + a_{m2}x_2 + \cdots + a_{mn}x_n &= y_n \end{aligned}$$

for the values of $x_1, x_2, \ldots, x_n$.

In order to discuss the general properties of the solutions of simultaneous linear equations it is useful to develop the algebra of vectors and matrices.

Notes and references

Mathematical investigations of the equilibrium of interacting markets have a long history, dating from the second half of the nineteenth century. In 1874 Leon Walras, a Frenchman who was a professor at Lausanne, published the first part of *Éléments d'économie Politique Pure*, in which he discussed the determination of prices and outputs in a perfectly competitive economy with several commodity markets. The equilibrium conditions for this economy were a set of simultaneous (but not, in general, linear) equations in an equal number of unknowns. Walras and his immediate successors did not discuss the existence of a unique equilibrium; it was often implicitly assumed that the economy would necessarily have a unique equilibrium provided that the mathematical formulation was economically reasonable. For a review of Walras' work see Hicks,[57] pp. 1–4 and Ch. 4.

The application of this general equilibrium analysis was extended when, in 1936, Keynes' *General Theory of Employment, Interest and Money* was published, J. R. Hicks (now Sir John Hicks) was working on a theory similar to Keynes', but based on an extension of Walras' theory. Hicks put Keynes' theory into Walras' framework, or, more strictly, into the framework of Walras' follower Wicksell (see Hicks[58]). By analysing the economy in terms of the interaction of the goods market and the money market, Hicks obtained two conditions for economic equilibrium; equilibrium in the money market required the economy to be on the *LM* curve and equilibrium in the goods market required the economy to be on the *IS* curve. Equilibrium in the economy as a whole required the economy to be at the intersection of the two curves. Algebraically, the equations of the *LM* and *IS* curves provided two simultaneous equations which were to be solved for the two unknowns, the equilibrium income and the equilibrium rate of interest. The application of general equilibrium analysis to the study of money and interest was developed in greater detail by Patinkin.[98]

The monetary aspects of the simple Keynesian model are outlined in Brooman,[21] Ch. 7, 10, Dernburg and McDougall,[34] Ch. 7–10, 15 and Kurihara,[72], Ch. 3, 4.

A further extension of general equilibrium analysis, this time to the determination of international prices and the terms of trade, was made by Mosak[93] in 1944.

All the theories mentioned above involved simultaneous nonlinear equations. The restriction to the case of linear equations was pioneered by Leontief[76] in the study of interindustry transactions and by Metzler[85, 86] in the study of the international economy. It was the work of Leontief and Metzler which demonstrated the importance of matrix algebra to the economist.

For the economic background to international trade see Brooman,[21] Ch. 8, Lipsey,[81] Ch. 46 and Samuelson,[113] Ch. 33; further references are given at the end of Chapter 13.

The early work of Leontief stimulated the development of 'input-output analysis'. A very readable survey is Miernyk;[89] this book provides a good background to this chapter and to Chapter 13 (see also Samuelson,[113] Ch. 38 Appendix). The application of input-output analysis to the specific case of interindustry transactions is described in Chenery and Clark.[25] The pioneering work in this field is Leontief.[76] Tables of input-output coefficients are usually produced by official bodies (government departments, United Nations, etc.) but several are reproduced in well-known text books: see Allen,[7] pp. 346, 355, for UK (1935), US (1947), Griffin and Enos,[45] p. 32, for Tanzania 1961, Klein,[71] p. 132, for UK (1954), Lange,[73] pp. 335–338, for UK (1935), US (1947), Poland (1956–59). The use of input-output tables for national economic planning is described in

Stone,[117] and more recently in Stone.[118] Applications of input-output analysis to particular regions are described in Hansen and Tiebout[50] (California), Moore and Petersen[91] (Utah), Nevin[96] (Wales), Parker[97] (Western Australia), Rasul[109] (Pakistan) and Wright[125] (Alberta). One of the most fruitful applications of input-output analysis has been to urban areas: see Artle[10] (Stockholm), Chatterji[24] (Calcutta), Hirsch[59] (St. Louis) and Isard, Langford and Romanoff[63] (Philadelphia). For a selection of readings see Barna;[11] for other references see the Input-Output Bibliography.[61] The methods of input-output analysis are also used in industrial complex analysis: see Isard, Schooler and Vietorisz,[64] especially Ch. 3.

Problems

10.1 How do you think the market for beef interacts with the market for lamb? Explain using a simple dynamic model. Derive the equilibrium conditions for your model.

10.3 You are given the following information about trade between Britain (country 1) and the rest of the world (country 2). The marginal propensities to consume are $c_1 = 0{\cdot}6$, $c_2 = 1{\cdot}0$. The marginal propensities to import are $m_1 = 0{\cdot}2$, $m_2 = 0{\cdot}4$. Exogenous demand is £200m in Britain and £400m in the rest of the world. Find the equilibrium incomes in Britain and the rest of the world.

10.4 (**10.3** continued) (a) Government expenditure in the rest of the world is increased permanently by £100m. How does this change the equilibrium incomes in Britain and the rest of the world?

(b) What is the effect of this change on the British balance of trade?

(c) Suppose that Britain pays foreign aid at a rate of £100m per annum to the rest of the world for expenditure on capital projects. How does this foreign aid influence the British balance of payments?

10.7.1 To produce 1 lorry requires 0·5 tons of steel. To produce 1 ton of steel requires 0·2 lorries. If the final demand for lorries is 1,000 per week and the final demand for steel is 4,000 tons per week, then (a) what would you, as an economic planner, set as the target outputs of lorries and steel? (b) according to your plan, what would be the supply of lorries to the steel industry? Illustrate your answers graphically.

10.6 The rate of interest in the liquidity trap is $2\frac{1}{2}\%$. Above this the speculative demand for money (in £m) is a function, $150/r$, of the rate of interest, $r\%$. The transactions demand for money is equal to a quarter of the national income. Investment is a function, $75/r$, of the rate of interest, and the marginal propensity to consume is $\frac{3}{4}$. Show that if government expenditure is £5m and the money supply is £100m, the economy is in the liquidity trap and the equilibrium income is £140m. Show that if government expenditure is increased by £20m the equilibrium income is £200m and the equilibrium rate of interest is 3%.

10.7.2 The economy of a small country is divided for planning purposes into three sectors: extractive industries, manufacturing industries and service industries. The output of any one of these sectors requires as inputs a certain amount of the output of the other two. To produce one unit of output in the extractive industries requires 0·1 units of manufacturing output and 0·1 units of service output. One unit of manufactures needs 0·2 units of extractive output and 0·2 units of service output. One unit of service output needs 0·1 units of extractive output and 0·2 units of manufacturing output. If an economic plan requires 924m units of extractive products, 1,386m units of manufactures and 462m units of service products, how much should each sector produce?

10.7.3 A, B, and C are three countries which trade together. A has a highly developed technology and exports sophisticated durable goods to B and C. B has large resources of oil and exports partly refined oil to A and C. C has the facility to generate large amounts of electric power which it exports by transmission cables to B and C. In the next year final demand by government and consumers is expected to be as follows.

		Final demand		
		Country A	*Country* B	*Country* C
Products (number of units)	Durable goods	750	500	500
	Oil	1,000	1,500	1,000
	Electricity	1,500	0	2,000

Each unit of durable goods output requires 0·3 units of oil and 0·3 units of electricity. Each unit of oil output requires 0·1 units of durable goods and 0·2 units of electricity. Each unit of electric power output requires 0·2 units of durable goods and 0·1 units of oil.

(a) What outputs of durable goods, oil and electricity are required to meet final demand?

(b) Each industry has certain fixed costs independent of the level of output. For durable goods, oil and electricity these costs are respectively £17·64m, £8·85m and £19·32m. The only other costs incurred are due to the products of other industries which are used up in production. If price = average cost for each commodity find the prices of durable goods, oil and electricity. (*Hint:* formulate a set of simultaneous equations in the unknown prices.)

(c) Find each country's balance of trade [= Value of exports − Value of imports].

10.9.1 The demand for skilled car workers, D_s (in units of 1,000 men) depends on the price of cars, P (in units of £1,000), the wage rate for skilled car workers, W_s (in £1,000 per annum) and the wage rate for unskilled car workers, W_u (in £1,000 per annum). The supply of skilled workers depends on the price of cars, P, the wage for unskilled workers, W_u, and the wage rate for skilled workers, W_s. The supply of unskilled workers depends on the wage rate, W_u.

If the demand and supply functions are

$$\begin{aligned} D_s &= 28 + 14P + 5W_u - 10W_s \\ S_s &= 6 + 12W_s \\ D_u &= 40 + 20P - 15W_u + 2W_s \\ S_u &= 8 + 20W_u \end{aligned}$$

and the price of cars is £1,000, find the equilibrium wage rates for skilled and unskilled workers and the total employment in the car industry.

10.9.2 Patients in the surgical ward of a hospital are classified into two types according to the amount of nursing care they need. Those needing intensive care are in beds in the main area of the ward. When they no longer need such intensive care they are moved into peripheral beds. A hospital has 60 intensive care beds and 165 peripheral beds. Patients are admitted to the ward as emergencies or as booked admissions. Emergency patients stay in the ward an average number of 25 days, averaging 10 days in intensive care beds. Booked admissions also stay in the ward an average of 25 days but average only 5 days in intensive care beds. How many emergency cases should be sent to this particular hospital if all the beds are to be fully occupied?

10.9.3 Solve the following equations for x_1, x_2, x_3:

$$\begin{aligned} x_1 + x_2 + x_3 &= 6 \\ 2x_1 + x_2 + 3x_3 &= 8 \\ x_1 + 2x_2 + 4x_3 &= 12 \end{aligned}$$

Can you find x_1, x_2 from the equations

$$\begin{aligned} 3x_1 + 2x_2 &= 6 \\ 6x_1 + 4x_2 &= 12 \end{aligned}$$

Elucidate your answer graphically.

Chapter 11

Introduction to matrix algebra

11.1 Vectors and matrices

The simultaneous linear equations derived in the first part of the previous chapter are special cases of the general form

$$a_{11}x_1 + a_{12}x_2 = y_1$$
$$a_{21}x_1 + a_{22}x_2 = y_2$$

in which x_1 and x_2 are unknowns to be found by solving the equations. In the notation of vectors and matrices these equations become

$$\begin{bmatrix} a_{11} & a_{12} \\ a_{21} & a_{22} \end{bmatrix} \begin{bmatrix} x_1 \\ x_2 \end{bmatrix} = \begin{bmatrix} y_1 \\ y_2 \end{bmatrix}$$

We say that

$$\begin{bmatrix} a_{11} & a_{12} \\ a_{21} & a_{22} \end{bmatrix}$$

is a '2 × 2 matrix', i.e., it is a matrix with 2 rows and 2 columns; we say that

$$\begin{bmatrix} x_1 \\ x_2 \end{bmatrix} \quad \text{and} \quad \begin{bmatrix} y_1 \\ y_2 \end{bmatrix}$$

are '2-element column vectors', the elements being, respectively, x_1, x_2 and y_1, y_2. The matrix

$$\begin{bmatrix} a_{11} & a_{12} \\ a_{21} & a_{22} \end{bmatrix}$$

(which we shall call 'the matrix **A**') may be regarded as two column vectors

$$\begin{bmatrix} a_{11} \\ a_{21} \end{bmatrix} \quad \text{and} \quad \begin{bmatrix} a_{12} \\ a_{22} \end{bmatrix}$$

put side by side, or as two 'row vectors'

$$\begin{bmatrix} a_{11} & a_{12} \end{bmatrix} \quad \text{and} \quad \begin{bmatrix} a_{21} & a_{22} \end{bmatrix}$$

put on top of one another. By convention, the elements of a matrix are labelled so that the first subscript indicates the row and the second subscript indicates the column in which the element appears.

Vectors and matrices at this stage are only a notation for simultaneous equations. Given the three equations

$$0{\cdot}5x_1 - 0{\cdot}2x_2 + 0{\cdot}1x_3 = y_1$$

$$0{\cdot}3x_1 + 0{\cdot}4x_2 - 0{\cdot}5x_3 = y_2$$

$$0{\cdot}1x_1 + 0{\cdot}2x_2 + 0{\cdot}2x_3 = y_3$$

these are written in matrix notation simply by moving the repeated row of subscripted x's over to the right-hand side and arranging them downwards in a column thus:

$$\begin{bmatrix} 0{\cdot}5 & -0{\cdot}2 & 0{\cdot}1 \\ 0{\cdot}3 & 0{\cdot}4 & -0{\cdot}5 \\ 0{\cdot}1 & 0{\cdot}2 & 0{\cdot}2 \end{bmatrix} \begin{bmatrix} x_1 \\ x_2 \\ x_3 \end{bmatrix} = \begin{bmatrix} y_1 \\ y_2 \\ y_3 \end{bmatrix}$$

We put the arrays of numbers in brackets, and use only one equals sign.

If we regard vectors and matrices as mathematical entities, then we may interpret the expression above as just one equation relating to vectors and matrices; in this case we should say that 'the 3×3 matrix of coefficients is multiplied into the 3-element column vector $\mathbf{x}$ and the result is equal to the 3-element column vector $\mathbf{y}$'. The use of the phrase 'multiplied into' is explained by the definition below.

11.2 Multiplication of vectors and matrices

A vector is a special case of a matrix; a column vector is a matrix with only one column, a row vector is a matrix with only one row. A general definition of matrix multiplication will apply, therefore, not only to the multiplication of one matrix into another but to the multiplication of a matrix into a vector, a vector into a matrix, and a vector into a vector.

The principles of matrix multiplications are illustrated by the multiplication of a 2×2 matrix $\mathbf{A}$ into a 2×2 matrix $\mathbf{B}$.

Definition Let $\mathbf{A}$ and $\mathbf{B}$ be the matrices

$$\mathbf{A} = \begin{bmatrix} a_{11} & a_{12} \\ a_{21} & a_{22} \end{bmatrix}, \qquad \mathbf{B} = \begin{bmatrix} b_{11} & b_{12} \\ b_{21} & b_{22} \end{bmatrix}$$

and let $\mathbf{C}$ be the result of multiplying $\mathbf{A}$ into $\mathbf{B}$. The matrix equation

$$\mathbf{AB} = \mathbf{C}$$

means that $\mathbf{C}$ is a 2×2 matrix

$$\mathbf{C} = \begin{bmatrix} c_{11} & c_{12} \\ c_{21} & c_{22} \end{bmatrix}$$

in which

$$c_{11} = a_{11}b_{11} + a_{12}b_{21}; \qquad c_{12} = a_{11}b_{12} + a_{12}b_{22}$$

$$c_{21} = a_{21}b_{11} + a_{22}b_{21}; \qquad c_{22} = a_{21}b_{12} + a_{22}b_{22}$$

While it is difficult to remember the exact expressions for the elements of **C** it is very easy to remember the rule by which these expressions are obtained.

To obtain the element in the *first row* and *first column* of **C** consider only the *first row* of **A** and the *first column* of **B**. Working progressively along the row of **A** and down the column of **B**, pair off the first term in the row with the first term in the column, and the second term in the row with the second term in the column. Multiply the paired terms together, add the resulting products, and set the sum equal to c_{11}. To obtain the element in the *first row* and *second column* of **C** consider the *first row* of **A** and the *second column* of **B**. Working along the row of **A** and down the column of **B**, pair off the terms in the way described above, multiply the paired terms together, sum the products and set the answer equal to c_{12}. The top row of the matrix **C** is now complete. To obtain the element in the *second row* and *first column* of **C**, consider the *second row of* **A** and the *first column* of **B**. Pair off the terms, multiply the paired terms together and set the sum of the products equal to c_{21}. Finally, to obtain the element in the *second row* and *second column* of **C**, pair off and multiply the terms in the *second row* of **A** and the *second column* of **B**, and set the sum of the products equal to c_{22}. To simplify further discussion, the operation of taking a row and a column, multiplying paired terms and summing the products, will be called, for short, 'multiplying a row into a column'.

Suppose that **A** is a matrix with m rows and n columns, and that **B** is a matrix with p rows and q columns. Multiplication of **A** into **B** is defined only when the pairing of terms described above can be carried out. Now the rows of **A** are to be multiplied into the columns of **B**; for exact pairing to be possible it is necessary that the number of terms in each row of **A** is equal to the number of terms in each column of **B**. The number of terms in each row of **A** is the number of columns in **A**, which is n. The number of terms in each column of **B** is the number of rows in **B**, which is p. For the matrix multiplication to be defined it is therefore necessary that $n = p$.

Let the result of multiplying the matrix **A** into the matrix **B** be the matrix **C**. According to the general rule for matrix multiplication, the elements of **C** may be calculated using the following table.

Table 11.1 Table to find the elements of the matrix **C**

c_{11}		1st		1st		1st		1st	
⋮		⋮		⋮		⋮		⋮	
c_{1q}		1st		qth	column	1st		qth	
c_{21}	is the	2nd		1st	of **C**;	2nd	row of	1st	column
⋮	element	⋮	row and	⋮	to find it,	⋮	**A** into	⋮	of **B**
c_{2q}	in the	2nd		qth	multiply	2nd	the	qth	
⋮		⋮		⋮	the	⋮		⋮	
c_{p1}		pth		1st		pth		1st	
⋮		⋮		⋮		⋮		⋮	
c_{pq}		pth		qth		pth		qth	

It is seen from the table that **C** is a matrix of m rows and q columns. We are now prepared for the formal definition of matrix multiplication.

Definition Let $\mathbf{A}$ be a $m \times n$ matrix; let $\mathbf{B}$ be a $p \times q$ matrix. The multiplication of $\mathbf{A}$ into $\mathbf{B}$ is defined if and only if $n = p$. If $\mathbf{C}$ is the result of multiplying $\mathbf{A}$ into $\mathbf{B}$

$$\mathbf{AB} = \mathbf{C}$$

then $\mathbf{C}$ is a $m \times q$ matrix whose elements are

$$c_{ij} = \sum_{k=1}^{n} a_{ik}b_{kj} \qquad (i = 1, 2, \ldots, m; j = 1, 2, \ldots, q)$$

where Σ denotes summation with respect to the repeated subscript k (see section 2.3).

The best way to understand the rules of matrix algebra is to practise using them. It is instructive to use the following selection of vectors and matrices:

$$\mathbf{A} = \begin{bmatrix} 3 & -1 \\ 2 & 4 \end{bmatrix} \quad \mathbf{B} = \begin{bmatrix} 5 & 1 \\ 2 & 6 \end{bmatrix} \quad \mathbf{E} = \begin{bmatrix} 2 & 4 & 6 \\ 1 & 3 & 5 \end{bmatrix} \quad \mathbf{f} = \begin{bmatrix} 7 \\ 8 \\ 9 \end{bmatrix} \quad \mathbf{I} = \begin{bmatrix} 1 & 0 \\ 0 & 1 \end{bmatrix}$$

$\mathbf{A}$ and $\mathbf{B}$ are known as 'square matrices' because each has the same number of rows and columns. $\mathbf{E}$ is a 2×3 matrix; it has 2 rows and 3 columns and is an example of a 'rectangular matrix'. $\mathbf{f}$ is a column vector. Vectors are denoted by lower case letters, matrices by upper case letters. $\mathbf{I}$ is a very special matrix, known as the 'identity matrix'. It is an example of a 'square matrix' since it has the same number of rows and columns, and of a 'diagonal matrix' since all its non-zero elements lie on the upper left to lower right diagonal.

Example 1 Evaluate $\mathbf{AB}$. To evaluate $\mathbf{AB}$ multiply each row of the left-hand matrix $\mathbf{A}$ into each column of the right-hand matrix $\mathbf{B}$ and place the result in the appropriate row and column of the resulting matrix $\mathbf{C}$.

$$\begin{aligned} \mathbf{C} = \mathbf{AB} &= \begin{bmatrix} 3 & -1 \\ 2 & 4 \end{bmatrix} \begin{bmatrix} 5 & 1 \\ 2 & 6 \end{bmatrix} \\ &= \begin{bmatrix} 3 \times 5 + (-1) \times 2 & 3 \times 1 + (-1) \times 6 \\ 2 \times 5 + 4 \times 2 & 2 \times 1 + 4 \times 6 \end{bmatrix} \\ &= \begin{bmatrix} 13 & -3 \\ 18 & 26 \end{bmatrix} \end{aligned}$$

Example 2 Evaluate $\mathbf{Ef}$. Regard $\mathbf{f}$ as a 2×1 matrix. Multiply each row of the left-hand matrix $\mathbf{E}$ into the single column of the vector $\mathbf{f}$, on the right, and place the result in the appropriate row of the resulting column vector $\mathbf{g}$.

$$\mathbf{g} = \mathbf{Ef} = \begin{bmatrix} 2 & 4 & 6 \\ 1 & 3 & 5 \end{bmatrix} \begin{bmatrix} 7 \\ 8 \\ 9 \end{bmatrix}$$

$$= \begin{bmatrix} 2 \times 7 + 4 \times 8 + 6 \times 9 \\ 1 \times 7 + 3 \times 8 + 5 \times 9 \end{bmatrix} = \begin{bmatrix} 100 \\ 76 \end{bmatrix}$$

Example 3 Evaluate **fE**. To evaluate **fE** is a different operation from evaluating **Ef**. This is because in matrix multiplication the rows of the left-hand matrix are multiplied into the columns of the right-hand matrix. In Example 2, **E** is on the left and **f** is on the right: in Example 3, **f** is on the left and **E** is on the right. Although the operations are different we still might get the same answer. It turns out, however, that we cannot even evaluate **fE**, because with **f** on the left and **E** on the right it is necessary to pair off the terms in the rows of **f** and the columns of **E**. In each row of **f** there is only one term, while in each column of **E** there are two terms. Consequently, the multiplication of **f** into **E** is not defined, even though the multiplication of **E** into **f** gives a definite answer.

$$\mathbf{fE} = \begin{bmatrix} 7 \\ 8 \\ 9 \end{bmatrix} \begin{bmatrix} 2 & 4 & 6 \\ 1 & 3 & 5 \end{bmatrix} \quad \text{is not defined}$$

An immediate test of whether or not multiplication is defined is given by the formal definition of matrix multiplication above. If the left-hand matrix is a $m \times n$ matrix and the right-hand matrix is a $p \times q$ matrix, then for multiplication to be defined it is necessary that $n = p$. The reader should verify that while **AE** can be calculated, **EA** is not defined.

Example 4 Evaluate **BA**. We know that this is a different operation from evaluating **AB**. It is readily seen that **BA** is defined. In fact, if **A** and **B** are square matrices then **BA** is defined if and only if **AB** is defined. Do we get the same answer for **BA** as we do for **AB**? Surprisingly we do not. We find that

$$\mathbf{D} = \mathbf{BA} = \begin{bmatrix} 5 & 1 \\ 2 & 6 \end{bmatrix} \begin{bmatrix} 3 & -1 \\ 2 & 4 \end{bmatrix}$$

$$= \begin{bmatrix} 5 \times 3 + 1 \times 2 & 5 \times (-1) + 1 \times 4 \\ 2 \times 3 + 6 \times 2 & 2 \times (-1) + 6 \times 4 \end{bmatrix}$$

$$= \begin{bmatrix} 17 & -1 \\ 18 & 22 \end{bmatrix}$$

In fact, it is usually the case with matrix multiplication that

$$\mathbf{AB} \neq \mathbf{BA}$$

However, different results are not always obtained. Those cases in which the same results are obtained are of particular importance.

Example 5 Show that **AI** = **IA**. The calculations are given below.

$$\mathbf{AI} = \begin{bmatrix} 3 & -1 \\ 2 & 4 \end{bmatrix} \begin{bmatrix} 1 & 0 \\ 0 & 1 \end{bmatrix} = \begin{bmatrix} 3 & -1 \\ 2 & 4 \end{bmatrix}$$

$$\mathbf{IA} = \begin{bmatrix} 1 & 0 \\ 0 & 1 \end{bmatrix} \begin{bmatrix} 3 & -1 \\ 2 & 4 \end{bmatrix} = \begin{bmatrix} 3 & -1 \\ 2 & 4 \end{bmatrix}$$

Not only is the answer the same whatever the order of multiplication but the answer is, in fact, equal to the matrix **A**. Indeed, for any square matrix **A** it is true that

$$\mathbf{AI} = \mathbf{A} = \mathbf{IA}$$

Since multiplication by **I** preserves the identity of the matrix **A**, the matrix **I** is known as the 'identity matrix'.

We have explained in some detail the process of matrix multiplication. We have seen that only in certain cases is the multiplication of matrices analogous to the multiplication of real numbers. We shall now define the processes of matrix addition and matrix subtraction and compare these processes with the addition and subtraction of real numbers.

11.3 Addition and subtraction of vectors and matrices

Addition of matrices

To add the matrix **A** to the matrix **B** add each element of **A** to the corresponding element of **B**. Two matrices can be added only if they both have the same number of rows and the same number of columns.

Definition Let **A** and **B** be $m \times n$ matrices. Then the sum of **A** and **B** is the $m \times n$ matrix **C**

$$\mathbf{C} = \mathbf{A} + \mathbf{B}$$

Each element of **C** is the sum of the corresponding elements in the matrices **A** and **B**:

$$c_{ij} = a_{ij} + b_{ij} \qquad (i = 1, 2, \ldots, m; j = 1, 2, \ldots, n).$$

If the matrix **A** is added to itself then we obtain a matrix in which each element is double that of the similar element in **A**. It seems reasonable to write such a matrix as 2**A**. This leads to the following definition.

Definition Let **A** be a $m \times n$ matrix and let λ be a real number. The matrix

$$\mathbf{D} = \lambda\mathbf{A}$$

is such that each element in **D** is equal to the corresponding element in **A** scaled by a factor λ:

$$d_{ij} = \lambda a_{ij} \qquad (i = 1, 2, \ldots, m; j = 1, 2, \ldots, n)$$

A real number which scales all the elements of a matrix in this way is referred to as a 'scalar'.

Subtraction of matrices

To subtract the matrix **B** from the matrix **A** subtract each element of **B** from the corresponding element of **A**.

Definition If the $m \times n$ matrix **B** is subtracted from the $m \times n$ matrix **A**,

$$\mathbf{C} = \mathbf{A} - \mathbf{B} = \mathbf{A} + (-1)\mathbf{B}$$

then the result is the $m \times n$ matrix **C** in which

$$c_{ij} = a_{ij} - b_{ij} \qquad (i = 1, 2, \ldots, m; j = 1, 2, \ldots, n)$$

Examples

$$\mathbf{A} + \mathbf{B} = \begin{bmatrix} 3 & -1 \\ 2 & 4 \end{bmatrix} + \begin{bmatrix} 5 & 1 \\ 2 & 6 \end{bmatrix} = \begin{bmatrix} 3+5 & 1-1 \\ 2+2 & 4+6 \end{bmatrix} = \begin{bmatrix} 8 & 0 \\ 4 & 10 \end{bmatrix}$$

$$\mathbf{A} - \mathbf{B} \quad \begin{bmatrix} 3 & -1 \\ 2 & 4 \end{bmatrix} - \begin{bmatrix} 5 & 1 \\ 2 & 6 \end{bmatrix} = \begin{bmatrix} 3-5 & -1-1 \\ 2-2 & 4-6 \end{bmatrix} \quad \begin{bmatrix} -2 & -2 \\ 0 & -2 \end{bmatrix}$$

It is readily seen that $\mathbf{A} + \mathbf{B} = \mathbf{B} + \mathbf{A}$ and that $\mathbf{A} - \mathbf{B} = \mathbf{B} - \mathbf{A}$. So far as addition and subtraction are concerned, therefore, the algebra of vectors and matrices is the same as the algebra of real numbers. The mathematician who specializes in algebra deals with many algebras besides those of matrices and real numbers; consequently, he finds it useful to classify algebras by whether or not they have certain important properties. Some of the ways in which an algebra is classified are shown below.

Table 11.2 Classification of algebras

Property of the algebra	*Does the algebra of matrices have this property?*	*Does the algebra of real numbers have this property?*
Commutation: AB = BA	No	Yes
Association: A(BC) = (AB)C	Yes	Yes
Distribution: A(B + C) = AB + AC	Yes	Yes

The associative property indicates that while it is always necessary to multiply the rows of a matrix on the left into the columns of a matrix immediately to the right it is not necessary, when multiplying a sequence of matrices together, to begin with the matrix on the extreme left and end with the matrix on the extreme right.

11.4 Inverse of a square matrix

Having discussed the addition, subtraction and multiplication of matrices, we turn to matrix division. However, before discussing matrix division it is useful to examine carefully what happens in ordinary division. The relation between the multiplication and the division of ordinary numbers may be explained as follows.

Suppose we have the equation

$$ax = y$$

where a, x and y are real numbers. Given the values of a and y we wish to find the value of x:

$$x = ?$$

Suppose, furthermore, that the concept of division has yet to be invented: we know only about addition, subtraction and multiplication. How would we set about determining x? First of all, we know that there is a number 1 such that

$$1x = x$$

Secondly, suppose that there is a number, denoted a^{-1}, such that

$$a^{-1}a = 1$$

a^{-1} is called the 'inverse' of a. Let us now multiply both sides of the equation by a^{-1}:

$$a^{-1}(a.x) = a^{-1}y$$

where the bracket indicates the order of multiplication. Using the property of association, which is valid for real numbers, it follows that

$$(a^{-1}a)x = a^{-1}y$$

Since a^{-1} is the inverse of a (i.e., $a^{-1}a = 1$) it follows that

$$1x = a^{-1}y$$

Because of the property of the number 1,

$$x = a^{-1}y$$

We have solved the equation for x *using only the concept of multiplication*. We can now define what is meant by division by saying that $a^{-1}y$ will be written y/a and called 'y divided by a'.

In the discussion above we had only the concepts of addition, subtraction and multiplication at our disposal. This is exactly the situation we are in with regard to matrix algebra. It will be instructive to recast the discussion in terms of matrices.

Suppose we have a set of n simultaneous linear equations

$$\begin{aligned}
a_{11}x_1 + a_{12}x_2 + \cdots + a_{1n}x_n &= y_1 \\
a_{21}x_1 + a_{22}x_2 + \cdots + a_{2n}x_n &= y_2 \\
\vdots \qquad \vdots \qquad\quad & \vdots \quad \vdots \\
a_{n1}x_1 + a_{n2}x_2 + \cdots + a_{nn}x_n &= y_n
\end{aligned}$$

to be solved for the n unknowns $x_1, x_2, \ldots, x_n$. These equations, when written in matrix notation, are of the form

$$\mathbf{Ax} = \mathbf{y}$$

where $\mathbf{A}$ is a $n \times n$ matrix, $\mathbf{x}$ is an n-element column vector which is to be determined and $\mathbf{y}$ is an n-element column vector which is known. Let us apply the above reasoning to this matrix equation. We first of all enquire whether there is a matrix $\mathbf{I}$ such that

$$\mathbf{Ix} = \mathbf{x}$$

In fact, we know that the identity matrix has this property. We must then enquire whether there is a matrix, denoted $\mathbf{A}^{-1}$, such that

$$\mathbf{A}^{-1}\mathbf{A} = \mathbf{I}$$

Suppose for a moment that there is such a matrix. Multiplying $\mathbf{A}^{-1}$ into both sides of the matrix equation, we get

$$\mathbf{A}^{-1}(\mathbf{Ax}) = \mathbf{A}^{-1}\mathbf{y}$$

Since matrix multiplication has the associative property,

$$(\mathbf{A}^{-1}\mathbf{A})\mathbf{x} = \mathbf{A}^{-1}\mathbf{y}$$

Since $\mathbf{A}^{-1}$ is the inverse of $\mathbf{A}$, it follows that

$$\mathbf{Ix} = \mathbf{A}^{-1}\mathbf{y}$$

Because of the property of the identity matrix,

$$\mathbf{x} = \mathbf{A}^{-1}\mathbf{y}$$

The matrix equation $\mathbf{Ax} = \mathbf{y}$ represents a set of simultaneous equations in which $\mathbf{x}$ is the vector of unknowns and the elements of $\mathbf{y}$ are known. Consequently if we can find $\mathbf{A}^{-1}$ then since the elements of $\mathbf{y}$ are known we can evaluate the expression $\mathbf{A}^{-1}\mathbf{y}$ and thereby determine the vector $\mathbf{x}$. In other words, if we can find the 'inverse matrix', $\mathbf{A}^{-1}$, then we can solve the simultaneous equations for the unknowns $x_1, x_2, \ldots, x_n$.

In fact, there is a general rule by which one can write down the inverse of a matrix; for a 2×2 matrix this rule is a very simple one.

Theorem 11.1 The inverse of the matrix

$$\mathbf{A} = \begin{bmatrix} a_{11} & a_{12} \\ a_{21} & a_{22} \end{bmatrix}$$

is the matrix

$$\mathbf{A}^{-1} = \frac{1}{a_{11}a_{22} - a_{12}a_{21}} \begin{bmatrix} a_{22} & -a_{12} \\ -a_{21} & a_{11} \end{bmatrix}$$

Furthermore, when $\mathbf{A}^{-1}$ is the inverse matrix not only is it true that

$$\mathbf{A}^{-1}\mathbf{A} = \mathbf{I}$$

but it is also true that

$$\mathbf{A}\mathbf{A}^{-1} = \mathbf{I}$$

so that the matrix $\mathbf{A}$ and its inverse commute (i.e. have the property of commutation).

PROOF The theorem can be proved by direct calculation using the rules of matrix multiplication. Note, however, that if

$$a_{11}a_{22} - a_{12}a_{21} = 0$$

then the inverse does not exist.

Example In the discussion of international trade (see Section 10.3) we were led to the equations

$$\begin{aligned} 0{\cdot}5x_1 \quad - 0{\cdot}5x_2 &= 10 \\ -0{\cdot}25x_1 + 0{\cdot}5x_2 &= 10 \end{aligned}$$

which were to be solved for the unknowns x_1, x_2. In matrix notation, these equations become

$$\begin{bmatrix} 0{\cdot}5 & -0{\cdot}5 \\ -0{\cdot}25 & 0{\cdot}5 \end{bmatrix} \begin{bmatrix} x_1 \\ x_2 \end{bmatrix} = \begin{bmatrix} 10 \\ 10 \end{bmatrix}$$

The inverse matrix is

$$\mathbf{A}^{-1} = \begin{bmatrix} 4 & 4 \\ 2 & 4 \end{bmatrix}$$

and the reader may verify that

$$\mathbf{A}^{-1}\mathbf{A} = \mathbf{I}$$

It follows that

$$\mathbf{x} = \mathbf{A}^{-1}\mathbf{y} = \begin{bmatrix} 4 & 4 \\ 2 & 4 \end{bmatrix} \begin{bmatrix} 10 \\ 10 \end{bmatrix} = \begin{bmatrix} 80 \\ 60 \end{bmatrix}$$

Consequently, $x_1 = 80$, $x_2 = 60$. In Section 10.3 we calculated the equilibrium incomes in countries 1 and 2 to be £80m and £60m respectively. We have now reached the same result by using the methods of matrix algebra.

To a certain extent, the formula for the inverse of a matrix is rather surprising. Had the reader been asked to guess the form of the inverse he might have suggested

$$\mathbf{A}^{-1} = \begin{bmatrix} 1/a_{11} & 1/a_{12} \\ 1/a_{21} & 1/a_{22} \end{bmatrix}$$

because of the analogy with the reciprocal of an ordinary number. In fact, although this suggestion is wrong, the analogy with the reciprocal of an ordinary number is not misplaced. Suppose that the matrix **A** is a diagonal matrix

$$\mathbf{A} = \begin{bmatrix} a_{11} & 0 \\ 0 & a_{22} \end{bmatrix}$$

The formula for the inverse indicates that

$$\mathbf{A}^{-1} = \frac{1}{a_{11}a_{22}} \begin{bmatrix} a_{22} & 0 \\ 0 & a_{11} \end{bmatrix}$$

$$= \begin{bmatrix} 1/a_{11} & 0 \\ 0 & 1/a_{22} \end{bmatrix}$$

so that for the diagonal matrix the inverse is obtained by taking the reciprocals of the diagonal elements. In fact, the following statement is true.

Theorem 11.2 Let the $n \times n$ matrix **A** be such that each element on the diagonal is a non-zero real number and each element elsewhere is zero. Then the inverse $\mathbf{A}^{-1}$ is found by replacing each diagonal element by its reciprocal:

$$\mathbf{A} = \begin{bmatrix} \lambda_1 & & 0 \\ & \lambda_2 & \\ 0 & & \lambda_n \end{bmatrix} \qquad \mathbf{A}^{-1} = \begin{bmatrix} 1/\lambda_1 & & 0 \\ & 1/\lambda_2 & \\ 0 & & 1/\lambda_n \end{bmatrix}$$

$$(\lambda_i \neq 0, i = 1, 2, \ldots, m)$$

PROOF Direct confirmation that $\mathbf{A}^{-1}\mathbf{A} = \mathbf{I}$ will suffice.

The reader who wishes to see some economic application of the elementary matrix operations with 2×2 matrices is referred to Chapter 13. For the moment, we pursue the more tedious task of stating the formula for the inverse of an arbitrary $n \times n$ matrix. When we have done this we shall know the general solution of n linear equations in n unknowns, and we shall be able to deduce a general formula to describe the equilibrium in an economy with n interacting markets.

The formula for the inverse of an arbitrary $n \times n$ matrix necessitates the evaluation of 'determinants' and 'cofactors' and involves the 'transposing' of a matrix.

11.5 Transpose of a matrix

Definition The transpose of a matrix is formed by interchanging the rows and the columns of the matrix. To form the transpose of a matrix, put the *first* row of the transpose equal to the *first* column of the original matrix, the *second* row of the transpose equal to the *second* column of the original matrix, and so on.

Examples

1 The transpose of the matrix

$$\mathbf{A} = \left[\begin{array}{c|c|c} a_{11} & a_{12} & a_{13} \\ a_{21} & a_{22} & a_{23} \\ a_{31} & a_{32} & a_{33} \end{array}\right]$$

is

$$\mathbf{A}^T = \left[\begin{array}{ccc} a_{11} & a_{21} & a_{31} \\ \hline a_{12} & a_{22} & a_{32} \\ \hline a_{13} & a_{23} & a_{33} \end{array}\right]$$

Notice that when **A** is a square matrix the transpose can be formed by leaving the elements on the diagonal unchanged and 'reflecting' the other elements in the diagonal.

2 The transpose of a column vector is a row vector and the transpose of a row vector is a column vector; for example, the transpose of

$$\mathbf{x} = \begin{bmatrix} x_1 \\ x_2 \\ x_3 \end{bmatrix}$$

is

$$\mathbf{x}^T = [x_1 \quad x_2 \quad x_3]$$

and the transpose of $\mathbf{x}^T$ is

$$(\mathbf{x}^T)^T = \begin{bmatrix} x_1 \\ x_2 \\ x_3 \end{bmatrix} = \mathbf{x}$$

3 For any matrix the transpose of the transpose is equal to the original:

$$(\mathbf{A}^T)^T = \mathbf{A}$$

For example, the transpose of

$$\mathbf{A} = \left[\begin{array}{c|c|c} a_{11} & a_{12} & a_{13} \\ a_{21} & a_{22} & a_{23} \end{array}\right]$$

is

$$\mathbf{A}^T = \begin{bmatrix} a_{11} & a_{21} \\ \hline a_{12} & a_{22} \\ \hline a_{13} & a_{23} \end{bmatrix} = \left[\begin{array}{c|c} a_{11} & a_{21} \\ a_{12} & a_{22} \\ a_{13} & a_{23} \end{array}\right]$$

so that

$$(\mathbf{A}^T)^T = \begin{bmatrix} a_{11} & a_{12} & a_{13} \\ \hline a_{21} & a_{22} & a_{23} \end{bmatrix} = \mathbf{A}$$

It follows that if $\mathbf{A}^T = \mathbf{B}$ then $\mathbf{B}^T = (\mathbf{A}^T)^T = \mathbf{A}$. Also it is easily seen that a matrix can be transposed just as well by transforming rows into columns as by transforming columns into rows.

4 If $\mathbf{Ax}$ is defined, then $\mathbf{x}^T\mathbf{A}^T$ is defined and $(\mathbf{x}^T\mathbf{A}^T)^T = \mathbf{Ax}$ (or $\mathbf{x}^T\mathbf{A}^T = (\mathbf{Ax})^T$, which is the same thing). For example, if

$$\mathbf{Ax} = \begin{bmatrix} a_{11} & a_{12} & a_{13} \\ a_{21} & a_{22} & a_{23} \end{bmatrix} \begin{bmatrix} x_1 \\ x_2 \\ x_3 \end{bmatrix} = \begin{bmatrix} a_{11}x_1 + a_{12}x_2 + a_{13}x_3 \\ a_{21}x_1 + a_{22}x_2 + a_{23}x_3 \end{bmatrix}$$

then

$$\mathbf{x}^T\mathbf{A}^T = \begin{bmatrix} x_1 & x_2 & x_3 \end{bmatrix} \begin{bmatrix} a_{11} & a_{21} \\ a_{12} & a_{22} \\ a_{13} & a_{23} \end{bmatrix}$$

$$\begin{bmatrix} a_{11}x_1 + a_{12}x_2 + a_{13}x_3 & a_{21}x_1 + a_{22}x_2 + a_{23}x_3 \end{bmatrix}$$

It follows immediately that

$$(\mathbf{x}^T\mathbf{A}^T)^T = \mathbf{Ax}$$

11.6 Determinants

The determinant is always a single number.

Definition For a 1×1 matrix, define

$$\det \begin{bmatrix} a_{11} \end{bmatrix} = a_{11}$$

For a 2×2 matrix, define

$$\det \begin{bmatrix} a_{11} & a_{12} \\ a_{21} & a_{22} \end{bmatrix} = a_{11} \det \begin{bmatrix} a_{22} \end{bmatrix} - a_{12} \det \begin{bmatrix} a_{21} \end{bmatrix}$$

For a 3 × 3 matrix, define

$$\det\begin{bmatrix} a_{11} & a_{12} & a_{13} \\ a_{21} & a_{22} & a_{23} \\ a_{31} & a_{32} & a_{33} \end{bmatrix} = a_{11}\det\begin{bmatrix} a_{22} & a_{23} \\ a_{32} & a_{33} \end{bmatrix} - a_{12}\det\begin{bmatrix} a_{21} & a_{23} \\ a_{31} & a_{33} \end{bmatrix} + a_{13}\det\begin{bmatrix} a_{21} & a_{22} \\ a_{31} & a_{32} \end{bmatrix}$$

For a 4 × 4 matrix, define

$$\det\begin{bmatrix} a_{11} & a_{12} & a_{13} & a_{14} \\ a_{21} & a_{22} & a_{23} & a_{24} \\ a_{31} & a_{32} & a_{33} & a_{34} \\ a_{41} & a_{42} & a_{43} & a_{44} \end{bmatrix} = a_{11}\det\begin{bmatrix} a_{22} & a_{23} & a_{24} \\ a_{32} & a_{33} & a_{34} \\ a_{42} & a_{43} & a_{44} \end{bmatrix} - a_{12}\det\begin{bmatrix} a_{21} & a_{23} & a_{24} \\ a_{31} & a_{33} & a_{34} \\ a_{41} & a_{43} & a_{44} \end{bmatrix} + a_{13}\det\begin{bmatrix} a_{21} & a_{22} & a_{24} \\ a_{31} & a_{32} & a_{34} \\ a_{41} & a_{42} & a_{44} \end{bmatrix} - a_{14}\det\begin{bmatrix} a_{21} & a_{22} & a_{23} \\ a_{31} & a_{32} & a_{33} \\ a_{41} & a_{42} & a_{43} \end{bmatrix}$$

In general, for the square $n \times n$ matrix **A**, define

$$\begin{aligned} \det[\mathbf{A}] &= a_{11}\det[\mathbf{A} \text{ with 1st row and 1st column deleted}] \\ &- a_{12}\det[\mathbf{A} \text{ with 1st row and 2nd column deleted}] \\ &+ a_{13}\det[\mathbf{A} \text{ with 1st row and 3rd column deleted}] \\ &\quad\vdots \\ &+ (-1)^{n+1}\det[\mathbf{A} \text{ with 1st row and } n\text{th column deleted}] \end{aligned}$$

This type of definition is known as 'recursive'. The definition of the determinant of an $n \times n$ matrix is expressed in terms of the determinants of $(n - 1) \times (n - 1)$ matrices. The determinant of an $(n - 1) \times (n - 1)$ matrix is defined in terms of the determinants of $(n - 2) \times (n - 2)$ matrices. The only determinant not defined in terms of the determinant of a smaller matrix is the determinant of a 1×1 matrix, which is equal to the element of the matrix itself. Notice that in the general formula for the determinant of an $n \times n$ matrix there is a correspondence, in each of the n terms, between the row and the column deleted, and the row index and the column index of the element multiplied into the determinant.

Theorem 11.3 From the definition of the determinant it follows that *for any i* $(i = 1, 2, \ldots, n)$

$$\begin{aligned} \det[\mathbf{A}] &= a_{i1}(-1)^{i+1}\det[\mathbf{A} \text{ with } i\text{th row and 1st column deleted}] \\ &+ a_{i2}(-1)^{i+2}\det[\mathbf{A} \text{ with } i\text{th row and 2nd column deleted}] \\ &\quad\vdots \\ &+ a_{in}(-1)^{i+n}\det[\mathbf{A} \text{ with } i\text{th row and } n\text{th column deleted}] \end{aligned}$$

The original definition is the special case, $i = 1$, of this general result.

Theorem 11.3 describes a whole family of definitions of a determinant, all of which are equivalent. But the definitions in Theorem 11.3 do not exhaust all the possible definitions of a determinant. The most usual definition of a determinant is described in Theorem 11.4. Theorem 11.4 will not be referred to in the future, and may be omitted on a first reading.

Theorem 11.4 To evaluate the determinant of an $n \times n$ matrix follow the following rules.

(i) Write out all the possible sequences of matrix elements which can be obtained by selecting one element from each row of the matrix; the selection must be made in such a way that no two elements are from the same column. For an $n \times n$ matrix there are $n \times (n-1) \times \cdots \times 2 \times 1$ (factorial n) such sequences.

Example The sequences obtained from a 3×3 matrix

$$\mathbf{A} = \begin{bmatrix} a_{11} & a_{12} & a_{13} \\ a_{21} & a_{22} & a_{23} \\ a_{31} & a_{32} & a_{33} \end{bmatrix}$$

are a_{11}, a_{22}, a_{33}

a_{11}, a_{23}, a_{32}

a_{12}, a_{21}, a_{33}

a_{12}, a_{23}, a_{31}

a_{13}, a_{21}, a_{32}

a_{13}, a_{22}, a_{31}

Each of these sequences is obtained by selecting any one element from the first row of **A**, then an element from the second row (an element that is not in the same column as the element in the first row) and finally an element from the third row (an element that is not in the same column as either the element in the first row or the element in the second row). For the 3×3 matrix **A** there are $3 \times 2 \times 1 = 6$ ways in which such a sequence can be obtained. It is a consequence of this procedure that in each sequence the row subscripts are ordered 1, 2, 3 when reading from left to right. However, the column subscripts are ordered differently in each sequence. In the six sequences the subscripts are ordered from left to right in the following way:

1, 2, 3; 1, 3, 2; 2, 1, 3; 2, 3, 1; 3, 1, 2; 3, 2, 1

Each of these sequences is a 'permutation' of the sequence 1, 2, 3. 1, 3, 2 is obtained by interchanging 2 and 3 in the sequence 1, 2, 3; 2, 1, 3 is obtained by interchanging 1 and 2 in the sequence 1, 2, 3; 2, 3, 1 is obtained from the sequence 1, 2, 3 by first interchanging 1 and 2 and then interchanging 3 and 1; and so on. An 'odd permutation' is made by making an odd number of interchanges; an 'even permutation' involves an even number of interchanges. For example, the sequences 1, 3, 2 and 2, 1, 3 are odd permutations of the sequence 1, 2, 3; the sequence 2, 3, 1 is an even permutation of the sequence 1, 2, 3.

(ii) For each sequence, form the product of the elements, and multiply the product by -1 if the column subscripts in the sequence are an odd permutation of the sequence $1, 2, \ldots, n$. Leave the product unchanged if the column subscripts in the sequence are an even permutation of $1, 2, \ldots, n$.

Example For the 3×3 matrix **A** the six product terms are, respectively,

$$a_{11}a_{22}a_{33}$$
$$-a_{11}a_{23}a_{32}$$
$$-a_{12}a_{21}a_{33}$$
$$a_{12}a_{23}a_{31}$$
$$a_{13}a_{21}a_{32}$$
$$-a_{13}a_{22}a_{31}$$

(iii) Sum the products to form the determinant.

Example For the 3×3 matrix **A**,

$$\begin{aligned}\det[\mathbf{A}] &= a_{11}a_{22}a_{33} - a_{11}a_{23}a_{32} \\ &- a_{12}a_{21}a_{33} + a_{12}a_{23}a_{31} \\ &+ a_{13}a_{21}a_{32} - a_{13}a_{22}a_{31}\end{aligned}$$

11.7 Cofactors

In Theorem 11.3 the expression

$$(-1)^{i+j} \det[\mathbf{A} \text{ with } i\text{th row and } j\text{th column deleted}]$$

occurred n times ($j = 1, 2, \ldots, n$). If this expression is denoted c_{ij}, then Theorem 11.3 can be written

$$\det[\mathbf{A}] = a_{i1}c_{i1} + a_{i2}c_{i2} + \cdots + a_{in}c_{in}$$

for any i ($i = 1, 2, \ldots, n$).

Definition

$$c_{ij} = (-1)^{i+j} \det[\mathbf{A} \text{ with } i\text{th row and } j\text{th column deleted}]$$

is the cofactor of the element a_{ij}.

The definition of a cofactor provides a very concise way of stating theorems such as the following:

Theorem 11.5 A determinant can be expanded not only by the cofactors of any row but also by the cofactors of any column; i.e., not only is it true, from Theorem 11.3, that for any row i,

$$\det[\mathbf{A}] = \sum_{j=1}^{n} a_{ij}c_{ij} \qquad (i = 1, 2, \ldots, n)$$

but it is also true that, for any column j,

$$\det[\mathbf{A}] = \sum_{i=1}^{n} a_{ij}c_{ij} \qquad (j = 1, 2, \ldots, n)$$

11.8 The $n \times n$ inverse matrix

We are now prepared for the general formula for the matrix inverse to the $n \times n$ matrix **A**. It can be shown by patient algebraic manipulation that

Theorem 11.6 The matrix inverse to the $n \times n$ matrix **A** ($n > 1$) is the transpose of the matrix of the cofactors, divided by $\det[\mathbf{A}]$.

$$\mathbf{A}^{-1} = \frac{1}{\det[\mathbf{A}]}\begin{bmatrix} c_{11} & c_{21} & \cdots & c_{n1} \\ c_{12} & c_{22} & \cdots & c_{n2} \\ \vdots & \vdots & \ddots & \vdots \\ c_{1n} & c_{2n} & \cdots & c_{nn} \end{bmatrix}$$

The inverse of the 1×1 matrix a_{11} is $1/a_{11}$.

Example Find the inverse of the matrix

$$\mathbf{A} = \begin{bmatrix} a_{11} & a_{12} & a_{13} \\ a_{21} & a_{22} & a_{23} \\ a_{31} & a_{32} & a_{33} \end{bmatrix} = \begin{bmatrix} 1 & 2 & 4 \\ 8 & 6 & 5 \\ 3 & 9 & 10 \end{bmatrix}$$

1st step Calculate the cofactors

$$c_{11} = (-1)^2 \det\begin{bmatrix} a_{22} & a_{23} \\ a_{32} & a_{33} \end{bmatrix} = +(a_{22}a_{33} - a_{32}a_{23}) = +(60 - 45) = 15$$

$$c_{12} = (-1)^3 \det\begin{bmatrix} a_{21} & a_{23} \\ a_{31} & a_{33} \end{bmatrix} = -(a_{21}a_{33} - a_{31}a_{23}) = -(80 - 15) = -65$$

Similarly,

$$
\begin{aligned}
c_{13} &= +(a_{21}a_{32} - a_{31}a_{22}) = (72 - 18) = 54 \\
c_{21} &= -(a_{12}a_{33} - a_{32}a_{13}) = -(20 - 36) = 16 \\
c_{22} &= +(a_{11}a_{33} - a_{31}a_{13}) = (10 - 12) = -2 \\
c_{23} &= -(a_{11}a_{32} - a_{31}a_{12}) = -(\;9 - \;6) = -3 \\
c_{31} &= +(a_{12}a_{23} - a_{22}a_{13}) = (10 - 24) = -14 \\
c_{32} &= -(a_{11}a_{23} - a_{21}a_{13}) = -(\;5 - 32) = 27 \\
c_{33} &= +(a_{11}a_{22} - a_{21}a_{12}) = (\;6 - 16) = -10
\end{aligned}
$$

The matrix of cofactors can be written down as follows:

$$
\begin{bmatrix} 15 & -65 & 54 \\ 16 & -2 & -3 \\ -14 & 27 & -10 \end{bmatrix}
$$

2nd step Evaluate the determinant. It follows from the definition of the determinant of a 3×3 matrix that

$$
\begin{aligned}
\det[\mathbf{A}] &= a_{11}c_{11} + a_{12}c_{12} + a_{13}c_{13} \\
&= 1 \times 15 + 2 \times -65 + 4 \times 54 \\
&= 101
\end{aligned}
$$

It is possible to check this calculation since, according to Theorem 11.3, it is also true that

$$
\begin{aligned}
\det[\mathbf{A}] &= a_{21}c_{21} + a_{22}c_{22} + a_{23}c_{23} \\
&= 8 \times 16 + 6 \times -2 + 5 \times -3 \\
&= 101
\end{aligned}
$$

It is also true that

$$
\begin{aligned}
\det[\mathbf{A}] &= a_{31}c_{31} + a_{32}c_{32} + a_{33}c_{33} \\
&= 3 \times -14 + 9 \times 27 + 10 \times -10 \\
&= 101
\end{aligned}
$$

3rd step Compute the inverse. The inverse of **A** is the transpose of the matrix of cofactors (known as the 'adjoint' or 'adjugate' of **A**) divided by $\det[\mathbf{A}]$; i.e.,

$$
\mathbf{A}^{-1} = \frac{1}{101}\begin{bmatrix} 15 & 16 & -14 \\ -65 & -2 & 27 \\ 54 & -3 & -10 \end{bmatrix}
$$

CHECK Does $\mathbf{A}^{-1}\mathbf{A} = \mathbf{I}$?

$$\frac{1}{101}\begin{bmatrix} 15 & 16 & -14 \\ -65 & -2 & 27 \\ 54 & -3 & -10 \end{bmatrix}\begin{bmatrix} 1 & 2 & 4 \\ 8 & 6 & 5 \\ 3 & 9 & 10 \end{bmatrix} = \begin{bmatrix} 1 & 0 & 0 \\ 0 & 1 & 0 \\ 0 & 0 & 1 \end{bmatrix}$$

The reader can easily satisfy himself that the formula for the inverse of a 2×2 matrix, given in Theorem 11.1, is a special case of Theorem 11.6.

A corollary of Theorem 11.6 is Cramer's rule, which has considerable historical significance but is little used for practical calculations. When solving a set of n simultaneous linear equations by evaluating the inverse matrix, the unknowns $x_1, x_2, \ldots, x_n$ are obtained from the matrix equation $\mathbf{A}^{-1}\mathbf{x} = \mathbf{y}$ which, in the light of Theorem 11.6, may be written

$$\begin{bmatrix} x_1 \\ x_2 \\ \vdots \\ x_n \end{bmatrix} = \frac{1}{\det[\mathbf{A}]}\begin{bmatrix} c_{11} & c_{21} & \cdots & c_{n1} \\ c_{12} & c_{22} & \cdots & c_{n2} \\ \vdots & \vdots & \ddots & \vdots \\ c_{1n} & c_{2n} & \cdots & c_{nn} \end{bmatrix}\begin{bmatrix} y_1 \\ y_2 \\ \vdots \\ y_n \end{bmatrix}$$

Multiplying out this expression it is seen that, for each x_j,

$$x_j = (c_{1j}y_1 + c_{2j}y_2 + \cdots + c_{nj}y_j)/\det[\mathbf{A}] \qquad (j = 1, 2, \ldots, n)$$

The expression in brackets on the right-hand side is equal to what det [**A**] would be *were the jth column of* **A** *replaced by the column vector* **y**. (This can be seen from Theorem 11.5.) This observation is the basis of Cramer's rule.

Theorem 11.7 (Cramer's rule) Let $\mathbf{B}_j$ be the matrix obtained from **A** by replacing the jth column of **A** by the column vector **y**; then the solution of the matrix equation

$$\mathbf{Ax} = \mathbf{y}$$

is

$$\begin{aligned} x_1 &= \det[\mathbf{B}_1]/\det[\mathbf{A}] \\ x_2 &= \det[\mathbf{B}_2]/\det[\mathbf{A}] \\ &\;\vdots \\ x_n &= \det[\mathbf{B}_n]/\det[\mathbf{A}] \end{aligned}$$

Example In Section 10.3 and again in Section 11.4 we discussed the solution of the equations

$$\begin{aligned} 0{\cdot}5x_1 - 0{\cdot}5x_2 &= 10 \\ -0{\cdot}25x_1 + 0{\cdot}5x_2 &= 10 \end{aligned}$$

According to Cramer's rule, the solution is

$$x_1 = \det\begin{bmatrix} 10 & -0{\cdot}5 \\ 10 & 0{\cdot}5 \end{bmatrix} \Big/ \det\begin{bmatrix} 0{\cdot}5 & -0{\cdot}5 \\ -0{\cdot}25 & 0{\cdot}5 \end{bmatrix}$$

$$= 10/0{\cdot}125$$

$$= 80$$

$$x_2 = \det\begin{bmatrix} 0{\cdot}5 & 10 \\ -0{\cdot}25 & 10 \end{bmatrix} \Big/ \det\begin{bmatrix} 0{\cdot}5 & -0{\cdot}5 \\ -0{\cdot}25 & 0{\cdot}5 \end{bmatrix}$$

$$= 7{\cdot}5/0{\cdot}125$$

$$= 60$$

which agrees with the solutions previously obtained.

11.9 Minors and rank

It is often the case when solving problems by the methods of matrix algebra that the nature of the solution depends on some general characteristic of a matrix. Many such characteristics do not depend on the individual elements of the matrix, but on certain quantities which are functions of the individual elements; these quantities may be thought of as describing how the values of various elements are related to one another. Some of these quantities are defined below, beginning with the most elementary one, the 'minor'.

Definition A minor of the $m \times n$ matrix $\mathbf{A}$ is a determinant of a square matrix formed from $\mathbf{A}$ by deleting either rows, or columns, or both (or possibly, if $\mathbf{A}$ is square, by taking $\mathbf{A}$ itself).

Example The minors of the 2×3 matrix

$$\mathbf{A} = \begin{bmatrix} a_{11} & a_{12} & a_{13} \\ a_{21} & a_{22} & a_{23} \end{bmatrix}$$

are the following:

$$\det\begin{bmatrix} a_{11} & a_{12} \\ a_{21} & a_{22} \end{bmatrix}, \quad \det\begin{bmatrix} a_{11} & a_{13} \\ a_{31} & a_{33} \end{bmatrix}$$

$$\det\begin{bmatrix} a_{12} & a_{13} \\ a_{22} & a_{23} \end{bmatrix}, \quad \det[a_{11}], \quad \det[a_{12}], \quad \det[a_{13}]$$

$$\det[a_{21}], \quad \det[a_{22}], \quad \det[a_{23}]$$

These are all the minors that can be formed from the matrix $\mathbf{A}$; they are the determinants of the matrices formed from $\mathbf{A}$ by deleting, respectively, the third column, the second column, the first column, the second row and the second and third columns, the second row and the first and third columns, the second row and the first and second columns, the first row and the second and third columns, the first row and the first and third columns and, finally, the first row and the first and second columns. It is easily verified that the minors formed in this way are the determinants of all the square matrices that can possibly be formed from the matrix **A**.

The reader will appreciate that to evaluate all the minors of a matrix is very tedious. Fortunately it is not usually necessary to evaluate all the minors, for in most cases the evaluation of minors is performed in order to determine the 'rank' of the matrix, and the 'rank' of the matrix is determined as soon as the first nonzero minor in a sequence of minors has been found. The concept of the 'rank' of a matrix will now be elucidated.

Definition The rank of the $m \times n$ matrix **A**, $r(\mathbf{A})$, is the dimension of the largest square matrix *with a nonzero determinant* which can be formed from **A** by deleting either rows, or columns, or both (or possibly, if **A** is square, by taking **A** itself).

To determine the rank of the matrix **A** one evaluates a sequence of minors of **A**, beginning with the set of minors corresponding to the largest square matrices that can be formed from **A** and continuing with sets of minors corresponding to successively smaller and smaller square matrices formed from **A**, until the first nonzero minor in the sequence is found. The dimension of the matrix corresponding to this first nonzero minor is the rank of the matrix **A**.

Example 1 Find the rank of the matrix

$$\mathbf{A} = \begin{bmatrix} 2 & 5 \\ -4 & -10 \\ 10 & 25 \end{bmatrix}$$

The largest square matrices that can be formed from **A** are the 2×2 matrices

$$\begin{bmatrix} 2 & 5 \\ -4 & -10 \end{bmatrix}, \begin{bmatrix} 2 & 5 \\ 10 & 25 \end{bmatrix} \text{ and } \begin{bmatrix} -4 & -10 \\ 10 & 25 \end{bmatrix}$$

for which the corresponding minors are

$$\det \begin{bmatrix} 2 & 5 \\ -4 & -10 \end{bmatrix} = 2 \times (-10) - (-4) \times 5 = 0,$$

$$\det \begin{bmatrix} 2 & 5 \\ 10 & 25 \end{bmatrix} = 2 \times 25 - 10 \times 5 = 0$$

and

$$\det \begin{bmatrix} -4 & -10 \\ 10 & 25 \end{bmatrix} = (-4) \times 25 - 10 \times (-10) = 0$$

Since all these minors are zero we proceed to the minors of the next largest square matrices that can be formed from **A**; these are the 1×1 matrices [2], [5], [−4], [−10], [10] and [25]. The minor corresponding to the first of these matrices is det [2] = 2, and this is the first nonzero minor we have found. Since the dimension of the square matrix corresponding to this first nonzero minor is 1 (i.e. the matrix is 1×1), the rank of the matrix **A** is 1.

Example 2 Find the rank of the matrix

$$\mathbf{A} = \begin{bmatrix} 3 & 5 \\ 6 & 7 \end{bmatrix}$$

Since the matrix **A** is square, the largest square matrix that can be formed from **A** is **A** itself. The corresponding minor is equal to the determinant of the matrix **A** and is

$$\det \begin{bmatrix} 3 & 5 \\ 6 & 7 \end{bmatrix} = 3 \times 7 - 6 \times 5 = -9$$

which is nonzero. Since the matrix corresponding to the first nonzero minor is a square matrix with dimension 2 (i.e. it is a 2×2 matrix) the rank of the matrix **A** is 2.

Square matrices are used to analyse many special problems for which rectangular matrices are quite inappropriate. For problems involving square matrices, the nature of the solution to the problem often depends critically on the values of the 'principal minors' of the square matrix; and if the square matrix is symmetric (see Section 16.5) then certain properties of the solution depend only on the 'leading principal minors' of the square matrix. 'Principal minors' and 'leading principal minors' are defined only for square matrices, whereas the definition of a minor applies to both square and rectangular matrices.

Definition The $(i, j, \ldots, m)$th principal minor, $\mathbf{A}_{ij\ldots m}$ of the matrix **A** is the determinant of the matrix formed from **A** by deleting first of all the ith row and the ith column of **A**, then the jth row and the jth column of **A**, and so on, until the mth row and mth column of **A** are deleted. The number of rows and columns which are deleted from the $n \times n$ matrix **A** can be any number up to $n - 1$.

Example The (1, 3)th principal minor, $\mathbf{A}_{13}$, of the 4×4 matrix

$$\mathbf{A} = \begin{bmatrix} a_{11} & a_{12} & a_{13} & a_{14} \\ a_{21} & a_{22} & a_{23} & a_{24} \\ a_{31} & a_{32} & a_{33} & a_{34} \\ a_{41} & a_{42} & a_{43} & a_{44} \end{bmatrix}$$

is the determinant of the matrix formed from **A** by deleting the first row and column and the third row and column, viz:

$$\mathbf{A}_{13} = \det \begin{bmatrix} a_{22} & a_{24} \\ a_{42} & a_{44} \end{bmatrix}$$

The difference between a minor and a principal minor is that, in forming a minor the rows and columns to be deleted may be chosen quite arbitrarily, while in forming a principal minor there is a correspondence between the rows and columns which are deleted, namely, that if the ith, jth, ..., mth rows of **A** are deleted then the ith, jth, ..., mth columns of **A** are also deleted.

A special case of a principal minor is a 'leading principal minor'.

Definition The mth leading principal minor $\mathbf{A}_m$ of the $n \times n$ square matrix **A** is the minor obtained by deleting the $m + 1$th, ..., nth rows and columns of the matrix **A** (i.e. by deleting all but the first m rows and columns of **A**).

The leading principal minors of the $n \times n$ square matrix **A** form the sequence

$$\det [a_{11}]$$

$$\det \begin{bmatrix} a_{11} & a_{12} \\ a_{21} & a_{22} \end{bmatrix}$$

$$\det \begin{bmatrix} a_{11} & a_{12} & a_{13} \\ a_{21} & a_{22} & a_{23} \\ a_{31} & a_{32} & a_{33} \end{bmatrix}$$

$$\vdots$$

$$\det \begin{bmatrix} a_{11} & \cdots & a_{1n-1} \\ \vdots & \ddots & \vdots \\ a_{n-11} & \cdots & a_{n-1n-1} \end{bmatrix}$$

$$\det [\mathbf{A}]$$

Example The leading principal minors of the matrix

$$\mathbf{A} = \begin{bmatrix} 3 & 0 & 1 \\ 0 & 2 & 5 \\ 1 & 3 & 6 \end{bmatrix}$$

form the sequence

$$\det [3] = 3$$

$$\det \begin{bmatrix} 3 & 0 \\ 0 & 2 \end{bmatrix} = 6$$

$$\det \begin{bmatrix} 3 & 0 & 1 \\ 0 & 2 & 5 \\ 1 & 3 & 6 \end{bmatrix} = -11$$

Appendix: Computational methods for finding the inverse

To find the inverse of an $n \times n$ matrix $\mathbf{A}$ by the method of Theorem 11.6 involves evaluating the determinant and all the cofactors of $\mathbf{A}$. This can be tedious. Fortunately there are alternative methods of finding the inverse which are sometimes quicker.

(i) Method of pivoting

This method is a useful way of minimizing rounding errors when the calculations are carried out in decimals. The essence of the pivotal method is to multiply a sequence of square matrices $\mathbf{E}_1, \mathbf{E}_2, \ldots, \mathbf{E}_m$ into the matrix $\mathbf{A}$, the matrices $\mathbf{E}_i$ being chosen so that

$$\mathbf{E}_m\mathbf{E}_{m-1}\ldots\mathbf{E}_2\mathbf{E}_1\mathbf{A} = \mathbf{I}$$

where $\mathbf{I}$ is the $n \times n$ identity matrix. Since by definition

$$\mathbf{A}^{-1}\mathbf{A} = \mathbf{I}$$

it follows from the uniqueness of the inverse (see lemma 1 of Chapter 12) that

$$\mathbf{E}_m\mathbf{E}_{m-1}\ldots\mathbf{E}_2\mathbf{E}_1 = \mathbf{A}^{-1}$$

We require one $\mathbf{E}$-matrix for every element of $\mathbf{A}$ which has to be converted to the corresponding element of the identity matrix. Since a $n \times n$ matrix has n^2 elements we generally require $m = n^2$ $\mathbf{E}$-matrices. The way in which the $\mathbf{E}$-matrices are chosen is illustrated by the following example.

Example 1 Find the inverse of

$$\mathbf{A} = \begin{bmatrix} 3 & 2 \\ 1 & 6 \end{bmatrix}$$

We shall convert in turn each element of $\mathbf{A}$ into the corresponding element of the identity matrix. Since $\mathbf{A}$ is a 2×2 matrix we shall require $2^2 = 4$ $\mathbf{E}$-matrices.

The first step is to convert the diagonal element in the first column of $\mathbf{A}$ to unity. To do this we form a suitable matrix, $\mathbf{E}_1$, which is to be multiplied into $\mathbf{A}$:

$$\mathbf{E}_1\mathbf{A} = \begin{bmatrix} \frac{1}{3} & 0 \\ 0 & 1 \end{bmatrix}\begin{bmatrix} 3 & 2 \\ 1 & 6 \end{bmatrix} = \begin{bmatrix} 1 & \frac{2}{3} \\ 1 & 6 \end{bmatrix}$$

We now convert the remaining element in the first column to zero. Since $\mathbf{A}$ is a 2×2 matrix there is only one other element in the column. This element is converted to zero by multiplying $\mathbf{E}_1\mathbf{A}$ by a suitably chosen matrix $\mathbf{E}_2$:

$$\mathbf{E}_2(\mathbf{E}_1\mathbf{A}) = \begin{bmatrix} 1 & 0 \\ -1 & 1 \end{bmatrix}\begin{bmatrix} 1 & \frac{2}{3} \\ 1 & 6 \end{bmatrix} = \begin{bmatrix} 1 & \frac{2}{3} \\ 0 & 5\frac{1}{3} \end{bmatrix}$$

The next step is to convert the diagonal element in the second column to zero, using a suitably chosen matrix $\mathbf{E}_3$:

$$\mathbf{E}_3(\mathbf{E}_2\mathbf{E}_1\mathbf{A}) = \begin{bmatrix} 1 & 0 \\ 0 & \frac{3}{16} \end{bmatrix}\begin{bmatrix} 1 & \frac{2}{3} \\ 0 & 5\frac{1}{3} \end{bmatrix} = \begin{bmatrix} 1 & \frac{2}{3} \\ 0 & 1 \end{bmatrix}$$

Since $\mathbf{A}$ has only two columns the process is completed by converting the remaining element in the second column to zero with a suitably chosen $\mathbf{E}_4$:

$$\mathbf{E}_4(\mathbf{E}_3\mathbf{E}_2\mathbf{E}_1\mathbf{A}) = \begin{bmatrix} 1 & -\frac{2}{3} \\ 0 & 1 \end{bmatrix}\begin{bmatrix} 1 & \frac{2}{3} \\ 0 & 1 \end{bmatrix} = \begin{bmatrix} 1 & 0 \\ 0 & 1 \end{bmatrix}$$

The inverse $\mathbf{A}^{-1}$ is then given by

$$\mathbf{E}_4\mathbf{E}_3\mathbf{E}_2\mathbf{E}_1 = \begin{bmatrix} 1 & \frac{2}{3} \\ 0 & 1 \end{bmatrix}\begin{bmatrix} 1 & 0 \\ 0 & \frac{3}{16} \end{bmatrix}\begin{bmatrix} 1 & 0 \\ -1 & 1 \end{bmatrix}\begin{bmatrix} \frac{1}{3} & 0 \\ 0 & 1 \end{bmatrix}$$

$$= \begin{bmatrix} \frac{3}{8} & -\frac{1}{8} \\ -\frac{1}{16} & \frac{3}{16} \end{bmatrix}$$

This example illustrates the general procedure for finding the inverse of an $n \times n$ matrix: work through the matrix column by column, beginning each column by converting the diagonal element to unity and then converting the remaining elements to zero. There is some advantage in working through the matrix in two stages, the first stage being to convert all the below-diagonal elements and the second stage to convert the remaining (diagonal and above-diagonal) elements. The advantage of the two-stage procedure is that when the inverse does not exist the situation will be diagnosed in the first stage, so that unnecessary second stage calculations may be avoided.

It is interesting to note that in the example above the effect of multiplying by an odd-numbered **E**-matrix is to convert a diagonal element to unity *by scaling all the elements in the appropriate row by the reciprocal of the diagonal element*. The effect of multiplying by an even-numbered **E**-matrix is to convert an off-diagonal element to zero *by adding to the appropriate row a suitable multiple of another row*. It follows from these observations that the matrix

$$\mathbf{E}_m\mathbf{E}_{m-1}\ldots\mathbf{E}_2\mathbf{E}_1\mathbf{A}$$

is the outcome of a sequence of arithmetical operations on the rows of the matrix **A** and, in a similar way, the matrix

$$\mathbf{E}_m\mathbf{E}_{m-1}\ldots\mathbf{E}_2\mathbf{E}_1 = \mathbf{E}_m\mathbf{E}_{m-1}\ldots\mathbf{E}_2\mathbf{E}_1\mathbf{I}$$

is the outcome of the same sequence of arithmetical operations on the rows of the identity matrix **I**. Because the operations with **E**-matrices described above are equivalent to a sequence of arithmetical operations on the rows of **A** and **I** it is possible to evaluate the inverse by the purely arithmetical procedure illustrated in the example below.

Example 2 Find the inverse of

$$\mathbf{A} = \begin{bmatrix} 3 & 2 \\ 1 & 6 \end{bmatrix}$$

Since **A** is a 2 × 2 matrix there are $2^2 = 4$ steps.

STEP 1 Convert the diagonal element in the first column to zero by scaling the first row by $\frac{1}{3}$. Apply the same operation to the 2 × 2 identity matrix **I**:

$$\mathbf{A}(1) = \begin{bmatrix} \frac{1}{3} & \frac{2}{3} \\ 1 & 6 \end{bmatrix} \qquad \mathbf{I}(1) = \begin{bmatrix} \frac{1}{3} & 0 \\ 0 & 1 \end{bmatrix}$$

(N.B. In terms of Example 1, $\mathbf{A}(1) = \mathbf{E}_1\mathbf{A}$, $\mathbf{I}(1) = \mathbf{E}_1$.)

STEP 2 Convert the element in the first column and second row to zero by adding $-1 \times$ the first row to the second row. Apply the same operation to **I**(1):

$$\mathbf{A}(2) = \begin{bmatrix} 1 & \frac{2}{3} \\ 0 & 5\frac{1}{3} \end{bmatrix} \qquad \mathbf{I}(2) = \begin{bmatrix} \frac{1}{3} & 0 \\ -\frac{1}{3} & 1 \end{bmatrix}$$

(N.B. In terms of Example 1, $\mathbf{A}(2) = \mathbf{E}_2\mathbf{E}_1\mathbf{A}$, $\mathbf{I}(2) = \mathbf{E}_2\mathbf{E}_1$.)

STEP 3 Convert the diagonal element in the second column to zero by scaling the second row by $\frac{3}{16}$. Apply the same operation to **I**(2):

$$\mathbf{A}(3) = \begin{bmatrix} 1 & \frac{2}{3} \\ 0 & 1 \end{bmatrix} \qquad \mathbf{I}(3) = \begin{bmatrix} \frac{1}{3} & 0 \\ -\frac{1}{16} & \frac{3}{16} \end{bmatrix}$$

(N.B. In terms of Example 1, $\mathbf{A}(3) = \mathbf{E}_3\mathbf{E}_2\mathbf{E}_1\mathbf{A}$, $\mathbf{I}(3) = \mathbf{E}_3\mathbf{E}_2\mathbf{E}_1$.)

STEP 4 Convert the element in the second column and first row to zero by adding $-\frac{2}{3} \times$ the second row to the first row. Apply the same operation to **I**(3):

$$\mathbf{A}(4) = \begin{bmatrix} 1 & 0 \\ 0 & 1 \end{bmatrix} \qquad \mathbf{I}(4) = \begin{bmatrix} \frac{3}{8} & -\frac{2}{16} \\ -\frac{1}{16} & \frac{3}{16} \end{bmatrix}$$

(N.B. In terms of Example 1, $\mathbf{A}(4) = \mathbf{E}_4\mathbf{E}_3\mathbf{E}_2\mathbf{E}_1\mathbf{A}$, $\mathbf{I}(4) = \mathbf{E}_4\mathbf{E}_3\mathbf{E}_2\mathbf{E}_1$.)

The final step is to set $\mathbf{A}^{-1} = \mathbf{I}(4)$.

Example 3 Find the inverse of

$$\mathbf{A} = \begin{bmatrix} 3 & 0 & 2 \\ 0 & 1 & 0 \\ 5 & 0 & 4 \end{bmatrix}$$

We shall employ the two-stage method in which we first convert the below-diagonal elements and then the remaining (diagonal and above-diagonal) elements.

STAGE 1: STEP 1 The top below-diagonal element in the first column is the element in the second row. Since this element is already zero no further operations are required.

STEP 2 The only other below-diagonal element in the first column is the element in the third row. To convert this element to zero add $-\frac{5}{3}\times$ the first row to the third row. Apply the same operation to the 3×3 identity matrix $\mathbf{I}$:

$$\mathbf{A}(2) = \begin{bmatrix} 3 & 0 & 2 \\ 0 & 1 & 0 \\ 0 & 0 & \frac{2}{3} \end{bmatrix} \qquad \mathbf{I}(2) = \begin{bmatrix} 1 & 0 & 0 \\ 0 & 1 & 0 \\ -\frac{5}{3} & 0 & 1 \end{bmatrix}$$

STEP 3 The only below-diagonal element in the second column is the element in the third row, which is already zero. Since all the below-diagonal elements are zero the first stage is completed.

STAGE 2: STEP 4 Convert the diagonal element in the first column to unity by scaling the first row by $\frac{1}{3}$. Apply the same operation to $\mathbf{I}(2)$:

$$\mathbf{A}(4) = \begin{bmatrix} 1 & 0 & \frac{2}{3} \\ 0 & 1 & 0 \\ 0 & 0 & \frac{2}{3} \end{bmatrix} \qquad \mathbf{I}(4) = \begin{bmatrix} \frac{1}{3} & 0 & 0 \\ 0 & 1 & 0 \\ -\frac{5}{3} & 0 & 1 \end{bmatrix}$$

STEP 5 The diagonal element in the second column is already unity. No further operations are required.

STEP 6 The only above-diagonal element in the second column is the element in the first row. Since this element is already zero no further operations are required.

STEP 7 Convert the diagonal element in the third column to unity by scaling the third row by $1\frac{1}{2}$. Apply the same operation to $\mathbf{I}(4)$:

$$\mathbf{A}(7) = \begin{bmatrix} 1 & 0 & \frac{2}{3} \\ 0 & 1 & 0 \\ 0 & 0 & 1 \end{bmatrix} \qquad \mathbf{I}(7) = \begin{bmatrix} \frac{1}{3} & 0 & 0 \\ 0 & 1 & 0 \\ -2\frac{1}{2} & 0 & 1\frac{1}{2} \end{bmatrix}$$

STEP 8 Convert the top above-diagonal element in the third column to zero by adding $-\frac{2}{3}\times$ the third row to the first row. Apply the same operation to $\mathbf{I}(7)$:

$$\mathbf{A}(8) = \begin{bmatrix} 1 & 0 & 0 \\ 0 & 1 & 0 \\ 0 & 0 & 1 \end{bmatrix} \qquad \mathbf{I}(8) = \begin{bmatrix} 2 & 0 & -1 \\ 0 & 1 & 0 \\ -2\frac{1}{2} & 0 & 1\frac{1}{2} \end{bmatrix}$$

STEP 9 The only remaining above-diagonal element in the third column is the element in the second row which is already zero. Since $\mathbf{A}(8) = \mathbf{I}$ no further steps are required. It remains to identify $\mathbf{I}(8)$ with the inverse $\mathbf{A}^{-1}$.

CHECK Does $\mathbf{AI}(8) = \mathbf{I}$?

$$\begin{bmatrix} 3 & 0 & 2 \\ 0 & 1 & 0 \\ 5 & 0 & 4 \end{bmatrix} \begin{bmatrix} 2 & 0 & -1 \\ 0 & 1 & 0 \\ -2\frac{1}{2} & 0 & 1\frac{1}{2} \end{bmatrix} = \begin{bmatrix} 1 & 0 & 0 \\ 0 & 1 & 0 \\ 0 & 0 & 1 \end{bmatrix}$$

The only difficulty occurs when one of the diagonal elements is equal to zero, either in **A** itself or in one of the auxiliary matrices, $\mathbf{A}(i)$. If this occurs, add a suitable row of the matrix to the row in which the zero diagonal element appears, and apply the same operation to the matrix $\mathbf{I}(i)$. If no suitable row of the matrix can be found, or if the addition of a suitable row inevitably reverses one of the first stage steps (i.e. converts to a nonzero value a below-diagonal element which has previously been set equal to zero) then it is impossible to convert **A** into an identity matrix. In this case no inverse matrix exists. If the first stage is completed successfully, leaving all below-diagonal elements zero and all diagonal elements nonzero, then the second stage of the evaluation of the inverse is purely routine. On the other hand, if the first stage cannot be completed successfully then no inverse exists.

(ii) Method of partitioning

It is sometimes useful to regard a matrix as being built up out of submatrices. A particularly useful 'partitioning' is of the form

$$\mathbf{A} = \left[\begin{array}{c|c} \mathbf{A}_1 & \mathbf{A}_2 \\ (p \times p) & (p \times q) \\ \hline \mathbf{A}_4 & \mathbf{A}_3 \\ (q \times p) & (q \times q) \end{array}\right]$$

where $\mathbf{A}_1$ and $\mathbf{A}_3$ are square matrices. Suppose that the inverse is partitioned in the same way:

$$\mathbf{A}^{-1} = \left[\begin{array}{c|c} \boldsymbol{\alpha}_1 & \boldsymbol{\alpha}_2 \\ (p \times p) & (p \times q) \\ \hline \boldsymbol{\alpha}_4 & \boldsymbol{\alpha}_3 \\ (q \times p) & (q \times q) \end{array}\right]$$

Since $\mathbf{AA}^{-1}$ we find that

$$\left[\begin{array}{c|c} \mathbf{A}_1 & \mathbf{A}_2 \\ \hline \mathbf{A}_4 & \mathbf{A}_3 \end{array}\right] \left[\begin{array}{c|c} \boldsymbol{\alpha}_1 & \boldsymbol{\alpha}_2 \\ \hline \boldsymbol{\alpha}_4 & \boldsymbol{\alpha}_3 \end{array}\right] = \left[\begin{array}{c|c} \mathbf{I} & \mathbf{0} \\ (p \times p) & (p \times q) \\ \hline \mathbf{0} & \mathbf{I} \\ (q \times p) & (q \times q) \end{array}\right]$$

whence

$$(1) \qquad \mathbf{A}_1\boldsymbol{\alpha}_1 + \mathbf{A}_2\boldsymbol{\alpha}_4 = \mathbf{I}$$

$$(2) \qquad \mathbf{A}_1\boldsymbol{\alpha}_2 + \mathbf{A}_2\boldsymbol{\alpha}_3 = \mathbf{0}$$

$$(3) \qquad \mathbf{A}_4\boldsymbol{\alpha}_1 + \mathbf{A}_3\boldsymbol{\alpha}_4 = \mathbf{0}$$

$$(4) \qquad \mathbf{A}_4\boldsymbol{\alpha}_2 + \mathbf{A}_3\boldsymbol{\alpha}_3 = \mathbf{I}$$

Since $\mathbf{A}_1$, $\mathbf{A}_3$ are square $\mathbf{A}_1^{-1}$, $\mathbf{A}_3^{-1}$ are defined. Multiplying equation (2) throughout by $\mathbf{A}_1^{-1}$ and rearranging terms gives

$$(5) \qquad \boldsymbol{\alpha}_2 = -\mathbf{A}_1^{-1}\mathbf{A}_2\boldsymbol{\alpha}_3$$

Substituting (5) into (4) gives

$$(6) \qquad \boldsymbol{\alpha}_3 = (\mathbf{A}_3 - \mathbf{A}_4\mathbf{A}_1^{-1}\mathbf{A}_2)^{-1}$$

From the fact that $\mathbf{A}^{-1}\mathbf{A} = \mathbf{I}$ we can get four more equations, of which the two most useful are

$$(7) \qquad \boldsymbol{\alpha}_1\mathbf{A}_1 + \boldsymbol{\alpha}_2\mathbf{A}_4 = \mathbf{I}$$

$$(8) \qquad \boldsymbol{\alpha}_4\mathbf{A}_1 + \boldsymbol{\alpha}_3\mathbf{A}_4 = \mathbf{0}$$

From (7) we find

$$(9) \qquad \boldsymbol{\alpha}_1 = \mathbf{A}_1^{-1} - \boldsymbol{\alpha}_2\mathbf{A}_4\mathbf{A}_1^{-1}$$

From (8) we get

$$(10) \qquad \boldsymbol{\alpha}_4 = -\boldsymbol{\alpha}_3\mathbf{A}_4\mathbf{A}_1^{-1}$$

Equations (5), (6), (9) and (10) constitute four equations which determine the four partitions of the inverse $\mathbf{A}_1^{-1}$. A convenient way of evaluating $\mathbf{A}^{-1}$ is to first determine

$$(11) \qquad \boldsymbol{\beta} = \mathbf{A}_1^{-1}\mathbf{A}_2$$

and then set

$$(12) \qquad \boldsymbol{\alpha}_3 = (\mathbf{A}_3 - \mathbf{A}_4\boldsymbol{\beta})^{-1}$$

$$(13) \qquad \boldsymbol{\alpha}_2 = -\boldsymbol{\beta}\boldsymbol{\alpha}_3$$

$$(14) \qquad \boldsymbol{\alpha}_4 = -\boldsymbol{\alpha}_3\mathbf{A}_4\mathbf{A}_1^{-1}$$

$$(15) \qquad \boldsymbol{\alpha}_1 = \mathbf{A}_1^{-1} - \boldsymbol{\beta}\boldsymbol{\alpha}_4$$

Notes and references

A very readable introduction to matrix algebra is Mills,[90] Ch. 1–3, 5; another excellent introductory book, containing interesting economic examples, is Peston,[100] Ch. 1–5. There is a lively introduction to matrix algebra in Lewis,[79] Ch. 29, 30. For a more comprehensive treatment of the subject see Aitken,[4] §1–21, and Hadley,[46] Ch. 3. Additional material, particularly relevent to economics, is covered in Allen,[7] Ch. 12, 13.

Problems

11.1 Write the following set of equations in matrix notation:

$$3x_1 + 5x_2 = 16$$

$$4x_1 + 8x_2 = 28$$

11.2 Given the row vector **r**, the column vector **s** and the rectangular matrix **T**,

$$\mathbf{r} = [2 \quad 3], \qquad \mathbf{s} = \begin{bmatrix} 4 \\ 1 \end{bmatrix}, \qquad \mathbf{T} = \begin{bmatrix} 4 & -2 \\ 0 & \frac{1}{2} \\ 3 & 3 \end{bmatrix}$$

evaluate, if possible, (i) **rs**, (ii) **sr**, (iii) **Tr**, (iv) **rT**, (v) **Ts**

11.3.1 Given the square matrices

$$\mathbf{A} = \begin{bmatrix} 2 & 4 \\ 0 & 1 \end{bmatrix}, \qquad \mathbf{B} = \begin{bmatrix} 3 & 4 \\ -2 & 2 \end{bmatrix}, \qquad \mathbf{C} = \begin{bmatrix} 2 & 1 \\ 3 & 1 \end{bmatrix}$$

(a) evaluate $5(\mathbf{A} - \mathbf{B} + \mathbf{C})$;

(b) show that (i) the matrices **A** and **B** do not commute: $\mathbf{AB} \neq \mathbf{BA}$, (ii) the multiplication of the matrices **A**, **B**, **C** is associative: $\mathbf{A}(\mathbf{BC}) = (\mathbf{AB})\mathbf{C}$, (iii) that the distributive property holds: $\mathbf{A}(\mathbf{B} + \mathbf{C}) = \mathbf{AB} + \mathbf{AC}$.

11.3.2 Given the square matrices

$$\mathbf{A} = \begin{bmatrix} a_{22} & a_{12} \\ a_{21} & a_{22} \end{bmatrix}, \qquad \mathbf{Z} = \frac{1}{a_{11}a_{22} - a_{12}a_{21}} \begin{bmatrix} a_{22} & -a_{12} \\ -a_{21} & a_{11} \end{bmatrix}, \qquad \mathbf{I} = \begin{bmatrix} 1 & 0 \\ 0 & 1 \end{bmatrix}$$

show that $\mathbf{AZ} = \mathbf{I}$ and that $\mathbf{ZA} = \mathbf{I}$.

11.4.1 Find the inverse of

$$\text{(a) } \mathbf{A} = \begin{bmatrix} 5 & 19 \\ 4 & 15 \end{bmatrix} \qquad \text{(b) } \mathbf{B} = \begin{bmatrix} 3 & 0 & 0 \\ 0 & 5 & 0 \\ 0 & 0 & 7 \end{bmatrix}$$

Check your answers.

11.4.2 Solve the equations in Problem 11.1 by finding the inverse of the appropriate matrix. Check your answer by solving the equations directly.

11.4.3 You are asked to plan the output of coal (commodity 1), steel (commodity 2) and lorries (commodity 3). To produce one ton of coal requires 0·4 tons of steel and 0·2 lorries. To produce 1 ton of steel requires 0·2 tons of coal and 0·1 lorries. To produce one lorry requires 0·6 tons of coal and 0·4 tons of steel. Consumers demand 10m tons of coal, 20m tons of steel and 10m lorries. Calculate what should be the total output of coal, steel and lorries by the following method.

(i) Write down three simultaneous equations expressing equilibrium in the coal, steel and lorry industries respectively.

(ii) Verify that the inverse of the matrix

$$\begin{bmatrix} 1{\cdot}0 & -0{\cdot}2 & -0{\cdot}6 \\ -0{\cdot}4 & 1{\cdot}0 & -0{\cdot}4 \\ -0{\cdot}2 & -0{\cdot}1 & 1{\cdot}0 \end{bmatrix} \text{ is } \frac{1}{36}\begin{bmatrix} 48 & 13 & 34 \\ 24 & 44 & 32 \\ 12 & 7 & 46 \end{bmatrix}$$

(iii) Hence solve the three simultaneous equations to find the outputs of coal, steel and lorries.

11.5.1 Let

$$\mathbf{A} = \begin{bmatrix} 3 & 2 & 4 \\ 1 & 6 & 6 \end{bmatrix} \qquad \mathbf{x} = \begin{bmatrix} 1 \\ 3 \end{bmatrix}$$

Evaluate, if possible,

(i) $\mathbf{x}^T\mathbf{A}$ (ii) $\mathbf{A}^T\mathbf{x}$ (iii) $\mathbf{x}\mathbf{x}^T$

(iv) $\mathbf{x}^T\mathbf{x}$ (v) $\mathbf{A}^T\mathbf{A}$ (vi) $\mathbf{A}\mathbf{A}^T$

11.5.2 The n-element unit vector is defined as

$$\mathbf{1} = \begin{bmatrix} 1 \\ 1 \\ \vdots \\ 1 \end{bmatrix}$$

Given the vector

$$\mathbf{x} = \begin{bmatrix} x_1 \\ x_2 \\ \vdots \\ x_n \end{bmatrix}$$

show that $\mathbf{1}^T\mathbf{x} = \mathbf{x}^T\mathbf{1} = \Sigma_{i=1}^{n} x_i$

11.6.1 Evaluate the determinants of the matrix

$$\mathbf{A} = \begin{bmatrix} 2 & 5 \\ 1 & 6 \end{bmatrix}$$

using each of the methods described in the text.

11.6.2 The determinant of the product of two matrices is equal to the product of the determinants.

(a) Verify this result for the matrices

$$\mathbf{A} = \begin{bmatrix} 1 & 4 \\ 1 & 8 \end{bmatrix}, \qquad \mathbf{B} = \begin{bmatrix} 2 & 5 \\ 6 & 10 \end{bmatrix}$$

(b) Use this result to prove that for the square matrices $\mathbf{A}_1, \mathbf{A}_2, \ldots, \mathbf{A}_n$,

$$\det[\mathbf{A}_1\mathbf{A}_2 \ldots \mathbf{A}_n] = \det[\mathbf{A}_1]\det[\mathbf{A}_2] \ldots \det[\mathbf{A}_n]$$

(*Hint:* Prove it by *induction.* Prove that if it is true for $n = k$ then it is true for $n = k + 1$; then, since it is true for $n = 2$, it must be true for any n.)

11.7.1 Expansion by alien cofactors If a determinant is expanded by multiplying a row or column into the cofactors of an alien row or (respectively) column then the result is equal to zero; e.g. expanding by the ith row of a matrix $\mathbf{A}$,

$$a_{i1}c_{j1} + a_{i2}c_{j2} + \cdots + a_{in}c_{jn} = \begin{cases} 0 \text{ for } i \neq j \\ \det[\mathbf{A}] \text{ for } i = j \end{cases}$$

Verify this result by taking in turn each of the three rows of the matrix

$$\begin{bmatrix} 2 & -5 & 4 \\ 1 & 0 & 7 \\ -3 & -3 & -1 \end{bmatrix}$$

11.7.2 Invariance of determinants If to any row or column of a matrix is added a sum of multiples of other rows or (respectively) columns of the matrix then the determinant of the resulting matrix is equal to the determinant of the original matrix; e.g. taking the first row of the matrix $\mathbf{A}$, for any real numbers $\xi_1, \xi_2, \ldots, \xi_{n-1}$,

$$(*) \qquad \det\begin{bmatrix} a_{11} + \xi_1 a_{12} + \xi_2 a_{13} + \cdots + \xi_{n-1}a_{1n} & a_{12} \cdots a_{1n} \\ a_{21} + \xi_1 a_{22} + \xi_2 a_{23} + \cdots + \xi_{n-1}a_{2n} & a_{22} \cdots a_{2n} \\ \vdots & \vdots \ddots \vdots \\ a_{n1} + \xi_1 a_{n2} + \xi_2 a_{n3} + \cdots + \xi_{n-1}a_{nn} & a_{n2} \cdots a_{nn} \end{bmatrix} = \det\begin{bmatrix} a_{11} & \cdots & a_{1n} \\ \vdots & \ddots & \vdots \\ a_{n1} & \cdots & a_{nn} \end{bmatrix}$$

(a) Verify that adding twice the second column to the first column does not change the determinant of the matrix

$$\mathbf{A} = \begin{bmatrix} 2 & 5 \\ 1 & 4 \end{bmatrix}$$

(b) Prove equation (*). (*Hint:* Think of expanding the left-hand determinant by the first column, and then make use of the result on alien cofactors given in Problem 11.7.1. These are the only two steps in the proof.)

11.7.3 Linear dependence A set of vectors is said to be 'linearly dependent' if one vector can be expressed as a sum of multiples of the other vectors, i.e. if in a set of vectors $\mathbf{x}_1, \mathbf{x}_2, \ldots, \mathbf{x}_n$, one vector, $\mathbf{x}_i$, is a weighted sum of the other vectors

$$\mathbf{x}_i = \alpha_1\mathbf{x}_1 + \cdots + \alpha_{i-1}\mathbf{x}_{i-1} + \alpha_{i+1}\mathbf{x}_{i+1} + \cdots + \alpha_n\mathbf{x}_n$$

where at least one $\alpha_j \neq 0$. If a set of vectors is not linearly dependent then it is said to be a 'linearly independent' set.

(a) Prove that if the column vectors which constitute the columns of a square matrix **A** are linearly dependent then det $[\mathbf{A}] = 0$ (use the result on the invariance of determinants).

(b) By similar reasoning, prove that if the rows of a square matrix **A** are linearly dependent then det $[\mathbf{A}] = 0$.

11.7.4 (**11.7.3** continued) The determinant of a square matrix **A** is zero if and only if the columns (or rows) of the matrix **A** are linearly dependent; also the columns of the matrix **A** are linearly dependent if and only if the rows are linearly dependent. Verify this result for the matrix

$$\mathbf{A} = \begin{bmatrix} 9 & 8 & 7 \\ -5 & -2 & 1 \\ 4 & 6 & 8 \end{bmatrix}$$

11.8.1 Evaluate the inverse of

$$\mathbf{A} = \begin{bmatrix} 6 & 0 & -2 \\ -1 & 5 & -1 \\ -1 & -1 & 7 \end{bmatrix}$$

and check that the inverse, $\mathbf{A}^{-1}$, satisfies

$$\mathbf{A}^{-1}\mathbf{A} = \mathbf{I}$$

11.8.2 Two countries, 1 and 2, engage in trade. Exogenous demand in country 1 increases by £ΔEm. The induced increases in income in countries 1 and 2 are £ΔY_1m, £ΔY_2m, respectively. Let c_1, c_2 be the marginal propensities to consume in countries 1 and 2, and let m_1, m_2 be the marginal propensities to import in countries 1 and 2. Denote the marginal propensities to save as

$$s_1 = 1 - c_1; \qquad s_2 = 1 - c_2$$

By using Cramer's rule, show that in country 1 the international trade multiplier for domestic income is

$$\Delta Y_1/\Delta E_1 = (s_2 + m_2)/(s_1 s_2 + m_1 s_2 + m_2 s_1)$$

and that the international trade multiplier for foreign income is

$$\Delta Y_2/\Delta E_1 = m_1/(s_1 s_2 + m_1 s_2 + m_2 s_1)$$

11.8.3 Verify that if an economy with n industries is of the kind described in Section 10.7 the equilibrium outputs satisfy the equations $\mathbf{Ax} = \mathbf{y}$ where **A** is an $n \times n$ matrix of input-output coefficients, **x** is an n-element column vector of outputs and **y** is an n-element column vector of final demands. Show that if the value added by production in the ith industry is £V_i per unit output then the prices of the n commodities are determined by the equation

$$\mathbf{p} = (\mathbf{I} - \mathbf{A}^T)^{-1}\mathbf{v}$$

where **p** is an n-element column vector of prices (in £) and **v** is an n-element column vector of value added per unit output. Show that for a square matrix $\mathbf{Z}$, $(\mathbf{Z}^T)^{-1} = (\mathbf{Z}^{-1})^T$. Hence show that in the n-industry economy the total cost of goods supplied to final demand, $\mathbf{p}^T\mathbf{y}$ is equal to the total value added in production, $\mathbf{v}^T\mathbf{x}$.

11.9.1 Evaluate all the minors of the matrix

$$\mathbf{A} = \begin{bmatrix} 3 & 2 \\ 1 & 6 \\ 2 & 4 \end{bmatrix}$$

11.9.2 The rank of the product of two matrices, $\mathbf{C} = \mathbf{AB}$, cannot exceed the rank of either of the matrices $\mathbf{A}$, $\mathbf{B}$. Verify this result for the matrices

$$\mathbf{A} = \begin{bmatrix} 3 & 4 & 5 \\ 2 & 6 & 1 \end{bmatrix} \qquad \mathbf{B} = \begin{bmatrix} 6 & 4 \\ 3 & 2 \\ 9 & 6 \end{bmatrix}$$

11.9.3 Evaluate all the principal minors of the matrix

$$\mathbf{A} = \begin{bmatrix} 3 & 5 & 7 \\ 1 & 2 & 4 \\ 1 & 1 & 3 \end{bmatrix}$$

Chapter 12

Simultaneous linear equations: existence, uniqueness and feasibility of the solution

12.1 Introduction

Having studied the elements of matrix algebra in the previous chapter we are now in a position to investigate the general properties of the solution of m simultaneous linear equations in n unknowns. The inquiry in this chapter is centred on three main questions:

(i) does a solution of the equations necessarily exist?
(ii) if a solution exists, is it unique?
(iii) if there is a solution, is it feasible?

These questions are not merely of academic importance. When simultaneous equations represent the equilibrium conditions of an economy, the nature of the solution indicates the nature of the equilibrium. If an equilibrium state is not unique the consequences can be very severe, not only economically, but socially and politically as well.[1] The consequences of there being no equilibrium at all, or no feasible equilibrium, can be catastrophic.[2]

We shall begin by analysing the case in which the number of equations is equal to the number of unknowns, $m = n$. This case is important in its own right and also highlights some of the problems encountered in the more general case.

1 For example, in the simple closed economy described in Section 3.8 the equilibrium will always be unique unless the marginal propensity to consume is exactly equal to one—which is not very likely. In this case, however, the consequence is severe, for income can be stabilized at a chosen level only when total exogenous demand is zero.

2 International monetary problems can often be analysed in terms of failure to adapt to circumstances in which there is no feasible solution to the equilibrium conditions of the world economy. The problem arises when several countries simultaneously pursue policies of full employment and balance of payments stability. A temporary solution to the problem is to float national currencies to make price levels flexible.

12.2 A necessary and sufficient condition for a unique solution to *n* equations in *n* unknowns

A set of n simultaneous linear equations in n unknowns is written in matrix notation

$$\mathbf{Ax} = \mathbf{y}$$

where $\mathbf{A}$ is a $n \times n$ matrix and $\mathbf{x}$ and $\mathbf{y}$ are n-element column vectors. This matrix equation is solved by finding the inverse $\mathbf{A}^{-1}$ and setting

$$\mathbf{x} = \mathbf{A}^{-1}\mathbf{y}$$

which determines the unknown vector $\mathbf{x}$ as a function of the inverse matrix $\mathbf{A}^{-1}$ and the vector $\mathbf{y}$. Since the elements of $\mathbf{y}$ are known constants, $\mathbf{y}$ certainly exists and is unique. Consequently $\mathbf{x}$ will also exist and be unique if and only if $\mathbf{A}^{-1}$ exists and is unique. Now the form of $\mathbf{A}^{-1}$ depends only on the form of $\mathbf{A}$; this shows that the existence of a unique solution to $\mathbf{Ax} = \mathbf{y}$ depends only on the matrix $\mathbf{A}$. By using the results of Chapter 11 it is easy to prove:

Theorem 12.1 A necessary and sufficient condition for a unique solution to a set of n simultaneous linear equations in n unknowns, $\mathbf{Ax} = \mathbf{y}$, is that $\det[\mathbf{A}] \neq 0$.

The proof is based on two lemmas.

Lemma 1 If the inverse of a square matrix exists then it is unique.

PROOF Firstly, note that if $\mathbf{A}^{-1}\mathbf{A} = \mathbf{I}$ then, since $\mathbf{A}$ is square and $\mathbf{I}$ is square and multiplication is defined, $\mathbf{A}^{-1}$ must be square and must have the same dimensions as $\mathbf{A}$. Consequently $\mathbf{AA}^{-1}$ is defined. However, if $\mathbf{AA}^{-1}$ is defined then, since

$$\mathbf{IA} = \mathbf{AI} = \mathbf{A}(\mathbf{A}^{-1}\mathbf{A}) = (\mathbf{AA}^{-1})\mathbf{A}$$

it follows that

$$\mathbf{AA}^{-1} = \mathbf{I}$$

Suppose there is another matrix, $\mathbf{Z}$, which is also the inverse of $\mathbf{A}$; $\mathbf{Z}$ must satisfy the equation defining the inverse,

$$\mathbf{ZA} = \mathbf{I}$$

It follows by the same argument as above that $\mathbf{Z}$ must also satisfy the equation

$$\mathbf{AZ} = \mathbf{I}$$

A little manipulation shows that

$$\mathbf{Z} = \mathbf{ZI} = \mathbf{Z}(\mathbf{AA}^{-1}) = (\mathbf{ZA})\mathbf{A}^{-1} = \mathbf{IA}^{-1} = \mathbf{A}^{-1}$$

so that the two inverses, $\mathbf{Z}$ and $\mathbf{A}^{-1}$, are identical. It follows that the inverse is unique.

Lemma 2 The inverse of a square matrix $\mathbf{A}$ exists if and only if $\det[\mathbf{A}] \neq 0$.

PROOF Since the inverse matrix is unique it must be of the form described in Theorem 11.6, in which each of the elements is scaled by a factor 1/det [**A**]; this scalar has a finite value if and only if det [**A**] $\neq 0$. It follows that det [**A**] $\neq 0$ is a necessary and sufficient condition for the existence of a unique inverse.

Since the inverse of a square matrix exists if and only if det [**A**] $\neq 0$, and the inverse is unique, it follows that the equations $\mathbf{Ax} = \mathbf{y}$ have a unique solution if and only if det [**A**] $\neq 0$.

12.3 The case of no unique solution to n equations in n unknowns

It is sometimes alleged that whenever there are an equal number of equations and unknowns there must be a unique solution. Theorem 12.1 shows this to be wrong; there is a unique solution only if the determinant of the appropriate matrix is nonzero. It is not necessarily true that a set of linear equations in an equal number of unknowns has any solution at all, let alone a unique solution. The point is illustrated by the simple examples invoiving linear equations which are given on the next page. These examples also illustrate special cases of Theorem 12.1.

One linear equation in one unknown

Does there necessarily exist a solution to the equation

$$a_{11}x = y?$$

No. If $a_{11} = 0$ then, whatever the value of x, the left-hand side of the equation is zero. If the right-hand side is nonzero, $y \neq 0$, so that there cannot be a solution, since there is no value of x which will equate the left-hand side to the right-hand side.

Even if a solution does exist, it may not be unique. Suppose that $a_{11} = 0$ and that $y = 0$ as well. Whatever the value of x, both the left-hand side and the right-hand side of the equation are equal to zero. In other words, when $a_{11} = 0$ and $y = 0$ any value of x will solve the equation so that there is no unique solution.

It follows that a necessary condition for there to be a unique solution to the equation

$$a_{11}x = y$$

is that $a_{11} \neq 0$. This confirms the result of Theorem 12.1, that the determinant of the matrix $[a_{11}]$ must be nonzero.

Two linear equations in two unknowns

Consider the two equations

$$x_1 + 3x_2 = 5$$

$$2x_1 + 6x_2 = 11$$

The equations are inconsistent and have no solution. By doubling the first equation we obtain

$$2x_1 + 6x_2 = 10$$

and this is inconsistent with the second equation. Consequently there can be no values of x_1 and x_2 which satisfy both equations, i.e. a solution does not exist. The position is illustrated in Fig. 12A. Because the left-hand side of one equation is a simple multiple of the left-hand side of the other, the graphs of the two equations must be parallel lines. Because the right-hand sides are not in the same ratio as the left-hand sides, the parallel lines do not coincide. Since the lines are distinct and parallel they do not meet, so that there is no point (x_1, x_2) which lies on both lines, and hence there is no solution (x_1, x_2) which satisfies both equations.

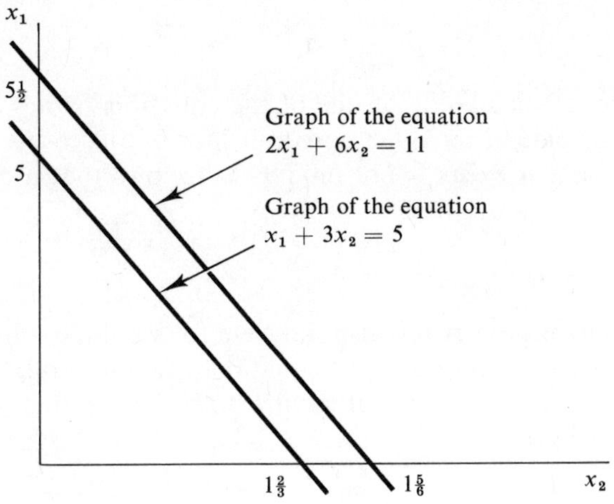

Fig. 12A

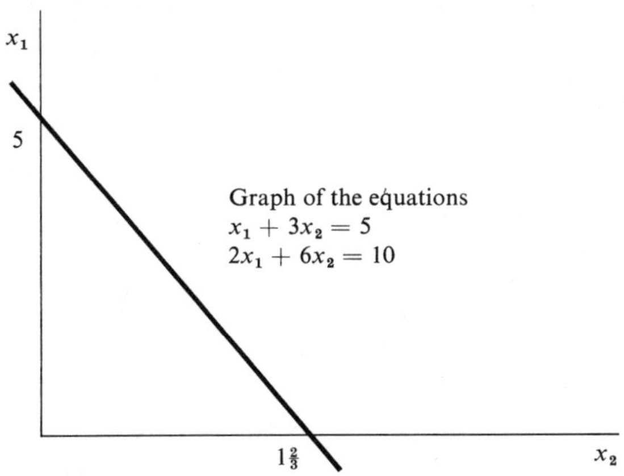

Fig. 12B

Even if a solution does exist it may not be unique. Suppose that the right-hand sides of the equations are in the same ratio as the left-hand sides. For example, if the two equations are

$$x_1 + 3x_2 = 5$$

$$2x_1 + 6x_2 = 10$$

then the second equation is a simple multiple of the first, so that if the first equation is satisfied then the second equation is satisfied as well. In other words, there is really only one equation, not two. This is illustrated in Fig. 12B where the graphs of the two equations coincide. All the points (x_1, x_2) on the straight line graph represent solutions of the equations.

It follows that for a unique solution to the two simultaneous linear equations

$$a_{11}x_1 + a_{12}x_2 = y_1$$

$$a_{21}x_1 + a_{22}x_2 = y_2$$

it is necessary that the left-hand side of one of the equations is not a simple multiple of the left-hand side of the other equations, for in this case a solution either does not exist, or if it exists is not unique. It follows that a necessary condition for a unique solution is that

$$a_{11}/a_{21} \neq a_{12}/a_{22}$$

This condition is not only necessary but also sufficient for a unique solution, for it implies that the straight-line graphs of the equations are not parallel, so that they must meet at a unique point. On multiplying both sides of this condition throughout by $a_{21}a_{22}$ we get

$$a_{11}a_{22} \neq a_{12}a_{21}$$

In other words, it is necessary and sufficient for a unique solution that

$$a_{11}a_{22} - a_{12}a_{21} \neq 0$$

which we may write

$$\det \begin{bmatrix} a_{11} & a_{12} \\ a_{21} & a_{22} \end{bmatrix} \neq 0$$

This confirms the result of Theorem 12.1, that the determinant of the matrix associated with the equations must be nonzero.

An interesting result emerges from the examples above, namely, that when there is no solution to the equations $\mathbf{Ax} = \mathbf{y}$ then a solution either does not exist, or is not unique, *depending on the relationship between the elements of the vector* $\mathbf{y}$ *and the elements of the matrix* $\mathbf{A}$. The way in which this relationship determines the category of the solution is described in Theorem 12.2 below. The theorem is expressed most elegantly by using the concept of the 'rank' of a matrix.

12.4 Necessary and sufficient conditions for existence and uniqueness of a solution

The concept of rank is fundamental in matrix algebra. Rank was defined in Section 11.9 as follows:

Definition The rank of a $m \times n$ matrix **A**, $r(\mathbf{A})$, is the dimension of the largest square matrix with a nonzero determinant which can be formed from **A** by deleting either rows, or columns, or both (or possibly, if **A** is square, by taking **A** itself).

The definition of rank applies to rectangular as well as to square matrices. It is an immediate consequence of the definition that

(i) a square $n \times n$ matrix **A** has a rank equal to n or less than n depending on whether $\det[\mathbf{A}] \neq 0$ or $\det[\mathbf{A}] = 0$.

(ii) a rectangular $m \times n$ matrix cannot have a rank exceeding the smaller of m and n.

By using the concept of the rank of a matrix it is possible to provide a general statement of the conditions under which a set of m simultaneous linear equations in n unknowns have either a unique solution, a solution which is not unique, or no solution at all.

Theorem 12.2 The nature of the solution of a set of m simultaneous linear equations in n unknowns

$$\mathbf{Ax} = \mathbf{y}$$

depends on the rank of the matrix **A** and on the rank of the augmented matrix

$$\mathbf{A}^* = \begin{bmatrix} a_{11}a_{12} & \cdots & a_{1n}y_1 \\ a_{21}a_{22} & \cdots & a_{2n}y_2 \\ \vdots\ \vdots & \ddots & \vdots \\ a_{m1}a_{m2} & \cdots & a_{mn}y_m \end{bmatrix} = [\mathbf{A}, \mathbf{y}]$$

There is a unique solution if $r(\mathbf{A}^*) = r(\mathbf{A}) = n$, there are an infinite number of solutions if $r(\mathbf{A}^*) = r(\mathbf{A}) < n$ and there is no solution if $r(\mathbf{A}^*) > r(\mathbf{A})$. These conditions are necessary and sufficient; they exhaust all the possibilities.

A close examination of Theorem 12.2 reveals a number of salient points.

(I) The *existence* of a solution to a set of m linear equations in n unknowns depends on the relationship between the rank of the matrix A and the rank of the augmented matrix $\mathbf{A}^*$; the *uniqueness* of a solution depends only on the rank of the matrix **A**.

(II) A set of m linear equations in n unknowns has a unique solution only if the number of equations is greater than or equal to the number of unknowns (i.e. if $m \geqslant n$)

An intuitive proof can be given as follows.

To determine one unknown, x_1, it is clearly necessary to have at least one equation of the form

$$a_{11}x_1 = y_1$$

However, such an equation is not always *sufficient* to determine x_1 since, as we saw in Section 13.3, when $a_{11} = 0$ the equation cannot be solved.

To determine two unknowns x_1, x_2 it is necessary to have at least the two equations

$$a_{11}x_1 + a_{12}x_2 = y_1$$

$$a_{21}x_1 + a_{22}x_2 = y_2$$

The first equation requires only that when x_1 takes on a value x^*, x_2 takes on the value $y_1/a_{11} - a_{12}x^*/a_{11}$. This is not, in itself, sufficient to determine both x_1 and x_2. Similarly, the second equation, by itself, is not sufficient to determine both x_1 and x_2. It should be noted that the two equations together do not necessarily determine unique values for x_1 and x_2, for it was seen in Section 12.3 that if $a_{11}/a_{21} = a_{12}/a_{22}$ the equations have no unique solution.

By extending this argument to cases involving more than two unknowns it is readily established that to solve a set of equations for n unknowns it is necessary that there are at least n equations. An illustration of the theorem is given by the following example.

Example Solve two equations in the three unknowns x_1, x_2, x_3:

$$3x_1 + 2x_2 + 5x_3 = 10$$

$$6x_1 + 4x_2 + 9x_3 = 18$$

Multiply the first equation throughout by 2 and subtract from it the second equation; this gives

$$x_3 = 2$$

Substituting back this result, we obtain

$$3x_1 + 2x_2 = 0$$

$$6x_1 + 4x_2 = 0$$

These equations tell us only that $x_1 = (\frac{2}{3})x_2$. Consequently there is no unique solution for x_1 and x_2.

A further consequence of Theorem 12.2 is

(III) If a set of simultaneous linear equations has a solution which is not unique, there is necessarily an infinite number of solutions.

This result may at first appear remarkable, but in fact its proof is quite elementary. Suppose that there are two solutions of the equation

(1) $\quad \mathbf{Ax} = \mathbf{y}$

Let the two solutions be represented by the vectors $\mathbf{x}_1, \mathbf{x}_2$. Since both $\mathbf{x}_1, \mathbf{x}_2$ are solutions of equation (1),

(2) $\mathbf{A}\mathbf{x}_1 = \mathbf{y}, \quad \mathbf{A}\mathbf{x}_2 = \mathbf{y}$

Let λ be some arbitrary real number. We shall show that any vector $\mathbf{z}$ of the form

(3) $\mathbf{z} = \lambda\mathbf{x}_1 + (1 - \lambda)\mathbf{x}_2$

is also a solution of equation (1). Write

$$\mathbf{A}\mathbf{z} = \mathbf{A}[\lambda\mathbf{x}_1 + (1 - \lambda)\mathbf{x}_2]$$

and use the distributive law of matrix multiplication to put the right-hand side into the form

$$\mathbf{A}\mathbf{z} = \mathbf{A}\lambda\mathbf{x}_1 + \mathbf{A}(1 - \lambda)\mathbf{x}_2$$

Since λ and $(1 - \lambda)$ are scalars the terms on the right-hand side may be written

$$\mathbf{A}\mathbf{z} = \lambda\mathbf{A}\mathbf{x}_1 + (1 - \lambda)\mathbf{A}\mathbf{x}_2$$

By using equations (2) we have

$$\begin{aligned} \mathbf{A}\mathbf{z} &= \lambda\mathbf{y} + (1 - \lambda)\mathbf{y} \\ &= \mathbf{y} \end{aligned}$$

which proves that the vector $\mathbf{z}$ is a solution of equation (1). Since there are an infinite number of vectors $\mathbf{z}$ corresponding to different values of λ there are an infinite number of solutions to equation (1).

In Problem 12.4.11 the reader is asked to demonstrate that Theorem 12.1 is a special case ($m = n$) of Theorem 12.2.

The application of Theorem 12.2 is illustrated by the following examples.

Example 1 The equilibrium conditions of an economy are

$$\begin{aligned} 0{\cdot}6x_1 - 0{\cdot}4x_2 &= 20 \\ -0{\cdot}3x_1 + 0{\cdot}2x_2 &= 40 \end{aligned}$$

Is there an equilibrium state and, if so, is it unique?

(i) *Examine the rank of* **A**. The 2×2 matrix **A** is

$$\mathbf{A} = \begin{bmatrix} 0{\cdot}6 & -0{\cdot}4 \\ -0{\cdot}3 & 0{\cdot}2 \end{bmatrix}$$

To determine the rank of **A** we must find the dimension of the largest square matrix with a nonzero determinant which can be formed from **A**, and to do this it is sufficient to find the first nonzero minor in a sequence of minors; this sequence contains all the minors of the matrix **A** ordered by the size of the square matrix to which the minor corresponds, beginning with the minor corresponding to the largest square matrix that can be formed from **A** (see Section 11.9). The largest square matrix that can be formed from **A** is **A** itself; consequently the first minor in the sequence of minors is the determinant of **A**, which is equal to zero:

$$\det \begin{bmatrix} 0{\cdot}6 & -0{\cdot}4 \\ -0{\cdot}3 & 0{\cdot}2 \end{bmatrix} = 0$$

Since the first minor in the sequence is zero we proceed to examine further minors in the sequence. The next minors in the sequence are the determinants of the 1×1 matrices formed from **A**; each of these minors is equal to an element of the matrix **A**. Since, by inspection, the elements of **A** are nonzero, each of these minors is nonzero, and so the first nonzero minor in the sequence of minors corresponds to a 1×1 matrix; hence the rank of **A** is equal to 1.

(ii) *Examine the rank of* $\mathbf{A}^*$. The augmented matrix $\mathbf{A}^* = [\mathbf{A}, \mathbf{y}]$ is

$$\mathbf{A}^* = \begin{bmatrix} 0{\cdot}6 & -0{\cdot}4 & 20 \\ -0{\cdot}3 & 0{\cdot}2 & 40 \end{bmatrix}$$

The largest square matrix that can be formed from $\mathbf{A}^*$ is a 2×2 matrix; hence the sequence of minors begins with the minors which correspond to each of the matrices that can be formed from $\mathbf{A}^*$. These minors are the determinants of the matrices

$$\begin{bmatrix} 0{\cdot}6 & -0{\cdot}4 \\ -0{\cdot}3 & 0{\cdot}2 \end{bmatrix}, \begin{bmatrix} 0{\cdot}6 & 20 \\ -0{\cdot}3 & 40 \end{bmatrix}, \begin{bmatrix} -0{\cdot}4 & 20 \\ 0{\cdot}2 & 40 \end{bmatrix}$$

and we know from part (i) that the determinant of the first of these matrices is zero. However, it is easily verified that the determinant of the second of the matrices is equal to 30; since this is the first nonzero minor in the sequence of minors, the dimension of the matrix to which it corresponds determines the rank of $\mathbf{A}^*$. Since the minor corresponds to a 2×2 matrix the rank of $\mathbf{A}^*$ is equal to 2.

Compare the ranks. Since $r(\mathbf{A}) = 1$ and $r(\mathbf{A}^*) = 2$,

$$r(\mathbf{A}^*) > r(\mathbf{A})$$

which implies that the equilibrium conditions have no solution and so there is no equilibrium state.

When a set of linear equations, such as the equilibrium conditions above, has no solution it is because the equations are inconsistent. It is easy to demonstrate the inconsistency in this example by multiplying the second equation through by -2 to give

$$0{\cdot}6x_1 - 0{\cdot}4x_2 = -80$$

and comparing the result with the first equation,

$$0{\cdot}6x_1 - 0{\cdot}4x_2 = 20$$

The left-hand sides of the equations are the same but the right-hand sides are not.

Example 2 The equilibrium conditions of an economy are

$$0{\cdot}5x_1 + 0{\cdot}2x_2 + 0{\cdot}4x_3 = 10$$

$$0{\cdot}8x_1 + 0{\cdot}4x_2 + 0{\cdot}5x_3 = 30$$

$$0{\cdot}3x_1 + 0{\cdot}2x_2 + 0{\cdot}1x_3 = 20$$

Is there an equilibrium state and, if so, is it unique?

(i) *Examine the rank of* **A**. The 3 × 3 matrix **A** is

$$\mathbf{A} = \begin{bmatrix} 0{\cdot}5 & 0{\cdot}2 & 0{\cdot}4 \\ 0{\cdot}8 & 0{\cdot}4 & 0{\cdot}5 \\ 0{\cdot}3 & 0{\cdot}2 & 0{\cdot}1 \end{bmatrix}$$

The largest square matrix that can be formed from **A** is **A** itself and so the first minor in the sequence of minors is the determinant of **A**, which is equal to zero. Since the first minor in the sequence of minors is equal to zero, we proceed to examine the next minors in the sequence, which correspond to the 2 × 2 matrices that can be formed from **A**. By deleting the last row and last column we can form the 2 × 2 matrix

$$\begin{bmatrix} 0{\cdot}5 & 0{\cdot}2 \\ 0{\cdot}8 & 0{\cdot}4 \end{bmatrix}$$

and the determinant of this matrix is 0·04. This is the first nonzero minor in the sequence of minors; since the minor corresponds to a 2 × 2 matrix the rank of **A** is 2.

(ii) *Examine the rank of* **A***. The augmented matrix **A*** = [**A**, **y**] is

$$\mathbf{A}^* = \begin{bmatrix} 0{\cdot}5 & 0{\cdot}2 & 0{\cdot}4 & 10 \\ 0{\cdot}8 & 0{\cdot}4 & 0{\cdot}5 & 30 \\ 0{\cdot}3 & 0{\cdot}2 & 0{\cdot}1 & 20 \end{bmatrix}$$

The largest square matrix that can be formed from **A** is a 3 × 3 matrix. There are four 3 × 3 matrices that can be formed from **A** and each has a zero determinant, which means that the first four minors in the sequence of minors are equal to zero. The next minors in the sequence correspond to 2 × 2 matrices formed from **A***, and within this set of 2 × 2 matrices formed from **A*** are all the 2 × 2 matrices that can be formed from **A**. We already know that one of the 2 × 2 matrices formed from **A** has a nonzero determinant; since this matrix can also be formed from **A***, it follows that one of the matrices formed from **A*** has a nonzero determinant. We conclude that the first nonzero minor in the sequence of minors formed from **A*** will be a minor corresponding to a 2 × 2 matrix. This determines the rank of **A*** as equal to 2. It is, in fact, a general rule that the rank of **A*** cannot be less than the rank of **A**; this is a consequence of the way the matrix **A*** is formed from the matrix **A**.

(iii) *Compare the ranks.* Since $r(\mathbf{A}) = 2$ and $r(\mathbf{A}^*) = 2$ the ranks are equal, but they are equal to a number less than the number of unknowns, $n = 3$.

Hence

$$r(\mathbf{A}^*) = r(\mathbf{A}) < n$$

which implies that the equilibrium conditions have an infinite number of solutions, which means that there are an infinite number of equilibrium states.

It is easy to understand intuitively why in this example the equilibrium conditions have an infinite number of solutions. Essentially, the reason is that the three linear equations representing the equilibrium conditions are not independent of one another, because given the first two equations one can deduce the third equation by subtracting the first equation from the second equation (or, alternatively, one can deduce the second equation by adding the first equation and the third equation, or one can deduce the first equation by subtracting the third equation from the second equation). Any two of the equations contain all the restrictions imposed on the values of the variables x_1, x_2, x_3; the other equation is quite redundant. If the redundant equation is removed, it is seen that there are in effect only two equations in three unknowns; the infinite number of solutions arise because two equations are not sufficient to determine uniquely the values of three unknowns.

Although there are an infinite number of solutions it is not, of course, the case that any arbitrary values of x_1, x_2, x_3 will provide a solution to the equations. By taking the first two equations, multiplying the first equation by two and subtracting the second we get

$$0{\cdot}2x_1 + 0{\cdot}3x_3 = -10$$

and by multiplying the first equation by 8, multiplying the second equation by 5 and subtracting the first equation from the second equation we get

$$0{\cdot}4x_2 - 0{\cdot}7x_3 = 70$$

These equations can be written in the form

$$x_1 = -50 - 1{\cdot}5x_3$$

$$x_2 = 175 + 1{\cdot}75x_3$$

These two equations describe the solutions to the equilibrium conditions; any one of the infinite number of solutions may be found by setting x_3 equal to some arbitrary value and using these equations to find the corresponding values of x_1 and x_2. For example, setting $x_3 = 100$ gives the solution

$$x_1 = -200, x_2 = 350, x_3 = 100$$

Example 3 The equilibrium conditions of an economy are

$$0{\cdot}2x_1 + 0{\cdot}4x_2 = 12$$

$$0{\cdot}5x_1 + 1{\cdot}0x_2 = 30$$

$$0{\cdot}4x_1 - 0{\cdot}1x_2 = 6$$

Is there a unique equilibrium state, and if so, what is it?

(i) *Examine the rank of* **A**. The 3 × 2 matrix **A** is

$$\mathbf{A} = \begin{bmatrix} 0{\cdot}2 & 0{\cdot}4 \\ 0{\cdot}5 & 1{\cdot}0 \\ 0{\cdot}4 & -0{\cdot}1 \end{bmatrix}$$

The largest square matrix that can be formed from **A** is a 2 × 2 matrix. Take the last two rows and columns of **A** to form a submatrix. It is readily seen that

$$\det \begin{bmatrix} 0{\cdot}5 & 1{\cdot}0 \\ 0{\cdot}4 & -0{\cdot}1 \end{bmatrix} = -0{\cdot}45$$

so that $r(\mathbf{A}) = 2$. Since there are two unknowns, and $r(\mathbf{A}) = 2$, it follows that the solution, if it exists, is unique.

(ii) *Examine the rank of* **A***. The augmented matrix $\mathbf{A}^* = [\mathbf{A}, \mathbf{y}]$ is

$$\mathbf{A}^* = \begin{bmatrix} 0{\cdot}2 & 0{\cdot}4 & 12 \\ 0{\cdot}5 & 1{\cdot}0 & 30 \\ 0{\cdot}4 & -0{\cdot}1 & 6 \end{bmatrix}$$

It is readily seen that $\det[\mathbf{A}^*] = 0$. Consequently $r(\mathbf{A}^*) \neq 3$. Now the rank of **A*** cannot possibly exceed 3, nor can it be less than the rank of **A**; it follows that $r(\mathbf{A}^*) = 2$.

(iii) *Compare the ranks.* Since

$$r(\mathbf{A}^*) = r(\mathbf{A}) = 2$$

it follows that the three equations are uniquely soluble.

(iv) *Use two of the three equations to solve for* x_1 *and* x_2. Using the last two equations it is found that $x_1 = 20$, $x_2 = 20$. This solution describes the unique equilibrium state.

In this example it is easy to see why the three equations in two unknowns are uniquely soluble. Essentially, there are really only two equations in two unknowns, because the first equation is a simple multiple of the second. Given that the last two equations are consistent this is another way of saying that all three equations are consistent, which is reflected in the fact that $r(\mathbf{A}) = r(\mathbf{A}^*)$. On taking the last two equations in two unknowns it is seen that they have a unique solution, since the determinant of the appropriate 2 × 2 matrix formed from **A** is nonzero.

12.5 Principle of least squares

The discussion in the previous section leads to the general conclusion that, given m simultaneous linear equations in n unknowns,

(i) there will never be a unique solution if $m < n$;

(ii) there will almost always be a unique solution if $m = n$ (since when the number of equations and unknowns are equal the condition for a unique solution is simply that a determinant is nonzero);

(iii) there will almost never be a unique solution if $m > n$ (since for a unique solution it is necessary that conditions must be satisfied which ensure that $m - n$ of the equations are merely disguised versions of the other n equations).

Conclusion (iii) suggests that the following practical problem will frequently arise: Given $m > n$ equations to which there is no exact solution, can we find an approximate solution which, in some sense, 'almost satisfies' the equations: i.e. are there values $x_1^*, x_2^*, \ldots, x_n^*$ such that each of the equations is satisfied to within some acceptable margin of error? One of the earliest examinations of this question is due to the Swiss mathematician Gauss, who is usually regarded, together with Archimedes and Sir Isaac Newton, as one of the three greatest mathematicians who ever lived.

In order to tackle this problem it is necessary to have a precise idea of what is meant by 'an acceptable margin of error', and of how we should decide that an approximate solution $x_1^*, x_2^*, \ldots, x_n^*$ is better than another approximate solution $x_1^{**}, x_2^{**}, \ldots, x_n^{**}$.

The criterion proposed by Gauss was that the most preferable approximate solution is that which minimizes the sum of the squares of the errors in each equation: in other words, given the equations

$$\begin{array}{ccccccc} a_{11}x_1 & + & a_{11}x_2 & + \cdots + & a_{1n}x_n & = & y_1 \\ a_{21}x_1 & + & a_{22}x_2 & + \cdots + & a_{2n}x_n & = & y_2 \\ \vdots & & \vdots & \ddots & \vdots & & \vdots \\ a_{m1}x_1 & + & a_{m2}x_2 & + \cdots + & a_{mn}x_n & = & y_m \end{array}$$

the best approximate solution, $x_1^*, x_2^*, \ldots, x_m^*$ is that for which

$$V = (y_1^* - y_1)^2 + (y_2^* - y_2)^2 + \cdots + (y_m - y_m^*)^2$$

is at a minimum. The terms $y_1^*, y_2^*, \ldots, y_m^*$ are the values of the left-hand sides of the equations as given by the approximate solution:

$$\begin{array}{ccccccc} y_1^* & = & a_{11}x_1^* & + & a_{12}x_2^* & + \cdots + & a_{1n}x_n^* \\ y_2^* & = & a_{21}x_1^* & + & a_{22}x_2^* & + \cdots + & a_{2n}x_n^* \\ \vdots & & \vdots & & \vdots & \ddots & \vdots \\ y_m^* & = & a_{m1}x_1^* & + & a_{m2}x_2^* & + \cdots + & a_{mn}x_n^* \end{array}$$

The difference between these values and the values on the right-hand sides of the equations are the errors in the equations, i.e., the errors in the equations are

$$y_1^* - y_1, y_2^* - y_2, \ldots, y_m^* - y_m$$

The Gaussian criterion is to minimize the sum of the squares of these errors, i.e. to minimize V. This deserves some comment.

It is desirable that V should equal the *sum* of the squares of the errors in each equation because this means that when V is minimized the error in each equation will, to a certain extent, be minimized as well. It is desirable that the errors be squared because if the errors were not squared before they were summed to obtain V, then it is possible that an error of $-e$ in one equation would cancel out an error of $+e$ in another equation. The result would be that the sum of the errors was zero although some of the errors themselves were not zero; the sum of the squares of the errors is the simplest expression which does not have this shortcoming: the sum of the squares of the errors is zero only when each one of the errors is zero.

The problem, therefore, is to minimize

$$V = \sum_{i=1}^{m} (y_i - y_i^*)^2$$

where

$$y_i^* = \sum_{j=1}^{n} a_{ij} x_j^*$$

the minimization to be made with respect to $x_1^*, x_2^*, \ldots, x_n^*$. By expanding the expression for V,

$$V = \sum_{i=1}^{m} y_i^2 - 2 \sum_{i=1}^{m} y_i y_i^* + \sum_{i=1}^{m} y_i^{*2}$$

and on substituting into it the expression for y^*, we get

$$V = \sum_{i=1}^{m} y_i^2 - 2 \sum_{i=1}^{m} y_i \sum_{j=1}^{n} a_{ij} x_j^* + \sum_{i=1}^{m} \left(\sum_{j=1}^{n} a_{ij} x_j^* \right)^2$$

This expresses V as a function of $x_1^*, x_2^*, \ldots, x_n^*$. Recall from Section 6.8 that a necessary condition for V to be a minimum with respect to $x_1^*, x_2^*, \ldots, x_m^*$ is that all the partial derivatives of V are zero:

$$\partial V/\partial x_1^* = \partial V/\partial x_2^* = \cdots = \partial V/\partial x_n^* = 0$$

Setting, in turn, each of these partial derivatives equal to zero gives the following equations

$$\sum_{j=1}^{n} \left(\sum_{i=1}^{m} a_{ij} a_{i1} \right) x_j^* = \sum_{i=1}^{m} y_i a_{i1}$$

$$\sum_{j=1}^{n} \left(\sum_{i=1}^{m} a_{ij} a_{i2} \right) x_j^* = \sum_{i=1}^{m} y_i a_{i2}$$

$$\vdots \qquad\qquad \vdots$$

$$\sum_{j=1}^{n} \left(\sum_{i=1}^{m} a_{ij} a_{in} \right) x_j^* = \sum_{i=1}^{m} y_i a_{in}$$

These are n simultaneous linear equations in the n unknowns $x_1^*, x_2^*, \ldots, x_n^*$. It can be shown that if the original $m > n$ equations are inconsistent, so that not all of them can be satisfied exactly, then we can be sure that these n equations have a unique solution. This has the important implication that if the original equations are inconsistent then there is always a unique solution to the problem of finding the values $x_1^*, x_2^*, \ldots, x_n^*$ which minimize the sum of the squares of the errors in the equations. This result is sometimes known as Gauss' theorem.

It will be useful to derive an exact expression for the approximate solution $x_1^*, x_2^*, \ldots, x_n^*$. If the n linear equations in n unknowns, derived above, are written in matrix notation as

$$\mathbf{B}\mathbf{x}^* = \mathbf{d}$$

then it is readily seen that the (j, k)th element of the matrix **B** is $b_{jk} = \sum_{i=1}^{m} a_{ij}a_{ik}$ and the kth element of the column vector **d** is $d_k = \sum_{i=1}^{m} y_i a_{ik}$. It follows, on inspection of these expressions, that in matrix notation the vector **B** is

$$\mathbf{B} = \mathbf{A}^T\mathbf{A}$$

and the vector d is

$$\mathbf{d} = \mathbf{A}^T\mathbf{y}$$

The matrix **A** is the $m \times n$ matrix associated with the original $m > n$ equations and **y** is the m-element column vector in the original equations. By using the equations for **B** and **d** we can obtain a matrix expression for the vector **x** in terms of the original matrix, **A**, and the original vector, **y**:

$$(\mathbf{A}^T\mathbf{A})\mathbf{x}^* = \mathbf{A}^T\mathbf{y}$$

Premultiplying both sides of the equation by the inverse $(\mathbf{A}^T\mathbf{A})^{-1}$, we obtain

$$\mathbf{x}^* = (\mathbf{A}^T\mathbf{A})^{-1}\mathbf{A}^T\mathbf{y}$$

The elements of the vector $\mathbf{x}^*$ are the values $x_1^*, x_2^*, \ldots, x_n^*$ which minimize the sum of the squares of the errors in the equations.

Example Let us return to the example of international trade between two countries which was given in Section 10.3. The marginal propensities to consume in countries 1 and 2 are 0·75 and 1·0 respectively; the marginal propensities to import in countries 1 and 2 are 0·25 and 0·5 respectively.

As before, let exogenous demand in each country be £10m. Suppose that the net movement of capital between the two countries is zero. Equilibrium of aggregate supply and aggregate demand in country 1 requires that

$$0{\cdot}5Y_1 - 0{\cdot}5Y_2 = 10$$

Equilibrium of aggregate supply and aggregate demand in country 2 requires that

$$-0{\cdot}25Y_1 + 0{\cdot}5Y_2 = 10$$

If we require that the balance of payments between the two countries is zero then it is also necessary that

$$-0{\cdot}25Y_1 + 0{\cdot}5Y_2 = 0$$

It is readily verified (using Theorem 12.2) that these three equations in two unknowns are inconsistent. We shall obtain an approximate solution using the principle of least squares (as Gauss' criterion is often called).

If the equations are written in matrix notation as

$$\mathbf{Ax} = \mathbf{y}$$

then it follows that

$$\mathbf{A} = \begin{bmatrix} 0{\cdot}5 & -0{\cdot}5 \\ -0{\cdot}25 & 0{\cdot}5 \\ 0{\cdot}25 & -0{\cdot}5 \end{bmatrix} \quad \mathbf{x} = \begin{bmatrix} X_1 \\ X_2 \end{bmatrix} \quad \mathbf{y} = \begin{bmatrix} 10 \\ 10 \\ 0 \end{bmatrix}$$

We have seen that the approximate solution is given by the matrix equation

$$\mathbf{x}^* = (\mathbf{A}^T\mathbf{A})^{-1}\mathbf{A}^T\mathbf{y}$$

It is readily verified that

$$\mathbf{A}^T\mathbf{A} = \begin{bmatrix} 0{\cdot}375 & -0{\cdot}5 \\ -0{\cdot}5 & 0{\cdot}75 \end{bmatrix}$$

and

$$\mathbf{A}^T\mathbf{y} = \begin{bmatrix} 2{\cdot}5 \\ 0 \end{bmatrix}$$

so that

$$\begin{aligned} \mathbf{x}^* &= \begin{bmatrix} 0{\cdot}375 & -0{\cdot}5 \\ -0{\cdot}5 & 0{\cdot}75 \end{bmatrix}^{-1} \begin{bmatrix} 2{\cdot}5 \\ 0 \end{bmatrix} \\ &= \begin{bmatrix} 24 & 16 \\ 16 & 12 \end{bmatrix} \begin{bmatrix} 2{\cdot}5 \\ 0 \end{bmatrix} \\ &= \begin{bmatrix} 60 \\ 40 \end{bmatrix} \end{aligned}$$

The approximate solution is $x_1^* = 60$, $x_2^* = 40$ and the errors in the equations are

$$y_1 - y_1^* = 10 - (0{\cdot}5 \times 60 - 0{\cdot}5 \times 40) = 0$$

$$y_2 - y_2^* = 10 - (-0{\cdot}25 \times 60 + 0{\cdot}5 \times 40) = 5$$

$$y_3 - y_3^* = -(0{\cdot}25 \times 60 + 0{\cdot}5 \times 40) = -5$$

It will be recalled from Section 10.3 that the equilibrium incomes in countries 1 and 2 are £80m and £60m respectively, when it is required only that aggregate demand and aggregate supply are in equilibrium in each country. In these circumstances the balance of payments in country 1 has a surplus of £10m and the balance of payments in country 2 has a deficit of £10m.

The approximate solution derived above suggests that the incomes in countries 1 and 2 should be £60m and £40m respectively; this will reduce the balance of payments surplus of country 1 to £5m, but will, at the same time, cause aggregate demand to fall short of aggregate supply by £5m in country 2.

This illustrates a result which is already widely appreciated on qualitative grounds: that to induce an equilibrium in the balance of payments between two countries it is usually necessary for the incomes in both these countries to be reduced. This exemplifies the well-known trade-off between balance of payments equilibrium and the aggregate level of employment.

12.6 Generalized least squares

The least squares criterion has been introduced as a way of obtaining an approximate solution to a set of $m > n$ simultaneous equations in n unknowns. It is important to appreciate that there are value judgements implicit in the use of this technique to solve problems of economic policy such as 'What levels of employment are consistent with an acceptable deficit in the balance of payments?'.

The most important value judgement concerns what is known as the 'weighting' of the squares of the errors in the expression for V. Each of the terms $(y_i - y_i^*)^2$ in the expression for V has the same 'weight': in other words, we can write

$$V = 1.(y_1 - y_1^*)^2 + 1.(y_2 - y_2^*)^2 + \cdots$$
$$\cdots + 1.(y_m - y_m)^2$$

where each of the numbers 1 represents a unit weight. Writing V in this way emphasizes the fact that the error in the first equation is of the same importance as the error in the second equation which, in turn, is just as important as the error in the third equation, and so on. So far as economic policy is concerned, these errors in the equations represent disequilibria in the various markets within the economy. On social grounds we might be especially concerned that there should be very little disequilibrium in one or two particular markets (such as the labour market) and for this reason we should require minimal error in the equations of equilibrium for these particular markets. But such a state of affairs will not be ensured by minimizing the measure V defined above, for in this measure the error in any one equation has just as much weight as the error in any other equation. If the aim of social policy is to ensure that there is very little disequilibrium in one particular market, then we should not expect the approximate solution $x_1^*, x_2^*, \ldots, x_n^*$ obtained by minimizing V, as defined above, to represent a particularly satisfactory way of implementing this policy. If, however, the measure of V is generalized to

$$V^* = w_1(y_1 - y_1^*)^2 + w_2(y_2 - y_2^*)^2 + \cdots$$
$$\cdots + w_m(y_m - y_m^*)^2$$

in which the ith weight, w_i, is large if an error in the ith equation represents a socially undesirable state of affairs, then the minimization of V^* will lead to an approximate solution $x_1^*, x_2^*, \ldots, x_n^*$ which will represent more closely the implementation of the desired social policy. The criterion that one should minimize V^* is known as 'the principle of generalized least squares'. The weights w_i represent explicitly the value judgements inherent in the minimization of V or V^*.

12.7 Conditions for an equilibrium to be feasible

In the remainder of this chapter we shall discuss the third of the questions posed at the beginning, namely, if there is an equilibrium for a system of interacting markets, is this equilibrium necessarily feasible? An equilibrium state which is not feasible would be one which involved, for example, negative prices, a negative stock of capital or an output of some commodity in excess of what can be achieved by a full employment of resources. To begin with, we shall examine the implications of the requirement that the values of certain economic variables should be either positive or zero.

It was shown in Chapter 10 that the equilibrium conditions for a system of interacting markets can often be expressed as simultaneous linear equations, written in matrix notation as

$$\mathbf{Ax} = \mathbf{y}$$

In the example of international trade the vector $\mathbf{y}$ represents exogenous demands; in the example of interindustry transactions the vector $\mathbf{y}$ represents the final demand for industrial products; and in the Keynesian economy the elements of the vector $\mathbf{y}$ are government expenditure and the stock of money. In each of these examples the elements of $\mathbf{y}$ are non-negative. A vector in which all the elements are non-negative is said to be a non-negative vector; a non-negative vector $\mathbf{y}$ is written $\mathbf{y} \geqslant 0$. In each of the examples above we should also require, on grounds of feasibility, that the vector $\mathbf{x}$ is non-negative, for the elements of the vector $\mathbf{x}$ are, respectively, the national incomes in different countries, the outputs of different commodities and, in the Keynesian economy, the national income and the reciprocal of the rate of interest. Quite clearly, in all these examples it is necessary for the equilibrium to be feasible that the equilibrium values which constitute the elements of the vector $\mathbf{x}$ should be non-negative.

Let us suppose that this is the only constraint imposed on the elements of the vector $\mathbf{x}$. In this case the position can be summarized as follows. The equilibrium conditions of the economy are of the form $\mathbf{Ax} = \mathbf{y}$, the vector $\mathbf{y}$ is non-negative in all realistic circumstances, and the equilibrium is feasible only if the vector of equilibrium values, $\mathbf{x}$, is non-negative. Under these circumstances the question 'is the equilibrium feasible?' is formally identical with the mathematical question 'if $\mathbf{Ax} = \mathbf{y}$ and the vector $\mathbf{y}$ is non-negative, $\mathbf{y} \geqslant 0$, is it always the case that the vector $\mathbf{x}$ is non-negative, $\mathbf{x} \geqslant 0$?' This question is answered by the following elementary argument.

Since $\mathbf{Ax} = \mathbf{y}$, it follows that if the inverse exists then $\mathbf{x} = \mathbf{A}^{-1}\mathbf{y}$; if all the elements of $\mathbf{A}^{-1}$ are non-negative, and also all the elements of the vector $\mathbf{y}$ are non-negative, it follows immediately from the rules of matrix multiplication that the elements of the vector $\mathbf{x}$ must also be non-negative. In other words, if all the elements of $\mathbf{A}^{-1}$ are non-negative, then $\mathbf{y} \geqslant 0$ implies $\mathbf{x} \geqslant 0$. On the other hand, if there is just one element of the inverse which is *negative*, say a_{ij}^{-1}, then by setting to zero all but one of the elements of y (the element y_j being positive) we can generate a vector $\mathbf{x} = \mathbf{A}^{-1}\mathbf{y}$ in which the element x_i is negative; i.e., if there is just one element of $\mathbf{A}^{-1}$ which is negative then it is no longer true that $\mathbf{y} \geqslant 0$ implies $\mathbf{x} \geqslant 0$. This proves

Theorem 12.3 Given n simultaneous linear equations in n unknowns, $\mathbf{Ax} = \mathbf{y}$, a necessary and sufficient condition that $\mathbf{y} \geqslant 0$ implies $\mathbf{x} \geqslant 0$ is that every element of the inverse matrix is non-negative, $\mathbf{A}^{-1} \geqslant 0$.

To illustrate the theorem we refer to the examples in Chapter 10.

Example 1 (see Section 10.3) Countries 1 and 2 engage in trade. The marginal propensities to consume are respectively 0·75 and 1·0, and the marginal propensities to import are 0·25 and 0·5. If an equilibrium exists, is it feasible?

In matrix notation the equilibrium conditions are

$$\begin{bmatrix} 0{\cdot}5 & -0{\cdot}5 \\ -0{\cdot}25 & 0{\cdot}5 \end{bmatrix} \begin{bmatrix} Y_1 \\ Y_2 \end{bmatrix} = \begin{bmatrix} E_1 \\ E_2 \end{bmatrix}$$

where Y_1, Y_2 are the equilibrium incomes and E_1, E_2 are exogenous demands. The inverse of the 2×2 matrix is

$$\begin{bmatrix} 4 & 4 \\ 2 & 4 \end{bmatrix}$$

Since the inverse is non-negative the equilibrium is feasible (if it exists).

Example 2 (see Section 10.6) Suppose that the equilibrium conditions for a Keynesian economy are

$$\begin{bmatrix} 0{\cdot}5 & 200 \\ 0{\cdot}25 & -100 \end{bmatrix} \begin{bmatrix} Y \\ 1/r \end{bmatrix} = \begin{bmatrix} M \\ G \end{bmatrix}$$

where Y is the equilibrium income, r is the equilibrium rate of interest, M is the stock of money and G is government expenditure. If an equilibrium exists, is it feasible?

The solution of the equilibrium conditions is

$$\begin{bmatrix} Y \\ 1/r \end{bmatrix} = \begin{bmatrix} 1 & 2 \\ 0{\cdot}0025 & -0{\cdot}005 \end{bmatrix} \begin{bmatrix} M \\ G \end{bmatrix}$$

Since the inverse has a negative element, the equilibrium may not be feasible. It can be seen from the solution that when M is small relative to G the equilibrium rate of interest becomes negative; the economic explanation is that the transactions demand for money exceeds the total stock of money.

Example 3 To produce one ton of coal requires 0·1 tons of steel. To produce one ton of steel requires 0·4 tons of coal. Is there a feasible set of equilibrium outputs for coal and steel?

The equilibrium conditions are

$$\begin{bmatrix} 1{\cdot}0 & -0{\cdot}1 \\ -0{\cdot}4 & 1{\cdot}0 \end{bmatrix} \begin{bmatrix} X_1 \\ X_2 \end{bmatrix} = \begin{bmatrix} F_1 \\ F_2 \end{bmatrix}$$

where X_1, X_2 are the equilibrium outputs of steel and coal, and F_1, F_2 are the final demands. The inverse of the 2×2 matrix is

$$\frac{1}{0{\cdot}96} \begin{bmatrix} 1{\cdot}0 & 0{\cdot}1 \\ 0{\cdot}4 & 1{\cdot}0 \end{bmatrix}$$

Since the inverse is non-negative the equilibrium set of outputs is feasible.

12.8 The Hawkins–Simon conditions

It is often useful to know whether a solution is feasible before deciding whether to evaluate the inverse; for if the solution is not feasible there is little point in calculating it. Specifically, it would be useful to be able to test whether all the elements of the inverse, $\mathbf{A}^{-1}$, are non-negative before evaluating the inverse itself. Fortunately it is possible, under certain circumstances, to test whether the inverse is non-negative without explicitly evaluating its elements. The test can be made by using the following result, due essentially to Hawkins and Simon.

Theorem 12.4 Suppose that there are n equations in n unknowns

$$\mathbf{Ax} = \mathbf{y}$$

where

$$\mathbf{A} = \mathbf{I} - \mathbf{M} \quad \text{and} \quad \mathbf{M} \geqslant 0$$

The matrix $\mathbf{A}$ is equal to the difference between an identity matrix and a matrix of non-negative elements. If all the leading principal minors of $\mathbf{A}$ are strictly positive, the inverse matrix $\mathbf{A}^{-1}$ exists and every element of $\mathbf{A}^{-1}$ is non-negative; hence $\mathbf{y} \geqslant 0$ implies $\mathbf{x} \geqslant 0$.

The conditions on the principal minors of the matrix are known as the 'Hawkins–Simon conditions'.

Example To illustrate the use of Theorem 12.4 we refer to Problem 11.4.3. In this problem you are asked to determine the equilibrium outputs of coal, steel and lorries (indexed 1, 2 and 3 respectively). In matrix notation the equilibrium conditions for the three markets are

$$\mathbf{Ax} = \mathbf{y}$$

where $\mathbf{x}$ is the vector of equilibrium outputs, $\mathbf{y}$ is the vector of final demands and

$$\mathbf{A} = \begin{bmatrix} 1 & -0{\cdot}2 & -0{\cdot}6 \\ -0{\cdot}4 & 1 & -0{\cdot}4 \\ -0{\cdot}2 & -0{\cdot}1 & 1 \end{bmatrix}$$

If the matrix **A** is written in the form **I** − **M** where **I** is the identity matrix

$$\mathbf{I} = \begin{bmatrix} 1 & 0 & 0 \\ 0 & 1 & 0 \\ 0 & 0 & 1 \end{bmatrix}$$

then it follows that the matrix **M** is

$$\mathbf{M} = \begin{bmatrix} 0 & 0{\cdot}2 & 0{\cdot}6 \\ 0{\cdot}4 & 0 & 0{\cdot}4 \\ 0{\cdot}2 & 0{\cdot}1 & 0 \end{bmatrix}$$

The elements of **M** are the 'input-output coefficients' for the three industries. The coefficient m_{ij} measures the quantity of the ith product required to produce one unit of the jth product. Since $\mathbf{M} \geqslant 0$ it follows immediately from Theorem 12.4 that the equilibrium outputs of coal, steel and lorries are feasible provided that all the leading principal minors of the matrix **A** are positive. The leading principal minors are

$$\mathbf{A}_{(1)} = \det [1] > 0$$

$$\mathbf{A}_{(2)} = \det \begin{bmatrix} 1 & -0{\cdot}2 \\ -0{\cdot}4 & 1 \end{bmatrix} = 0{\cdot}92 > 0$$

$$\mathbf{A}_{(3)} = \det [\mathbf{A}] = 0{\cdot}72 > 0$$

Since all the leading principal minors are positive, the Hawkins–Simon conditions are satisfied and so the equilibrium outputs are feasible. This decision is reached without explicitly checking that the inverse is non-negative (the inverse is given in Problem 11.4.3).

The matrix of coefficients shown in Table 12.1 is obtained from the inverse of the matrix (**I** − **M**) corresponding to the 1972 input-output matrix **M**. Because the matrix **M** satisfies the Hawkins–Simon conditions, the inverse matrix $(\mathbf{I} - \mathbf{M})^{-1}$ is non-negative. It follows that the final demands of the United Kingdom economy can be satisfied by the equilibrium outputs of United Kingdom industries.

In most applications the condition that all the principal minors of a matrix must be positive has a straightforward economic interpretation.

Example (continued) In terms of inter-industry transactions (see above and also Section 10.7) the Hawkins–Simon conditions require the output of each industry not to be exhausted by the demands of the industries which supply the inputs used up in production. In other words, after each industry has satisfied the input requirements of the industries which supply its inputs, it must have some output left over to satisfy a final demand for its product.

Consider, for example, the transactions between two industries, industry 1 and industry 2. Suppose that **M** is the matrix of input-output coefficients; industry 1 requires m_{11} units of its own products to produce a unit of output. If the requirements of industry 1 for its own products are not to exhaust its output then it is necessary that $m_{11} < 1$. Similarly, if industry 2 requires m_{22} units of its own products to produce a unit of output then it is necessary that $m_{22} < 1$. Let us now examine the transactions between the two industries. Suppose that one unit of output is produced in industry 1. Of this output, m_{11} units are used up as an input by industry 1 and some must go to final demand, so that less than $1 - m_{11}$ units are available to industry 2 as an input. Will this be sufficient to meet industry 2's input requirements, given that industry 2 must supply its output as an input to industry 1? Let us evaluate the output of industry 2 which is necessary to meet the input requirements of industry 1. To produce one unit of industry 1's output, m_{21} units of industry 2's output are required. Now in order for one unit of industry 2's output to be available to industry 1 it is necessary that $1/(1 - m_{22})$ units of industry 2's output should be produced (because $m_{22}/(1 - m_{22})$ units will be used up as an input by industry 2, leaving only one unit for industry 1). Consequently, to make available m_{21} units of industry 2's output to industry 1, the total output of industry 2 must be $m_{21}/(1 - m_{22})$. We can now evaluate industry 2's requirements from industry 1. To produce one unit of industry 2's output, m_{12} units of industry 1's output are required. It follows that industry 2's requirements of industry 1's output are $m_{12}m_{21}/(1 - m_{22})$. The amount of ir dustry 1's output available to industry 2 is less than $1 - m_{11}$. For production in industry 1 to be feasible it is clearly necessary that

$$1 - m_{11} > m_{12}m_{21}/(1 - m_{22})$$

i.e. it is necessary that

$$(1 - m_{11})(1 - m_{22}) - m_{12}m_{21} > 0$$

The condition that industry 2 shall be able to satisfy a final demand for its products is given by this same inequality. As a result we have three conditions for the productive processes in both industries to be capable of satisfying final demands. These conditions are

(1) $$1 - m_{11} > 0$$

(2) $$1 - m_{22} > 0$$

(3) $$(1 - m_{11})(1 - m_{22}) - m_{12}m_{21} > 0$$

If the elements m_{12}, m_{21} are non-negative the conditions (1) and (3) together imply condition (2). Since $\mathbf{A} = \mathbf{I} - \mathbf{M}$ we have $a_{11} = 1 - m_{11}, a_{22} = 1 - m_{22}$, $a_{12} = -m_{12}, a_{21} = -m_{21}$ so that the two independent conditions (1) and (3) may be written

(4) $$a_{11} > 0$$

(5) $$a_{11}a_{22} - a_{12}a_{21} > 0$$

In terms of leading principal minors the conditions (4) and (5) are

$$\mathbf{A}_{(1)} > 0, \quad \mathbf{A}_{(2)} > 0$$

Table 12.1 Coefficients of direct and indirect requirements of input per unit output

Commodities	Agricultural products n.e.s.	Coal	Mining products n.e.s.	Processed food n.e.s.	Drink	Refined mineral oil	Chemicals n.e.s.	Iron and steel	Non-ferrous metals
Agricultural products n.e.s.	1028	3	2	205	35	2	30	2	1
Coal	7	1008	14	10	10	3	21	36	12
Mining products n.e.s.	4	3	1005	5	4	5	20	4	11
Processed food n.e.s.	10	1	1	1113	67	0	7	1	1
Drink	0	0	1	5	1057	0	2	0	0
Refined mineral oil	38	13	59	26	40	1052	32	59	33
Chemicals n.e.s.	125	62	75	174	126	67	1506	101	46
Iron and steel	27	63	21	44	25	7	34	1426	50
Non-ferrous metals	14	15	12	25	15	4	27	51	1666
Engineering products	46	68	69	50	44	15	43	60	55
Metal goods n.e.s.	36	29	15	74	39	10	44	53	33
Textiles n.e.s.	9	22	7	15	8	1	16	10	9
Leather, clothing and footwear	1	4	1	1	1	0	2	2	1
Building materials	8	15	4	5	4	6	8	15	5
Timber, furniture etc.	8	23	12	14	12	2	16	12	8
Paper, printing and publishing n.e.s.	15	12	24	62	20	5	34	15	18
Rubber products	6	29	8	5	4	1	7	6	4
Manufactures n.e.s.	8	7	4	9	8	1	13	6	6
Construction	37	53	8	19	18	7	17	18	10
Gas	29	7	7	18	13	9	43	56	18
Electricity	28	37	53	29	29	19	45	58	42
Water	1	1	1	1	2	1	2	1	1
Transport and communications	68	44	144	75	48	13	75	95	54
Distribution	53	31	50	53	39	6	42	52	70
Services n.e.s.	52	41	44	80	52	16	79	66	91

These are the Hawkins–Simon conditions for the 2×2 matrix **A**. It follows that for the transactions between two industries we have shown by economic reasoning that the Hawkins–Simon conditions are necessary and sufficient to ensure the existence of a feasible equilibrium of inter-industry transactions.

12.9 Additional constraints on the solution of equations

We conclude by discussing briefly the case in which conditions other than non-negativity are imposed on a solution. For example, there may be a constraint on equilibrium output because of the physical limitation of productive capacity or

for 25 UK industries, projected to 1972

Engineering products	Metal goods n.e.s.	Textiles n.e.s.	Leather, clothing & footwear	Building materials	Timber, furniture etc.	Paper, printing & publishing n.e.s	Rubber products	Manufactures n.e.s.	Construction	Gas	Electricity	Water	Transport & communications	Distribution	Services n.e.s.
2	2	6	41	2	5	3	52	9	2	1	1	1	2	2	1
11	18	9	7	32	7	14	16	13	10	38	128	16	4	6	6
4	4	8	4	100	4	7	10	9	31	3	2	2	2	3	2
1	1	4	2	1	2	4	3	2	1	0	0	0	6	1	1
0	0	1	0	0	1	0	1	1	0	0	0	0	2	3	0
23	38	45	29	94	24	22	30	24	31	122	129	51	31	38	18
80	64	183	107	83	101	101	512	339	92	45	31	19	32	42	29
179	459	23	27	30	42	16	39	55	98	114	28	84	23	17	22
131	198	21	17	16	25	27	28	28	55	15	13	19	10	11	14
1218	58	56	40	64	39	40	54	52	75	56	74	23	22	19	54
83	1151	26	43	22	76	15	52	64	45	20	15	9	13	18	26
19	9	1951	725	12	95	14	250	90	14	4	6	2	10	24	12
2	2	12	1154	1	7	2	5	5	2	1	1	0	2	3	1
10	8	5	5	1059	7	4	9	11	141	9	9	13	6	6	4
26	19	9	14	17	1465	18	13	25	69	6	8	3	10	15	6
27	18	26	33	67	21	1064	39	46	29	9	9	11	9	45	93
10	9	9	16	6	19	5	1077	9	6	3	7	2	14	9	12
17	14	7	28	5	9	6	20	1014	12	3	5	2	9	19	10
11	12	23	20	16	17	13	22	18	1217	14	13	13	25	27	19
18	33	14	15	9	15	17	25	26	11	1216	39	8	4	14	13
13	43	45	33	55	33	29	58	46	25	31	1073	87	9	29	29
1	1	2	2	3	1	1	2	2	2	1	2	1035	1	6	1
49	65	81	63	72	72	55	74	60	68	53	55	30	1110	47	22
37	47	63	54	44	87	48	58	52	50	30	27	14	30	1041	21
64	71	76	73	72	107	80	78	71	83	32	35	44	39	45	1037

SOURCE *A Programme for Growth, No. 9: Exploring 1972*, Department of Applied Economics, University of Cambridge, and Chapman and Hall, London 1970, Appendix 2.

NOTE The coefficient in the *i*th row and *j*th column of the table measures the value of the input (in £) from the *i*th industry which is required to satisfy a final demand of £1,000 for the output of the *j*th industry. Notice that all the diagonal terms exceed 1,000: this indicates that to satisfy a final demand of £1,000 for any commodity the output of that commodity must exceed £1,000, because the output must satisfy not only the final demand but also the input requirements of the industries which contribute inputs to the production of the output. All the coefficients in the table are non-negative. This indicates that an increase in the final demand for any one commodity, other final demands remaining constant, cannot reduce the output requirements for any commodity.

because of scarcity of labour. As a result, the non-negativity constraint on output, $X > 0$, is augmented by a constraint $X^* > X$ where X^* is the output produced with full employment of resources.

There is no general method for solving problems involving such constraints. It is sufficient to note the following general principles.

1 If a solution exists and is unique then to determine whether it is feasible it is usually necessary to see by inspection whether it satisfies the constraints.

2 If a solution exists and is not unique then it is possible to impose inequality constraints. If the constraints are consistent with the equations then a feasible solution can be obtained.

Notes and references

Useful references on the existence and uniqueness of the solution of simultaneous linear equations are Aitken,[4] §29, 30, Allen,[7] §14.1, 14.2, Cohn,[29] Hadley,[46] Ch. 4, 5, Lewis,[79] Ch. 31, 32, and Mills,[90] Ch. 4, 6. In some cases an economically feasible solution is one in which variables take on integer values: see Mills,[90] Ch. 7. For further details of the principle of least squares see Johnston,[66] Ch. 2, 4 and Wonnacott and Wonnacott,[124] Ch. 1, 13.

Problems

12.1 The marginal propensity to consume in a closed economy (such as that described in Section 3.2(b)) is equal to 1·1 and investment and government expenditure are exogenous. Is the equilibrium income of the economy always feasible?

12.2.1 The marginal propensity to consume of the developing countries is $1\frac{1}{4}$. Their marginal propensity to import from the developed countries is $\frac{1}{2}$. The marginal propensity to consume of the developed countries is $\frac{3}{4}$. Their marginal propensity to import from the undeveloped countries is $\frac{1}{4}$. Are there unique equilibrium incomes in the developed and undeveloped countries?

12.2.2 Four students and their girls go to the union bar together one evening. The first round is four pints of bitter, one of lager, and one of cider (the girls are drinking halfpints); the round costs 74p. The next round is 3 pints of bitter, 2 of lager, and one of cider, costing 77p. The third round is 2 pints of bitter, 2 of lager and 2 of cider, costing 76p. The fourth student goes to the bar to order his round, which is 2 pints of bitter and 4 of lager. He feels for his money and realizes that he has not got as much as he thought he had. Can he work out in advance how much his round will come to? In fact he has 83p. Will this be enough to avoid embarrassment?

12.3.1 (**12.2.1** continued) Suppose that exogenous demand in the developed countries is £4 billion and exogenous demand in the undeveloped countries is £2 billion. Are there *any* unique equilibrium incomes for the developed and undeveloped countries? (Illustrate your answer graphically.) How, if at all, is the answer changed if exogenous demand in the developed countries is increased to £6m?

12.3.2 Solve, if possible, the following sets of equations

(a) $$\begin{aligned} 6x_1 + 2x_2 &= 0 \\ -2x_1 - \tfrac{2}{3}x_2 &= 0 \end{aligned}$$

(b) $$\begin{aligned} 6x_1 + 2x_2 &= 0 \\ -2x_1 - \tfrac{2}{3}x_2 &= 1 \end{aligned}$$

(c) $$\begin{aligned} 5x_1 + 4x_2 - 5x_3 &= 15 \\ -2x_1 + 10x_2 \qquad &= 5 \\ 58x_2 - 10x_3 &= 55 \end{aligned}$$

(d) $$\begin{aligned} 7x_1 - 5x_2 &= 12 \\ x_1 + 2x_2 &= 10 \\ 2x_1 - 15x_2 &= 6 \end{aligned}$$

12.4.1 Three countries trade with one another and each country requires its balance of payments to be in equilibrium and the aggregate supply of its products to meet the aggregate demand. How many equations are there to determine the equilibrium set of incomes? If the governments adopt a common fiscal policy will they, as a rule, be able to achieve a state of equilibrium?

12.4.2 (a) From the equations

$$\begin{aligned} 3x_1 - 6x_2 + x_3 &= 15 \\ 8x_1 + 2x_2 + 4x_3 &= 16 \end{aligned}$$

determine the relationship between x_1 and x_3.

(b) Solve, if possible,

$$\begin{aligned} 7x_1 - 5x_2 &= 12 \\ x_1 + 2x_2 &= 10 \\ 2x_1 - 15x_2 &= 6 \end{aligned}$$

How is the answer changed if the last equation is $2x_1 - 15x_2 = -38$?

12.4.3 An animal foodstuff is made up of two ingredients. The first ingredient contains vitamins and proteins in the ratio 1:1 and the second ingredient contains them in the ratio 1:3. If the animal food must contain vitamins and proteins in the ratio 1:2 in what proportion must the ingredients be blended?

Vitamin C accounts for half the vitamins in the first ingredient and a quarter of the vitamins in the second ingredient. Is it possible for the animal food to satisfy the additional requirement that $\frac{1}{3}$ of the vitamins should be vitamin C?

12.4.4 Urbanville has four local bus services. No. 1 runs from Grasslands through the town centre to Sunnyside; No. 2 runs from Whiteoaks through Grasslands to the town centre; No. 3 runs from Whiteoaks through Grasslands to Sunnyside (avoiding the town centre) and No. 4 runs from Whiteoaks to Sunnyside via the town centre (avoiding Grasslands). It is required to run a service between Grasslands and the town centre 4 times an hour, a service from Grasslands to Sunnyside 3 times an hour and a service from Whiteoaks to Sunnyside 3 times an hour. Do these requirements determine the frequencies of the services? Which service is more frequent: No. 2 or No. 3? Is it possible to arrange that the frequency of the service between Sunnyside and the town centre is 3 times an hour? If so, how?

12.4.5 The manager of a small workshop has available 18 unskilled men, 14 skilled men, and 8 machines. He wishes to employ fully his productive capacity by producing three products. To produce one unit of the first product needs one unskilled man, one skilled man and one machine. The second product needs 3 unskilled men, 2 skilled men and 2 machines. The third needs 4 unskilled men, 3 skilled men and one machine. How many units of each product should he produce?

Each day's output has to be stored overnight in his dispatch department. The dispatch department has only 1,000 square feet of storage space. If one unit of either product 1 or product 3 requires 150 square feet of space and 1 unit of product 2 requires 100 square feet of space, can he ensure that there is no wasted storage space?

12.4.6 The council parks department has 9,000 square yards of land which it wants to allocate between bowling greens which require 600 square yards and tennis courts which require 300 square yards. It also has available 800 square feet of pavilion space, and it estimates that each tennis court will require 50 square feet of pavilion space and each bowling green 20 square feet. It's evening work force is restricted to 30; each tennis court needs one person on hand and each bowling green two.

(a) Given that the council wish to make full use of all available resources, formulate this problem as a set of simultaneous equations.

(b) Does this problem have a unique solution?

12.4.7 Luigi runs a hotel in Majorca. He receives requests for accommodation from three organizations who are holding conferences in the area. Luigi has a degree of flexibility in his staffing and catering arrangements but he considers that the maximum his hotel can supply over a week is 290 lunches and 530 evening meals, and he can serve 240 people in the hotel bar. Luigi studies the three groups' agendas and reservation requests, and, after first making sure that none of his hotel's services will be in heavy demand from all groups on one day, assesses that the first group's members will require 4 evening meals, 2 lunches and will spend 1 evening in the bar, the second group will need 6 evening meals, 3 lunches and spend two evenings in the bar, and the third group will require 5 evening meals, 3 lunches and will spend 3 evenings in the bar. Can Luigi take a number from each group such that his facilities are completely utilized? How many should he take?

If Luigi's hotel has 120 beds can he make sure all these beds are taken?

12.4.8 A metallurgist needs a nickel/tin/copper alloy with 20% nickel, 30% tin and 50% copper. He has on hand 3 different alloys; A which is 10% nickel, 40% tin and 50% copper, B which is 30% nickel and 70% copper, and C which is 30% nickel, 40% tin and 30% copper. In what proportions should he mix A, B and C in order to obtain his required alloy?

12.4.9 The manager of a television station has available each week up to 13·5 hours of transmission time from his outside broadcast team, up to 21 hours of studio time and up to 2,100 man hours of film-crew time. He wants to employ fully all these resources because if he does not they will be reallocated to somebody else. He classifies programmes into sport, current affairs and light entertainment. Each hour of sport requires 0·5 hours of outside broadcast, 0·3 hours of studio time and 20 man hours of film-crew time. Each hour of current affairs requires 0·2 hours of outside broadcast,

0·6 hours of studio time and 20 man hours of film-crew time. Each hour of light entertainment requires 0·3 hours outside broadcast, 0·4 hours studio time and 30 man hours of film-crew time. How many hours of each type of programme should he aim to produce?

12.4.10 The planners of a large city have decided to impose severe penalties upon private car users within the city. Anticipating a large scale switch from private to public transport they have decided to introduce a number of new bus services. The city has four railway stations (denoted A, B, C and D) and around each there is a large concentration of shops and offices. At the moment the planners have budgeted for four bus services: the first starts at station C and runs to D, then to A and B; the second goes on a circular run from A via B, C and D back to A; the third runs from C to D to A; and the fourth from D to A to B to C. Traffic data indicates to the planners that there is an optimum number of *direct* bus links between each two stations. These are: stations A and B should be linked 26 times an hour, B and C 20 times an hour, and D and A 34 times an hour. Can these conditions be met by using the planned bus services? If so, determine the optimum number of trips for each service per hour.

12.4.11 Demonstrate that Theorem 12.1 is a special case ($m = n$) of Theorem 12.2.

12.4.12 A linear equation with no constant term is known as a homogeneous linear equation. A set of homogeneous linear equations may be written in matrix notation

$$\mathbf{Ax} = 0$$

where $\mathbf{A}$ is a $m \times n$ matrix, $\mathbf{x}$ is a n-element column vector and $\mathbf{0}$ is the m-element null vector. Show that a set of homgeneous linear equations always has a solution. What is the solution?

12.5 The problem of fitting a line $y = a + bx$ to a scatter of n points whose coordinates are $(X_1, Y_1), (X_2, Y_2), \ldots, (X_n, Y_n)$ may be regarded as a problem of solving the n linear equations

$$\begin{aligned} Y_1 &= a + bX_1 \\ Y_2 &= a + bX_2 \\ \vdots\ & \quad \vdots \quad\ \ \vdots \\ Y_n &= a + bX_n \end{aligned}$$

for the two unknowns a, b. An approximate solution of these equations may be obtained using the principle of least squares.

(a) Show that the approximate solution is obtained by solving the equations

$$na + \left(\sum_{i=1}^{n} X_i\right) b = \sum_{i=1}^{n} Y_i$$

$$(\Sigma X_i)a + \left(\sum_{i=1}^{n} X_i^2\right) b = \sum_{i=1}^{n} X_i Y_i$$

for a and b.

(b) Show that equations in (a) are equivalent to

$$\begin{bmatrix} 1 & 1 & 1 & \cdots & 1 \\ X_1 & X_2 & X_3 & \cdots & X_n \end{bmatrix} \begin{bmatrix} 1 & X_1 \\ 1 & X_2 \\ 1 & X_3 \\ \vdots & \vdots \\ 1 & X_n \end{bmatrix} \begin{bmatrix} a \\ b \end{bmatrix} = \begin{bmatrix} 1 & 1 & 1 & \cdots & 1 \\ X_1 & X_2 & X_3 & \cdots & X_n \end{bmatrix} \begin{bmatrix} Y_1 \\ Y_2 \\ Y_3 \\ \vdots \\ Y_n \end{bmatrix}$$

(c) Putting $\mathbf{X} = \begin{bmatrix} 1 & X_1 \\ 1 & X_2 \\ 1 & X_3 \\ \vdots & \vdots \\ 1 & X_n \end{bmatrix}$, $\mathbf{y} = \begin{bmatrix} Y_1 \\ Y_2 \\ Y_3 \\ \vdots \\ Y_n \end{bmatrix}$ show that

(**) $$\begin{bmatrix} a \\ b \end{bmatrix} = (\mathbf{X}^T\mathbf{X})^{-1}\mathbf{X}^T\mathbf{y}$$

(d) Given the three pairs of observations (y, x): (3, 3), (2, 6), (7, 9) use equation (**) to find the approximate values for a and b.

(e) If x represents national income (measured at three dates) and y represents consumption (measured at these dates), what do you infer from (d) about (i) the marginal propensity to consume (ii) the size of the multiplier?

12.6.1 (**12.5** continued) Show that the principle of generalized least squares is to minimize $V^* = (\mathbf{y} - \mathbf{X}\boldsymbol{\beta})^T\mathbf{W}^T\mathbf{W}(\mathbf{y} - \mathbf{X}\boldsymbol{\beta})$

where $\boldsymbol{\beta} = \begin{bmatrix} a \\ b \end{bmatrix}$ and $\mathbf{W} = \begin{bmatrix} w_1 & & & 0 \\ & w_2 & & \\ & & \ddots & \\ 0 & & & w_n \end{bmatrix}$

Using the fact that a scalar is equal to its transpose, show that this is the same thing as minimizing

$$\mathbf{u}^T\mathbf{u} - 2\boldsymbol{\beta}^T\mathbf{Z}^T\mathbf{u} - \boldsymbol{\beta}^T\mathbf{Z}^T\mathbf{Z}\boldsymbol{\beta}$$

where $\mathbf{u} = \mathbf{W}\mathbf{y}$, $\mathbf{Z} = \mathbf{W}\mathbf{X}$. By writing out this expression in full, differentiating it, and then setting the partial derivatives equal to zero, $\partial V^*/\partial a, \partial V^*/\partial b = 0$, show that the necessary conditions for a minimum of V^* are two simultaneous equations whose solution may be expressed in matrix notation as

(***) $\qquad \boldsymbol{\beta} = (\mathbf{Z}^T\mathbf{Z})^{-1}\mathbf{Z}^T\mathbf{u} = (\mathbf{X}^T\mathbf{W}^T\mathbf{W}\mathbf{X})^{-1}\mathbf{X}^T\mathbf{W}^T\mathbf{y}$

12.6.2 Let $\mathbf{a}$ and $\mathbf{x}$ be n-element column vectors and let V be the scalar quantity $V = \mathbf{a}^T\mathbf{x}$. Let the column vector of the partial derivatives of V with respect to the elements of $\mathbf{x}$ be

$$\partial V/\partial \mathbf{x} = \begin{bmatrix} \partial V/\partial x_1 \\ \partial V/\partial x_2 \\ \vdots \\ \partial V/\partial x_n \end{bmatrix}$$

(a) Show that $\partial V/\partial \mathbf{x} = \mathbf{a}$

(b) Let $\mathbf{B}$ be a $n \times n$ matrix and let $V = \mathbf{x}^T\mathbf{B}\mathbf{x}$. Show that $\partial V/\partial \mathbf{x} = 2\mathbf{B}\mathbf{x}$ if and only if $b_{ij} = b_{ji}$ $(i, j = 1, \ldots, n)$

(c) If $V = V_1 + V_2$ then $\partial V/\partial \mathbf{x} = \partial V_1/\partial \mathbf{x} + \partial V_2/\partial \mathbf{x}$. Use this result and the results of (a) and (b) to deduce that the necessary conditions for a minimum of V^* in exercise 12.6.1 are given by equation (***).

12.7.1 What are the likely consequences of the infeasibility of equilibrium in the economy described in Problem 12.1.1?

12.7.2 If $\mathbf{A}\mathbf{x} = \mathbf{y}$, what is the necessary and sufficient condition that if every element in $\mathbf{y}$ is strictly positive ($\mathbf{y} > 0$) then every element in $\mathbf{x}$ is strictly positive ($\mathbf{x} > 0$)?

12.7.3 Three countries trade with one another; they have marginal propensities to consume of 0·6, 0·7 and 1·1 respectively. Each country has a marginal propensity to import from each of the other countries of 0·3. Is the equilibrium of the international economy necessarily feasible?

12.7.4 The equations of the *LM* and *IS* curves of an economy (see Section 10.6) are

$$0{\cdot}4Y + 100(1/r) = 100$$
$$0{\cdot}3Y - 75(1/r) = 45$$

and the rate of interest in the liquidity trap is 4% p.a. Is the equilibrium of the economy feasible if the income at full employment is (a) 240 (£m), (b) 180 (£m)? If the equilibrium is not feasible, what do you think will be the consequences?

12.8.1 Suppose that the input-output relationships between the manufacturing sector, the agricultural sector and the service sector are as follows.

To produce one unit of manufactures requires 0·9 units of manufactures, 0·2 units of agricultural products and 0·1 units of services; to produce one unit of agricultural products requires 0·4 units of manufactures, 0·4 units of agricultural products and 0·2 units of services; to produce one unit of services 0·1 units of manufactures, 0·6 units of agricultural products and 0·8 units of services.

(a) Are the Hawkins–Simon conditions satisfied?

(b) By evaluating the inverse, find the outputs necessary to satisfy a final demand for 20 units of manufactures, 10 units of agricultural products and 80 units of services. (Ignore the answer to part (a).)

12.8.2 Elucidate by economic reasoning the relationship between the answers to parts (a) and (b) of Problem 12.8.1.

Chapter 13

The matrix multiplier and the stability of equilibrium

This chapter explains how it is possible to gain insight into the behaviour of a system of interacting markets by applying the powerful techniques of matrix algebra to comparative static and dynamic analyses of the system. It will be shown that the behaviour of interacting markets over time depends critically on the properties of a certain matrix.

13.1 Use of matrix algebra in comparative static analysis

Comparative static analysis is concerned with the effect of a change in the values of exogenous variables on the equilibrium values of endogenous variables. Suppose that the equilibrium values are determined by n simultaneous linear equations in n unknowns, represented by the matrix equation

(1) $\mathbf{Ax} = \mathbf{y}$

The elements of the vector $\mathbf{x}$ are the equilibrium values of the endogenous variables and the elements of the vector $\mathbf{y}$ are the values of the exogenous variables. The elements of the matrix $\mathbf{A}$ are the parameters of the system of interacting markets. Throughout this chapter we shall only consider the case in which there exists a unique solution to equation (1). This solution is written in terms of the inverse matrix $\mathbf{A}^{-1}$:

(2) $\mathbf{x} = \mathbf{A}^{-1}\mathbf{y}$

According to Chapter 12 it is not strictly necessary for a unique solution that the equilibrium conditions originally given should consist of the same number of equations as unknowns. It is possible to have more equations than unknowns, provided that all the equations are consistent and that there are exactly as many redundant equations as there are equations in excess of unknowns. If this condition is met, all the information in the equilibrium conditions can be condensed into a set of n equations in n unknowns, of the same form as (1).

Equation (2) is a fundamental result in the comparative static analysis of interacting markets. To appreciate why this is so, consider the effect of a small change in the value of any one of the exogenous variables, e.g. suppose that the value of the jth exogenous variable is increased by Δy_j. Let the resulting change in the value of the ith endogenous variable be Δx_i. According to equation

(2) the equilibrium values of the endogenous variables are changed from

$$\begin{bmatrix} x_1 \\ \vdots \\ x_i \\ \vdots \\ x_n \end{bmatrix} = \begin{bmatrix} & & \\ & \mathbf{A}^{-1} & \\ & & \end{bmatrix} \begin{bmatrix} y_1 \\ \vdots \\ y_j \\ \vdots \\ y_n \end{bmatrix}$$

to

$$\begin{bmatrix} x_1 + \Delta x_1 \\ \vdots \\ \vdots \\ x_i + \Delta x_i \\ \vdots \\ \vdots \\ x_n + \Delta x_n \end{bmatrix} = \begin{bmatrix} & & \\ & \mathbf{A}^{-1} & \\ & & \end{bmatrix} \begin{bmatrix} y_1 \\ \vdots \\ y_{j-1} \\ y_j + \Delta y_j \\ y_{j+1} \\ \vdots \\ y_n \end{bmatrix}$$

Using the associative law of matrix multiplication we find

(3) $$\begin{bmatrix} x_1 + \Delta x_1 \\ \vdots \\ \vdots \\ x_i + \Delta x_i \\ \vdots \\ \vdots \\ x_n + \Delta x_n \end{bmatrix} = \begin{bmatrix} & & \\ & \mathbf{A}^{-1} & \\ & & \end{bmatrix} \begin{bmatrix} y_1 \\ \vdots \\ \vdots \\ y_j \\ \vdots \\ \vdots \\ y_n \end{bmatrix} + \begin{bmatrix} & & \\ & \mathbf{A}^{-1} & \\ & & \end{bmatrix} \begin{bmatrix} 0 \\ \vdots \\ 0 \\ \Delta y_j \\ 0 \\ \vdots \\ 0 \end{bmatrix}$$

Applying equation (2) to the first term on the right-hand side of (3) and multiplying out the second term gives

(4) $$\begin{bmatrix} x_1 + \Delta x_1 \\ \vdots \\ x_i + \Delta x_i \\ \vdots \\ x_n + \Delta x_n \end{bmatrix} = \begin{bmatrix} x_1 \\ \vdots \\ x_i \\ \vdots \\ x_n \end{bmatrix} + \begin{bmatrix} a_{1j}^{-1} \Delta y_j \\ \vdots \\ a_{ij}^{-1} \Delta y_j \\ \vdots \\ a_{nj}^{-1} \Delta y_j \end{bmatrix}$$

where a_{ij}^{-1} is the element in the ith row and jth column of $\mathbf{A}^{-1}$. Taking out the factor Δy_j in the second term on the right-hand side of (4) and subtracting the vector x from both sides gives

$$\begin{bmatrix} \Delta x_1 \\ \vdots \\ \Delta x_i \\ \vdots \\ \Delta x_n \end{bmatrix} = \Delta y_j \begin{bmatrix} a_{1j}^{-1} \\ \vdots \\ a_{ij}^{-1} \\ \vdots \\ a_{nj}^{-1} \end{bmatrix}$$

Taking the ith equation of this set of equations we get

$$(5) \qquad \Delta x_i/\Delta y_j = a_{ij}^{-1}$$

The left-hand side of equation (5) measures the rate of change of the equilibrium value of the ith endogenous variable with respect to a change in the value of the jth exogenous variable. In the terminology of Section 3.5, $\Delta x_i/\Delta y_j$ is the multiplier relating the ith endogenous variable and the jth exogenous variable. Our conclusions are embodied in the following theorem.

Theorem 13.1 The element in the ith row and jth column of the inverse matrix associated with a set of equilibrium conditions is the multiplier relating the ith endogenous variable to the jth exogenous variable; it measures the rate at which the equilibrium value of the ith endogenous variable changes with respect to a change in the value of the jth exogenous variable.

We describe below three important applications of Theorem 13.1.

(1) A generalization of the model of Section 10.2 to a trading bloc of n countries

Let the marginal propensity to consume in the ith country be c_i and the marginal propensity of the jth country to import from the ith country be m_{ij} (the order of the subscripts indicates the direction of the flow of goods). The total marginal propensity to import for each country is the sum of the marginal propensities to import from individual countries, i.e. $m_i = \Sigma_{j=1}^{n} m_{ji}$ where m_i is the total marginal propensity to import for the ith country. Exogenous demand in the ith country is E_i and the equilibrium income is Y_i. The conditions for planned aggregate supply to equal planned aggregate demand in each country within the bloc constitute a set of n simultaneous linear equations in n unknowns:

$$\begin{bmatrix} 1 - c_1 + m_1 & -m_{12} & \cdots & -m_{1n} \\ -m_{21} & 1 - c_2 + m_2 & \cdots & -m_{2n} \\ \vdots & \vdots & & \vdots \\ -m_{n1} & -m_{n2} & \cdots & 1 - c_n + m_n \end{bmatrix} \begin{bmatrix} Y_1 \\ Y_2 \\ \vdots \\ Y_n \end{bmatrix} = \begin{bmatrix} E_1 \\ E_2 \\ \vdots \\ E_n \end{bmatrix}$$

More compactly, we may write

$$\mathbf{Ay} = \mathbf{e}$$

(One way of memorizing the form of the matrix **A** is to note that the sum of the elements in the ith column is equal to $1 - c_i$). The element in the ith row and jth column of the inverse, a_{ij}^{-1}, is the multiplier relating exogenous demand in the jth country to the equilibrium income in the ith country; it measures the rate of change of equilibrium income in country i with respect to a change in exogenous demand in country j. A dynamic analysis of the way in which trade flows adjust to bring the individual economies into equilibrium is given in the next section.

Example Consider the two country trading bloc discussed in Example 1 of Section 12.7. Since there are only two countries, in each country the total marginal propensity to import is equal to the marginal propensity to import from the other country, i.e. $m_{12} = m_2$, $m_{21} = m_1$. Since $c_1 = 0{\cdot}75$, $c_2 = 1{\cdot}0$, $m_1 = 0{\cdot}25$, $m_2 = 0{\cdot}5$ the equilibrium conditions are $\mathbf{Ay} = \mathbf{e}$ with

$$\mathbf{A} = \begin{bmatrix} (1 - 0{\cdot}75 + 0{\cdot}25) & -0{\cdot}5 \\ -0{\cdot}25 & (1 - 1 + 0{\cdot}5) \end{bmatrix} = \begin{bmatrix} 0{\cdot}5 & -0{\cdot}5 \\ -0{\cdot}25 & 0{\cdot}5 \end{bmatrix}$$

The solution $\mathbf{y} = \mathbf{A}^{-1}\mathbf{e}$ is

$$\begin{bmatrix} Y_1 \\ Y_2 \end{bmatrix} = \begin{bmatrix} 4 & 4 \\ 2 & 4 \end{bmatrix} \begin{bmatrix} E_1 \\ E_2 \end{bmatrix}$$

The reader can easily verify that the multiplier relating domestic exogenous demand to domestic income in country 1 is $\Delta Y_1/\Delta E_1 = a_{11}^{-1} = 4$. This confirms the result arrived at in Section 10.4. The multiplier relating exogenous demand in country 1 to income in country 2 is $\Delta Y_2/\Delta E_1 = a_{21}^{-1} = 2$. This result was also deduced in Section 10.4. The interpretation of the other two elements of the inverse should be self-evident. It is clear from this example that a change in exogenous demand in one country can have quite a strong effect on equilibrium incomes in other countries.

(2) The multipliers of a Keynesian model

The equilibrium conditions for the Keynesian model described in Section 10.5 are

$$\begin{bmatrix} e & f \\ 1 - c & -d \end{bmatrix} \begin{bmatrix} Y \\ 1/r \end{bmatrix} = \begin{bmatrix} M \\ G \end{bmatrix} \qquad r > r_{\min} > 0$$

where Y is equilibrium income, r is the equilibrium rate of interest, M is the stock of money and G is government expenditure; c is the marginal propensity to consume, d measures the strength of investment demand, e is the reciprocal of the velocity of circulation of money for transactions purposes and f measures the strength of the speculative demand for money. The solution of the equilibrium conditions is

$$\begin{bmatrix} Y \\ 1/r \end{bmatrix} = \frac{1}{de + f(1 - c)} \begin{bmatrix} d & f \\ 1 - c & -e \end{bmatrix} \begin{bmatrix} M \\ G \end{bmatrix}$$

It can be seen that the multiplier relating government expenditure and income is $\Delta Y/\Delta G = f/[de + f(1 - c)] = 1/[(1 - c) + de/f]$. In the simple closed economy of Section 3.5, in which there was no money market, the multiplier was equal to $1/(1 - c)$. Normally $d, e, f > 0$ so that the multiplier relating government expenditure to income is reduced by the action of the money market. The economic explanation is that the direct effect of a change in government expenditure on aggregate demand, and hence on income, is modified because the induced change in income alters the transactions demand for money, which in turn affects the rate of interest and hence investment demand. If $d, e, f > 0$ then the direction of the resulting change in investment demand is opposite to the initiating change in government expenditure, so that the initial effect on income is partly offset by repercussions acting through the money market.

The reader should appreciate that in the Keynesian model there is not only a 'government expenditure multiplier' but a 'money multiplier' as well.

Example What are the multipliers of a Keynesian economy in which $c = 0{\cdot}8$, $d = 40$, $e = 0{\cdot}4$ and $f = 120$?

The multipliers are the elements of the matrix

$$\frac{1}{40 \times 0{\cdot}4 + 120(1 - 0{\cdot}8)}\begin{bmatrix} 40 & 120 \\ (1 - 0{\cdot}8) & -0{\cdot}4 \end{bmatrix}$$

$$= \begin{bmatrix} 1 & 3 \\ 0{\cdot}005 & -0{\cdot}01 \end{bmatrix}$$

It can be seen that the multiplier relating government expenditure to income is three times the multiplier relating the stock of money to income. This suggests that fiscal policy will be more effective than monetary policy in adjusting income to a target value. The multiplier relating government expenditure and the *reciprocal* of the rate of interest is negative; this means that an increase in government expenditure will *increase* the rate of interest (because a reduction in $1/r$ means an increase in r). Similar reasoning shows that an increase in the stock of money *reduces* the rate of interest.

(3) A generalization of the model of Section 10.7 to transactions between *n* industries

Let X be planned output, F final demand, and let a subscript denote the industry. Suppose that to produce one unit of output in the jth industry requires m_{ij} units of the output of the ith industry. In the ith industry

$$\text{Planned supply} = X_i$$

$$\text{Planned demand} = m_{i1}X_1 + m_{i2}X_2 + \cdots + m_{in}X_n + F_i$$

where the terms $m_{ij}X_j$ are the requirements of the jth industry for the products of the ith industry. If planned supply equals planned demand in each industry then there are n equations in the n unknown outputs $X_1, \ldots, X_n$:

$$\begin{bmatrix} X_1 \\ X_2 \\ \vdots \\ X_n \end{bmatrix} = \begin{bmatrix} m_{11} & m_{12} & \cdots & m_{1n} \\ m_{21} & m_{22} & \cdots & m_{2n} \\ \vdots & \vdots & \ddots & \vdots \\ m_{n1} & m_{n2} & \cdots & m_{nn} \end{bmatrix} \begin{bmatrix} X_1 \\ X_2 \\ \vdots \\ X_n \end{bmatrix} + \begin{bmatrix} F_1 \\ F_2 \\ \vdots \\ F_n \end{bmatrix}$$

In more compact notation

(1) $\mathbf{x} = \mathbf{M}\mathbf{x} + \mathbf{f}$

To solve we must first collect terms in $\mathbf{x}$. It is a property of the $n \times n$ identity matrix $\mathbf{I}$ that $\mathbf{I}\mathbf{x} = \mathbf{x}$, so that equation (1) may be written

(2) $\mathbf{I}\mathbf{x} = \mathbf{M}\mathbf{x} + \mathbf{f}$

Subtracting $\mathbf{M}\mathbf{x}$ from both sides of (2) and using the distributed law of matrix multiplication gives

(3) $(\mathbf{I} - \mathbf{M})\mathbf{x} = \mathbf{f}$

Setting $\mathbf{A} = \mathbf{I} - \mathbf{M}$ in (3) gives

(4) $\mathbf{A}\mathbf{x} = \mathbf{f}$

and solving (4) we get

(5) $\mathbf{x} = \mathbf{A}^{-1}\mathbf{f}$

Equation (5) shows that the element in the ith row and jth column of the inverse $\mathbf{A}^{-1}$ is the multiplier relating the equilibrium output of the ith commodity to the final demand for the jth commodity; it measures the rate at which the output of the ith commodity must be changed as a result of a change in the final demand for the jth commodity if all the requirements of industries for one another's output are to be satisfied.

Example In the example in Section 12.8 we examined transactions between the coal, steel and lorry industries (indexed 1, 2 and 3 respectively). The matrix of input-output coefficients $\mathbf{M}$ is

$$\mathbf{M} = \begin{bmatrix} 0 & 0{\cdot}2 & 0{\cdot}6 \\ 0{\cdot}4 & 0 & 0{\cdot}4 \\ 0{\cdot}2 & 0{\cdot}1 & 0 \end{bmatrix}$$

The equilibrium conditions are $\mathbf{A}\mathbf{x} = \mathbf{f}$ where

$$\mathbf{A} = \mathbf{I} - \mathbf{M} = \begin{bmatrix} 1 & -0{\cdot}2 & -0{\cdot}6 \\ -0{\cdot}4 & 1 & -0{\cdot}4 \\ -0{\cdot}2 & -0{\cdot}1 & 1 \end{bmatrix}$$

The multipliers are the elements of

$$\mathbf{A}^{-1} = \tfrac{1}{36}\begin{bmatrix} 48 & 13 & 34 \\ 24 & 44 & 32 \\ 12 & 7 & 46 \end{bmatrix}$$

The elements on the north-west to south-east diagonal of the inverse are the multipliers relating to final demand for a commodity to the equilibrium output *of the same commodity*; it is interesting to note that each of these multipliers exceeds unity. This means that for each commodity the effect of an increase in the final demand is to increase the equilibrium output of that commodity by more than the change in final demand. The economic explanation is that the additional output is needed to supply the other industries so that they in turn can step up their output to meet the new requirements of the industry whose final demand has risen.

13.2 Dynamic analysis using matrix algebra

The application of matrix algebra to the dynamic analysis of interacting markets illustrates very clearly the way in which the use of matrices simplifies the analysis of complex economic situations. The simplicity effected by the use of matrices helps to illuminate general principles underlying the analysis. We give below just one example; another can be found in Section 13.3.

The dynamics of international trade

Consider the dynamic model of the world economy described in Section 10.2:

$$\begin{aligned} Y_1(t) &= (c_1 - m_1)Y_1(t-1) + m_2 Y_2(t-1) + E_1(t) \\ Y_2(t) &= m_1 Y_1(t-1) + (c_2 - m_2)Y_2(t-1) + E_2(t) \end{aligned}$$

where Y denotes income, E exogenous demand and a subscript denotes the country. Without the use of matrix algebra it is difficult to study the evolution of the world economy over time. For example, let us see how far simple economic reasoning can analyse the effect of a change in exogenous demand in one or other of the countries.

Suppose that in period 0 the world economy is in equilibrium and that in period 1 there is a permanent increase in exogenous demand of £1m in country 1. The immediate impact of this is to increase aggregate demand in country 1 by £1m, and hence to increase factor incomes in country 1 by £1m. This is shown in the first column of Table 13.1 below. In the following period (period 2) the impact of this increase in income in country 1 is felt in both country 1 and country 2. The increase in income of £1m calls forth additional consumer demand of £c_1 million in country 1, of which £$(c_1 - m_1)$ million is spent on home products and £m_1 million on imports, i.e., on the exports of country 2. As a result, aggregate demand in country 1 increases by a total of £$(1 + c_1 - m_1)$ million and, because of the increase in demand for country 2's exports, aggregate demand in country 2 increases by £m_1 million. These increases in exogenous demand are transformed into increases in factor income (see the second column of the table).

Table 13.1 Time path of income in countries 1 and 2 for $t = 1, 2, 3$

	Period		
Increase in (£m)	*1*	*2*	*3*
C_1	0	c_1	$c_1(1 + c_1 - m_1)$
I_1	0	0	0
G_1	1	1	1
X_1	0	0	$m_2 m_1$
M_1	0	m_1	$m_1(1 + c_1 - m_1)$
Y_1	1	$1 + c_1 - m_1$	$1 + (c_1 - m_1)(1 + c_1 - m_1) + m_2 m_1$
C_2	0	0	$c_2 m_1$
I_2	0	0	0
G_2	0	0	0
X_2	0	m_1	$m_1(1 + c_1 - m_1)$
M_2	0	0	$m_2 m_1$
Y_2	0	m_1	$m_1(1 + c_1 - m_1) + (c_2 - m_2)m_1$

In period 3 the increased income in country 1 calls forth additional consumption of £$c_1(1 + c_1 - m_1)$ million, of which £$(c_1 - m_1)(1 + c_1 - m_1)$ million is spent at home and £$m_1(1 + c_1 - m_1)$ million is spent abroad; the income of country 2 has increased by £m_1 million and this calls forth additional consumption of £$c_2 m_1$ million, of which £$(c_2 - m_2)m_1$ million is spent on the products of country 2 and £$m_2 m_1$ million on the products of country 1. As a result of these repercussions, aggregate demand in country 1 is increased by a total of £$[1 + (c_1 - m_1)(1 + c_1 - m_1) + m_2 m_1]$ million and aggregate demand in country 2 is increased by a total of £$[m_1(1 + c_1 - m_1) + (c_2 - m_2)m_1]$ million. These increases in aggregate demand lead to corresponding increases in the factor incomes (see the third column of the table). By this stage, the analysis of the time paths of income has become rather cumbersome, and it seems advisable to search for another method.

By using the algebra of vectors and matrices it is easy to see that the dynamic analysis of a system of interacting markets is a simple generalization of the dynamic analysis of a single market. The same formulae apply in both cases, but in one case the elements in the formulae are ordinary numbers, in the other case they are vectors and matrices.

Suppose that in period 0 the world economy is in equilibrium and that in period 1 there is a permanent increase in exogenous demand of £ΔE_1 million in country 1 and £ΔE_2 million in country 2. The time path of income in each country may be calculated as follows.

Let us write the dynamic equations in matrix notation:

(1) $$\mathbf{y}(t) = \mathbf{M}\mathbf{y}(t - 1) + \mathbf{e}(t)$$

where

$$\mathbf{y}(t) = \begin{bmatrix} Y_1(t) \\ Y_2(t) \end{bmatrix}, \quad \mathbf{e}(t) = \begin{bmatrix} E_1(t) \\ E_2(t) \end{bmatrix} \quad \text{and} \quad \mathbf{M} = \begin{bmatrix} c_1 - m_1 & m_2 \\ m_1 & c_2 - m_2 \end{bmatrix}$$

In period 1 there is a permanent change in the vector of exogenous demands, so we set

(2) $\mathbf{e}(t) = \mathbf{e}(0) + \Delta\mathbf{e} \qquad (t > 0)$

where $\Delta\mathbf{e}$ is the vector of the initial changes in exogenous demands.

If the world economy is in equilibrium in period 0 then the equilibrium conditions (see Section 10.3) imply

(3) $\mathbf{y}(0) = \mathbf{M}\mathbf{y}(0) + \mathbf{e}(0)$

It follows by setting $t = 1$ in equation (1) and using (2) and (3) that

(4) $\mathbf{y}(1) = \mathbf{y}(0) + \Delta\mathbf{e}$

Setting $t = 2$ in equation (1) and using (2) and (4) gives

(5) $$\begin{aligned} \mathbf{y}(2) &= \mathbf{y}(0) + \mathbf{M}\Delta\mathbf{e} + \Delta\mathbf{e} \\ &= \mathbf{y}(0) + (\mathbf{I} + \mathbf{M})\Delta\mathbf{e} \end{aligned}$$

[the second line of (5) is obtained by putting $\Delta\mathbf{e} = \mathbf{I}\Delta\mathbf{e}$ and grouping terms.] Quite generally, it follows from (1) and (2) that if, for any $t > 0$,

(6) $\mathbf{y}(t) = \mathbf{y}(0) + (\mathbf{I} + \mathbf{M} + \cdots + \mathbf{M}^{t-1})\,\Delta\mathbf{e}$

then[1]

(7) $\mathbf{y}(t+1) = \mathbf{y}(0) + (\mathbf{I} + \mathbf{M} + \cdots + \mathbf{M}^{t})\,\Delta\mathbf{e}$

Since (6) is certainly true for $t = 2$ it follows by induction that income N periods after the increase in exogenous demand is given by

(8) $\mathbf{y}(N+1) = \mathbf{y}(0) + (\mathbf{I} + \mathbf{M} + \cdots + \mathbf{M}^{N})\,\Delta\mathbf{e}$

Subtracting $\mathbf{y}(0)$ from both sides of equation (8) and setting $\Delta\mathbf{y}(N+1) = \mathbf{y}(N+1) - \mathbf{y}(0)$ gives

(9) $\Delta\mathbf{y}(N+1) = (\mathbf{I} + \mathbf{M} + \cdots + \mathbf{M}^{N})\,\Delta\mathbf{e}$

1 The proof is a matter of straightforward algebra. From equation (1)

$\mathbf{y}(t+1) = \mathbf{M}\mathbf{y}(t) + \mathbf{e}(t+1)$

Since by assumption $\mathbf{y}(t) = \mathbf{y}(0) + (\mathbf{I} + \mathbf{M} + \cdots + \mathbf{M}^{t-1})\,\Delta\mathbf{e}$, and since also $\mathbf{e}(t+1) = \mathbf{e}(0) + \Delta\mathbf{e}$,

$\mathbf{y}(t+1) = \mathbf{M}\mathbf{y}(0) + \mathbf{M}(\mathbf{I} + \mathbf{M} + \cdots + \mathbf{M}^{t-1})\,\Delta\mathbf{e} + \mathbf{e}(0) + \Delta\mathbf{e}$

Since $\mathbf{M}(\mathbf{I} + \mathbf{M} + \cdots + \mathbf{M}^{t-1}) = \mathbf{M} + \mathbf{M}^2 + \cdots + \mathbf{M}^t$ we get, on grouping terms in $\Delta\mathbf{e}$,

$\mathbf{y}(t+1) = \mathbf{M}\mathbf{y}(0) + \mathbf{e}(0) + (\mathbf{I} + \mathbf{M} + \cdots + \mathbf{M}^{t})\,\Delta\mathbf{e}$

Applying equation (3) gives equation (7).

Equation (9) shows that the effect of a permanent change, $\boldsymbol{\Delta e}$, in the vector of exogenous demands is to change the vector of incomes N periods afterwards by an amount equal to the product of the sum of a geometric series in the matrix **M** and the vector $\boldsymbol{\Delta e}$. Equation (9) should be compared with the result obtained in Section 3.6 for a single closed economy; the effect of an increase of £ΔI million in investment in a closed economy is to increase income after N periods by an amount

$$(10) \qquad \Delta Y(N+1) = (1 + c + \cdots + c^N)\,\Delta I$$

where c is the marginal propensity to consume. Equation (9) may be obtained from equation (10) by replacing the number ΔI by the vector $\boldsymbol{\Delta e}$, the number $\Delta Y(N+1)$ by the vector $\boldsymbol{\Delta y}(N+1)$, the number c by the matrix **M** and the number one by the identity matrix **I**.

Example Continuing example 1 of Section 12.7, consider the dynamics of trade between countries 1 and 2. In country 1 the marginal propensity to consume is $c_1 = 0{\cdot}75$ and the marginal propensity to import is $m_1 = 0{\cdot}25$; in country 2 the marginal propensity to consume is $c_2 = 1{\cdot}0$ and the marginal propensity to import is $m_2 = 0{\cdot}5$. If there are simultaneous changes in exogenous demand of $\Delta E_1 = 10$ (£m) in country 1 and $\Delta E_2 = 20$ (£m) in country 2, what will be the resulting change in income in each country after 3 periods?

Suppose that changes in exogenous demand take place in period 1; then $Y_1(4)$, $Y_2(4)$ are the respective incomes 3 periods afterwards. From the notation explained in the text we have

$$\boldsymbol{\Delta y}(4) = \begin{bmatrix} Y_1(4) - Y_1(0) \\ Y_2(4) - Y_2(0) \end{bmatrix}, \qquad \boldsymbol{\Delta e} = \begin{bmatrix} \Delta E_1 \\ \Delta E_2 \end{bmatrix} = \begin{bmatrix} 10 \\ 20 \end{bmatrix},$$

$$\mathbf{M} = \begin{bmatrix} c_1 - m_1 & m_2 \\ m_1 & c_2 - m_2 \end{bmatrix} = \begin{bmatrix} 0{\cdot}5 & 0{\cdot}5 \\ 0{\cdot}25 & 0{\cdot}5 \end{bmatrix}$$

Equation (9) with $N = 3$ shows that

$$\boldsymbol{\Delta y}(4) = (\mathbf{I} + \mathbf{M} + \mathbf{M}^2 + \mathbf{M}^3)\,\boldsymbol{\Delta e}$$

Powers of a matrix are defined in the usual way: $\mathbf{M}^2 = \mathbf{MM}$, $\mathbf{M}^3 = \mathbf{MMM}$, etc. It follows that

$$\mathbf{I} = \begin{bmatrix} 1 & 0 \\ 0 & 1 \end{bmatrix}, \qquad \mathbf{M} = \begin{bmatrix} 0{\cdot}5 & 0{\cdot}5 \\ 0{\cdot}25 & 0{\cdot}5 \end{bmatrix},$$

$$\mathbf{M}^2 = \mathbf{MM} = \begin{bmatrix} 0{\cdot}375 & 0{\cdot}5 \\ 0{\cdot}25 & 0{\cdot}375 \end{bmatrix}$$

$$\mathbf{M}^3 = \mathbf{M}^2\mathbf{M} = \begin{bmatrix} 0{\cdot}3125 & 0{\cdot}4375 \\ 0{\cdot}21875 & 0{\cdot}3125 \end{bmatrix}$$

whence

$$\mathbf{I} + \mathbf{M} + \mathbf{M}^2 + \mathbf{M}^3 = \begin{bmatrix} 2{\cdot}1875 & 1{\cdot}4375 \\ 0{\cdot}71875 & 2{\cdot}1875 \end{bmatrix}$$

and

$$\Delta\mathbf{y}(4) = (\mathbf{I} + \mathbf{M} + \mathbf{M}^2 + \mathbf{M}^3)\,\Delta\mathbf{e} = \begin{bmatrix} 50{\cdot}625 \\ 51{\cdot}9375 \end{bmatrix}$$

We conclude that after three periods income in country 1 will have risen by £50·625m and income in country 2 by £51·9375.

13.3 Analysis of stability by using matrix algebra

The comparative static analysis of Section 13.1 can be combined with the dynamic analysis of Section 13.2 to examine the stability of equilibrium in a system of interacting markets. In Section 3.7 it was shown how comparative static analysis and dynamic analysis can be combined to examine the stability of equilibrium in a single market. By using the techniques of matrix algebra it is very easy to investigate the stability of interacting markets. In many cases a result which holds for a single market has an exact counterpart among the results for a system of interacting markets. The correspondence between the two sets of results is brought out by developing the theory of interacting markets in terms of matrix algebra.

Many dynamic models of interacting markets are of the form

(1) $\mathbf{y}(t) = \mathbf{M}\mathbf{y}(t-1) + \mathbf{e}(t)$

The equilibrium condition is usually

(2) $\mathbf{y}(t) = \mathbf{y}(t-1)$

$\mathbf{y}(t)$ is a vector of measurements on the endogenous variables in period t, $\mathbf{e}(t)$ is a vector of measurements on exogenous variables in period t and $\mathbf{M}$ is a matrix of fixed coefficients. Substituting equation (2) into equation (1) and grouping terms in $\mathbf{y}(t)$ gives an alternative form of the equilibrium condition:

(3) $(\mathbf{I} - \mathbf{M})\mathbf{y}(t) = \mathbf{e}(t)$

Comparative static analysis applied to equation (3) shows that a change, $\Delta\mathbf{e}$, in the vector of exogenous variables changes the equilibrium values of the endogenous variables by

(4) $\Delta\mathbf{y} = (\mathbf{I} - \mathbf{M})^{-1}\,\Delta\mathbf{e}$

Dynamic analysis applied to equation (1) shows that the effect of a permanent increase $\Delta\mathbf{e}$ in the vector of exogenous variables is to change the vector of endogenous variables after $\mathbf{N}$ periods by

(5) $\Delta\mathbf{y}(N+1) = (\mathbf{I} + \mathbf{M} + \cdots + \mathbf{M}^N)\,\Delta\mathbf{e}$

In Section 3.7 an equilibrium was defined to be stable if a market adjusts to it from any initial state when all exogenous variables are stationary. The stability equilibrium in a system of interacting markets may be defined in a similar way. It is a consequence of such a definition that in the dynamic model above the equilibrium is stable if

$$\lim_{N \to \infty} \Delta \mathbf{y}(N + 1) = \Delta \mathbf{y} \tag{6}$$

Equation (6) requires the actual change in the vector **y**—as indicated by the dynamic analysis—to be just sufficient to adjust the system from the old equilibrium to the new—as indicated by the comparative static analysis.

The limit in equation (6) concerns a vector rather than an ordinary number; we say that a vector is equal in the limit to another vector if and only if each element in the vector is equal in the limit to the corresponding element in the other vector.

Substituting equations (4) and (5) into (6) shows that the stability condition is

$$\lim_{N \to \infty} (\mathbf{I} + \mathbf{M} + \cdots + \mathbf{M}^N)\, \Delta \mathbf{e} = (\mathbf{I} - \mathbf{M})^{-1}\, \Delta \mathbf{e}$$

Since $\Delta \mathbf{e}$ is arbitrary the condition becomes

$$\lim_{N \to \infty} (\mathbf{I} + \mathbf{M} + \cdots + \mathbf{M}^N) = (\mathbf{I} - \mathbf{M})^{-1} \tag{7}$$

There is a very close analogy between the stability condition (7) and the stability condition for a single market; for example, in Section 3.7 it was shown that the stability condition for a simple closed economy is

$$\lim_{N \to \infty} (1 + c + \cdots + c^N) = 1/(1 - c) \tag{8}$$

Both equations (7) and (8) involve the convergence of a geometric series. Equation (7) may be obtained from equation (8) by (i) replacing the number c by the matrix **M**. (ii) replacing the number one by the identity matrix **I** and (iii) using the correspondence between the inverse of a matrix and the reciprocal of a real number (as explained in Section 11.4).

Example 1 Consider the trading relations between two countries described in example 1 of Section 12.7. The comparative statics of this model were discussed in example 1 of Section 13.1 and the dynamics at the end of Section 13.2. The model satisfies equations (1) and (2) in the text if $\mathbf{y}(t)$ is a vector of incomes, $\mathbf{e}(t)$ is a vector of exogenous demands and

$$\mathbf{M} = \begin{bmatrix} 0{\cdot}5 & 0{\cdot}5 \\ 0{\cdot}25 & 0{\cdot}5 \end{bmatrix}$$

According to equation (8) the stability of equilibrium depends upon whether

$$\mathbf{I} + \mathbf{M} + \mathbf{M}^2 + \cdots = (\mathbf{I} - \mathbf{M})^{-1}$$

Using the calculations given in Section 13.2, we see that

$$\mathbf{I} + \mathbf{M} = \begin{bmatrix} 1{\cdot}5 & 0{\cdot}5 \\ 0{\cdot}25 & 1{\cdot}5 \end{bmatrix}$$

$$\mathbf{I} + \mathbf{M} + \mathbf{M}^2 = \begin{bmatrix} 1{\cdot}875 & 1{\cdot}0 \\ 0{\cdot}5 & 1{\cdot}875 \end{bmatrix}$$

$$\mathbf{I} + \mathbf{M} + \mathbf{M}^2 + \mathbf{M}^3 = \begin{bmatrix} 2{\cdot}1875 & 1{\cdot}4375 \\ 0{\cdot}71875 & 2{\cdot}1875 \end{bmatrix}$$

and from Section 13.1, example 1, we have

$$(\mathbf{I} - \mathbf{M})^{-1} = \begin{bmatrix} 4 & 4 \\ 2 & 4 \end{bmatrix}$$

Looking at the relative sizes of the elements in the sequence of matrix sums it is possible to detect a trend toward the form of the inverse. As we shall see in Section 14.6, it is easy to confirm that this trend continues as more terms are added to the sequence of sums.

Example 2: Planning of output in related industries Let us return to the example of the economic planning of industrial output described in Section 10.7. The problem was to determine the outputs of coal and steel which together would meet a given pattern of final demand and at the same time provide the necessary inputs to production in the other industry. The problem was solved by assuming that the economic planner knew the coefficients of input per unit output in each industry (the 'input-output coefficients'). By using this information, he could determine the conditions for simultaneous equilibrium in the coal market and the steel market. Suppose now that he is not in a position to know the input-output coefficients in each industry, so that the coal industry and the steel industry must solve the problem by negotiation. If neither industry knows the other industry's input-output coefficients, the negotiations will proceed as follows.

To begin with, the planned output of each industry will be set equal to the final demand for the products of that industry. In terms of the example in Section 11.7, the planned output of steel will be 200m tons and the planned output of coal will be 160m tons. But the steel industry requires 0·4 tons of coal to produce one ton of steel. In the first round of negotiations, therefore, the steel industry will order from the coal industry the $0{\cdot}4 \times 200 = 80$m tons of coal required to produce the 200m tons of steel for final demand. The coal industry requires 0·1 tons of steel to produce one ton of coal. In the first round of negotiations, therefore, the coal industry will order from the steel industry the $0{\cdot}1 \times 160 = 16$m tons of steel required to produce the 160m tons of coal for final demand. As a result of this round of negotiations the planned output of coal will be 240m tons and the planned output of steel will be 216m tons (see the second column of Table 13.2 below).

Table 13.2 Solution of the planning problem by negotiation

	Negotiating rounds			
	0	*1*	*2*	*3*
Steel industry				
Production for final demand	200	200	200	200
Production for coal industry	0	16	24	24·64
Total production (units of million tons)	200	216	224	224·64
Coal industry				
Production for final demand	160	160	160	160
Production for steel industry	0	80	86·4	89·6
Total production (units of million tons)	160	240	246·4	249·6

Each industry will then calculate a new set of input requirements, and these requirements will form the basis for the second round of negotiations. The first three rounds of the negotiations are shown in the table above.

It is seen from the table that by the end of the third round of negotiations the planned outputs of the two industries are almost equal to the equilibrium outputs, which are 225m tons of steel and 250m tons of coal. This suggests that the process of negotiation is an effective method for evaluating the equilibrium outputs.

When the process of negotiation is formalized it is seen to be a special case of the model described by equations (1) and (2). Let t index the round of negotiations; the planned output of steel after round t is denoted $X_1(t)$ and the planned output of coal after round t is denoted $X_2(t)$. The final demand for steel is Y_1 and the final demand for coal is Y_2. The negotiations are then described by the equations

$$X_1(t) = 0{\cdot}1X_2(t-1) + Y_1$$

$$X_2(t) = 0{\cdot}4X_1(t-1) + Y_2$$

The dynamics of the process of negotiation can be studied by writing these equations in matrix notation:

$$\mathbf{x}(t) = \mathbf{M}\mathbf{x}(t-1) + \mathbf{y}$$

where $\mathbf{x}(t)$, $\mathbf{x}(t-1)$ and $\mathbf{y}$ are 2-element column vectors and $\mathbf{M}$ is the matrix

$$\mathbf{M} = \begin{bmatrix} 0 & 0{\cdot}1 \\ 0{\cdot}4 & 0 \end{bmatrix}$$

Substituting successively $t = 1, t = 2, \ldots$ in the matrix equation and using the initial condition that

$$\mathbf{x}(0) = \mathbf{y}$$

we find that, in any period N,

$$\mathbf{x}(N) = (\mathbf{I} + \mathbf{M} + \mathbf{M}^2 + \cdots + \mathbf{M}^N)\mathbf{y} \tag{9}$$

This equation expresses the dynamics of the process of negotiation in terms of a geometric series in the matrix $\mathbf{M}$.

The conditions for simultaneous equilibrium in the coal and steel markets are, in matrix notation,

$$\mathbf{x} = \mathbf{M}\mathbf{x} + \mathbf{y}$$

i.e.,

$$(\mathbf{I} - \mathbf{M})\mathbf{x} = \mathbf{y}$$

so that

$$\mathbf{x} = (\mathbf{I} - \mathbf{M})^{-1}\mathbf{y} \tag{10}$$

Comparing equations (9) and (10) shows that the process of negotiation will lead to the equilibrium values of output if and only if the infinite geometric series in the matrix $\mathbf{M}$ converges to the inverse $(\mathbf{I} - \mathbf{M})^{-1}$,

$$\mathbf{I} + \mathbf{M} + \mathbf{M}^2 + \cdots = (\mathbf{I} - \mathbf{M})^{-1}$$

13.4 Geometric series in a matrix

The analysis of stability in the previous section suggests that it may be useful to make a systematic study of geometric series involving matrices. Within the scope of this book it is not possible to develop the subject very far. We shall do no more than present the matrix analogues of Theorems 2.1 and 2.2 of Section 2.5, which concern the sums of geometric series, both finite and infinite.

Theorem 13.2 The sum of the first N terms of a geometric series $\mathbf{I}, \mathbf{M}, \mathbf{M}^2, \ldots$ is equal to

$$\mathbf{I} + \mathbf{M} + \cdots + \mathbf{M}^{N-1} = (\mathbf{I} - \mathbf{M}^N)(\mathbf{I} - \mathbf{M})^{-1}$$

provided that the inverse matrix $(\mathbf{I} - \mathbf{M})^{-1}$ exists.

It should be obvious that there is a close analogy with Theorem 2.1, which states that

$$1 + c + \cdots + c^{N-1} = (1 - c^N)/(1 - c)$$

provided that $c \neq 1$. The analogy can be made to look even closer by using the notation $(1 - c^N)/(1 - c) = (1 - c^N)(1 - c)^{-1}$.

PROOF The proof is elementary. Note that

$$\begin{aligned}(\mathbf{I} + \mathbf{M} + \cdots + \mathbf{M}^{N-1})(\mathbf{I} - \mathbf{M}) &= \mathbf{I} + \mathbf{M} + \mathbf{M}^2 + \cdots + \mathbf{M}^{N-1} \\ &\quad - \mathbf{M} - \mathbf{M}^2 - \cdots - \mathbf{M}^{N-1} - \mathbf{M}^N \\ &= \mathbf{I} - \mathbf{M}^N\end{aligned}$$

Suppose that the inverse $(\mathbf{I} - \mathbf{M})^{-1}$ exists. Multiplying both sides of the equation into the inverse gives

$$(\mathbf{I} + \mathbf{M} + \ldots + \mathbf{M}^N)(\mathbf{I} - \mathbf{M})(\mathbf{I} - \mathbf{M})^{-1} = (\mathbf{I} - \mathbf{M}^N)(\mathbf{I} - \mathbf{M})^{-1}$$

By the definition of the inverse $(\mathbf{I} - \mathbf{M})(\mathbf{I} - \mathbf{M})^{-1} = \mathbf{I}$; since $\mathbf{I}$ is the identity matrix the left-hand side of the equation becomes simply $\mathbf{I} + \mathbf{M} + \cdots + \mathbf{M}^{N-1}$ and the theorem is proved. The following one is a consequence of it.

Theorem 13.3 The sum of an infinite geometric series exists if and only if every element of the matrix $\mathbf{M}^N$ converges to zero as N becomes infinitely large, i.e. if and only if

$$\lim_{N \to \infty} \mathbf{M}^N = \mathbf{0}$$

where $\mathbf{0}$ is a null matrix in which every element is zero. If this condition is satisfied then the sum of the series is equal to

$$\mathbf{I} + \mathbf{M} + \mathbf{M}^2 + \cdots = (\mathbf{I} - \mathbf{M})^{-1}$$

Unfortunately, Theorem 13.3 is not of much value unless we can test whether the matrix $\mathbf{M}$ satisfies the condition

$$\lim_{N \to \infty} \mathbf{M}^N = \mathbf{0}$$

For certain types of matrix it is relatively easy to test whether this condition is satisfied; of particular interest to the economist is the class of 'non-negative' matrices. Non-negative matrices are matrices in which all the elements are non-negative.

Theorem 13.4 If $\mathbf{M}$ is a $n \times n$ matrix in which every element is non-negative and less than one

$$0 \leqslant m_{ij} < 1$$

and every 'column sum' in $\mathbf{M}$ is also less than one

$$\sum_{j=1}^{n} m_{ji} < 1$$

then

$$\lim_{N \to \infty} \mathbf{M}^N = \mathbf{0}$$

where $\mathbf{0}$ is the null matrix whose every element is zero.

Note that the inequality on the column sums is a sufficient *but not necessary* condition for the powers of a non-negative matrix to converge to $\mathbf{0}$. A necessary *and* sufficient condition is given in Section 14.5.

PROOF Consider the column sums of $\mathbf{M}^2$. By the rules of matrix algebra, the ith column sum of $\mathbf{M}^2$ is the result of multiplying each row of $\mathbf{M}$ into the ith column of $\mathbf{M}$ and then adding the products. But this result can also be obtained by multiplying the jth column sum of $\mathbf{M}$ into the element in the jth row of the ith column of $\mathbf{M}$ and adding the results for the different j's. Now each of the column sums of $\mathbf{M}$ is less than one, so that the column sum of $\mathbf{M}^2$ is certainly less than the sum of the elements in the ith column of $\mathbf{M}$; in fact, if $s < 1$ is the largest column sum of $\mathbf{M}$, then the column sum of $\mathbf{M}^2$ is certainly less than or equal to s times the sum of the elements in the ith column of $\mathbf{M}$. But the sum of the elements in the ith column of $\mathbf{M}$ is also less than or equal to $s < 1$. Hence the ith column sum of $\mathbf{M}_2$ is less than or equal to s multiplied into a quantity less than or equal to s, so that it is less than or equal to s^2. It follows that each column sum of $\mathbf{M}^2$ is less than or equal to s^2.

Because each element of $\mathbf{M}$ is non-negative, each element of $\mathbf{M}^2$ is also non-negative. It follows that since each column sum of $\mathbf{M}^2$ is less than or equal to s^2 each element of $\mathbf{M}^2$ is less than or equal to s^2.

Repeating this argument for $\mathbf{M}^3$, $\mathbf{M}^4, \ldots$ and so on it is seen that in $\mathbf{M}^N$ each element is less than or equal to s^N. But $s < 1$, so that $\lim_{N\to\infty} s^N = 0$. Hence as N tends to infinity every element in $\mathbf{M}^N$ tends to zero, i.e. as N tends to infinity, $\mathbf{M}^N$ tends to the null matrix, $\mathbf{0}$.

Example The conditions of Theorem 13.4 are satisfied by the matrix $\mathbf{M}$ in example 2 of the previous section and also by the matrices

$$\begin{bmatrix} 0{\cdot}2 & 0{\cdot}5 \\ 0{\cdot}6 & 0 \end{bmatrix}, \quad \begin{bmatrix} 0 & 0 \\ 0 & 0{\cdot}9 \end{bmatrix}, \quad \begin{bmatrix} 0{\cdot}2 & 0{\cdot}6 & 0{\cdot}5 \\ 0{\cdot}5 & 0{\cdot}3 & 0{\cdot}1 \\ 0{\cdot}1 & 0{\cdot}05 & 0{\cdot}1 \end{bmatrix}$$

The conditions are not satisfied by the matrix $\mathbf{M}$ in example 1 of the previous section, nor by any of the following:

$$\begin{bmatrix} 1 & 0 \\ 0 & 1 \end{bmatrix}, \quad \begin{bmatrix} 0{\cdot}3 & 0{\cdot}5 \\ 0{\cdot}1 & 0{\cdot}6 \end{bmatrix}, \quad \begin{bmatrix} 0{\cdot}4 & 0{\cdot}3 & 0{\cdot}2 \\ 0{\cdot}1 & 0{\cdot}2 & -0{\cdot}1 \\ 0{\cdot}3 & 0{\cdot}1 & 0{\cdot}1 \end{bmatrix}$$

Theorems 13.3 and 13.4 together imply that for a sum of a geometric matrix series to converge it is sufficient that the matrix is non-negative and all its column sums are less than one. Referring to equation (7) of Section 13.3 we obtain the following result.

Theorem 13.5 Consider an economy characterized by the matrix equation

$$\mathbf{y}(t) = \mathbf{M}\mathbf{y}(t-1) + \mathbf{e}(t)$$

with the equilibrium condition

$$\mathbf{y}(t) = \mathbf{y}(t-1)$$

The equilibrium is stable if $\mathbf{M}$ is non-negative and every column sum of $\mathbf{M}$ is less than one.

Example In the dynamic model of trading relations between n countries the matrix $\mathbf{M}$ is of the form

$$\begin{bmatrix} c_1 - m_1 & m_{12} & m_{13} & \cdots & m_{1n} \\ m_{21} & c_2 - m_2 & m_{23} & \cdots & m_{2n} \\ m_{31} & m_{32} & c_3 - m_3 & \cdots & m_{3n} \\ \vdots & \vdots & \vdots & \ddots & \vdots \\ m_{n1} & \cdots & \cdots & \cdots & c_n - m_n \end{bmatrix}$$

where c_i is the marginal propensity to consume in country i, m_i is the marginal propensity to import in country i and m_{ij} is the marginal propensity for country j to import from country i. (The order of the subscripts i, j indicates the direction of the flow of goods from country i to country j.) It is necessary that for each country the total marginal propensity to import is equal to the sum of the individual marginal propensities to import from other countries, $m_i = \sum_{i=1}^{n} m_{ji}$. Simple arithmetic then shows that the sum of the elements in the ith column of the matrix is equal to c_i, which is the marginal propensity to consume in the ith country. Theorem 13.5 therefore implies that *if the marginal propensity to import of any one country from any other is non-negative and less than one, and if in every country the marginal propensity to consume is non-negative and less than one, then the world economy is stable.*

Now if the marginal propensity to consume is less than one in every country, every economy is stable if it does not engage in trade. As a general rule, therefore, *if every economy in the world is stable in isolation, the world economy will also be stable. This assumes that the marginal propensities to consume and to import are ordinarily non-negative.* If this is the case, the following proposition is also true. *When the world economy is stable, an increase in the world total of exogenous demand will necessarily cause the world economy to adjust to a new equilibrium in which world income is higher than before.* This result is analogous to the result for a single market, which was illustrated by Figs 3A and 3B. Furthermore, it can be shown that under certain circumstances the multiplier for the world economy is completely independent of the patterns of trade between the various countries. *If the marginal propensity to consume is the same in every country,*

$$c_1 = c_2 = \cdots = c_n = c$$

then the equilibrium income in the world economy depends only on the world total of exogenous demand, and not on the distribution of exogenous demand between the various countries, or on the values of the marginal propensities to import. As a corollary, if the world total of exogenous demand is increased by £ΔE million then whatever the distribution of this increase between the various countries, and whatever the pattern of world trade, the world total of income will increase by £$[1/(1 - c)]\, \Delta E$ million.

This last result is of considerable importance. To appreciate its significance, suppose that the countries involved are England, Wales, Scotland and Northern Ireland. It is reasonable to suppose that the marginal propensity to consume is the same in each of these countries. It follows from the result above that a multiplier analysis can be carried out for the United Kingdom as a whole, and that the multiplier effect of a change in total exogenous demand in the United Kingdom on the United Kingdom national income is entirely independent of the structure of trade between England, Wales, Scotland and Northern Ireland. It is therefore possible to make an aggregate study of the United Kingdom without examining the transactions taking place within the country.

Notes and references

The use of matrix algebra in comparative static analysis is demonstrated in an elementary textbook by Ames.[9]

The earliest discussion of the dynamics of the world economy is by Machlup;[82] for a more mathematical approach see Metzler,[88] Neisser and Modigliani[95] and Polak.[105] The systematic application of matrix algebra to economic dynamics began with Chipman[26] and Goodwin,[41] who simultaneously developed the theory of the 'matrix multiplier'. The theory was not developed without some controversy about the nature of the time paths of income in the world economy; see Chipman[27] and Goodwin.[42] The moral of the discussion in these articles is that whether or not there are oscillations in the time path of income in one or more countries depends on the nature of the changes in exogenous demand: in particular, on how the changes in exogenous demand are distributed between the various countries, and on whether the changes are temporary or permanent. The theory of the matrix multiplier has been used, amongst other things, to calculate the effect of foreign aid on the balance of payments; see, for example, Hopkin.[60] The matrix multiplier is also used in regional economics; see, for example, Airov.[3]

Problems

13.1.1 In a trading bloc of two countries the marginal propensity to consume in the first country is 0·7 and the marginal propensity to import is 0·3. In the second country the marginal propensity to consume is 0·9 and the marginal propensity to import is 0·2. What is the multiplier relating exogenous demand in country 1 to income in country 2? Which country has the greater influence on the other's income?

13.1.2 Find the expenditure and money multipliers for a closed Keynesian economy in which

$$C(t) = 10 + 0{\cdot}8\,Y(t-1)$$
$$I(t) = 50/r(t)$$
$$L_1(t) = 0{\cdot}5\,Y(t)$$
$$L_2(t) = 100/r(t) \qquad r(t) > r_{\min}$$

If the investment function changes to

$$I(t) = 40 + 10/r(t)$$

what difference does this make to the relative sizes of the expenditure and money multipliers? What are the policy implications of the change?

13.2.1 Suppose that the economy described in Section 13.2 is initially in equilibrium and that in period 1 there is an exogenous switch in investment expenditure of £ΔE million from country 1 to country 2. Trace the effect on the income in each country from period 1 until period 3. Verify your calculations for period 3 using the matrix equation $\Delta\mathbf{y}(3) = (\mathbf{I} + \mathbf{M} + \mathbf{M}^2)\Delta\mathbf{e}$

13.2.2 For the trading bloc in Problem 13.1.1 find the change in income after three periods if there is a simultaneous increase in exogenous demand in each country of £10m.

13.3.1 Determine the time path of negotiations (up to the third round) in the planning problem described in Problem 11.4.3.

13.3.2 Three nationalized industries are meeting to plan their outputs for the next year. Final demand for industry 1's product is estimated at 2,625 units of output, for industry 2 final demand is 1,750, and for industry 3 it is 3,500 units. To produce one unit of industry 1's product requires 0·3 units of industry 2's product and 0·3 units of industry 3's product. Industry 2 needs 0·1 units of industry 1's product and 0·2 units of industry 3's product. Industry 3 needs 0·2 units of industry 1's product and 0·1 units of industry 2's product.

(a) Find each industry's planned output after three rounds of negotiations.

(b) To what values must these planned outputs converge if a set of equilibrium outputs is to result from the negotiation process?

13.3.3 For the trading bloc in Problems 13.1.1 and 13.2.2 find the values to which income in each country must tend for the multiplier process to be stable.

13.4.1 Find the sum of the first four terms of the series **I**, **M**, $\mathbf{M}^2$, ... by direct computation and then by use of Theorem 13.2, for the matrix

$$\mathbf{M} = \begin{bmatrix} 2 & 1 \\ 1 & 3 \end{bmatrix}$$

13.4.2 Show that if **M** is a diagonal matrix then

$$\mathbf{I} + \mathbf{M} + \mathbf{M}^2 + \cdots = (\mathbf{I} - \mathbf{M})^{-1}$$

if and only if each of the diagonal terms in **M** lies between -1 and $+1$.

13.4.3 Without using Theorem 13.3 prove that if

$$\mathbf{M} = \begin{bmatrix} 0 & \frac{1}{2} \\ \frac{1}{2} & 0 \end{bmatrix}$$

then

$$\mathbf{I} + \mathbf{M} + \mathbf{M}^2 + \cdots = (\mathbf{I} - \mathbf{M})^{-1}$$

13.4.4 Evaluate the sum of the first eight terms of the series **I**, **M**, $\mathbf{M}^2$, ... where

$$\mathbf{M} = \begin{bmatrix} 2 & 1 \\ 1 & 1 \end{bmatrix}$$

[*Hint:* Use Theorem 13.2 and note that $\mathbf{M}^8 = ((\mathbf{M}^2)^2)^2$.]

13.4.5 Suppose that Britain and Germany have the same marginal propensity to consume, $\frac{3}{4}$. The marginal propensity of Britain to import from Germany is $\frac{3}{8}$, and the marginal propensity of Germany to import from Britain is $\frac{1}{2}$. All other countries are excluded from the analysis.

(a) Is the world economy stable?

(b) Suppose there is an increase in world exogenous demand of £5m. Show that the increase in the equilibrium value of world income is the same when (a) the whole of the £5m increase occurs in Britain, (b) the whole of the £5m increase occurs in Germany and (c) there is a £2m increase in Britain and a £3m increase in Germany.

(c) What is the multiplier relating world exogenous demand to world income?

(d) If the world economy is initially in equilibrium and there is an increase in exogenous demand in Germany of £1m in period 1, evaluate the time path of income in each country for periods 1, 2 and 3.

(e) How far is the world economy from equilibrium in period 3?

Chapter 14
Characteristic values

14.1 A matrix as a linear operator

This chapter explores the consequences of the fact that a matrix is a 'linear operator'. The mathematical methods which we shall develop are applicable not only to the analysis of systems of interacting markets, but to many other problems, both economic and noneconomic. Two important economic applications are to the study of the distribution of income and to the solution of difference equations which arise in the study of the trade cycle (see Chapter 20).

It is a most important property of matrix multiplication that it is a linear operation. A linear operation, L, has two characteristics:

(a) it is additive; for any two mathematical entities, x, z,

$$L(x + z) = L(x) + L(z)$$

(b) it is homogeneous; for any mathematical entity, x, and any real number, g,

$$L(g.x) = g.L(x)$$

It is easily verified that matrix multiplication is a linear operation. Let $\mathbf{M}$ be a matrix and let $\mathbf{x}$ and $\mathbf{z}$ be column vectors for which matrix multiplication by $\mathbf{M}$ is defined. It is an immediate consequence of the rules of matrix algebra that matrix multiplication is additive, since $\mathbf{M}(\mathbf{x} + \mathbf{z}) = \mathbf{Mx} + \mathbf{Mz}$ and that matrix multiplication is homogeneous since, for any real number g, $\mathbf{M}(g\mathbf{x}) = g(\mathbf{Mx})$.

From the linearity of matrix multiplication it is easy to deduce a further property. Consider any set of vectors, $\mathbf{y}_1, \mathbf{y}_2, \ldots, \mathbf{y}_n$ and a corresponding set of weights $a_1, a_2, \ldots, a_n$. It can be shown that the result of multiplying the matrix $\mathbf{M}$ into a weighted sum of n vectors, $\mathbf{x} = a_1\mathbf{y}_1 + a_2\mathbf{y}_2 + \cdots + a_n\mathbf{y}_n$, is the same as the result of first multiplying the matrix $\mathbf{M}$ into each of the vectors $\mathbf{y}_1, \mathbf{y}_2, \ldots, \mathbf{y}_n$ and then taking the weighted sum, i.e. that

$$\begin{aligned}\mathbf{Mx} &= \mathbf{M}(a_1\mathbf{y}_1 + a_2\mathbf{y}_2 + \cdots + a_n\mathbf{y}_n)\\ &= a_1(\mathbf{My}_1) + a_2(\mathbf{My}_2) + \cdots + a_n(\mathbf{My}_n)\end{aligned}$$

We can take the consequences of linearity even further. Suppose we substitute the matrix $\mathbf{M}^N$ for the matrix $\mathbf{M}$ in the equation above, where $\mathbf{M}^N$ is the matrix $\mathbf{M}$ multiplied by itself N times; the equation then becomes

$$\begin{aligned}&\mathbf{M}^N(a_1\mathbf{y}_1 + a_2\mathbf{y}_2 + \cdots + a_n\mathbf{y}_n)\\ &= a_1\mathbf{M}^N\mathbf{y}_1 + a_2\mathbf{M}^N\mathbf{y}_2 + \cdots + a_n\mathbf{M}^N\mathbf{y}_n\end{aligned}$$

There is one particular case in which this equation acquires great significance. This is the case in which the vectors $\mathbf{y}_1, \mathbf{y}_2, \ldots, \mathbf{y}_n$ are nontrivial solutions of the equation

$$\mathbf{My} = h\mathbf{y}$$

where $\mathbf{M}$ is an $n \times n$ matrix and h is a real number. Let us suppose that the values of h for which this equation has a solution are $h_1, h_2, \ldots, h_n$ and that the vectors which solve the equation are respectively $\mathbf{y}_1, \mathbf{y}_2, \ldots, \mathbf{y}_n$, i.e. the vectors $\mathbf{y}_1, \mathbf{y}_2, \ldots, \mathbf{y}_n$ satisfy the equations

$$\begin{aligned} \mathbf{My}_1 &= h_1\mathbf{y}_1 \\ \mathbf{My}_2 &= h_2\mathbf{y}_2 \\ &\vdots \\ \mathbf{My}_n &= h_n\mathbf{y}_n \end{aligned}$$

The ith equation ($i = 1, 2, \ldots, n$) shows that the result of multiplying the matrix $\mathbf{M}$ into the vector $\mathbf{y}_i$ is simply to scale the vector $\mathbf{y}_i$ by the factor h_i. An important corollary of this result is deduced as follows. Multiplying the ith equation by the matrix $\mathbf{M}$ gives

$$\mathbf{M}^2\mathbf{y}_i = \mathbf{M}(\mathbf{My}_i) = \mathbf{M}(h_i\mathbf{y}_i)$$

and from the property of homogeneity in matrix multiplication it follows that

$$\mathbf{M}(h_i\mathbf{y}_i) = h_i\mathbf{My}_i$$

Since it is already known that $\mathbf{My}_i = h_i\mathbf{y}_i$ it follows that

$$h_i\mathbf{My}_i = h_i(h_i\mathbf{y}_i) = h_i^2\mathbf{y}_i$$

Hence $\quad \mathbf{M}^2\mathbf{y}_i = h_i^2\mathbf{y}_i$

and in general, for $N = 0, 1, 2, \ldots$

$$\mathbf{M}^N\mathbf{y}_i = h_i^N\mathbf{y}_i$$

Substituting this result into the equation

$$\mathbf{M}^N\mathbf{x} = a_1\mathbf{M}^N\mathbf{y}_1 + a_2\mathbf{M}^N\mathbf{y}_2 + \cdots + a_n\mathbf{M}^N\mathbf{y}_n$$

gives $\quad \mathbf{M}^N\mathbf{x} = a_1h_1^N\mathbf{y}_1 + a_2h_2^N\mathbf{y}_2 + \cdots + a_nh_n^N\mathbf{y}_n$

The right-hand side of this equation is a weighted sum of the vectors $\mathbf{y}_1, \mathbf{y}_2, \ldots, \mathbf{y}_n$; the weights are, respectively, $a_1h_1^N, a_2h_2^N, \ldots, a_nh_n^N$. This result is of immense importance; it is summarized in the theorem below.

Theorem 14.1 Let $\mathbf{M}$ be a $n \times n$ matrix and let $\mathbf{y}_1, \ldots, \mathbf{y}_n$ be n-element vectors which are solutions of the equation

$$\mathbf{My} = h\mathbf{y}$$

for some value of h. Let h_i denote the value of h for which $\mathbf{y}_i$ is a solution. If an arbitrary vector $\mathbf{x}$ can be expressed as a weighted sum of the vectors $\mathbf{y}_1, \mathbf{y}_2, \ldots, \mathbf{y}_n$,

$$\mathbf{x} = a_1\mathbf{y}_1 + a_2\mathbf{y}_2 + \cdots + a_n\mathbf{y}_n$$

then the effect of multiplying the matrix $\mathbf{M}$ into the vector $\mathbf{x}$ N times in succession is simply to change the weights associated with the $\mathbf{y}_i$ from $a_1, a_2, \ldots, a_n$ to $a_1h_1^N, a_2h_2^N, \ldots, a_nh_n^N$, i.e.

$$\mathbf{M}^N\mathbf{x} = a_1h_1^N\mathbf{y}_1 + a_2h_2^N\mathbf{y}_2 + \cdots + a_nh_n^N\mathbf{y}_n$$

Theorem 14.1 shows that a process of multiplication by a $n \times n$ matrix is equivalent to a process of multiplication by n different scalars, which is a much simpler operation. This result is a direct consequence of the linearity of matrix multiplication; it is extremely useful for studying the behaviour of a geometric series in a matrix as the number of terms in the series becomes large.

Example Theorem 14.1 can be used to simplify the computations involved in the dynamic analysis of interacting markets. For example, in Sections 13.2 and 13.3 it was necessary to evaluate expressions of the form

$$(\mathbf{I} + \mathbf{M} + \cdots + \mathbf{M}^N)\mathbf{x}$$

where $\mathbf{M}$ is a square matrix and $\mathbf{x}$ is a vector. Setting $\mathbf{x} = a_1\mathbf{y}_1 + a_2\mathbf{y}_2 + \cdots + a_n\mathbf{y}_n$ where $\mathbf{y}_i$ satisfies $\mathbf{M}\mathbf{y}_i = h_i\mathbf{y}_i$ we find that

$$\begin{aligned}(\mathbf{I} + \mathbf{M} + \cdots + \mathbf{M}^N)\mathbf{x} = \quad & a_1(1 + h_1 + \cdots + h_1^N)\mathbf{y}_1 \\ & + a_2(1 + h_2 + \cdots + h_2^N)\mathbf{y}_2 \\ & \vdots \\ & + a_n(1 + h_n + \cdots + h_n^N)\mathbf{y}_n\end{aligned}$$

Summing the geometric series in the h_i by use of Theorem 2.1 gives

$$(\mathbf{I} + \mathbf{M} + \cdots + \mathbf{M}^N)\mathbf{x} = \sum_{i=1}^{n} [a_i(1 - h_i^{N+1})/(1 - h_i)]\mathbf{y}_i$$

The right-hand side is simply a weighted sum of the vectors $\mathbf{y}_i$, the weights being functions of the a_i (which are determined by the vector $\mathbf{x}$) and the h_i (which depend only on the matrix $\mathbf{M}$). Moreover, if all the h_i have an absolute value less than one, $-1 < h_i < 1$ $(i = 1, \ldots, n)$ then $\lim_{N\to\infty} h_i^{N+1} = 0$ $(i = 1, \ldots, n)$ and so

$$\begin{aligned}\lim_{N\to\infty} (\mathbf{I} + \mathbf{M} + \cdots + \mathbf{M}^N)\mathbf{x} &= \lim_{N\to\infty} \sum [a_i(1 - h_i^{N+1})/(1 - h_i)]\mathbf{y}_i \\ &= [\lim_{N\to\infty} \sum a_i(1 - h_i^{N+1})/(1 - h_i)]\mathbf{y}_i \\ &= \sum [a_i/(1 - h_i)]\mathbf{y}_i\end{aligned}$$

The result is very useful for examining the behaviour of a system of interacting markets over a long period of time.

14.2 Characteristic values of a matrix

In order to apply the results of the previous section it is necessary first to solve the matrix equation

$$\mathbf{My} = h\mathbf{y}$$

where $\mathbf{M}$ is an $n \times n$ matrix, $\mathbf{y}$ is an n-element column vector and h is a scalar. In this section we shall study in detail the solutions of this equation.

Let $\mathbf{I}$ denote the $n \times n$ identity matrix and let $\mathbf{0}$ denote the n-element null column vector in which every element is zero. Subtracting $h\mathbf{y}$ from both sides of the equation $\mathbf{My} = h\mathbf{y}$ and grouping terms in $\mathbf{y}$ gives

$$(\mathbf{M} - h\mathbf{I})\mathbf{y} = \mathbf{0}$$

When written out in full this matrix equation takes the form

$$\begin{aligned}
(m_{11} - h)Y_1 + m_{12}Y_2 \qquad + \cdots + m_{1n}Y_n \qquad &= 0 \\
m_{21}Y_1 \qquad + (m_{22} - h)Y_2 + \cdots + m_{2n}Y_n \qquad &= 0 \\
\vdots \qquad\qquad \vdots \qquad\qquad \ddots \qquad \vdots \qquad & \\
m_{n1}Y_1 \qquad + m_{n2}Y_2 \qquad + \cdots + (m_{nn} - h)Y_n &= 0
\end{aligned}$$

where $Y_1, Y_2, \ldots, Y_n$ are the elements of the column vector $\mathbf{y}$. It is readily seen that whatever the value of h these equations have the solution $Y_1 = 0$, $Y_2 = 0, \ldots, Y_n = 0$. This is known as the 'trivial solution'. We shall now determine whether there is another solution to these equations, a solution which is more suitable for our purposes.

First of all notice that our problem is essentially to solve a set of n simultaneous linear equations in n unknowns, $Y_1, Y_2, \ldots, Y_n$. We know from Theorem 12.1 that if the determinant associated with these equations is nonzero then the solution is unique, i.e. if $\det[\mathbf{M} - h\mathbf{I}] \neq 0$ then the solution $Y_1 = 0$, $Y_2 = 0, \ldots, Y_n = 0$ is unique. Consequently, it is possible for there to be another (nontrivial) solution only when $\det[\mathbf{M} - h\mathbf{I}] = 0$. Now when $\det[\mathbf{M} - h\mathbf{I}] = 0$ it follows either that the equations have an indefinite number of solutions, or that the equations are inconsistent and have no solution at all. Since the equations have at least one solution (the trivial one) they cannot be inconsistent. It follows that when $\det[\mathbf{M} - h\mathbf{I}] = 0$ the equations

$$(\mathbf{M} - h\mathbf{I})\mathbf{y} = \mathbf{0}$$

are consistent, and that there are an indefinite number of solutions.

The values of h for which these solutions exist are therefore the values of h which equate the determinant of $(\mathbf{M} - h\mathbf{I})$ to zero, i.e. to find the values of h it is necessary to solve the equation

$$\det[\mathbf{M} - h\mathbf{I}] = 0$$

If we evaluate the determinant of the $n \times n$ matrix $(\mathbf{M} - h\mathbf{I})$ then the result is always an nth degree polynomial in h; in other words, the condition $\det[\mathbf{M} - h\mathbf{I}] = 0$ may be written

$$b_0 + b_1h + b_2h^2 + \cdots + b_{n-1}h^{n-1} + h^n = 0$$

where the coefficients $b_0, b_1, b_2, \ldots, b_{n-1}$ depend on the elements of the matrix $\mathbf{M}$, and the coefficient of h^n is always unity. The solution of this equation is described by the roots $h_1, h_2, \ldots, h_n$. When any one of these roots is substituted back into the equation $(\mathbf{M} - h\mathbf{I})\mathbf{y} = 0$ then the result is a set of n simultaneous linear equations from which the ratio between any two elements in the vector $\mathbf{y}$ can be determined (the equations do not have a unique solution because their determinant is zero). Substituting back in succession the roots $h_1, h_2, \ldots, h_n$ generates the vectors $\mathbf{y}_1, \mathbf{y}_2, \ldots, \mathbf{y}_n$; these vectors are not known exactly, but the ratio between any two elements in a given vector is known. In this way we can determine the values $h_1, h_2, \ldots, h_n$ and the vectors $\mathbf{y}_1, \mathbf{y}_2, \ldots, \mathbf{y}_n$ for which

$$\begin{aligned} \mathbf{M}\mathbf{y}_1 &= h_1\mathbf{y}_1 \\ \mathbf{M}\mathbf{y}_2 &= h_2\mathbf{y}_2 \\ &\vdots \\ \mathbf{M}\mathbf{y}_n &= h_n\mathbf{y}_n \end{aligned}$$

The values of $h_1, h_2, \ldots, h_n$ are known as the *characteristic values* of the matrix $\mathbf{M}$; the vectors $\mathbf{y}_1, \mathbf{y}_2, \ldots, \mathbf{y}_n$ are known as the *characteristic vectors* of the matrix $\mathbf{M}$. The equation

$$\det[\mathbf{M} - \mathbf{hI}] = 0$$

is known as the *characteristic equation* of the matrix $\mathbf{M}$.

Example Find the characteristic values and the characteristic vectors of the matrix

$$\mathbf{M} = \begin{bmatrix} 0{\cdot}5 & 0{\cdot}2 & 0{\cdot}1 \\ 0 & 0{\cdot}3 & 0{\cdot}2 \\ 0{\cdot}1 & 0{\cdot}1 & 0{\cdot}3 \end{bmatrix}$$

Hence evaluate $\mathbf{M}^{12}\mathbf{x}$ where $\mathbf{x}$ is the vector

$$\mathbf{x} = \begin{bmatrix} 16 \\ 1 \\ 7 \end{bmatrix}$$

The characteristic values of the matrix $\mathbf{M}$ are the values of h for which there is a nontrivial solution to the equation

$$(\mathbf{M} - h\mathbf{I})\mathbf{y} = 0$$

This equation has a nontrivial solution only when the value of h satisfies the characteristic equation

$$\det[\mathbf{M} - h\mathbf{I}] = 0$$

The roots of this equation are the characteristic values $h_1, h_2, \ldots, h_n$. Expanding the determinant gives

$$\det \begin{bmatrix} 0{\cdot}5 - h & 0{\cdot}2 & 0{\cdot}1 \\ 0 & 0{\cdot}3 - h & 0{\cdot}2 \\ 0{\cdot}1 & 0{\cdot}1 & 0{\cdot}3 - h \end{bmatrix} = 0{\cdot}036 - 0{\cdot}36h + 1{\cdot}1h^2 - h^3$$

so that the characteristic equation is

$$0{\cdot}036 - 0{\cdot}36h + 1{\cdot}1h^2 - h^3 = 0$$

This equation may be factorized as follows

$$(0{\cdot}6 - h)(0{\cdot}3 - h)(0{\cdot}2 - h) = 0$$

so that the roots of the characteristic equation are 0·6, 0·3, 0·2. These are the characteristic values of the matrix **M**.

The characteristic vectors of the matrix **M** are found by substituting the characteristic values back into the equation

$$(\mathbf{M} - h\mathbf{I})\mathbf{y} = 0$$

For example, substituting the first characteristic value back into this equation gives the equation

$$(\mathbf{M} - h_1\mathbf{I})\mathbf{y} = \mathbf{0}$$

This matrix equation represents a set of n simultaneous linear equations in n unknowns. Since $\det [\mathbf{M} - h_1\mathbf{I}] = 0$ there is no unique solution to these equations; however, as a rule it is possible to determine uniquely the ratio of any two elements in the vector **y**. The vector so determined is the first characteristic vector of the matrix **M**.

In this numerical example the first characteristic value is $h_1 = 0{\cdot}6$; the equation $(\mathbf{M} - h_1\mathbf{I})\mathbf{y} = \mathbf{0}$ takes the form

$$\begin{bmatrix} -0{\cdot}1 & 0{\cdot}2 & 0{\cdot}1 \\ 0 & -0{\cdot}3 & 0{\cdot}2 \\ 0{\cdot}1 & 0{\cdot}1 & -0{\cdot}3 \end{bmatrix} \begin{bmatrix} Y_1 \\ Y_2 \\ Y_3 \end{bmatrix} = \begin{bmatrix} 0 \\ 0 \\ 0 \end{bmatrix}$$

The second of the equations in this set of 3 simultaneous equations is

$$0{\cdot}3Y_2 - 0{\cdot}2Y_3 = 0$$

from which it follows that $Y_3 = 1{\cdot}5Y_2$. Substituting this result into the first of the simultaneous equations gives

$$-0{\cdot}1Y_1 + 0{\cdot}2Y_2 + (0{\cdot}1 \times 1{\cdot}5)Y_2 = 0$$

i.e. $$0{\cdot}35Y_2 = 0{\cdot}1Y_1$$

so that $Y_1 = 3{\cdot}5Y_2$. It follows that the elements of the vector $\mathbf{y}_1$ are in the ratio $3{\cdot}5:1:1{\cdot}5$. This specifies the first characteristic vector as

$$\mathbf{y}_1 = \begin{bmatrix} 3{\cdot}5 \\ 1 \\ 1{\cdot}5 \end{bmatrix}$$

(or as some multiple of this vector).

The second and third characteristic vectors are found in a similar way. The second characteristic vector is determined by the equation

$$(\mathbf{M} - h_2\mathbf{I})\mathbf{y} = 0$$

which, when written out in full, becomes

$$\begin{bmatrix} 0{\cdot}2 & 0{\cdot}2 & 0{\cdot}1 \\ 0 & 0 & 0{\cdot}2 \\ 0{\cdot}1 & 0{\cdot}1 & 0 \end{bmatrix} \begin{bmatrix} Y_1 \\ Y_2 \\ Y_3 \end{bmatrix} = \begin{bmatrix} 0 \\ 0 \\ 0 \end{bmatrix}$$

By using the second of the simultaneous equations it can be deduced that $Y_3 = 0$; from the third equation it follows that $Y_1 = -Y_2$. The elements of the vector $\mathbf{y}_2$ are therefore in the ratio $1:-1:0$. This specifies the second characteristic vector as

$$\mathbf{y}_2 = \begin{bmatrix} 1 \\ -1 \\ 0 \end{bmatrix}$$

(or as some multiple of this vector). The third characteristic vector is the solution of the equation

$$(\mathbf{M} - h_3\mathbf{I})\mathbf{y} = \mathbf{0}$$

where $h_3 = 0{\cdot}2$. It is readily deduced the ratios $Y_1:Y_2:Y_3$ are $1:-2:1$. This specifies the third characteristic vector as

$$\mathbf{y}_3 = \begin{bmatrix} 1 \\ -2 \\ 1 \end{bmatrix}$$

(or as some multiple of this vector).

The final stage of the calculation is to evaluate $\mathbf{M}^{12}\mathbf{x}$. Applying Theorem 14.1 with $n = 3$ and $N = 12$ gives

$$\mathbf{M}^{12}\mathbf{x} = a_1h_1^{12}\mathbf{y}_1 + a_2h_2^{12}\mathbf{y}_2 + a_3h_3^{12}\mathbf{y}_3$$

where the characteristic values are $h_1 = 0{\cdot}6$, $h_2 = 0{\cdot}3$, $h_3 = 0{\cdot}2$, and the characteristic vectors are

$$\mathbf{y}_1 = \begin{bmatrix} 3{\cdot}5 \\ 1{\cdot}0 \\ 1{\cdot}5 \end{bmatrix}, \quad \mathbf{y}_2 = \begin{bmatrix} 1 \\ -1 \\ 0 \end{bmatrix}, \quad \mathbf{y}_3 = \begin{bmatrix} 1 \\ -2 \\ 1 \end{bmatrix}$$

It remains to determine the weights a_1, a_2, a_3; these are determined by the equation

$$\mathbf{x} = a_1\mathbf{y}_1 + a_2\mathbf{y}_2 + a_3\mathbf{y}_3$$

which, when written out in full, becomes

$$\begin{bmatrix} 16 \\ 1 \\ 7 \end{bmatrix} = a_1 \begin{bmatrix} 3{\cdot}5 \\ 1{\cdot}0 \\ 0{\cdot}5 \end{bmatrix} + a_2 \begin{bmatrix} 1 \\ -1 \\ 0 \end{bmatrix} + a_3 \begin{bmatrix} 1 \\ -2 \\ 1 \end{bmatrix}$$

or, dropping the matrix notation,

$$\begin{aligned} 16 &= 3{\cdot}5a_1 + a_2 + a_3 \\ 1 &= a_1 - a_2 - 2a_3 \\ 7 &= 1{\cdot}5a_1 \qquad + a_3 \end{aligned}$$

Solving these equations gives $a_1 = 4$, $a_2 = 1$, $a_3 = 1$. It follows that

$$\mathbf{M}^{12}\mathbf{x} = 4 \times 0{\cdot}6^{12} \begin{bmatrix} 3{\cdot}5 \\ 1{\cdot}0 \\ 1{\cdot}5 \end{bmatrix} + 0{\cdot}3^{12} \begin{bmatrix} 1 \\ -1 \\ 0 \end{bmatrix} + 0{\cdot}2^{12} \begin{bmatrix} 1 \\ -2 \\ 1 \end{bmatrix}$$

The reader could, if he wished, verify this result by multiplying the matrix **M** into the vector **x** twelve times in succession.

Some further developments of the mathematical analysis described above will be outlined in Section 14.5.

14.3 Concept of a basis

The discussion of the linearity of matrix multiplication raises the important question: under what circumstances can an arbitrary vector **x** be expressed as a weighted sum of the characteristic vectors $\mathbf{y}_1, \mathbf{y}_2, \ldots, \mathbf{y}_n$ of a matrix **M**? The following result gives a partial answer to this question.

Theorem 14.2 If the characteristic values of a matrix are distinct, there is a unique set of weights by which an arbitrary vector is expressed as a sum of the characteristic vectors.

PROOF Firstly, note that the null vector, **0**, represents the trivial solution of the equation $\mathbf{My} = h\mathbf{y}$ and by convention is not a characteristic vector.

Suppose that there is not a unique set of weights by which an arbitrary vector is expressed as a sum of the characteristic vectors: this case arises only if at least one of the characteristic vectors, say $\mathbf{y}_n$, is already a weighted sum of the other characteristic vectors, in which case a vector which cannot be expressed as a weighted sum of the $n - 1$ vectors $\mathbf{y}_1, \mathbf{y}_2, \ldots, \mathbf{y}_{n-1}$ cannot be expressed as a weighted sum of the n vectors either.[1] The vector $\mathbf{y}_n$, expressed as a weighted sum of the other $n - 1$ vectors, is

$$\mathbf{y}_n = b_1\mathbf{y}_1 + b_2\mathbf{y}_2 + \cdots + b_{n-1}\mathbf{y}_{n-1}$$

where at least one of the coefficients $b_1, b_2, \ldots, b_n$ is nonzero (since $\mathbf{y}_n \neq \mathbf{0}$). Multiplying this equation through by the matrix $\mathbf{M}$ gives

$$\begin{aligned}\mathbf{My}_n &= b_1\mathbf{My}_1 + b_2\mathbf{My}_2 + \cdots + b_{n-1}\mathbf{My}_{n-1}\\ &= b_1h_1\mathbf{y}_1 + b_2h_2\mathbf{y}_2 + \cdots + b_{n-1}h_{n-1}\mathbf{y}_{n-1}\end{aligned}$$

But we also know that

$$\begin{aligned}\mathbf{My}_n &= h_n\mathbf{y}_n\\ &= b_1h_n\mathbf{y}_1 + b_2h_n\mathbf{y}_2 + \cdots + b_{n-1}h_n\mathbf{y}_{n-1}\end{aligned}$$

Subtracting the two equations shows that

$$\mathbf{0} = b_1(h_1 - h_n)\mathbf{y}_1 + b_2(h_2 - h_n)\mathbf{y}_2 + \cdots + b_{n-1}(h_{n-1} - h_n)\mathbf{y}_{n-1}$$

Since the characteristic values are distinct none of the terms $(h_i - h_n)$ $(i = 1, 2, \ldots, n - 1)$ is zero, and at least one of the coefficients b_i is nonzero. Hence either one of the vectors $\mathbf{y}_1, \mathbf{y}_2, \ldots, \mathbf{y}_n$ is the null vector, $\mathbf{0}$, which is ruled out, or one of these vectors, say $\mathbf{y}_{n-1}$, can be expressed as a weighted sum of the other vectors. Hence if $\mathbf{y}_n$ is a weighted sum of $n - 1$ vectors then $\mathbf{y}_{n-1}$ is a weighted sum of the other $n - 2$ vectors. Repeating this argument for $\mathbf{y}_{n-1}, \mathbf{y}_{n-2}, \ldots, \mathbf{y}_2$ shows that if $\mathbf{y}_n$ is a weighted sum of $n - 1$ vectors then the characteristic vector $\mathbf{y}_1$ is the null vector, which is a contradiction in terms. Hence $\mathbf{y}_n$ is not a weighted sum of $n - 1$ vectors, and so the weights $a_1, a_2, \ldots, a_n$ are unique.

The case in which a set of vectors can be used to express an arbitrary vector as a weighted sum is of such importance that it has led to a special terminology.

Definition If an arbitrary n-element vector $\mathbf{x}$ can be expressed as a weighted sum of the n vectors $\mathbf{y}_1, \mathbf{y}_2, \ldots, \mathbf{y}_n$ then the set of vectors $\mathbf{y}_1, \mathbf{y}_2, \ldots, \mathbf{y}_n$ is said to constitute a 'basis' of order n.

There are certain classes of matrix for which the characteristic vectors always form a basis of the same order as the dimension of the matrix. One very important example is the class of symmetric matrices (see Chapter 16). The characteristic values of an $n \times n$ symmetric matrix are not always distinct but nevertheless the characteristic vectors form a basis of order n. It is not necessarily true that there is a *unique* characteristic vector associated with each characteristic value of a symmetric matrix, but it is always possible to select a set of n characteristic vectors which together form a basis of order n.

1 The reader who has studied Problem 11.7.3 will appreciate that this is the case in which the set of vectors $\mathbf{y}_1, \mathbf{y}_2, \ldots, \mathbf{y}_n$ is linearly dependent. According to the problem, if the vectors $\mathbf{y}_1, \mathbf{y}_2, \ldots, \mathbf{y}_n$ are linearly dependent then the determinant associated with the equations for the weights $a_1, a_2, \ldots, a_n$ is zero, and so the equations may not have a solution i.e. it is possible that the vector $\mathbf{x}$ cannot be expressed as a weighted sum of the vectors $\mathbf{y}_1, \mathbf{y}_2, \ldots, \mathbf{y}_n$.

14.4 Note on complex numbers

So far we have implicitly assumed that an $n \times n$ matrix has exactly n characteristic values and n characteristic vectors. If the characteristic values and the elements of the characteristic vectors are taken to be real numbers, this assumption is unfortunately not always true. For example, to find the characteristic values of the matrix

$$\mathbf{M} = \begin{bmatrix} 0 & 1 \\ -1 & 0 \end{bmatrix}$$

it is necessary to solve the equation

$$\det[\mathbf{M} - h\mathbf{I}] = \det\begin{bmatrix} -h & 1 \\ -1 & -h \end{bmatrix} = h^2 + 1 = 0$$

The solution of this equation is a number h, which when squared is equal to minus one. But the square of a real number cannot be negative and so there is no solution. We conclude that no real number is a characteristic value of **M**.

Is it possible to generalize the concept of a number in such way that an $n \times n$ matrix always has exactly n characteristic values? To be effective, the generalization must avoid the problem encountered above, which is essentially that there is no real number whose square is negative. One way of avoiding the problem is to *define* a number whose square is negative! We define the number i to be the number whose square is minus one:

$$\mathrm{i}^2 = -1$$

Another way of putting this is to say that i is the square root of minus one:

$$\mathrm{i} = \sqrt{(-1)}$$

The number i is not a real number, otherwise i^2 would be positive. Because i is not a real number it is known as an *imaginary number*. By multiplying or dividing i by real numbers and adding or subtracting real numbers from the result it is possible to form a whole family of numbers. Each number of this family is of the form $x + \mathrm{i}y$ where x and y are real numbers. Numbers of the form $x + \mathrm{i}y$ are known as *complex numbers*. Setting $y = 0$ shows that the real number x is a special case of the complex number $x + \mathrm{i}y$.

It can be shown that the generalization to complex numbers 'works' in the sense that *if the characteristic values of a matrix are taken to be complex numbers, an $n \times n$ matrix has exactly n characteristic values*. To prove this result requires a knowledge of the algebra of complex numbers (see Chapter 19).

The absolute value of a real number has an analogue in the *modulus* of a complex number. The modulus of a complex number $x + \mathrm{i}y$ is the quantity $\sqrt{(x^2 + y^2)}$. It is a measure of the size of a complex number. The modulus of a complex number has all the properties of the absolute value of a real number. In particular, if the modulus of a complex number exceeds unity then the modulus of the Nth power of the number increases as N is raised, whereas if the modulus is less than unity then the modulus of the Nth power decreases as N is raised.

14.5 Asymptotic behaviour of $\mathbf{M}^N\mathbf{x}$

Let the characteristic values of the matrix $\mathbf{M}$ be $h_1, h_2, \ldots, h_n$ and let the corresponding characteristic vectors be $\mathbf{y}_1, \mathbf{y}_2, \ldots, \mathbf{y}_n$. It was established in Section 14.1 that if an arbitrary vector $\mathbf{x}$ can be expressed as a weighted sum of the characteristic vectors of the matrix $\mathbf{M}$,

$$\mathbf{x} = a_1\mathbf{y}_1 + a_2\mathbf{y}_2 + \cdots + a_n\mathbf{y}_n$$

then

$$\mathbf{M}^N\mathbf{x} = a_1h_1^N\mathbf{y}_1 + a_2h_2^N\mathbf{y}_2 + \cdots + a_nh_n^N\mathbf{y}_n$$

This result can be used not only to simplify computations but also to deduce the asymptotic behaviour of the expression $\mathbf{M}^N\mathbf{x}$ as N becomes large. This second application is often more useful than the first.

Suppose that the modulus of one of the characteristic values, say h_1, is larger than the moduli of the others (if the characteristic value is real then the modulus is the same thing as the absolute value of the number). As N increases, the modulus of the term h_1^N will become very large compared with the moduli of the terms $h_2^N, \ldots, h_n^N$, so that as N tends to infinity the modulus of each of these terms will be negligible compared with the modulus of h_1^N. It follows that unless $a_1 = 0$, when N is large the modulus of each of the weights $a_2h_2^N, \ldots, a_nh_n^N$ will be negligible compared with the modulus of the weight $a_1h_1^N$. Since the modulus of a complex number is a measure of its size, it follows that

$$\lim_{N\to\infty} \mathbf{M}^N\mathbf{x} = a_1h_1^N\mathbf{y}_1 \text{ (often written } \mathbf{M}^N\mathbf{x} \approx a_1h_1^N\mathbf{y}_1\text{)}$$

where the limit is understood to mean that equality holds only for large values of N and that equality holds only in the sense that the error in the equation is proportionately (but not absolutely) small. The equation shows that if the characteristic vectors of an $n \times n$ matrix $\mathbf{M}$ form a basis of order n then the effect of multiplying the matrix $\mathbf{M}$ repeatedly into an arbitrary vector $\mathbf{x}$ is to transform the vector $\mathbf{x}$ into a multiple of the first characteristic vector of the matrix $\mathbf{M}$ (i.e. the characteristic vector corresponding to the characteristic value of largest modulus). It follows that when the matrix $\mathbf{M}$ has a unique characteristic value of largest modulus the result of repeatedly multiplying the matrix $\mathbf{M}$ into an arbitrary vector is independent of the vector itself (apart from a constant of proportionality). This result is of great importance and is summarized below.

Theorem 14.3 Let $\mathbf{M}$ be an $n \times n$ matrix with characteristic values $h_1, h_2, \ldots, h_n$. Suppose that the characteristic vectors of $\mathbf{M}$ form a basis of order n. If $\mathbf{M}$ has a unique characteristic value of largest modulus, say h_1, with corresponding characteristic vector $\mathbf{y}_1$ then for an arbitrary vector $\mathbf{x}$

$$\lim_{N\to\infty} \mathbf{M}^N\mathbf{x} = a_1h_1^N\mathbf{y}_1$$

where a_1 is a constant of proportionality determined by the vector $\mathbf{x}$.

It is worth noting that if there is a unique characteristic value of largest modulus then it must be real rather than complex. This follows from

Section 19.5 where it is shown that complex numbers occur in pairs in which each number has the same modulus.

Example Given

$$\mathbf{M} = \begin{bmatrix} 0 & 1 & 0{\cdot}5 \\ 0{\cdot}25 & 0 & 0 \\ 0 & 0 & 1 \end{bmatrix} \qquad \mathbf{x} = \begin{bmatrix} 2 \\ 5 \\ 3 \end{bmatrix}$$

discuss the behaviour of $\mathbf{M}^N\mathbf{x}$ as N becomes large.

The characteristic values of $\mathbf{M}$ are the roots of the equation

$$\det[\mathbf{M} - h\mathbf{I}] = (1 - h)(h^2 + \tfrac{1}{4}) = 0$$

from which it is seen that $h_1 = 1$, $h_2 = \frac{1}{2}\mathrm{i}$, $h_3 = -\frac{1}{2}\mathrm{i}$.[2] Since the roots are distinct, it follows from Theorem 14.2 that the vector $\mathbf{x}$ can be expressed as a weighted sum of the characteristic vectors $\mathbf{y}_1, \mathbf{y}_2, \mathbf{y}_3$. The moduli of the characteristic values are, respectively, $1, \frac{1}{2}, \frac{1}{2}$. Since there is a unique characteristic value of largest modulus it follows that

$$\lim_{N\to\infty} \mathbf{M}^N\mathbf{x} = a_1 h_1^N \mathbf{y}_1$$

where $h_1 = 1$, a_1 is constant determined by the vector $\mathbf{x}$ and $\mathbf{y}_1$ is the characteristic vector obtained from the equation $(\mathbf{M} - h_1\mathbf{I}) = \mathbf{0}$. Written out in full, this equation becomes, with $h_1 = 1$,

$$\begin{aligned} -Y_1 + Y_2 + 0{\cdot}5Y_3 &= 0 \\ 0{\cdot}25Y_1 - Y_2 \qquad &= 0 \\ 0 \;+ 0 \;+ 0 \qquad &= 0 \end{aligned}$$

where Y_1, Y_2, Y_3 are the elements of the vector $\mathbf{y}_1$. From the second equation it follows that $Y_1 = 4Y_2$ and substituting this result into the first equation shows that $Y_3 = -5/2Y_2$. It follows that the elements of the vector $\mathbf{y}_1$ are in the ratio $8:2:-5$. Since the largest characteristic value is unity, for very large values of N

$$\mathbf{M}^{N+1}\mathbf{x} = \mathbf{M}(\mathbf{M}^N\mathbf{x}) \approx \mathbf{M}(a_1\mathbf{y}_1) = a_1\mathbf{M}\mathbf{y}_1 = a_1\mathbf{y}_1$$

whence

$$\mathbf{M}^{N+1}\mathbf{x} \approx \mathbf{M}^N\mathbf{x}$$

We conclude that for large values of $\mathbf{N}$, the vector $\mathbf{M}^N\mathbf{x}$ is proportional to the vector

$$\begin{bmatrix} 8 \\ 2 \\ -5 \end{bmatrix}$$

and is entirely independent both of $\mathbf{x}$ and of N.

2 The factorization of the equation shows that the roots occur when $h - 1 = 0$ and when $h^2 + \frac{1}{4} = 0$. It follows immediately that one of the roots is $h_1 = 1$. Applying the formula for the solution of a quadratic (Section 2.4b) shows that the roots of $h^2 + \frac{1}{4} = 0$ are $\pm\frac{1}{2}\sqrt{(-1)}$. According to Section 14.4 the imaginary number i is defined by $\mathrm{i} = \sqrt{(-1)}$. Consequently the other two roots of the characteristic equation are $h_2 = \frac{1}{2}\mathrm{i}$, $h_3 = -\frac{1}{2}\mathrm{i}$. The modulus of each of these complex numbers is $\frac{1}{2}$.

A useful application of this mathematical method is to the analysis of the distribution of income.

Example The determinants of the distribution of income can be analysed in the following way. A number of size classes of income are distinguished, such as the classes shown in the first column of Table 14.1.

The distribution of income at any one time is described by the proportion of the households in the economy which have incomes within each of these classes. A typical distribution of income is shown in the first column of the table. The entries in this column indicate the proportion of the households whose income is in each particular class. Since every household must have an income which falls within one of the classes shown in the table, all the households in the economy are included in the table. As a result, the sum of the proportions shown in the second column is equal to one.

Table 14.1

		Transition matrix Income class				
Income class	*Proportion of households within the income class*	*Below £500 p.a.*	*£500–£999 p.a.*	*£1,000–£1,999 p.a.*	*£2,000–£3,999 p.a.*	*£4,000 p.a. and above*
Below £500 p.a.	0·2	0·7	0·3	0·1	0	0
£500–999 p.a.	0·4	0·2	0·5	0·3	0·1	0·05
£1,000–1,999 p.a.	0·2	0·1	0·1	0·4	0·2	0·05
£2,000–3,999 p.a.	0·1	0	0·1	0·2	0·5	0·2
£4,000 p.a. and above	0·1	0	0	0	0·2	0·7
Sum of entries in column	1·0	1·0	1·0	1·0	1·0	1·0

The income of the typical household will not remain constant over time. The head of the household may perhaps increase his income through statutory increments in his salary, or through promotion, or he may reduce his income through retirement. When other members of the household grow up to working age they may bring in additional income; or they may grow up and leave the household altogether. As a result, over a period of, say, a year, some households will move to a higher income class and some will move to a lower one. The proportion of households likely to move to a different income class may be characterized as follows. For each income class a column is entered in Table 14.1 showing the proportion of the households in that income class which, over a year, will move into each of the other income classes. For example, the entries in the second column of the table show the proportion of the households earning below £500 p.a. which will move, within a year, into the various income classes shown in the first column. The first entry in the column shows that 0·7 of these households (i.e. 70% of them) will, after one year, continue to earn below £500 p.a. The second entry in the column shows that, of the remaining 30% of households, 20% will, after one year, be earning an income in the range £500–£999 p.a. The third entry shows that the final 10% of households will all earn an income in the range £1,000–£1,999 p.a. The fourth and fifth entries show that none of the households will be earning above £2,000 p.a. after one year. That the entries in the column are consistent with one another is shown by the fact that the sum of the entries is equal to one; this indicates that all the households in the income class have been accounted for.

The third column in the table concerns households which, to begin with, are earning an income in the range £500–£999 p.a. The entries in the third column show that, after one year, 30% of these households will be earning less than £500 p.a., 50% of the households will be earning about the same amount as before, 10% will be earning between £1,000–£1,999 p.a. and the final 10% will earn more than £4,000. The interpretation of the remaining three columns of the table should be obvious to the reader.

The entries in columns 2–6 of Table 14.1 constitute a 5×5 matrix of coefficients. Let us denote this matrix $\mathbf{P}$. Each of the 'column sums' of the matrix $\mathbf{P}$ is equal to one. In the same way, the entries in the first column of Table 1 constitute the elements of a 5-element column vector; let us denote this by vector $\mathbf{x}$. The elements of the vector $\mathbf{x}$ describe the distribution of income.

The information contained in the table can be used to determine the distribution of income one year later. To illustrate the calculations involved, let us determine what proportion of households will be earning less than £500 p.a. after one year. At the beginning of the year, the distribution of income is described by the first column of the table (i.e. by the elements of the vector $\mathbf{x}$). The households earning below £500 p.a. after one year will consist of 0·7 of those households earning below £500 p.a. to begin with, 0·3 of the households earning between £500–£999 p.a. to begin with and 0·1 of the households earning between £1,000–£1,999 to begin with (this is seen by reading along the first row of the matrix $\mathbf{P}$). The households earning below £500 p.a. to begin with constitute 0·2 of all the households in the economy, the households earning between £500–£999 p.a. constitute 0·4 of all households and the households earning between £1,000–£1,999 p.a. constitute 0·2 of all households (this can be seen by reading down the column vector $\mathbf{x}$). It follows that the households earning less than £500 p.a. after one year will constitute a proportion $0{\cdot}7 \times 0{\cdot}2 + 0{\cdot}3 \times 0{\cdot}4 + 0{\cdot}1 \times 0{\cdot}2 = 0{\cdot}28$ of the total households in the economy. This calculation illustrates that to evaluate the proportion of households earning less than £500 p.a. it is necessary to multiply the first row of the matrix $\mathbf{P}$ into the column vector $\mathbf{x}$. A similar calculation will show that to evaluate the proportion of households earning between £500–£999 p.a. it is necessary to multiply the second row of the matrix $\mathbf{P}$ into the column vector $\mathbf{x}$. In general, to evaluate the proportion of the households in the ith income class it is necessary to multiply the ith row of the matrix $\mathbf{P}$ into the column vector $\mathbf{x}$. In this way it is possible to determine the distribution of income after one year. This distribution of income is shown in Table 14.2.

The entries in Table 14.2 constitute a column vector with five elements. Denote this column vector $\mathbf{x}(1)$ to indicate that it characterizes the

Table 14.2 Distribution of income after one year

Income class	*Proportion of households within the income class*
Below £500 p.a.	0·280
£500–999 p.a.	0·315
£1,000–1,999 p.a.	0·165
£2,000–3,999 p.a.	0·150
£4,000 p.a. and above	0·090
Sum of entries in column	1·000

distribution of income after one year. The calculations made above illustrate that

$$\mathbf{x}(1) = \mathbf{P}\mathbf{x}$$

i.e. the vector $\mathbf{x}(1)$ is evaluated by multiplying the matrix $\mathbf{P}$ into the vector $\mathbf{x}$.

Let the vector $\mathbf{x}(2)$ characterize the distribution of income after two years. It is readily established that

$$\mathbf{x}(2) = \mathbf{P}\mathbf{x}(1)$$

and substituting for $\mathbf{x}(1)$ gives

$$\mathbf{x}(2) = \mathbf{P}^2\mathbf{x}$$

It is not surprising to note that after N years the distribution of income is characterized by the vector

$$\mathbf{x}(N) = \mathbf{P}^N\mathbf{x}$$

We shall now demonstrate how mathematical analysis can be used to determine very simply the distribution of income after an arbitrary length of time. We shall show that as N becomes large the distribution of income becomes independent of the vector $\mathbf{x}$—which describes the initial distribution of income—and depends only on the form of the matrix $\mathbf{P}$—which describes the frequency of transition from one income class to another.

By using the theorems given in Chapter 15 it is possible to show that the characteristic values of

$$\mathbf{P} = \begin{bmatrix} 0{\cdot}7 & 0{\cdot}3 & 0{\cdot}1 & 0 & 0 \\ 0{\cdot}2 & 0{\cdot}5 & 0{\cdot}3 & 0{\cdot}1 & 0{\cdot}05 \\ 0{\cdot}1 & 0{\cdot}1 & 0{\cdot}4 & 0{\cdot}2 & 0{\cdot}05 \\ 0 & 0{\cdot}1 & 0{\cdot}2 & 0{\cdot}5 & 0{\cdot}2 \\ 0 & 0 & 0 & 0{\cdot}2 & 0{\cdot}7 \end{bmatrix}$$

are all distinct and that there is a unique characteristic value of largest modulus equal to unity, $h_1 = 1$. Theorem 14.1 tells us that because all the characteristic values are distinct, the characteristic vectors of $\mathbf{P}$ form a basis of order 5. Since the characteristic vectors form a basis of order 5 and in addition there is a unique characteristic vector of largest modulus, $h_1 = 1$, it follows from Theorem 14.3 that

$$\lim_{N \to \infty} \mathbf{P}^N \mathbf{x} = a_1 \mathbf{y}_1$$

where $\mathbf{y}_1$ is the characteristic vector corresponding to h_1 and a_1 is a coefficient determined by the vector $\mathbf{x}$. Since a_1 appears only as a constant of proportionality, we conclude that ultimately the proportion of income distributed to each group is determined solely by the vector $\mathbf{y}_1$. By using the fact that

$$(\mathbf{M} - h_1\mathbf{I})\mathbf{y}_1 = \mathbf{0}$$

where $h_1 = 1$, we obtain a set of simultaneous equations for the elements of $\mathbf{y}_1$:

$$\begin{aligned}
-0{\cdot}3Y_1 + 0{\cdot}3Y_2 + 0{\cdot}1Y_3 &= 0\\
0{\cdot}2Y_1 - 0{\cdot}5Y_2 + 0{\cdot}3Y_3 + 0{\cdot}1Y_4 + 0{\cdot}05Y_5 &= 0\\
0{\cdot}1Y_1 + 0{\cdot}1Y_2 - 0{\cdot}6Y_3 + 0{\cdot}2Y_4 + 0{\cdot}05Y_5 &= 0\\
0{\cdot}1Y_2 + 0{\cdot}2Y_3 - 0{\cdot}5Y_4 + 0{\cdot}2Y_5 &= 0\\
0{\cdot}2Y_4 - 0{\cdot}3Y_5 &= 0
\end{aligned}$$

Solving these equations it is found that the ratio $Y_1 : Y_2 : Y_3 : Y_4 : Y_5$ is 6:5:3:3:2. It follows from this that ultimately 31·6% of all households will be in the first income group earning below £500 p.a., 26·3% of all households in the second income group, earning between £500–£999 p.a., 15·8% in the third income group, earning between £1,000–£1,999 p.a., 15·8% in the fourth income group, earning between £2,000–£3,999 p.a., and 10·5% in the fifth income group, earning above £4,000 p.a.

The reader should appreciate that by using the theory of characteristic values it has been possible to establish the eventual distribution of income in the economy without any need for a repeated process of matrix multiplication. Two further points should be made. Firstly, once this ultimate distribution of income has been reached there is no propensity whatsoever for the distribution to change. This is an immediate consequence of the fact that the characteristic vector $\mathbf{y}_1$ is a solution of the equation

$$(\mathbf{P} - \mathbf{I})\mathbf{y}_1 = \mathbf{0}$$

which implies that

$$\mathbf{P}\mathbf{y}_1 = \mathbf{y}_1$$

so that

$$\mathbf{P}^2\mathbf{y}_1 = \mathbf{P}(\mathbf{P}\mathbf{y}_1) = \mathbf{P}\mathbf{y}_1 = \mathbf{y}_1$$

and that, in general, after any length of time, say N periods,

$$\mathbf{P}^N\mathbf{y}_1 = \mathbf{y}_1$$

This equation indicates that once the distribution of income is characterized by the vector $\mathbf{y}_1$, the vector characterizing the distribution of income remains unchanged even though individual households continue to move from one income class to another. The second point is that the final distribution of income is independent of the initial distribution of income. This is a simple consequence of the fact that the final distribution of income depends only on the characteristic vector $\mathbf{y}_1$, which in turn depends only on the form of the matrix $\mathbf{P}$.

The analytical method illustrated above can also be used to examine the distribution of wealth; other applications are to the size distribution of firms and to the time variation of the demand for durable goods. The type of process studied above is widely known as a Markoff process.[3] Essentially, a Markoff process of income distribution is one in which the distribution of income in any year is dependent only on the distribution of income in the previous year.

14.6 Asymptotic behaviour of $\mathbf{M}^N$

There is obviously a close relationship between the asymptotic behaviour of $\mathbf{M}^N$ and the asymptotic behaviour of $\mathbf{M}^N\mathbf{x}$. The following result, although rather abstract, is very useful.

Lemma Let $\mathbf{M}$ be a $n \times n$ matrix, $\mathbf{y}_1$ a n-element vector and a_1, h_1 real numbers. A necessary and sufficient condition that

$$\lim_{N\to\infty} \mathbf{M}^N\mathbf{x} = a_1 h_1^N \mathbf{y}_1$$

for all vectors $\mathbf{x}$ is that

$$\lim_{N\to\infty} \mathbf{M}^N = h_1^N \mathbf{y}_1 \mathbf{u}_1^T$$

where $a = \mathbf{u}_1^T\mathbf{x}$ and $\mathbf{u}^T$ is the transpose of an n-element vector $\mathbf{u}$.

PROOF Since $\mathbf{x}$ is independent of N, $\lim_{N\to\infty} \mathbf{M}^N\mathbf{x} = (\lim_{N\to\infty} \mathbf{M}^N)\mathbf{x}$. Consequently, if $\lim_{N\to\infty} \mathbf{M}^N = h_1^N\mathbf{y}_1\mathbf{u}^T$ where $\mathbf{u}_1^T\mathbf{x} = a_1$ then

$$\lim_{N\to\infty} \mathbf{M}^N\mathbf{x} = (h_1^N\mathbf{y}_1\mathbf{u}_1^T)\mathbf{x} = h_1^N\mathbf{y}_1(\mathbf{u}_1^T\mathbf{x}) = h_1^N\mathbf{y}_1 a_1 = a_1 h_1^N \mathbf{y}_1$$

since a_1 is a scalar. This proves sufficiency. To prove necessity, suppose that $\lim_{N\to\infty} \mathbf{M}^N = h_1^N\mathbf{y}_1\mathbf{u}_1^T + \mathbf{E}$ where $\mathbf{E} \neq \mathbf{0}$ is an $n \times n$ matrix. Then

$$\lim_{N\to\infty} \mathbf{M}^N\mathbf{x} = (h_1^N\mathbf{y}_1\mathbf{u}_1^T + \mathbf{E})\mathbf{x} = a_1 h_1^N \mathbf{y}_1 + \mathbf{E}\mathbf{x}$$

Since $\mathbf{E} \neq 0$ and $\mathbf{x}$ is arbitrary it follows that in general $\mathbf{E}\mathbf{x} \neq \mathbf{0}$. This proves necessity.

Taking this lemma together with Theorem 14.3 demonstrates the following theorem.

Theorem 14.4 Let $\mathbf{M}$ be an $n \times n$ matrix whose characteristic vectors form a basis of order n.[4] If $\mathbf{M}$ has a unique characteristic value of largest modulus, say h_1, with corresponding characteristic vector $\mathbf{y}_1$, then

$$\lim_{N\to\infty} \mathbf{M}^N = h_1^N \mathbf{y}_1 \mathbf{z}_1^T$$

3 More strictly speaking, the year to year sequence of income distributions is an example of a Markoff chain.

4 The requirement imposed on the basis is not strictly necessary.

where $\mathbf{z}_1$ is the characteristic vector of $\mathbf{M}^T$ corresponding to the characteristic value h_1.

PROOF The proof is obvious apart from the identification of $\mathbf{z}_1$ with a characteristic vector of the transpose $\mathbf{M}^T$. By using the fact that a determinant can be expanded by the cofactors of either a row or a column, it can be shown that $\det[\mathbf{M} - h\mathbf{I}] = \det[\mathbf{M}^T - h\mathbf{I}]$, whence $\det[\mathbf{M} - h\mathbf{I}] = 0$ if and only if $\det[\mathbf{M}^T - h\mathbf{I}] = 0$. It follows that the characteristic values of $\mathbf{M}$ are also the characteristic values of $\mathbf{M}^T$. Since h_1 is the characteristic value of largest modulus not only for $\mathbf{M}$ but also for $\mathbf{M}^T$, we find by using Theorem 14.3 that

$$\lim_{N\to\infty} (\mathbf{M}^T)^N \mathbf{x} = b_1 h_1^N \mathbf{z}_1$$

where b_1 is a constant of proportionality and $\mathbf{z}_1$ is the characteristic vector of $\mathbf{M}^T$ corresponding to h_1. From the lemma we get

$$\text{(1)} \qquad \lim_{N\to\infty} (\mathbf{M}^T)^N = h_1^N \mathbf{z}_1 \mathbf{w}_1^T$$

where $\mathbf{w}_1$ is an n-element vector. On using the result $(\mathbf{AB})^T = \mathbf{B}^T\mathbf{A}^T$ with $\mathbf{A} = \mathbf{M}, \mathbf{B} = \mathbf{M}$ it can be shown that $(\mathbf{M}^T)^N = (\mathbf{M}^N)^T$. Now it is a consequence of Theorem 14.3 and the lemma that

$$\text{(2)} \qquad \lim_{N\to\infty} (\mathbf{M}^N)^T = h_1^N(\mathbf{y}_1\mathbf{u}_1^T)^T = h_1^N \mathbf{u}_1 \mathbf{y}_1^T$$

Comparing equations (1) and (2) shows that $\mathbf{u}_1 = \mathbf{z}_1$ and $\mathbf{w}_1 = \mathbf{y}_1$.

It may be helpful to summarize Theorem 14.4 in the following way:

$$\left[\; \lim_{N\to\infty} \mathbf{M}^N \;\right] = \left(\begin{matrix}\text{Characteristic vector of}\\ \text{largest modulus}\end{matrix}\right)^N \cdot \left[\; \mathbf{y}_1 \;\right] \left[\; \mathbf{z}_1 \;\right]$$

where $\mathbf{y}_1$ is a characteristic vector of $\mathbf{M}$, $\mathbf{z}_1$ is a characteristic vector of $\mathbf{M}^T$ and both $\mathbf{y}_1$, $\mathbf{z}_1$ correspond to the characteristic value of largest modulus. It is assumed that the constants of proportionality in the characteristic vectors have been suitably chosen. It can be seen that all the rows of $\lim_{N\to\infty} \mathbf{M}^N$ are multiples of the vector $\mathbf{z}_1$, each row being scaled by the corresponding element of the vector $\mathbf{y}_1$. A consequence of this is that the rank of the matrix $\lim_{N\to\infty} \mathbf{M}^N$ is equal to one.

Example Determine the asymptotic form of $\mathbf{M}^N$ where

$$\mathbf{M} = \begin{bmatrix} 0{\cdot}6 & 0{\cdot}4 \\ 0{\cdot}6 & 1{\cdot}6 \end{bmatrix}$$

The characteristic values of $\mathbf{M}$ are the roots of

$$\det[\mathbf{M} - h\mathbf{I}] = \det\begin{bmatrix} 0{\cdot}6 - h & 0{\cdot}4 \\ 0{\cdot}6 & 1{\cdot}6 - h \end{bmatrix} = h^2 + 2{\cdot}2h + 0{\cdot}72 = 0$$

whence $h_1 = 1{\cdot}8$, $h_2 = 0{\cdot}4$. The unique characteristic value of largest modulus is 1·8. The corresponding characteristic vector of $\mathbf{M}$ is the solution of $(\mathbf{M} - 1{\cdot}8\mathbf{I})\mathbf{y}_1 = \mathbf{0}$. Let the elements of $\mathbf{y}_1$ be Y_1, Y_2. Then

$$-1{\cdot}2Y_1 + 0{\cdot}4Y_2 = 0$$

$$0{\cdot}6Y_1 - 0{\cdot}2Y_2 = 0$$

Using the first equation we get $Y_2 = 3Y_1$. Since the second equation is necessarily redundant we have

$$\mathbf{y}_1 = \begin{bmatrix} 1 \\ 3 \end{bmatrix}$$

(or some multiple of this). The characteristic vector of $\mathbf{M}^T$ corresponding to $h_1 = 1{\cdot}8$ is the solution of $(\mathbf{M}^T - 1{\cdot}8\mathbf{I})\mathbf{z}_1 = \mathbf{0}$. Let the elements of $\mathbf{z}_1$ be Z_1, Z_2. Then

$$-1{\cdot}2Z_1 + 0{\cdot}6Z_2 = 0$$

$$0{\cdot}4Z_1 - 0{\cdot}2Z_2 = 0$$

Using the first equation we get $Z_2 = 2Z_1$. Since the second equation is necessarily redundant we have

$$\mathbf{Z}_1 = \begin{bmatrix} 1 \\ 2 \end{bmatrix}$$

(or some multiple of this). Applying Theorem 14.4 we find

$$\lim_{N\to\infty} \mathbf{M}^N = 1{\cdot}8^N \begin{bmatrix} 1 \\ 3 \end{bmatrix} [1 \quad 2]$$

$$= 1{\cdot}8^N \begin{bmatrix} 1 & 2 \\ 3 & 6 \end{bmatrix}$$

(or some multiple of this).

To assess how quickly $\mathbf{M}^N$ converges to this asymptotic form we can evaluate the first few terms in the sequence $\mathbf{M}, \mathbf{M}^2, \mathbf{M}^3, \ldots$. We get

$$\mathbf{M}^2 = \begin{bmatrix} 0{\cdot}60 & 0{\cdot}88 \\ 1{\cdot}32 & 2{\cdot}80 \end{bmatrix}$$

$$\mathbf{M}^3 = \begin{bmatrix} 0{\cdot}89 & 1{\cdot}25 \\ 2{\cdot}47 & 5{\cdot}01 \end{bmatrix}$$

$$\mathbf{M}^4 = \begin{bmatrix} 1{\cdot}28 & 2{\cdot}35 \\ 4{\cdot}49 & 9{\cdot}01 \end{bmatrix}$$

It can be seen that the relative sizes of the elements in $\mathbf{M}^4$ are approximately the same as in $\lim_{N\to\infty} \mathbf{M}^N$. Furthermore the rate at which the elements increase in size between $\mathbf{M}^3$ and $\mathbf{M}^4$ is approximately equal to 1·8, the characteristic value of largest modulus. For example, on looking at the bottom right-hand corner elements we see that $9{\cdot}01/5{\cdot}01 = 1{\cdot}8$.

Another important result on the asymptotic behaviour of $\mathbf{M}^N$ is the following.

Theorem 14.5 A necessary and sufficient condition that

$$\lim_{N\to\infty} \mathbf{M}^N = \mathbf{0}$$

is that all the characteristic values of $\mathbf{M}$ have a modulus less than unity.

Taking this result together with Theorem 13.3 shows immediately that the characteristic values provide a condition for the convergence of a sum of a geometric series.

Theorem 14.6 A necessary and sufficient condition that

$$\mathbf{I} + \mathbf{M} + \mathbf{M}^2 + \cdots = (\mathbf{I} - \mathbf{M})^{-1}$$

is that all the characteristic values of $\mathbf{M}$ have a modulus less than unity.

Example By referring to Example 1 of Section 13.3, determine whether the equilibrium of trade between countries 1 and 2 is stable. The condition for stability (see Section 13.3) is that

$$\mathbf{I} + \mathbf{M} + \mathbf{M}^2 + \cdots = (\mathbf{I} - \mathbf{M})^{-1}$$

where

$$\mathbf{M} = \begin{bmatrix} 0{\cdot}5 & 0{\cdot}5 \\ 0{\cdot}25 & 0{\cdot}5 \end{bmatrix}$$

To apply Theorem 14.6 it is necessary to determine the characteristic values of $\mathbf{M}$. Solving

$$\det[\mathbf{M} - h\mathbf{I}] = \det\begin{bmatrix} 0{\cdot}5 - h & 0{\cdot}5 \\ 0{\cdot}25 & 0{\cdot}5 - h \end{bmatrix} = h_2 - h + 0{\cdot}125 = 0$$

we get $h_1 = 0{\cdot}85$, $h_2 = 0{\cdot}15$. Since the modulus of each characteristic value is less than unity, $\mathbf{I} + \mathbf{M} + \mathbf{M}^2 + \cdots = (\mathbf{I} - \mathbf{M})^{-1}$ and so the equilibrium is stable.

Notes and references

The theory of characteristic values and characteristic vectors is usually discussed from a much more advanced point of view. Simple treatments are given in Allen,[7] §14.4 and Hadley,[46] Ch. 7. For a lucid discussion of powers of a matrix see Peston,[103] Ch. 3, 5.

Simple economic applications of the theory are to the study of the growth of firms—see Adelman[2] and Hart[53]—and to forecasting demand for consumer goods—see Pyatt.[108] The theory has been used by Blumen, Kogan and McCarthy[19] to analyse the industrial mobility of labour and by Prais,[106, 107] to analyse social mobility. Bartholomew[12] has surveyed the applications to socioeconomic problems.

Problems

14.1.1 Verify that the operation of differentiation, as applied to a function, is a linear operation.

14.1.2 Verify that the operation of raising a number to a power is not a linear operation unless the power is equal to one.

14.2.1 Given the matrix **M** and the vector **x**

$$\mathbf{M} = \begin{bmatrix} 3 & 2 \\ 2 & 6 \end{bmatrix} \qquad \mathbf{x} = \begin{bmatrix} -8 \\ 4 \end{bmatrix}$$

(a) Find the characteristic values and the characteristic vectors of the matrix **M**
(b) Hence evaluate $\mathbf{M}^{10}\mathbf{x}$
(c) Denote the characteristic vectors by $\mathbf{y}_1$, $\mathbf{y}_2$ and prove that

$$\mathbf{y}_1^T\mathbf{y}_2 = 0$$

[This is true whenever the matrix **M** is symmetric about the diagonal.]

14.2.2 Find the characteristic values of the following matrices

(a) $$\mathbf{A} = \begin{bmatrix} 5 & 0 & 1 \\ 0 & 5 & 0 \\ -2 & 0 & 2 \end{bmatrix}$$

[*Hint:* Expand the appropriate determinant by the cofactors of the second row or the second column.]

(b) $$\mathbf{B} = \begin{bmatrix} 1 & 1 \\ 1 & 1 \end{bmatrix}$$

(c) $$\mathbf{C} = \begin{bmatrix} 3 & 0 & 0 \\ 0 & -8 & 0 \\ 0 & 0 & 16 \end{bmatrix}$$

(d) $$\mathbf{I} = \begin{bmatrix} 1 & 0 & 0 & 0 \\ 0 & 1 & 0 & 0 \\ 0 & 0 & 1 & 0 \\ 0 & 0 & 0 & 1 \end{bmatrix}$$

14.2.3 Given the matrices

$$\mathbf{B} = \begin{bmatrix} 1 & 0 \\ 1 & 1 \end{bmatrix} \qquad \mathbf{C} = \begin{bmatrix} 0 & 1 \\ 1 & 0 \end{bmatrix} \qquad \mathbf{D} = \begin{bmatrix} 2 & 3 \\ 4 & 6 \end{bmatrix}$$

verify the following statements

(a) **B** has two characteristic values which are equal
(b) **C** has two characteristic values which are distinct but have the same modulus
(c) **D** is a matrix whose determinant is zero; it also has a characteristic value which is zero.

14.2.4 Find the characteristic values and characteristic vectors of

$$\mathbf{M} = \begin{bmatrix} 7 & 4 \\ -1 & 2 \end{bmatrix}$$

Hence evaluate $(\mathbf{I} + \mathbf{M} + \cdots + \mathbf{M}^5)\mathbf{x}$ where

$$\mathbf{x} = \begin{bmatrix} 3 \\ -1 \end{bmatrix}$$

14.2.5 The trace of a matrix is defined to be the sum of its diagonal elements. It is a general rule that the sum of the characteristic values of a matrix is equal to its trace. Verify this result for the matrices in Problems 14.2.1 and 14.2.2.

14.2.6 (**14.2.5** continued) The trace of a matrix **M** is denoted tr (**M**). Prove that for the square matrices **A, B, C**

$$\text{tr}(\mathbf{ABC}) = \text{tr}(\mathbf{BCA}) = \text{tr}(\mathbf{CAB})$$

14.3.1 Do the vectors below constitute a basis?

$$\mathbf{x}_1 = \begin{bmatrix} 3 \\ 0 \\ 5 \end{bmatrix} \quad \mathbf{x}_2 = \begin{bmatrix} -2 \\ 2 \\ 1 \end{bmatrix} \quad \mathbf{x}_3 = \begin{bmatrix} -1 \\ 4 \\ 7 \end{bmatrix}$$

[*Hint:* Write out the equations to determine the weights associated with an arbitrary vector **x** and show that there always exists a solution to these equations.]

14.3.2 Without using Theorem 14.2, show that the characteristic vectors of **M** in Problem 14.2.4 form a basis of order 2.

14.3.3 Find the order of the basis formed by the characteristic vectors of

$$\mathbf{M} = \begin{bmatrix} 1 & 2 \\ 0 & 1 \end{bmatrix}$$

14.3.4 Find the order of the basis formed by the characteristic vectors of the matrix **A** in Problem 14.2.2.

14.3.5 Show that any vector is a characteristic vector of

$$\mathbf{I} = \begin{bmatrix} 1 & 0 & 0 \\ 0 & 1 & 0 \\ 0 & 0 & 1 \end{bmatrix}$$

corresponding to a characteristic value of unity. Show that the set of three characteristic vectors

$$\mathbf{y}_1 = \begin{bmatrix} 1 \\ 0 \\ 0 \end{bmatrix} \quad \mathbf{y}_2 = \begin{bmatrix} 0 \\ 1 \\ 0 \end{bmatrix} \quad \mathbf{y}_3 = \begin{bmatrix} 0 \\ 0 \\ 1 \end{bmatrix}$$

form a basis of order 3.

14.3.6 Find the characteristic values and characteristic vectors of the matrix

$$\mathbf{M} = \begin{bmatrix} 5 & 0 & 0 \\ 2 & 3 & 4 \\ 1 & 2 & 1 \end{bmatrix}$$

Do the characteristic vectors form a basis of order 3?

14.4.1 Find the moduli of (i) $3 + 4i$, (ii) $12 - 5i$, (iii) $-i$

14.5.1 Given

$$\mathbf{M} = \begin{bmatrix} 6 & 3 \\ 3 & -2 \end{bmatrix} \quad \mathbf{x} = \begin{bmatrix} 4 \\ 7 \end{bmatrix} \quad \text{and} \quad \mathbf{y} = \begin{bmatrix} -2 \\ 8 \end{bmatrix}$$

examine and compare the asymptotic behaviour of $\mathbf{M}^N\mathbf{x}$ and $\mathbf{M}^N\mathbf{y}$.

14.5.2 Firms are classified as large or small depending on whether their fixed assets exceed £0·1m. Each year 20% of the small firms become large firms (because of their fast growth) and 10% of the large firms become small firms (because, for example, they are so unprofitable that they are unable to replace depreciated fixed assets). The remaining 80% of small firms continue as small firms, and the remaining 90% of large firms continue as large firms.

Suppose that in 1973 40% of firms are small and 60% are large.

(a) By repeated matrix multiplication find the relative proportions of large firms and small firms in 1975.

(b) Verify your answer to (a) by finding the characteristic values and the characteristic vectors of the matrix in (a).

(c) Use the answer to (b) and show that eventually two-thirds of all firms will be large and one third will be small.

14.6.1 Given

$$\mathbf{M} = \begin{bmatrix} 0{\cdot}5 & 0{\cdot}4 \\ 0{\cdot}2 & 0{\cdot}7 \end{bmatrix}$$

determine the asymptotic form of $\mathbf{M}^N$ up to a constant of proportionality. By evaluating powers up to $\mathbf{M}^4$ assess how quickly $\mathbf{M}^N$ converges to its asymptotic form. Does $\lim_{N\to\infty} \mathbf{M}^N = \mathbf{0}$?

Chapter 15

Non-negative matrices

15.1 Introduction

A non-negative matrix is a matrix in which all the elements are non-negative.

The theory of non-negative matrices has wide applicability in economics. Many of the examples of previous chapters have involved matrices which are normally non-negative, for example, the matrix of input-output coefficients used in the study of inter-industry transactions (Section 10.7, especially Table 10.2), the matrix **M** used in the dynamic analysis of international trade (Section 13.4) and the matrix of transitional frequencies, **P**, used in the study of the distribution of income (Section 14.5).

In Chapter 14 it was shown how important properties of a matrix depend upon the characteristic values and characteristic vectors. For example, the convergence of a sum of a geometric series in a matrix depends upon the characteristic values of the matrix and the asymptotic form of the power of a matrix depends upon the characteristic vectors. In this chapter and the next we describe how the properties of characteristic values and characteristic vectors are related to corresponding properties of the elements of a matrix. These results are very useful because they enable us to infer important properties of a matrix from a superficial examination of its elements. In this chapter we give results relevant to non-negative matrices; in Chapter 16 we do the same thing for symmetric matrices.

15.2 Characteristics of an arbitrary non-negative matrix

The following result is fundamental to the theory of non-negative matrices.

Theorem 15.1 If **M** is a non-negative matrix then there is a real[1] non-negative characteristic value, $h_1 \geqslant 0$, with which a non-negative characteristic vector $\mathbf{y}_1 \geqslant 0$ is associated; there is no characteristic value larger than h_1.

We shall use this result to outline a proof of the following theorem.

Theorem 15.2 If **M** is a non-negative matrix, $\mathbf{M} \geqslant 0$, then

$$\mathbf{I} + \mathbf{M} + \mathbf{M}^2 + \cdots = (\mathbf{I} - \mathbf{M})^{-1}$$

is a necessary and sufficient condition that

$$(\mathbf{I} - \mathbf{M})^{-1} \geqslant 0$$

1 The value is real as opposed to complex: see Chapter 19.

PROOF The proof of sufficiency is simple. If $\mathbf{M} \geqslant 0$ then for any $n = 1, 2, \ldots, \mathbf{M}^n \geqslant 0$, so that $\mathbf{I} + \mathbf{M} + \mathbf{M}^2 + \cdots \geqslant \mathbf{0}$. Hence if $\mathbf{I} + \mathbf{M} + \mathbf{M}^2 + \cdots = (\mathbf{I} - \mathbf{M})^{-1}$ then $(\mathbf{I} - \mathbf{M})^{-1} \geqslant \mathbf{0}$.

The proof of necessity is more complicated, and only an outline will be given.(2) Firstly, we shall establish that if $\mathbf{y}_i$ is a characteristic vector of $\mathbf{M}$, corresponding to a characteristic value h_i, then $\mathbf{y}_i$ is also a characteristic vector of $(\mathbf{I} - \mathbf{M})^{-1}$, corresponding to a characteristic value $1/(1 - h_i)$. To see this, note that since $\mathbf{M}\mathbf{y}_i = h_i\mathbf{y}_i$ it follows, on multiplying the equation through by -1 and adding $\mathbf{y}_i$, that $(\mathbf{I} - \mathbf{M})\mathbf{y}_i = (\mathbf{I} - h_i\mathbf{I})\mathbf{y}_i = (1 - h_i)\mathbf{y}_i$. If $(\mathbf{I} - \mathbf{M})^{-1}$ exists then $\mathbf{y}_i = (\mathbf{I} - \mathbf{M})^{-1}(\mathbf{I} - \mathbf{M})\mathbf{y}_i = (1 - h_i)(\mathbf{I} - \mathbf{M})^{-1}\mathbf{y}_i$ and dividing through by $(1 - h_i)$ gives $(\mathbf{I} - \mathbf{M})^{-1}\mathbf{y}_i = [1/(1 - h_i)]\mathbf{y}_i$. Hence if $(\mathbf{I} - \mathbf{M})^{-1}$ exists, $\mathbf{y}_i$ is a characteristic vector of $(\mathbf{I} - \mathbf{M})^{-1}$ corresponding to the characteristic value $1/(1 - h_i)$. Secondly, we shall show that the theorem is vacuously true if some $h_i = 1$. If some $h_i = 1$ then $\mathbf{M}\mathbf{y}_i = h_i\mathbf{y}_i = \mathbf{y}_i$ and $(\mathbf{I} - \mathbf{M})\mathbf{y}_i = \mathbf{0}$; since $\mathbf{y}_i \neq \mathbf{0}$ by convention it follows that $\det[\mathbf{I} - \mathbf{M}] = 0$ and hence that $(\mathbf{I} - \mathbf{M})^{-1}$ does not exist. Hence the theorem is vacuously true. Finally, we show that if $0 \leqslant h_1 < 1$ then $\mathbf{I} + \mathbf{M} + \mathbf{M}^2 + \cdots$ converges and $(\mathbf{I} - \mathbf{M})^{-1}$ is non-negative, while if $h_1 > 1$ then $\mathbf{I} + \mathbf{M} + \mathbf{M}^2 + \cdots$ does not converge and $(\mathbf{I} - \mathbf{M})^{-1}$ is not non-negative.(3) Write out an arbitrary vector $\mathbf{x}$ as a weighted sum of the characteristic vectors, $\mathbf{x} = a_1\mathbf{y}_1 + a_2\mathbf{y}_2 + \cdots + a_n\mathbf{y}_n$. From the linearity of matrix multiplication it follows that

$$
\begin{aligned}
&(\mathbf{I} + \mathbf{M} + \mathbf{M}^2 + \cdots)\mathbf{x} \\
&= (\mathbf{I} + \mathbf{M} + \mathbf{M}^2 + \cdots)(a_1\mathbf{y}_1 + a_2\mathbf{y}_2 + \cdots + a_n\mathbf{y}_n) \\
&= a_1(\mathbf{I} + \mathbf{M} + \mathbf{M}^2 + \cdots)\mathbf{y}_1 + a_2(\mathbf{I} + \mathbf{M} + \mathbf{M}^2 + \cdots)\mathbf{y}_2 + \cdots \\
&\quad + a_n(\mathbf{I} + \mathbf{M} + \mathbf{M}^2 + \cdots)\mathbf{y}_n \\
&= a_1(1 + h_1 + h_1^2 + \cdots)\mathbf{y}_1 + a_2(1 + h_2 + h_2^2 + \cdots)\mathbf{y}_2 + \cdots \\
&\quad + a_n(1 + h_n + h_n^2 + \cdots)\mathbf{y}_n
\end{aligned}
$$

From the theory of geometric series we know that if $-1 < h_1 < 1$ then $1 + h_1 + h_1^2 + \cdots = 1/(1 - h_1)$; it follows that if $0 \leqslant h_1 < 1$ is the largest characteristic value then each of the summed geometric series in $h_1, h_2, \ldots, h_n$ converges, so that the last line above becomes $a_1[1/(1 - h_1)]\mathbf{y}_1 + a_2[1/(1 - h_2)]\mathbf{y}_2 + \cdots + a_n[1/(1 - h_n)]\mathbf{y}_n$. But we know that $(\mathbf{I} - \mathbf{M})^{-1}\mathbf{y}_i = [1/(1 - h_i)]\mathbf{y}_i$, so that this expression is equal to

$$
\begin{aligned}
&a_1(\mathbf{I} - \mathbf{M})^{-1}\mathbf{y}_1 + a_2(\mathbf{I} - \mathbf{M})^{-1}\mathbf{y}_2 + \cdots + a_n(\mathbf{I} - \mathbf{M})^{-1}\mathbf{y}_n \\
&= (\mathbf{I} - \mathbf{M})^{-1}(a_1\mathbf{y}_1 + a_2\mathbf{y}_2 + \cdots + a_n\mathbf{y}_n) \\
&= (\mathbf{I} - \mathbf{M})^{-1}\mathbf{x}
\end{aligned}
$$

Hence if $0 \leqslant h_1 < 1$ then $\mathbf{I} + \mathbf{M} + \mathbf{M}^2 + \cdots = (\mathbf{I} - \mathbf{M})^{-1}$, and since $\mathbf{M} \geqslant \mathbf{0}$, $\mathbf{I} + \mathbf{M} + \mathbf{M}^2 + \cdots \geqslant \mathbf{0}$, and so $(\mathbf{I} - \mathbf{M})^{-1} \geqslant 0$. Suppose now that $h_1 > 1$;

2 The discussion is oversimplified because it ignores the possibility that the characteristic values are not distinct.

3 The argument given below is not valid in the limiting case $h_1 = 0$ unless $\mathbf{M}$ is a 1×1 matrix, for if $h_1 = 0$ then $h_2 = \cdots = h_n = 0$ and the characteristic values are not distinct.

then the expression $1 + h_1 + h_1^2 + \cdots$ does not converge, so that $\mathbf{I} + \mathbf{M} + \mathbf{M}^2 + \cdots$ does not converge either; furthermore, since $(\mathbf{I} - \mathbf{M})^{-1}\mathbf{y}_1 = [1/(1 - h_1)]\,\mathbf{y}_1$ with $\mathbf{y}_1 \geqslant 0$, it follows that if $h_1 > 1$ then $(\mathbf{I} - \mathbf{M})^{-1}\mathbf{y}_1 \leqslant 0$, with at least one element negative, so that $(\mathbf{I} - \mathbf{M})^{-1} \leqslant 0$.

The economic significance of this result should not be overlooked. In an economy described by the dynamic model

$$\mathbf{y}(t) = \mathbf{M}\mathbf{y}(t - 1) + \mathbf{e}(t)$$

the condition for stability of equilibrium is that

$$\mathbf{I} + \mathbf{M} + \mathbf{M}^2 + \cdots = (\mathbf{I} - \mathbf{M})^{-1}$$

(see Section 13.3). If the equilibrium condition is $\mathbf{y}(t) = \mathbf{y}(t - 1)$, then assuming $\mathbf{e}(t) \geqslant 0$ the equilibrium is feasible if and only if

$$(\mathbf{I} - \mathbf{M})^{-1} \geqslant \mathbf{0}$$

(see Section 12.7). It is a consequence of Theorem 15.2 that *when the matrix* $\mathbf{M}$ *is non-negative the condition for stability of equilibrium is also the condition for feasibility of equilibrium.* Simple logic shows that the converse is also true.

The connection between stability and feasibility suggests that it may be instructive to compare Theorem 15.2 with Theorem 12.4. According to Theorem 12.4, when $\mathbf{M} \geqslant \mathbf{0}$ a necessary and sufficient condition for $(\mathbf{I} - \mathbf{M})^{-1} \geqslant \mathbf{0}$ is that the Hawkins–Simon conditions are satisfied. According to Theorem 15.2, when $\mathbf{M} \geqslant \mathbf{0}$ a necessary and sufficient condition for $(\mathbf{I} - \mathbf{M})^{-1} \geqslant \mathbf{0}$ is that $\mathbf{I} + \mathbf{M} + \mathbf{M}^2 + \cdots = (\mathbf{I} - \mathbf{M})^{-1}$. It follows that the Hawkins–Simon conditions are necessary and sufficient not only for $(\mathbf{I} - \mathbf{M}) \geqslant 0$ but also for $\mathbf{I} + \mathbf{M} + \mathbf{M}^2 + \cdots = (\mathbf{I} - \mathbf{M})^{-1}$. In economic terms, the Hawkins–Simon conditions are not only conditions for feasibility but also conditions for stability.

A similar sort of comparison between Theorem 15.2 and Theorem 14.6 reveals that when $\mathbf{M} \geqslant \mathbf{0}$ a necessary and sufficient condition both for $\mathbf{I} + \mathbf{M} + \mathbf{M}^2 + \cdots = (\mathbf{I} - \mathbf{M})^{-1}$ and for $(\mathbf{I} - \mathbf{M}) \geqslant \mathbf{0}$ is that all the characteristic values of $\mathbf{M}$ have a modulus less than unity. Finally, a comparison of this result with the result in the previous paragraph shows that a necessary and sufficient condition for all the characteristic values of a non-negative matrix to have a modulus less than unity is that the Hawkins–Simon conditions are satisfied. This establishes a useful connection between the elements of a non-negative matrix and its characteristic values: all the characteristic values of a non-negative matrix $\mathbf{M}$ have a modulus less than unity if and only if all the leading principal minors of $\mathbf{I} - \mathbf{M}$ are positive.

Example Determine whether all the characteristic vectors of the matrix $\mathbf{M}$ have a modulus less than unity.

$$\mathbf{M} = \begin{bmatrix} 0{\cdot}2 & 0{\cdot}4 & 0 \\ 0{\cdot}1 & 0{\cdot}1 & 0{\cdot}1 \\ 1{\cdot}2 & 0 & 0{\cdot}2 \end{bmatrix}$$

Since $\mathbf{M}$ is non-negative the Hawkins–Simon conditions are applicable. Form the matrix

$$\mathbf{A} = \mathbf{I} - \mathbf{M} = \begin{bmatrix} 0{\cdot}8 & -0{\cdot}4 & 0 \\ -0{\cdot}1 & 0{\cdot}9 & -0{\cdot}1 \\ -1{\cdot}2 & 0 & 0{\cdot}8 \end{bmatrix}$$

The sequence of leading principal minors of $\mathbf{A}$ is

$$\mathbf{A}_{(1)} = \det [0{\cdot}8] = 0{\cdot}8 > 0$$

$$\mathbf{A}_{(2)} = \det \begin{bmatrix} 0{\cdot}8 & -0{\cdot}4 \\ -0{\cdot}1 & 0{\cdot}9 \end{bmatrix} = 0{\cdot}68 > 0$$

$$\mathbf{A}_{(3)} = \det [A] = 0{\cdot}556 > 0$$

Since all the leading principal minors of $\mathbf{A}$ are positive the Hawkins–Simon conditions are satisfied and so all the characteristic values of $\mathbf{M}$ are of less than unit modulus.

15.3 Stochastic matrices

A stochastic matrix is a non-negative matrix in which the sum of the elements in each column is equal to unity. An example of a stochastic matrix is

$$\mathbf{P} = \begin{bmatrix} 0{\cdot}1 & 0{\cdot}3 & 0{\cdot}3 \\ 0{\cdot}9 & 0{\cdot}5 & 0{\cdot}3 \\ 0 & 0{\cdot}2 & 0{\cdot}4 \end{bmatrix}$$

The elements of a stochastic matrix usually represent transition probabilities; the element p_{ij} measures the probability, or relative frequency, with which a member of class j moves to class i.

Stochastic matrices have the following useful property.

Theorem 15.3 A stochastic matrix has at least one characteristic value equal to unity.

PROOF Consider the transpose of the matrix $\mathbf{P}$. Since the column sums of $\mathbf{P}$ are equal to one, the row sums of the transpose, $\mathbf{P}^T$ will be equal to one. It is then easily verified that if the transpose $\mathbf{P}^T$ is multiplied into a column vector in which all the elements are equal to one, then the result is a column vector in which all the elements are equal to one; i.e. if

$$\mathbf{x} = \begin{bmatrix} 1 \\ 1 \\ \vdots \\ 1 \end{bmatrix}$$

then

$$\mathbf{P}^T\mathbf{x} = \mathbf{x}$$

It follows that

$$(\mathbf{P}^T - \mathbf{I})\mathbf{x} = \mathbf{0}$$

so that when $h = 1$ the equation

$$(\mathbf{P}^T - h\mathbf{I})\mathbf{x} = \mathbf{0}$$

has a nontrivial solution for the vector **x**. Because this solution is nontrivial it follows that $h = 1$ must be a solution of the equation

$$\det [\mathbf{P}^T - h\mathbf{I}] = 0$$

But this equation, when the determinant is expanded, is seen to be identical with the equation

$$\det [\mathbf{P} - h\mathbf{I}] = 0$$

Hence $h = 1$ is a solution of this equation, and is therefore a characteristic value of the matrix **P**.

Example Find the characteristic values of

$$\mathbf{P} = \begin{bmatrix} 0{\cdot}4 & 0{\cdot}2 & 0 \\ 0{\cdot}3 & 0{\cdot}5 & 0{\cdot}6 \\ 0{\cdot}3 & 0{\cdot}3 & 0{\cdot}4 \end{bmatrix}$$

Expanding $\det [\mathbf{P} - h\mathbf{I}]$ shows that the characteristic values are the roots of the equation

$$h^3 - 1{\cdot}3h^2 + 0{\cdot}32h - 0{\cdot}02 = 0$$

Since **P** is stochastic it has at least one characteristic value equal to unity. Consequently we can factorize the left-hand side of the characteristic equation to get

$$(h - 1)(h^2 - 0{\cdot}3h + 0{\cdot}02) = 0$$

The roots of the quadratic are 0·1, 0·2 so that the characteristic values are $h_1 = 1{\cdot}0$, $h_2 = 0{\cdot}2$, $h_3 = 0{\cdot}1$.

Considering Theorem 15.1 and Theorem 15.3 together shows that a stochastic matrix has no root of modulus exceeding unity. In order to be able to apply Theorem 14.4 to analyse the asymptotic behaviour of $\mathbf{P}^N$ we must be sure that the root $h_1 = 1$ is the *only* root of modulus equal to unity. Unfortunately, it is quite possible for a stochastic matrix to have several roots of unit modulus. The situation is not too bad, however, because the cases in which there are several roots of unit modulus can be identified by a simple examination of the elements of the stochastic matrix. We describe how to recognize the symptoms in the following sections.

15.4 Decomposable matrices

A matrix **M** is decomposable if by interchanging its rows (and at the same time interchanging its columns) it can be put into the form

$$\mathbf{M} = \begin{bmatrix} \mathbf{M}_1 & \mathbf{N}_1 & \cdots & \cdots & \mathbf{Z} \\ & \mathbf{M}_2 & \mathbf{N}_2 & & \vdots \\ & & \ddots & \ddots & \mathbf{N}_{r-1} \\ & & & \ddots & \mathbf{M}_r \end{bmatrix}$$

where the $\mathbf{M}_i$ ($i = 1, 2, \ldots, r$) are submatrices whose diagonal elements lie on the diagonal of **M** and the $\mathbf{N}_j, \ldots, \mathbf{Z}$ are submatrices lying to the right of and above the matrices $\mathbf{M}_i$. All elements to the left of and below the submatrices **M** are zero.

The matrix **M** is completely decomposable if it can be put into the form

$$\mathbf{M} = \begin{bmatrix} \mathbf{M}_1 & & & \mathbf{0} \\ & \mathbf{M}_2 & & \\ & & \ddots & \\ \mathbf{0} & & & \mathbf{M}_r \end{bmatrix}$$

Complete decomposability is a special case of decomposability in which the elements of the submatrices $\mathbf{N}_j, \ldots, \mathbf{Z}$ are all zero.

The matrix **M** is indecomposable if it is not decomposable.

Example Is the matrix below decomposable?

$$\mathbf{M} = \begin{bmatrix} 0{\cdot}4 & 0 & 0{\cdot}6 \\ 0{\cdot}5 & 0{\cdot}3 & 0{\cdot}2 \\ 0{\cdot}1 & 0 & 0{\cdot}1 \end{bmatrix}$$

The best way of performing row and column interchanges is to note that an interchange can be considered as a transformation of subscripts. However, the transformation of the subscripts is the *reverse* of the transformation of the rows and columns. For example, to transform the first row and first column into the third row and third column, the second row and second column into the first row and first column, and the third row and third column into the second row and second column, make the respective transformations $3 \rightarrow 1$, $1 \rightarrow 2$ and $2 \rightarrow 3$ on the subscripts. Applying this transformation to a matrix

$$\mathbf{A} = \begin{bmatrix} a_{11} & a_{12} & a_{13} \\ a_{21} & a_{22} & a_{23} \\ a_{31} & a_{32} & a_{33} \end{bmatrix}$$

gives

$$\mathbf{A}\dagger = \begin{bmatrix} a_{22} & a_{23} & a_{21} \\ a_{32} & a_{33} & a_{31} \\ a_{12} & a_{13} & a_{11} \end{bmatrix}$$

The transformation applied to the matrix **M** gives

$$\mathbf{M}\dagger = \begin{bmatrix} 0{\cdot}3 & 0{\cdot}2 & 0{\cdot}5 \\ 0 & 0{\cdot}1 & 0{\cdot}1 \\ 0 & 0{\cdot}6 & 0{\cdot}4 \end{bmatrix}$$

It can be seen that $\mathbf{M}\dagger$ is of the form

$$\mathbf{M}\dagger = \left[\begin{array}{c|c} \mathbf{M}_1 & \mathbf{N} \\ \hline \mathbf{0} & \mathbf{M}_2 \end{array}\right]$$

where

$$\mathbf{M}_1 = [0{\cdot}3] \qquad \mathbf{M}_2 = \begin{bmatrix} 0{\cdot}1 & 0{\cdot}1 \\ 0{\cdot}6 & 0{\cdot}4 \end{bmatrix} \qquad \mathbf{N} = [0{\cdot}2 \quad 0{\cdot}5] \qquad \mathbf{0} = \begin{bmatrix} 0 \\ 0 \end{bmatrix}$$

We conclude that **M** is decomposable.

Indecomposable matrices have a number of important properties which do not apply to decomposable matrices. Within the scope of this book it is impossible to give a comprehensive discussion of the subject. We shall do no more than state a theorem from which many of the most useful properties of indecomposable matrices can be deduced.

Theorem 15.4 A non-negative indecomposable square matrix has a positive and distinct real characteristic value, $h_1 > 0$, which is as large as any other characteristic value; associated with h_1 is a strictly positive characteristic vector $\mathbf{y}_1$ and there is no non-negative characteristic vector which is linearly independent of $\mathbf{y}_1$.

Theorem 15.4 shows that it is possible to strengthen Theorem 15.1 quite significantly in the case of an indecomposable matrix. However, even when a matrix is indecomposable it is not necessarily true that there is a unique characteristic value of largest modulus. A sufficient condition is given in the next section; the condition involves not only indecomposability but also the 'aperiodicity' of a matrix.

The economic significance of the concept of decomposability may be explained as follows.

An economy whose intersectoral relationships are described by a decomposable matrix is one in which not all the sectors are 'connected up' either directly or indirectly. An exogenous change in one (or possibly more than one) of the sectors fails to induce a change in some other sector, even if repercussions throughout the economy are taken into account. If the economy is stable then it follows that the matrix multiplier relating exogenous changes to equilibrium values has at least one element equal to zero, indicating that an exogenous change in one sector does not influence the equilibrium value in some other sector. These remarks are illustrated in the following example.

Example Suppose that trading relations between Britain, India and the Argentine are such that the Argentine sells meat to Britain and Britain sells cars to the Argentine; Britain also sells cars to India, and India sells textiles to both Britain and the Argentine. However, the Argentine does not export to India. The trade flows are illustrated schematically in Fig. 15A. An arrow indicates the direction of the flow of goods.

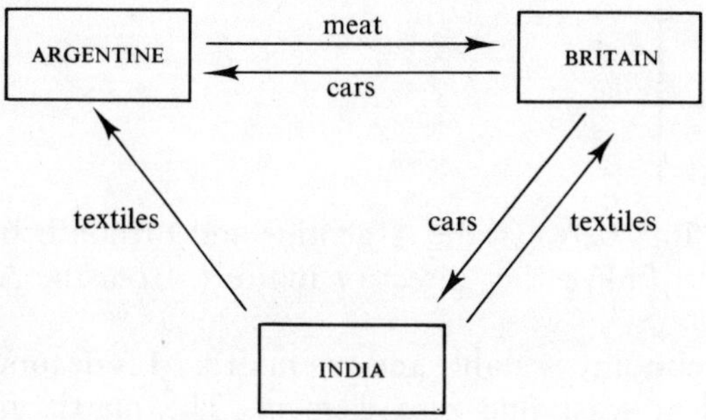

Fig. 15A Directed graph of trade flows

The structure of intersectoral relationships within the trading bloc is described by the matrix

$$\mathbf{M} = \begin{bmatrix} c_1 - m_1 & m_{12} & m_{13} \\ m_{21} & c_2 - m_2 & m_{23} \\ m_{31} & m_{32} & c_3 - m_3 \end{bmatrix}$$

The interpretation of this matrix is given in Example 1 of Section 13.1. The element in the ith row and jth column is the marginal propensity of country j to import from country i; the diagonal elements represent the marginal propensity of a country to consume its own products. Let Britain be indexed 1, India 2 and the Argentine 3. Figure 15A shows that the Argentine does not export to Germany, which implies that the element m_{32} is zero. Assuming that each country consumes some of its own products it follows from the figure that all the other elements are positive. Consequently **M** is of the form

$$(1)\quad \mathbf{M} = \begin{bmatrix} + & + & + \\ + & + & + \\ + & 0 & + \end{bmatrix}$$

It is easily verified that **M** is not decomposable. The reason is that although the Argentine does not export *directly* to India it does export *indirectly* to India, since the Argentine exports to Britain and Britain exports to India.

If either $m_{12} = 0$ or $m_{31} = 0$, in addition to $m_{32} = 0$, then $\mathbf{M}$ is decomposable. Suppose, for example, that India raises the import duty on cars to a prohibitive level, so that Britain no longer exports cars to India. This sets $m_{12} = 0$:

$$(2)\quad \mathbf{M} = \begin{bmatrix} + & 0 & + \\ + & + & + \\ + & 0 & + \end{bmatrix}$$

The indirect link between India and the Argentine is now broken. Neither Britain nor the Argentine exports to India *either directly or indirectly*. A similar result applies if $m_{31} = 0$:

$$(3)\quad \mathbf{M} = \begin{bmatrix} + & + & + \\ + & + & + \\ 0 & 0 & + \end{bmatrix}$$

In this case the export link between the Argentine and Britain is broken; as a result there is no export link, either direct or indirect, from the Argentine to either Britain or India.

When the economy is stable and the matrix $\mathbf{M}$ is decomposable the matrix multiplier has at least one zero element. The matrix multiplier is $(\mathbf{I} - \mathbf{M})^{-1}$, which certainly exists if the economy is stable. We shall demonstrate that if $\mathbf{M}$ has the form of either (2) or (3) the multiplier relating exogenous demand in India to equilibrium income in the Argentine is equal to zero.

The multiplier concerned is the element in the third row and second column of $(\mathbf{I} - \mathbf{M})^{-1}$. Since the inverse is equal to the transpose of the matrix of the cofactors scaled by the reciprocal of the determinant it follows that an element of the inverse is zero if the cofactor of the corresponding element *in the transpose* is equal to zero. It is therefore sufficient to demonstrate that the cofactor of the element in the *second row* and *third column* of $(\mathbf{I} - \mathbf{M})$ is equal to zero. Since the off-diagonal elements of $\mathbf{I} - \mathbf{M}$ are equal to the off-diagonal elements of $\mathbf{M}$, apart from sign, equation (2) implies

$$(4)\quad \mathbf{I} - \mathbf{M} = \begin{bmatrix} ? & 0 & - \\ - & ? & - \\ - & 0 & ? \end{bmatrix}$$

and equation (3) implies

$$(5)\quad \mathbf{I} - \mathbf{M} = \begin{bmatrix} ? & - & - \\ - & ? & - \\ 0 & 0 & - \end{bmatrix}$$

Inspection of equations (4) and (5) shows that in both cases the cofactor of the element in the second row and third column is equal to zero, which proves the point.

15.5 Periodic matrices

The condition that a matrix has a unique characteristic vector of largest modulus involves the periodicity of the matrix.

Definition A matrix **P** is periodic if, by interchanging the rows (and at the same time interchanging the corresponding columns) it can be put into the form

$$\mathbf{P} = \begin{bmatrix} \mathbf{0} & \mathbf{P}_{12} & \mathbf{0} & \cdots & \mathbf{0} \\ \vdots & \mathbf{0} & \mathbf{P}_{13} & & \mathbf{0} \\ \mathbf{0} & \vdots & & \ddots & \mathbf{P}_{k-1k} \\ \mathbf{P}_{k1} & \mathbf{0} & \cdots & & \mathbf{0} \end{bmatrix} \quad (k > 1)$$

with square matrices on the diagonal. A matrix which is not periodic is said to be aperiodic.

The fundamental theorem on aperiodic matrices is as follows.

Theorem 15.5 A sufficient condition that a non-negative matrix **M** has a unique characteristic value of largest modulus is that it is indecomposable and aperiodic. Corresponding to this characteristic value is a unique characteristic vector in which every element is positive.

This result has a very useful application to stochastic matrices. It was shown in Section 15.3 that a stochastic matrix **P** always has a characteristic value of unity, and no other root of modulus exceeding unity. Theorem 15.5 tells us that if the stochastic matrix **P** is indecomposable and aperiodic then the characteristic value of unity is the unique characteristic value of largest modulus. Consequently the asymptotic form of $\mathbf{P}^N\mathbf{x}$ for arbitrary $\mathbf{x} \neq \mathbf{0}$ is given by the characteristic vector corresponding to the characteristic value of unity. Because the characteristic value is unity this characteristic vector is the solution of the equation

$$(\mathbf{P} - \mathbf{I})\mathbf{y} = 0$$

If **P** is an $n \times n$ matrix then when written out in full the equation constitutes a set of n equations for the n unknown elements of the vector **y**. Theorem 15.5 indicates that **y** is uniquely determined (up to a constant of proportionality) and has every element positive. By using this result it is possible to determine the asymptotic behaviour of $\mathbf{P}^N\mathbf{x}$ without solving the characteristic equation of the matrix **P**, provided that **P** is indecomposable and aperiodic.

Notes and references

The properties of non-negative square matrices are conveniently summarized in Morishima,[92] Appendix §1; for further references see Burmeister and Dobell,[23] Appendix. The Hawkins–Simon conditions were first stated in an economic context by Hawkins and Simon[54]; the most comprehensive reference on the subject is Gantmacher.[38]

One of the most readable discussions of the economic stability of interacting markets is Solow[115]; Solow demonstrates the formal equivalence of several different economic models, and explains the economic significance of decomposability.

The stability of the international economy is discussed from the theoretical point of view in Metzler,[86,88] and from the empirical point of view in Beckerman.[15] The correspondence between the conditions for stability and the conditions for feasibility was first demonstrated by Samuelson,[112] though in a slightly different context; this is sometimes known as 'the correspondence principle'.

More advanced discussions of stochastic matrices are given by Kemeny and Snell[70] and Lindley.[80] A definitive work is Cox and Miller.[31] For applications see the references to Chapter 14.

Problems

15.2.1 Verify Theorem 15.1 for the following matrices:

$$\mathbf{A} = \begin{bmatrix} 5 & 3 \\ 2 & 4 \end{bmatrix}, \quad \mathbf{B} = \begin{bmatrix} 5 & 0 & 2 \\ 0 & 4 & 0 \\ 6 & 0 & 1 \end{bmatrix}, \quad \mathbf{C} = \begin{bmatrix} 0 & 0 & 1 \\ 1 & 0 & 0 \\ 0 & 1 & 0 \end{bmatrix}$$

15.2.2 The matrix of input-output coefficients of a three-sector economy is

$$\mathbf{M} = \begin{bmatrix} 0{\cdot}2 & 0{\cdot}4 & 0{\cdot}4 \\ 0{\cdot}6 & 0{\cdot}1 & 0{\cdot}4 \\ 0{\cdot}3 & 0{\cdot}1 & 0{\cdot}2 \end{bmatrix}$$

If the vector of outputs, $\mathbf{y}$, is planned by a process of negotiation in which the vector of planned outputs after t rounds is $\mathbf{y}(t) = \mathbf{M}\mathbf{y}(t-1) + \mathbf{e}$, where $\mathbf{e}$ is the vector of final demands, will the negotiations lead to an equilibrium output in each sector? Are the equilibrium outputs feasible?

15.2.3 The marginal propensity of country j to import from country i is shown by the element m_{ij} in the following matrix:

$$\mathbf{M} = \begin{bmatrix} 0{\cdot}4 & 0{\cdot}1 & 0{\cdot}2 \\ 0{\cdot}3 & 0{\cdot}3 & 0{\cdot}3 \\ 0{\cdot}4 & 0{\cdot}4 & 0{\cdot}4 \end{bmatrix}$$

The diagonal elements show the marginal propensity of each country to consume its own output. If trade between the three countries is governed by the matrix equation $\mathbf{y}(t) = \mathbf{M}\mathbf{y}(t-1) + \mathbf{e}$, where $\mathbf{y}$ is the vector of incomes and $\mathbf{e}$ is the vector of exogenous demands, is the international economy stable?

15.2.3 Suppose that for trade between two countries the matrix of marginal propensities is

$$\mathbf{M} = \begin{bmatrix} 0{\cdot}7 & -0{\cdot}05 \\ 0{\cdot}2 & 0{\cdot}9 \end{bmatrix}$$

Is the international economy stable?

15.3 Find the characteristic values of the following matrices:

$$\mathbf{A} = \begin{bmatrix} 0{\cdot}5 & 0{\cdot}4 \\ 0{\cdot}5 & 0{\cdot}6 \end{bmatrix}, \quad \mathbf{B} = \begin{bmatrix} 0{\cdot}5 & 0{\cdot}5 \\ 0{\cdot}4 & 0{\cdot}6 \end{bmatrix},$$

$$\mathbf{C} = \begin{bmatrix} 0{\cdot}2 & 0{\cdot}1 & 0 \\ 0{\cdot}4 & 0{\cdot}7 & 0 \\ 0{\cdot}4 & 0{\cdot}2 & 1{\cdot}0 \end{bmatrix}, \quad \mathbf{D} = \begin{bmatrix} 0{\cdot}5 & 0{\cdot}3 & 0{\cdot}2 \\ 0{\cdot}1 & 0{\cdot}6 & 0{\cdot}3 \\ 0{\cdot}2 & 0{\cdot}7 & 0{\cdot}1 \end{bmatrix}$$

15.4.1 Is the matrix $\mathbf{M}$ decomposable?

$$\mathbf{M} = \begin{bmatrix} 0{\cdot}2 & 0{\cdot}4 & 0{\cdot}1 \\ 0{\cdot}5 & 0{\cdot}2 & 0 \\ 0{\cdot}1 & 0{\cdot}2 & 0 \end{bmatrix}$$

15.4.2 Show that the matrix **B** is decomposable and that $(\mathbf{I} - \mathbf{B})^{-1}$ has at least one element equal to zero.

$$\mathbf{B} = \begin{bmatrix} 0{\cdot}2 & 0 & 0{\cdot}2 \\ 0{\cdot}4 & 0{\cdot}1 & 0{\cdot}4 \\ 0{\cdot}1 & 0 & 0{\cdot}2 \end{bmatrix}$$

15.4.3 Given the matrix of marginal propensities for the world economy

$$\mathbf{M} = \begin{bmatrix} 0{\cdot}6 & 0{\cdot}2 & 0 & 0 \\ 0{\cdot}3 & 0{\cdot}5 & 0 & 0 \\ 0 & 0 & 0{\cdot}4 & 0{\cdot}3 \\ 0 & 0 & 0{\cdot}1 & 0{\cdot}4 \end{bmatrix}$$

show that equilibrium incomes in countries 1 and 2 are independent of exogenous demands in countries 3 and 4, and vice versa.

15.5.1 Show that the periodic matrix

$$\mathbf{P} = \begin{bmatrix} 0 & 1 \\ 1 & 0 \end{bmatrix}$$

has no unique characteristic value of largest modulus.

15.5.2 Find the steady state distribution of income for an economy in which the matrix of transition frequencies between income classes is

$$\mathbf{P} = \begin{bmatrix} 0{\cdot}5 & 0{\cdot}4 & 0{\cdot}2 & 0 \\ 0{\cdot}4 & 0{\cdot}4 & 0{\cdot}2 & 0 \\ 0{\cdot}1 & 0{\cdot}2 & 0{\cdot}5 & 0{\cdot}3 \\ 0 & 0 & 0{\cdot}1 & 0{\cdot}7 \end{bmatrix}$$

Chapter 16
Symmetric matrices

16.1 Introduction

Symmetric matrices are an important class of matrices; they are defined as follows.

Definition A symmetric matrix is a square matrix in which the element in the ith row and jth column is equal to the element in the jth row and ith column, i.e. a symmetric matrix $\mathbf{M}$ is an $n \times n$ matrix in which

$$m_{ij} = m_{ji} \quad (i, j = 1, 2, \ldots, n)$$

Each element in a symmetric matrix is equal to the element which represents its reflection in the upper left to lower right diagonal (the 'main' diagonal) of the matrix. An example of a symmetric matrix is

$$\mathbf{M} = \begin{bmatrix} 5 & 7 & 2 \\ 7 & 4 & -8 \\ 2 & -8 & 9 \end{bmatrix}$$

Symmetric matrices have properties which are shared by few other types of matrix. The most important properties relate to the characteristic values and characteristic vectors of a symmetric matrix.

Theorem 16.1 If $\mathbf{M}$ is an $n \times n$ symmetric matrix then

(i) all the characteristic values $h_1, h_2, \ldots, h_n$ are real numbers—none of them are complex;

(ii) the characteristic vectors $\mathbf{y}_1, \mathbf{y}_2, \ldots, \mathbf{y}_n$ form a basis of order n—if the characteristic vectors are not unique then it is always possible to find a set which forms a basis of order n;

(iii) the characteristic vectors satisfy the equations

$$\left.\begin{array}{ll} \mathbf{y}_i^T\mathbf{y}_j = 0 & (i \neq j) \\ \mathbf{y}_i^T\mathbf{y}_i \neq 0 & \end{array}\right\} \quad (i, j = 1, \ldots, n)$$

If the characteristic vectors are not unique it is always possible to find a set of n characteristic vectors with this property.

This third property is quite remarkable. It tells us that if the transpose of one characteristic vector is multiplied into any *different* characteristic vector the result is always equal to *zero*, whereas if the transpose is multiplied into the *same* characteristic vector, the result is a *nonzero* value.

Definition The result of multiplying the transpose of one vector into another vector is known as the *scalar product* of the two vectors. The scalar product of the vectors *a* and *b* is

$$[\ \mathbf{a}^T\ ]\begin{bmatrix} \\ \mathbf{b} \\ \\ \end{bmatrix} = \mathbf{a}^T\mathbf{b}$$

The scalar product is a 1 × 1 matrix. Since the algebra of 1 × 1 matrices is the same as the algebra of real numbers the scalar product is regarded as just a number. Since

$$\mathbf{a}^T\mathbf{b} = A_1B_1 + A_2B_2 + \cdots + A_nB_n = B_1A_1 + B_2A_2 + \cdots + B_nA_n = \mathbf{b}^T\mathbf{a}$$

it does not matter in which order the vectors **a**, **b** are taken.

The properties in Theorem 16.1 are illustrated by the following example.

Example Consider the symmetric matrix

$$\mathbf{M} = \begin{bmatrix} 2 & 1 \\ 1 & 2 \end{bmatrix}$$

The characteristic values of **M** are $h_1 = 3$, $h_2 = 1$. Both are real numbers. The corresponding characteristic vectors are proportional to

$$\mathbf{y}_1 = \begin{bmatrix} 1 \\ 1 \end{bmatrix} \quad \text{and} \quad \mathbf{y}_2 = \begin{bmatrix} 1 \\ -1 \end{bmatrix}$$

Multiplying the transpose of any one characteristic vector into some other characteristic vector gives the set of scalar products

$$\mathbf{y}_1^T\mathbf{y}_1 = [1 \quad 1]\begin{bmatrix} 1 \\ 1 \end{bmatrix} = 2$$

$$\mathbf{y}_1^T\mathbf{y}_2 = [1 \quad 1]\begin{bmatrix} 1 \\ -1 \end{bmatrix} = 0$$

$$\mathbf{y}_2^T\mathbf{y}_1 = [1 \quad -1]\begin{bmatrix} 1 \\ 1 \end{bmatrix} = 0$$

$$\mathbf{y}_2^T\mathbf{y}_2 = [1 \quad -1]\begin{bmatrix} 1 \\ -1 \end{bmatrix} = 2$$

The scalar products formed from *different* characteristic vectors are *zero* ($\mathbf{y}_1^T\mathbf{y}_2 = \mathbf{y}_2^T\mathbf{y}_1 = 0$) whereas the scalar products formed from the *same* characteristic vector are nonzero ($\mathbf{y}_1^T\mathbf{y}_1 = \mathbf{y}_2^T\mathbf{y}_2 = 2$).

16.2 Orthogonality

The third property of symmetric matrices described in the previous section is of really fundamental importance and it is the object of the next three sections to explore its ramifications.

First of all, we shall formally introduce the concept of orthogonality, which was implicit in the discussion of the previous section.

Definition Two vectors **a**, **b** are said to be orthogonal if their scalar product is zero, $\mathbf{a}^T\mathbf{b} = 0$.

It is also convenient at this stage to introduce the definition of a 'normalized characteristic vector'. Recall from Section 14.3 that a characteristic vector has an arbitrary constant of proportionality, reflecting the fact that the ratios of the elements in a characteristic vector are determinate but that the actual values of the elements are not. A normalized characteristic vector is formed from a characteristic vector by choosing this constant of proportionality so that the sum of the squares of the elements of the normalized characteristic vector is equal to one. The reason why the normalizing value of the constant of proportionality is chosen in this way will become evident later on. It should be appreciated that the normalization fixes the elements of the normalized characteristic vector to precise values (apart from sign).

Definition A normalized characteristic vector $\mathbf{u}_i$ is formed by scaling a characteristic vector $\mathbf{y}_i$ so that $\mathbf{u}_i^T\mathbf{u}_i = 1$. The easiest way to find the normalized characteristic vectors of a matrix is demonstrated in the example below.

Example Find the normalized characteristic vectors of the matrix

$$\mathbf{M} = \begin{bmatrix} 3 & 1 \\ 1 & 3 \end{bmatrix}$$

It is easily verified that the characteristic vectors of this matrix are proportional to

$$\mathbf{y}_1 = \begin{bmatrix} 1 \\ 1 \end{bmatrix} \quad \text{and} \quad \mathbf{y}_2 = \begin{bmatrix} 1 \\ -1 \end{bmatrix}$$

Neither of these vectors are normalized characteristic vectors since in the first vector the sum of the squares of the elements is $(1)^2 + (1)^2 = 2$ and in the second vector the sum of the squares of the elements is $(1)^2 + (-1)^2 = 2$. In order to normalize any vector it is sufficient to divide through the vector by the square root of the sum of the squares of the elements. For both the vectors in this example the sum of the squares of the elements is equal to 2, so that for both vectors the required divisor is $\sqrt{2}$. Dividing through each element in each of the vectors by $\sqrt{2}$ gives the normalized characteristic vectors

$$\mathbf{u}_1 = \begin{bmatrix} 1/\sqrt{2} \\ 1/\sqrt{2} \end{bmatrix} \quad \text{and} \quad \mathbf{u}_2 = \begin{bmatrix} 1/\sqrt{2} \\ -1/\sqrt{2} \end{bmatrix}$$

16.3 The latent matrix

The first stage in analysing the consequences of the orthogonality of the characteristic vectors of a symmetric matrix $\mathbf{M}$, is to construct a new matrix, $\mathbf{L}$, from the normalized characteristic vectors. Let $\mathbf{M}$ be an $n \times n$ symmetric matrix with characteristic values $h_1, h_2, \ldots, h_n$ and normalized characteristic vectors $\mathbf{u}_1, \mathbf{u}_2, \ldots, \mathbf{u}_n$. Let $\mathbf{L}$ be the $n \times n$ matrix formed by placing side by side the n normalized characteristic vectors of the matrix $\mathbf{M}$; $\mathbf{L}$ is of the form

$$\mathbf{L} = \left[\begin{array}{c|c|c|c} \mathbf{u}_1 & \mathbf{u}_2 & \cdots & \mathbf{u}_n \end{array}\right]$$

We shall refer to $\mathbf{L}$ as the 'latent matrix'.

Theorem 16.2 If $\mathbf{M}$ is symmetric then the corresponding latent matrix $\mathbf{L}$ has an inverse equal to its own transpose,

$$\mathbf{L}^{-1} = \mathbf{L}^T$$

PROOF Quite obviously $\mathbf{L}^T$ is of the form

$$\mathbf{L}^T = \left[\begin{array}{c} \mathbf{u}_1^T \\ \mathbf{u}_2^T \\ \hline \vdots \\ \hline \mathbf{u}_n^T \end{array}\right]$$

where $\mathbf{u}_1^T, \mathbf{u}_2^T, \ldots, \mathbf{u}_n^T$ are the transposes of the normalized characteristic vectors, i.e. they are the normalized characteristic vectors written in row rather than column form. From the structure of the matrices $\mathbf{L}$ and $\mathbf{L}^T$ it follows that the result of multiplying the transpose matrix $\mathbf{L}^T$ into the original matrix $\mathbf{L}$ is a matrix in which the element in the ith row and jth column is equal to $\mathbf{u}_i^T\mathbf{u}_j$:

$$\mathbf{L}^T\mathbf{L} = \left[\begin{array}{c} \mathbf{u}_1^T \\ \hline \mathbf{u}_2^T \\ \hline \vdots \\ \hline \mathbf{u}_n^T \end{array}\right] \left[\begin{array}{c|c|c|c} \mathbf{u}_1^T & \mathbf{u}_2^T & \cdots & \mathbf{u}_n^T \end{array}\right]$$

$$= \begin{bmatrix} \mathbf{u}_1^T\mathbf{u}_1 & \mathbf{u}_1^T\mathbf{u}_2 & \cdots & \mathbf{u}_1^T\mathbf{u}_n \\ \mathbf{u}_2^T\mathbf{u}_1 & \mathbf{u}_2^T\mathbf{u}_2 & \cdots & \mathbf{u}_2^T\mathbf{u}_n \\ \vdots & \vdots & \ddots & \vdots \\ \mathbf{u}_n^T\mathbf{u}_1 & \mathbf{u}_n^T\mathbf{u}_2 & \cdots & \mathbf{u}_n^T\mathbf{u}_n \end{bmatrix}$$

But the vectors $\mathbf{u}_i$ are simply normalized versions of the characteristic vectors $\mathbf{y}_i$ and we know, from the orthogonality of the characteristic vectors of a symmetric matrix, that $\mathbf{y}_i^T\mathbf{y}_j = 0$ if $i \neq j$; it follows that $\mathbf{u}_i^T\mathbf{u}_j = 0$ if $i \neq j$ and hence that all the off-diagonal elements in the matrix $\mathbf{L}^T\mathbf{L}$ are equal to zero. Since the $\mathbf{u}_i$ are normalized characteristic vectors $\mathbf{u}_i^T\mathbf{u}_i = 1$ and hence each diagonal element in the matrix $\mathbf{L}^T\mathbf{L}$ is equal to unity. We conclude that $\mathbf{L}^T\mathbf{L}$ is equal to the $n \times n$ identity matrix $\mathbf{I}$,

$$\mathbf{L}^T\mathbf{L} = \mathbf{I}$$

But according to the definition of the inverse

$$\mathbf{L}^{-1}\mathbf{L} = \mathbf{I}$$

If the inverse exists it is unique (see Section 12.2), consequently $\mathbf{L}^T$ must be identical with $\mathbf{L}^{-1}$, i.e.

$$\mathbf{L}^T = \mathbf{L}^{-1}$$

16.4 Diagonalization of symmetric matrices

In this section we shall describe a method by which a symmetric matrix can be transformed with a diagonal matrix. The method involves multiplying the symmetric matrix by the latent matrix and by the transpose of the latent matrix. Some applications of the method will be explained in this and in the following sections. A symmetric matrix, **M**, can be transformed into a diagonal matrix, **D**, by multiplying the matrix **M** into the latent matrix, **L**, and multiplying the result by the transpose of the latent matrix, $\mathbf{L}^T$. The diagonal elements of **D** are the characteristic values of **M**.

Theorem 16.3 Let **M** be an $n \times n$ symmetric matrix with characteristic values $h_1, h_2, \ldots, h_n$ and normalized characteristic vectors $\mathbf{u}_1, \mathbf{u}_2, \ldots, \mathbf{u}_n$ (normalized so that $\mathbf{u}_i^T\mathbf{u}_i = 1$, $i = 1, 2, \ldots, n$). If the normalized characteristic values are not uniquely determined, let $\mathbf{u}_1, \mathbf{u}_2, \ldots, \mathbf{u}_n$ be any set of normalized characteristic vectors which forms a basis of order n. Define the latent matrix **L** as the matrix whose columns are the normalized characteristic vectors $\mathbf{u}_1, \mathbf{u}_2, \ldots, \mathbf{u}_n$,

$$\mathbf{L} = \left[\begin{array}{c|c|c|c} \mathbf{u}_1 & \mathbf{u}_2 & \cdots & \mathbf{u}_n \end{array}\right]$$

Let **D** be a diagonal matrix in which the diagonal elements are the characteristic values of **M**,

$$\mathbf{D} = \begin{bmatrix} h_1 & & & 0 \\ & h_2 & & \\ & & \ddots & \\ 0 & & & h_n \end{bmatrix}$$

Then

$$\mathbf{L}^T\mathbf{M}\mathbf{L} = \mathbf{D}$$

PROOF From the rules of matrix multiplication, the result of multiplying **M** into **L** is

$$\mathbf{ML} = \left[\begin{array}{c|c|c|c} \mathbf{Mu}_1 & \mathbf{Mu}_2 & \cdots & \mathbf{Mu}_n \end{array}\right]$$

Since $\mathbf{u}_1, \mathbf{u}_2, \ldots, \mathbf{u}_n$ are normalized characteristic vectors of **M**, the result of multiplying **M** into each $\mathbf{u}_i$ is simply to scale each $\mathbf{u}_i$ by the corresponding characteristic value h_i: $\mathbf{Mu}_i = h_1 \mathbf{u}_i$ $(i = 1, 2, \ldots, n)$; hence

$$\mathbf{ML} = \left[\begin{array}{c|c|c|c} h_1\mathbf{u}_1 & h_2\mathbf{u}_2 & \cdots & h_n\mathbf{u}_n \end{array}\right]$$

Again, from the rules of matrix multiplication

$$\mathbf{L}^T\mathbf{ML} = \left[\begin{array}{c} \mathbf{u}_1^T \\ \hline \mathbf{u}_2^T \\ \hline \vdots \\ \hline \mathbf{u}_n^T \end{array}\right] \left[\begin{array}{c|c|c|c} h_1\mathbf{u}_1 & h_2\mathbf{u}_2 & \cdots & h_n\mathbf{u}_n \end{array}\right]$$

$$= \begin{bmatrix} h_1\mathbf{u}_1^T\mathbf{u}_1 & h_2\mathbf{u}_1^T\mathbf{u}_2 & \cdots & h_n\mathbf{u}_1^T\mathbf{u}_n \\ h_1\mathbf{u}_2^T\mathbf{u}_1 & h_2\mathbf{u}_2^T\mathbf{u}_2 & \cdots & h_n\mathbf{u}_2^T\mathbf{u}_n \\ \vdots & \vdots & \ddots & \vdots \\ h_1\mathbf{u}_n^T\mathbf{u}_1 & h_2\mathbf{u}_n^T\mathbf{u}_2 & \cdots & h_n\mathbf{u}_n^T\mathbf{u}_n \end{bmatrix}$$

Since the h_i are scalars, it follows from the orthogonality of the characteristic vectors, $\mathbf{u}_i^T\mathbf{u}_j = 0\ (i \neq j)$ that $h_j\mathbf{u}_i^T\mathbf{u}_j = 0\ (i \neq j)$ and from the normalization of the characteristic vectors, $\mathbf{u}_i^T\mathbf{u}_i = 1$, that $h_i\mathbf{u}_i^T\mathbf{u}_i = h_i$. Hence the expression for the matrix $\mathbf{L}^T\mathbf{ML}$ simplifies to

$$\mathbf{L}^T\mathbf{ML} = \begin{bmatrix} h_1 & & & 0 \\ & h_2 & & \\ & & \ddots & \\ 0 & & & h_n \end{bmatrix}$$

which is equal to the diagonal matrix **D**.

Example Consider the symmetric matrix

$$\mathbf{M} = \begin{bmatrix} 5 & 2 \\ 2 & 5 \end{bmatrix}$$

The characteristic values of $\mathbf{M}$ are $h_1 = 7, h_2 = 3$ and the corresponding normalized characteristic vectors are

$$\mathbf{u}_1 = \begin{bmatrix} 1/\sqrt{2} \\ 1/\sqrt{2} \end{bmatrix} \quad \text{and} \quad \mathbf{u}_2 = \begin{bmatrix} -1/\sqrt{2} \\ 1/\sqrt{2} \end{bmatrix}$$

The latent matrix and its transpose are, respectively,

$$\mathbf{L} = \begin{bmatrix} 1/\sqrt{2} & -1/\sqrt{2} \\ 1/\sqrt{2} & 1/\sqrt{2} \end{bmatrix} \quad \text{and} \quad \mathbf{L}^T = \begin{bmatrix} 1/\sqrt{2} & 1/\sqrt{2} \\ -1/\sqrt{2} & 1/\sqrt{2} \end{bmatrix}$$

Multiplying $\mathbf{M}$ into $\mathbf{L}$ and multiplying the result by $\mathbf{L}^T$ gives

$$\begin{aligned} \mathbf{L}^T\mathbf{ML} &= \begin{bmatrix} 1/\sqrt{2} & 1/\sqrt{2} \\ -1/\sqrt{2} & 1/\sqrt{2} \end{bmatrix} \begin{bmatrix} 5 & 2 \\ 2 & 5 \end{bmatrix} \begin{bmatrix} 1/\sqrt{2} & -1/\sqrt{2} \\ 1/\sqrt{2} & 1/\sqrt{2} \end{bmatrix} \\ &= \begin{bmatrix} 1/\sqrt{2} & 1/\sqrt{2} \\ -1/\sqrt{2} & 1/\sqrt{2} \end{bmatrix} \begin{bmatrix} 7/\sqrt{2} & -3/\sqrt{2} \\ 7/\sqrt{2} & 3/\sqrt{2} \end{bmatrix} \\ &= \begin{bmatrix} 7 & 0 \\ 0 & 3 \end{bmatrix} = \mathbf{D} \end{aligned}$$

where the diagonal elements of $\mathbf{D}$ are the characteristic values of $\mathbf{M}$.

An important consequence of Theorem 16.3 is the following.

Theorem 16.4 Let $\mathbf{M}$ be an $n \times n$ symmetric matrix and let $\mathbf{x}$ be an arbitrary n-element column vector; then there exists an $n \times n$ matrix $\mathbf{J}$ such that the vector

$$\mathbf{z} = \mathbf{Jx}$$

satisfies the equation

$$\mathbf{x}^T\mathbf{Mx} = \mathbf{z}^T\mathbf{Dz}$$

where $\mathbf{D}$ is a diagonal matrix in which the diagonal elements are the characteristic values of $\mathbf{M}$.

PROOF The proof is elementary. We know from Theorem 16.3 that if $\mathbf{M}$ is symmetric then there is a matrix $\mathbf{L}$ such that

$$\mathbf{L}^T\mathbf{ML} = \mathbf{D}$$

Substituting for $\mathbf{D}$ in the expression $\mathbf{z}^T\mathbf{Dz}$ gives

$$\mathbf{z}^T\mathbf{Dz} = \mathbf{z}^T\mathbf{L}^T\mathbf{MLz}$$

and since $\mathbf{z}^T\mathbf{L}^T = (\mathbf{Lz})^T$ this can be written

$$\mathbf{z}^T\mathbf{Dz} = (\mathbf{Lz})^T\mathbf{M}(\mathbf{Lz})$$

If we set $\mathbf{x} = \mathbf{Lz}$ then we get

$$\mathbf{z}^T\mathbf{Dz} = \mathbf{x}^T\mathbf{Mx}$$

The transformation $\mathbf{x} = \mathbf{Lz}$ can be written in the form $\mathbf{z} = \mathbf{Jx}$ setting $\mathbf{J} = \mathbf{L}^T$ and recalling that $\mathbf{L}^T = \mathbf{L}^{-1}$ so that $\mathbf{z} = \mathbf{L}^{-1}\mathbf{x} = \mathbf{L}^T\mathbf{x} = \mathbf{Jx}$.

Finally, we state an important consequence of Theorem 16.4.

Theorem 16.5 Let $\mathbf{M}$ be an $n \times n$ symmetric matrix, and let $\mathbf{x}$ be an n-element column vector. The only restriction placed on $\mathbf{x}$ is that it is not equal to the null vector. The quantity $\mathbf{x}^T\mathbf{Mx}$ is positive (negative) whatever the vector $\mathbf{x}$ if and only if all the characteristic values of $\mathbf{M}$ are positive (negative).

PROOF Firstly, note that $\mathbf{x}^T\mathbf{Mx}$ is necessarily a 1×1 matrix and hence may be regarded as a real numbered quantity. From Theorem 16.4 the quantity $\mathbf{x}^T\mathbf{Mx}$ may be written in the form $\mathbf{z}^T\mathbf{Dz}$ where $\mathbf{z}$ is an n-element column vector and $\mathbf{D}$ is a diagonal matrix whose diagonal elements are the characteristic values of $\mathbf{M}$. Now

$$\mathbf{x}^T\mathbf{Mx} = \mathbf{z}^T\mathbf{Dz} = [Z_1\, Z_2 \cdots Z_n] \begin{bmatrix} h_1 & & & 0 \\ & h_2 & & \\ & & \ddots & \\ 0 & & & h_n \end{bmatrix} \begin{bmatrix} Z_1 \\ Z_2 \\ \vdots \\ Z_n \end{bmatrix}$$

$$= h_1Z_1^2 + h_2Z_2^2 + \cdots + h_nZ_n^2$$

$$= \sum_{i=1}^{n} h_iZ_i^2$$

The elements Z_i are real numbers and not all of them are zero. Since $Z_i^2 \geqslant 0$ for all i and $Z_i^2 > 0$ for some i it follows that if all the characteristic values h_i are positive then $\sum_{i=1}^n h_iZ_i^2$ is positive and so $\mathbf{x}^T\mathbf{Mx}$ is positive for any vector $\mathbf{x}$. If, however, one of the characteristic values is either zero or negative then it is possible that $\sum_{i=1}^n h_iZ_i^2$ is either zero or negative and in this case we cannot be sure that $\mathbf{x}^T\mathbf{Mx}$ is positive for an arbitrary vector $\mathbf{x}$. This proves both the necessity and the sufficiency of the characteristic values being positive. Similarly, if all characteristic values h_i are negative then $\sum_{i=1}^n h_iZ_i^2$ is negative (since each term in the sum is a negative quantity multiplied into a positive or zero quantity) and so $\mathbf{x}^T\mathbf{Mx}$ is negative for any vector $\mathbf{x}$. However, if one of the characteristic vectors is either zero or positive, it is possible that $\sum_{i=1}^n h_iZ_i^2$ is either zero or positive and hence we cannot be sure that $\mathbf{x}^T\mathbf{Mx}$ is negative for an arbitrary vector $\mathbf{x}$. This proves the necessity and sufficiency of the characteristic values being negative.

Example Given the symmetric matrix

$$\mathbf{M} = \begin{bmatrix} 5 & \sqrt{2} \\ \sqrt{2} & 6 \end{bmatrix}$$

and an arbitrary 2-element vector $\mathbf{x} \neq \mathbf{0}$, show that $\mathbf{x}^T\mathbf{Mx} > 0$.

The characteristic values of $\mathbf{M}$ are $h_1 = 7, h_2 = 4$. Since $h_1, h_2 > 0$ it follows from the theorem that $\mathbf{x}^T\mathbf{Mx} > 0$ for any $\mathbf{x} \neq \mathbf{0}$.

16.5 Quadratic forms

A quadratic form in the variables $X_1, X_2, \ldots, X_2$ is a quantity which can be written in the form

$$(1) \qquad \begin{aligned} V = c_{11}X_1^2 + c_{12}X_1X_2 + \cdots & & + c_{1n}X_1X_n \\ c_{22}X_2^2 \quad + \cdots & & + c_{2n}X_2X_n \\ \ddots & & \vdots \\ & + c_{n-1\,n-1}X_{n-1}^2 & + c_{n-1\,n}X_{n-1}X_n \\ & & + c_{nn}X_n^2 \end{aligned}$$

where the c_{ij} $(i = 1, \ldots, n; j \geqslant i)$ are constants. A quadratic form in n variables contains only terms which are squares or crossproducts of the variables.

It is possible to establish a correspondence between a quadratic form and a symmetric matrix. Consider the matrix

$$(2) \quad \mathbf{M} = \begin{bmatrix} c_{11} & c_{12}/2 & \cdots & c_{1n}/2 \\ c_{12}/2 & c_{22} & \ddots & \vdots \\ \vdots & \ddots & \ddots & c_{n-1\,n}/2 \\ c_{1n}/2 & \cdots & c_{n-1\,n}/2 & c_{nn} \end{bmatrix}$$

in which the ith diagonal element is equal to the constant c_{ii} and the above-diagonal element in the ith row and the jth column is equal to $c_{ij}/2$, the below-diagonal elements being determined by the symmetry condition. It is easy to see that the symmetric matrix $\mathbf{M}$ is uniquely determined by the constants in the quadratic form.

If $\mathbf{x}$ is the n-element column vector

$$\mathbf{x} = \begin{bmatrix} X_1 \\ X_2 \\ \vdots \\ X_n \end{bmatrix}$$

then (1) may be written

$$(3) \qquad V = \mathbf{x}^T\mathbf{M}\mathbf{x}$$

where $\mathbf{M}$ is given by (2). This result can be verified by multiplying out the right-hand side of (3) and pairing off the corresponding terms.

Example Write the following quadratic form in matrix notation:

$$V = X_1^2 + 3X_1X_2 + 3X_2^2$$

Form the matrix

$$\mathbf{M} = \begin{bmatrix} 1 & \frac{3}{2} \\ \frac{3}{2} & 3 \end{bmatrix}$$

and the vector

$$\mathbf{x} = \begin{bmatrix} X_1 \\ X_2 \end{bmatrix} \quad \text{and set} \quad V = \mathbf{x}^T\mathbf{M}\mathbf{x}$$

To verify the result multiply out the expression

$$\begin{aligned}
\mathbf{x}^T\mathbf{M}\mathbf{x} &= [X_1 \quad X_2] \begin{bmatrix} 1 & \frac{3}{2} \\ \frac{3}{2} & 3 \end{bmatrix} \begin{bmatrix} X_1 \\ X_2 \end{bmatrix} \\
&= [X_1 \quad X_2] \begin{bmatrix} X_1 + (\frac{3}{2})X_2 \\ (\frac{3}{2})X_1 + 3X_2 \end{bmatrix} \\
&= X_1[X_1 + (\tfrac{3}{2})X_2] + X_2[(\tfrac{3}{2})X_1 + 3X_2] \\
&= X_1^2 + (\tfrac{3}{2})X_1X_2 + (\tfrac{3}{2})X_1X_2 + 3X_2^2
\end{aligned}$$

Grouping terms in X_1X_2 gives

$$\mathbf{x}^T\mathbf{M}\mathbf{x} = X_1^2 + 3X_1X_2 + 3X_2^2$$

It is often useful to determine whether the sign of a quadratic form V is independent of the values of the variables $X_1, X_2, \ldots, X_n$. However, we are not usually interested in the trivial case in which all the variables are equal to zero (and in which V is therefore equal to zero). We specifically exclude this case from the discussion.

Definition If a quadratic form is positive for all values of the variables (except in the case where all the variables are equal to zero) it is said to be *positive definite*; if it is negative for all values of the variables (provided not all the variables are zero) it is said to be *negative definite*. If a quadratic form is either positive or zero for all the values of the variables, and it is zero at least once when not all the variables are zero, it is said to be *positive semi-definite*; if it is either negative or zero for all values of the variables, and it is zero at least once when not all the variables are zero, it is said to be *negative semi-definite*.[1]

Formally, a quadratic form $V = \mathbf{x}^T\mathbf{M}\mathbf{x}$ is

(i) positive definite if $\mathbf{x}^T\mathbf{M}\mathbf{x} > 0$ for any non-null vector $\mathbf{x} \neq 0$;
(ii) negative definite if $\mathbf{x}^T\mathbf{M}\mathbf{x} < 0$ for any non-null vector $\mathbf{x} \neq 0$;
(iii) positive semi-definite if $\mathbf{x}^T\mathbf{M}\mathbf{x} \geqslant 0$ and there is at least one non-null vector, $\mathbf{x} \neq 0$, such that $\mathbf{x}^T\mathbf{M}\mathbf{x} = 0$;
(iv) negative semi-definite if $\mathbf{x}^T\mathbf{M}\mathbf{x} \leqslant 0$ and there is at least one non-null vector, $\mathbf{x} \neq 0$, such that $\mathbf{x}^T\mathbf{M}\mathbf{x} = 0$

The following result is an immediate consequence of the results on the diagonalization of symmetric matrices given in the previous section.

1 The reader is warned that the definition of semi-definite forms is not standard; different authors use different definitions.

Theorem 16.6 Let $\mathbf{M}$ be an $n \times n$ symmetric matrix and let $\mathbf{x}$ be an n-element column vector. A necessary and sufficient condition that the quadratic form $V = \mathbf{x}^T\mathbf{M}\mathbf{x}$ is

(i) positive definite is that all the characteristic values of $\mathbf{M}$ are positive;
(ii) negative definite is that all the characteristic values of $\mathbf{M}$ are negative;
(iii) positive semi-definite is that all the characteristic values of $\mathbf{M}$ are non-negative and at least one is equal to zero;
(iv) negative semi-definite is that all the characteristic values of $\mathbf{M}$ are nonpositive and at least one is equal to zero.

PROOF Parts (i) and (ii) of the theorem are simply a restatement of Theorem 16.5. To prove parts (iii) and (iv) it is sufficient to show that if a characteristic value is zero $\mathbf{x}^T\mathbf{M}\mathbf{x} = 0$ for some non-null vector $\mathbf{x} \neq 0$. Now if a characteristic value is zero, say $h_n = 0$, there is a corresponding characteristic vector $\mathbf{u}_n$ such that $\mathbf{M}\mathbf{u}_n = h_n\mathbf{u}_n = \mathbf{0}$ where $\mathbf{0}$ denotes the null vector. Since $\mathbf{M}\mathbf{u}_n = \mathbf{0}$ it follows that $\mathbf{u}_n^T\mathbf{M}\mathbf{u}_n = 0$. By definition a characteristic vector is non-null, so that there exists a non-null vector $\mathbf{x} = \mathbf{u}_n \neq \mathbf{0}$ such that $\mathbf{x}^T\mathbf{M}\mathbf{x} = 0$.

Theorem 16.6 indicates that the signs of the characteristic values of a symmetric matrix reflect important properties of the quadratic forms with which the matrix is associated. Fortunately, there are simple criteria for determining whether all the characteristic values of a symmetric matrix are either positive, negative, non-negative or nonpositive. These criteria concern the leading principal minors of the symmetric matrix (see Section 12.9). Because of the correspondence established in Theorem 16.6 between the properties of the characteristic values of $\mathbf{M}$ and the properties of the quadratic form $V = \mathbf{x}^T\mathbf{M}\mathbf{x}$, the criteria are immediately applicable to a determination of the properties of a quadratic form. It is in this context that we state them.

Theorem 16.7 A necessary and sufficient condition for the quadratic form $V = \mathbf{x}^T\mathbf{M}\mathbf{x}$ to be

(i) positive definite is that all the leading principal minors of M are positive,

$$\mathbf{M}_{(1)} > 0, \mathbf{M}_{(2)} > 0, \ldots, \mathbf{M}_{(n)} > 0;$$

(ii) negative definite is that the leading principal minors of M alternate in sign (beginning with a negative sign),

$$\mathbf{M}_{(1)} < 0, \mathbf{M}_{(2)} > 0, \ldots, (-1)^n\mathbf{M}_{(n)} > 0;$$

(iii) positive semi-definite is that the determinant of M is zero and the other leading principal minors of M are non-negative,

$$\mathbf{M}_{(1)} \geqslant 0, \mathbf{M}_{(2)} \geqslant 0, \ldots, \mathbf{M}_{(n-1)} \geqslant 0, \mathbf{M}_{(n)} = 0;$$

(iv) negative semi-definite is that the determinant of $\mathbf{M}$ is zero and the other leading principal minors of $\mathbf{M}$ are alternately nonpositive and non-negative (the first being nonpositive),

$$\mathbf{M}_{(1)} \leqslant 0, \mathbf{M}_{(2)} \geqslant 0, \ldots, (-1)^{n-1}\mathbf{M}_{(n-1)} \geqslant 0, \mathbf{M}_{(n)} = 0$$

Example Show that the quadratic form $V = X_1^2 + 3X_1X_2 + 3X_2^2$ is positive definite (i.e. show that for any $X_1, X_2 \neq 0$, $X_1^2 + 3X_1X_2 + 3X_2^2 > 0$).

We can write V in the form $V = \mathbf{x}^T\mathbf{M}\mathbf{x}$ where

$$\mathbf{x} = \begin{bmatrix} X_1 \\ X_2 \end{bmatrix} \quad \text{and} \quad \mathbf{M} = \begin{bmatrix} 1 & \frac{3}{2} \\ \frac{3}{2} & 3 \end{bmatrix}$$

The leading principal minors of $\mathbf{M}$ are

$$\mathbf{M}_{(1)} = \det [1] = 1$$

$$\mathbf{M}_{(2)} = \det \begin{bmatrix} 1 & \frac{3}{2} \\ \frac{3}{2} & 3 \end{bmatrix} = \frac{3}{4}$$

Since $\mathbf{M}_{(1)} > 0$, $\mathbf{M}_{(2)} > 0$ all the leading principal minors of $\mathbf{M}$ are positive and so the quadratic form V is positive definite.

Because of the correspondence between symmetric matrices and quadratic forms, a symmetric matrix is often referred to in terms of the type of quadratic form to which it corresponds, e.g. a symmetric matrix associated with a positive definite quadratic form is sometimes known as a 'positive definite matrix'. A symmetric matrix which does not fall into a definite category is known as an 'indefinite matrix'.

16.6 Necessary and sufficient conditions for maxima and minima of a function of several variables

The elements of the theory of quadratic forms have been reviewed in the previous section; in this section we describe an important application of the theory. The properties of a quadratic form are referred to, implicitly, when stating a condition for a function of several variables to have a maximum (or a minimum). Recall from Section 6.9 that the function of several variables $y = f(x_1, x_2, \ldots, x_n)$ is at a maximum if and only if the second derivative of $f(x_1 + k\Delta x_1, x_2 + k\Delta x_2, \ldots, x_n + k\Delta x_n)$ with respect to k is negative whatever the values of $\Delta x_1, \Delta x_2, \ldots, \Delta x_n$ and that $y = f(x_1, x_2, \ldots, x_n)$ is at a minimum if and only if this second derivative is positive whatever the values of $\Delta x_1, \Delta x_2, \ldots, \Delta x_n$. It was shown in Section 6.9. that the second derivative of $f(x_1 + k\Delta x_1, x_2 + k\Delta x_2, \cdots, x_n + k\Delta x_n)$ is equal to

$$\begin{aligned}
&\frac{\partial^2 y}{\partial x_1^2}\Delta x_1^2 + \frac{\partial^2 y}{\partial x_1\,\partial x_2}\Delta x_1\,\Delta x_2 + \cdots + \frac{\partial^2 y}{\partial x_1\,\partial x_n}\Delta x_1\,\Delta x_n \\
&+ \frac{\partial^2 y}{\partial x_2\,\partial x_1}\Delta x_2\,\Delta x_1 + \frac{\partial^2 y}{\partial x_2^2}\Delta x_2^2 + \cdots + \frac{\partial^2 y}{\partial x_2\,\partial x_n}\Delta x_2\,\Delta x_n \\
&+ \cdots \\
&\quad \vdots \qquad\qquad \vdots \qquad\qquad \vdots \\
&+ \cdots \\
&+ \frac{\partial^2 y}{\partial x_n\,\partial x_1}\Delta x_n\,\Delta x_1 + \frac{\partial^2 y}{\partial x_n\,\partial x_2}\Delta x_n\,\Delta x_2 + \cdots + \frac{\partial^2 y}{\partial x_n^2}\Delta x_n^2
\end{aligned}$$

This is a quadratic form in the variables $\Delta x_1, \Delta x_2, \ldots, \Delta x_n$ and may be written in matrix notation as

$$\mathbf{x}^T \mathbf{M} \mathbf{x}$$

where $\mathbf{x}$ is the n-element column vector

$$\mathbf{x} = \begin{bmatrix} \Delta x_1 \\ \Delta x_2 \\ \vdots \\ \Delta x_n \end{bmatrix}$$

and $\mathbf{M}$ is an $n \times n$ matrix of the second partial derivatives of the function $y = f(x_1, x_2, \ldots, x_n)$,

$$\mathbf{M} = \begin{bmatrix} \dfrac{\partial^2 y}{\partial x_1^2} & \dfrac{\partial^2 y}{\partial x_1 \, \partial x_2} & \cdots & \dfrac{\partial^2 y}{\partial x_1 \, \partial x_n} \\ \dfrac{\partial^2 y}{\partial x_2 \, \partial x_1} & \dfrac{\partial^2 y}{\partial x_2^2} & \cdots & \dfrac{\partial^2 y}{\partial x_2 \, \partial x_n} \\ \vdots & \vdots & \ddots & \vdots \\ \dfrac{\partial^2 y}{\partial x_n \, \partial x_1} & \dfrac{\partial^2 y}{\partial x_n \, \partial x_2} & \cdots & \dfrac{\partial^2 y}{\partial x_n^2} \end{bmatrix}$$

The matrix $\mathbf{M}$ is the *Hessian matrix* of the function y. Since $\partial^2 y/\partial x_i \, \partial x_j = \partial^2 y/\partial x_j \, \partial x_i$ $(i, j = 1, 2, \ldots, n)$ the matrix $\mathbf{M}$ is symmetric.

The condition for a maximum of y is that this quadratic form in the variables $\Delta x_1, \Delta x_2, \ldots, \Delta x_n$ must be negative whatever the values of $\Delta x_1, \Delta x_2, \ldots, \Delta x_n$, i.e. the condition for a maximum is that the quadratic form $\mathbf{x}^T \mathbf{M} \mathbf{x}$ is negative definite. The condition for a minimum of y is that the quadratic form must be positive independently of the values of $\Delta x_1, \Delta x_2, \ldots, \Delta x_n$ i.e. the condition for a minimum is that $\mathbf{x}^T \mathbf{M} \mathbf{x}$ is positive definite. Necessary and sufficient conditions for a maximum and minimum can be obtained from Theorem 16.7: it is an immediate consequence of this theorem that the function y is at a maximum if and only if the leading principal minors of the Hessian matrix of y are alternately negative and positive (the first principal minor being negative, the second positive, and so on) and y is at a minimum if and only if all the principal minors of the Hessian matrix of y are positive. These conditions have been summarized in Section 6.9 and they are spelt out in detail below.

Theorem 16.8 The function $y = f(x_1, x_2, \ldots, x_n)$ is at a maximum if and only if

$$\det \, [\partial^2 y/\partial x_1^2] < 0$$

$$\det \begin{bmatrix} \dfrac{\partial^2 y}{\partial x_1^2} & \dfrac{\partial^2 y}{\partial x_1\, \partial x_2} \\ \dfrac{\partial^2 y}{\partial x_2\, \partial x_1} & \dfrac{\partial^2 y}{\partial x_2^2} \end{bmatrix} > 0$$

$$\vdots$$

$$(-1)^n \det \begin{bmatrix} \dfrac{\partial^2 y}{\partial x_1^2} & \dfrac{\partial^2 y}{\partial x_1\, \partial x_2} & \cdots & \dfrac{\partial^2 y}{\partial x_1\, \partial x_n} \\ \dfrac{\partial^2 y}{\partial x_n\, \partial x_2} & \dfrac{\partial^2 y}{\partial x_2^2} & \cdots & \dfrac{\partial^2 y}{\partial x_2\, \partial x_n} \\ \vdots & \vdots & \ddots & \vdots \\ \dfrac{\partial^2 y}{\partial x_n\, \partial x_1} & \dfrac{\partial^2 y}{\partial x_n\, \partial x_2} & \cdots & \dfrac{\partial^2 y}{\partial x_n^2} \end{bmatrix} > 0$$

The function y is at a minimum if and only if

$$\det\, [\partial^2 y/\partial x_1] > 0$$

$$\det \begin{bmatrix} \dfrac{\partial^2 y}{\partial x_1^2} & \dfrac{\partial^2 y}{\partial x_1\, \partial x_2} \\ \dfrac{\partial^2 y}{\partial x_2\, \partial x_1} & \dfrac{\partial^2 y}{\partial x_2^2} \end{bmatrix} > 0$$

$$\vdots$$

$$\det \begin{bmatrix} \dfrac{\partial^2 y}{\partial x_1^n} & \dfrac{\partial^2 y}{\partial x_1\, \partial x_2} & \cdots & \dfrac{\partial^2 y}{\partial x_1\, \partial x_n} \\ \dfrac{\partial^2 y}{\partial x_2\, \partial x_1} & \dfrac{\partial^2 y}{\partial x_2^2} & \cdots & \dfrac{\partial^2 y}{\partial x_2\, \partial x_n} \\ \vdots & \vdots & \ddots & \vdots \\ \dfrac{\partial^2 y}{\partial x_n\, \partial x_1} & \dfrac{\partial^2 y}{\partial x_n\, \partial x_2} & \cdots & \dfrac{\partial^2 y}{\partial x_n^2} \end{bmatrix} > 0$$

No special significance attaches to the labelling of the variables. The conditions still apply if the subscripts are interchanged.

An example of the use of these conditions is given at the end of Section 6.9.

Notes and references

Symmetric matrices are important in statistics and econometrics, where they appear as covariance matrices, dispersion matrices and moment matrices. The special properties of symmetric matrices are used to derive statistical tests of hypotheses—see Johnston,[66] and Wonnacott and Wonnacott.[124] For further developments of the 'second order' conditions for maxima and minima see Henderson and Quandt[56] and Samuelson.[112]

Problems

16.1 Verify Theorem 16.1 for each of the following matrices:

$$\mathbf{A} = \begin{bmatrix} 3 & 2 \\ 2 & 6 \end{bmatrix}, \quad \mathbf{B} = \begin{bmatrix} 1 & 0 \\ 0 & 1 \end{bmatrix}, \quad \mathbf{C} = \begin{bmatrix} 5 & 0 & 0 \\ 0 & 3 & 2 \\ 0 & 2 & 6 \end{bmatrix}$$

16.2.1 Which of the following vectors are orthogonal to one another?

$$\mathbf{a} = \begin{bmatrix} 1 \\ 1 \end{bmatrix}, \quad \mathbf{b} = \begin{bmatrix} 1 \\ -1 \end{bmatrix}, \quad \mathbf{c} = \begin{bmatrix} 2 \\ 0 \end{bmatrix}$$

16.2.2 Find the normalized characteristic vectors of the matrix

$$\mathbf{M} = \begin{bmatrix} 4 & \sqrt{2} \\ \sqrt{2} & 2 \end{bmatrix}$$

16.4 Verify Theorem 16.3 for the three matrices in Problem 16.1.

16.5 Classify each of the following matrices as either (i) positive definite, (ii) positive semidefinite, (iii) negative definite, (iv) negative semidefinite or (v) indefinite.

$$\mathbf{A} = \begin{bmatrix} 5 & 1 & 3 \\ 1 & 8 & 1 \\ 3 & 1 & 9 \end{bmatrix} \quad \mathbf{B} = \begin{bmatrix} 6 & 1 & 7 \\ 1 & 1 & 2 \\ 7 & 2 & 1 \end{bmatrix} \quad \mathbf{C} = \begin{bmatrix} -3 & 5 & 2 \\ 5 & -9 & 6 \\ 2 & 6 & -5 \end{bmatrix}$$

16.6 Locate the maxima and minima of $y = 3x_1^2 - 6x_1x_2 + 4x_2^2 - 8x_1$.

Part 4

Difference and differential equations

Chapter 17

Difference and differential equations of the first order

17.1 Differences

Consider a variable $Y(t)$ which takes on different values for different t. Suppose that t varies over the integers $\ldots -2, -1, 0, 1, 2, \ldots$. The *first difference* of $Y(t)$ is the difference between successive values of $Y(t)$; in conventional notation

$$\Delta Y(t) = Y(t+1) - Y(t)$$

The *second* difference is the difference between successive first differences,

$$\begin{aligned} \Delta^2 Y(t) &= \Delta Y(t+1) - \Delta Y(t) \\ &= [Y(t+2) - Y(t+1)] - [Y(t+1) - Y(t)] \\ &= Y(t+2) - 2Y(t+1) + Y(t) \end{aligned}$$

The *third* difference is the difference between successive second differences,

$$\begin{aligned} \Delta^3 Y(t) &= \Delta^2 Y(t+1) - \Delta^2 Y(t) \\ &= \Delta Y(t+2) - 2\Delta Y(t+1) + \Delta Y(t) \\ &= Y(t+3) - 3Y(t+2) + 3Y(t+1) - Y(t) \end{aligned}$$

In general, the nth difference is the difference between successive $(n-1)$th differences,

$$\Delta^n Y(t) = \Delta^{n-1} Y(t+1) - \Delta_{n-1} Y(t)$$

Elementary algebra shows that

$$\begin{aligned} (1) \qquad \Delta^n Y(t) &= Y(t+n) - n!\,Y(t+n-1) + \frac{n!}{2!(n-2)!} Y(t+n-2) \\ &\quad \cdots + (-1)^{n-2} \frac{n!}{(n-2)!2!} Y(t+2) + (-1)^{n-1} n!\,Y(t+1) \\ &\quad + (-1)^n Y(t) \\ &= \sum_{i=0}^{n} (-1)^{n-i} \frac{n!}{i!(n-i)!} Y(t+i) \end{aligned}$$

where $n!$ denotes factorial n,

$$n! = \begin{cases} n \times (n-1) \times (n-2) \times \cdots \times 2 \times 1 & (n > 0) \\ 1 & (n = 0) \end{cases}$$

The coefficients in equation (1) can be determined by using Pascal's triangle, which is illustrated in Table 17.1.

$Y(t)$	1					
$\Delta Y(t)$	1	1				
$\Delta^2 Y(t)$	1	2	1			
$\Delta^3 Y(t)$	1	3	3	1		
$\Delta^4 Y(t)$	1	4	6	4	1	
$\Delta^5 Y(t)$	1	5	10	10	5	1
	$+Y(t+5)$	$-Y(t+4)$	$+Y(t+3)$	$-Y(t+2)$	$+Y(t+1)$	$-Y(t)$

NOTE Each coefficient in the triangle is the sum of two coefficients in the previous line, the coefficient directly above and the coefficient above and to the left. Only six lines of the table are shown; further lines can be added indefinitely by using this formula. To evaluate, say, $\Delta^4 Y(t)$, write the relevant entry in the left-hand column and pair off each coefficient in the same row of the table with the corresponding term at the bottom of the table. Multiply together each coefficient and its corresponding term and sum the resulting products. This gives, for example,
$\Delta^4 Y(t) = Y(t) - 4Y(t-1) + 6Y(t-2) - 4Y(t-3) + Y(t-4)$.

Table 17.1 Pascal's triangle, for use in evaluating high-order differences

17.2 Difference equations

A difference equation is an equation relating differences. The general form of a difference equation is

(2) $$f(Y(t), \Delta Y(t), \ldots, \Delta^n Y(t)) = g(t)$$

Usually $g(t)$ is a known function of t and the problem is to solve for $Y(t)$.

The *order* of a difference equation is the highest index associated with the differences, i.e. an equation containing differences up to and including the nth difference, but no higher, is an equation of the nth order. For example,

$$\Delta^3 Y(t) - \Delta Y(t) = g(t)$$

and

$$2\Delta^3 Y(t) + 3\Delta^2 Y(t) - Y(t) = g(t)$$

are both difference equations of the third order.

A difference equation is said to be *homogeneous* if only terms in $Y(t)$ and its successive differences appear. The general form of a homogeneous difference equation is obtained by setting $g(t) = 0$ in equation (2):

(3) $$f(Y(t), \Delta Y(t), \ldots, \Delta^n Y(t)) = 0$$

An equation which is linear in $Y(t)$ and its differences is known as a *linear difference equation*. The general form of a linear difference equation is

$$\Delta^n Y(t) + a_1(t)\,\Delta^{n-1} Y(t) + \cdots + a_{n-1}(t)\,\Delta Y(t) + a_n(t) Y(t) = g(t)$$

In this book we shall be concerned only with *linear difference equations with constant coefficients*, of which the general form is

(4) $$\Delta^n Y(t) + a_1\,\Delta^{n-1} Y(t) + \cdots + a_{n-1}\,\Delta Y(t) + a_n Y(t) = g(t)$$

17.3 Simple and compound growth

The simplest form of difference equation is the linear difference equation of the first order

(5) $$\Delta Y(t) + a_1 Y(t) = g(t)$$

Equation (5) is obtained by setting $n = 1$ in equation (4). There are two important special cases of (5). One is when $a_1 = 0$ and $g(t)$ is a constant, which is the case of *simple growth*; the other is when $a_1 \neq 0$ and $g(t) = 0$, which is the case of *compound growth*.

Simple growth

The equation of simple growth is most conveniently written

(6) $$\Delta Y(t) = b$$

To solve (6), note that by definition $\Delta Y(t) = Y(t+1) - Y(t)$ so that we have $Y(t+1) - Y(t) = b$ or, adding $Y(t)$ to both sides,

(7) $$Y(t+1) = Y(t) + b$$

Setting $t = 0, 1, 2, \ldots, N-1$ successively in equation (7) shows that the solution of (6) is

(8) $$Y(N) = Y(0) + bN$$

Equation (8) describes the time path of a quantity under conditions of simple growth. $Y(N)$ is a linear function of N with gradient b and intercept $Y(0)$. It follows that if a quantity Y grows in a simple fashion then it is a linear function of time.

Example 1 Suppose that total passenger miles travelled on British Rail increase by 0·2 million each year. If total passenger miles travelled this year is 30 million, what will be the total 15 years hence?

Let t be the index of the years, with $t = 0$ indicating the present.

The equation of growth is

$$\Delta Y(t) = 0{\cdot}2$$

and the solution is

$$Y(N) = Y(0) + 0{\cdot}2N$$

Setting $N = 15$ and $Y(0) = 30$ gives

$$Y(15) = 30 + 0{\cdot}2 \times 15$$
$$= 33$$

We conclude that 15 years hence total passenger miles travelled on British Rail will be 33 million.

Example 2 Suppose that the maximum possible output of an economy is directly proportional to the size of its capital stock. Technological factors determine the ratio of the capital stock to output to be a constant v; v is known as the 'capital–output' ratio. Suppose that aggregate investment[1] in the economy each year is equal to £I million. By how much can output increase after N years?

Let $K(t)$ denote the capital stock at the beginning of year t, and $Y(t)$ denote the maximum attainable output that year. Technological factors determine that

(9) $$K(t) = vY(t)$$

Let $I(t)$ denote investment during year t. Since investment is a measure of the change in the capital stock

(10) $$I(t) = \Delta K(t)$$

Now it follows from equation (9) that

(11) $$\begin{aligned}\Delta K(t) &= K(t+1) - K(t) = vY(t+1) - vY(t)\\ &= v[Y(t+1) - Y(t)] = v\,\Delta Y(t)\end{aligned}$$

Substituting (11) on the right-hand side of (10) and applying $I(t) = I$ to the left-hand side gives

(12) $$I = v\,\Delta Y(t)$$

Dividing both sides of (12) by v gives

(13) $$\Delta Y(t) = I/v$$

The solution of (13) is

(14) $$Y(N) = Y(0) + NI/v$$

We conclude from (14) that after N years output can increase by £NI/v million.

1 It is assumed that capital equipment lasts for ever so that there is no depreciation: it follows that there is no need to distinguish between gross investment and net investment.

Compound growth

The equation of compound growth is most conveniently written

$$(15)\qquad \Delta Y(t) = rY(t)$$

To solve (15) note that by definition $\Delta Y(t) = Y(t+1) - Y(t)$ so that we have $Y(t+1) - Y(t) = rY(t)$ or, adding $Y(t)$ to both sides,

$$(16)\qquad Y(t+1) = (1+r)Y(t)$$

Substituting successively $t = 0, 1, 2, \ldots, N-1$ into (16) shows that

$$(17)\qquad Y(N) = (1+r)^N Y(0)$$

Equation (17) describes the time path of a quantity under conditions of compound growth.

When evaluating quantities of the form $(1+r)^N$ it is often convenient to use the binomial approximation.

Binomial approximation

When r and N are both small, a good approximation to $(1+r)^N$ is

$$1 + Nr$$

A better approximation is

$$1 + Nr + \frac{N!}{2!(N-2)!}r^2$$

Further approximations, each better than the last, are obtained by taking the first four, five, six, etc., terms in the expression

$$(18)\qquad 1 + Nr + \frac{N!}{2!(N-2)!}r^2 + \cdots + \frac{N!}{i!(N-i)!}r^i + \cdots$$

$$\cdots + \frac{N!}{(N-2)!2!}r^{N-2} + N!r^{N-1} + r^N$$

The coefficients in (18) may be obtained from the rows of Pascal's triangle, shown in Table 17.1. They are known as 'binomial coefficients'. The complete expression (18) is exactly equal to $(1+r)^N$, as the reader may verify by multiplying out $(1+r) \times \cdots \times (1+r)$ N times. The reason the approximations are satisfactory when r and N are small is that when r is small the higher powers of r, e.g. r^4, are negligible compared with the lower powers of r, e.g. r itself, and when N is small the number of neglected terms in (18)—and the binomial coefficients associated with them—are also small.

Example 3 A man invests £1,000 in an annuity and earns a rate of interest of 8% per annum. How much will his investment be worth in 5 years?

To begin with let us analyse this question as economists rather than as mathematicians. If a man invests £1,000 at 8% per annum then at the end of the first year he will have the right to the principal of £1,000 and will in addition receive an interest payment of £80. If the interest payment is added to the investment of £1,000 then the total amount invested during the second year will be £1,080. If £1,080 is invested at 8% per annum then at the end of the year the man will have the right to the £1,080 and he will receive an interest payment of £(0·08 × 1,080) = £86·4. The interest payment received in the second year is larger than the interest payment received in the first year because the amount invested in the second year is larger than the amount invested in the first year (this is the particular characteristic of compound growth which distinguishes it from simple growth). If this interest payment is added to the original investment then the amount invested for the third year is £1,166·4. Quite clearly, to calculate the value of the investment at the end of 5 years is going to be a laborious business (see Table 17.2).

Table 17.2

Year	*Value of the investment* (£)	*Interest payment* (£)
0	1,000	80
1	1,080	86·4
2	1,166·4	93·312
3	1,259·712	100·77696
4	1,360·48896	108·8391168
5	1,469·3280768	

The problem may be analysed mathematically as follows. Let $Y(t)$ be the value of the investment at the beginning of period t. The interest payment received at the end of period t is equal to $0{\cdot}08\,Y(t)$. Since this interest payment is added on to the principal it follows that

$$\Delta Y(t) = 0{\cdot}08\,Y(t)$$

The solution is

$$Y(N) = Y(0)(1 + 0{\cdot}08)^N$$

Since $Y(0) = 1{,}000$ and $N = 5$ we find that after five years

$$Y(5) = 1{,}000(1{\cdot}08)^5$$

Using the binomial approximation with $c = 0{\cdot}08$ and $N = 5$ we obtain the successive approximations

$$1{,}000(1 + 5 \times 0{\cdot}08) = 1{,}400$$

$$1{,}000\left[1{\cdot}4 + \frac{5}{2!3!}(0{\cdot}08)^2\right] = 1{,}464$$

$$1{,}000\left[1{\cdot}464 + \frac{5}{3!2!}(0{\cdot}08)^3\right] = 1{,}469{\cdot}12$$

$$1{,}000[1{\cdot}46912 + 5(0{\cdot}08)^4] = 1{,}469{\cdot}3248$$

The exact value is

$$1{,}000[1{\cdot}4693248 + (0{\cdot}08)^5] = 1{,}469{\cdot}3280768$$

It can be seen that the third approximation gives a reasonably accurate value for the investment after 5 years.

Example 4 A firm has assets of £20m which earn a rate of return of 15% per annum. As a matter of policy the firm distributes 60% of its profits as dividends or as interest payments and the remainder of the profits are retained and used to purchase new assets. By how much will (a) assets and (b) profits increase over a 10-year period?

Let the assets at the beginning of the year be $Y(t)$. Since the return on assets is 15% per annum, total profit during year t is $0{\cdot}15\,Y(t)$. Since 60% of profits are distributed, it follows that 40% are retained and invested. Consequently investment during year t is $0{\cdot}4(0{\cdot}15)\,Y(t) = 0{\cdot}06\,Y(t)$. Since investment is equal to the change in assets during the year,

$$\Delta Y(t) = 0{\cdot}06\,Y(t)$$

The solution is

$$Y(N) = (1{\cdot}06)^N\,Y(0)$$

Setting $Y(0) = 20$ and $N = 10$ shows that after 10 years the assets of the firm are

$$Y(10) = 20(1{\cdot}06)^{10}$$

Since the rate of return is 15%, profits after 10 years are equal to

$$0{\cdot}15\,Y(10) = 3(1{\cdot}06)^{10}$$

From the first three terms in the binomial expansion the increase in assets is approximately

$$20\left[1 + 10 \times 0{\cdot}06 + \frac{10!}{2!8!}(0{\cdot}06)^2\right] - 20$$

$$= 20(0{\cdot}762)$$

$$= 15{\cdot}24 \text{ (£m)}$$

The increase in profits is

$$0{\cdot}15 \times 15{\cdot}24 = 2{\cdot}286 \text{ (£m)}$$

17.4 Dynamic models and first-order linear difference equations

In Section 3.2 we developed two simple dynamic models: (i) a macroeconomic model in which income $Y(t)$ is determined by the previous period's income $Y(t - 1)$ and current investment $I(t)$,

(19) $$Y(t) = b + cY(t - 1) + I(t)$$

and (ii) a microeconomic model in which the price of frozen food $P(t)$ is determined by the previous period's price of frozen food $P(t-1)$ and consumer income $Y(t)$,

(20) $$P(t) = (c - a)/d - (b/d)P(t-1) + (e/d)Y(t-1)$$

Equations (19) and (20) can both be expressed as first-order linear difference equations. Substituting $t + 1$ for t in equation (19) gives

(21) $$Y(t+1) = b + cY(t) + I(t+1)$$

Subtracting $Y(t)$ from both sides of (21) gives

$$Y(t+1) - Y(t) = b + (c-1)Y(t) + I(t+1)$$

By using the notation $\Delta Y(t) = Y(t+1) - Y(t)$ we get

(22) $$\Delta Y(t) = b + (c-1)Y(t) + I(t+1)$$

Equation (22) is a special case of equation (5) with $a_1 = 1 - c$ and $g(t) = b + I(t+1)$. Similar reasoning shows that equation (20) can be put into the form

(23) $$\Delta P(t) = (c-a)/d - [1 + (b/d)]P(t) + (e/d)Y(t)$$

Equation (23) is obtained from equation (5) by setting $a_1 = 1 + (b/d)$ and $g(t) = (c-a)/d + (e/d)Y(t)$.

Theorem 17.1 The solution of the first-order difference equation

(24) $$\Delta Y(t) + a_1 Y(t) = g(t)$$

is

(25) $$Y(N) = \sum_{i=0}^{N-1} (1 - a_1)^i g(N-1-i) + (1-a_1)^N Y(0)$$

PROOF Equation (24) can be written in the form

$$Y(t+1) = (1-a_1)Y(t) + g(t)$$

Substituting successively $t = 1, 2, \ldots, N-1$ establishes (25).

Equation (25) shows that the time path of Y depends on the time path of g and also on the initial value $Y(0)$. However, if $-2 < a_1 < 0$ then $\lim_{N\to\infty} (1-a_1)^N = 0$ and so the effect of the initial value $Y(0)$ on the time path of Y dies out as time passes.

Example 5 Consider an economy in which investment grows by 5% per annum. The marginal propensity to consume is $c = 0{\cdot}84$. Exogenous consumer demand is $b = 32$ (£m). In 1972 investment is £40m and income is £200m. What will be the value of income (a) in 1982, (b) ultimately?

Since investment grows at 5% per annum

$$\Delta I(t) = 0{\cdot}05I(t)$$

and so

$$I(N) = (1{\cdot}05)^N I(0)$$

If 1972 is taken as the base year then $I(0) = 40$, so that

$$I(N) = 40(1{\cdot}05)^N$$

Since $b = 20$ and $c = 0{\cdot}84$ equation (22) becomes

(26) $$\Delta Y(t) = 32 - 0{\cdot}16Y(t) + 40(1{\cdot}05)^{t+1}$$

Comparing (26) with the general form (24) shows that $a_1 = 0{\cdot}16$ and $g(t) = 32 + 40(1{\cdot}05)^{t+1}$. Substituting these values into equation (25) and using the fact that $Y(0) = 200$ gives

$$Y(N) = \sum_{i=0}^{N-1} (0{\cdot}84)^i[32 + 40(1{\cdot}05)^{N-i}] + 200(0{\cdot}84)^N$$

Multiplying out the bracket gives

$$Y(N) = 32 \sum_{i=0}^{N-1} (0{\cdot}84)^i + 40(1{\cdot}05)^N \sum_{i=0}^{N-1} (0{\cdot}8)^i + 200(0{\cdot}84)^N$$

Using the formula for the sum of a geometric series,

$$\sum_{i=0}^{N-1} c^i = (1 - c^N)/(1 - c)$$

we get after simplifying

$$Y(N) = 200 + 200(1{\cdot}05)^N[1 - (0{\cdot}8)^N]$$
$$= 200[1 + (1{\cdot}05)^N - (0{\cdot}84)^N]$$

Using the first three terms of the binomial expansion shows that income in 1982 is approximately

$$200[1 + 1{\cdot}6125 + 0{\cdot}552] = 632{\cdot}9 \quad (\text{£m})$$

As N becomes large the term $(1{\cdot}05)^N$ becomes very large compared with the terms $(0{\cdot}84)^N$ and 1, so that

$$\lim_{N\to\infty} Y(N) = 200(1{\cdot}05)^N$$

where the limit is defined in a proportional, not absolute, sense. We conclude that ultimately income becomes indefinitely large and increases at 5% per annum, the same rate of increase as for investment.

17.5 Differential equations

A differential equation is an equation involving the derivatives of a function. The derivatives appearing in a differential equation have the same role as the differences in a difference equation. The general form of an nth order differential equation is

(27) $$f(Y(t), dY/dt, \ldots, d^nY/dt^n) = g(t)$$

where t varies continuously over some prescribed range of values. A differential equation is homogeneous if only terms in $Y(t)$ and its derivatives appear. The general form of a homogeneous differential equation is obtained by setting $g(t) = 0$ in equation (27). A *linear differential equation* of the nth order with constant coefficients has the form

(28) $$\frac{d^nY(t)}{dt^n} + a_1\frac{d^{n-1}Y(t)}{dt^{n-1}} + \cdots + a_{n-1}\frac{dY(t)}{dt} + a_nY(t) = g(t)$$

17.6 Continuous growth

The simplest form of differential equation is the linear differential equation of the first order

(29) $$\frac{dY(t)}{dt} + a_1Y(t) = g(t)$$

which is obtained by setting $n = 1$ in (28). There are two important special cases of (29). One is when $a_1 = 0$ and $g(t)$ is a constant, which is the case of *continuous simple growth*; the other is when $a_1 \neq 0$ and $g(t) = 0$, which is the case of *continuous compound growth.*

Continuous simple growth

The equation of continuous simple growth is

(30) $$dY(t)/dt = b$$

It is easily verified that the solution of (30) is

(31) $$Y(t) = Y(0) + bt$$

The proof is simply that only when $Y(t)$ is given by (31) does $dY(t)/dt = b$. The very close analogy between equation (8) and equation (31) should be evident. In both equations Y is a linear function of time; the only difference is that in equation (8) N is integer-valued, whereas in equation (31) t is a real number.

Example 6 The rate of output of a newly-commissioned oil refinery working round the clock is 20,000 gallons a day. How long will it take to build up stocks of oil equal to 125,000 gallons?

Let $Y(t)$ be the number of gallons of oil produced by time t after the commissioning of the refinery. Since the output of oil is continuous, the rate of output is measured by the derivative $dY(t)/dt$. If the rate of output is 20,000 gallons per day,

(32) $$dY(t)/dt = 20{,}000$$

The general solution of (32) is

(33) $Y(t) = Y(0) + 20{,}000t$

Since the oil refinery is commissioned at date 0, $Y(0) = 0$. Consequently the stock of oil will be 125,000 gallons when

$$125{,}000 = 20{,}000t$$

i.e. when

$$t = 125{,}000/20{,}000 = 6{\cdot}25$$

We conclude that the stock of oil will be 125,000 gallons after 6 days and 6 hours.

Continuous compound growth

The equation of continuous compound growth is

(34) $dY(t)/dt = rY(t)$

The discovery of the solution of equation (34) was one of the most important mathematical discoveries ever made; it is attributed to Sir Isaac Newton. The solution involves the exponential function, which is discussed in detail in the next chapter. If exp ( ) denotes the exponential function then the solution of (34) is

(35) $Y(t) = Y(0) \exp(rt)$

The following example illustrates the principle of continuous compound growth.

Example 7 In Example 3 a man invested £1,000 in an annuity and received an annual interest payment of 8% per annum. Show that if his interest is paid continuously instead of at discrete intervals the value of his investment increases exponentially.

Let $Y(t)$ be the value of the principal at date t. When payments were annual the equation of growth was

$$Y(t + 1) - Y(t) = 0{\cdot}08\,Y(t)$$

Suppose that instead of a payment of 8% every year he receives a payment of 4% every 6 months; the equation of growth becomes

$$Y(t + \tfrac{1}{2}) - Y(t) = [0{\cdot}08 \times \tfrac{1}{2}]\,Y(t)$$

If payments were 2% every 3 months then the equation of growth would be

$$Y(t + \tfrac{1}{4}) - Y(t) = [0{\cdot}08 \times \tfrac{1}{4}]\,Y(t)$$

In general, if payments are $0{\cdot}08\,\Delta t$% at intervals of Δt, the equation of growth is

$$Y(t + \Delta t) - Y(t) = [0{\cdot}08\,\Delta t]\,Y(t)$$

Dividing through by Δt gives

$$\frac{Y(t + \Delta t) - Y(t)}{\Delta t} = 0{\cdot}08\,Y(t)$$

Suppose now that the frequency of payments becomes so great that payment is effectively continuous; then the interval between payments, Δt, tends to zero and the equation of growth becomes

$$(36) \qquad \lim_{\Delta t \to 0} \frac{Y(t + \Delta t) - Y(t)}{\Delta t} = 0{\cdot}08\,Y(t)$$

But the left-hand side of (36) is just the derivative of Y with respect to t; consequently (36) may be written

$$(37) \qquad dY(t)/dt = 0{\cdot}08\,Y(t)$$

The solution of (37) is

$$(38) \qquad Y(t) = Y(0) \exp(0{\cdot}08t)$$

Consequently the value of the investment increases exponentially.

17.7 Dynamic models and first-order linear differential equations

In Section 17.4 we discussed two simple dynamic models which could be formulated as difference equations. Other dynamic models are most naturally formulated as differential equations (see the example below)

The general solution of the first-order linear differential equation

$$(39) \qquad dY(t)/dt + a_1 Y(t) = g(t)$$

is

$$(40) \qquad Y(t) = Y(0) \exp(-a_1 t) + \int_0^t \exp(a_1(T - t))g(T)\,dT$$

In the special case where $g(t)$ is constant, say $g(t) = b$, the solution (40) simplifies to

$$(41) \qquad Y(t) = [Y(0) - b/a_1] \exp(-a_1 t) + b/a_1$$

Example 8 Consider the determination of the wages of nonunion labour in, say, the construction industry. Theory suggests that the demand for labour at time t, $D(t)$, depends on the amount of work contracted for, $C(t)$,

$$D(t) = kC(t)$$

where k is a constant of proportionality. The supply of labour, $S(t)$, depends on the wage rate, $W(t)$,

$$S(t) = l + mW(t)$$

The 'excess demand for labour' is defined as

$$E(t) = D(t) - S(t)$$

By elementary algebra the excess demand for labour is a function of the wage rate and the amount of work contracted for,

(41) $E(t) = -l - mW(t) + kC(t)$

If there is positive excess demand for labour then competition for labour between employers will tend to raise the wage rate, whereas if the excess demand is negative, competition between workmen will tend to reduce the wage rate. This suggests that the rate of change of wages is a function of the excess demand for labour, e.g.

(42) $dW(t)/dt = pE(t)$

where p is a constant, sometimes known as the 'speed of adjustment' coefficient. Taking equations (41) and (42) together shows that

(43) $dW(t)/dt = -mpW(t) - lp + kpC(t)$

Equation (43) is a special case of (39) with $a_1 = mp$ and $g(t) = -lp + kpC(t)$. Substituting these values into equation (40) shows that the solution of (43) is

(44) $$W(t) = W(0)\exp(-mpt) + \int_0^t \exp(mp(T - t))[-lp + kpC(T)]dT$$

Equation (44) explains how the initial value of wages, $W(0)$, and the time path of work contracted for, $C(t)$, combine to determine the time path of wages, $W(t)$. In order to study the time path of wages in more detail it is necessary to know the properties of the exponential function, to which we turn in the next chapter.

Notes and references

For social scientists the most useful reference on difference equations is Goldberg.[40] Elementary difference and differential equations are lucidly discussed by Lewis,[79] Ch. 25, 26. The examples on economic growth stem from the work of Harrod.[51, 52] For further details of Harrod–Domar growth theory see Ackley,[1] Ch. 18, Allen,[8] Ch. 11, and Jones.[6] First-order differential equations are widely used in the theory of market adjustment; for microeconomic applications see Henderson and Quandt[56] and for application to inflation theory see Phillips.[103]

Problems

17.1.1 Using Pascal's triangle, express $\Delta^7 Y(t)$ as a function of $Y(t)$, $Y(t - 1), \ldots, Y(t - 7)$.

17.1.2 The element in the jth row and kth column of Pascal's triangle is $t_{jk} = n!/[i!(n - i)!]$ where $n = j - 1$, $i = k - 1$. By using the formula for a factorial, prove the recurrence relation on which the triangle is based: $t_{jk} = t_{j-1\,k-1} + t_{j-1\,k}$.

17.2 Determine the order of the following equations and classify them as either homogeneous or inhomogeneous and as either linear or nonlinear.

(a) $\Delta^4 Y(t) - 2\Delta^2 Y(t) = 0$
(b) $(\Delta^2 Y(t) - 5Y(t))^2 = 0$
(c) $(\Delta Y(t) - 4)^3 = 0$
(d) $1/(\Delta Y(t) - 4)^3 = 0$
(e) $\Delta^3 Y(t) - t^2 Y(t) + t^3 = 0$

Which of the equations have constant coefficients?

17.3.1 £500 is invested at 8% and is compounded annually. How much will the investment be worth after 8 years? (Use a suitable binomial approximation.) Suppose that instead of being reinvested the interest payments had been placed in a current account at the bank on which no interest was paid. What would be the value of the investment after 8 years? What is the financial gain due to reinvesting the interest payments at 8%?

17.3.2 A man contributes £250 per annum to a pension fund. If he retires after six years, what will be the value of the fund, assuming the rate of interest to be 5%?

17.3.3 Given the function $A(t)$, $t = 0, 1, 2, 3, \ldots$, the first difference is defined as $\Delta A(t) = A(t+1) - A(t)$, the second difference is $\Delta^2 A(t) = \Delta A(t+1) - \Delta A(t)$ and the third difference is $\Delta^3 A(t) = \Delta^2 A(t+1) - \Delta^2 A(t)$.

(a) If $A(t)$ grows in a compound fashion at a rate of $100r\%$, show that

$$\Delta^3 A(t) = r^3 A(t)$$

(b) If $A(t)$ grows in a simple fashion at $100r\%$, show that

$$\Delta^2 A(t) = 0$$

and that

$$\Delta^3 A(t) = 0$$

17.3.4 An economy has a capital–output ratio of v. Investment goods account for a proportion ω of the total output; the capital stock does not depreciate; at the end of each year the investment goods are added to the capital stock of the economy. In period 0 the output is £20m.

(a) Show that after N years the value of output, $Y(N)$ is

$$£20(1 + \omega/v)^N \text{ million}$$

(b) Suppose now that the capital stock depreciates in such a way that a proportion, d, of the capital assets becomes useless each year. At what rate will the economy grow?

(c) Suppose now that investment goods are added to the capital stock of the economy every 6 months instead of only once a year. Ignore depreciation. What will be the value of output after N years? Will the output be larger or smaller or the same as in (a). (Give reasons for your answer.)

17.3.5 The value of GNP in 1950 was £21,000m (approximately) and in 1970 it was £37,000m (approximately). Both figures are in constant prices. If the economy grew in a compound fashion at a rate of $100r\%$ per annum find the annual growth rate by using the binomial approximation with terms in r and r^2 only. Compare your result with the simple growth rate.

17.4.1 An economy has a marginal propensity to consume of 0·5. Both exogenous consumer demand and investment grow by 2% per annum. Initially exogenous consumer demand is £37m, investment is £63m and income is £160m. What will be the value of income (a) after 2 years, (b) ultimately? Check your answer to (a) by direct economic reasoning.

17.4.2 The demand for frozen peas is equal to

$$D(t) = 40 - 5P(t) + Y(t)$$

and the supply is equal to

$$S(t) = 20 + 15P(t-1)$$

where P is price, Y is consumers' income and t is an index of time (in years). Initially $P = 2$ (£ per cwt) and consumers' income is 20 (£m). If consumers' income increases by 5% per annum, what will be the price of peas (a) after 2 years, (b) ultimately. Explain your answer to (a) with the aid of graphs.

17.6.1 A dam discharges water through its sluices at the rate of 20,000 gallons an hour. A river flows into the dam at the rate of 35,000 gallons an hour. Each foot depth of water in the dam corresponds to 180,000 gallons. How long will it take the water level to rise three feet?

17.6.2 Investment goods are added to the capital stock of an economy as soon as they are produced. Production is continuous and one fifth of the goods produced are investment goods. Show that if the capital–output ratio is 8 then the output of the economy increases exponentially at a rate of 2·5% per annum.

17.7 In the antiquarian book market the demand for first editions of Adam Smith's *Wealth of Nations* is a linear function of the auction price,

$$D(t) = 9 - 5P(t)$$

where $D(t)$ is the rate at which copies are demanded in year t and $P(t)$ is the price in year t (£,000). The rate at which books come onto the market in year t is

$$S(t) = 1{\cdot}3 + 0{\cdot}5P(t)$$

The rate at which the price changes depends on the excess demand is

$$dP(t)/dt = 400E(t)$$

At a poorly attended auction at the beginning of 1970 a copy sells for only £600. Express subsequent auction prices as a function of time.

Chapter 18

Exponentials and logarithms

18.1 Exponential function

The exponential function is defined by the series expansion

$$\exp(x) = 1 + x + \frac{x^2}{2!} + \frac{x^3}{3!} + \frac{x^4}{4!} + \cdots$$

where $$n! = \begin{cases} n(n-1)(n-2)\ldots 2.1 & n > 0 \\ 1 & n = 0 \end{cases}$$

Although the series expansion of the exponential function contains an infinite number of terms, the sum of these terms is nevertheless finite. The proof is given in the following paragraph, which may be omitted on a first reading.

Recall from Theorem 2.2 that the sum of the infinite geometric series $1, c, c^2, \ldots$ converges to a definite value if $-1 < c < 1$. If we can prove that there exists an infinite geometric series in which every term is greater than the corresponding term in the series expansion of the exponential function, and which nevertheless is such that its sum has a definite value, it follows that the series expansion of the exponential function must also converge to a definite value. If beyond a certain term in the exponential series the size of the terms decays faster than the size of the terms in a convergent geometric series, a convergent geometric series can always be found in which all the terms exceed the corresponding terms in the exponential series.[(1)]. Now in a convergent geometric series the size of the terms decays in such a way that the ratio of consecutive terms is equal to c, where $-1 < c < 1$. Consequently, if beyond a certain point the size of the terms in the series expansion of the exponential function decays in such a way that the ratio of consecutive terms is less that c, $-1 < c < 1$, then a convergent geometric series exists in which each term is greater than the corresponding term in the series expansion of the exponential function; in this case the series expansion of the exponential function must converge to a definite value. Now the ratio of consecutive terms in the series expansion of the exponential function is such that

$$\begin{aligned}(n+1)\text{th term}/n\text{th term} &= (r^n/n!)/(r^{n-1}(n-1)!) \\ &= r/n\end{aligned}$$

1 This is the principle of d'Alembert's ratio for the convergence of series.

Noting that

$$\lim_{n \to \infty} r/n = 0$$

it is seen that for the more remote terms in the exponential series the ratio of consecutive terms is arbitrarily close to zero; hence beyond a certain term the ratio of consecutive terms in the series expansion of the exponential function lies between -1 and $+1$. Consequently the series expansion of the exponential function converges to a definite value.

18.2 Properties of the exponential function

The most important properties of the exponential function are catalogued below for easy reference. When describing the first two properties it is most convenient to make the substitution $x = rt$ and examine the function

(1) $$\exp(rt) = 1 + rt + \frac{r^2t^2}{2!} + \frac{r^3t^3}{3!} + \frac{r^4t^4}{4!} + \cdots$$

where t is a variable and r is a parameter.

(1a) *The first derivative is proportional to the value of the function:*

(2) $$\frac{d}{dt}\exp(rt) = r\exp(rt)$$

PROOF Differentiating the right-hand side of (1) term by term shows that

$$\frac{d}{dt}\exp(rt) = r + \frac{2r^2t}{2!} + \frac{3r^3t^2}{3!} + \frac{4r^4t^3}{4!} + \cdots$$

$$= r + r^2t + \frac{r^3t^2}{2!} + \frac{r^4t^3}{3!} + \cdots$$

$$= r\exp(rt)$$

(1b) The second derivative is proportional to the value of the function:

$$\frac{d^2}{dt^2}\exp(rt) = r^2\exp(rt)$$

PROOF By using equation (2) it is seen that

$$\frac{d^2}{dt^2}\exp(rt) = \frac{d}{dt}\left(\frac{d}{dt}\exp(rt)\right)$$

$$= \frac{d}{dt}(r\exp(rt))$$

$$= r^2\exp(rt)$$

The two properties described above are special cases of the property given below.

(1c) Every derivative is proportional to the value of the function:

(3) $$\frac{d^m}{dt^m} \exp(rt) = r^m \exp(rt) \qquad (m = 0, 1, 2, 3, \ldots)$$

PROOF By successive application of equation (2) it is seen that

$$\begin{aligned} \frac{d^m}{dt^m} \exp(rt) &= r \frac{d^{m-1}}{dt^{m-1}} \exp(rt) \\ &= r^2 \frac{d^{m-2}}{dt^{m-2}} \exp(rt) \\ &\vdots \\ &= r^{m-1} \frac{d}{dt} \exp(rt) \\ &= r^m \exp(rt) \end{aligned}$$

(2) *Whatever the values of p, q*

(4) $$\exp(r(p+q)) = \exp(rp).\exp(rq)/\exp(0)$$

PROOF The proof is most conveniently demonstrated by making the substitution $u = rp$, $v = rq$, noting that $\exp(0) = 1$, and then proving that

(5) $$\exp(u + v) = \exp(u).\exp(v)$$

The right-hand side of equation (5) is the product of two functions each of which is the sum of an infinite series of terms. The result of multiplying these two series of terms into one another is shown in Table 18.1. The terms in the ith row of Table 18.1 are the result of multiplying the ith term in the series for $\exp(u)$ into the series for $\exp(v)$; the terms in the jth column of Table 18.1 are the result of multiplying the jth term in the series for $\exp(v)$ into the series for $\exp(u)$. The sum of all the terms in the first m rows and columns of the table

Table 18.1 Multiplication of the series $\exp(u) = 1 + u + u^2/2 + u^3/6 + u^4/24 + \cdots$ into the series $\exp(v) = 1 + v + v^2/2 + v^3/6 + v^4/24 + \cdots$

Column	*1*	*2*	*3*	*4*	*5*	...
Row						
1	1	v	$v^2/2$	$v^3/6$	$v^4/24$	...
2	u	uv	$uv^2/2$	$uv^3/6$	$uv^4/24$	...
3	$u^2/2$	$u^2v/2$	$u^2v^2/4$	$u^2v^3/12$	$u^2v^4/48$	...
4	$u^3/6$	$u^3v/6$	$u^3v^2/12$	$u^3v^3/36$	$u^3v^4/144$	...
5	$u^4/24$	$u^4v/24$	$u^4v^2/48$	$u^4v^3/144$	$u^4v^4/576$	...
⋮	⋮	⋮	⋮	⋮	⋮	⋱

is the result of multiplying the first m terms in the series for $\exp(u)$ into the first m terms in the series for $\exp(v)$. If the terms in the table are added up in a particular order then it can be shown that the sum of the terms is equal to the series for $\exp(u + v)$. The particular order in which the terms must be added is indicated in Table 18.2: the terms are taken in successive groups, indicated A, B, C, ... in Table 18.2; each group of terms lies on a particular diagonal in the table.

Table 18.2 Order of summation of the terms in Table 18.1

Column	*1*	*2*	*3*	*4*	*5*	...
Row						
1	*A*	*B*	*C*	*D*	*E*	
2	*B*	*C*	*D*	*E*		
3	*C*	*D*	*E*			
4	*D*	*E*				
5	*E*					
⋮						

The first group of terms, A, is simply the number 1. This is the first term in the series for $\exp(u + v)$. The second group of terms, B, when added together gives $u + v$; this is the second term in the series for $\exp(u + v)$. The sum of the third group of terms, C, is

$$(u^2/2) + uv + (v^2/2) = \tfrac{1}{2}(u^2 + 2uv + v^2) = \tfrac{1}{2}(u + v)^2$$

this is the third term in the series for $\exp(u + v)$. The reader can verify that the sum of the fourth group of terms, D, is equal to $(u + v)^3/6$; this is the fourth term in the series for $\exp(u + v)$. If the grouping of terms is carried on in this way then it can be shown that the sum of the nth group of terms is

$$\frac{(u + v)^{n-1}}{(n - 1)!}$$

which is the nth term in the series for $\exp(u + v)$. This completes the proof.

Equation (5) may be used to give an alternative proof of equation (2). Substitute $u = rt$, $v = r\,\Delta t$ in equation (5). It follows that

$$\exp(r(t + \Delta t)) = \exp(rt).\exp(r\,\Delta t)$$

Simple manipulation shows that

$$\frac{\exp(r(t + \Delta t)) - \exp(rt)}{\Delta t} = \exp(rt)\,\frac{(\exp(r\,\Delta t) - 1)}{\Delta t}$$

Expanding $\exp(r\,\Delta t)$ in series form gives

$$\frac{\exp(r(t + \Delta t)) - \exp(rt)}{\Delta t} = \exp(rt)\left(r + \frac{r^2\,\Delta t}{2} + \frac{r^3\,\Delta t^2}{3!} + \frac{r^4\,\Delta t^3}{4!} + \cdots\right)$$

As t tends to zero the left-hand side of this equation tends to $d \exp(rt)/dt$, and the right-hand side tends to $r \exp(rt)$. Hence, in the limit,

$$\frac{d}{dt} \exp(rt) = r \exp(rt)$$

(3) *The exponential function is always positive.*

PROOF Putting $u = -x$, $v = x$ in equation (5) it follows that

(6) $$\exp(x) . \exp(-x) = \exp(0)$$

But from the series expansion for the exponential function it follows that $\exp(0) = 1$; hence, dividing both sides of equation (6) by $\exp(-x)$ gives

(7) $$\exp(x) = 1/\exp(-x)$$

If x is positive then it is readily seen from the series expansion that $\exp(x)$ is also positive. If x is negative then $-x$ is positive, so that the right-hand side of equation (7) is positive; hence the left-hand side of equation (7), $\exp(x)$, is also positive even when x is negative. Consequently $\exp(x)$ is always positive.

(4) *The exponential function is always increasing.*

PROOF It follows immediately from equation (2) that

$$d \exp(x)/dx = \exp(x)$$

Since $\exp(x)$ is always positive it follows that $d \exp(x)/dx$ is also always positive so that $\exp(x)$ is always increasing.

(5) *When $x = 1$ the value of the exponential function is e; e is an irrational number and to 10 places of decimals is equal to*

$$\exp(1) = e = 2{\cdot}7182818285$$

(6) *As x tends to infinity the exponential function*, $\exp(x)$, *also tends to infinity: as x tends to minus infinity the exponential function tends to zero.*

PROOF It is readily seen from the series expansion of the exponential function that as x tends to infinity $\exp(x)$ also tends to infinity. Equation (7) shows that as $\exp(x)$ tends to infinity, $\exp(-x)$ tends to zero.

Properties 3–6 are illustrated by the graph of the exponential function shown in Fig. 18A.

(7) *The exponential function may be evaluated as*

(8) $$\exp(r) = \lim_{n \to \infty} (1 + r/n)^n$$

Equation (8) was used as a definition of the exponential function by the nineteenth century French mathematician Cauchy.

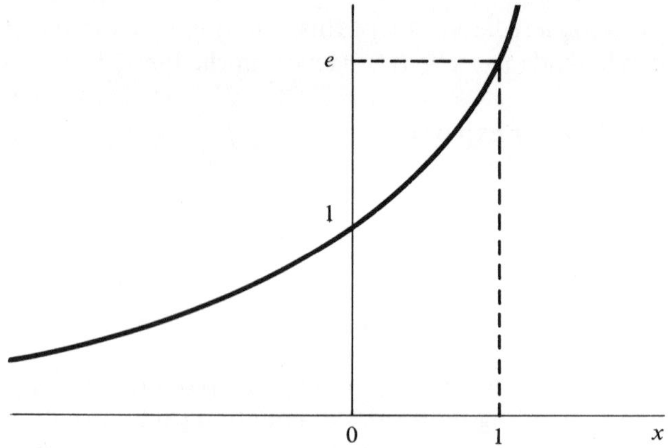

Fig. 18A The exponential function exp(x)

18.3 Exponential function as a formula for continuous compound growth

The exponential function was introduced in Section 17.6 as the solution of an equation of continuous compound growth. Many of the properties catalogued in the previous section are continuous analogues of properties of compound growth. In order to demonstrate this we shall first of all deduce some of the properties of discrete compound growth and then show that as the discrete intervals become arbitrarily small these properties tend to corresponding properties of the exponential function.

(1) *If $Y(t)$ grows in a compound fashion the nth difference of Y is proportional to the value of Y, i.e. if*

(9) $$\Delta Y(t) = rY(t) \qquad \text{for all } t = \ldots -2, -1, 0, 1, 2, \ldots$$

then

(10) $$\Delta^n Y(t) = r^n Y(t) \qquad \text{for all } n = 1, 2, \ldots \text{ and all } t = -2, -1, 0, 1, 2, \ldots$$

PROOF It follows from equation (9) that

$$\Delta^2 Y(t) = \Delta Y(t+1) - \Delta Y(t)$$
$$= rY(t+1) - rY(t)$$
$$= r\,\Delta Y(t)$$

(11) $$= r^2 Y(t)$$

In general, if $\Delta^{n-1} Y(t) = r^{n-1} Y(t)$ then $\Delta^n Y(t) = r^n Y(t)$ since

$$\Delta^n Y(t) = \Delta^{n-1} Y(t+1) - \Delta^{n-1} Y(t-1)$$
$$= r^{n-1} Y(t+1) - r^{n-1} Y(t)$$
$$= r^{n-1}\,\Delta Y(t)$$

(12) $$= r^n Y(t)$$

The principle of induction applied to (11) and (12) shows that for any value $n = 1, 2, \ldots, \Delta^n Y(t) = r^n Y(t)$.

(2) *If $Y(t)$ grows in a compound fashion then*

(13) $$Y(p + q) = Y(p)Y(q)/Y(0)$$

for any $p, q = \cdots -2, -1, 0, 1, 2, \ldots$

PROOF The solution of the equation of compound growth (9) is

(14) $$Y(N) = Y(0)(1 + r)^N$$

Setting in turn $N = p$, $N = q$ and $N = p + q$ in (14) shows that

$$Y(p) = Y(0)(1 + r)^p$$

$$Y(q) = Y(0)(1 + r)^q$$

$$Y(p + q) = Y(0)(1 + r)^{p+q}$$

Since $(1 + r)^{p+q} = (1 + r)^p(1 + r)^q$ we find

$$\begin{aligned} Y(p + q) &= Y(0)(1 + r)^p(1 + r)^q \\ &= Y(0)(1 + r)^p Y(0)(1 + r)^q/Y(0) \\ &= Y(p)Y(q)/Y(0) \end{aligned}$$

(3) *If Y is compounded by $100r/n\%$ at discrete intervals of length $1/n$ then*

(15) $$Y(1) = Y(0)(1 + r/n)^n$$

PROOF The equation of growth is

$$Y(t + 1/n) - Y(t) = (r/n)Y(t)$$

The solution is easily verified to be

$$Y(N) = Y(0)(1 + r/n)^{nN}$$

Setting $N = 1$ shows that

$$Y(1) = Y(0)(1 + r/n)^n$$

The continuous analogues of equations (9) and (10) are the equations (2) and (3) satisfied by the exponential function. To appreciate this, consider the sequence of ratios

(16) $$\Delta^n Y(t)/\Delta t = [\Delta^{n-1} Y(t + \Delta t) - \Delta^{n-1} Y(t)]/\Delta t \qquad (n = 1, 2, \ldots)$$

the differences being measured with reference to an interval of length Δt. When $\Delta t = 1$ (16) is the same as the left-hand side of (10). Equation (10) shows that when compounding is at unit intervals the nth difference (16) is proportional to the value of $Y(t)$. As Δt tends to zero (16) converges to the nth derivative of Y with respect to t,

(17) $$\lim_{\Delta t \to 0} [\Delta^{n-1} Y(t + \Delta t) - \Delta^{n-1} Y(t)]/\Delta t = d^n Y(t)/dt^n$$

and hence equation (10) converges to equation (3). Equation (3) shows that as the interval between compounding tends to zero the nth difference (16) remains proportional to the value of $Y(t)$, where $Y(t) = \exp(rt)$.

The continuous analogue of equation (13) is equation (4) of the exponential function. This follows immediately on setting $Y(t) = \exp(rt)$.

The continuous analogue of equation (15) is equation (8) of the exponential function. This follows immediately on taking the limit as n tends to infinity and setting $Y(t) = \exp(rt)$ with $t = 1$.

Table 18.3 Table of the exponential function for the range $-1 < x < 1$

x	$\exp(x)$	$\exp(-x)$
0·00	1·0000	1·0000
0·05	1·0513	0·9512
0·10	1·1052	0·9048
0·15	1·1618	0·8607
0·20	1·2214	0·8187
0·25	1·2840	0·7788
0·30	1·3499	0·7408
0·35	1·4191	0·7047
0·40	1·4918	0·6703
0·45	1·5683	0·6376
0·50	1·6487	0·6065
0·55	1·7333	0·5769
0·60	1·8221	0·5488
0·65	1·9155	0·5220
0·70	2·0138	0·4966
0·75	2·1170	0·4724
0·80	2·2255	0·4493
0·85	2·3396	0·4274
0·90	2·4596	0·4066
0·95	2·5857	0·3867
1·00	2·7183	0·3679

Example Technological factors determine that the capital–output ratio of an economy is equal to 4. 20% of all output is in the form of investment goods. If the capital stock is initially £200m, and investment goods are continuously added to the capital stock, what will be value of output after 10 years?

Let $Y(t)$ be the rate of output at date t, $K(t)$ the capital stock and $I(t)$ the rate of investment. Since the capital–output ratio is 4,

$$K(t) = 4Y(t)$$

Since investment goods account for 20% of all output

$$I(t) = 0{\cdot}2Y(t)$$

Since new capital goods are continuously added to the capital stock

$$dK/dt = I(t)$$

Combining these three equations shows that

$$dK/dt = [0{\cdot}2/4]K(t) = 0{\cdot}05K(t)$$

The solution of this differential equation is

$$K(t) = K(0) \exp (0{\cdot}05t)$$

where $K(0) = 200$ (£m). It follows that when $t = 10$,

$$K(10) = 200 \exp (0{\cdot}5)$$

From Table 18.3, $\exp (0{\cdot}5) = 1{\cdot}6487$, so that

$$K(10) = 329{\cdot}74$$

Since $Y(10) = K(10)/4$ we get

$$Y(10) = 82{\cdot}435$$

We conclude that after 10 years the rate of output is £82·435m per annum.

18.4 Logarithmic function

The exponential function and the logarithmic function are closely related; in fact the function log (y) is defined by the equation

(18) $$\exp (\log (y)) = y$$

In other words, if one is given a number y and asked to find the number x such that $\exp (x) = y$ then the answer is defined to be $x = \log (y)$. To illustrate this point, refer to the table of the exponential function, Table 18.3. Suppose we are told that $\exp (x) = 1{\cdot}3499$, and are asked to find x; by using Table 18.3 it is readily seen that $\exp (0{\cdot}30) = 1{\cdot}3499$: it follows that $\log (1{\cdot}3499) = 0{\cdot}30$. Thus a table of the logarithmic function can be based on the table of the exponential function: only instead of reading from the left-hand column, x, to the right-hand column, exp (x) you read from the right-hand column, y, to the left-hand column, log (y).

It follows from this close correspondence between the exponential function and the logarithmic function that all the properties of the logarithmic function can be deduced immediately from the properties of the exponential function.

(1) *The most important property of the logarithmic function is that the logarithm of the product of any two numbers is simply equal to the sum of the logarithms of the two numbers* (it is because this property is so useful that the logarithmic function is tabulated to facilitate its widespread use). This property may be formalized as follows: for any two real numbers, r, s,

(19) $$\log (rs) = \log (r) + \log (s)$$

It was mentioned above that all the properties of the logarithmic function are simple corollaries of the properties of the exponential function. Equation (19) follows immediately from equation (5):

$$\exp(u + v) = \exp(u).\exp(v)$$

Substitute $u = \log(r)$, $v = \log(s)$ into equation (5):

$$\exp[\log(r) + \log(s)] = \exp[\log(r)].\exp[\log(s)]$$

From the definition of the logarithm given in equation (18), $\exp(\log(r)) = r$ and $\exp(\log(s)) = s$; hence the right-hand side of the equation above becomes

$$\exp[\log(r)].\exp[\log(s)] = rs \tag{20}$$

It follows again from equation (18) that $rs = \exp[\log(rs)]$ so that equation (20) becomes

$$\exp[\log(r) + \log(s)] = \exp[\log(rs)] \tag{21}$$

Since the exponential function is always increasing, to each value of the exponential function, $\exp(x)$, there corresponds a unique value of x; it therefore follows from equation (21) that

$$\log(r) + \log(s) = \log(rs)$$

which is the result we wished to deduce.

(2) *The logarithm of the ratio of any two numbers is equal to the logarithm of the numerator minus the logarithm of the denominator:*

$$\log(r/s) = \log(r) - \log(s) \tag{22}$$

PROOF From equation (18) it follows that

$$r/s = \exp[\log(r/s)], \qquad r = \exp[\log(r)], \qquad s = \exp[\log(s)]$$

so that

$$\exp[\log(r/s)] = \exp[\log(r)]/\exp[\log(s)] \tag{23}$$

Since $1/\exp(x) = \exp(-x)$ (from equation (7)), the right-hand side of (23) is equal to

$$\exp[\log(r)].\exp[-\log(s)]$$

and this simplifies, by using equation (5), to

$$\exp[\log(r) - \log(s)]$$

Substituting this expression back into the right-hand side of equation (23) gives

$$\exp[\log(r/s)] = \exp[\log(r) - \log(s)]$$

from which equation (22) follows.

(3) *If $Y(t)$ is an exponential function of t then $\log[Y(t)]$ is a linear function of t.*

PROOF Suppose, quite generally, that $Y(t) = Y(0)\exp(rt)$ where

r is a constant. Dividing through by $Y(0)$ gives

$$Y(t)/Y(0) = \exp(rt)$$

from which it follows that

$$\begin{aligned} rt &= \log[Y(t)/Y(0)] && \text{(by using equation (18))} \\ &= \log[Y(t)] - \log[Y(0)] && \text{(by using equation (22))} \end{aligned}$$

so that

$$\log[Y(t)] = \log Y(0) + rt$$

Thus $\log[Y(t)]$ is a linear function of t with an intercept $\log Y(0)$ and gradient r.

(4) *The logarithmic function, log (y), is defined only for positive values of y.* This is an immediate corollary of the fact that the value of the exponential function $y = \exp(x)$ is always positive.

(5) *The derivative of the logarithmic function is the reciprocal function:*

(24) $$d\log(y)/dy = 1/y$$

PROOF By the ordinary definition of a derivative,

$$\frac{d}{dy}\log(y) = \lim_{\Delta y \to 0} \frac{\log(y + \Delta y) - \log(y)}{\Delta y}$$

By using equation (18) we can make the substitutions

$$\log(y) = x, \qquad \log(y + \Delta y) = x + \Delta x,$$

$$\Delta y = (y + \Delta y) - y = \exp(x + \Delta x) - \exp(x)$$

Since the exponential function is differentiable, it follows that as $\Delta y \to 0$ so $\Delta x \to 0$, whence, the expression for the derivative can be written

$$\lim_{\Delta x \to 0} \frac{(x + \Delta x) - x}{\exp(x + \Delta x) - \exp(x)} = \lim_{\Delta x \to 0} \frac{1}{[\exp(x + \Delta x) - \exp(x)]/\Delta x}$$

As $\Delta x \to 0$, the denominator of this expression tends to the derivative of $\exp(x)$; the derivative of $\exp(x)$ is $\exp(x)$ itself, so that the right-hand side becomes

$$1/\exp(x) = 1/y$$

(6) *For the range of values* $0 < y \leqslant 2$, *the value of* $\log(y)$ *is the sum of the infinite series*

$$\log(y) = (y-1) - (y-1)^2/2 + (y-1)^3/3 - \cdots$$
$$\cdots + (-1)^{n-1}(y-1)^n/n + \cdots$$

PROOF From equation (24) it follows that

$$\log(y) = \int_1^y (1/y)\, dy$$

[the lower limit of the integration is unity because log (1) = 0]. If $0 < y < 2$ then $-1 < 1 - y < 1$ so that

$$\log(y) = \int_1^y \frac{1}{1-(1-y)}\,dy$$

$$= \int_1^y [1 + (1-y) + (1-y)^2 + \cdots + (1-y)^{n-1} + \cdots]\,dy$$

$$= [y - (1-y)^2/2 - (1-y)^3/3 - \cdots (1-y)^n/n - \cdots]_1^y$$

$$= (y-1) - (y-1)^2/2 + (y-1)^3/3 - \cdots + (-1)^{n-1}(y-1)^n/n + \cdots$$

It can be shown that this expression converges to a definite value whenever

$$-1 \leqslant y < 1$$

The graph of the logarithmic function is shown in Fig. 18B. This graph is obtained from Fig. 18A by making the substitutions

$$\exp(x) = y, \qquad x = \log(y)$$

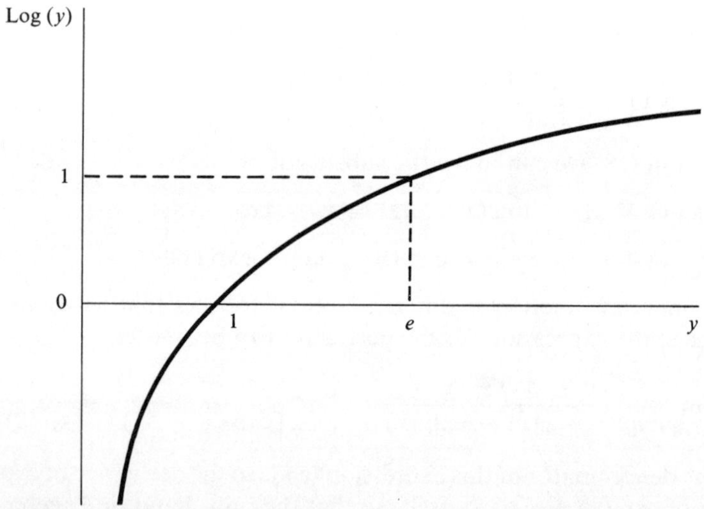

Fig. 18B The logarithmic function

18.5 Base of a logarithm

The logarithmic function, log (y), is often referred to as the 'natural logarithm' or as the 'logarithm to the base of e' of y. This terminology is based on an alternative and more general definition of a logarithm; this definition of a logarithm involves the concept of a base; *the logarithm to the base z of the number y is the power to which z must be raised in order that* $z^x = y$, i.e. the logarithm to the base z, denoted $\log_z(y)$, is defined by the equation

(25) $$z^{\log_z(y)} = y$$

An example will illustrate this concept of a logarithm: substituting $z = 10$ in the definition above gives the definition of a logarithm to the base 10—the logarithm to the base 10 is the power, x, to which 10 must be raised in order that $10^x = y$. It follows that the logarithm to the base 10, denoted $\log_{10}(y)$, satisfies the equation

$$10^{\log_{10}(y)} = y$$

For example, since $10^2 = 100$ it follows that $\log_{10}(100) = 2$; i.e. since 10 must be raised to the power 2 in order that it shall be equal to 100, so the logarithm of 100 to the base 10 is equal to 2.

We shall now show that the logarithmic function, $\log(y)$, can, in terms of this more general definition of a logarithm, be identified with the logarithm of y to the base e.

The first step in the proof of this proposition is to recall that the number e is the special value of the exponential function, $e = \exp(1)$. Using the properties of the exponential function it is readily seen that

$$\exp(1) = e$$

$$\exp(2) = \exp(1).\exp(1) = [\exp(1)]^2 = e^2$$

$$\exp(3) = \exp(1).\exp(2) = [\exp(1)]^3 = e^3$$

and, in general, it can be shown that for any integers, p, q,

$$\exp(p/q) = \sqrt[q]{e^p}$$

where $\sqrt[q]{e^p}$ denotes the qth root of the pth power of e. If the qth root of the pth power of e is denoted $e^{p/q}$ then we may write instead

$$\exp(p/q) = e^{p/q}$$

or, expressing this equation in a different way,

$$\exp(x) = e^x \tag{26}$$

where $x = p/q$ and p and q are integers. If the value of x is not equal to the ratio of two integers, then equation (26) is used as a definition of what is meant by e^x.

Now it follows immediately from equation (26), by making the substitution $x = \log(y)$, that

$$\exp[\log(y)] = e^{\log(y)}$$

and since, from equation (18), $\exp[\log(y)] = y$, it follows that

$$e^{\log(y)} = y$$

Comparing this equation with equation (25) in the special case $z = e$,

$$e^{\log_e(y)} = y$$

it is seen that the function $\log(y)$ is equivalent to the function $\log_e(y)$. Hence the function $\log(y)$ is often written $\log_e(y)$ and is known as the 'logarithm of y to the base e'.

18.6 Change of base

As suggested by the definition of equation (25), the base of a logarithm is quite arbitrary: it can be any positive real number. Let us consider the logarithms of the number 64. Suppose that the base is 8; the logarithm to the base 8 of the number 64 is the power, x, to which 8 must be raised in order that $8^x = 64$: it follows that $x = 2$, so that $\log_8(64) = 2$. Suppose now that the base is 4; then the logarithm to the base 4 of the number 64 is the power, x, to which 4 must be raised in order that $4^x = 64$: it follows immediately that $x = 3$, so that $\log_4(64) = 3$. A table of four-figure common logarithms (common logarithms are logarithms to the base 10) will tell us that $\log_{10}(64) = 1{\cdot}8062$: in other words, 1·8062 is the power to which 10 must be raised in order that it should equal 64. The following proposition is easily established.

For any number, y, the logarithm to the base a and the logarithm to the base b are related by the equation

(27) $$\log_b(y) = \log_b(a)\log_a(y)$$

PROOF From the general definition of a logarithm given by equation (25) it follows that

(28) $$a^{\log_a(y)} = y = b^{\log_b(y)}$$

and that

(29) $$a = b^{\log_b a}$$

Substituting equation (29) into equation (28) gives

$$(b^{\log_b(a)})^{\log_a(y)} = b^{\log_b(y)}$$

and by using the law of the multiplication of indices, that $(b^r)^s = b^{rs}$, it follows that

$$b^{\log_b(a)\log_a(y)} = b^{\log_b(y)}$$

whence

$$\log_b(a)\log_a(y) = \log_b(y)$$

It follows from equation (27) that to convert from logarithms in base a to logarithms in base b it is necessary only to multiply the logarithm in base a by the appropriate constant, $\log_b(a)$. For example, to convert from logarithms in base 10 (as given in tables of the common logarithm) to logarithms in base e it is necessary only to multiply the common logarithm by $\log_e(10)$. The value of this constant is usually given as a footnote to tables of the common logarithm.

Because logarithms to different bases are simple multiples of one another it is readily established that the properties 1–4 of the logarithmic function—i.e. of logarithms to the base e—are valid for logarithms of any base whatsoever. A consequence of properties 1 and 2 is the 'rule for taking logarithms': if

$$y = Ax_1^{a_1}x_2^{a_2}\ldots x_n^{a_n}$$

then for any base $z > 0$ and for any real numbers $a_1, a_2, \ldots, a_n$,

$$\log_z(y) = \log_z(A) + a_1 \log_z(x_1) + a_2 \log_z(x_2) + \cdots + a_n \log_z(x_n)$$

from which it follows that

$$y = \text{antilog}_z [\log_z(A) + a_1 \log_z(x_1) + a_2 \log_z(x_2) + \cdots + a_n \log_z(x_n)]$$

Example 1 The graphical determination of the rate of growth of exponentially growing quantities.

Suppose that you are given a number of different measurements, taken at different times, of the exponentially growing quantity, $A(t)$,

$$A(t) = B \exp(rt)$$

where the parameters B and r are unknown, and that, on the basis of these sample measurements you are asked to determine the rate of growth, $100r\%$, of A. The most straightforward way to answer this question is to fit an exponential function to the sample measurements and then to evaluate the parameter r of the fitted function. However, the graph of an arbitrary exponential function is similar to the graph shown in Fig. 18A, which is by no means easy to plot; as a result, it is difficult to obtain an accurate measure of r by this graphical method.

By using the properties of the logarithmic function an accurate measurement of r can be obtained very easily. This is a result of the third property of the logarithmic function: if $A(t)$ grows exponentially then $\log(A(t))$ is a linear function of t, i.e. if

$$A(t) = B \exp(rt)$$

then

$$\log[A(t)] = \log(B) + rt$$

Changing the base of the logarithms from base e to base 10 by the formula

$$\log_{10}[A(t)] = \log_{10}(e) \log_e[A(t)] = \log_{10}(e) \log[A(t)]$$

it follows that

$$\log_{10}[A(t)] = \log_{10}(B) + \log_{10}(e)\, rt$$

To four decimal places, $\log_{10}(e) = 0{\cdot}4343$ so that

$$\log_{10}[A(t)] = \log_{10}(B) + 0{\cdot}4343rt$$

It follows from this that the graph of $\log_{10}[A(t)]$ is a linear function of t with a gradient $0{\cdot}4343r$. If the common logarithms of the sample measurements of $A(t)$ are plotted against time then they will all lie on a straight line; consequently, if a straight line is drawn through these plotted points then the gradient of this line will be equal to $0{\cdot}4343r$. The value of r can then be determined by the equation

$$r = \text{gradient}/0{\cdot}4343 = 2{\cdot}3026 \times \text{gradient}$$

Example 2 The specification of demand curves of constant elasticity In order to see how a demand curve of constant elasticity can be specified by using logarithms, it is useful, as a preliminary, to demonstrate that for a demand curve, $Q = f(P)$, *the elasticity of demand*

$$\eta = -\frac{dQ}{dP}\cdot\frac{P}{Q}$$

is equal to the negative of the derivative of the logarithm of the quantity demanded with respect to the logarithm of the price,

$$\text{(30)} \qquad \eta = -\frac{d\log_z(Q)}{d\log_z(P)}$$

where the logarithms are taken to any base, $z > 0$.

The first step in the proof is to note that if the proposition is true for the 'natural base', base e, then it is true for any base, $z > 0$. This can be seen as follows. Converting from base z to the base e gives, for any $z > 0$,

$$\frac{d\log_z(Q)}{d\log_z(P)} = \frac{\mathrm{d}\,[\log_z(e).\log_e(Q)]}{d\,[\log_z(e).\log_e(P)]}$$

Since $\log_z(e)$ is a constant, the right-hand side is equal to

$$\log_z(e)\left\{\frac{d\log_e(Q)}{d\,[\log_z(e)\log_e(P)]}\right\}$$

If the derivative is written out using the function of a function rule, this expression becomes

$$\log_z(e)\left\{\frac{d\log_e(Q)}{d\log_e(P)}\cdot\frac{d\log_e(P)}{d\,[\log_z(e).\log_e(P)]}\right\}$$

$$= \log_z(e)\left\{\frac{d\log_e(Q)}{d\log_e(P)}\cdot\frac{d\,[\log_e(P).\log_z(e)/\log_z(e)]}{d\,[\log_z(e).\log_e(P)]}\right\}$$

$$= \log_z(e)\left\{\frac{d\log_e(Q)}{d\log_e(P)}\cdot 1/\log_z(e)\right\}$$

$$= \frac{d\log(Q)}{d\log(P)}$$

Consequently if the proposition is true for $d\log(Q)/d\log(P)$, it is true for $d\log_z(Q)/d\log_z(P)$, $z > 0$.

It remains to prove that

$$-\frac{d\log(Q)}{d\log(P)} = \eta$$

where η is the elasticity of demand. By using the function of a function rule,

$$\text{(31)} \qquad \frac{d\log(Q)}{d\log(P)} = \frac{d\log(Q)}{dP}\cdot\frac{dP}{d\log(P)}$$

Substituting $P = \exp(u)$ shows that

$$\frac{dP}{d\log(P)} = \frac{d\exp(u)}{du} = \exp(u) = P$$

Since the derivative of the logarithmic function is the reciprocal function it follows, by using the function of a function rule, that

$$\frac{d\log(Q)}{dP} = \frac{1}{Q} \cdot \frac{dQ}{dP}$$

Substituting these equations into the right-hand side of equation (31) gives

$$\frac{d\log(Q)}{d\log(P)} = \left(\frac{1}{Q} \cdot \frac{dQ}{dP}\right) \cdot P$$

$$= -\eta$$

which proves equation (30).

We have shown that for any base, $z > 0$, the negative of the derivative of the logarithm of the quantity demanded with respect to the logarithm of the price is equal to the elasticity of demand. An immediate consequence of this is that if the demand curve is such that the derivative of the logarithm of the quantity demanded with respect to the logarithm of the price is a constant, the elasticity of demand is also a constant. The derivative of the logarithm of the quantity demanded with respect to the logarithm of the price will be a constant if and only if the logarithm of the quantity demanded is a linear function of the logarithm of the price. Consequently the set of all demand curves for which the elasticity is a constant is described by the equation

$$\log_z(Q) = a - b\log_z(P) \qquad (z > 0)$$

where the parameters a and b can have any real values. Differentiating this equation with respect to $\log_z(P)$ shows that the parameter b is equal to the elasticity of demand.

The graph of a typical demand curve of constant elasticity is shown in Fig. 18C.

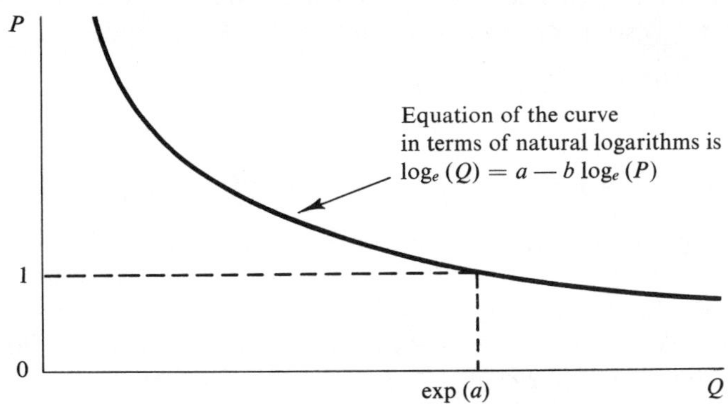

Fig. 18C A typical demand curve of constant elasticity

Example 3 The estimation of the parameters of the Cobb-Douglas production function

The general form of the Cobb-Douglas production is

(32) $$Y = AL^{\alpha}K^{\beta}$$

where Y is output, L is labour input, K is capital input, A is a constant of proportionality (which depends both on the units in which Y, L and K are measured and partly on the technology of production) and α and β are parameters which describe the technical nature of production.

As it stands it is very difficult to calculate from empirical data the values of the parameters, A, α and β. Computations are made much easier by taking logarithms to the base 10, which gives

(33) $$\log_{10}(Y) = \log_{10}(A) + \alpha \log_{10}(L) + \beta \log_{10}(K)$$

Equation (33) expresses $\log_{10}(Y)$ as a linear function of $\log_{10}(L)$ and $\log_{10}(K)$ [in fact it can be shown that for any base, $z > 0$, $\log_z(Y)$ is a linear function of $\log_z(L)$ and $\log_z(K)$].

The fact that equation (33) can be deduced from equation (32) is a considerable help in calculating the parameters of the Cobb–Douglas production function, for the parameters in the linear equation (33) are much easier to calculate from empirical data than are the parameters of the non-linear equation (32).

18.7 Special rule for evaluating logarithms to the base 10

Logarithms to the base 10 are known as common logarithms. An important advantage of working in logarithms to the base 10 may be deduced as follows. Any positive number, y, can be written in the form

$$y = 10^n.x$$

where n is some integer, $n = \ldots -2, -1, 0, 1, 2, \ldots$ and x is some number between 1 and 10. A moment's consideration will make it clear that if $y = 10^n.x$ and $1 \leqslant x \leqslant 10$ then there must be $n + 1$ figures to the left of the decimal point in the number y. Now when x is some number between 1 and 10 it follows that if $x = 10^z$ then z is some number between 0 and 1; furthermore

$$y = 10^n.x = 10^n 10^z = 10^{n+z}$$

so that

$$\log_{10}(y) = n + z$$

where n is an integer and z is some number between 0 and 1. It follows from the fact that $x = 10^z$ and $y = 10^n.x$ that z is the logarithm of the number $10^{-n}y$. By assumption, z lies between 0 and 1, so that $z = \log_{10}(10^{-n}y)$ can always be found from a table of common logarithms ranging from 0 to 1. In other words, *if there are $n + 1$ figures to the left of the decimal point in the number y then*

$$\log_{10}(y) = n + \log_{10}(10^{-n}y)$$

where $\log_{10}(10^{-n}y)$ *may be found from tables of the common logarithm ranging from* 0 *to* 1.

Example Let us return to Example 3 of Section 17.3 and see how common logarithms can be used to find the value after 5 years of £1,000 invested at 8% per annum. The amount to be evaluated is

$$Y(5) = 1{,}000(1{\cdot}08)^5$$

Taking logarithms to the base 10 shows that

$$\log_{10}(Y(5)) = 3 + 5\log_{10}(1{\cdot}08)$$

The evaluation of $Y(5)$ is shown in Table 18.4. The first stage is to evaluate $\log_{10}(Y(5))$: from four-figure tables it is seen that $\log_{10}(1{\cdot}08) = 0{\cdot}0334$, so that $\log_{10}(Y(5)) = 3 + 5 \times 0{\cdot}0334 = 3{\cdot}1670$. It follows that $Y(5)$ is the number whose logarithm is 3·1670. This number can be found from a table of 'antilogarithms' in the following way. The table of antilogarithms to the base 10 is

Table 18.4

Number		*Logarithm*
1·08	→	0·0334
		5 ×
		0·1670
		+ 3·0000
1,469	←	3·1670 ($\log_{10}(Y(5))$

usually given only for logarithms between 0 and 1. To find the numbers whose logarithms are outside this range it is necessary to use the fact that for any two numbers, r, s, $10^{r+s} = 10^r . 10^s$. Substituting $r = 3$, $s = 0{\cdot}1670$ it follows that

$$10^{3{\cdot}1670} = 10^3 . 10^{0{\cdot}1670}$$

so that the number whose logarithm is 3·1670 is equal to the number whose logarithm is 3 multiplied by the number whose logarithm is 0·1670. The number whose logarithm to the base 10 is 3 is 1,000, and, from tables of the antilogarithm, the number whose logarithm to the base 10 is 0·1670 is 1·469. Consequently, the number whose logarithm is 3·1670 is 1,469. It follows that the value of the investment after 5 years is £1,469. This approximate value compares with the exact value, deduced in Section 17.3 of £1,469·3280768 (the approximation is due to the rounding of the logarithms to four figures).

Notes and references

Exponentials and logarithms are discussed in all the standard texts on mathematics for economists, see Allen,[6] Ch. 9, Lewis,[79] Ch. 13, 14, and Yamane,[126] Ch. 3, 7. For economic applications see the references to Chapter 17 and Chapter 20.

Problems

18.1 Find an approximate value for exp (1) by taking the first six terms of the series expansion of the exponential function.

18.2.1 Differentiate with respect to x (a) $y = x \exp(x)$, (b) $y = 2x^2 \exp(3x)$, (c) $\exp x/x^2$.

18.2.2 The Poisson distribution is defined as follows. The probability, $p(x)$, of obtaining the sample measurement x ($x = 0, 1, 2, \ldots$) is

$$p(x) = \exp(-m)m^x/x!$$

where m is a parameter of the distribution. Show that the Poisson distribution is a probability distribution, i.e. show that the sum of the probabilities is equal to unity,

$$\sum_{i=0}^{\infty} p(i) = 1$$

[*Hint:* Compare the sum of the probabilities with the series expansion of exp (m); then use equation (7) in the text.]

18.2.3 The normal probability density function with zero mean and unit standard deviation is

$$\phi(x) = (1/\sqrt{(2\pi)}) \exp(-\tfrac{1}{2}x^2)$$

(a) By substituting $u = -\frac{1}{2}x^2$ into the series expansion of exp (u), show that

$$\exp(-\tfrac{1}{2}x^2) = 1 - \tfrac{1}{2}x^2 + x^4/(2!2^2) - x^6/(3!2^3) + \cdots$$

(b) Given that $1/\sqrt{(2\pi)} = 0{\cdot}40$ to 2 decimal places, evaluate $\phi(1)$ using the first four terms of the series expansion of $\exp(-\frac{1}{2}x^2)$.

(c) Compare your answer to (b) with the true value $\phi(1) = 0{\cdot}2420$.

(d) Graph $\phi(x)$, paying particular attention to the location of its maximum and its points of inflection as well as to its behaviour for large positive and negative values of x.

18.3.1 What is the value in 10 years of £600 invested at 7% per annum when compounding is continuous?

18.3.2 What sum invested at 8% per annum and compounded continuously will be worth £1,000 in 10 years time?

18.3.3 (Problem 17.6.2 continued) If output is initially at the rate of £20m per annum, what will be the rate of output after (i) 4 years (ii) 20 years?

18.4.1 If world population is growing continuously at 3·5% per annum, approximately how many years will it take for the population to double?

18.4.2 (Problem 18.3.3 continued) Approximately how many years will it take for output to increase by 50%?

18.4.3 A man receives a lump sum legacy of £200 and saves up to buy a car which costs £600. If he invests his legacy at a rate of interest of 10%, and if compounding is continuous, how long will it be before he can buy the car? (Use the fact that log (3) = 1·10 to 2 decimal places.)

18.5 The definition $x^\alpha = \exp(\alpha \log(x))$, $x > 0$, defines x^α for *any real number* α. Using this definition, prove that

$$dx^\alpha/dx = \alpha x^{\alpha - 1}$$

This formula for differentiation generalizes to any power the rule proved in Chapter 5 for integer values of α.

18.6 Verify that the demand curve whose equation is

$$Q = A/P^\beta$$

(Q is demand, P is price, A and β are constants) has a constant elasticity of demand equal to β. Show this

(a) by taking logs and then differentiating;

(b) by differentiating directly.

18.7 The population of the United Kingdom in 1970 was 55 million. Suppose that the population is expected to grow exponentially at 4% per annum over the next 10 years.

(a) Find the projected population in 1980.

(b) If the government wishes to expand the capacity of the higher education sector from 2% of the population to 4% by 1980, find the yearly percentage increase in higher education places necessary to meet the government's target (additions to the number of places can take place only once a year).

Chapter 19
Complex numbers

19.1 Introduction

In many problems particular interest centres on the values of the roots of a polynomial; for example, if the polynomial is an expansion of the determinant det [M $-$ hI] of the $n + n$ matrix (M $-$ hI), then the roots $h_1, h_2, \ldots h_n$ are the characteristic values of the matrix M (see Section 14.2). These characteristic values are important for the dynamic analysis of interacting markets and for the theory of income distribution. Characteristic values also play a vitally important part in the theory of linear difference and differential equations described in Chapter 20.

When expanded, det [M $-$ hI] is a polynomial of degree n in h, i.e. an equation of the form

$$f(h) = b_0 + b_1 h + b_2 h^2 + \cdots + b_{n-1} h^{n-1} + h^n = 0$$

The values of h which satisfy this equation are known as the roots of the polynomial $f(h)$. If the roots are $h_1, h_2, \ldots, h_n$ then the polynomial can be factorized in the form

$$f(h) = (h - h_1)(h - h_2)\ldots(h - h_n)$$

so that setting $h = h_i (i = 1, 2, \ldots, n)$ sets $f(h) = 0$.

It is not necessarily true that a polynomial of degree n has n real roots. Indeed, it is quite possible that a polynomial $f(h)$ has no real roots at all. If the reader plots the graph of the polynomial $f(h) = h^2 - 2h + 5$ he will see at once that the graph never crosses the h axis, so that there is no real value of h for which $f(h) = 0$. For the present purpose, the importance of complex numbers lies in the fact that an arbitrary polynomial of degree n, which may have no real roots at all, always has exactly n complex roots (i.e. roots which are complex numbers). For this reason it is often more convenient to work in terms of complex numbers rather than in terms of real numbers.

19.2 Complex numbers

The theory of complex numbers is, to a mathematician, one of the most fascinating, ingenious and aesthetically pleasing branches of mathematics. To an economist, the theory of complex numbers is somewhat abstract, usually bewildering and occasionally useful. This chapter will be confined mainly to the useful aspects of complex numbers, though a certain amount of background material will be covered as well.

How do complex numbers arise? Perhaps the simplest way in which a complex number can arise is in the solution of a quadratic equation. For example, to solve the quadratic equation

(1) $$x^2 + 1 = 0$$

it is necessary to find a number x, such that x^2 is equal to -1. Now if x is a real number, then when x is positive, x^2 is positive and when x is negative, x^2 is again positive. When $x = 0$ then $x^2 = 0$. It follows that for any real number x, $x^2 \geqslant 0$. Hence the quadratic equation $x^2 = -1$ cannot have a solution which is a real number. To avoid the embarrassment of not having a solution it is expedient to *define* a solution of the equation (1). It is customary to call the solution 'the square root of minus one' since the solution, when squared, must be equal to minus one. The square root of minus one cannot be a real number, as noted above; it is therefore known as an imaginary number, and denoted i.

The imaginary number i can be used together with real numbers to give a formal solution to any quadratic equation. Consider, for example, the solution of the equation

(2) $$x^2 - 2x + 5 = 0$$

The formula for the solution of a quadratic shows that

$$x = \frac{2 \pm \sqrt{-16}}{2}$$

The expression for x can be put into the form

$$x = \frac{2 \pm \sqrt{16}\sqrt{-1}}{2}$$

Noting that $\sqrt{16} = 4$ and that, by definition, $\mathrm{i} = \sqrt{-1}$, it follows that

$$x = \frac{2 \pm 4\mathrm{i}}{2} = 1 \pm 2\mathrm{i}$$

Thus the formal solution of the quadratic equation (2) is given by the two roots,

$$x_1 = 1 + 2\mathrm{i}, \qquad x_2 = 1 - 2\mathrm{i}$$

The roots x_1 and x_2 are examples of complex numbers: a complex number contains both a real part and an imaginary part. For example, the real part of x_1 is the number 1 and the imaginary part is 2i; the real part of x_2 is the number 1, the imaginary part is $-2\mathrm{i}$.

As a check that x_1 and x_2 are the roots of equation (2) it is easily verified that the equation factorizes in the form

(3) $$x^2 - 2x + 5 = (x - 1 - 2\mathrm{i})(x - 1 + 2\mathrm{i})$$

To demonstrate this it is necessary to understand the algebra of complex numbers. This algebra is really no more than a commonsense extension of the algebra of real numbers. Multiplying out the brackets in equation (3) in the usual way (i.e. multiplying the terms in the first bracket successively into the whole of the second bracket) gives

$$x^2 - x + 2ix - x + 1 - 2i - 2ix + 2i - (2i)^2$$

Cancelling and grouping terms gives

$$x^2 - 2x + 1 - (2i)^2$$

Now $(2i)^2 = 2^2 \times i^2 = 2^2 \times -1 = -4$ so that the final result is

$$x^2 - 2x + 5$$

which is the left-hand side of equation (3).

Another example should help clear up any difficulty with the addition, subtraction and multiplication of complex numbers.

Example Evaluate $(3 + 2i)(5 - 4i) - 6i$. Taking the first term and multiplying out the brackets in the usual way gives

$$(3 + 2i)(5 - 4i) = 15 - 12i + 10i - (2i)(4i)$$

Now $-(2i)(4i) = -8i^2 = -8 \times -1 = 8$ so that

$$(3 + 2i)(5 - 4i) = 15 - 12i + 10i + 8$$

Grouping terms we get

$$(3 + 2i)(5 - 4i) = 23 - 2i$$

Now taking the second term into account gives

$$(3 + 2i)(5 - 4i) - 6i = 23 - 2i - 6i$$

and on grouping terms the right-hand side is seen to equal

$$23 - 8i$$

which is the answer required.

19.3 The Argand diagram

There is a very useful way of representing complex numbers geometrically. This is to represent each number by a point in a plane; the plane is known as the complex plane. The two coordinates of a point in the complex plane are, respectively, the real part and the coefficient of the imaginary part of the complex number.

In Fig. 19A two axes are drawn for reference. The horizontal axis is the *real axis*, along which is measured the real part of the complex number. The vertical axis is the *imaginary axis*, along which is measured the imaginary part of the complex number. The point representing the complex number $z = x + iy$ is such that its coordinate, when referred to the real axis, is equal to x, and its coordinate, when referred to the imaginary axis, is equal to y. For

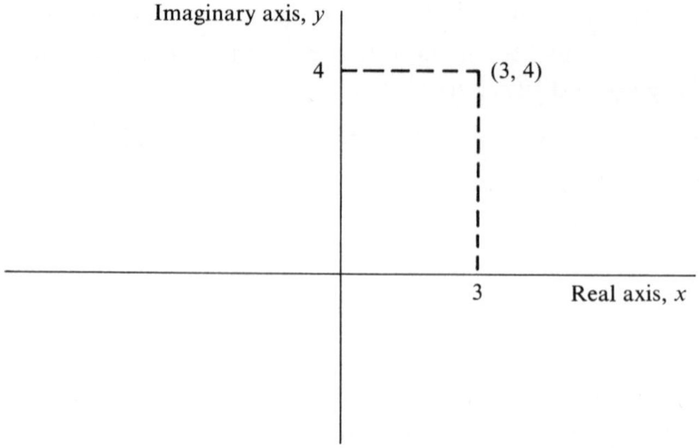

Fig. 19A Argand diagram showing the geometric representation of the number 3+4i

illustration, the point representing the complex number 3 + 4i is shown in Fig. 19A.

There is more than one way of describing the location of a point in the complex plane. It can be done in the way described above, using the coordinates of the point referred to the real axis and to the imaginary axis. It can also be done by taking the length of the line joining the point to the origin, together with the angle this line makes with the real axis. In Fig. 19B the location of the point A is described uniquely by the length, r, of the line OA, together with the angle, θ, which the line OA makes with the real axis. This second description of the point A is often more useful than the first. It is therefore interesting to see how this second specification can be obtained from the first specification.

The connection between the two specifications is a matter of simple geometry. Consider the right-angled triangle OAB shown in Fig. 19C. The length of the line AB is equal to the coordinate of A referred to the imaginary

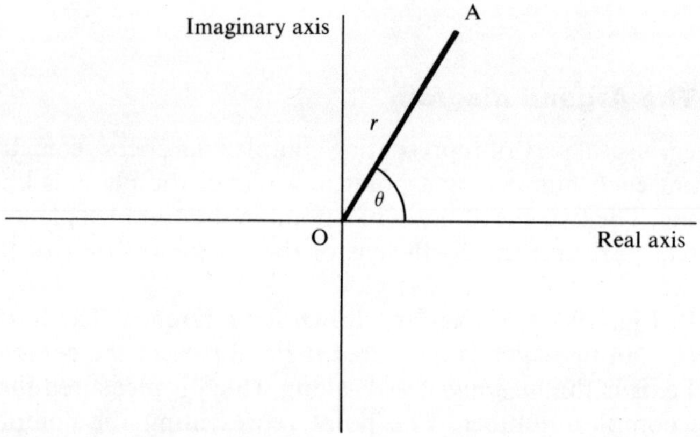

Fig. 19B Argand diagram showing how the point A can be described by the parameters r and θ

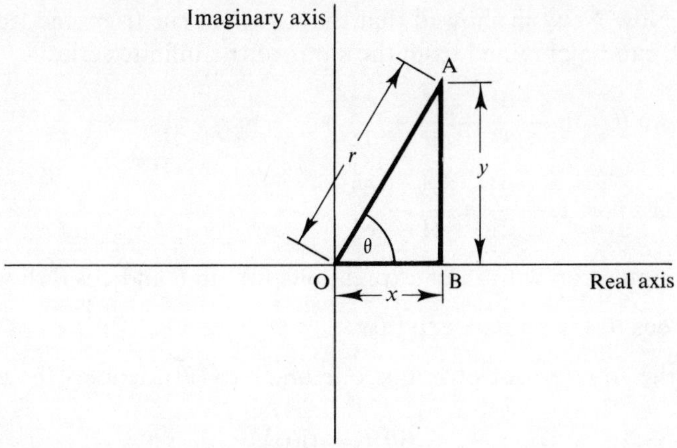

Fig. 19C Connection between coordinates (x,y) and coordinates (r,θ)

axis, i.e. the length of AB is equal to y; similarly, the length of the line OB is equal to the coordinate of A referred to the real axis, i.e. the length of OB is equal to x. The length of the line OA has already been given as r. The lines AB and OB are two sides of the right-angled triangle OAB, whose hypotenuse is OA. It follows from Pythagoras' theorem that

$$\text{OA} = \sqrt{(\text{OB}^2 + \text{AB}^2)}$$

i.e. that

$$r = \sqrt{(x^2 + y^2)}$$

Since OAB is a right-angled triangle it follows from elementary trigonometry that

$$\sin\theta = \frac{\text{AB}}{\text{OA}} = \frac{y}{r}$$

(4)

$$\cos\theta = \frac{\text{OB}}{\text{OA}} = \frac{x}{r}$$

Multiplying the equations (4) throughout by r gives

$$y = r\sin\theta$$

$$x = r\cos\theta$$

This establishes a relationship between the description of the point A by the coordinates (x, y) and the description of A by the distance from the origin, r, and the angle made with the real axis, θ. The variables r, θ are sometimes described as the 'polar coordinates' of the point A, to distinguish them from the 'Cartesian coordinates', x, y. Since the point A is simply a geometric representation of the complex number $z = x + \mathrm{i}y$, it follows from equations (4) that the number z can also be written in the form

(5) $$z = x + \mathrm{i}y = r\cos\theta + \mathrm{i}r\sin\theta = r(\cos\theta + \mathrm{i}\sin\theta)$$

Now Newton showed that the values of the trignometric functions, sin θ, cos θ, can be obtained from the sums of the infinite series

(6)
$$\sin\theta = \theta - \frac{\theta^3}{3!} + \frac{\theta^5}{5!} - \frac{\theta^7}{7!} + \cdots$$
$$\cos\theta = 1 - \frac{\theta^2}{2!} + \frac{\theta^4}{4!} - \frac{\theta^6}{6!} + \cdots$$

A little manipulation with these expressions for sin θ and cos θ shows that

(7) $$\cos\theta + \mathrm{i}\sin\theta = \exp(\mathrm{i}\theta)$$

where i is the square root of minus one and exp (iθ) denotes the exponential series

(8) $$\exp(\mathrm{i}\theta) = 1 + \mathrm{i}\theta + \frac{(\mathrm{i}\theta)^2}{2!} + \frac{(\mathrm{i}\theta)^3}{3!} + \cdots$$

The reader can easily verify equation (7) for himself; it is necessary only to multiply out equation (8) using the fact that $\mathrm{i}^2 = -1$, and then to compare the result with the expressions for the sine and cosine in equations (6).

Substituting equation (7) into equation (5), it is seen that

(9) $$z = r\exp(\mathrm{i}\theta)$$

This is known as the polar form of the complex number z, and in many cases it is the most convenient form in which a complex number can be written. It has been established above that when the number z is plotted as a point, A, in the complex plane, the distance of A from the origin is equal to r, and the line from A to the origin makes an angle θ with the real axis.

19.4 Modulus and argument of a complex number

In the polar form of the complex number, given by equation (9), the angle θ is measured in radians and not in degrees. A radian is simply an alternative way of measuring an angle; it is defined as follows. One radian is equal to the angle subtended at the origin of a circle by an arc formed by measuring off the radius of the circle along the circumference. In Fig. 19D the length of the circumference between the points X and Y is equal to the radius of the circle, r. The angle, θ, made by the lines OX and OY is equal to one radian. This defines a radian. One radian is equal to approximately 57·296 degrees.

The reader is expected to be familiar with the fact that the length of the circumference of a circle is 2π times the radius of the circle, where $\pi = 3{\cdot}1416$ to 4 decimal places. It follows from this that if the line OX is rotated through 2π radians then it will completely circumscribe the origin O, and the point X will return to its original position on the circumference of the circle; it follows that an angle of 2π radians is equivalent to an angle of 360 degrees.

In the theory of the complex number, the angle θ, when measured in radians, is said to be the *argument*[1] of the complex number $z = r\exp(\mathrm{i}\theta)$;

1 Also known as the *amplitude* or *phase*.

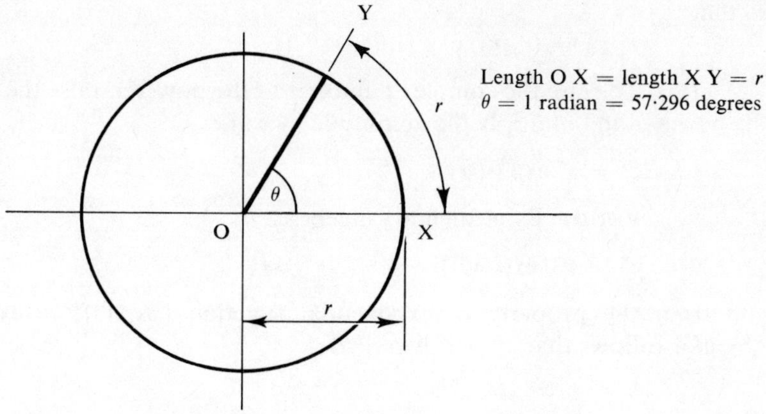

Fig. 19D Definition of a radian

the radius, r, is said to be the *modulus* of the complex number $z = r \exp(i\theta)$. It is easy to establish the following results.

(i) To multiply two complex numbers, multiply the moduli and add the arguments; i.e. if

$$z_1 = r_1 \exp(i\theta), \qquad z_2 = r_2 \exp(i\theta_2)$$

then

$$z_1 z_2 = r_1 r_2 \exp[i(\theta_1 + \theta_2)]$$

PROOF By elementary algebra

$$z_1 z_2 = r_1 r_2 \exp(i\theta_1) \exp(i\theta_2)$$

Substituting $u = i\theta_1$, $v = i\theta_2$ and using the property of the exponential function that

$$\exp(u) \exp(v) = \exp(u + v)$$

we get

$$z_1 z_2 = r_1 r_2 \exp[i(\theta_1 + \theta_2)]$$

(ii) To divide two complex numbers, divide the moduli and subtract the arguments; i.e. if

$$z_1 = r_1 \exp(i\theta_1), \qquad z_2 = r_2 \exp(i\theta_2)$$

then

$$z_1/z_2 = (r_1/r_2) \exp[i(\theta_1 - \theta_2)]$$

PROOF By elementary algebra

$$z_1/z_2 = (r_1/r_2)[\exp(i\theta_1)/\exp(i\theta_2)]$$

From the properties of the exponential function it follows that

$$1/\exp(i\theta_2) = \exp(-i\theta_2)$$

and that

$$\exp(i\theta_1) \exp(-i\theta_2) = \exp(i\theta_1 - i\theta_2)$$

Hence

$$\exp(i\theta_1)/\exp(i\theta_2) = \exp[i(\theta_1 - \theta_2)]$$

so that

$$z_1/z_2 = (r_1/r_2) \exp [i(\theta_1 - \theta_2)]$$

(iii) To raise the complex number z to the power α, raise the modulus to the power α and multiply the amplitude by α; i.e.

$$z^\alpha = r^\alpha \exp (i\theta\alpha)$$

PROOF By elementary algebra

$$z^\alpha = r^\alpha [\exp (i\theta)]^\alpha$$

and from the property of exponential function $[\exp (s)]^\alpha = \exp (s\alpha)$ with $s = i\theta$ it follows that $z^\alpha = r^\alpha \exp (i\theta\alpha)$.

19.5 Conjugate of a complex number

Complex numbers generally occur in pairs. This is always the case, for instance, when complex numbers occur as the roots of a polynomial with real coefficients. Each pair consists of a complex number and its conjugate. The conjugate of the general complex number $z = x + iy$ is the number $\bar{z} = x - iy$; i.e. the conjugate, $\bar{z}$, of a complex number, z, is obtained simply by changing the sign of the imaginary part. For example, the conjugate of the number $5 - 3i$ is the number $5 + 3i$, and vice versa.[2]

We have already seen that complex numbers occur in conjugate pairs when they are the roots of a quadratic equation. For example, the roots of the equation (2) are $1 + 2i$, $1 - 2i$, and the reader can easily satisfy himself that the roots of equation (1) are i and $-i$. Since complex numbers always occur in pairs when they are the roots of a polynomial, it follows, for example, that the three roots of a cubic equation must either all be real, or two must be complex and one real; there is no other possibility. The following argument explains why this must be true.

Elementary algebra shows that the conjugate of the sum of two numbers is the sum of the conjugates,

$$\overline{(z_1 + z_2)} = \overline{z_1} + \overline{z_2}$$

and that the conjugate of the product of two numbers is the product of the conjugates,

$$\overline{(z_1 z_2)} = \overline{z_1}\,\overline{z_2}$$

from which it follows that if

$$f(z) = a_0 + a_1 z_1 + a_2 z^2 + \cdots a_n z^n$$

then

$$\overline{f(z)} = \overline{a_0} + \overline{a_1 z_1} + \overline{a_2 z^2} + \cdots + \overline{a_n z^n}$$

2 It is usually the case in economic problems that where the solution involves complex numbers the imaginary parts of the complex numbers cancel one another out, i.e. if the solution is a formula in complex numbers then the formula, when evaluated, is necessary equal to a real number. An example is given in the next chapter.

When the coefficients $a_0, a_1, a_2, \ldots a_n$ are real it follows that

$$a_0 = \overline{a_0}, \qquad a_1 = \overline{a_1}, \qquad a_2 = \overline{a_2}, \qquad \ldots, a_n = \overline{a_n}$$

so that

$$\overline{f(z)} = a_0 + a_1\bar{z}_1 + a_2\bar{z}^2 + \cdots + a_n\bar{z}^n = f(\bar{z})$$

It is a trivial point that if $f(z) = 0$ then $\overline{f(z)} = 0$, and since $\overline{f(z)} = f(\bar{z})$ it follows that $f(\bar{z}) = 0$ as well. Hence any solution of the equation $f(z) = 0$ is a solution of the equation $f(\bar{z}) = 0$, so that if any number is a root of $f(z)$ then its conjugate is also a root of $f(z)$. For this reason the roots of the polynomial with real coefficients, $f(z)$ must either be real, or must occur in conjugate pairs.

A useful property is that the product of a complex number and its conjugate is equal to the square of the modulus

$$z\bar{z} = (x + \mathrm{i}y)(x - \mathrm{i}y) = x^2 + \mathrm{i}xy - \mathrm{i}xy - (\mathrm{i}y)^2 = x^2 + y^2$$

(10) $$= [\sqrt{(x^2 + y^2)}]^2$$

By using this result it can be shown that the reciprocal of a complex number is equal to the conjugate divided by the square of the modulus.

(PROOF The reciprocal z^{-1} is defined by the equation $zz^{-1} = 1$. Setting

(11) $$z^{-1} = \bar{z}/(z\bar{z})$$

shows that $zz^{-1} = z\bar{z}/(z\bar{z}) = 1$. Substituting (10) into the denominator of (11) completes the proof.)

Example Find the reciprocal of $z = 0{\cdot}5 - 1{\cdot}5\mathrm{i}$.

The conjugate is $\bar{z} = 0{\cdot}5 + 1{\cdot}5\mathrm{i}$ and the square of the modulus is $0{\cdot}5^2 + 1{\cdot}5^2 = 2{\cdot}5$, whence

$$\bar{z} = (0{\cdot}5 + 1{\cdot}5\mathrm{i})/2{\cdot}5 = 0{\cdot}2 - 0{\cdot}6\mathrm{i}$$

CHECK $$z\bar{z} = (0{\cdot}5 - 1{\cdot}5\mathrm{i})(0{\cdot}2 + 0{\cdot}6\mathrm{i})$$

$$= 0{\cdot}1 + 0{\cdot}3\mathrm{i} - 0{\cdot}3\mathrm{i} + 0{\cdot}9$$

$$= 1$$

19.6 Fundamental theorem of algebra

The importance of complex numbers in mathematical analysis is largely accounted for by a result known as the fundamental theorem of algebra.

Theorem 19.1 A polynomial of degree n with complex numerical coefficients has exactly n complex roots.

An example of a fifth degree polynomial with complex numerical coefficients is

$$f(z) = 3 - (2{\cdot}5 + \mathrm{i})z + (4 - 3\mathrm{i})z^2 + \mathrm{i}z^5$$

Complex numbers include, as special cases, both real numbers and imaginary numbers. Consequently a special case of the theorem tells us that any equation of the form

$$f(z) = b_0 + b_1 z + b_2 z^2 + \cdots + b_n z^n = 0$$

where $b_0, b_1, \ldots, b_n$ are real numbers, has exactly n roots. It is important to appreciate that these roots are not necessarily distinct.

This fundamental theorem illustrates one of the advantages of working in complex numbers. Most equations in complex numbers have solutions which are complex numbers, whereas many equations in real numbers do not have solutions which are real numbers. For this reason it is often more convenient to work in terms of complex numbers.

Notes and references

Two very lucid little books on complex numbers are Lederman[75] and Phillips.[104] There is a fairly extensive treatment of complex numbers in Lewis,[79] Ch. 24.

Problems

19.2.1 Solve the following equations and verify your answers.
(a) $x^2 + 2x + 10 = 0$
(b) $x^2 + x + \frac{1}{2} = 0$
(c) $x^2 + 6x + 10 = 0$
(d) $x^3 - 4x^2 - 7x + 4 = 0$

19.2.2 Express the following in the form $x + iy$.
(a) $(3 + 6i)(2 - i)$
(b) $(\frac{1}{2} - i)^2$
(c) $(3 + i) - (6 - 3i)$
(d) $(2 + 3i)(3 - 4i) + (1 + i)^2$
(e) $i^3(1 + 3i)$

19.3.1 Plot the following complex numbers on an Argand diagram and express them in polar form.

(a) $5 + 12i$ (b) $\sqrt{3} + i$ (c) $1 + i$ (d) $3 + 4i$

19.3.2 Using the first seven terms of the series expansion of $\exp(i\theta)$ verify that

$$\exp(i\theta) = \cos\theta + i\sin\theta$$

19.3.3 By using the first four terms of the series expansion of $\cos\theta$ and $\sin\theta$ verify that

$$\frac{d}{d\theta}\sin\theta = \cos\theta$$

$$\frac{d}{d\theta}\cos\theta = -\sin\theta$$

19.4 Find the moduli of the following numbers.

(a) $-3 + 4i$ (b) $4 + 3i$ (c) 5 (d) $1 + 2i$ (e) $3 + 2i$

19.5 Express the following in the form $x + iy$.
(a) $(2 + 3i)/(3 + 2i)$
(b) $1/i^5$
(c) $3i/(4 - 5i)^2$

19.6 By using the formula for the solution of a quadratic verify Theorem 19.1 for the case

$$x^2 + (5 - 3i)x - 8 - 4i = 0$$

[HINT Use the fact that $(7 - i)^2 = 48 - 14i$]

Chapter 20

Linear difference and differential equations of the second order and above

The subject of difference and differential equations is very large. In a single chapter of an elementary textbook it is impossible to do more than discuss a few special cases. The cases examined below have been selected on account of their relevance to economics. Unfortunately, when applying difference and differential equations the sophistication of the economics is often greater than the sophistication of the mathematical techniques, so it is not always possible to elucidate results with a simple application.

20.1 Linear difference equations of the second order

A linear difference equation of the second order has the general form

$$\Delta^2 Y(t) + a_1 \Delta Y(t) + a_2 Y(t) = g(t)$$

It is often convenient to make the substitutions

$$\Delta Y(t) = Y(t+1) - Y(t), \qquad \Delta^2 Y(t) = Y(t+2) - 2Y(t+1) - Y(t)$$

and write

(1) $$Y(t+2) + b_1 Y(t+1) + b_2 Y(t) = g(t)$$

where $b_1 = a_1 - 2$, $b_2 = a_2 - a_1$. The solution of equation (1) is complicated by the fact that $g(t)$ is an arbitrary function of t. When $g(t)$ is a constant the solution of equation (1) is relatively simple.

Theorem 20.1 The solution of

(2) $$Y(t+2) + b_1 Y(t+1) + b_2 Y(t) = E$$

is

(3) $$Y(N) = A_1 h_1^N + A_2 h_2^N + B$$

where h_1, h_2 are the roots of the quadratic

(4) $$h^2 + b_1 h + b_2 = 0$$

If three values of $Y(t)$ are known, say for $t = 0, 1, 2$, then A_1, A_2, B are determined by the simultaneous linear equations

$$\begin{aligned} A_1 \quad + A_2 \quad + B &= Y(0) \\ A_1h_1 + A_2h_2 + B &= Y(1) \\ A_1h_1^2 + A_2h_2^2 + B &= Y(2) \end{aligned}$$

If the roots of (4) are equal (which occurs only if $b_2 = b_1^2/4$) then the solution is of the form

(5) $$Y(N) = A_1h^{*N} + A_2Nh^{*N} + B$$

where h^* is the solution of (4) and A_1, A_2, B are determined by the equations

$$\begin{aligned} A_1 \qquad\qquad + B &= Y(0) \\ A_1h^* + A_2h^* + B &= Y(1) \\ A_1h^{*2} + 2A_2h^{*2} + B &= Y(2) \end{aligned}$$

PROOF It is useful to consider equation (2) in conjunction with the dummy equation $Y(t + 1) = Y(t + 1)$:

$$\begin{aligned} Y(t + 2) &= -b_1Y(t + 1) - b_2Y(t) + E \\ Y(t + 1) &= \qquad Y(t + 1) \end{aligned}$$

This pair of equations may be written in matrix notation as

(6) $$\mathbf{y}(t + 1) = \mathbf{M}\mathbf{y}(t) + \mathbf{e}$$

where

$$\mathbf{y}(t) = \begin{bmatrix} y(t + 1) \\ y(t) \end{bmatrix}, \qquad \mathbf{M} = \begin{bmatrix} -b_1 & -b_2 \\ 1 & 0 \end{bmatrix}, \qquad \mathbf{e} = \begin{bmatrix} E \\ 0 \end{bmatrix}$$

Setting successively $t = 0, 1, 2, \ldots, N - 1$ in equation (6) it is seen that

$$\mathbf{y}(N) = M^N\mathbf{y}(0) + (\mathbf{I} + \mathbf{M} + \cdots + \mathbf{M}^{N-1})\mathbf{e}$$

Let us now suppose that the characteristic vectors of the matrix $\mathbf{M}$ are, respectively,

$$\mathbf{m}_1 = \begin{bmatrix} m_{11} \\ m_{12} \end{bmatrix}, \qquad \mathbf{m}_2 = \begin{bmatrix} m_{21} \\ m_{22} \end{bmatrix}$$

and that there are weights $a_{11}, a_{12}, a_{21}, a_{22}$ such that

$$\begin{aligned} \mathbf{y}(0) &= a_{11}\mathbf{m}_1 + a_{12}\mathbf{m}_2 \\ \mathbf{e} &= a_{21}\mathbf{m}_1 + a_{22}\mathbf{m}_2 \end{aligned}$$

i.e. there are weights such that both the vector $\mathbf{y}(0)$ and the vector $\mathbf{e}$ can be expressed as weighted sums of the characteristic vectors $\mathbf{m}_1$, $\mathbf{m}_2$. Equation (6) may then be written

(7) $$\mathbf{y}(N) = \mathbf{M}^N(a_{11}\mathbf{m}_1 + a_{12}\mathbf{m}_2) + (\mathbf{I} + \mathbf{M} + \cdots + \mathbf{M}^{N-1}) \\ (a_{21}\mathbf{m}_1 + a_{22}\mathbf{m}_2)$$

Using the linearity of matrix multiplication equation (7) becomes

$$\text{(8)} \qquad \mathbf{y}(N) = a_{11}\mathbf{M}^N\mathbf{m}_1 + a_{12}\mathbf{M}^N\mathbf{m}_2 + a_{21}\mathbf{m}_1 + a_{21}\mathbf{M}\mathbf{m}_1 + \cdots + a_{21}\mathbf{M}^{N-1}\mathbf{m}_1 + a_{22}\mathbf{m}_2 + a_{22}\mathbf{M}\mathbf{m}_2 + \cdots + a_{22}\mathbf{M}^{N-1}\mathbf{m}_2$$

Now in equation (8) the matrix $\mathbf{M}$ is always multiplied into its characteristic vectors, and we know from Chapter 14 that the effect of multiplying $\mathbf{M}$ into one of its characteristic vector is simply to scale the vector by the corresponding characteristic value. It follows that equation (8) simplifies to

$$\text{(9)} \qquad \mathbf{y}(N) = a_{11}h_1^N\mathbf{m}_1 + a_{12}h_2^N\mathbf{m}_2 + a_{21}\mathbf{m}_1 + a_{21}h_1\mathbf{m}_1 + \cdots + a_{21}h_1^{N-1}\mathbf{m}_1 + a_{22}\mathbf{m}_2 + a_{22}h_2\mathbf{m}_2 + \cdots + a_{22}h_2^{N-1}\mathbf{m}_2$$

where h_1, h_2 are the characteristic values of the matrix $\mathbf{M}$. Grouping terms in equation (9) gives

$$\text{(10)} \qquad \mathbf{y}(N) = [a_{11}h_1^N + a_{21}(1 + h_1 + \cdots + h_1^{N-1})]\mathbf{m}_1 + [a_{12}h_2^N + a_{22}(1 + h_2 + \cdots + h_2^{N-1})]\mathbf{m}_2$$

Equation (10) expresses the vector $\mathbf{y}(N)$ as a weighted sum of the characteristic vectors $\mathbf{m}_1$ and $\mathbf{m}_2$. It follows that, in particular, the second element of the vector $\mathbf{y}(N)$, which is $Y(N)$, is a weighted sum of the second elements of the characteristic vectors $\mathbf{m}_1$ and $\mathbf{m}_2$; these elements are, respectively, m_{12} and m_{22}: i.e. the vector equation (10) implies the equation

$$\text{(11)} \qquad Y(N) = m_{12}[a_{11}h_1^N + a_{21}(1 + h_1 + \cdots + h_1^{N-1})] + m_{22}[a_{12}h_2^N + a_{22}(1 + h_2 + \cdots + h_2^{N-1})]$$

Using the formula for the sum of the first N terms of a geometric series,

$$1 + h + \cdots + h^{N-1} = (1 - h^N)/(1 - h)$$

equation (11) simplifies to

$$Y(N) = m_{12}[a_{11} - a_{21}/(1 - h_1)]h_1^N + m_{22}[a_{12} - a_{22}/(1 - h_2)]h_2^N + [m_{12}a_{21}/(1 - h_1) + m_{22}a_{22}/(1 - h_2)]$$

Making the substitutions

$$\text{(12)} \qquad \begin{aligned} A_1 &= m_{12}[a_{11} - a_{21}/(1 - h_1)] \\ A_2 &= m_{22}[a_{12} - a_{22}/(1 - h_2)] \\ B &= m_{12}a_{21}/(1 - h_1) + m_{22}a_{22}/(1 - h_2) \end{aligned}$$

it follows that $Y(N)$ can be written in the form

$$Y(N) = A_1h_1^N + A_2h_2^N + B$$

which is the same as (3). However, there is no need to use the formulae (12) in order to evaluate the constants in (3), for the constants A_1, A_2 and B can be determined directly once the first three measurements are known. This can be seen by setting $t = 0, 1, 2$ successively in equation (3); one obtains three simultaneous linear equations for A_1, A_2 and B

$$Y(0) = A_1 + A_2 + B$$

$$Y(1) = A_1 h_1 + A_2 h_2 + B$$

$$Y(2) = A_1 h_1^2 + A_2 h_2^2 + B$$

As a rule these three equations can be solved uniquely for the values of A_1, A_2 and B, once the 'initial conditions', $Y(0)$, $Y(1)$, $Y(2)$, are known. It follows that while it is necessary to determine the characteristic values, it is not necessary to determine the characteristic vectors in order to solve equation (2).

There is a very quick way of finding the characteristic equation associated with a difference equation. Writing out in full the characteristic equation $\det [\mathbf{M} - h\mathbf{I}] = 0$ gives

$$h^2 + b_1 h + b_2 = 0$$

This equation can be determined directly from (2) by writing h^2 for $Y(t + 2)$, h for $Y(t + 1)$, $h^0 = 1$ for $Y(t)$ and setting the right-hand side equal to zero. The characteristic equation associated with a difference equation is sometimes known as the 'auxiliary equation'.

The special case is which $h_1 = h_2$ is analysed as follows. It is a consequence of the formula for the solution of a quadratic that the roots of (4) are identical only if $b_2 = b_1^2/4$, in which case both roots are equal to $-b_1/2$. Direct calculation using (2) with $t = 0, 1, 2, \ldots, N$ establishes (5).

Economic application

Linear difference equations frequently arise in economics. One important application is to macroeconomics, where difference equations are used to examine the effect of the interaction of consumer demand and investment demand on the level of aggregate income.

Consider a single sector economy in which there are three components of aggregate demand: consumption, investment and government expenditure.

(a) Consumption in year t, $C(t)$, depends on income in the previous year, $Y(t - 1)$. It is a linear function of income and there is an exogenous component of consumer demand equal to £b million

$$C(t) = b + cY(t - 1)$$

(b) Investment during year t is determined by the businessmen's policy of adjusting the capital stock of the economy from its initial value, $K(t)$, to the stock required to meet the expected aggregate demand in year $t + 1$.

Let the expected aggregate demand in year $t + 1$ be denoted $\hat{Y}(t + 1)$. If the optimal capital–output ratio is v, the capital stock required to meet expected aggregate demand in year $t + 1$ is equal to $v\hat{Y}(t + 1)$. Consequently, the capital stock at the beginning of year $t + 1$ is

$$K(t + 1) = v\hat{Y}(t + 1)$$

Substituting t for $t + 1$ in the equation above it can be seen that, at the beginning of any year t, the capital stock is equal to

$$K(t) = v\hat{Y}(t)$$

If depreciation is ignored, then investment in year t is equal to

$$I(t) = K(t + 1) - K(t)$$

so that

$$I(t) = v(\hat{Y}(t + 1) - \hat{Y}(t))$$

Suppose that there is a one period lag between the ordering of investment goods and their construction and installation (this is known as a gestation lag). Investment goods to be installed in period t must then be ordered in period $t - 1$, when only the value of aggregate demand, $Y(t - 1)$, is known. If businessmen expect aggregate demand in the future to be equal to aggregate demand in the present then

$$\hat{Y}(t + 1) = Y(t - 1)$$

It follows that

$$I(t) = v[Y(t - 1) - Y(t - 2)]$$

This equation describes the determination of investment when there is a gestation lag of one period.

(c) Government expenditure is exogenous and remains constant from period to period,

$$G(t) = G$$

Assumptions (a)–(c) together imply that aggregate demand in period t is equal to

$$cY(t - 1) + v[Y(t - 1) - Y(t - 2)] + b + G$$

Suppose that in the short run aggregate supply is adjusted to meet aggregate demand; then in any period t aggregate demand is equal to aggregate income, $Y(t)$, so that

$$Y(t) = cY(t - 1) + v[Y(t - 1) - Y(t - 2)] + b + G$$

This equation determines the time path of income in the economy. It may be simplified by grouping terms and by denoting the exogenous demand by E, viz:

(13) $$Y(t) - (c + v)Y(t - 1) + vY(t - 2) = E$$

Equation (13) is an example of a second-order linear difference equation because it can be put into the form

$$\Delta^2 Y(t - 2) + (2 - c - v)\,\Delta Y(t - 2) + (1 - c)Y(t - 2) = E$$

Example 1 Let the marginal propensity to consume be 0·5 and let the capital–output ratio be 5. Government expenditure is £12m and exogenous consumer demand is £4m. Examine the time path of income when the first two values of income are £26m and £28m respectively.

Equation (13) becomes

$$Y(t) - 5{\cdot}5Y(t-1) + 5{\cdot}0Y(t-2) = 16$$

It is necessary first to evaluate the characteristic values h_1, h_2, which are the solutions of the characteristic equation

$$\det[\mathbf{M} - h\mathbf{I}] = 0$$

When this equation is written out the coefficients are the same as in the difference equation above; i.e. the characteristic equation is

$$h^2 - 5{\cdot}5h + 5{\cdot}0 = 0$$

This quadratic equation has the approximate solution

$$h_1 = 4{\cdot}35, \qquad h_2 = 1{\cdot}15$$

It follows that the solution of the difference equation has the form

(14) $$Y(N) = A_1 4{\cdot}35^N + A_2 1{\cdot}15^N + B$$

To find the solution it is necessary to evaluate the three unknowns A_1, A_2 and B. To do this, note that we are given the information that $Y(0) = 26$, $Y(1) = 28$ (£m), and since we also know that exogenous demand is 16 (£m) we can calculate the value of $Y(2)$.

$$Y(2) = 5{\cdot}5Y(1) - 5{\cdot}0Y(0) + 16$$
$$= 40 \quad (\text{£m})$$

Knowing the values of $Y(0)$, $Y(1)$ and $Y(2)$ enables us to write down the equations from which the three unknown constants can be determined. Setting $t = 0$, $t = 1$, $t = 2$ successively in equation (14) gives three simultaneous linear equations in the three unknowns A_1, A_2, B:

$$26 = A_1 + A_2 + B$$

$$28 = 4{\cdot}35A_1 + 1{\cdot}15A_2 + B$$

$$40 = 18{\cdot}93A_1 + 1{\cdot}32A_2 + B$$

The solution of these equations is

$$A_1 = 0{\cdot}91, \qquad A_2 = -6{\cdot}91, \qquad B = 32{\cdot}00$$

Substituting these values into (14) gives

$$Y(N) = (0{\cdot}91)4{\cdot}35^N - (6{\cdot}91)1{\cdot}15^N + 32{\cdot}00$$

This result indicates that as N becomes large the income in the economy will tend to grow in a fashion which will be dominated entirely by the term $0{\cdot}91(4{\cdot}35)^N$. For large values of N the income may therefore be approximated by the formula

$$\lim_{N \to \infty} Y(N) = 0{\cdot}91(4{\cdot}35)^N$$

where the limit must be interpreted to mean that for large values of N the error in the equation is proportionately (but not absolutely) small.

What this result means in economic terms is that the economy will be dominated by a need to satisfy the induced demand for investment goods. To appreciate this, consider the time path of income in the first few periods. The initial increase in income from £26m to £28m induces a demand for investment goods of £10m in the following year. When this demand is added to consumer demand and to exogenous demand, the total aggregate demand in the following year is £40m. The resulting increase in demand from £28m to £40m induces a demand for investment goods of £60m in the year after. This increases aggregate demand even further. The reader may suspect that if the capital–output ratio were much lower then the influence of investment on aggregate demand would be much smaller and the economy might behave in a more stable fashion. That this conjecture is correct is illustrated by the following example, in which the capital–output ratio is only 0·25.

Example 2 Consider the economy described in Example 1. Suppose that the marginal propensity to consume is now 0·75 and that the capital–output ratio is now 0·25; determine the time path of income under the same conditions as before.

Equation (13) becomes

$$Y(t) - Y(t-1) + 0{\cdot}25\,Y(t-2) = 16$$

The characteristic equation is

$$h^2 - h + 0{\cdot}25 = 0$$

and the characteristic values are found to be $h_1 = 0{\cdot}5$, $h_2 = 0{\cdot}5$.

Because the characteristic values are not distinct the solution is of the form

$$Y(N) = A_1 0{\cdot}5^N + A_2 N 0{\cdot}5^N + B$$

where the constants are determined by the equations

$$\begin{aligned} 26 &= A_1 + B \\ 28 &= 0{\cdot}5\,A_1 + 0{\cdot}5A_2 + B \\ 37{\cdot}5 &= 0{\cdot}25A_1 + 0{\cdot}5A_2 + B \end{aligned}$$

The solution for $Y(N)$ is found to be

$$Y(N) = -38(0{\cdot}5)^N - 34N(0{\cdot}5)^N + 64$$

It can be established that when N becomes large both the terms in N become arbitrarily close to zero, so that as N becomes large the value of $Y(N)$ converges to £64m. In this case the investment demand, induced as a result of changes in income, does not prevent the income from converging to a stable level.

Example 3 Suppose that the marginal propensity to consume, $c = 0{\cdot}5$, and the capital–output ratio, $v = 1{\cdot}0$. Suppose that the initial income is zero and that after one year exogenous demand is increased from zero to £4m. What is the time path of income?

The characteristic equation is

$$h^2 - h + \tfrac{1}{2} = 0$$

and the characteristic values are obtained by the formula

$$h = \frac{1 \pm \sqrt{(1 - 2)}}{2}$$

from which $h_1 = \tfrac{1}{2} + \tfrac{1}{2}\mathrm{i}$, $h_2 = \tfrac{1}{2} - \tfrac{1}{2}\mathrm{i}$. The value of $Y(N)$ is given by the formula

$$Y(N) = A_1(\tfrac{1}{2} + \tfrac{1}{2}\mathrm{i})^N + A_2(\tfrac{1}{2} - \tfrac{1}{2}\mathrm{i})^N + B$$

where the constants, A_1, A_2, B are obtained from the initial conditions. We already know that $Y(0) = 0$ and it is readily found that $Y(1) = 4$, $Y(2) = 8$. Hence the constants A_1, A_2, B are determined by the equations

(15.1) $$0 = A_1 + A_2 + B$$

(15.2) $$4 = (\tfrac{1}{2} + \tfrac{1}{2}\mathrm{i})A_1 + (\tfrac{1}{2} - \tfrac{1}{2}\mathrm{i})A_2 + B$$

(15.3) $$8 = (\tfrac{1}{2} + \tfrac{1}{2}\mathrm{i})^2 A_1 + (\tfrac{1}{2} - \tfrac{1}{2}\mathrm{i})^2 A_2 + B$$

Multiplying out the squared terms in equation (15.3) gives

$$8 = \tfrac{1}{2}\mathrm{i}A_1 - \tfrac{1}{2}\mathrm{i}A_2 + B$$

These three equations are really six equations, since each equates the real part of the left-hand side to the real part of the right-hand side and also the imaginary part of the left-hand side to the imaginary part of the right-hand side. In the special case where A_1, A_2, B are all real the three equations when written out with the real parts and imaginary parts kept distinct are

(16.1)	$0 = A_1 + A_2 + B$	real part of (15.1)
(16.2)	$0 = 0 + 0 + 0$	imaginary part of (15.1)
(16.3)	$4 = \tfrac{1}{2}A_1 + \tfrac{1}{2}A_2 + B$	real part of (15.2)
(16.4)	$0 = \tfrac{1}{2}A_1 - \tfrac{1}{2}A_2$	imaginary part of (15.2)
(16.5)	$8 = B$	real part of (15.3)
(16.6)	$0 = \tfrac{1}{2}A_1 - \tfrac{1}{2}A_2$	imaginary part of (15.3)

Equation (16.5) shows that $B = 8$, and from equation (16.6) it follows that $A_1 = A_2$. Substituting these results into equation (16.1) shows that $A_1 = A_2 = -4$. Hence the arbitrary constants are

$$A_1 = -4, \qquad A_2 = -4, \qquad B = 8$$

and the time path of income is given by the equation

(17) $$Y(t) = -4(\tfrac{1}{2} + \tfrac{1}{2}\mathrm{i})^N - 4(\tfrac{1}{2} - \tfrac{1}{2}\mathrm{i})^N + 8$$

Equation (17) can be checked against Table 20.1, which is derived by straightforward economic reasoning.

Table 20.1 shows that income oscillates over time, but eventually becomes close to £8m. When exogenous demand is £4m and the marginal propensity to consume is $\frac{1}{2}$, the stationary value of income is £8m. Consequently income oscillates over time and converges to a stationary value.

Table 20.1 Time path of income

Year t	*Consumption* $C(t) = cY(t-1)$	*Investment* $I(t) = v[Y(t-1) - Y(t-2)]$	*Exogenous demand* $E(t)$	*Income* $Y(t)$
0	0·0	0·0	0·0	0·0
1	0·0	0·0	4·0	4·0
2	2·0	2·0	4·0	8·0
3	4·0	2·0	4·0	10·0
4	5·0	1·0	4·0	10·0
5	5·0	0·0	4·0	9·0
6	4·5	−0·5	4·0	8·0
7	4·0	−0·5	4·0	7·5
8	3·75	−0·25	4·0	7·5
9	3·75	0·0	4·0	7·75
10	3·875	0·125	4·0	8·0
11	4·0	0·125	4·0	8·125
12	4·0625	0·0625	4·0	8·125
13	4·0625	0·0	4·0	8·0625
14	4·03025	−0·03025	4·0	8·0

Although equation (17) involves complex numbers, the value of income is nevertheless a real quantity. This exemplifies the fact that a formula involving complex numbers is often no more than a convenient way of calculating the values of a real number. It is for this reason that there are no conceptual problems in using complex numbers in economics.

20.2 Linear difference equations of the nth order

A natural generalization of the proof of Theorem 20.1 can be used to establish the following result on the solution of linear difference equations of the nth order. To state this result it is convenient to transform the equation

$$\Delta^n Y(t) + a_1 \Delta^{n-1} Y(t) + \cdots + a_{n-1} \Delta Y(t) + a_n Y(t) = g(t)$$

into the equivalent form

$$Y(t+n) + b_1 Y(t+n-1) + \cdots + b_{n-1} Y(t+1) + b_n Y(t) = g(t)$$

Theorem 20.2 To solve the nth order linear difference equation

(18) $$Y(t+n) + b_1 Y(t+n-1) + \cdots + b_{n-1} Y(t+1) + b_n Y(t) = E$$

it is necessary only to find the characteristic values $h_1, h_2, \ldots, h_n$ which solve the characteristic equation

$$h^n + b_1 h^{n-1} + \cdots + b_{n-1} h + b_n = 0 \tag{19}$$

and then to set

$$Y(N) = A_1 b_1^N + A_2 h_2^N + \cdots + A_n h_n^N + B \tag{20}$$

where the $A_1, A_2, \ldots, A_n, B$ are obtained by solving the $n + 1$ simultaneous linear equations

$$\begin{aligned}
Y(0) &= A_1 + A_2 + \cdots + A_n + B \\
Y(1) &= A_1 h_1 + A_2 h_2 + \cdots + A_n h_n + B \\
Y(2) &= A_1 h_1^2 + A_2 h_2^2 + \cdots + A_n h_n^2 + B \\
&\vdots \\
Y(n) &= A_1 h_1^n + A_2 h_2^n + \cdots + A_n h_n^n + B
\end{aligned} \tag{21}$$

There is one important restriction on the generality of the solution (20): it is necessary for the characteristic values $h_1, h_2, \ldots, h_n$ to be distinct. If the characteristic values $h_k, h_{k+1}, \ldots, h_n$ are not distinct, say $h_k = h_{k+1} = \cdots = h_n = h^*$, then the general solution has the form

$$\begin{aligned}
Y(N) = {} & A_1 h_1^N + A_2 h_2^N + \cdots + A_{k-1} h_{k-1}^N \\
& + (A_k + A_{k+1} N + A_{k+2} N^2 \ldots \\
& + A_n N^{n-k}) h^{*N}
\end{aligned} \tag{22}$$

where the arbitrary constants can be evaluated from the initial conditions as before.

An important question concerns the conditions under which the value of $Y(N)$ converges to a fixed value as N becomes large. A necessary and sufficient condition for convergence can be deduced from an inspection of equation (20). If the initial conditions are arbitrary, the constants $A_1, A_2, \ldots, A_n$ are also arbitrary [since they are determined by the initial conditions, as shown by equation (21)]. It follows that the value of $Y(t)$ may become infinitely large if any one of the terms $h_1^N, h_2^N, \ldots, h_n^N$ becomes infinitely large. On the other hand, if all the terms $h_1^N, h_2^N, \ldots, h_n^N$ converge to zero then the value of $Y(N)$ will converge to B, which is a fixed and finite value. We conclude that when the initial conditions are arbitrary $Y(N)$ converges to a definite value as N becomes large if and only if all the terms $h_1^N, h_2^N, \ldots, h_n^N$ converge to zero. The results of Section 19·4 show that the modulus of h_i^N converges to zero if and only if the modulus of h_i is less than unity. Consequently a necessary and sufficient condition for the convergence of $Y(N)$ is that the modulus of each of the characteristic values $h_1, h_2, \ldots, h_n$ is less than unity. The condition for the modulus of each of the characteristic values to be less than unity is given in the theorem below.

Theorem 20.3 A necessary and sufficient condition that all the roots of the polynomial

$$(23) \qquad b_0 h^n + b_1 h^{n-1} + \cdots + b_{n-1} h + b_n = 0$$

have a modulus less than unity is that for $k = 1, 2, \ldots, n$

$$(24) \qquad \begin{cases} \det\,[\mathbf{Q}_k] < 0 & \text{when } k \text{ is odd} \\ \det\,[\mathbf{Q}_k] > 0 & \text{when } k \text{ is even} \end{cases}$$

where

$$(25)\ \mathbf{Q}_k = \left[\begin{array}{cccc|cccc}
b_n & & & 0 & b_0 & b_1 & \cdots & b_{k-1} \\
b_{n-1} & b_n & & & & b_0 & & b_{k-2} \\
\vdots & \vdots & \ddots & & & & \ddots & \vdots \\
 & & & & \cdot & 0 & & \\
b_{n-k+1} & b_{n-k+2} & \cdots & b_n & & & & b_0 \\
\hline
b_0 & & & & b_n & b_{n-1} & \cdots & b_{n-k+1} \\
b_1 & b_0 & & 0 & & b_n & \cdots & b_{n-k+2} \\
\vdots & \vdots & \ddots & & & & \ddots & \vdots \\
 & & & & & 0 & & \\
b_{k-1} & b_{k-2} & \cdots & b_0 & & & & b_n
\end{array}\right]$$

The criterion given by this theorem can be simplified, but even the simplification is rather complicated.

20.3 Linear differential equations of the nth order

The general form of an nth order linear differential equation is

$$(26) \qquad \frac{d^n Y}{dt^n} + a_1 \frac{d^{n-1} Y}{dt^{n-1}} + \cdots + a_{n-1} \frac{dY}{dt} + a_n Y(t) = g(t)$$

The solution of (26) when $g(t)$ is a constant is given by the theorem below.

Theorem 20.4 The solution of (26) with $g(t) = $ constant is

$$(27) \qquad Y(t) = A_0 + A_1 \exp(\lambda_1 t) + A_2 \exp(\lambda_2 t) + \cdots + A_n \exp(\lambda_n t)$$

where $\lambda_1, \lambda_2, \ldots, \lambda_n$ are roots of the equation

$$(28) \qquad \lambda^n + a_1 \lambda^{n-1} + \cdots + a_{n-1}\lambda + a_n = 0$$

The left-hand side of (28) is obtained by substituting λ^j for dY^j/dt^j in the left-hand side of (26). If the roots of (28) are not all distinct, say

$$\lambda_k = \lambda_{k+1} = \cdots = \lambda_n = \lambda^*,$$

then the solution is of the form

$$(29) \qquad Y(t) = A_1 \exp(\lambda_1 t) + \cdots + A_{k-1} \exp(\lambda_{k-1} t) + [A_k + A_{k+1}\lambda^* + \cdots + A_n \lambda^{*n-k}] \exp(\lambda^* t)$$

A rigorous proof of equations (27) and (29) can be based on the fact that differentiation is a *linear operation* (in the sense of Chapter 14). A nonrigorous proof of equation (27) for the special case $n = 2$ is given in the following paragraph.

When $n = 2$ equation (27) becomes

$$(30) \qquad Y(t) = A_0 + A_1 \exp(\lambda_1 t) + A_2 \exp(\lambda_2 t)$$

Differentiating gives

$$(31) \qquad \begin{aligned} dY/dt &= A_1\lambda_1 \exp(\lambda_1 t) + A_2\lambda_2 \exp(\lambda_2 t) \\ d^2Y/dt^2 &= A_1\lambda_1^2 \exp(\lambda_1 t) + A_2\lambda_2^2 \exp(\lambda_2 t) \end{aligned}$$

Using (30) and (31) we find

$$\begin{aligned} &d^2y/dt^2 + a_1\, dy/dt + a_2 y(t) \\ &= A_1(\lambda_1^2 + a_1\lambda_1 + a_2) \exp(\lambda_1 t) \\ &\quad + A_2(\lambda_2^2 + a_1\lambda_2 + a_2) \exp(\lambda_2 t) \\ &\quad + A_0 a_2 \end{aligned}$$

But since λ_1, λ_2 are roots of $\lambda^2 + a_1\lambda + a_2 = 0$,

$$\lambda_1^2 + a_1\lambda_1 + a_2 = 0 \quad \text{and} \quad \lambda_2^2 + a_1\lambda_2 + a_2 = 0$$

whence

$$d^2Y/dt^2 + a_1\, dY/dt + a_2 Y(t) = A_0 a_2$$

Consequently, if $g(t) = k$ then setting $A_0 = k/a_2$ we find that

$$d^2Y/dt^2 + a_1\, dY/dt + a_2 Y(t) = k$$

In order to determine the A_i it is necessary to have additional information, e.g. initial conditions.

A necessary and sufficient condition that $Y(t)$ converges to a fixed value as t becomes large whatever the initial conditions is that all the roots of equation (28), $\lambda_1, \lambda_2, \ldots, \lambda_n$, have negative real parts, i.e. if λ_j is expressed as a complex number $x_j + iy_j$ then $x_j < 0$. A necessary and sufficient condition that all the roots of equation (28) have negative real parts is given in Theorem 20.5 below.

Theorem 20.5 The roots of the nth degree polynomial

$$a_0\lambda^n + a_1\lambda^{n-1} + \cdots + a_{n-1}\lambda + a_n = 0$$

all have negative real parts if and only if the first n of the determinants in the following sequence are strictly positive

$$\det [a_1]$$

$$\det\begin{bmatrix} a_1 & a_3 \\ a_0 & a_2 \end{bmatrix}$$

$$\det\begin{bmatrix} a_1 & a_3 & a_5 \\ a_0 & a_2 & a_4 \\ 0 & a_1 & a_3 \end{bmatrix}$$

$$\det\begin{bmatrix} a_1 & a_3 & a_5 & a_7 \\ a_0 & a_2 & a_4 & a_6 \\ 0 & a_1 & a_3 & a_5 \\ 0 & a_0 & a_2 & a_4 \end{bmatrix}, \text{ etc.}$$

If an element does not exist it is replaced by a zero.

Notes and references

The mathematics of difference and differential equations is covered in Allen,[6] Ch. 16, Lewis,[79] Ch. 25, 26 and Yamane,[126] Ch. 12. The standard work on difference equations for economists is Goldberg.[40] Stability conditions for linear difference equations are reviewed by Jury,[68] Ch. 3, who gives a lucid discussion of alternative methods of solution.

The basic reference on macroeconomic difference equations is Samuelson;[110] see also Allen,[8] p. 336, Allen,[7] Ch. 6, 7. For macroeconomic applications of differential equations see Phillips,[101, 102] and the review in Allen,[8] Ch. 18, 19.

Problems

20.1.1 A country has a marginal propensity to consume of 0·75 and a capital–output ratio of 4. Total exogenous demand is £3m and income in the first two periods is £30m and £32m respectively.

(a) Show that in the absence of resource constraints the income in the tenth period is approximately £4,270m.

(b) To what value does income tend over a long period?

20.1.2 Find the value to which income tends over time in an economy where the capital–output ratio is 0·36, the marginal propensity to consume is 0·84, income in the first two periods is £40m and £42m, and exogenous demand is £10m.

20.1.3 In an economy where the marginal propensity to consume is 0·6 and the capital–output ratio is 0·4 income is stable at £25m. One year exogenous demand increases from £10m to £12m. What is the time path of income? Does income converge to a stationary value? If so, find the new stationary value of income.

20.2 For each of the following equations determine whether $Y(N)$ converges to a fixed value as N becomes large (assume the initial conditions are arbitrary).

(a) $Y(t + 2) - Y(t) = 5$

(b) $Y(t + 3) - 3Y(t + 2) + 2Y(t + 1) - Y(t) = 70$

(c) $3Y(t + 3) - 6Y(t + 1) - 27Y(t) = 67$

20.3.1 Solve each of the following equations, leaving the coefficients A_i undetermined. For each equation determine whether $Y(t)$ converges to a fixed value as t becomes large (assume the initial conditions are arbitrary).

(a) $d^2Y(t)/dt - 3dY(t)/dt + 2Y(t) = 30$

(b) $3d^2Y(t)/dt^2 + 3Y(t) = 40$

(c) $5d^2Y(t)/dt^2 + 6dY(t)/dt + 40Y(t) = 76$

20.3.2 Given the equation $Y(t) = d^3Y(t)/dt^3 - 6d^2Y(t)/dt^2 + 4Y(t) = 8$, determine whether $Y(t)$ converges to a fixed value as t becomes large.

Bibliography

1. Ackley, G., *Macroeconomic Theory*, New York: Macmillan, 1961.
2. Adelman, I. G., A stochastic analysis of the size distribution of firms, *Journal of the American Statistical Association*, **53**, 1958, 893–904.
3. Airov, J., The construction of interregional business cycle models, in H. W. Richardson (ed.), *Regional Economics, A Reader*, London: Macmillan, 1970.
4. Aitken, A. C., *Determinants and Matrices*, 9th edn., Edinburgh: Oliver and Boyd, 1956.
5. Alexander, S. S., Opposition to deficit spending for the prevention of unemployment, in Hansen [49], pp. 177–198.
6. Allen, R. G. D., *Mathematical Analysis for Economists*, London: Macmillan, 1938.
7. Allen, R. G. D., *Mathematical Economics*, London: Macmillan, 1956.
8. Allen, R. G. D., *Macroeconomic Theory*, London: Macmillan, 1967.
9. Ames, E., *Introduction to Macroeconomic Theory*, New York: Holt, Rinehart and Winston, 1968.
10. Artle, R., *The Structure of the Stockholm Economy*, Ithaca, New York: Cornell University Press, 1965.
11. Barna, T. (ed.), *Structural Interdependence and Economic Development*, London: Macmillan, 1963.
12. Bartholomew, D. J., *Stochastic Models for Social Processes*, London: Wiley, 1967.
13. Baumol, W. J., *Economic Theory and Operations Analysis*, 2nd edn., Englewood Cliffs, N.J.: Prentice-Hall, 1965.
14. Beale, E. M. L., *Mathematical Programming in Practice*, London: Pitmans, 1968.
15. Beckerman, W., The world trade multiplier and the stability of world trade, 1938 to 1953, *Econometrica*, **24**, 1956, 239–252.
16. Bellman, R., *Dynamic Programming*, Princeton, N.J.: Princeton University Press, 1957.
17. Bellman, R., *Introduction to Matrix Analysis*, New York: McGraw-Hill, 1960.
18. Bishop, R. L., Alternative expansionist fiscal policies, in Hansen [49], pp. 317–340.
19. Blumen, I., M. Kogan, and P. J. McCarthy, *The Industrial Mobility of Labour as a Probability Process*, Ithaca, New York: Cornell University Press, 1960.
20. Boot, J. C. G., *Quadratic Programming: Algorithms – Anomalies – Applications*, New York: North-Holland Publishing Co., 1964.
21. Brooman, F. S., *Macroeconomics*, 4th edn., London: Allen and Unwin, 1970.
22. Brown, M., *On the Theory and Measurement of Technical Change*, London: Cambridge University Press, 1966.
23. Burmeister, E. and R. Dobell, *Mathematical Theories of Economic Growth*, London: Collier Macmillan, 1971.
24. Chatterji, M. K., An input–output study of the Calcutta industrial region, *Regional Science Association Papers*, **13**, 1964, 93–105.
25. Chenery, H. B. and P. G. Clark, *Interindustry Economics*, New York: Wiley, 1959.
26. Chipman, J., The multisector multiplier, *Econometrica*, **18**, 1950, 355–373.
27. Chipman, J., Professor Goodwin's matrix multiplier, *Economic Journal*, **60**, 1950, 753–763.
28. Cohen, K. J. and R. M. Cyert, *Theory of the Firm*, Englewood Cliffs, N.J.: Prentice-Hall, 1965.
29. Cohn, P. M., *Linear Equations*, London: Routledge and Kegan Paul, 1958.
30. Courant, R., *Differential and Integral Calculus*, 2 vols., 2nd edn., London: Blackie, 1963.
31. Cox, D. R. and H. D. Miller, *The Theory of Stochastic Processes*, London: Methuen, 1965.
32. Dantzig, G. B., *Linear Programming and Extensions*, Princeton: Princeton University Press, 1955.

33. Dasgupta, A. K. and A. J. Hagger, *The Objectives of Macroeconomic Policy*, London: Macmillan, 1971.
34. Dernburg, T. F. and D. M. McDougall, *Macroeconomics*, 3rd edn., New York: McGraw-Hill, 1968.
35. Dorfman, R., P. A. Samuelson, and R. M. Solow, *Linear Programming and Economic Analysis*, New York: McGraw-Hill, 1958.
36. Duesenberry, J. S., Income-consumption relations and their implications, in Hansen [49], pp. 54–81.
37. Evans, M. K., *Macroeconomic Activity*, New York: Harper and Row, 1969.
38. Gantmacher, F. R., *Applications of the Theory of Matrices*, New York: Interscience Publishers, 1959.
39. Gale, D., *The Theory of Linear Economic Models*, New York: McGraw-Hill, 1960.
40. Goldberg, S., *Introduction to Difference Equations*, New York: Wiley, 1958.
41. Goodwin, R., The multiplier as matrix, *Economic Journal*, **59**, 1949, 537–555.
42. Goodwin, R., Does the matrix multiplier oscillate?, *Economic Journal*, **60**, 1950, 764–770.
43. Graves, R. L. and P. Wolfe, *Recent Advances in Mathematical Programming*, New York: McGraw-Hill, 1963.
44. Green, H. A. J., *Consumer Theory*, Harmondsworth: Penguin Books, 1972.
45. Griffin, K. B. and J. L. Enos, *Planning Development*, London: Addison-Wesley, 1970.
46. Hadley, G., *Linear Algebra*, Reading, Mass.: Addison-Wesley, 1961.
47. Hadley, G., *Linear Programming*, Reading, Mass.: Addison-Wesley, 1962.
48. Hadley, G., *Nonlinear and Dynamic Programming*, Reading, Mass.: Addison-Wesley, 1964.
49. Hansen, A. H., *Income, Employment and Public Policy: Essays in Honour of Alvin H. Hansen*, New York: Norton, 1948.
50. Hansen, W. L. and C. M. Tiebout, An intersectoral flows analysis of the California economy, *Review of Economics and Statistics*, **45**, 1963, 409–418.
51. Harrod, R. F., An essay in dynamic theory, *Economic Journal*, **49**, 1939, 14–33, reprinted in A. H. Hansen and R. V. Clemence (eds), *Readings in Business Cycles and National Income*, New York: Norton, 1953, pp. 200–219, also in A. K. Sen (ed.), *Growth Economics*, Harmondsworth: Penguin Books, 1970.
52. Harrod, R. F., *Towards a Dynamic Economics*, London: Macmillan, 1949.
53. Hart, P. E., The size and growth of firms, *Economica*, **29**, 1962, 29–39.
54. Hawkins, D. and H. A. Simon, Some conditions of macroeconomic stability, *Econometrica*, **17**, 1949, 245–248.
55. Heathfield, D. F., *Production Functions*, London: Macmillan, 1971.
56. Henderson, J. M. and R. E. Quandt, *Microeconomic Theory*, 2nd edn., New York: McGraw-Hill, 1971.
57. Hicks, J. R., *Value and Capital*, 2nd edn., Oxford: Clarendon Press, 1939.
58. Hicks, J. R., Mr. Keynes and the 'Classics'; a suggested interpretation, *Econometrica*, **5**, 1937, 147–159, reprinted in M. G. Mueller (ed.), *Readings in Macroeconomics*, New York: Holt, Rinehart and Winston, 1966.
59. Hirsch, W., Interindustry relations of a metropolitan area, *Review of Economics and Statistics*, **41**, 1959, 360–370.
60. Hopkin, B. and associates, Aid and the balance of payments, *Economic Journal*, **80**, 1970, 1–24.
61. *Input–Output Bibliography, 1963–66*, New York: United Nations Statistical Papers Series M, No. 46, 1967.
62. Intriligator, M. D., *Mathematical Optimisation and Economic Theory*, Englewood Cliffs, N.J.: Prentice-Hall, 1971.
63. Isard, W., T. W. Langford Jr., and E. Romanoff, *Philadelphia Region Input–Output Study*, Philadelphia, Penn.: Regional Science Research Institute (no date).
64. Isard, W., E. W. Schooler, and T. Vietorisz, *Industrial Complex Analysis and Regional Development*, London: Chapman and Hall, 1959.

65. Johnston, J., *Statistical Cost Analysis*, New York: McGraw-Hill, 1960.
66. Johnston, J., *Econometric Methods*, 2nd edn., New York: McGraw-Hill, 1972.
67. Jones, H., *Introduction to the Theory of Growth*, London: Nelson (in preparation).
68. Jury, E. I., *Theory and Application of the z-Transform Method*, New York: Wiley, 1964.
69. Kahn, R. F., The relation of home investment to unemployment, *Economic Journal*, **41**, 1931, 173–198.
70. Kemeny, J. G. and L. Snell, *Finite Markoff Chains*, New York: Van Nostrand, 1960.
71. Klein, L. R., *An Introduction to Econometrics*, Englewood Cliffs, N.J.: Prentice-Hall, 1962.
72. Kurihara, K. K., *Introduction to Keynesian Dynamics*, London: Allen and Unwin, 1956.
73. Lange, O., *Introduction to Econometrics*, Oxford: Pergamon Press, 1962.
74. Lange, O., *Optimal Decisions*, Oxford: Pergamon Press, 1971.
75. Ledermann, W., *Complex Numbers*, London: Routledge and Kegan Paul, 1960.
76. Leontief, W. W., *The Structure of the American Economy, 1919–1939*, 2nd edn., New York: Oxford University Press, 1951.
77. Lerner, A. B., The burden of the national debt, in Hansen [49], pp. 255–275.
78. Lesbourne, J., *Economic Analysis and Industrial Management*, Englewood Cliffs, N.J.: Prentice-Hall, 1960.
79. Lewis, J. Parry, *An Introduction to Mathematics for Students of Economics*, 2nd edn., London: Macmillan, 1969.
80. Lindley, D. V., *Introduction to Probability and Statistics from a Bayesian Viewpoint, Part I*, London: Cambridge University Press, 1965.
81. Lipsey, R. G., *An Introduction to Positive Economics*, 2nd edn., London: Weidenfeld and Nicolson, 1966.
82. Machlup, F., *International Trade and the National Income Multiplier*, Reprinted New York: Augustus M. Kelly, 1961.
83. Meier, R. C. and S. H. Archer, *An Introduction to Mathematics for Business Analysis*, New York: McGraw-Hill, 1960.
84. Merrill, W. C. and K. A. Fox, *Introduction to Economic Statistics*, New York: Wiley, 1970.
85. Metzler, L. A., Underemployment equilibrium and international trade, *Econometrica*, **10**, 1942, 97–112.
86. Metzler, L. A., The transfer problem reconsidered, *Journal of Political Economy*, **50**, 1942, 397–414.
87. Metzler, L. A., Three lags in the circular flow of income, in Hansen [49], pp. 11–32.
88. Metzler, L. A., A multiple-region theory of income and trade, *Econometrica*, **18**, 1950, 329–355.
89. Miernyk, W. H., *The Elements of Input–Output Analysis*, New York: Random House, 1967.
90. Mills, G., *Introduction to Linear Algebra for Social Scientists*, London: Allen and Unwin, 1969.
91. Moore, F. T. and J. W. Peterson, Interindustry model of Utah, *Review of Economics and Statistics*, **37**, 1955, 380–381.
92. Morishima, M., *Equilibrium, Stability and Growth*, London: Oxford University Press, 1964.
93. Mosak, J., *General Equilibrium Theory in International Trade*, Bloomington: Principia Press, 1944.
94. Musgrave, R. A., *The Theory of Public Finance*, New York: McGraw-Hill, 1959.
95. Neisser, H. and F. Modigliani, *National Incomes and International Trade*, New York: University of Illinois Press, Urbana, Ill., 1953.
96. Nevin, E. *et al.*, *The Social Accounts of the Welsh Economy, 1948–1956*, Cardiff: University of Wales Press, 1957.

97. Parker, M. L., *An Interindustry Study of the Western Australian Economy*, Perth: University of Western Australia Press, 1967.
98. Patinkin, D., *Money, Interest and Prices*, 2nd edn., New York: Harper and Row, 1965.
99. Peacock, A. T. and G. K. Shaw, *The Economic Theory of Fiscal Policy*, London: Allen and Unwin, 1971.
100. Peston, M. H., *Elementary Matrices for Economics*, London: Routledge and Kegan Paul, 1969.
101. Phillips, A. W., Stabilisation policy in a closed economy, *Economic Journal*, **64**, 1954, 290–323.
102. Phillips, A. W., Stabilisation policy and the time form of lagged responses, *Economic Journal*, **67**, 1957, 265–277.
103. Phillips, A. W., The relation between unemployment and the rate of change of money wage rates in the United Kingdom, 1861–1957, *Economica* (New Series), **25**, 1958, 283–299.
104. Phillips, E. G., *Functions of a Complex Variable*, 7th edn., Edinburgh: Oliver and Boyd, 1954.
105. Polak, J. J., *An International Economic System*, London: Allen and Unwin, 1954.
106. Prais, S. J., Measuring social mobility, *Journal of the Royal Statistical Society, Series A*, **118**, 1955, 56–66.
107. Prais, S. J., The formal theory of social mobility, *Population Studies*, **9**, 1955, 72–82.
108. Pyatt, F. G., *Priority Patterns and the Demand for Household Durable Goods*, London: Cambridge University Press, 1964.
109. Rasul, G., *Input–Output Relationships in Pakistan*, 1954, Rotterdam: Rotterdam University Press, 1964.
110. Samuelson, P. A., Interactions between the multiplier analysis and the principle of acceleration, *Review of Economics and Statistics*, **21**, 1939, 75–78.
111. Samuelson, P. A., The simple mathematics of income determination, in Hansen [49], pp. 135–155.
112. Samuelson, P. A., *Foundations of Economic Analysis*, Cambridge, Mass.: Harvard University Press, 1948.
113. Samuelson, P. A., *Economics*, 8th edn., New York: McGraw-Hill, 1970.
114. Sasieni, M., A. Yaspan, and L. Friedman, *Operations Research*, New York: Wiley, 1959.
115. Solow, R., On the structure of linear models, *Econometrica*, **20**, 1952, 29–46.
116. Stephenson, G., *Mathematical Methods for Science Students*, London: Longmans, 1961.
117. Stone, J. R. N., *Input–Output and National Accounts*, Brussels: O.E.C.D., 1961.
118. Stone, J. R. N. *et al.*, *A Programme for Growth No. 9: Exploring 1972*, London: Chapman and Hall, 1970.
119. Tinbergen, J., *Economic Policy: Principles and Design*, Amsterdam: North Holland Publishing Co., 1966.
120. Tintner, G., *Mathematics and Statistics for Economics*, New York: Holt, Rinehart and Winston, 1953.
121. Vajda, S., *Readings in Mathematical Programming*, 2nd edn., London: Pitman, 1962.
122. Vajda, S., *Mathematical Programming*, Reading, Mass.: Addison-Wesley, 1961.
123. Wolfe, P., The simplex method for quadratic programming, *Econometrica*, **27**, 1959, 382–398.
124. Wonnacott, R. J. and T. H. Wonnacott, *Econometrics*, New York: Wiley, 1970.
125. Wright, R. W., *The Alberta Economy: An Input–Output Analysis*, Calgary: University of Alberta, 1965.
126. Yamane, T., *Mathematics for Economists*, 2nd edn., Englewood Cliffs, N.J.: Prentice-Hall, 1968.

Index

Solutions to selected problems

Chapter 2

2.1 (a) 13, 0, (b) 13, $-8{\cdot}4$, 1/7, 0, (c) $\sqrt{2}$, (d) all.

2.2 Using obvious symbols: (a) $U > 1{,}000{,}000$, (b) $D \geqslant 150{,}000$, (c) $P_b > P_m$, (d) $S \leqslant 10$, (e) $J \leqslant 25{,}000$, (f) $30 < L < 35$, (g) $10 \leqslant M \leqslant 20$.

2.3.1 (a) 3, (b) 8, (c) $\frac{3}{8}$.

2.3.2 (a) $\sum_{i=1}^{4} x_i/N$, (b) $\sum_{i=1}^{5} x_i y_i$, (c) $\sum_{i=1}^{4} x_i^2 x_{i+2}$

2.3.3 (a) 1024, (b) $\frac{1}{4}$, (c) 64.

2.4.3 (i) 24, (ii) lower, (iii) not unless exchange rates are flexible.

2.5.2 $C = 100 + 0{\cdot}8Y$

2.7.1 (a) 2, (b) $\frac{1}{2}$.

2.7.2 2.

2.7.3 (a) 4, -7, (b) -3, (c) -2, 17, (d) $\frac{1}{3}$, 2.

2.7.4 20%.

2.7.5 (a) $x_1 = 1$, $x_2 = 2$, (b) $x_1 = 4$, $x_2 = 3$.

2.7.6 Sugar costs 10p per pound, milk 5p per bottle.

2.7.7 $M = 20{\cdot}5$.

2.8.2 (a) $1\frac{1}{4}$, (b) 10.

2.9 (a) 1, (b) 1.

Chapter 3

3.1.1 Static.

3.1.2 Dynamic.

3.2 $S(t) = f(r(t - \frac{1}{2}))$, $D(t) = f(r(t), n(t))$, $S(t) = D(t)$; Dynamic.

3.5.1 Productivity of labour is exogenous. The rate of growth of population, real income per head and the proportion of the population of working age are endogenous.

3.6.2 Repercussions die out if $-1 < c < 1$.

3.6.3 $(1 - c^{N+1})\Delta I/(1 - c)$; £63m.

3.8.1 2.

Chapter 4

4.3 (a) $6x$, (b) $12x + 4$, (c) $9x^2 + 12x + 1$, (d) $1/(2x^2)$.

4.4.1 Marginal cost $= \lim_{\Delta x \to 0} \Delta y/\Delta x = 9x^2 + 12x + 1$.

4.4.2 Rate of investment $= \lim_{\Delta t \to 0} \Delta K/\Delta t = 5{,}400 + 800t - 30t^2$.

4.4.3 (a) Revenue $= 200Q - Q^2$, (b) Marginal revenue $= 200 - 2Q$, (c) Marginal cost $= 2Q$, (d) $Q = 50$, (e) 4,900.

4.5.2 (a) $x = 0$, $y = 0$, (b) $x = -\frac{1}{3}$, $y = -\frac{2}{3}$.

4.6 (a) 6, 0, (b) $1/x^3$, $-3/x^4$, (c) $2/(x - 3)^3$, $-6/(x - 3)^4$.

4.7.2 (a) $N = 110$, Fee = £180, (b) No change in N, Fee = £200.

Chapter 5

5.2.1 (a) $30x^5 - 12x^2 + 2$, (b) $24x + 14$, (c) $15(5x + 4)^2$, (d) $(3x^2 + 8x)/(3x + 4)^2$.

5.2.2 (a) $-6/(3x - 2)^3$, (b) $-(7x^2 + 42x - 3)/(x - 3)^4$, (c) $-1/(2\sqrt{x^3})$, (d) $(5\sqrt{x^3})/2$, (e) $(13x^3\sqrt[3]{x})/3$, (f) $(5\sqrt[4]{x})/4$, (g) $-(3x + 13\frac{1}{2})/\{(x - 2)^2\sqrt{(x - 2)}\}$.

5.2.3 $20x(5x^2 + 4)$, $300x^2 + 80$, $600x$, 600, 0.

5.2.5 $x = 2, 3$.

Chapter 6

6.2 $Y = 96\sqrt[4]{L}$.

6.3.1 (a) x_2, (b) $6x_1x_2^2 + 1$, (c) $\frac{3}{4}x_1^{-1/4}x_2^{1/4}$.

6.4 $dY = 0{\cdot}375K^{3/4}L^{1/4}\{(dL/L) + 3(dK/K)\}$.

6.6 $K = 273/\sqrt[3]{L}$.

6.7.1 $\alpha + \beta - \gamma$, $\alpha \neq \gamma$.

Chapter 7

7.1 (a) $y_1^2 + 16y_2^2 = 1600$, (c) maximize $y_1 + 2y_2$ subject to (a).

7.2 $x = 20$, $y = 20$.

7.3.1 $x_1 = 2$, $x_2 = 2$, $\lambda = 4$, $y = 28$.

7.3.2 $x_1 = 13$, $x_2 = 8\frac{2}{3}$, $\lambda = 4\frac{1}{3}$, $y = 563\frac{1}{3}$.

7.3.4 $y_1 = 16\sqrt{5}$, $y_2 = 2\sqrt{5}$.

Chapter 8

8.2.1 (a) $x^3 + K$, (b) $\frac{1}{2}x^2 + \frac{2}{3}x^3 + (x^6/30) + K$, (c) $\frac{1}{3}x^3 + 2x^2 - 5x + K$, (d) $\frac{2}{5}x^5 + 1\frac{1}{4}x^4 - 3\frac{1}{3}x^3 - 12\frac{1}{2}x^2 + K$.

8.2.2 $100 + 4Q + 3Q^2 + 10Q^3$.

8.2.3 (a) 44, (b) $10\frac{1}{2}$, (c) 0, (d) 1954.

8.6.2 $24\frac{1}{4}$.

8.7.1 £26,920.

Chapter 9

9.2 (a) CEK, (b) DEH or DEJ.

9.3.1 toast, butter, sugar cubes, boiled egg, table mat.

9.3.2 $x = 1\frac{5}{8}$, $y = 0$.

9.3.4 $\lambda_1 = 0$, $\lambda_2 = 1\frac{1}{2}$.

Chapter 10

10.3 $Y_1 = 1500$, $Y_2 = 1750$.

10.4 (a) $Y_1 = 1750$, $Y_2 = 2125$, (b) Improves by £100m., (c) Balance of payments unchanged.

10.7.1 (a) 2000 lorries, 5000 tons of steel, (b) 1000 lorries.

10.9.1. $W_s = 2$, $W_u = 1{\cdot}6$, Total employment 70,000 men.

10.9.2 3 per day.

10.9.3 $x_1 = 2$, $x_2 = 3$, $x_3 = 1$; No.

Chapter 11

11.1 $\begin{bmatrix} 3 & 5 \\ 4 & 8 \end{bmatrix}\begin{bmatrix} x_1 \\ x_2 \end{bmatrix} = \begin{bmatrix} 16 \\ 28 \end{bmatrix}$

11.2 (i) 11, (ii) $\begin{bmatrix} 8 & 12 \\ 2 & 3 \end{bmatrix}$, (iii) Not defined, (iv) Not defined, (v) $\begin{bmatrix} 14 \\ \frac{1}{2} \\ 15 \end{bmatrix}$

11.4.1 (a) $\begin{bmatrix} -15 & 19 \\ 4 & -5 \end{bmatrix}$, (b) $\begin{bmatrix} \frac{1}{3} & 0 & 0 \\ 0 & \frac{1}{5} & 0 \\ 0 & 0 & \frac{1}{7} \end{bmatrix}$

11.5.1 (i) $[6 \quad 20 \quad 22]$, (ii) $\begin{bmatrix} 6 \\ 20 \\ 22 \end{bmatrix}$, (iii) $\begin{bmatrix} 1 & 3 \\ 3 & 9 \end{bmatrix}$, (iv) 10, (v) $\begin{bmatrix} 6 & 12 & 18 \\ 12 & 40 & 44 \\ 18 & 44 & 52 \end{bmatrix}$, (vi) $\begin{bmatrix} 29 & 39 \\ 39 & 73 \end{bmatrix}$

11.9.1 16, 8, −8, 3, 2, 1, 6, 2, 4.

Chapter 12

12.1 No.
12.2.1 No.
12.2.2 Yes, No.
12.3.1 No; not changed.
12.3.2 (a) Solution not unique, (b) No solution, (c) Solution not unique, (d) No solution.
12.4.1 Six, No.
12.4.2 (a) $27x_1 + 13x_3 = 63$, (b) Not possible, after the change $x_1 = 74/19$, $x_2 = 58/19$.

Chapter 13

13.1.1 2·5, Country 1.
13.1.2 $2\frac{2}{9}$, $1\frac{1}{9}$; Multipliers change to 4, $\frac{2}{5}$; Expenditure becomes a more efficient policy instrument and money supply becomes much less efficient.
13.2.2 Income increases by £23·92m. in country 1 and £36·28m. in country 2.
13.3.3 Income must increase by £41·7m. in country 1 and £75m. in country 2.
13.4.1 $\begin{bmatrix} 23 & 26 \\ 26 & 49 \end{bmatrix}$
13.4.4 $\begin{bmatrix} 987 & 609 \\ 609 & 378 \end{bmatrix}$

Chapter 14

14.2.1 (a) $\lambda_1 = 2, \lambda_2 = 7, \mathbf{y}_1 = \begin{bmatrix} 2 \\ -1 \end{bmatrix}$, $\mathbf{y}_2 = \begin{bmatrix} 1 \\ 2 \end{bmatrix}$, (b) $2^{12}\begin{bmatrix} -2 \\ 1 \end{bmatrix}$

14.2.2 (a) 3, 4, 5, (b) 0, 2, (c) 3, −8, 16, (d) 1, 1, 1, 1.

14.2.4 $\lambda_1 = 3, \lambda_2 = 6, \mathbf{y}_1 = \begin{bmatrix} 1 \\ -1 \end{bmatrix}$, $\mathbf{y}_2 = \begin{bmatrix} 4 \\ 1 \end{bmatrix}$, $\frac{1}{6}(1 - 3^6)\begin{bmatrix} -1 \\ 1 \end{bmatrix} + \frac{2}{15}(1 - 6^6)\begin{bmatrix} -4 \\ 1 \end{bmatrix}$

14.3.1 No.
14.3.3 1.
14.3.4 3.
14.3.6 −1, 5, 5; $\begin{bmatrix} 0 \\ 1 \\ -1 \end{bmatrix}$, $\begin{bmatrix} 0 \\ 2 \\ 1 \end{bmatrix}$; No.
14.4.1 (i) 5, (ii) 13, (iii) 1.
14.5.1 $\mathbf{M}^N\mathbf{x} \sim 1{\cdot}9(7^N)\begin{bmatrix} 3 \\ 1 \end{bmatrix}$, $\mathbf{M}^N\mathbf{y} \sim 0{\cdot}2(7^N)\begin{bmatrix} 3 \\ 1 \end{bmatrix}$

Chapter 15

15.2.2 Yes, Yes.
15.2.3 Yes.
15.2.4 Yes.
15.3 **A**: 1, 10, **B**: 1, 10, **C**: 10, $(3 - \sqrt{41})/2$, $(3 + \sqrt{41})/2$, **D**: $0{\cdot}1(1 - \sqrt{8})$, $0{\cdot}1(1 + \sqrt{8})$, 10.
15.4.1 No.

Chapter 16

16.2.1 **a** and **b**.
16.5 **A**: positive definite, **B**: indefinite, **C**: indefinite.
16.6 Minimum at $x_1 = 5\frac{1}{3}$, $x_2 = 4$.

Chapter 17

17.2 (a) 4th-order linear homogeneous, (b) 2nd-order nonlinear homogeneous, (c) first-order nonlinear inhomogeneous, (d) first-order nonlinear inhomogeneous, (e) 3rd-order linear homogeneous. Equations with constant coefficients are (a)–(d).
17.3.2 £925 using the first five terms; £820; £105.
17.6.1 36 hours.

Chapter 18

18.2.1 (a) $(x + 1)\exp(x)$, (b) $(6x^2 + 4x)\exp(3x)$, (c) $(x - 2)\exp(x)/x^3$.
18.3.1 £1208.
18.3.2 £449.
18.4.1 20.
18.4.3 11 years.

Chapter 19

19.2.1 (a) $1 + 3i$, $1 - 3i$, (b) $\frac{1}{2} + \frac{1}{2}i$, $\frac{1}{2} - \frac{1}{2}i$, (c) $-3 + i$, $-3 - i$, (d) 1, $(3 + \sqrt{7}i)/2$, $(3 - \sqrt{7}i)/2$.

19.2.2 (a) $12 + 9i$, (b) $-\frac{3}{4} - i$, (c) $-3 + 4i$, (d) $18 + 3i$, (e) $3 - i$.

19.4 (a) 5, (b) 5, (c) 5, (d) $\sqrt{5}$, (e) $\sqrt{13}$.

19.5 (a) $\frac{12}{13} + \frac{5}{13}i$, (b) $-i$, (c) $-(120 + 27\,i)/1681$.

Chapter 20

20.1.2 £62·5m.

20.2 (a) No, (b) No, (c) No.